Teach
Yourself
More C++
in 21 Days

Teach Yourself
More C++
in 21 Days

Jesse Liberty

SAMS
PUBLISHING

201 West 103rd Street
Indianapolis, Indiana 46290

Copyright© 1996 by Sams Publishing

FIRST EDITION

International Standard Book Number: 0-672-30657-3

Library of Congress Catalog Card Number: 94-69275

99 98 97 96   4 3 2 1

Interpretation of the printing code: the rightmost double-digit number is the year of the book's printing; the rightmost single-digit, the number of the book's printing. For example, a printing code of 96-1 shows that the first printing of the book occurred in 1996.

Composed in AGaramond and MCPdigital by Macmillan Computer Publishing

Printed in the United States of America

Trademarks

Publisher	*Richard K. Swadley*
Acquisitions Manager	*Greg Wiegand*
Development Manager	*Dean Miller*
Managing Editor	*Cindy Morrow*
Marketing Manager	*Gregg Bushyeager*

Acquistions Editor
Christopher Denny

Development Editor
Dean Miller

Copy Editor
Fran Blau

Technical Reviewers
Robert Bogue
Jeff Perkins
Vincent Mayfield

Editorial Coordinator
Bill Whitmer

Technical Edit Coordinator
Lynette Quinn

Formatter
Frank Sinclair

Editorial Assistants
Sharon Cox
Andi Richter
Rhonda Tinch-Mize

Cover Designer
Tim Amrhein

Book Designer
Alyssa Yesh

Production Team Supervisor
Brad Chinn

Production
Mary Ann Abramson
Angela Bannan, Carol Bowers
Georgiana Briggs, Michael Brumitt
Charlotte Clapp, Judy Everly
Jason Hand, Casey Price
Nancy Price, Brian-Kent Proffitt
Bobbi Satterfield, Andrew Stone
Jill Tompkins, Mark Walchle
Paul Wilson

Indexer
Brad Herriman

Overview

1	Getting Started	1
2	Templates	25
3	Strings and Lists	47
4	Sorting	73
5	Design	103
6	Command-Line Processing and the Environment	125
7	Complex Data Structures	151
8	Advanced Data Structures	193
9	Writing to Disk	227
10	Collection Classes and B-Trees	253
11	Building Indexes on Disk	279
12	Records and Parsing	305
13	ROBIN, V. 1	339
14	Advanced Data Manipulation	377
15	Iterators	399
16	Synonyms	433
17	Profiling and Optimization	473
18	Advanced Exceptions and Error Handling	493
19	Writing Solid Code	517
20	Debugging	535
21	Next Steps	557
A	Answers	567
B	Make Files	691
	Index	695

Contents

Day   **1   Getting Started**   **1**

Understanding Object-Oriented Programming 2
    Encapsulation 2
    Polymorphism 3
    Inheritance.. 3
    The Fundamentals 3
Understanding Memory 4
The Stack and Functions 5
Using Classes and Structures 6
Using Pointers 6
Using *new* and *delete* 8
Using References 9
Using *const*.. 10
Using Arrays 10
Examining Inheritance in Detail.. 11
    Using Abstract Data Types 12
    Using Multiple Inheritance 12
    Understanding Private Inheritance and Containment 12
Defining Operator Overloading 12
Using Static Data and Functions 13
Using Friend Functions and Classes 13
Using Streams.. 13
Using Exceptions 13
Writing Large Programs 14
    Looking At Style Guidelines 14
    Indenting 15
    Braces 15
    Long Lines 15
    Switch Statements 16
    Program Text.. 16
    Identifier Names 17
    Spelling and Capitalization of Names 17
    Comments 18
    Access 18
    Constants 19
The Project 19
    Understanding How ROBIN Works 20
    Reinventing the Wheel 21
    Relating ROBIN to Your Own Projects 21
Summary 22
Q&A 22

Workshop 22
   Quiz 23
   Exercises 23

Day   2   Templates   25

The Fundamentals 26
   Template Instances 27
   Template Definition 27
   Using the Name 29
   Implementing the Template 29
Template Functions 33
   Using Template Items 34
   Specialized Functions 38
Summary 44
Q&A 44
Workshop 45
   Quiz 45
   Exercises 45

Day   3   Strings and Lists   47

The String Class 48
Lists 57
   Linked Lists 57
   Creating Your First Linked List 58
Parameterizing the List 65
Summary 70
Q&A 70
Workshop 71
   Quiz 71
   Exercises 71

Day   4   Sorting   73

A Practical View 74
Selection Sort 74
Improving Efficiency 76
Did the Optimization Help? 78
Insertion Sort 79
Bubble Sort 81
   Improving the Bubble Sort 85
QuickSort() 88
Sorting Pointers Rather Than Records 92
Parameterizing the Sort 94
   Limitations of the *QuickSort()* Routine 97
Summary 100
Q&A 100

Workshop 101
    Quiz 101
    Exercises 101

Day 5 Design   **103**

The Specification 104
    The Functional Specification 104
    Storing Data 105
    Searching for Data 106
    Displaying Found Data 106
    Database Management 107
    Getting Help 108
    A Moving Target 108
The Technical Specification 108
    Iterative Design 109
Where Do I Start? 109
    What Are the Initial Classes? 110
    Event-Driven Programming 110
    Object Orientation 111
    Getting Started 111
Abstract Data Types 113
    Searching 113
    The Collections 113
Getting Started 114
    The rWord Class 115
Reviewing a Technical Specification 117
Next Steps 118
Other Designs: CLiDE 119
CLiDE's Functional Specifications 119
    Portability Issues 119
    The User Interface 119
    The Technical Specification 120
    What Are the Objects? 120
Prototyping 120
Sorting, Filtering, and Displaying 121
CLiDE's First Steps 121
Q&A 121
Workshop 123
    Quiz 123
    Exercises 124

Day 6 Command-Line Processing and the Environment   **125**

Command-Line Processing 126
Command-Line Flags 128

An Alternative to Flags 130
Sorting Command-Line Arguments 131
    Command-Line Arguments and Linked Lists 134
Using the Environment Variables 140
    Using *getenv* 144
    Using *putenv* 145
Summary 147
Q & A 147
Workshop 148
    Quiz 148
    Exercises 148

Day   7   Complex Data Structures   151

Laying the Groundwork 152
    Standard Definitions 152
    The List Class 153
    Strings and Notes 157
    Testing the Building Blocks 163
Using Hash Tables 164
Deciding When To Use Hash Tables 166
Using Trees and Other Powerful Data Structures 166
    Using Trees 167
    Using Binary Trees 168
    Finding a Node 168
    Inserting Nodes 169
    Deleting a Node 170
    Creating an rWord Object 171
    Using the Demonstration Program 173
Rewriting the Binary Tree 181
Summary 189
Q&A 189
Workshop 190
    Quiz 190
    Exercises 190

Day   8   Advanced Data Structure   193

Printing a Tree 194
Using FIFO Queues 194
    Using the Queue Class to Print 198
    Problems with This Approach 206
    Using Recursion to Print 206
Using Balanced Binary Trees 213
    Using AVL Trees 213
    Writing the AVL Tree 213

Looking At Other Binary Trees 224
Summary 224
Q&A 224
Workshop 225
    Quiz 225
    Exercises 225

Day   9   Writing to Disk   227

Writing Objects to Disk 228
Writing Data from an Object 230
    Object Persistence versus Data Persistence 231
    Storing Objects to Disk 231
Creating Classes to Handle Storage 240
What Have We Gained? 249
From Here to an Object Store 249
Summary 249
Q&A 249
Workshop 250
    Quiz 250
    Exercises 251

Day   10   Collection Classes and B-Trees   253

Collection Classes 254
    Sets 254
    Dictionaries 254
Creating the Sparse Array Class 255
    Implementation Issues 255
Tree Structures and Object Persistence 261
B-Trees 261
    Deleting a Node 264
    Implementing the B-Tree 264
Writing Pages To Disk (Not Yet) 276
Summary 276
Q & A 276
Workshop 276
    Quiz 277
    Exercises 277

Day   11   Building Indexes on Disk   279

Keeping It in Perspective 280
Real-World Considerations 280
Knowing What You Are Building 280
Using Disk-Based B-Trees 281
Caching 281
    Swapping Out 282
    Determining How Big Each Page Should Be 282
    Determining How Many Pages Can Be in Memory at Once 283

Swapping to Disk 283
Implementing the Tree 288
Connecting Nodes to Data 301
Deleting Notes 301
Implementing Performance Enhancements 302
Summary 302
Q&A 303
Workshop 303
        Quiz 303
        Exercises 303

Day   12   Records and Parsing   305

Putting the Notes into a Data File 306
        Storing the Notes 306
Improving the Code 306
        Recording Length and Data 307
        Case Insensitivity 307
        Very Small Words 308
        Statistics 308
The Final Preliminary Version 308
Summary 334
Q & A 335
Workshop 335
        Quiz 336
        Exercises 336

Day   13   ROBIN, V.1   339

Testing Your Program 340
Finishing ROBIN, V.1 341
Locking the Pages 341
Displaying Results 342
Exercising the Program 342
Getting It Out the Door 373
Looking At What You Didn't Fix 373
What's Ahead 374
Summary 374
Q&A 374
Workshop 375
        Quiz 375
        Exercises 375

Day   14   Advanced Data Manipulation   377

Bit Twiddling 378
        Operator AND 378
        Operator OR 379
        Operator Exclusive OR 379

The Complement Operator 379
Setting Bits 379
Clearing Bits 379
Flipping Bits 380
Bit Fields 380
Learning How Memory Works 383
Examining the Levels of Abstraction 383
Partitioning RAM 384
Using Registers and the Instruction Pointer 384
Using the Stack 385
Understanding How the Stack Works with Functions 385
Using the Heap 386
Working with Binary and Hexadecimal Values 387
What Are These Strange Numbers? 387
Using Other Bases 388
Working with Binary Values 390
Why Base 2? 390
Bits and Bytes 391
What Is a K? 391
Binary Numbers 391
Working with Hexadecimal Values 392
Summary 395
Q&A 395
Workshop 395
Quiz 395
Exercises 396

Day   15   Iterators   399

Using an Iterator 400
Understanding How the Iterator Works 400
Illustrating an Iterator over a B-Tree 401
Extending the Iterator 430
Examining Issues with Iterators 430
Summary 430
Q&A 431
Workshop 431
Quiz 431
Exercises 431

Day   16   Synonyms   433

Maintainable and Extensible Code 434
How Synonyms Work 434
Summary 470
Q&A 470
Workshop 471
Quiz 471
Exercises 471

Day	**17**	**Profiling and Optimization**	**473**
		Optimizing Your Code	474
		Programming Optimization	474
		Compiler Optimization	474
		Using Profilers	475
		Profiling Your Program	476
		Profiling Function Count	477
		Examining Time versus Occurrence	478
		Profiling by Line	479
		Using Coverage Profiling	481
		Putting the Profile to Use	482
		False Optimizations	487
		Applying the Lessons	490
		Summary	491
		Q&A	491
		Workshop	491
		Quiz	492
		Exercises	492
Day	**18**	**Advanced Exceptions and Error Handling**	**493**
		Reviewing Exceptions	494
		Seeing How Exceptions Are Used	495
		Using *Try* Blocks and *Catch* Blocks	500
		Catching Exceptions	500
		Using More Than One Catch Specification	500
		Using Exception Hierarchies	503
		Exception Objects	504
		Using Exceptions with Templates	510
		Using Exceptions without Errors	512
		Q&A	513
		Workshop	514
		Quiz	514
		Exercises	514
Day	**19**	**Writing Solid Code**	**517**
		Writing It Isn't the Hard Part	518
		Robustness	519
		Extensibility	519
		Maintainability	520
		Using Asserts	520
		Leave the Assert in There	521
		Beware of Side Effects	522
		Class Invariants	522
		Test the Return Value from *New*	523

Make Destructors Virtual 523
Initialize Pointers to Zero 523
Use *Const* Wherever You Can 524
Managing Object Creation 524
Initialize in the Order You Declare Your Member Variables 525
Never, Ever, Return a Reference to a Local Object. Ever. 525
Create a Consistent Style 525
    Braces 526
    Long Lines 526
    Switch Statements 526
    Program Text 527
    Identifier Names 527
    Spelling and Capitalization of Names 528
    Comments 528
    Access 529
    Class Definitions 529
    Include Files 530
    Evolve Your Own Rules and Write Them Down 530
Reviewing Your Code 530
    Design Reviews 530
    Code Reviews 531
    Documentation Reviews 532
Planning for Change 532
Summary 532
Q&A 532
Workshop 533
    Quiz 533
    Exercises 533

Day   20   Debugging   535

Examining Bugs, Errors, and Design Problems 536
Looking At the Cost of Bugs 536
    Writing a Good Specification 536
    Writing the Design Document 537
    Considering Reality and Schedules 537
Using Debuggers 538
    Use the Source, Luke 538
    Use TRACE Macros 538
    Use Logs 539
Using the Debugger 539
    Using Symbolic Debuggers 540
    Using Break Points 540
    Using Watch Points 540
    Examining Memory 540

		Using a Call Stack	541
		Turning Off Optimization	541
		Zen Mind, Debugging Mind	541
		Defining the Problem	541
		Locating, Isolating, and Destroying the Problem	542
		Knowing What to Look For	542
		Questioning Your Assumptions	543
		Looking At Logic Flaws	543
		Finding Bugs That Only Show Up in Release Code	543
		Watching for Some Common Bugs	544
		Making Fence-Post Errors	544
		Deleting Memory Twice, or Not at All	544
		Wrapping around an Integer	544
		Returning a Reference to a Local Variable	544
		Memory Checking	545
		A Word about Rest	545
		Looking At Some Debugging Examples	545
		Summary	551
		Q&A	551
		Workshop	552
		Quiz	552
		Exercises	552

Day 21 Next Steps — **557**

		Using Version Control	558
		Learning How Version Control Works	558
		Managing More Than One Programmer	559
		Understanding Branches and Trunks	559
		Understanding Release Branches	560
		Creating Dynamic Names	560
		Making Enhancements	560
		Using Shareware	561
		Writing Commercial Software	561
		Finding Help and Advice	562
		Required Reading	562
		Getting More Information about Object-Oriented Analysis and Design	562
		Writing for Windows or the Macintosh	563
		Writing Solid Code	563
		Getting More Information from Magazines	563
		Staying in Touch	564
		Summary	564
		Q&A	564

Workshop 564
    Quiz 564
    Exercises 565

A   Answers   **567**
    Answers for Day 1, "Getting Started" 568
    Quiz 568
    Exercises 569
    Answers for Day 2, "Templates" 574
    Quiz 574
    Exercises 574
    Answers to Day 3, "Strings and Lists" 577
    Quiz 577
    Exercises 578
    Answers to Day 4, "Sorting" 584
    Quiz 584
    Exercises 584
    Answers to Chapter 5, "Design" 588
    Quiz 588
    Exercises 589
    Answers to Day 6, "Command-Line Processing and the
      Environment" 591
    Quiz 591
    Exercises 591
    Answers to Day 7, "Complex Data Structures" 592
    Quiz 592
    Exercises 593
    Answers to Day 8, "Advanced Data Structures" 599
    Quiz 599
    Exercises 600
    Answers to Day 9, "Writing to Disk" 608
    Quiz 608
    Exercises 608
    Answers to Day 10, " Collection Classes and B-Trees" 630
    Quiz 630
    Exercises 630
    Answers for Day 11, "Building Indexes on Disk" 639
    Quiz 639
    Exercises 639
    Answers for Day 12, "Records and Parsing" 646
    Quiz 646
    Exercises 646
    Answers for Day 13, " ROBIN, V.1" 657
    Quiz 657
    Exercises 657

Answers for Day 14, " Advanced Data Manipulation" 659
    Quiz 659
    Exercises 659
Answers for Day 15, " Iterators" 662
    Quiz 662
    Exercises 663
Answers for Day 16, "Synonyms" 667
    Quiz 667
    Exercises 667
Answers for Day 17, " Profiling and Optimization" 674
    Quiz 674
    Exercises 674
Answers for Day 18, " Advanced Exceptions and Error Handling" 675
    Quiz 675
    Exercises 675
Answers for Day 19, "Writing Solid Code" 680
    Quiz 680
    Exercises 680
Answers for Day 20, "Debugging" 687
    Quiz 687
    Exercises 687
Answers for Day 21, " Next Steps" 688
    Quiz 688

B   Make Files   691
    Conditional Compilation 692
    Make Variables 693
    Built-In Variables 693
    Suffix Rules 693
    Next Steps 694

Index   695

Acknowledgments

Again, there are too many people to thank to write down all their names.

My wife and daughters deserve special thanks for their patience and their encouragement.

I'd like to thank the management and development team at AT&T Interchange Online Network for their help and support, and for teaching me what I know about C++; expecially Mike Kraley and Stephen Zagieboylo.

Chris Denny, Brad Jones, Cindy Morrow, Dean Miller, and many other editors at Sams deserve special mention for going above and beyond all expectations in ensuring that this book is far better than it was when I created it. Richard K. Swadley sets the standards of excellence. It was a pleasure working with them all.

Special thanks to those who bought my first book, and for those who helped me make it better.

Finally, I'd like to thank three very brave people: Jenny Levine, who will be 102 before this book prints; Ken Levine, for showing me there is always hope; and David Levine, who will never know what an inspiration he was.

About the Author

Jesse Liberty is a Distinguished Software Engineer with AT&T Interchange Online Network, where he was a founding member of the Software Development Team. He is the author of *Teach Yourself C++ in 21 Days* and is a former vice president of Citibank's Development Division. He lives with his wife and daughters Robin and Rachel in the suburbs of Cambridge, Massachusetts. He can be reached on the Internet at `jl@staff.ichange.com`.

Getting Started

Welcome to *Teach Yourself More C++ Programming in 21 Days!* This book assumes that you already have read an introductory book on C++ and are comfortable writing simple C++ programs. If this is not so, please take the time to read one of the many available C++ primers, such as *Teach Yourself C++ in 21 Days* by Jesse Liberty (ISBN: 0-672-30541-0), published by Sams Publishing, 1994.

Today you will review the fundamentals of C++. If the topics are new to you, read a comprehensive primer on the subject before proceeding. Take the time to answer the quiz questions and to do the review exercises at the end of this chapter. These will ensure that you are ready for the material presented in the rest of the book.

This review is different from the rest of the book in that very few examples are provided, and the explanations are quite terse. The idea is to double check that you are comfortable with the fundamentals of C++, rather than to learn anything new.

Understanding Object-Oriented Programming

C++ programs are concerned with the creation, management, and manipulation of objects. An *object* is an encapsulation of data and the methods, or *functions*, used to manipulate that data.

Traditional programming languages separated data from functionality. Typically, data was aggregated into structures that then were passed among various functions that created, read, altered, and otherwise managed that data.

Object-oriented programming focuses on the creation and manipulation of "things," such as people, cars, animals, employees, factories, televisions, cities, air traffic control systems, and so on. This type of programming gives you a greater level of abstraction; the programmer can concentrate on how the employee objects interact with the city objects without having to focus on the details of the implementation of either type.

Encapsulation

Encapsulation is the desirable trait of being able to treat an object as an entity without worrying about, or even knowing, how it works. Thus, in object-oriented programming, you can create, use, and destroy dialog boxes, for example, without knowing how they work. You can create and use strings, arrays, collections, or even more complex, user-defined types such as `employee` and `municipal worker`, without knowing anything about how they are implemented.

In C++, there is a strong distinction made between a class's interface and its implementation. The class interface tells you how objects of that class are used; the implementation tells you how they work. Clients (users) of the class do not need to know about the implementation; they care only about the interface, which tells what the objects can do, and how they are created and destroyed.

Polymorphism

Polymorphism refers to the capability to treat different types of objects in a common way by using only the abstract interface. You might write a function, for example, that manipulates different types of phones—dial phones, touch-tone phones, and ISDN (digital) phones, for example—without knowing or caring about the implementation differences between the different phone types.

Each phone is passed in as a parameter to your function, and you can tell the phone to ring by calling `thePhone->ring()`. The old-fashioned phone rings, the modern phone trills, and the picture phone flash a message. Your program doesn't need to know which type of phone it is working with; it calls `ring()`, and the right thing happens based on the real type of the phone.

Inheritance

The traditional object-oriented programming use of the term *inheritance* refers to the capability to create a new type based on an existing type, specifying only the ways in which the two types differ. The benefit of inheritance is that a well-tested type can be used as the basis of new types, taking advantage of all the work that went into the existing type.

In C++, inheritance is tightly tied to polymorphism; in C++, the principal way to invoke polymorphism is through inheritance.

> **Note:** You should be familiar with the following terms:
>
> **Encapsulation:** Bundling an entire process with its data into a single class.
>
> **Polymorphism:** The capability to treat many types as if they were all of one (base) type, or the capability for one object or function to change behavior based on context.
>
> **Inheritance:** Extending the behavior of an existing type in a new, derived type.
>
> **Object oriented:** Paying attention to types and their behavior, rather than to functions and the data on which they act.

The Fundamentals

C++ programs consist of classes—each can include member data and member functions. Additionally, C++ programs call upon nonmember (global) functions. You must be comfortable writing and using member functions and global functions, and you must understand in some depth the differences between passing by reference and passing by value.

The built-in data types such as int and double are augmented in C++ by user-defined types: classes. An essential principle of C++ is that user-defined types are at least as powerful and integrated into the language as the built-in types. Thus, virtually anything you can do with a built-in type—such as passing it to a function, getting it as a return type, using operators such as plus and indirection on it, and so on—you can do with a user-defined type.

Understanding Memory

Although it is possible to write simple C++ programs without understanding the stack and the heap, a full and rich understanding of the language requires a deep understanding of how memory is allocated and used.

When you begin your program, your operating system (such as DOS or Microsoft Windows) sets up various areas of memory based on the requirements of your compiler. The principle areas of memory covered in this section are global name space, the free store, the registers, the code space, and the stack.

Global variables are available to every function in the program. *Registers* are a special area of memory built right into the central processing unit (CPU). They take care of internal housekeeping. A great deal goes on in the registers that is beyond the scope of this book; we're concerned with the set of registers responsible for pointing, at any given moment, to the next line of code. We'll call these *registers* or, as a group, the *instruction pointer*. The instruction pointer keeps track of which line of code is to be executed next.

The code itself is in *code space*, which is the part of memory set aside to hold the binary form of the instructions you created in your program. Each line of source code is translated into a series of instructions, and each of these instructions is at a particular address in memory. The instruction pointer has the address of the next instruction to execute.

The *stack* is a special area of memory allocated for your program to hold the data required by each of the functions in your program. When data is "pushed" onto the stack, the stack grows; as data is "popped" off the stack, the stack shrinks.

A stack of dishes in a cafeteria is the common analogy, and it is fine as far as it goes, but it is wrong in a fundamental way. A closer mental picture is of a series of cubbyholes aligned top to bottom. The top of the stack is whatever cubby the "stack pointer" (which is another register) happens to be pointing to.

Each of the cubbies has a sequential address, and one of those addresses is kept, at any moment, in the stack pointer register. Everything below that magic address, known as the top of the stack, is considered to be on the stack. Everything above the top of the stack is considered off the stack and invalid.

When data is put on the stack, it is placed into a cubby above the stack pointer, and then the stack pointer is moved to the new data. When data is popped off the stack, all that really happens is that the address of the stack pointer changes.

The Stack and Functions

When your code branches to a function, here's what happens:

1. All the arguments to the function are placed on the stack.
2. The address in the instruction pointer is incremented to the next instruction past the function call. That address then is placed on the stack, and will be the return address when the function returns.
3. Room is made on the stack for the return type you've declared. On a system with two-byte integers, if the return type is declared to be an integer, another two bytes are added to the stack, but no value is placed in these bytes. Note that some compilers store small values in registers rather than using the stack.
4. The address of the called function is loaded into the instruction pointer, so the next instruction executed will be in the called function.
5. The instruction now in the instruction pointer is executed, thus executing the first instruction in the function.
6. The current top of the stack is noted and held in a special pointer called the *stack frame*. Everything added to the stack from now until the function returns will be considered "local" to the function.
7. Local variables are pushed onto the stack as they are defined.

When the function is ready to return, the return value is placed in the area of the stack reserved at step 2. The stack then is popped all the way up to the stack frame pointer, which effectively throws away all the local variables, calls their destructors, and removes the arguments to the function.

The return value is popped off the stack and assigned as the value of the function call, and the address stashed away in step one is retrieved and put into the instruction pointer. The program thus resumes immediately after the function call, with the value of the function retrieved.

Some of the details of this process are compiler dependent; that is, they change from compiler to compiler, but the essential idea is consistent across computers and compilers. When you call a function, the parameters and the return address are put on the stack. During the life of the function, local variables are added to the stack. When the function returns, these are all removed by popping the stack.

Using Classes and Structures

Classes are user-defined data types. The member data and functions of the class are accessible through objects of the class, with the exception of static members, which are described later. Member functions have an implicit `this` pointer, which operates as a pointer to the individual instance of the class. (Note that static functions don't have a `this` pointer.)

Classes differ from structures *only* in that their default inheritance and access is private, whereas structures inherit publicly by default and, by default, have public access. Other than this, there is *no difference* between classes and structures.

Classes with virtual functions maintain a virtual function table, known as the `vtable`. This table is used to allow polymorphism. Virtual functions can be overridden in derived classes. Pointers to base classes can also point to objects of derived classes (e.g., a pointer to Animal can point to a Dog object). When the member function is called, the overridden implementation is invoked by way of the `vtable` (e.g., when you call `speak()` on the Animal pointer, the Dog's overridden `speak()` function will be invoked).

Using Pointers

A *pointer* is a variable that holds in memory the address of an object. Pointers enable objects to be acted on indirectly; the pointer is used to access the object at the address stored in the pointer.

Pointers are declared by writing the type of object they point to, followed by the *indirection operator*(*), followed by the pointer name. Pointers should be initialized to point to an object or to point to zero.

> **Caution:** Some programmers, especially old C hackers, use the word NULL, but this is controversial in C++ and is *not* a keyword in the language. You are better off assigning the value 0 to your pointers.

You access the value at the address stored in a pointer by using the indirection operator (*). You can declare constant pointers, which can't be reassigned to point to other objects, and pointers to constant objects, which can't be used to change the objects to which they point. Using `const` and `nonconst` pointers is illustrated in Listing 1.1.

Listing 1.1 Constant and Nonconstant Pointers

```
1:    // Listing 1.1 - constant and nonconstant pointers
2:
3:    #include <iostream.h>
4:    int main()
```

```
5:      {
6:          int x = 5;
7:          int y = 90;
8:          int * pInt = &x;
9:          const int * ptrConstInt = &x;
10:         int * const ConstPtrInt = &x;
11:         const int * const ConstPtrConstInt = &x;
12:
13:         *pInt = 7;
14:      //    *ptrConstInt = 8;    // error, can't change value
15:         *ConstPtrInt = 9;
16:      //    *ConstPtrConstInt = 10;  // error, can't change value
17:
18:         cout << "pInt: " << pInt << " *pInt: " << *pInt << endl;
19:         cout << "ptrConstInt: " << (int*)ptrConstInt << " *ptrConstInt: "
            << *ptrConstInt << endl;
20:         cout << "ConstPtrInt: " << ConstPtrInt << " *ConstPtrInt: "
            << *ConstPtrInt << endl;
21:         cout << "ConstPtrConstInt: " << (int*)ConstPtrConstInt;
22:         cout << " *ConstPtrConstInt: " << *ConstPtrConstInt << endl;
23:
24:         pInt = &y;
25:         ptrConstInt = &y;
26:      //    ConstPtrInt = &y;       // error, can't reassign
27:      //    ConstPtrConstInt = &y;       // error, can't reassign
28:
29:         *pInt = 97;
30:      //    *ptrConstInt = 98;       // error, can't change value
31:         *ConstPtrInt = 99;
32:      //    *ConstPtrConstInt = 100;    // error, can't change value
33:
34:         cout << "pInt: " << pInt << " *pInt: " << *pInt << endl;
35:         cout << "ptrConstInt: " << (int*)ptrConstInt << " *ptrConstInt: " <<
*ptrConstInt << endl;
36:         cout << "ConstPtrInt: " << ConstPtrInt << " *ConstPtrInt: " <<
*ConstPtrInt << endl;
37:         cout << "ConstPtrConstInt: " << (int*)ConstPtrConstInt;
38:         cout << " *ConstPtrConstInt: " << *ConstPtrConstInt << endl;
39:
40:         return 0;
41:      }
```

```
pInt: 0x1ee30ffe *pInt: 9
ptrContInt: 0x1ee30ffe *ptrContInt: 9
ContPtrInt: 0x1ee30ffe *ContPtrInt: 9
ContPtrContInt: 0x1ee30ffe *ContPtrContInt: 9
pInt: 0x1ee30ffc *pInt: 97
ptrContInt: 0x1ee30ffc *ptrContInt: 97
ContPtrInt: 0x1ee30ffe *ContPtrInt: 99
ContPtrContInt: 0x1ee30ffe *ContPtrContInt: 99
```

Note: The exact values you receive might be different, depending on what segment of memory your program happens to use.

On lines 6 and 7, two local variables, x and y, are declared and initialized. On lines 8 through 10, four pointers are declared and initialized with the address of x. The first pointer, pInt is a pointer to an integer.

The second, ptrConstInt, is a pointer to a constant integer, and thus cannot be used to change the value of the integer to which it points.

The third, ConstPtrInt, is a constant pointer to an integer, and thus cannot be reassigned.

The final pointer, ConstPtrConstInt, is a constant pointer to a constant integer, and thus cannot be used to change the value of the integer to which it points, and also cannot be reassigned to point to a different integer.

Lines 14 and 16, if uncommented, would cause a compile-time error, in each case because you are attempting to change the integer pointed to. Because the pointer is defined to be a pointer to a constant integer, the compiler correctly balks.

Lines 26 and 27 would, if uncommented, create compile-time errors because you are attempting to reassign a constant pointer.

Note that on lines 19, 21, 35, and 37, the constness of the pointer must be cast away so that you can pass the pointer to the cout object.

Using *new* and *delete*

You create new objects on the free store by using the new keyword, and assigning the address that is returned to a pointer. You free the memory by calling the delete on that pointer. delete frees the memory but does not destroy the pointer; you must reassign the pointer after its memory is freed.

If you create an array of objects on the heap, you must signal delete that more than one object is to be destroyed; do this by including the brackets in the delete call. For example, if you create an array of integers with

```
int *myArray = new int[50];
```

you must delete this array by writing

```
delete [] myArray;
```

Using References

References are aliases to objects that already exist somewhere in memory. They often are implemented using pointers, but they are quite different in fundamental ways.

References must be initialized to refer to an existing object and cannot be reassigned to refer to anything else. Any action taken on a reference is in fact taken on the reference's target object; taking the address of a reference returns the address of the target. Listing 1.2 presents a simple program that illustrates the use of references.

 Listing 1.2 Using References

```
1:      // listing 1.2
2:
3:      #include <iostream.h>
4:
5:      int main()
6:      {
7:          int x = 5;
8:          int y = 7;
9:          // int &FirstRef; // error, must be initialized
10:         int &intRef = x;
11:
12:         cout << "x: " << x << " y: " << y << " intRef: " << intRef << endl;
13:
14:         intRef = 8;
15:
16:         cout << "x: " << x << " y: " << y << " intRef: " << intRef << endl;
17:
18:         intRef = y;   // not what you might expect!
19:
20:         cout << "x: " << x << " y: " << y << " intRef: " << intRef << endl;
21:
22:         return 0;
23:     }
```

```
x: 5 y: 7 intRef: 5
x: 8 y: 7 intRef: 8
x: 7 y: 7 intRef: 7
```

 On lines 7 and 8, two local variables are defined and initialized. If line 9 were uncommented, it would generate a compile-time error because references must be initialized.

Line 10 declares and initializes intRef, making it an alias for x. On line 12, the values of x, y, and intRef are printed, resulting in the first output line.

On line 14, intRef is assigned the value 8, and because intRef is an alias for x, the printout reflects that both have changed their value.

On line 18, the programmer meant to reassign intRef to point to y, but this is not possible with references. What happens instead is that intRef continues to act as an alias for x. Consequently, `intRef = y` becomes an alias for x = y, setting x (and therefore `intRef`) to the value of y, as reflected in the final line of the printout.

Passing objects by reference, either using references or pointers, can be far more efficient than passing by value. Passing by reference allows the called function to change the value in the arguments back in the calling function, unless the reference or pointer is declared to be constant (`const`).

Using *const*

As discussed earlier, constant pointers cannot be reassigned, references are always constant in this way and do not need to be declared as such. Pointers or references to constant objects cannot be used to change those objects. Member functions also can be declared constant, which indicates that the function does not change the object, and thus can be used with constant objects.

It is desirable to use the keyword `const` wherever appropriate because it enlists the compiler in the effort to find programming errors before they become runtime bugs. Bugs found at compile time are cheaper to fix than those found once the product ships.

Using Arrays

An *array* is a fixed-size collection of objects all of the same type. Arrays do not do bounds checking, so it is legal, even if disastrous to read or write past the end of an array. Arrays count from 0. Thus, a 10-member array will count from offset 0 to offset 9, and more generally an array of *n* values will be numbered from 0 to *n*-1. It is a common mistake to write to offset *n* of an *n*-member array, which is one past the end of the array.

Arrays can be single dimensional or multi-dimensional. In either case, the members of the array can be initialized, as long as the array contains either built-in types such as `int`, or objects of a class that has a default constructor.

Arrays and their contents can be on the free store or on the stack. If you delete an array on the free store, remember to use the brackets in the call to delete.

Array names are constant pointers to the first elements of the array. Pointers and arrays use pointer arithmetic to find the next element of an array.

Linked lists can be created to manage collections for which size cannot be known at compile time. From linked lists, any number of more complex data structures can be created.

Strings are arrays of characters (type `char`). C++ provides some special features for the management of character arrays, including the capability to initialize them with quoted strings.

Note: Character arrays typically are terminated with zero. These strings are called *null terminated* because old C programs declared the name NULL for the value zero. The traditional character array manipulation functions, such as strcpy() and strlen(), rely on this convention.

Examining Inheritance in Detail

New classes can be created by deriving from existing classes. The class derived *from* is referred to as the *base* class.

Derived classes inherit all the public and protected data and functions from their base classes. Protected access is public to derived classes and private to all other objects. Even derived classes cannot access private data or functions in their base classes.

Constructors can be initialized before the body of the constructor. It is at this time that base constructors are invoked and parameters can be passed to the base class.

Functions in the base class can be overridden in the derived class. If the base class functions are virtual, and if the object is accessed by pointer or reference, the derived class's functions will be invoked based on the runtime type of the object pointed to. This is the essence of polymorphism in C++; your function invokes a base class method, and based on the runtime type of the actual object referred to, the right method is called.

Methods in the base class can be invoked by explicitly naming the function with the prefix of the base class name and the scoping operator.

Tip: In classes with virtual methods, the destructor almost always should be made virtual. A virtual destructor ensures that the derived part of the object will be freed when delete is called on the pointer.

Tip: Although constructors cannot be virtual, a virtual copy constructor can be created by making a virtual member function, which then calls the copy constructor.

Using Abstract Data Types

C++ supports the creation of abstract data types (ADT) with pure virtual functions. A virtual function is made pure by initializing it with zero, as in the following:

```
virtual void Draw() = 0;
```

Any class with one or more pure virtual functions is an ADT. Attempting to instantiate an object of a class that is an ADT will cause a compile-time error. Putting a pure virtual function in your class signals two things to clients of your class: (1) don't make an object of this class—instead, derive from it and (2) make sure you override the pure virtual function.

Any class that derives from an ADT inherits the pure virtual function as pure, and so must override every pure virtual function if it wants to instantiate objects.

Using Multiple Inheritance

Classes can inherit from more than one base class: this is called *multiple inheritance*. When a class is multiply derived, it inherits all the member functions and data from all its base classes. Virtual inheritance can be used to avoid inheriting multiple copies of the *same* base class when a new class is derived from two classes, each of which shares a common ancestor class.

Understanding Private Inheritance and Containment

Private inheritance can be used to implement one class in terms of another. Thus, the implementation is inherited in whole or in part, but not the interface. Privately inherited methods and data are private in the derived class, regardless of their access status in the base class.

Functionality can be delegated to a second class, or implemented in terms of that class, by private inheritance or containment. When one class contains another, you obtain nearly all the benefits of private inheritance with two substantial differences: you cannot override methods of the contained class, but you can instantiate more than one instance.

Defining Operator Overloading

User-defined classes can override nearly all the built-in operators, such as the mathematical operators, the increment and decrement operators, and so on. Operator overloading enables user-defined classes to be used in much the same way as built-in classes.

Using Static Data and Functions

Class member data and member functions can be declared static. Static data is scoped to the class rather than to the object; only one instance of static data will exist, shared among all instances of the class. Access can be public, protected, or private—just as for any other class data.

Static methods provide access to private static data, and can be invoked without having an actual object of the class type by using the scoping operator. Static data and functions provide the flexibility of global data, while maintaining type safety.

Using Friend Functions and Classes

Classes can declare other classes or member functions of other classes to be friends. This extends the interface of the class to include the friends; the friend functions have access to the public, protected, and private members of the class as if they were member functions of that class.

At times, you will want to override operators so that an object of your class can be on the right side of the operator. To do this, you often must declare the operator to be a friend function, so that it can access private data members of your class.

Using Streams

Streams provide the basic input and output functionality to your program. The iostream libraries provided with every C++ compiler override the insertion and extraction operators for all the built-in types, although you are free to extend this to user-defined types as well. Manipulators and other member functions of this library provide for formatting and manipulating both input and output of text and binary data. The data can come from the keyboard or from the disk and can go out to the monitor or to permanent storage.

Using Exceptions

Exceptions are objects that can be created and "thrown" at points in the program where the executing code cannot handle the error or other exceptional condition that has arisen. Other parts of the program, higher in the call stack, implement catch *blocks*, which catch the exception and take appropriate action.

Exceptions are normal user-created objects and, as such, can be passed by value or by reference. They can contain data and methods, and the catch block can use that data to decide how to deal with the exception.

It is possible to create multiple catch blocks, but once an exception matches a catch block's signature, it is considered to be handled and is not given to the subsequent catch blocks. It is important to order the catch blocks appropriately, so that more specific catch blocks have first chance, and more general catch blocks handle those not otherwise handled.

Writing Large Programs

The goal of object-oriented programming is to provide the programmer with the tools needed to manage large, complex solutions to difficult programming problems. Although there are thousands of useful tiny utilities available on bulletin board systems nationwide, the truly interesting, commercially feasible programs are getting larger and more complicated every day.

In order to manage this complexity, the programmer must be able to move up and down through the different levels of abstraction and organization with the program. To make this more manageable, most C++ programmers use two files for every class they create: a header file for the interface to the class and a .cp file for the implementation of the class's methods. That is the style this book uses.

Compiling each of these files when they change and linking them together can become a major project. The classic solution to this problem is the make file.

Looking At Style Guidelines

Large programs, especially those worked on by more than one programmer, can become difficult to maintain if consistent programming style rules are not used. One programmer might write the following, for example.

```
while (someCondition){
    someAction(int x);
}
```

Another programmer might write this:

```
while ( some condition )
{
    someAction( int x );
};
```

With enough variation, it becomes difficult for a programmer to read through the code recognizing where conditions end, what variables refer to, and so on. It is important to adopt a consistent coding style, although in many ways it doesn't matter *which* style you adopt. A consistent style makes it easier to guess what you meant by a particular part of the code, and avoids having to look up whether you spelled the function with an initial cap or a lowercase letter the last time you invoked it.

Note: The following guidelines are *arbitrary*; they are based on the guidelines used in projects I've worked on in the past, and they've worked well. You can just as easily make up your own, but these will get you started.

Although Emerson said, "A foolish consistency is the hobgoblin of little minds," having some consistency in your code is a good thing. Make up your own, but then treat your code as if it were dispensed by the programming gods.

Indenting

A good size for tab spacing is three or four spaces; this keeps the listings narrow enough to print well. Where the editor allows it, use tabs rather than multiple spaces; this enables other programmers to reformat your code to their liking.

Braces

Matching braces should be aligned vertically. The outermost set of braces in a definition or declaration should be at the left margin. Statements within should be indented. All other sets of braces should be in line with their leading statement. No code should appear on the same line as a brace. An example of the correct use of code follows:

```
if ()
{
    j = k;
    foo();
}
m++;
```

Long Lines

Even though your editor will allow wider lines, keep lines to the width displayable on a single screen. Code that is off to the right easily is overlooked, and scrolling horizontally is annoying. When a single logical line is broken, indent the following lines. Try to break the line at a rational point, and try to leave the intervening operator at the end of the preceding line (rather than the beginning of the following line) so that it is clear that the line does not stand alone and that there is more code coming.

Switch Statements

Indent switches as follows, to conserve horizontal space:

```
switch(variable)
{
case ValueOne:
    ActionOne();
    break;
case ValueTwo:
    ActionTwo();
    break;
default:
    assert("bad Action");
    break;
}
```

Program Text

There are several tips you can use to create code that is easy to read. Easy-to-read code is easy to maintain.

- ☐ Use white space to help readability.

- ☐ Objects and arrays really are referring to one thing. Don't use spaces within object references (., ->, or [ ]).

- ☐ Unary operators are associated with their operand, so don't put a space between them. Do put a space on the side away from the operand. Unary operators include !, ~, ++, --, -, * (for pointers), & (casts), and sizeof.

- ☐ Binary operators should have spaces on both sides—for example, 6 + 7, x = 10, and so on.

- ☐ Don't use lack of spaces to indicate a precedence. For example, don't write: (4+ 3*2). Instead, write (4 + 3 * 2) or, ((4 + 3) * 2).

- ☐ Put a space *after* commas and semicolons rather than *before*.

- ☐ Parentheses should not have spaces on either side. For example x = (5 + 3).

- ☐ Keywords, such as if, should be set off by a space: if (a == b).

- ☐ The body of a comment should be set off from the // with a space.

- ☐ Place the pointer or reference indicator next to the type name, not the variable name. For example,

    ```
    char* foo;
    int& theInt;
    ```

    rather than

    ```
    char *foo;
    int &theInt;
    ```

☐ Do *not* declare more than one variable on the same line. For example rather than writing

```
int x, y;
```

write
```
int x;
int y;
```

Identifier Names

Here are some guidelines for working with identifiers:

☐ Identifier names should be long enough to be descriptive.

☐ Avoid cryptic abbreviations.

☐ Take the time and energy to spell things out.

☐ Do not use Hungarian notation. C++ is strongly typed, and there is no reason to put the type into the variable name. With user-defined types (classes), Hungarian notation quickly breaks down. The exception to this may be to use a prefix for pointers (p) and references (r), as well as for class member variables (its).

☐ Short names (i, p, x, and so on) should be used only where their brevity makes the code more readable *and* where the usage is so obvious that a descriptive name is not needed.

☐ The length of a variable's name should be proportional to its scope.

☐ Make sure that identifiers look and sound different from one another to minimize confusion.

☐ Function (or method) names usually are verbs or verb-noun phrases: Search(), Reset(), FindParagraph(), and ShowCursor(), for example. Variable names usually are abstract nouns, possibly with an additional noun: count, state, windSpeed, and windowHeight, for example. Boolean variables should be named appropriately: windowIconized and fileIsOpen, for example.

Spelling and Capitalization of Names

Spelling and capitalization should not be overlooked when creating your own style. Some tips for these areas include the following:

☐ Use all uppercase and underscore characters to separate the logical words of names, such as SOURCE_FILE_TEMPLATE. Note, however, that these are rare in C++. Consider using constants and templates in most cases.

All other identifiers should use mixed case—no underscores. Function names, methods, class, `typedef`, and `struct` names should begin with a capitalized letter. Elements, such as data members or locals, should begin with a lowercase letter.

Enumerated constants should begin with a few lowercase letters as an abbreviation for the `enum`. For example,

```
enum TextStyle
{
    tsPlain,
    tsBold,
    tsItalic,
    tsUnderscore,
};
```

Comments

Comments can make it much easier to understand a program. Often, you will not work on a program for several days or even months. After this amount of time, you can forget what certain code does or why it was included. Problems in understanding code also can occur when someone else reads your code. Comments that are applied in a consistent, well thought-out style can be well worth the effort. There are several tips to remember concerning comments:

Wherever possible, use C++ `//` comments rather than the `/* */` style.

Higher level comments are infinitely more important than process details. Add value; do not merely restate the code. For example,

```
n++;    // n is incremented by one
```

Concentrate on the semantics of functions and blocks of code. Say what a function does. Indicate side effects, types of parameters, and return values. Describe all assumptions that are made (or not made), such as "assumes n is non-negative" or "will return −1 if x is invalid." Within complex logic, use comments to indicate the conditions that exist at that point in the code.

Use complete English sentences with appropriate punctuation and capitalization. The extra typing is worth it. Don't be overly cryptic and don't abbreviate. What seems exceedingly clear to you as you write code will be amazingly obtuse in a few months.

Use blank lines freely to help the reader understand what is going on. Separate statements into logical groups.

Access

The way you access portions of your program also should be consistent. Some tips for access include the following:

- Always use public:, private:, and protected: labels; don't rely on the defaults.

- List the public members first, then protected, then private. This makes it easy to find each section when reading the declaration. List the data members in a group after the methods.

- Put the constructor(s) first in the appropriate section, followed by the destructor. List overloaded methods with the same name adjacent to each other. Group accessor functions together when possible.

- Consider alphabetizing the method names within each group and alphabetizing the member variables. Be sure to alphabetize the file names in include statements.

- Even though the use of the virtual keyword is optional when overriding, use it anyway; it helps to remind you that it is virtual, and also keeps the declaration consistent.

Constants

Use const wherever appropriate: for parameters, variables, and methods. Often, there is a need for both a const and a non-const version of a method; don't use this as an excuse to leave one out. Be very careful when explicitly casting from const to non-const and vice versa—there are times when this is the only way to do something—but be certain that it makes sense, and include a comment.

Note: The use of const in your code enlists the compiler in helping you find bugs in your code. Remember, bugs found at compile time are easier to find and fix than bugs found at runtime!

The Project

This book concentrates on a single project that serves as the departure point for a number of programming issues. Like many programmers, I collect a thousand notes during the course of a week. These include ideas for this book, tips on how to accomplish something with the local area network, programming ideas, bugs to fix, and so on.

I've often wished for a simple utility that would let me type in a note and then get it back quickly when I need it. Such a Personal Information Manager (PIM) makes an ideal project for this book, because it requires all the skills you'll be learning in the next three weeks.

The key idea behind this project is that the user will not have to provide a subject, keywords, or categories to the message until the messages are retrieved! The average PIM forces you to provide sort criteria when you save the message. This is unfortunate, because it slows you down and decreases the likelihood that you'll use the product.

This project, which we'll call ROBIN, does not have that requirement; you just type your note and forget it. When you save it, the note is indexed and stored, and ROBIN finds it when you need it.

ROBIN can be written for a non-graphical environment such as DOS or UNIX, and then the heart of the program easily can be ported to a GUI such as Windows or Mac. This book focuses on building the preliminary portable version. When you are done, you will have learned a great deal about databases and the more advanced aspects of C++. You also will have a program that you then can expand and enhance. Along the way, you will learn a lot about writing portable code and the fundamentals of event-driven programming.

The most effective way to work on a project is to design your program, write a bit of functionality, try it out, fix it, adjust your design, and then write some more. The project evolves and builds itself up in stages. But don't be fooled, this approach requires *more* up-front design—not less.

The ROBIN project anticipates a number of enhancements that you will not implement for version 1, such as a full-screen editor, a GUI interface complete with menus and display windows, and so on.

Prior even to version 1, there will be intermediate preliminary versions. For example, an early version will not sort the notes; later versions will sort them in increasingly efficient ways. Faster search algorithms will be added as you progress, and better ways to organize the data will be tried in turn. Early versions of ROBIN will not bother writing the data to the disk; all the data will be stored in memory. Later versions will explore approaches to writing the data to disk in a way that provides optimal retrieval speed.

You will refine and build the program as new skills and techniques are discussed. Each subsequent iteration of the program will provide real-world experience with new methodologies.

Understanding How ROBIN Works

When you invoke ROBIN version 1.0, you will do so with either the keywords Add or Find. Robin Add can be followed either by text on the command line, or by the switch -F followed by the name of a text file.

If a text file is provided, a new note will be created from that file. If a file is not provided, the text following the keyword Add will be used for the new note.

In either case, the note will be date stamped, numbered, indexed, and saved for later retrieval.

To find a note, you enter `Robin Find` followed by one or more terms. ROBIN will print a menu of matching notes, displaying the first few words of the message and the date of the note, like this:

```
C:>Robin find Using Member Functions of Classes
[1] Using Member Functions in C++       5/5/94
[2] Member Functions and Classes        10/1/94
[3] C++ Functions and Member Data       8/3/93
[4] Functions and C++ Member Access     7/10/89
```

In the preliminary version that you will develop in the next few weeks, only a brute force match will be made on all the terms entered; the messages will be ordered first by how many words match and then by date. Enhancements to ROBIN might include the capability to enter phrases rather than individual words, the capability to score results based on proximity (how close the words are to one another), and so on. You might want to add a thesaurus to the program, allowing for searches on synonyms, so that *member function* would match notes with the word *method*, and so on.

When and if you port the program to a graphical environment, such as Windows, you will have the option of adding a fancier and more flexible user interface. If a multitasking environment such as UNIX or Windows 95 is available, the indexing and searching can be done in the background.

Reinventing the Wheel

In a real-world project, you would constantly be evaluating the build/buy decision. Often, it makes more sense to buy a class library that does much of what you need, rather than writing your own. For the purposes of this book, however, you will write your own classes, starting with the string class.

Each "note" will have a number of strings of various lengths, and you will depend heavily on a good, robust, String class. You'll write your String class on day 3, "Strings and Lists," and it will be the linchpin of your project, which you will develop over the full three weeks.

Relating ROBIN to Your Own Projects

It is easy, in a programming book, to become overfocused on the demonstration program. The *point* of this book, however, is not to teach you how to create a Personal Information Manager, or even how to create a database, but how to apply a series of advanced techniques and skills to solve real-world problems. The program written here is a prototype of a design and creation *process* that you will be able to transfer to your own programs.

Summary

Today you reviewed the fundamentals of C++. This review included a quick survey of the basic object-oriented programming concepts of inheritance, encapsulation, and polymorphism.

You also reviewed how memory is allocated and used in C++ programs, how the stack works, and how pointers and references are manipulated. The core elements of the language were reviewed, including arrays, class constructors and destructors, as well as operator and function overloading.

Advanced topics reviewed included multiple inheritance, abstract data types, static members and friends, and exceptions. Finally, make files were reviewed and a set of somewhat arbitrary style guidelines were offered.

Q&A

Q What do I do if some of this is new material?

A It is imperative that you are comfortable with this material before going on. I strongly recommend picking up a good C++ Primer, such as *Teach Yourself C++ In 21 Days* by Jesse Liberty (ISBN: 0-672-30541-0), published by Sams Publishing, 1994.

Q What compiler is required for the rest of this book?

A The code in this book is designed to be platform independent, and should work with any compiler that supports iostreams.

Q What about Windows, Mac, and X Window programming?

A The graphical user interfaces (GUIs) are complex development environments. This book does not attempt to teach you how to write programs for the GUIs, but it does equip you with the advanced programming skills you'll need when you do write professional programs in these environments.

Workshop

In future chapters, the Workshop will provide quiz questions to help you solidify your understanding of the material covered and exercises to provide you with experience in using what you've learned. Today, however, use the Workshop quiz and exercises as a preliminary qualifying exam to prove to yourself that you understand all the aspects of C++ that you will need for the work to come. Try to answer the quiz and exercise questions before checking the answers in Appendix A, and make sure that you understand the answers before continuing to the next chapter.

Quiz

1. Provide the header for a constant member function getText() of the class String, which returns a constant pointer to a constant string of characters and takes no parameters.

2. What is the difference between const int * ptrOne and int * const ptrTwo?

3. How does the copy constructor differ from the assignment operator (=)?

4. What is the *this* pointer?

5. What is a v-table?

6. If you create two classes, Horse and Bird, and they inherit virtual public from the base class Animal, do their constructors initialize the Animal constructor? If you then create a new class, Pegasus, which inherits from both Horse and Bird, how does it initialize Animal's constructor?

7. What is the difference between *containment* and *delegation*?

8. What is the difference between *delegation* and *implemented in terms of*?

9. What is the difference between *public* and *private* inheritance?

10. What are the three forms of cin.get() and what are their differences?

11. What is the difference between cin.read() and cin.getline()?

Exercises

1. Write two small programs—one with recursion, and one using iteration—to print out the *n*th number in a Fibonnacci series. (The *Fibonnacci* series is 0,1,1,2,3,5,8... where each number is the sum of the previous two, except the first two, which are zero and one.)

2. Write a short program declaring a class with three member variables and one static member variable. Have the constructor initialize the member variables and increment the static member variable. Have the destructor decrement the static member variable.

   Write a short driver program that makes three objects of your class and then displays their member variables and the static member variable. Then destroy each object and show the effect on the static member variable.

3. Write a program that takes a file name as a parameter and opens the file for reading. Read every character of the file and display only the letters and punctuation to the screen (ignore all non-printing characters). Then close the file and exit.

4. Create a try block, a catch statement, and a hierarchy of exceptions. Put data into the exceptions, along with an accessor function, and use the data in the catch block. Test this with a driver program that uses three levels of function calls.

2

WEEK
1

Templates

The capability to create parameterized types is essential to advanced programming. Because this capability can be a source of enormous confusion, and because this book relies on templates to a great extent, today you will review templates in depth. You will learn

☐ What templates are and how to create them

☐ How to create `Template` classes, functions, and member functions

☐ How to specialize the functionality of template functions for particular types

☐ How to write template static functions and friend functions

Note: All modern C++ compilers now support templates and exceptions in one form or another. Although minor differences may exist in how exceptions are implemented, if your compiler has templates, they will work as described today. Check your documentation, however, because some older compilers do not implement templates at all (if you are working with an older compiler, you can read along but not try these exercises). In time, you may want to upgrade to a more up-to-date compiler.

Note: Visual C++ 1.52b does not support "templates." It uses a macro to implement templates and trick the compiler. Consult Technical Note #4 from the Visual C++ documentation for more information on how to work around templates in Visual C++ 2.

The Fundamentals

Templates are a built-in facility of C++ used to create *parameterized types*: types that change their behavior based on parameters passed in at creation. Using parameterized types is a way to reuse code safely and effectively.

NEW☞
TERM *Parameterized types* are classes that change their behavior based on parameters passed in at creation time.

In metal- or woodworking, a template is a mold used to turn out the same pattern again and again. A C++ template tells the compiler how to create a type of object, substituting the parameters you provide at compile time. A list template, for example, tells the compiler how to

create a list; then, at compile time you can specify a list of car parts, a list of children, a list of numbers, and a list of things to do. The template encapsulates the list-specific capabilities, and the parameters apply the list to different types of objects.

Unlike macros, templates are a built-in part of the language. Templates are type-safe, and parameterized types can be used wherever other types can be used.

Template Instances

Each time you declare an instance of a template, the compiler creates a declaration for the class and instantiates an actual object. These objects can be used like any other object—as a parameter to a function, as a return value, and so on.

`Template` classes can declare three types of friend functions: nontemplate, general template, and type-specific template. A template can declare static data members, in which case each instance of the template has its own set of static data.

Note: Templates are used throughout this book, so it is essential that you are fully comfortable with them.

Template Definition

You can declare a parameterized array object (a template for an array) by using the following code:

```
1:    template <class T>  // declare the template and the parameter
2:    class Array          // the class being parameterized
3:    {
4:    public:
5:      Array();
6:    // full class declaration here
7:    };
```

The keyword `template` is used at the beginning of every declaration and definition of a `Template` class. After the keyword `template` are the parameters of the template. The parameters are the items that will change with each instance. In the array template shown here, for example, the type of the objects stored in the array will change; one instance might store an array of integers, and another might store an array of controls (list boxes, buttons, and so on) in a window.

In this example, the keyword `class` is used, followed by the identifier `T`. The keyword `class` indicates that this parameter is a *type*. The identifier `T` is used throughout the rest of the template definition to refer to the parameterized type. One instance of this class will substitute `int` everywhere `T` appears; another will substitute `Window`.

To declare an int and a Window instance of the Parameterized Array class, use the following code:

```
Array<int> anIntArray;
Array<Window> aWindowArray;
```

The object anIntArray is of the type *array of integers*; the object aWindowArray is of the type *array of Windows*. You now can use the type Array<int> anywhere you normally would use a type—as the return value from a function, as a parameter to a function, and so on. Listing 2.1 provides the full declaration of this stripped-down array template.

Note: Although Microsoft's 32-bit (Visual C++ 2.0) compiler does support templates, the Microsoft 16-bit compiler used with DOS and Windows 3.1 (Visual C++ 1.5) does not support templates. Many other compilers for Windows 3.1 do support templates, however.

Listing 2.1 A Template of an Array Class

```
1:      #include <iostream.h>
2:
3:      const int DefaultSize = 10;
4:
5:      template <class T>  // declare the template and the parameter
6:      class Array          // the class being parameterized
7:      {
8:      public:
9:          // constructors
10:         Array(int itsSize = DefaultSize);
11:         Array(const Array &rhs);
12:         ~Array() { delete [] pType; }
13:
14:         // operators
15:         Array& operator=(const Array&);
16:         Type& operator[](int offSet) { return pType[offSet]; }
17:
18:         // accessors
19:         int getSize() { return itsSize; }
20:
21:      private:
22:          Type *pType;
23:          int  itsSize;
24:      };
```

     None.

 The definition of the template begins in line 5 with the keyword `template` followed by the parameter. In this case, the parameter is identified to be a type, by the keyword `class`, and the identifier T is used.

From line 6 until the end of the template in line 24, the rest of the declaration is like any other class declaration—except that wherever the type of the object normally would appear, the identifier T is used instead. For example, `operator[]` would be expected to return a reference to an object in the array and, in fact, it is declared to return a reference to a T.

When an instance of an `int` array is declared, the `operator=` provided to that array will return a reference to an integer. When an instance of an `Animal` array is declared, the `operator=` provided to the `Animal` array will return a reference to an `Animal`.

Using the Name

Within the class declaration, the word `Array` may be used without further qualification. Elsewhere in the program, this class will be referred to as `Array<T>`. If you do not write the constructor within class declaration, for example, you must write an implementation as shown in listing 2.2.

 Listing 2.2 An Array Class Constructor Template Definition

```
1:   template <class T>
2:   Array<T>::Array(int size):
3:   itsSize = size
4:   {
5:     pType = new T[size];
6:     for (int i = 0; i<size; i++)
7:         pType[i] = 0;
8:   }
```

 None.

 The declaration in line 1 is required to identify the type (`class T`). The template name is `Array<T>` and the function name is `Array(int size)`.

The remainder of the function is exactly the same as it would be for a nontemplate function. This is a common and preferred method to get the class and its functions working as a simple declaration before turning it into a template.

Implementing the Template

The full implementation of the `Template` class array requires implementing the copy constructor, `operator=`, and so on. Listing 2.3 provides a simple driver program to exercise this `Template` class.

Listing 2.3 Implementation of the Template Array

```
1:     #include <iostream.h>
2:
3:     const int DefaultSize = 10;
4:
5:     // declare a simple Animal class so that we can
6:     // create an array of animals
7:
8:     class Animal
9:     {
10:    public:
11:       Animal(int);
12:       Animal();
13:       ~Animal() {}
14:       int GetWeight() const { return itsWeight; }
15:       void Display() const { cout << itsWeight; }
16:    private:
17:       int itsWeight;
18:    };
19:
20:    Animal::Animal(int weight):
21:    itsWeight(weight)
22:    {}
23:
24:    Animal::Animal():
25:    itsWeight(0)
26:    {}
27:
28:
29:    template <class T>  // declare the template and the parameter
30:    class Array              // the class being parameterized
31:    {
32:    public:
33:       // constructors
34:       Array(int itsSize = DefaultSize);
35:       Array(const Array &rhs);
36:       ~Array() { delete [] pType; }
37:
38:       // operators
39:       Array& operator=(const Array&);
40:       T& operator[](int offSet) { return pType[offSet]; }
41:       const T& operator[](int offSet) const { return pType[offSet]; }
42:
43:       // accessors
44:       int GetSize() const { return itsSize; }
45:
46:    private:
47:       T *pType;
48:       int  itsSize;
49:    };
50:
51:    // implementations follow...
52:
53:    // implement the constructor
54:    template <class T>
```

```
55:    Array<T>::Array(int size):
56:    itsSize(size)
57:    {
58:        pType = new T[size];
59:        for (int i = 0; i<size; i++)
60:            pType[i] = 0;
61:    }
62:
63:    // copy constructor
64:    template <class T>
65:    Array<T>::Array(const Array &rhs)
66:    {
67:        itsSize = rhs.GetSize();
68:        pType = new T[itsSize];
69:        for (int i = 0; i<itsSize; i++)
70:            pType[i] = rhs[i];
71:    }
72:
73:    // operator=
74:    template <class T>
75:    Array<T>& Array<T>::operator=(const Array &rhs)
76:    {
77:        if (this == &rhs)
78:            return *this;
79:        delete [] pType;
80:        itsSize = rhs.GetSize();
81:        pType = new T[itsSize];
82:        for (int i = 0; i<itsSize; i++)
83:            pType[i] = rhs[i];
84:        return *this;
85:    }
86:
87:    // driver program
88:    void main()
89:    {
90:        Array<int> theArray;      // an array of integers
91:        Array<Animal> theZoo;     // an array of Animals
92:        Animal *pAnimal;
93:
94:        // fill the arrays
95:        for (int i = 0; i < theArray.GetSize(); i++)
96:        {
97:            theArray[i] = i*2;
98:            pAnimal = new Animal(i*3);
99:            theZoo[i] = *pAnimal;
100:       }
101:
102:       // print the contents of the arrays
103:       for (int j = 0; j < theArray.GetSize(); j++)
104:       {
105:           cout << "theArray[" << j << "]:\t" << theArray[j] << "\t\t";
106:           cout << "theZoo[" << j << "]:\t";
107:           theZoo[j].Display();
108:           cout << endl;
109:       }
110:   }
```

theArray[0]:	0	theZoo[0]:	0
theArray[1]:	2	theZoo[1]:	3
theArray[2]:	4	theZoo[2]:	6
theArray[3]:	6	theZoo[3]:	9
theArray[4]:	8	theZoo[4]:	12
theArray[5]:	10	theZoo[5]:	15
theArray[6]:	12	theZoo[6]:	18
theArray[7]:	14	theZoo[7]:	21
theArray[8]:	16	theZoo[8]:	24
theArray[9]:	18	theZoo[9]:	27

Lines 8 through 26 provide a minimal `Animal` class, created here so that there are objects of a user-defined type to add to the array. In lines 11 and 12, the constructors are declared; in line 13, the destructor is defined inline.

Lines 14 and 15 provide simple inline accessor functions, and lines 20 through 26 provide the implementations to the constructors.

Line 29 starts the template definition of the `Parameterized Array` class. The keyword `template` in line 29 declares that what follows is a template, and that the parameter to the template is a *type*, designated as `T`. The array class has two constructors as shown, the first of which takes a size and defaults to the constant int `DefaultSize`.

The assignment and offset operators are declared (lines 39 and 40), with the latter declaring both a `const` and a non-`const` variant. The only accessor provided is `GetSize()`, which returns the size of the array (line 44).

One certainly can imagine a fuller interface, and for any serious `Array` program, what has been supplied would be inadequate. A minimum requirement would be operators to remove elements, to expand the array, to pack the array, and so on.

The private data consists of the size of the array and a pointer to the actual in-memory array of objects.

The implementation of the parameterized methods follows, beginning in line 54. Note that each function begins with the `template` keyword, and everywhere the type would be used (`Animal`, in this case), the designation `T` is used instead.

The *type* of the `Array` can be thought of as *ArrayOfAnimal* or *ArrayOfInt*. The designation for this is `Array<T>`, which the compiler treats as `Array<Animal>` or `Array<int>` at runtime. Note that you *cannot* write `Array<Animal>` in your code—this is for illustration purposes only.

Note also that `T` becomes a synonym for the type. So that you see in line 47 that the pointer is declared to be a pointer to `T`, you allocate memory in line 68 by writing `new T[]`.

In lines 90 and 91 in the driver program, two *instances* of the parameterized `Array` type are declared. The first, in line 90, is an array of integers (`Array<int>`). This designates that everywhere the template had `T`, it now should use `int`.

In line 91, an array of the user-defined `Animal` type is declared, which works in *exactly* the same way as the array of `int` works.

In line 97, `theArray`, which is an array of integers, is filled with integers. In line 99, `theZoo`, which is an array of `Animals`, is initialized with `Animal` objects.

In line 105, the members of the integer array `theArray` each are accessed. In line 107, the members of the `Animal` array, `theZoo`, are accessed in turn *using the same parameterized offset accessor!*

DO	**DON'T**

Working with Parameterized Types

DO use parameterized types (templates) to create flexible containers and functions.

DO remember to use the parameterized type wherever the actual type should be used.

DON'T forget that at compile time, each instance of the parameterized type will be created by the compiler, just as if you had written it explicitly.

DO use templates to provide code reuse and type-safe flexibility in your programs.

DO consider using templates rather than inheritance, where applicable.

Template Functions

If you want to pass an array object to a function, you must pass a particular *instance* of the array—not a template. If `SomeFunction()` takes an integer array as a parameter, therefore, you may write

```
void SomeFunction(Array<int>&);    // ok
```

but you may not write

```
void SomeFunction(Array<T>&);    // error!
```

because there is no way to know what a `T&` is. You also may not write

```
void SomeFunction(Array &);    // error!
```

because there is no class `Array`—there just are the template and the instances.

To accomplish the more general approach, you must declare a function template:

```
template <class T>
void MyTemplateFunction(Array<T>&);    // ok
```

Here, the function `MyTemplateFunction()` is declared to be a template function by the declaration in the preceding line. Note that template functions can have any name, just as other functions can.

Template functions also can take instances of the template, in addition to the parameterized form. Here's an example:

```
template <class T>
void MyOtherFunction(Array<T>&, Array<int>&);     // ok
```

Note that this function takes two arrays: a parameterized array and an array of integers. The former can be an array of any object, but the latter is always an array of integers.

Using Template Items

You can treat template items as you would any other type. You can pass them as parameters, either by reference or by value, and you can return them as the return values of functions, also by value or by reference. Listing 2.4 demonstrates passing template objects.

Listing 2.4 Passing Template Objects to and from Functions

```
1:     // Listing 2.4 - Passing Template Objects to and from Functions
2:
3:     #include <iostream.h>
4:
5:     const int DefaultSize = 10;
6:
7:     // A trivial class for adding to arrays
8:     class Animal
9:     {
10:    public:
11:    // constructors
12:        Animal(int);
13:        Animal();
14:        ~Animal();
15:
16:        // accessors
17:        int GetWeight() const { return itsWeight; }
18:        void SetWeight(int theWeight) { itsWeight = theWeight; }
19:
20:         // friend operators
21:        friend ostream& operator<< (ostream&, const Animal&);
22:
23:    private:
24:        int itsWeight;
25:    };
26:
27:    // extraction operator for printing animals
28:    ostream& operator<< (ostream& theStream, const Animal& theAnimal)
29:    {
30:    theStream << theAnimal.GetWeight();
31:    return theStream;
```

```
32:        }
33:
34:        Animal::Animal(int weight):
35:        itsWeight(weight)
36:        {
37:            // cout << "Animal(int)\n";
38:        }
39:
40:        Animal::Animal():
41:        itsWeight(0)
42:        {
43:            // cout << "Animal()\n";
44:        }
45:
46:        Animal::~Animal()
47:        {
48:           // cout << "Destroyed an animal...\n";
49:        }
50:
51:        template <class T>  // declare the template and the parameter
52:        class Array          // the class being parameterized
53:        {
54:        public:
55:           Array(int itsSize = DefaultSize);
56:           Array(const Array &rhs);
57:           ~Array() { delete [] pType; }
58:
59:           Array& operator=(const Array&);
60:           T& operator[](int offSet) { return pType[offSet]; }
61:           const T& operator[](int offSet) const { return pType[offSet]; }
62:           int GetSize() const { return itsSize; }
63:
64:
65:        private:
66:           T *pType;
67:           int  itsSize;
68:        };
69:
70:        template <class T>
71:        ostream& operator<< (ostream& output, const Array<T>& theArray)
72:        {
73:           for (int i = 0; i<theArray.GetSize(); i++)
74:              output << "[" << i << "] " << theArray[i] << endl;
75:           return output;
76:        }
77:        // implement the constructor
78:        template <class T>
79:        Array<T>::Array(int size):
80:        itsSize(size)
81:        {
82:           pType = new T[size];
83:           for (int i = 0; i<size; i++)
84:              pType[i] = 0;
85:        }
86:
```

continues

Listing 2.4 continued

```
87:     // copy constructor
88:     template <class T>
89:     Array<T>::Array(const Array &rhs)
90:     {
91:         itsSize = rhs.GetSize();
92:         pType = new T[itsSize];
93:         for (int i = 0; i<itsSize; i++)
94:             pType[i] = rhs[i];
95:     }
96:
97:     // operator=
98:     template <class T>
99:     Array<T>& Array<T>::operator=(const Array &rhs)
100:    {
101:        if (this == &rhs)
102:            return *this;
103:        delete [] pType;
104:        itsSize = rhs.GetSize();
105:        pType = new T[itsSize];
106:        for (int i = 0; i<itsSize; i++)
107:            pType[i] = rhs[i];
108:        return *this;
109:    }
110:
111:
112:
113:    void IntFillFunction(Array<int>& theArray);
114:    void AnimalFillFunction(Array<Animal>& theArray);
115:    enum BOOL {FALSE, TRUE};
116:
117:    void main()
118:    {
119:        Array<int> intArray;
120:        Array<Animal> animalArray;
121:        IntFillFunction(intArray);
122:        AnimalFillFunction(animalArray);
123:        cout << "intArray...\n" << intArray;
124:        cout << "\nanimalArray...\n" << animalArray << endl;
125:    }
126:
127:    void IntFillFunction(Array<int>& theArray)
128:    {
129:        BOOL Stop = FALSE;
130:        int offset, value;
131:        while (!Stop)
132:        {
133:            cout << "Enter an offset (0-9) and a value. (-1 to stop): " ;
134:            cin >> offset >> value;
135:            if (offset < 0)
136:                break;
137:            if (offset > 9)
138:            {
139:                cout << "***Please use values between 0 and 9.***\n";
140:                continue;
```

```
141:          }
142:              theArray[offset] = value;
143:          }
144:      }
145:
146:
147:      void AnimalFillFunction(Array<Animal>& theArray)
148:      {
149:          Animal * pAnimal;
150:          for (int i = 0; i<theArray.GetSize(); i++)
151:          {
152:              pAnimal = new Animal;
153:              pAnimal->SetWeight(i*100);
154:              theArray[i] = *pAnimal;
155:              delete pAnimal;  // a copy was put in the array
156:          }
157:      }
```

Output

```
Enter an offset (0-9) and a value. (-1 to stop): 1 10
Enter an offset (0-9) and a value. (-1 to stop): 2 20
Enter an offset (0-9) and a value. (-1 to stop): 3 30
Enter an offset (0-9) and a value. (-1 to stop): 4 40
Enter an offset (0-9) and a value. (-1 to stop): 5 50
Enter an offset (0-9) and a value. (-1 to stop): 6 60
Enter an offset (0-9) and a value. (-1 to stop): 7 70
Enter an offset (0-9) and a value. (-1 to stop): 8 80
Enter an offset (0-9) and a value. (-1 to stop): 9 90
Enter an offset (0-9) and a value. (-1 to stop): 10 10
***Please use values between 0 and 9. ***
Enter an offset (0-9) and a value. (-1 to stop): -1 -1

intArray:...
[0] 0
[1] 10
[2] 20
[3] 30
[4] 40
[5] 50
[6] 60
[7] 70
[8] 80
[9] 90

animalArray:...
[0] 0
[1] 100
[2] 200
[3] 300
[4] 400
[5] 500
[6] 600
[7] 700
[8] 800
[9] 900
```

Analysis The `Animal` class is declared in lines 7 through 24. Although this is a minimal class declaration, it does provide its own insertion operator (<<) to allow printing of the animal's weight.

Note that `Animal` has a default constructor, declared in line 13 and defined in lines 40 through 44. This is necessary because when you add an object to an array, its default constructor is used to create the object. This creates some difficulties, as you will see.

In line 113, the function `IntFillFunction()` is declared. The prototype indicates that this function takes an *integer array*. Note that this is *not* a template function; it expects only one type of an array: an integer array. Similarly, in line 114, `AnimalFillFunction()` is declared to take an array of `Animals`.

The implementations for these functions are different from one another, because filling an array of integers does not have to be accomplished in the same way as filling an array of `Animals`.

The implementation for `IntFillFunction()` is provided in lines 127 through 144. The user is prompted for a value, and that value is placed directly into the array.

In lines 147 through 157, the `AnimalFillFunction()` is defined, and this is quite different. The value provided by the user cannot be placed directly into the array. Instead, in line 152, a new `Animal` is created, and its weight is set to the value given by the user in line 153. The animal then is placed into the array, and the temporary pointer is deleted because it no longer is needed.

In a real-world program, you might consider having an array of pointers to `Animals` (or other large objects), rather than having an array of the objects themselves. This method can save significant stack space if the array is created on the stack.

Specialized Functions

If you uncomment the print statements in `Animal`'s constructors and destructor (lines 37 and 43 in listing 2.4); you will find that there are unanticipated extra constructions and destructions of `Animals`.

When an object is added to an array, its default constructor is called. The `Array` constructor, however, goes on to assign 0 to the value of each member of the array, as shown in lines 85 and 86 of listing 2.4.

When you write `someAnimal = (Animal) 0;` you call the default `operator=` for `Animal`. This causes a temporary `Animal` object to be created, using the constructor that takes an integer (zero). That temporary object is used on the right-hand side of the operator equals, and then is destroyed.

This is an unfortunate waste of time; the `Animal` object already was initialized properly. You cannot remove this line, however, because integers are *not* automatically initialized to value 0.

The solution is to teach the template not to use this constructor for `Animals`, but to use a special `Animal` constructor.

You can provide an explicit implementation for the `Animal` class, as indicated in listing 2.5.

 Listing 2.5 Specializing Template Implementations

```
1:     #include <iostream.h>
2:
3:     const int DefaultSize = 3;
4:
5:     // A trivial class for adding to arrays
6:       class Animal
7:       {
8:       public:
9:        // constructors
10:         Animal(int);
11:         Animal();
12:         ~Animal();
13:
14:         // accessors
15:         int GetWeight() const { return itsWeight; }
16:         void SetWeight(int theWeight) { itsWeight = theWeight; }
17:
18:          // friend operators
19:         friend ostream& operator<< (ostream&, const Animal&);
20:
21:       private:
22:           int itsWeight;
23:       };
24:
25:        // extraction operator for printing animals
26:       ostream& operator<< (ostream& theStream, const Animal& theAnimal)
27:       {
28:        theStream << theAnimal.GetWeight();
29:        return theStream;
30:       }
31:
32:       Animal::Animal(int weight):
33:       itsWeight(weight)
34:       {
35:          cout << "animal(int)\n";
36:       }
37:
38:       Animal::Animal():
39:       itsWeight(0)
40:       {
41:          cout << "animal()\n";
42:       }
43:
44:       Animal::~Animal()
45:       {
```

continues

Listing 2.5 continued

```
46:          cout << "Destroyed an animal...\n";
47:        }
48:
49:    template <class T>   // declare the template and the parameter
50:    class Array              // the class being parameterized
51:    {
52:    public:
53:        // constructors
54:        Array(int itsSize = DefaultSize);
55:        Array(const Array &rhs);
56:        ~Array() { delete [] pType; }
57:
58:        // operators
59:        Array& operator=(const Array&);
60:        T& operator[](int offSet) { return pType[offSet]; }
61:        const T& operator[](int offSet) const { return pType[offSet]; }
62:
63:        // accessors
64:        int GetSize() const { return itsSize; }
65:
66:
67:    private:
68:        T *pType;
69:        int  itsSize;
70:    };
71:
72:    template <class T>
73:    Array<T>::Array(int size):
74:    itsSize(size)
75:    {
76:        pType = new T[size];
77:        for (int i = 0; i<size; i++)
78:          pType[i] = (T)0;
79:    }
80:
81:    template <class T>
82:    Array<T>& Array<T>::operator=(const Array &rhs)
83:    {
84:        if (this == &rhs)
85:           return *this;
86:        delete [] pType;
87:        itsSize = rhs.GetSize();
88:        pType = new T[itsSize];
89:        for (int i = 0; i<itsSize; i++)
90:           pType[i] = rhs[i];
91:        return *this;
92:    }
93:
94:    template <class T>
95:    Array<T>::Array(const Array &rhs)
96:    {
97:        itsSize = rhs.GetSize();
98:        pType = new T[itsSize];
99:        for (int i = 0; i<itsSize; i++)
100:          pType[i] = rhs[i];
```

```
101:    }
102:
103:    template <class T>
104:    ostream& operator<< (ostream& output, const Array<T>& theArray)
105:    {
106:        for (int i = 0; i<theArray.GetSize(); i++)
107:            output << "[" << i << "] " << theArray[i] << endl;
108:        return output;
109:    }
110:
111:    template<classT>
112:    Array<Animal>::Array(int AnimalArraySize):
113:    itsSize(AnimalArraySize)
114:    {
115:        pType = new T[AnimalArraySize];
116:    }
117:
118:
119:    void IntFillFunction(Array<int>& theArray);
120:    void AnimalFillFunction(Array<Animal>& theArray);
121:    enum BOOL {FALSE, TRUE};
122:
123:    void main()
124:    {
125:        Array<int> intArray;
126:        Array<Animal> animalArray;
127:        IntFillFunction(intArray);
128:        AnimalFillFunction(animalArray);
129:        cout << "intArray...\n" << intArray;
130:        cout << "\nanimalArray...\n" << animalArray << endl;
131:    }
132:
133:    void IntFillFunction(Array<int>& theArray)
134:    {
135:        BOOL Stop = FALSE;
136:        int offset, value;
137:        while (!Stop)
138:        {
139:            cout << "Enter an offset (0-9) and a value. (-1 to stop): " ;
140:            cin >> offset >> value;
141:            if (offset < 0)
142:                break;
143:            if (offset > 2)
144:            {
145:                cout << "***Please use values between 0 and 2.***\n";
146:                continue;
147:            }
148:            theArray[offset] = value;
149:        }
150:    }
151:
152:
153:    void AnimalFillFunction(Array<Animal>& theArray)
154:    {
155:        Animal * pAnimal;
```

continues

Listing 2.5 continued

```
156:        for (int i = 0; i<theArray.GetSize(); i++)
157:        {
158:            pAnimal = new Animal(i*10);
159:            theArray[i] = *pAnimal;
160:            delete pAnimal;
161:        }
162:    }
```

Note: Line numbers have been added to the input to make analysis easier. Your output will not have these line numbers.

```
1:      animal()
2:      animal()
3:      animal()
4:      Enter an offset (0-9) and a value. (-1 to stop): 0 0
5:      Enter an offset (0-9) and a value. (-1 to stop): 1 1
6:      Enter an offset (0-9) and a value. (-1 to stop): 2 2
7:      Enter an offset (0-9) and a value. (-1 to stop): 3 3
***Please use values between 0 and 2.***
8:      Enter an offset (0-9) and a value. (-1 to stop): -1 -1
9:      animal(int)
10:     Destroyed an animal...
11:     animal(int)
12:     Destroyed an animal...
13:     animal(int)
14:     Destroyed an animal...
15:     intArray...
16:     [0] 0
17:     [1] 1
18:     [2] 2
19:
20:     animalArray...
21:     [0] 0
22:     [1] 10
23:     [2] 20
24:
25:     Destroyed an animal...
26:     Destroyed an animal...
27:     Destroyed an animal...
28:
29:     << second run >>
30:
31:     animal()
32:     animal()
33:     animal()
34:     animal(int)
35:     Destroyed an animal...
36:     animal(int)
37:     Destroyed an animal...
```

```
38:    animal(int)
39:    Destroyed an animal...
40:    Enter an offset (0-9) and a value. (-1 to stop): 0 0
41:    Enter an offset (0-9) and a value. (-1 to stop): 1 1
42:    Enter an offset (0-9) and a value. (-1 to stop): 2 2
***Please use values between 0 and 2.***
43:    Enter an offset (0-9) and a value. (-1 to stop): 3 3
44:    Enter an offset (0-9) and a value. (-1 to stop): -1 -1
45:    animal(int)
46:    Destroyed an animal...
47:    animal(int)
48:    Destroyed an animal...
49:    animal(int)
50:    Destroyed an animal...
51:    intArray...
52:    [0] 0
53:    [1] 1
54:    [2] 2
55:
56:    animalArray...
57:    [0] 0
58:    [1] 10
59:    [2] 20
60:
61:    Destroyed an animal...
62:    Destroyed an animal...
63:    Destroyed an animal...
```

Listing 2.5 reproduces both classes in their entirety so that you can see the creation and destruction of temporary `Animal` objects. The value of `DefaultSize` has been reduced to 3 to simplify the output.

The `Animal` constructors and destructors in lines 32 through 47 each print a statement indicating when they are called.

In lines 72 through 79, the template behavior of an `Array` constructor is declared. In lines 112 through 116, the specialized constructor for an `Array` of `Animal`s is demonstrated. Note that in this special constructor, the default constructor is allowed to set the initial value for each animal, and no explicit assignment is performed.

The first time this program is run, the first set of output is shown. Lines 1 through 3 of the output show the three default constructors called by creating the array. The user enters three numbers, and these are entered into the integer array.

Execution jumps to `AnimalFillFunction()`. Here, a temporary animal is created on the heap in line 158, and its value is used to modify the `Animal` object in the array in line 159. In line 160, the temporary `Animal` is destroyed. This process is repeated for each member of the array, and is reflected in the output in lines 9 through 15.

At the end of the program, the arrays are destroyed; and when their destructors are called, all their objects are destroyed as well. This is reflected in the output in lines 25 through 27.

For the second set of output (lines 31 through 63), the special implementation of the Array of character constructor (shown in lines 112 through 116 of the program) is commented out. When the program is run again, the template constructor (shown in lines 72 through 79 of the program) is run when the Animal array is constructed.

This process causes temporary Animal objects to be called for each member of the array in lines 77 and 78 of the program and is reflected in the output in lines 26 through 29 of the output.

In all other respects, the output for the two runs is identical, as you would expect.

Summary

Today you learned how to create and use templates. *Templates* are a built-in facility of C++ to create *parameterized types*—types that change their behavior based on parameters passed in at creation. These types are a way to reuse code safely and effectively.

The definition of the template determines the parameterized type. Each instance of the template is an actual object, which can be used like any other object—as a parameter to a function, as a return value, and so on.

Template classes can declare three types of friend functions: nontemplate, general template, and type-specific template. A template can declare static data members—in which case, each instance of the template has its own set of static data.

If you need to specialize behavior for some template functions based on the actual type, you can override a template function with a particular type. This process works for member functions as well.

Q&A

Q Why use templates when macros will do?

A Templates are type-safe and built into the language.

Q What is the difference between the parameterized type of a template function and the parameters to a normal function?

A A regular function (nontemplate) takes parameters on which it may take action. A template function enables you to parameterize the type of a particular parameter to the function. In other words, you can pass an array of type to a function, and then have the type determined by the template instance.

Q When do you use templates and when do you use inheritance?

A Use templates when all the behavior or virtually all the behavior is unchanged, except in regard to the type of the item on which your class acts. If you find yourself copying a class and changing only the type of one or more of its members, it may be time to consider using a template.

Q When do you use general `Template Friend` classes?

A You use general `Template Friend` classes when every instance, regardless of type, should be a friend to this class or function.

Q When do you use type-specific `Template Friend` classes or functions?

A You use these classes or functions when you want to establish a one-to-one relationship between two classes. For example, `array<int>` should match `iterator<int>` but not `iterator<Animal>`.

Q Are templates portable?

A Yes, templates are portable across all modern C++ compilers.

Q Do all compilers support templates?

A Nearly all new compilers support templates. Templates have been a part of the language since C++ 2.0, and are an accepted part of the emerging ANSI/ISO specification.

Workshop

The Workshop provides quiz questions to help you solidify your understanding of the material covered and exercises to provide you with experience in using what you have learned. Try to answer the quiz and exercise questions before checking the answers in Appendix A, and make sure that you understand the answers before continuing to the next chapter.

Quiz

1. What is the difference between a template and a macro?
2. What is the difference between the parameter in a template and the parameter in a function?
3. What is the difference between a type-specific `Template Friend` class and a general `Template Friend` class?
4. Is it possible to provide special behavior for one instance of a template but not for other instances?
5. How many static variables are created if you put one static member into a `Template` class definition?

Exercises

1. Create a template based on this `List` class:
   ```
   class List
   {
   private:
   ```

```
        public:
            List():head(0),tail(0),theCount(0) {}
            virtual ~List();

            void insert( int value );
            void append( int value );
            int is_present( int value ) const;
            int is_empty() const { return head == 0; }
            int count() const { return theCount; }
        private:
            class ListCell
            {
            public:
                ListCell(int value, ListCell *cell = 0)
                :val(value),next(cell){}
                int val;
                ListCell *next;
            };
            ListCell *head;
            ListCell *tail;
            int theCount;
        };
```

2. Write the implementation for the List class (nontemplate) version.

3. Write the template version of the implementations.

4. Declare three list objects: a list of strings, a list of windows, and a list of integers.

5. **BUG BUSTER:** What is wrong with the following code (assume that the List template is defined and Window is the class defined earlier in the book):

```
        List<Window> Window_List;
        Window Felix;
        WindowList.append( Felix );
        cout << "Felix is " <<
            ( Window_List.is_present( Felix ) ) ? "" : "not " <<
            "present\n";
```

Tip: HINT (this is tough): What makes the Window type different from int?

6. Declare friend operator==for List.

7. Implement friend operator==for List.

8. Does operator==have the same problem as in question 5?

9. Implement a template function for "swap" that exchanges two variables.

Strings and Lists

This book focuses on the manipulation of complex and powerful data structures. The fundamental data structure, beyond arrays and other built-in types, is the *list*.

Before you begin work on the list, however, you will need a good String class. Strings, of course, are essential in building your messaging system as described on day 1, and they will be an integral component of many of the other classes you will see today and on future days.

Today you will learn

☐ How to write the first iteration of your String class

☐ What a list is and what it can do for your program

☐ How to create a linked list

☐ How to create a linked list template

The String Class

The fundamental building block of your Note class will be strings. *Strings* are blocks of text such as sentences or paragraphs.

Your String class will allow for the creation and manipulation of variable-length sequences of characters. You decide to allow strings of zero to 65,535 characters; that is, you will index the strings using an unsigned int, and your strings will all fit in one 64K segment if you run your program on an 80x86 machine.

Your String class will look to the user like a C-style array of characters, but it will provide its own memory management, bounds checking, and sophisticated set of operators. Your preliminary design calls for supporting string concatenation and comparison, copying, and dynamic reallocation of memory as required.

You will overload const char * conversion operators so that your strings can be used wherever C-style strings are required, such as in standard library function calls. Other operators will enable you to directly access a *non-constant* char * if required.

You will treat the String object as a string—not as a pointer to a char *. You can allocate String objects on the stack or the heap, but each string object will manage its own internal memory on the heap. Clients of your String class therefore get the convenience of stack-based objects without losing the flexibility of dynamic allocation. Because stack-based string objects will be destroyed automatically when exceptions are thrown, exception cleanup becomes trivial if you declare your string objects on the stack.

Listing 3.1 provides the interface to the string object, which you should save in a file called string.hpp. This file is used throughout the rest of the book.

Listing 3.1 Using the String Class Interface

```
1:      // Listing 3.1 - Using the String Class Interface
2:
3:      #include <iostream.h>
4:      #include <string.h>
5:      #define int unsigned int
6:      enum BOOL { FALSE, TRUE };
7:
8:      class xOutOfBounds {};
9:
10:     class String
11:     {
12:     public:
13:
14:             // constructors
15:             String();
16:             String(const char *);
17:             String (const char *, int length);
18:             String (const String&);
19:             ~String();
20:
21:             // helpers and manipulators
22:             int   GetLength() const { return itsLen; }
23:             BOOL IsEmpty() const { return (BOOL) (itsLen == 0); }
24:             void Clear();               // set string to 0 length
25:
26:             // accessors
27:             char operator[](int offset) const;
28:             char& operator[](int offset);
29:             const char * GetString()const  { return itsCString; }
30:
31:             // casting operators
32:              operator const char* () const { return itsCString; }
33:              operator char* () { return itsCString;}
34:
35:             // operators
36:             const String& operator=(const String&);
37:             const String& operator=(const char *);
38:
39:             void operator+=(const String&);
40:             void operator+=(char);
41:             void operator+=(const char*);
42:
43:             int operator<(const String& rhs)const;
44:             int operator>(const String& rhs)const;
45:             int operator<=(const String& rhs)const;
46:             int operator>=(const String& rhs)const;
47:             int operator==(const String& rhs)const;
48:             int operator!=(const String& rhs)const;
49:
50:
51:             // friend functions
52:             String operator+(const String&);
53:             String operator+(const char*);
```

Listing 3.1 continued

```
54:                String operator+(char);
55:
56:                friend ostream& operator<< (ostream&, const String&);
57:
58:        private:
59:                // returns 0 if same, -1 if this is less than argument,
60:                // 1 if this is greater than argument
61:                int StringCompare(const String&) const;  // used by Boolean
                   operators
62:
63:
64:                char * itsCString;
65:                int itsLen;
66:        };
67:
```

None.

String.hpp attempts to provide the fundamental features of a String class. It has four constructors, although more may be added later. Note that the String class explicitly provides a default constructor (line 15). Remember that if you provide *any* constructors, the *default constructor* (the constructor with no parameters) no longer is provided by the compiler; if you need one, you must write it explicitly.

A constructor is provided to create a String object from a C-style null-terminated string (henceforth called a *C-style string*). Another constructor creates a string of a maximum length based on a C-style string and, finally, a copy constructor is provided.

The destructor is explicitly provided, as are a number of helper functions: GetLength(), which returns the length of the string (not including the terminating null); IsEmpty(), which returns TRUE if the string has length 0; and Clear(), which removes the string and sets the length to 0.

The offset operator ([ ]) is twice overloaded—in line 27, it is the read-only version; and in line 28, it is the read-write (nonconstant) version.

The assignment operator (=) also is twice overloaded—once to provide assignment of Strings, and then again to provide assignment of C-style strings.

Operator plus-equals is overloaded to allow the addition of Strings to other Strings, to single characters, and to C-style strings. In lines 51 through 54, operator plus is overloaded three times to allow adding Strings to other Strings, to C-style strings, and to single characters.

The Boolean operators are overloaded in lines 43 through 48. Finally, the ostream insertion operator (<<) is overloaded on line 58. An extraction operator (>>) is not provided at this time, because its use is not anticipated, but this easily can be added later.

The helper function StringCompare() is designated as private, because only member functions of the class will ever need to call this function directly. It is used by the Boolean operators, as you will see in the next listing.

Finally, itsString is the C-style string that provides internal storage for the String's characters, and itsLen provides the current length of itsString.

Listing 3.2 provides the implementation of the string object, which you should save in a file called string.cpp. This file will be used throughout the rest of the book.

 Listing 3.2 Using String Class Implementation

```
1:      #include "string.hpp"
2:       // default constructor creates string of 0 bytes
3:      String::String()
4:      {
5:          itsCString = new char[1];
6:          itsCString[0] = '\0';
7:          itsLen=0;
8:      }
9:
10:     String::String(const char *rhs)
11:     {
12:         itsLen = strlen(rhs);
13:         itsCString = new char[itsLen+1];
14:         strcpy(itsCString,rhs);
15:     }
16:
17:     String::String (const char *rhs, int length)
18:     {
19:         itsLen = strlen(rhs);
20:         if (length < itsLen)
21:             itsLen = length;  // max size = length
22:         itsCString = new char[itsLen+1];
23:         memcpy(itsCString,rhs,itsLen);
24:         itsCString[itsLen] = '\0';
25:     }
26:
27:     // copy constructor
28:     String::String (const String & rhs)
29:     {
30:         itsLen=rhs.GetLength();
31:         itsCString = new char[itsLen+1];
32:         memcpy(itsCString,rhs.GetString(),itsLen);
33:         itsCString[rhs.itsLen]='\0';
34:     }
35:
36:     String::~String ()
37:     {
38:         Clear();
39:     }
40:
41:     void String::Clear()
```

continues

3

Listing 3.2 continued

```
42:        {
43:            delete [] itsCString;
44:            itsLen = 0;
45:        }
46:
47:        //non constant offset operator
48:        char & String::operator[](int offset)
49:        {
50:            if (offset > itsLen)
51:            {
52:                // throw xOutOfBounds();
53:                 return itsCString[itsLen-1];
54:            }
55:            else
56:                return itsCString[offset];
57:        }
58:
59:        // constant offset operator
60:        char String::operator[](int offset) const
61:        {
62:            if (offset > itsLen)
63:            {
64:                // throw xOutOfBounds();
65:                return itsCString[itsLen-1];
66:            }
67:            else
68:                return itsCString[offset];
69:        }
70:
71:        // operator equals
72:        const String& String::operator=(const String & rhs)
73:        {
74:            if (this == &rhs)
75:                return *this;
76:            delete [] itsCString;
77:            itsLen=rhs.GetLength();
78:            itsCString = new char[itsLen+1];
79:            memcpy(itsCString,rhs.GetString(),itsLen);
80:            itsCString[rhs.itsLen]='\0';
81:            return *this;
82:        }
83:
84:        const String& String::operator=(const char * rhs)
85:        {
86:            delete [] itsCString;
87:            itsLen=strlen(rhs);
88:            itsCString = new char[itsLen+1];
89:            memcpy(itsCString,rhs,itsLen);
90:            itsCString[itsLen]='\0';
91:            return *this;
92:        }
93:
94:
95:        // changes current string, returns nothing
96:        void String::operator+=(const String& rhs)
```

```
97:     {
98:         unsigned short rhsLen = rhs.GetLength();
99:         unsigned short totalLen = itsLen + rhsLen;
100:        char *temp = new char[totalLen+1];
101:        for (int i = 0; i<itsLen; i++)
102:            temp[i] = itsCString[i];
103:        for (int j = 0; j<rhsLen; j++, i++)
104:            temp[i] = rhs[j];
105:        temp[totalLen]='\0';
106:        *this = temp;
107:        delete temp;
108:    }
109:
110:    int String::StringCompare(const String& rhs) const
111:    {
112:            return strcmp(itsCString, rhs.GetString());
113:    }
114:
115:    String String::operator+(const String& rhs)
116:    {
117:
118:        char * newCString = new char[GetLength() + rhs.GetLength() + 1];
119:        strcpy(newCString,GetString());
120:        strcat(newCString,rhs.GetString());
121:        String newString(newCString);
122:        return newString;
123:    }
124:
125:
126:    String String::operator+(const char* rhs)
127:    {
128:
129:        char * newCString = new char[GetLength() + strlen(rhs)+ 1];
130:        strcpy(newCString,GetString());
131:        strcat(newCString,rhs);
132:        String newString(newCString);
133:        return newString;
134:    }
135:
136:
137:    String String::operator+(char rhs)
138:    {
139:        int oldLen = GetLength();
140:        char * newCString = new char[oldLen + 2];
141:        strcpy(newCString,GetString());
142:        newCString[oldLen] = rhs;
143:        newCString[oldLen+1] = '\0';
144:        String newString(newCString);
145:        return newString;
146:    }
147:
148:
149:
150:    int String::operator==(const String& rhs) const
151:    { return (StringCompare(rhs) == 0); }
```

continues

Listing 3.2 continued

```
152:    int String::operator!=(const String& rhs)const
153:        { return  (StringCompare(rhs) != 0); }
154:    int String::operator<(const String& rhs)const
155:        { return StringCompare(rhs) < 0;  }
156:    int String::operator>(const String& rhs)const
157:        { return  (StringCompare(rhs) > 0); }
158:    int String::operator<=(const String& rhs)const
159:        { return  (StringCompare(rhs) <= 0); }
160:    int String::operator>=(const String& rhs)const
161:        { return (StringCompare(rhs) >= 0); }
162:
163:    ostream& operator<< (ostream& ostr, const String& str)
164:    {
165:        ostr << str.itsCString;
166:        return ostr;
167:    }
```

 None.

 Listing 3.2 provides the implementation for the String class. The default constructor in lines 5 through 11 initializes itsString to zero length and itsLen to zero.

The second constructor takes a C-style string, sets itsLen to the length of that string, and then allocates memory for itsString. Finally, the contents of the C-style string are copied into itsString.

The third constructor is much like the first, except that strncpy() is used, setting a maximum size of the new itsString member variable. Note that itsLen is set to the actual size of the new string, because that may be smaller than the length parameter. This member function might be called with String("hello", 20), for example. Even though the maximum length of the new String is set to 20, only 5 bytes are required.

The copy constructor is implemented in lines 31 through 39. Note that each character of the old string is copied to the corresponding character of the new string, and then the string is null terminated. Memcpy is used for greater speed and efficiency.

The destructor (lines 36 through 38) calls Clear() (lines 44 through 48), which deletes the space allocated for the itsString, and sets itsLen to zero.

The String class overrides the offset operator ([]) to allow its clients ready access to the individual characters of the string. Some clients will want to be able to modify a single character, using the array accessor as an l-value in expressions such as myString[5]='*';. Other clients will want to access the character as an R-Value (char theChar = myString[5];, for example).

Two versions of the accessor thus are supplied. The first, in lines 50 through 60, returns a nonconstant reference to the character. The second, in lines 62 through 72, returns a character by value; the method itself therefore is `const`.

Note that because a character is small (no larger than four bytes, and often only one) there is no advantage to returning a `const char &`. You could do so, but you don't gain anything, and returning by value is simpler.

Because the `String` class allocates and manages dynamic memory (the pointer to the character array), it requires a copy constructor (lines 32 through 39) and operator equals (lines 87 through 96). The latter is overloaded on lines 90 through 99 to allow assignment to a `String` from a `const` character array.

The (private) `StringCompare()` function (lines 112 through 118) examines the current string against a second string by passing their internal strings to the standard library `strncmp`. This method acts as an interface between the user-defined `String` class and the standard string library function, and is used by the various comparison operators on lines 121 through 137.

Finally, in lines 139 through 143, a non-member insertion operator (`<<`) is defined that inserts a String object into a Stream buffer.

Listing 3.3 provides a simple driver program to exercise some of the `String` class functionality.

Listing 3.3 Using a Driver Program to Exercise the String Class

```
1:     // Listing 3.3 - Using a Driver Program to Exercise the String Class
2:
3:     #include "string.hpp"
4:     #include <iostream.h>
5:     void main()
6:     {
7:         char buffer[255];
8:         String helloStr("Hello");
9:         String worldStr(" world");
10:        cout << helloStr << endl;
11:        cout << worldStr << endl;
12:        helloStr+=worldStr;
13:        cout << helloStr << endl;
14:
15:        String t1 = worldStr + worldStr;
16:        String t2 = worldStr + " series";
17:        String t3 = worldStr + '!';
18:
19:        cout << "t1: " << t1 << endl;
20:        cout << "t2: " << t2 << endl;
21:        cout << "t3: " << t3 << endl;
22:
23:        cout << "\nEnter string 1: ";
```

continues

Listing 3.3 continued

```
24:        cin >> buffer;
25:        String S1(buffer);
26:        cout << "Enter string 2: ";
27:        cin >> buffer;
28:        String S2(buffer);
29:        cout << "\n";
30:        if (S1 < S2)
31:            cout << "S1 is less" << endl;
32:        else if ( S1 == S2)
33:            cout << "They are the same!" << endl;
34:        else
35:            cout << "S1 is greater" << endl;
36:        try   // if your compiler doesn't support templates, comment this out
37:        {
38:            char theChar = S1[(int)3];
39:            cout << "The fourth character of S1 is " << theChar << endl;
40:        }
41:        catch(...)   // if your compiler doesn't support templates, comment this
                       out
42:        {
43:            cout << "Unable to display the fourth character!" << endl;
44:        }
45:    }
```

```
Hello
 world
Hello world
t1:   world world
t2:   world series
t3:   world!
Enter string 1: this
Enter string 2: thin
S1 is greater
The fourth character of S1 is s
```

Note: If your compiler does not support exceptions, change lines 36 through 44 to the following:

```
36:        if (strlen(S1) >= 4)
37:        {
38:            char theChar = S1[3];
39:            cout << "The fourth character of S1 is " << theChar << endl;
40:        }
41:        else
42:        {
43:            cout << "Unable to display the fourth character!" << endl;
44:        }
```

 In lines 8 and 9, Strings helloStr and worldStr are created and then concatenated and printed. In lines 15 through 17, three temporary strings are created to exercise the overloaded addition operator, and then are printed in lines 19 through 21.

The user is prompted for two words in lines 23 and 24—in this case, this and thin—and the words are compared. Because this ends with s and thin ends with n, and because s is later in the alphabet, this is considered to be "greater" than thin.

Finally, the fourth character (s) is accessed using the offset operator ([ ]).

DO	DON'T

When Creating a Class

DO put the declaration in a header file (.hpp).

DO put the definition in an implementation file.

DO get all the essential functionality into the class.

DON'T assume that you must provide every imaginable function for the class even before you need it.

Lists

Now that you have a good, working String class with which to build your notes and other objects in ROBIN, it is time to turn your attention to issues of data management. Over time, you will need to create an entire database of notes, which are indexed and storable on disk. The next few days will introduce many of the concepts and classes you will need for this project, but today you will start by examining how data can be managed and manipulated in memory.

Linked Lists

A linked list is one way to implement a dynamic array of objects. The significant limitation of arrays is that you must decide, at compile time, how many objects you will hold in the array. But what if you don't know? You have only two choices with an array: you can take a reasonable guess and risk running out of room, or you can create a very large array and risk wasting a lot of memory.

A linked list provides much of the functionality of an array, but it enables you to size the list at run time, adding nodes (elements or members of the list) and removing them at will. Linked lists can be searched, sorted, and otherwise manipulated as needed. Simple linked lists, however,

provide poor performance when quick access to an individual node is needed. During the next few days, you will explore more complex cousins of the linked list to overcome this limitation.

Figure 3.1 illustrates a simple, singly linked list. The list is singly linked because each node points only to the *next* node in the list—not to any other nodes.

Figure 3.1
A singly linked list.

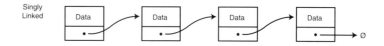

Note: A *linked list* provides the functionality of an array without the restriction of having a fixed size. You can provide the best of both worlds by creating an `Array` class with `Array` syntax, which grows and shrinks as your needs change. To create such an array, store the data in a linked list.

Creating Your First Linked List

You might be tempted to create a linked list of notes, and then perhaps another linked list of `Strings`, and so on. It quickly will become apparent, however, that linked lists are so fundamental that you will be using them in many different places. A template offers the flexibility you need, without significant overhead.

Creating a template always is easiest if you start with a well-debugged working example. You therefore will create a linked list of notes, get it working, and then parameterize it. Listing 3.4 provides the header for a linked list of notes. Listing 3.5 provides the implementation for the linked list, and listing 3.6 provides a simple driver program.

Listing 3.4 Declaring a Message, Node, and Linked List

```
 1:    // Listing 3.4 - Declaring a Message, Node, and Linked List
 2:
 3:    #include <iostream.h>
 4:    #include "String.hpp"  // string class
 5:
 6:    typedef  unsigned long  ULONG;
 7:    typedef unsigned short USHORT;
 8:
 9:    // minimal Note class
10:    class Note
11:    {
12:     public:
13:        Note(const String& text):
14:        itsText(text), itsDate(0L)
15:           {itsNoteNumber = theNoteNumber++;}
```

```
16:          ~Note(){}
17:          const String& GetText()const { return itsText; }
18:          long GetDate() const { return itsDate; }
19:          ULONG GetNoteNumber() const { return itsNoteNumber; }
20:          int operator<(const Note& rhs) { return itsNoteNumber
             < rhs.GetNoteNumber(); }
21:          void Display() const
22:             { cout << "Note #: " << itsNoteNumber;
23:             cout <<    "  Text: " << itsText << endl; }
24:          static ULONG theNoteNumber;
25:       private:
26:          String itsText;
27:          ULONG itsDate;
28:          ULONG itsNoteNumber;
29:       };
30:
31:       // *************** Note Node class ************
32:       class Node
33:       {
34:       public:
35:          Node (Note*);
36:          ~Node();
37:          void InsertAfter(Node*);
38:          Node * GetNext() { return itsNext; }
39:          void SetNext(Node * next) { itsNext = next; }
40:          Note * GetNote() const;
41:          int operator<(const Node &rhs) {return itsNote < (rhs.GetNote());}
42:
43:       private:
44:
45:          Note *itsNote;
46:          Node * itsNext;
47:       };
48:
49:
50:       // *************** Note List ************
51:       class NoteList
52:       {
53:       public:
54:          NoteList();
55:          ~NoteList();
56:          ULONG   GetCount() const { return itsCount; }
57:          void    Insert(Note *);
58:          void    Iterate(void (Note::*f)()const) ;
59:          Note*   operator[](ULONG) ;
60:          Note*   FindNote(ULONG & NoteNumber )  ;
61:
62:       private:
63:          Node   itsHead;
64:          ULONG itsCount;
65:       };
```

 None. This is the class declaration.

The declarations begin, in lines 3 and 4, by including two necessary header files. The first, `iostream.h`, is provided by the compiler vendor and declares all the iostream objects. The second, `String.hpp`, is the header for the `String` class you built earlier.

In lines 9 through 29, a minimal `Note` class is declared. This provides a convenient object to store in your linked list. Each note object consists of a `String`, a date, and a unique identification number. For now, the date is stored as an `unsigned long` and is set to 0. This serves as a placeholder for information you will need in later versions of the `Note` object.

Each `Note` is numbered sequentially using a static member variable, `theMsgNumber`, which is incremented as each `Message` is instantiated.

The `Note` object is instantiated with a string representing the note the user wants to record. The body of the constructor (line 15) initializes the individual note's sequential number while incrementing the static counter.

The `Display()` member function prints the note number and the text of its `String` object to the console, taking advantage of the fact that the `String` class overloaded the insertion operator to allow writing `String` objects directly to `cout`.

Note that all member functions are declared inline; again this class exists, for now, only to provide an object to store in the lists.

A `Node` class is declared in lines 31 through 42 and, again, this is specific to the `Note` class. When you write the template version of this class later today, you will see how to generalize this type. For now, a `Node` class is constructed with a pointer to a `Note` and is responsible for pointing to the next `Node` in the list, as well as for returning the `Note` pointer on demand.

The `NoteList` is declared in lines 51 through 65. Each `NoteList` object consists of a `Node` object and a running count of all the `Nodes` in the list. The count, of course, could be computed as needed, but it is a small amount of data to store and doing so optimizes how quickly the class can return its count. Note that the contained `Node` does not hold data for the list; it provides a convenient entry point for accessing the other nodes in the list, thereby simplifying inserting new nodes and walking the list.

In line 58, the member function `Iterate()` is declared. This function is used to call any member function of the `Note` class that matches the appropriate signature (taking no parameters, returning void, and having a constant to this pointer). `Iterate()` is used to iterate over each `Node` in the list, calling the appropriate function in its `Note` object.

Listing 3.5 Implementing Note, Node, and List Classes

```
1:      #include "0304.hpp"
2:
3:      // Listing 3.5 - Implementing Note, Node, and List Classes
4:
5:      // *** node implementations ****
```

```
6:
7:        Node::Node(Note* pNote):
8:        itsNote(pNote),
9:        itsNext(0)
10:       {}
11:
12:       Node::~Node()
13:       {
14:          delete itsNote;
15:          itsNote = 0;
16:          delete itsNext;
17:          itsNext = 0;
18:       }
19:
20:       void Node::InsertAfter(Node* newNode)
21:       {
22:        newNode->SetNext(itsNext);
23:        itsNext=newNode;
24:       }
25:
26:       Note * Node::GetNote() const
27:       {
28:          if (itsNote)
29:             return itsNote;
30:          else
31:             return NULL; //error
32:       }
33:
34:        // Implementations for Lists...
35:
36:       NoteList::NoteList():
37:          itsCount(0),
38:          itsHead(0)  // initialize head node to have no note
39:          {}
40:
41:       NoteList::~NoteList()
42:       {
43:       }
44:
45:
46:       Note *  NoteList::operator[](ULONG offSet)
47:       {
48:          Node* pNode = itsHead.GetNext();
49:
50:          if (offSet+1 > itsCount)
51:             return NULL; // error
52:
53:          for (ULONG i=0;i<offSet; i++)
54:             pNode = pNode->GetNext();
55:
56:         return    pNode->GetNote();
57:       }
58:
59:       Note*    NoteList::FindNote(ULONG & NoteNumber )
60:       {
```

continues

Listing 3.5 continued

```
61:            for (Node * pNode = itsHead.GetNext();
62:                    pNode!=NULL;
63:                    pNode = pNode->GetNext()
64:                )
65:            {
66:                if (pNode->GetNote()->GetNoteNumber() == NoteNumber)
67:                    break;
68:            }
69:            if (pNode == NULL)
70:                return NULL;
71:            else
72:                return pNode->GetNote();
73:        }
74:
75:        void NoteList::Insert(Note* pNote)
76:        {
77:            Node * NewNode = new Node(pNote);
78:            itsCount++;
79:            for (Node * pNode = &itsHead;;pNode = pNode->GetNext())
80:            {
81:                if (pNode->GetNext() == NULL || *(pNode->GetNext()) < *NewNode)
82:                {
83:                    pNode->InsertAfter(NewNode);
84:                    break;
85:                }
86:            }
87:        }
88:
89:        void NoteList::Iterate(void (Note::*func)()const)
90:        {
91:          for (Node* pNode = itsHead.GetNext();
92:                    pNode;
93:                    pNode=pNode->GetNext()
94:                )
95:                (pNode->GetNote()->*func)();
96:
97:        }
```

None.

In line 3, the header file (as shown in the previous listing) is included. Lines 7 through 10 represent the very simple constructor for the Node class, and lines 12 through 18 show the destructor.

The implementation of InsertAfter() occurs in lines 20 through 24. This takes a pointer to a node and inserts it into the list after the current node.

The implementation for the linked list itself begins in line 34.

The insert method in lines 76 through 87 provides the capability to add a Note and have it inserted in the correct position based on the note's number.

Here's how it works: a new node is created in line 77 and initialized with the new note. The list's counter is incremented in line 79. A for loop is started, and a pointer is initialized to point to the itsHead member of the list. There is no test condition in the loop, and each time through the pointer pNode is reset to point to the next node in the list.

At each node point, a test is conducted in line 81. If there is no following node, or if the note attached to the following node has a higher number than the new note's number, the new note is inserted into the list. The actual insertion is accomplished by the node after which you are inserting the new node.

The accessor function ([ ]) shown in lines 46 through 57 returns the Note object associated with the Node at the offset provided. Note that if the offset is beyond the end of the list, no exception is thrown—a Null pointer simply is returned. This is not considered an error in this case, and so there is no need for an exception. You might decide to implement your list so that this *is* considered an error, in which case you might throw an exception if there are no nodes in your list (line 51).

Note also that in this linked list, there is no way to jump directly to a given offset. Instead, you must *walk the list*, as shown in lines 53 and 54. This is a severe limitation of simple linked lists, and one that will be addressed in coming days when you learn about more complex data structures such as Trees.

The FindNote() function walks the list looking for a Note object in which the itsNumber member matches the number provided. This is accomplished by walking the list and asking each node to ask its associated note what its number is by calling GetNoteNumber() (line 66).

Finally, in lines 89 through 95, the member function NoteList::Iterate() is defined. This takes as its only parameter a pointer to a member function of class Note, which itself takes no parameters, is constant, and returns void. The Iterate() member function itself is constant as well. For every Node in the list, the member function pointed to by the parameter is invoked on the Note object held by the Node.

Listing 3.6 Using the Driver Program for the Linked List

```
1:    // Listing 3.6 - Using the Driver Program for the Linked List
2:
3:    #include "0304.hpp"
4:    #include <stdlib.h>
5:
6:    ULONG Note::theNoteNumber = 0;
7:    void main()
```

continues

Listing 3.6 continued

```
8:      {
9:          NoteList pl;
10:         Note * pNote = 0;
11:         ULONG choice;
12:         char buffer[256];
13:
14:         while (1)
15:         {
16:            cout << "\n(0)Quit (1)Add Note ";
17:            cin >> choice;
18:            if (!choice)
19:                break;
20:
21:            cin.ignore(255,'\n');
22:            cout << "\nText: ";
23:            cin.getline(buffer,255);
24:            pNote = new Note(buffer);
25:            pl.Insert(pNote);
26:         }
27:
28:         cout << "\n\nResults: \n" << endl;
29:         void (Note::*pFunc)()const = Note::Display;
30:         pl.Iterate(pFunc);
31:
32:         cin.ignore(255,'\n');
33:         cout << "\nFind Note: ";
34:         cin.getline(buffer,255);
35:         ULONG position = atol(buffer);
36:         pNote =  pl.FindNote(position);
37:         if (pNote)
38:          cout << "\nFound! " << endl;
39:          pNote->Display();
40:     }
```

```
(0)Quit (1)Add Note 1
Text: Wash the car
(0)Quit (1)Add Note 1
Text: Write the next chapter
(0)Quit (1)Add Note 0
Results:
Note #: 0  Text: Wash the car
Note #: 1  Text: Write the next chapter
Find Note: 1
Found!
Note #: 1  Text: Write the next chapter
```

The driver program exists only to ensure that you have created a valid and working linked list. The program initializes the static member theNoteNumber in line 6, outside of the main() function, as required. It then, in line 9, instantiates a NoteList object.

The user repeatedly is prompted to enter a new note in the while loop in lines 14 through 26. Each time the user does create a new note, the user is prompted to enter the text. A new note then is created and inserted into the linked list.

The extraction operator (>>) is not used, because the user may want to enter a multiword note. The new line from the choice therefore is eaten in line 21, and `getline` is used to take the user's entire input into the character buffer that was declared in line 12.

In lines 28 through 30, the results are printed by assigning the `Display()` method of `Note` to the pointer to member function `pFunc`. This pointer then is passed to the `Iterate()` function of the linked list, and each member of the list is printed.

In line 33, the user is prompted to enter a number, and that note is retrieved. Remember that this list counts from zero, as an array would.

NEW☞ A *node* is an entry in a list. The node contains either the data for the list or
TERM a pointer to the data for the list, and it acts as an interface between the list and the objects contained in the list.

Parameterizing the List

Now that you have a working list class, it is fairly straightforward to parameterize it by using templates. The goal is to be able to separate the `Node` and `List` concepts from the particular objects stored in each. Listing 3.7 provides the declarations of a `Node` and `List` template and their implementations, as well as a driver program that declares two simple classes designed to show the flexibility of the `List` template.

Listing 3.7 Using a Parameterized List Class

```
1:      #include <iostream.h>
2:      #include "String.hpp"  // string class
3:      #include <stdlib.h>
4:
5:      typedef  unsigned long  ULONG;
6:      typedef unsigned short USHORT;
7:
8:      // minimal Note class
9:     class Note
10:    {
11:    public:
12:       Note(const String& text):
13:       itsText(text), itsDate(0L)
14:          {itsNoteNumber = theNoteNumber++;}
15:       ~Note(){}
16:
17:       const String& GetText()const { return itsText; }
18:       long GetDate() const { return itsDate; }
```

continues

Listing 3.7 continued

```
19:            ULONG GetNoteNumber() const { return itsNoteNumber; }
20:
21:            int operator<(const Note& rhs)
22:             { return itsNoteNumber < rhs.GetNoteNumber(); }
23:            BOOL operator==(const Note& rhs)
24:             {(BOOL)(return itsText == rhs.GetText()); }
25:
26:            operator long() { return itsNoteNumber; }
27:
28:            void Display() const
29:               { cout << "Note #: " << itsNoteNumber;
30:               cout <<   " Text: " << itsText << endl; }
31:
32:            static ULONG theNoteNumber;
33:         private:
34:            String itsText;
35:            ULONG itsDate;
36:            ULONG itsNoteNumber;
37:         };
38:
39:
40:         // *************** Node class ************
41:         template <class T>
42:         class Node
43:         {
44:         public:
45:            Node (T*);
46:            ~Node();
47:            void InsertAfter(Node *);
48:            Node * GetNext() const            { return itsNext; }
49:            void SetNext(Node * next)         { itsNext = next; }
50:            T & GetObject() const             { return *itsObject; }
51:            BOOL operator<(const Node &rhs) const;
52:            BOOL operator==(const T& rhs) const;
53:
54:         private:
55:            T * itsObject;
56:            Node * itsNext;
57:         };
58:
59:         // *************** Object List ************
60:         template <class T>
61:         class List
62:         {public:
63:         public:
64:            List();
65:            ~List();
66:            ULONG       GetCount() const { return itsCount; }
67:            void        Insert(T &);
68:            void        Iterate(void (T::*f)()const);
69:            T &          operator[](ULONG);
70:            T *          FindObject(const T& target );
71:
72:         private:
73:            Node<T>  itsHead;
```

```
74:           ULONG itsCount;
75:        };
76:
77:     // *** node implementations ****
78:
79:        template <class T>
80:        Node<T>::Node(T * pObject):
81:        itsObject(pObject),
82:        itsNext(0)
83:        {}
84:
85:         template <class T>
86:         Node<T>::~Node()
87:         {
88:            delete itsObject;
89:            itsObject = 0;
90:            delete itsNext;
91:            itsNext = 0;
92:         }
93:
94:         template <class T>
95:         void Node<T>::InsertAfter(Node* newNode)
96:         {
97:          newNode->SetNext(itsNext);
98:          itsNext=newNode;
99:         }
100:
101:        template <class T>
102:        BOOL Node<T>::operator<(const Node &rhs) const
103:        {
104:        return(BOOL)(*itsObject < rhs.GetObject());
105:        }
106:
107:        template <class T>
108:        BOOL Node<T>::operator==(const T& target) const
109:        {
110:           return (BOOL)(*itsObject == target);
111:        }
112:
113:         // Implementations for Lists...
114:
115:        template<class T>
116:        List <T>::List():
117:           itsCount(0),
118:           itsHead(0)  // initialize head node to have no Object
119:           {}
120:
121:        template<class T>
122:        List <T>::~List()
123:        {
124:        }
125:
126:        template<class T>
127:        T &  List<T>::operator[](ULONG offSet)
128:        {
```

continues

Listing 3.7 continued

```
129:            if (offSet+1 > itsCount)
130:                return itsHead.GetObject(); // error
131:
132:            Node<T>* pNode = itsHead.GetNext();
133:
134:            for (ULONG i=0;i<offSet; i++)
135:                pNode = pNode->GetNext();
136:
137:          return   pNode->GetObject();
138:        }
139:
140:        template<class T>
141:        T*  List<T>::FindObject(const T& target )
142:        {
143:            for (Node<T> * pNode = itsHead.GetNext();
144:                    pNode!=NULL;
145:                    pNode = pNode->GetNext()
146:                  )
147:            {
148:                if ( *pNode == target)
149:                    break;
150:            }
151:            if (pNode == NULL)
152:                return 0;
153:            else
154:                return &(pNode->GetObject());
155:        }
156:
157:        template<class T>
158:        void List<T>::Insert(T & Object)
159:        {
160:            Node<T> * NewNode = new Node<T>(&Object);
161:
162:            for (Node<T> * pNode = &itsHead;;pNode = pNode->GetNext())
163:            {
164:                if (pNode->GetNext() == NULL ¦¦ *NewNode < *(pNode->GetNext()) )
165:                {
166:                    pNode->InsertAfter(NewNode);
167:                    itsCount++;
168:                    break;
169:                }
170:            }
171:        }
172:
173:        template<class T>
174:        void List<T>::Iterate(void (T::*func)()const)
175:        {
176:          for (Node<T>* pNode = itsHead.GetNext();
177:                  pNode;
178:                  pNode=pNode->GetNext()
179:                )
180:                (pNode->GetObject().*func)();
181:        }
182:
```

```
183:    ULONG Note::theNoteNumber = 0;
184:    void main()
185:    {
186:        List<Note> pl;
187:        Note * pNote = 0;
188:        ULONG choice;
189:        char buffer[256];
190:
191:        while (1)
192:        {
193:            cout << "\n(0)Quit (1)Add Note ";
194:            cin >> choice;
195:            if (!choice)
196:                break;
197:
198:            cin.ignore(255,'\n');
199:            cout << "\nText: ";
200:            cin.getline(buffer,255);
201:            pNote = new Note(buffer);
202:            pl.Insert(*pNote);
203:        }
204:
205:        cout << "\n\nResults: \n" << endl;
206:        void (Note::*pFunc)()const = Note::Display;
207:        pl.Iterate(pFunc);
208:
209:        cin.ignore(255,'\n');
210:        cout << "\nFind Note with text: ";
211:        cin.getline(buffer,255);
212:        Note target(buffer);
213:        pNote=0;
214:        pNote =  pl.FindObject(target);
215:        if (pNote)
216:        {
217:         cout << "\nFound! " << endl;
218:         pNote->Display();
219:        }
220:        else
221:            cout << "Note not found." << endl;
222:    }
```

Output

```
(0)Quit (1)Add Note 1
Text: Walk the walk
(0)Quit (1)Add Note 1
Text: Talk the talk
(0)Quit (1)Add Note 0
Results:
Note #: 0   Text: Walk the walk
Note #: 1   Text: Talk the talk
Find Note with text: Talk the talk
Found!
Note #: 1   Text: Talk the talk
```

The implementation for the Node and List classes is similar to the previous example. Because the list was undergoing parameterization, a few additional changes were made to allow the list

Analysis to be used with a wide variety of objects.

In listing 3.6, matches are made based on a specific characteristic of notes (the note number). In listing 3.7, for the more generalized template, matches are made on the basis of the overloaded `operator==()` in the object itself.

In lines 23 and 24, the `Note` implements its new `operator==()`, which allows the List to compare two `Note` objects. This is critical to building a generalized `List` class; other objects now can be stored in this type of list if they implement both `operator<()` and `operator==()`.

The `Node` class also implements `operator<()` and `operator==()`, and this time is careful *not* to make these inline, because the client may need to override these templates with specific functions for some instances of `Node`.

The `FindObject()` method of `List`, in line 70, changes to take a reference to the parameterized type object, so that the object itself can determine an accurate match on any particular characteristic of that object.

Note that the implementation of `Node`'s overloaded operators (lines 111 through 121) pass on the comparison and equate operations to the objects themselves. Also, carefully note that the decision on when to use references and when to use pointers now is made with more consistency; use pointers when the pointer might be null—otherwise, use references.

Summary

Today you learned how to create a `String` object to allow flexible handling of text. You also learned how to create a simple linked list and to manipulate the nodes in the list. Finally, you reviewed creating a template based on a well-tested existing class; in this case, the linked list was parameterized to hold any object that can be treated as a ULONG.

Q&A

Q Is this the final design for the `String` class?

A The goal of a good early design is to provide a nearly-complete class. As work on your program continues, other functionality may be added, but the more complete the early design, the better. A weak, early class exposes you to the danger that you will have to go back and rework early code as your design changes.

Q Why bother having a `String` class? Why not use C-style strings?

A The `String` class protects the user from several bugs that are common even to experienced programmers, such as forgetting to allocate space for the trailing NULL, and writing past the end of the buffer.

Q What else does the `String` class provide that C-style strings don't provide?

A With a user-defined class such as String, you can add useful operators such as operator+ for concatenation and operator< for alphabetization.

Q **Why did you first write the List class without making it a template, instead of just making a template?**

A Debugging a Template class is much harder than debugging a simple class, and many debuggers don't support templates at all. After you have a specific example of a class, making a template out of it is relatively straightforward.

Q **Why was the entire node object included inside the list, rather than just including a pointer to the first node in the list?**

A Including the node simplifies the insertion and removal code. Without the included node, you would have to include special handling for insertions before the first node, and insertions into an empty list.

3

Workshop

The Workshop provides quiz questions to help you solidify your understanding of the material covered, and exercises to provide you with experience in using what you have learned. Try to answer the quiz and exercise questions before checking the answers in Appendix A, and make sure that you understand the answers before continuing to the next chapter.

Quiz

1. What is a C-style string?

2. Is there a difference between a C-style string and a char* or char array?

3. What is the purpose of the iterate function in the list?

4. Why does the declaration of the List template include the line Node<T> itsHead rather than simply Node itsHead?

5. What features are required of a class if it is to be used with the list template?

Exercises

1. Using the String class and the list template, create a list of strings. Write a test program that enables you to enter strings to be put on the list and prints out the list when it is complete.

2. Modify your test program from exercise 1 to enable the user to ask for a particular entry by numeric index.

3. Try to use the template to create a list of type int. Why doesn't this work? (Hint:

Look at the arguments to the different functions in `List`.) Modify the list template so that you can create a list of type int.

4. Using the modified list template from exercise 3, write a test program that enables the user to create a list of doubles, and then prints them back.

5. Write a class `Text` that contains a string but does not have an `operator ==` or an `operator <`. Instead, give it the methods `IsEqualTo` and `IsLessThan`. (These should just use the appropriate comparisons in the `String` class.) Use the list template to make a list of Text objects. (Hint: You have to replace the methods `Node<Text>::operator ==` and `Node<Text>::operator <` with your own versions. Don't let the template define these two.)

Sorting

Object-oriented programs deal with objects, which in turn consist of data and the methods of operating on that data. Although having objects all in a jumble often is fine, at other times it is convenient, or even required that the objects be given some sort of order. Perhaps you need to examine the objects in chronological order, by size, or in alphabetical order.

The job of imposing order on a group of objects or a set of data is called *sorting*. A number of techniques exist for sorting data, each of which may be optimized for some type of trait—for example, ease of use, speed, or size. Today you will learn

- [ ] The fundamentals of sorting
- [ ] Various simple sorts and some more complex sorts
- [ ] How to evaluate sorts

A Practical View

Many books have been written on sorting algorithms, and most take what I would call an *academic* view of the subject. These books are filled with formulae showing that one sort or another is faster, and examining the mathematics of sorting.

All that is required for a practical approach, however, is to know how fast your sort is, and for what it is optimized. Sorts break down into slow, quick, and wicked-fast. In this book, I'll leave out the slow sorts, show you a few fast sorts, and then show you one or two wicked-fast sorts.

If you are interested in a more rigorous approach to the speed and efficiency of sorting (one that tells you how well the particular sort approximates the goal of N log(2) of N compares, where N is the number of elements to be sorted), I recommend *Algorithms in C++* by Sedgewick as a good starting point.

Selection Sort

One of the simplest sorts available is the selection sort. Like the insertion and bubble sorts, this is a reasonably fast sort, and it is easy to implement.

Imagine that you have a set of children's blocks in front of you, as shown in figure 4.1.

Figure 4.1.
Blocks to sort.

Follow this technique: Separate the first block (x) from the others and call it the *target*. Of the remaining blocks, you can see that a is the smallest (earliest in the alphabet), so swap a with the target. That finishes round 1 of the sort, and your array looks like figure 4.2.

Figure 4.2.
Blocks to sort after the first round.

For each subsequent round, start with the next block (in this case, r). Examine the remaining blocks and establish which is smallest; again, in this case, b. Once again, swap them; after round 2, the blocks will be in the order shown in figure 4.3.

Figure 4.3.
Blocks to sort after the second round.

This process continues until the entire array is sorted. Listing 4.1 illustrates this technique.

Type **Listing 4.1 Using a Selection Sort**

```
1:     // Listing 4.1 - Using a Selection Sort
2:
3:     #include <iostream.h>
4:     #include <string.h>
5:
6:     void Swap( char *Array, int index1, int index2);
7:     void SelectionSort(char *Array);
8:
9:     int main()
10:    {
11:        char buffer[100];
12:        cout << "Enter up to 100 characters: ";
13:        cin.getline(buffer,100);
14:        cout << "Unsorted:\t" << buffer << endl;
15:        SelectionSort(buffer);
16:        cout << "Sorted:\t\t" << buffer << endl;
17:        return 0;
18:    }
19:
20:    // Read through each member of the array in turn
21:    // For every member, examine every remaining member and
22:    // swap with smallest
23:    void SelectionSort(char *Array)
24:    {
25:        int ArrayLen = strlen(Array);
26:        for (int i = 0; i<ArrayLen; i++)
27:        {
28:            int min = i;
29:            for (int j = i+1; j< ArrayLen; j++)
30:                if (Array[j] < Array[min])
31:                    min = j;
32:            Swap(Array,min,i);
33:        }
34:    }
```

continues

Listing 4.1 continued

```
35:
36:    void Swap( char *Array, int left, int right)
37:    {
38:        char tmp = Array[left];
39:        Array[left]=Array[right];
40:        Array[right]=tmp;
41:    }
```

```
Enter up to 100 characters: jdk;ayf4eyiapuvhia;jfkda;jdajdjkewnzc
Unsorted:          jdk;ayf4eyiapuvhia;jfkda;jdajdjkewnzc
Sorted:            4;;;aaaaacddddeeffhiijjjjjkkknpuvwyyz

Enter up to 100 characters: Eternal vigilance is the price of liberty
Unsorted:          Eternal vigilance is the price of liberty
Sorted:                   Eaabcceeeeefghiiiiilllnnoprrrstttvy
```

The user is prompted, in line 12, to enter up to 100 characters. An array is created and passed to SelectionSort(), which ticks through each member of the array in the outer loop, as shown in line 26.

For each time through the loop, the smallest remaining element in the array is selected in the inner loop in lines 28 through 31. Swap() then is called to swap the smaller element into position.

Although this is an inefficient sort in many ways, it does work quickly on a modern computer and may be all you need for many sorts. Also, it has the advantage that every member of the array is filled with (at most) one swap, which works well when you are swapping large objects.

Note that the program was run twice, and the second time a number of spaces were introduced. These are all pushed to the front of the array, so in the sorted output there are seven spaces before the first letter. Capital letters evaluate to lower values than lowercase, so the first printable letter is the uppercase E, which does *not* sort in with the lowercase es.

Improving Efficiency

The program in listing 4.1 calls swap on each member of the array. Careful examination reveals, however, that many times a swap is unnecessary; the current member of the array already is the smallest. Listing 4.2 illustrates how testing for this condition can reduce the number of calls to Swap and thus potentially improve the efficiency of the program.

Listing 4.2 Demonstrating Potential Optimization

```
1:    // Listing 4.2 - Demonstrating Potential Optimization
2:
3:    #include <iostream.h>
4:    #include <string.h>
5:
```

```
6:     void Swap( char *Array, int min, int i);
7:     void SelectionSort(char *Array);
8:     int NumberSwaps = 0;
9:     int NumberExaminations = 0;
10:    int WouldSwap=0;
11:
12:    int main()
13:    {
14:       char buffer[100];
15:       cout << "Enter up to 100 characters: ";
16:       cin.getline(buffer,100);
17:       cout << "Unsorted:\t" << buffer << endl;
18:       SelectionSort(buffer);
19:       cout << "Sorted:\t\t" << buffer << endl;
20:
21:       cout << "\nExamined: " <<  NumberExaminations;
22:       cout << " Would Swap: " <<  WouldSwap << endl;
23:       cout << " Did Swap: " <<  NumberSwaps;
24:
25:
26:       return 0;
27:    }
28:
29:    enum BOOL {FALSE, TRUE};
30:    // Read through each member of the array in turn
31:    // For every member, examine every remaining member and
32:    // swap with smallest
33:    void SelectionSort(char *Array)
34:    {
35:       int ArrayLen = strlen(Array);
36:       for (int i = 0; i<ArrayLen; i++)
37:       {
38:          int min = i;
39:          for (int j = i+1; j< ArrayLen; j++)
40:          {
41:             NumberExaminations++;
42:
43:             if (Array[j] < Array[min])
44:                min = j;
45:          }
46:          WouldSwap++;
47:          if (i != min)
48:          {
49:             NumberSwaps++;
50:             Swap(Array,min,i);
51:          }
52:       }
53:    }
54:
55:    void Swap( char *Array, int min, int i)
56:    {
57:       char tmp = Array[min];
58:       Array[min]=Array[i];
59:       Array[i]=tmp;
60:    }
```

4

Output

```
Enter up to 100 characters: jdk;ayf4eyiapuvhia;jfkda;jdajdjkewnzc
Unsorted:       jdk;ayf4eyiapuvhia;jfkda;jdajdjkewnzc
Sorted:         4;;;aaaaacddddeeffhiijjjjjkkknpuvwyyz
Examined: 666 Would Swap: 37 Did Swap: 32

Enter up to 100 characters: Eternal vigilance is the price of liberty
Unsorted:       Eternal vigilance is the price of liberty
Sorted:             Eaabcceeeeefghiiiiilllnnoprrrstttvy
Examined: 820 Would Swap: 41 Did Swap: 38

Enter up to 100 characters: abcdefghijklmnopqrstuvwxyz
Unsorted:       abcdefghijklmnopqrstuvwxyz
Sorted:         abcdefghijklmnopqrstuvwxyz
Examined: 325 Would Swap: 26 Did Swap: 0
```

Analysis

Listing 4.2 is much like listing 4.1, but some external counter variables are declared. Although externals are shunned in any large program, they are convenient in a quick-and-dirty demonstration like this.

NumberExaminations keeps track of how many letters are examined in the inner loop. WouldSwap keeps track of how many times Swap() would be called if there were no check to make sure that it is needed, and NumberSwaps keeps track of the actual count of calls to Swap().

The check on need is performed in line 47, by examining whether the conditions for the swap have been met. The variable i will be equal to min if no swap is needed; otherwise, a value to swap has been found.

As you can see, in an array that already is in order or nearly in order, this examination can reduce dramatically the number of swaps.

Did the Optimization Help?

In the most extreme examination, where the original array was fully sorted before processing began, the number of swaps was reduced from 26 to 0. This appears to be a fantastic savings, because Swap() did not have to be called for any of its potential 26 function calls. The price, however, was 26 additional comparisons. Assuming that you made the Swap() function inline, it is not clear whether you have saved much, if anything, by adding these compares.

When it is time to optimize your program, as discussed on day 17, you will examine the actual assembler output of both the inline Swap() function and the comparison to really determine which version is more efficient. You will do this examination *only* if you first can demonstrate that much of the efficiency of your program depends on getting this right, however.

Tip: Although you can optimize your sorts with a variety of approaches, you first should be sure that you need an optimization. Then, you should be able to prove that the optimization is in fact making a significant improvement.

Insertion Sort

An alternative to the selection sort is the insertion sort. The insertion sort generally is a bit quicker than the selection sort and can be represented by the way most people add cards to their poker hands. Each element is picked up in turn and inserted into its place in the array.

Suppose that you start with the children's blocks shown in figure 4.4.

Figure 4.4.
Blocks to sort.

The insertion sort examines each value and pushes each into order. First, r is moved before x. Next, a is moved before r. Then, c is moved in after a but before r, and so on. Listing 4.3 illustrates this idea.

Type   **Listing 4.3 Using an Insertion Sort**

```
1:      // Listing 4.3 - Using an Insertion Sort
2:
3:      #include <iostream.h>
4:      #include <string.h>
5:      void InsertionSort(char *Array);
6:
7:      // Ask for a buffer full of characters
8:      // Use the insertion sort to sort 'em
9:      int main()
10:     {
11:        char buffer[100];
12:
13:        cout << "Enter up to 100 characters: ";
14:        cin.getline(buffer,100);
15:
16:        cout << "Unsorted:\t" << buffer << endl;
17:
18:        InsertionSort(buffer);
19:
20:        cout << "Sorted:\t\t" << buffer << endl;
21:
22:        return 0;
23:     }
24:
25:     enum BOOL {FALSE, TRUE};
26:     // Examine each member in turn, inserting into place
27:     // any smaller member
28:     void InsertionSort(char *Input)
29:     {
30:        const int iLen = strlen(Input)+1; // length of input string
31:        char *Array = new char[iLen];       // array on which we'll work
32:        Array[0]=-1;                       // force sentinel
33:        for (int i = 0; i<iLen; i++)       // fill in from input buffer
```

continues

Listing 4.3 continued

```
34:            Array[i+1]=Input[i];
35:        Array[iLen]='\0';                // null terminate our working array
36:        int ArrayLen = strlen(Array);    // ArrayLen = N (number to sort)
37:
38:        for (int ctr = 2; ctr < ArrayLen; ctr++)
39:        {
40:            int val = Array[ctr];
41:
42:            for (int ctrTwo = ctr; Array[ctrTwo-1] > val; ctrTwo--)
43:                Array[ctrTwo]=Array[ctrTwo-1];
44:
45:            Array[ctrTwo]=val;
46:        }
47:
48:        for (i = 0; i<strlen(Input); i++)    // ready the return buffer
49:            Input[i]=Array[i+1];
50:    }
```

```
Enter up to 100 characters: xracdbsb
Unsorted:       xracdbsb
Sorted:         abbcdrsx

Enter up to 100 characters: jkdfsla;jfaisuvioaie;jiqopu7vzm,zC>320akweuioa
Unsorted:       jkdfsla;jfaisuvioaie;jiqopu7vzm,zC>320akweuioa
Sorted:         ,0237;;>Caaaaadeeffiiiiijjjkklmooopqssuuuvvwzz

d:\bc4\book2\exe>proj0000
Enter up to 100 characters: Eternal vigilance is the price of liberty
Unsorted:       Eternal vigilance is the price of liberty
Sorted:             Eaabcceeeeefghiiiiiilllnnoprrrstttvy
```

Once again, the user is prompted to enter a string in line 13, and the string is passed to InsertionSort() in line 18.

The very first thing InsertionSort() does, in lines 30 through 36, is to create a copy of the array, inserting the value -1 as the very first value (Array[0]). If the original buffer was x, r, a, c, d, b, s, b, the array now is -1, x, r, a, c, d, b, s, b.

In line 38, a counter (ctr) is created and a for loop ticks through every element in the array beginning at offset 2 (in this case, the value r). The local variable var is set to point to that value; and another counter, ctrTwo, is set to the value of ctr). For each element to the left of the value at ctr (in this case, x and -1), a comparison is made. If the value to the left is greater than the target value, a swap is performed. In this case, x is moved to the position formerly held by r. Finally, when r's place is found, it is swapped in, leaving the array -1, r, x, a, c, d, b, s, b.

This process is repeated for each member in the array, so after the next round, a has been moved into place, leaving -1, a, r, x, c, d, b, s, b.

When the array is sorted fully, the new array (without the sentinel) is copied back into the buffer, returned to the calling function, and printed.

Bubble Sort

The bubble sort is popular because it is easy to implement, easy to understand, and has the desirable trait of quickly moving the smallest element to the top of the list. The bubble sort also is quite efficient with data that already is nearly sorted; it wastes little time on resorting already sorted data.

The name *bubble sort* comes from the fact that smaller values bubble up through the array to the top, much like gas bubbles in a glass of soda (you may know this as pop, fizz, or some other bizarre regional variant). Listing 4.4 illustrates a simple bubble sort.

Listing 4.4 Using a Bubble Sort

```
1:     // Listing 4.4 - Using a Bubble Sort
2:
3:     #include <iostream.h>
4:     #include <string.h>
5:     void BubbleSort(char *Array);
6:     void swap(char& i, char& j);
7:
8:     // Ask for a buffer full of characters
9:     // Use the bubble sort to sort 'em
10:    int main()
11:    {
12:        char buffer[100];
13:
14:        cout << "Enter up to 100 characters: ";
15:        cin.getline(buffer,100);
16:
17:        cout << "Unsorted:\t" << buffer << endl;
18:
19:        BubbleSort(buffer);
20:
21:        cout << "Sorted:\t\t" << buffer << endl;
22:
23:        return 0;
24:    }
25:
26:    enum BOOL {FALSE, TRUE};
27:    // Examine each member in turn, bubbling into place
28:    // any smaller member
29:    void BubbleSort(char *Input)
30:    {
31:        int N = strlen(Input);
32:        for (int i = 0; i< N; i++)
33:            for (int j = N-1; j>0; j--)
34:                if (Input[j-1] > Input[j])
35:                    swap(Input[j-1],Input[j]);
36:    }
37:
38:    void swap(char& i, char& j)
```

continues

Listing 4.4 continued

```
39:     {
40:         char temp;
41:         temp = j;
42:         j = i;
43:         i = temp;
44:     }
```

```
Enter up to 100 characters: 54321
Unsorted:        54321
Sorted:          12345
```

The body of the program, in lines 8 through 24, is essentially identical to the previous programs, except that BubbleSort() is called.

The sort itself is fairly simple. Each member of the array is visited left to right in the outer loop in line 32. For each of these members, the inner loop is visited right to left in lines 33 through 35. Smaller values are bubbled up. This process can be seen most clearly by adding a print statement, as shown in listing 4.5.

Listing 4.5 Using a Bubble Sort with a Print Listing

```
1:      // Listing 4.5 - Using a Bubble Sort with a Print Listing
2:
3:      #include <iostream.h>
4:      #include <string.h>
5:      void BubbleSort(char *Array);
6:      void swap(char& i, char& j);
7:
8:      // Ask for a buffer full of characters
9:      // Use the bubble sort to sort 'em
10:     int main()
11:     {
12:         char buffer[100];
13:
14:         cout << "Enter up to 100 characters: ";
15:         cin.getline(buffer,100);
16:
17:         cout << "Unsorted:\t" << buffer << endl;
18:
19:         BubbleSort(buffer);
20:
21:         cout << "Sorted:\t\t" << buffer << endl;
22:
23:         return 0;
24:     }
25:
26:     enum BOOL {FALSE, TRUE};
27:     // Examine each member in turn, bubbling into place
28:     // any smaller member
29:     void BubbleSort(char *Input)
30:     {
```

```
31:        int N = strlen(Input);
32:        for (int i = 0; i< N; i++)
33:        {
34:           cout << "i: " << i << " buffer: " << Input << endl;
35:           for (int j = N-1; j>0; j--)
36:               if (Input[j-1] > Input[j])
37:                   swap(Input[j-1],Input[j]);
38:        }
39:    }
40:
41:    void swap(char& i, char& j)
42:    {
43:        char temp;
44:        temp = j;
45:        j = i;
46:        i = temp;
```

Note: Line numbers have been added to the input to make analysis easier. Your output will not have these line numbers.

```
1:  Enter up to 100 characters: 54321
2:  Unsorted:        54321
3:  i: 0 buffer: 54321
4:  i: 1 buffer: 15432
5:  i: 2 buffer: 12543
6:  i: 3 buffer: 12354
7:  i: 4 buffer: 12345
8:  Sorted:          12345
```

Listing 4.5 is just like listing 4.4, except that in line 34 the value of i is printed each time it changes. The output has been numbered to make analysis easier, although your actual output will *not* be numbered.

Line 3 of the output shows the buffer before the inner loop runs, and the numbers are in the sequence as entered: 5,4,3,2,1. After the first complete run of the inner loop, the variable i is incremented to 1; and the lowest value in the buffer, 1, has bubbled up to the top, as shown in line 4. After another run of the inner buffer, i is incremented to 2; and the second lowest value, 2, has bubbled up to the second position. This process continues until the entire array has been walked through in the outer loop, by which time the array is in order.

Tip: Although the bubble sort often is derided for being slow and inefficient, if you need to get the first results of a sort quickly, the bubble sort often can be the best option.

The bubble sort can be very convenient when you need to move values quickly to the top of the array. In fact, with a minor change, the flow can be reversed. Listing 4.6 shows the effect of bubbling downward, moving the highest values into the end of the array.

Listing 4.6 Bubbling Downward

```
1:    // Listing 4.6 - Bubbling Downward
2:
3:    #include <iostream.h>
4:    #include <string.h>
5:    void BubbleSort(char *Array);
6:    void swap(char& i, char& j);
7:
8:    // Ask for a buffer full of characters
9:    // Use the insertion sort to sort 'em
10:   int main()
11:   {
12:      char buffer[100];
13:
14:      cout << "Enter up to 100 characters: ";
15:      cin.getline(buffer,100);
16:
17:      cout << "Unsorted:\t" << buffer << endl;
18:
19:      BubbleSort(buffer);
20:
21:      cout << "Sorted:\t\t" << buffer << endl;
22:
23:      return 0;
24:   }
25:
26:   enum BOOL {FALSE, TRUE};
27:   // Examine each member in turn, bubbling highest values
28:   // down into place
29:   void BubbleSort(char *Input)
30:   {
31:      int N = strlen(Input);
32:      for (int i = N; i>=1; i--)
33:      {
34:         cout << "i: " << i << " buffer: " << Input << endl;
35:         for (int j = 1; j<i; j++)
36:            if (Input[j-1] > Input[j])
37:               swap(Input[j-1],Input[j]);
38:      }
39:   }
40:
41:   void swap(char& i, char& j)
42:   {
43:      char temp;
44:      temp = j;
45:      j = i;
46:      i = temp;
47:   }
```

Output

```
1: Enter up to 100 characters: 54321
2: Unsorted:        54321
3: i: 5 buffer: 54321
4: i: 4 buffer: 43215
5: i: 3 buffer: 32145
6: i: 2 buffer: 21345
7: i: 1 buffer: 12345
8: Sorted:         12345
```

Analysis

Listing 4.6 differs from listing 4.5 only in the logic of the bubble sort itself. Line 32 of listing 4.5 shows the outer loop counting upward from 0—for (int i = 0; i< N; i++)—whereas listing 4.6 sets i to the value of N and then counts down while i is greater than or equal to 1. Listing 4.5 counts from left to right, and listing 4.6 counts from right to left.

Listing 4.5's inner loop starts at the far right and moves left; listing 4.6's inner loop starts at the far left and moves right. The net effect of this is that the higher values are bubbled downward.

In line 3 of the output, i has been initialized to 5 (the value of N), and the array is fully unsorted. In line 4 of the output, i has been decremented and the value 5 has fallen to the bottom of the array. In line 4, i again has been decremented, and now the second highest value, 4, has fallen to the next-to-last position. In this way, the array is sorted in low-to-high order by pushing down the values in the order high to low.

Bubble sorts can be very convenient, even though they are somewhat less efficient than other sorts. If you were to take a directory listing and sort it using the bubble sort, each entry could be shown as it is made available (at each iteration of the outer loop). Although the overall sort might be marginally slower, preliminary results could be provided earlier than with some other sorts.

Improving the Bubble Sort

You might make two observations about the bubble sort. The first is that if you are sorting upward, after you move a value into position, there is no reason to compare other values with that value ever again. That is, if you bubble the lowest number to the top of the array, there is no reason to compare other numbers to see whether they are lower than that number. After all, that is what a bubble sort does—it moves the lowest number up into position, and then it moves the second lowest, and so on.

The second observation is that if you make no swaps in any comparison all the way through one iteration, you are done; no future iterations will create swaps either. Listing 4.7 illustrates these improvements.

Type | Listing 4.7 Improving the Bubble Sort

```
1:      // listing 4.7 - Improving the Bubble Sort
2:
3:      #include <iostream.h>
4:      #include <string.h>
5:      void BubbleSort(char *);
6:      void BetterBubble(char *);
7:      void swap(char& i, char& j);
8:
9:      // Ask for a buffer full of characters
10:     // Use the bubble sort to sort 'em
11:     int main()
12:     {
13:         char buffer[100];
14:         char buff2[100];
15:
16:         cout << "Enter up to 100 characters: ";
17:         cin.getline(buffer,100);
18:         strcpy(buff2,buffer);
19:
20:         cout << "Unsorted:\t" << buffer << endl;
21:
22:         BubbleSort(buffer);
23:
24:         cout << "Sorted:\t\t" << buffer << endl;
25:
26:         cout << "press Enter to continue";
27:         cin.getline(buffer,10);
28:
29:         BetterBubble(buff2);
30:
31:         cout << "Sorted:\t\t" << buff2 << endl;
32:
33:         return 0;
34:     }
35:
36:     enum BOOL {FALSE, TRUE};
37:     // Examine each member in turn, bubbling into place
38:     // any smaller member
39:     void BubbleSort(char *Input)
40:     {
41:         int N = strlen(Input);
42:         int compare = 0;
43:         int didSwap = 0;
44:         for (int i = 0; i< N; i++)
45:         {
46:             for (int j = N-1; j>0; j--)
47:             {
48:               compare++;
49:               if (Input[j-1] > Input[j])
50:               {
51:                   didSwap++;
52:                   swap(Input[j-1],Input[j]);
53:               }
54:             }
```

```
55:            }
56:            cout << compare << " compares; " << didSwap << " swaps" << endl;
57:     }
58:
59:    void BetterBubble(char *Input)
60:    {
61:       int n = strlen(Input);
62:        int compare = 0;
63:        int didSwap = 0;
64:       BOOL swapped = TRUE;
65:
66:       for (int i=0; swapped; i++)
67:       {
68:          swapped = FALSE;
69:          for (int j=n-1;j>i; j--)
70:          {
71:             compare++;
72:             if (Input[j-1] > Input[j])
73:             {
74:                swap(Input[j-1], Input[j]);
75:                swapped = TRUE;
76:                didSwap++;
77:             }
78:          }
79:       }
80:        cout << compare << " compares; " << didSwap << " swaps" << endl;
81:    }
82:
83:     void swap(char& i, char& j)
84:     {
85:        char temp;
86:        temp = j;
87:        j = i;
88:        i = temp;
89:     }
```

```
Enter up to 100 characters: asdfghjklzxcvbnmpoiuytrewq
Unsorted:         asdfghjklzxcvbnmpoiuytrewq
650 compares; 108 swaps
Sorted:           abcdefghijklmnopqrstuvwxyz
press Enter to continue
297 compares; 108 swaps
Sorted:           abcdefghijklmnopqrstuvwxyz

d:\bc4\book2\exe>proj0001
Enter up to 100 characters: abcdefghijklmnopqrstuvwxyz
Unsorted:         abcdefghijklmnopqrstuvwxyz
650 compares; 0 swaps
Sorted:           abcdefghijklmnopqrstuvwxyz
press Enter to continue
25 compares; 0 swaps
Sorted:           abcdefghijklmnopqrstuvwxyz
```

Analysis Listing 4.7 runs two versions of the BubbleSort(). The first version is just like listing 4.4, except that it keeps track of comparison in line 48; if there is a swap, it counts that as well in line 51. After the array is sorted, it prints these counts as a metric of how hard the sort worked.

The second version of BubbleSort() implements the two optimizations described in the preceding paragraph. The outer for loop in line 66 ends if nothing was swapped. The inner for loop is modified to check whether j is greater than i rather than 0; that is, it doesn't check those items already sorted. The count of comparisons and swaps is printed in line 80.

As you can see from the output, a nearly random array of characters falls from 650 compares and 108 swaps to 297 compares and 108 swaps. A sorted array falls from 650 compares and no swaps to 25 compares and no swaps. This optimization, therefore, is very much worth the tiny extra effort.

> **Tip:** The correct optimization can save you significant processing time. The trick is to make sure that you are fixing a real problem. The fix must not make other conditions worse, and the problem you are solving must matter in your program. There is no sense in fixing a part of the code that you almost never call and that doesn't take very long in the first place.

QuickSort()

The most popular sort among computer programmers may well be QuickSort(). This approach, invented in 1960 by C.A.R. Hoare, is probably not the quickest sort (despite its name) available, but it is easy to implement, it works well for many needs, and it has been adopted by many compiler vendors. The standard C library calls for a Qsort, which does *not* guarantee that the QuickSort() will be used, but many programmers assume that QuickSort() is the implementation nonetheless.

To see how QuickSort() works, assume that you have the array shown in figure 4.5.

Figure 4.5.
An initial array.

	left					right	
	i					j	target
(position)	0	1	2	3	4	5	6	7
(value)	b	r	d	h	c	g	e	f

The first time you call QuickSort(), you pass in the array and ask it to sort starting at position 0, which is given the name left. You also ask it to sort the entire array by telling it the size of the array, in this case 8, called right.

On each call to QuickSort(), the right parameter (8) is compared with the left parameter (0). If right is not greater than left, the function exits.

The value of the entry in the rightmost position (Array[right-1]) is saved as target. (In this case, target holds the value f.) Two local variables (i and j) are initialized. i is initialized to point to the extreme left (b), and j is initialized to point to the rightmost value other than the target (in this case, e).

An inner loop is created in which i will be incremented and j will be decremented. When the letters cross over, the inner loop will end.

Each time through the inner loop, i is incremented until it points to a value that is greater than or equal to the target. In this case, it will end up pointing to r and have the value 1 (remembering that arrays count from 0).

j is decremented each time through the inner loop, and moves left until it finds a value that is less than or equal to the target. Because in this case j was initialized to position 6 and holds the value e, it will not move at all.

If the letters have not crossed over, the values they point to are swapped. The result of this is shown in figure 4.6.

Figure 4.6.
After the first swap.

				i			j	target
(position)	0	1	2	3	4	5	6	7
(value)	b	e	d	h	c	g	r	f

The second time through the inner loop, i starts out with the value 1 and continues looking for a value greater than or equal to the target, thus moving right to position 3. j starts out with the value 6, pointing to r, and moves left until it finds a value less than or equal to the target. It stops at position 4 and i stops at position 3, and these are swapped. The result is shown in figure 4.7.

Figure 4.7.
After the second swap.

				i	j			
(position)	0	1	2	3	4	5	6	7
(value)	b	e	d	c	h	g	r	f

The variables i and j look again, but this time when they stop, i is pointing to position 4 and j is pointing to position 3, and they have crossed over one another. This terminates the inner loop, without an additional swap.

Sorting

The outer loop now swaps the value at i with the target. The result is shown in figure 4.8.

Figure 4.8.

After the outer loop swap.

						j	i			
(position)	0	1	2	3	4	5	6	7
(value)	b	e	d	c	f	g	r	h

Note that at this point the target, F, is at position 4. Everything to the left of the target now is smaller than it, and everything to its right now is larger. The array has been broken into two parts around the target.

At this point, QuickSort() is called again, twice. The first call sets left to 0 and right to the value of i (4), and the second call sets left to the value of i+1 (5) and right to the value of right (8). This is illustrated in figure 4.9.

Figure 4.9.

Ready for the next
QuickSort().

	left				right	left		right
(position)	0	1	2	3	4	0	1	2
(value)	b	e	d	c	f	g	r	h

Each of these arrays then will be sorted recursively, as shown in listing 4.8.

Listing 4.8 Using QuickSort()

```
1:    // Listing 4.8 - Using QuickSort()
2:
3:    #include <iostream.h>
4:    #include <string.h>
5:    void QuickSort(char*, int, int);
6:    void swap(char& i, char& j);
7:
8:    // Ask for a buffer full of characters
9:    // Use Quicksort to sort 'em
10:   int main()
11:   {
12:       char buffer[100];
13:
14:       cout << "Enter up to 100 characters: ";
15:       cin.getline(buffer,100);
16:
17:       cout << "Unsorted:\t" << buffer << endl;
18:
19:       int len = strlen(buffer);
20:       QuickSort(buffer,0,len);
21:
22:       cout << "Sorted:\t\t" << buffer << endl;
23:
24:       return 0;
25:   }
26:
```

```
27:     enum BOOL {FALSE, TRUE};
28:     // Sort each part, then recursively call
29:     // the Quicksort procedure
30:     void QuickSort(char *Input, int left, int right)
31:     {
32:         if (right > left)
33:         {
34:             char target = Input[right-1];
35:             int i = left-1;
36:             int x = right-1;
37:             for (;;)
38:             {
39:                 while (Input[++i] < target)
40:                     ;
41:                 while (Input[--x] > target)
42:                     ;
43:                 if (i >= x)
44:                     break;
45:                 swap(Input[i], Input[x]);
46:             }
47:             swap(Input[i], Input[right-1]);
48:             QuickSort(Input,left,i);
49:             QuickSort(Input,i+1,right);
50:         }
51:     }
52:
53:     void swap(char& i, char& j)
54:     {
55:         char temp;
56:         temp = j;
57:         j = i;
58:         i = temp;
59:     }
```

4

Enter up to 100 characters: jaskl;jfdk;a3uioapvjiasd
Unsorted: jaskl;jfdk;a3uioapvjiasd
Sorted: 3;;aaaaddfiijjjkklopssuv

Enter up to 100 characters: Eternal vigalence is the price of liberty
Unsorted: Eternal vigalence is the price of liberty
Sorted: Eaabcceeeeeefghiiiilllnnoprrrstttvy

Once again, the body of the main program differs from the previous programs only in that QuickSort() is called. Initially, Quicksort() is called with 0 and N—that is the entire array is to be sorted.

In line 32, the end condition for the recursion is tested, the second parameter must be greater than the first, or you have "crossed over" and it is time to return. In line 34, the last letter in the array is set as the target. In lines 35 and 36, two local variables are initialized to the leftmost and rightmost entries in the array *not counting the target*.

The leftmost pointer (`Input[i]`) is incremented to point to the first letter that is *not* less in value than the target, and the rightmost pointer (`Input[x]`) is decremented until it points to a letter that is not greater than the target. If the letters have crossed over, the loop is exited as shown in lines 43 and 44. Otherwise, not having crossed over, the letters now are swapped.

In either case, the value at the left pointer then is swapped with the target. The array then is divided (unevenly) into everything up to where i now is pointing and everything after that point, and `QuickSort()` then is called recursively on the remaining arrays.

> **Note:** `QuickSort()` is a very popular sort, but it is important to note that the QSORT provided by ANSI standard libraries is *not* guaranteed to use `QuickSort()`.

Sorting Pointers Rather Than Records

Until now, you have been sorting letters in an array. It is possible, however, that your objects to be sorted are substantially larger than letters. You might, for example, have a collection of strings to sort.

Each string might be hundreds of bytes large, and exchanging two strings might entail significant overhead. Because each of these sorting algorithms involves multiple swaps, it would be best if it were possible to avoid more than N swaps. In other words, you will want to swap each string no more than once.

To accomplish this, you create an array of pointers to your objects, and then swap the pointers. After the array of pointers is fully sorted, you then can rearrange your array of objects into the sorted order. Listing 4.9 illustrates this technique by using `QuickSort()` on an array of string objects.

Listing 4.9 Sorting Pointers

```
1:     // Listing 4.9 - Sorting Pointers
2:
3:     #include <iostream.h>
4:     #include <string.h>
5:     #include "string.hpp"
6:
7:     void QuickSort(String**, int, int);
8:     void swap(String*& i, String*& j);
9:
10:    // Ask for a buffer full of characters
11:    // Use the insertion sort to sort 'em
12:    int main()
13:    {
14:       char buffer[100];
15:       String *pArray[5];
```

```
16:        for (int i = 0; i<5; i++)
17:        {
18:            cout << "Enter the string: ";
19:            cin.getline(buffer,100);
20:            pArray[i] = new String(buffer);
21:        }
22:
23:        cout << "\nUnsorted: "<< endl;
24:        for (i = 0; i < 4; i++)
25:            cout << *pArray[i] << ", ";
26:        cout << *pArray[4] << endl;
27:
28:        QuickSort(pArray,0,5);
29:
30:        cout << "\nSorted: "<< endl;
31:        for (i = 0; i < 4; i++)
32:            cout << *pArray[i] << ", ";
33:        cout << *pArray[4] << endl;
34:
35:        return 0;
36:    }
37:
38:    // QuickSort method modified to take pointers.
39:    // Examine each member in turn, inserting into place
40:    // any smaller member
41:    void QuickSort(String** Input, int left, int right)
42:    {
43:        if (right > left)
44:        {
45:            String* target = Input[right-1];
46:            int i = left-1;
47:            int x = right-1;
48:            for (;;)
49:            {
50:                while (*Input[++i] < *target)
51:                    ;
52:                while (*Input[--x] > *target)
53:                    ;
54:
55:                if (i >= x)
56:                    break;
57:                swap(Input[i], Input[x]);
58:            }
59:            swap(Input[i], Input[right-1]);
60:            QuickSort(Input,left,i);
61:            QuickSort(Input,i+1,right);
62:        }
63:    }
64:
65:    // note reference to pointers!
66:    void swap(String*& i, String*& j)
67:    {
68:        String* temp;
69:        temp = j;
70:        j = i;
71:        i = temp;
72:    }
```

```
Enter the string: eternal
Enter the string: vigalence
Enter the string: is the
Enter the string: price of
Enter the string: liberty

Unsorted:
eternal, vigalence, is the, price of, liberty

Sorted:
eternal, is the, liberty, price of, vigalence
```

Listing 4.8 is similar to listing 4.7, except that in this case, *pointers* to the strings are sorted, rather than the strings themselves.

This requires a change to the signatures of both QuickSort() and Swap(). QuickSort() now receives an array of pointers to strings, which can be represented as String*[], or equally well as String**.

What is passed to Swap() now will be a pointer to a String, which is itself passed by reference, so the signature is a reference to pointer and thus Swap(String*& i, String*& j).

The array of pointers to strings is initialized in lines 16 through 21. The user repeatedly is prompted to enter a string, which is placed in a C-style string buffer. This then is used as a parameter to the constructor of a String object created on the heap, and the unnamed pointer returned by the operator new is stored in pArray.

The unsorted contents of this array are printed in lines 23 through 26, and then the array is passed to QuickSort() in line 28. The returned values, now sorted, are printed in lines 30 through 33.

Careful examination of lines 57 and 59 of QuickSort() reveal that only the pointers are swapped within the array, rather than the strings themselves. Note, however, that the comparisons in lines 50 and 52 involve the strings and not the pointers. The idea is to sort by the value of the strings, but to swap only the pointers.

As discussed, Swap() takes as its parameters *references* to the two String pointers to swap. It could well have taken pointers to these pointers, but then all the pointers would have had to be dereferenced. This way, the clean interface is preserved. Note, in line 68, that temp must be declared as a pointer to String because, of course, that is what it must hold.

Parameterizing the Sort

Now that QuickSort() is working well for you, you will want to parameterize it to take pointers to any objects. This process is fairly straightforward; simply create a template form of both QuickSort() and Swap().

In the body of each of these functions, you must replace the specific type (String*) with a parameterized type (T*). You do *not* need to instantiate a particular instance of the template (you don't write QuickSort<String*>), because function overloading will take care of that for you. Listing 4.10 illustrates parameterizing the QuickSort() function and then using it with an array of String pointers and an array of int pointers.

Listing 4.10 Using a Parameterized QuickSort

```
1:     // Listing 4.10 - Using a Parameterized QuickSort
2:
3:     #include <iostream.h>
4:     #include <string.h>
5:     #include <stdlib.h>
6:
7:     #include "string.hpp"
8:
9:     template <class T> void QuickSort(T*, int, int);
10:    template <class T> void Swap(T& i, T& j);
11:
12:    // Ask for a buffer full of characters
13:    // Use the insertion sort to sort 'em
14:    int main()
15:    {
16:        char buffer[100];
17:        String *pArray[5];
18:        for (int i = 0; i<5; i++)
19:        {
20:            cout << "Enter the string: ";
21:            cin.getline(buffer,100);
22:            pArray[i] = new String(buffer);
23:        }
24:
25:        cout << "\nUnsorted: "<< endl;
26:        for (i = 0; i < 4; i++)
27:            cout << *pArray[i] << ", ";
28:        cout << *pArray[4] << endl;
29:
30:        QuickSort(pArray,0,5);
31:
32:        cout << "\nSorted: "<< endl;
33:        for (i = 0; i < 4; i++)
34:            cout << *pArray[i] << ", ";
35:        cout << *pArray[4] << endl;
36:
37:        int *intArray[10];
38:        for (i = 0; i < 10; i++)
39:        {
40:            intArray[i] = new int;
41:            *intArray[i] = rand();
42:        }
43:
44:        cout << "\nUnsorted: "<< endl;
```

continues

Listing 4.10 continued

```
45:        for (i = 0;  i < 9;  i++)
46:            cout << *intArray[i] << ", ";
47:        cout << *intArray[9] << endl;
48:
49:        QuickSort(intArray,0,10);
50:
51:        cout << "\nSorted: "<< endl;
52:        for (i = 0;  i < 9;  i++)
53:            cout << *intArray[i] << ", ";
54:        cout << *intArray[9] << endl;
55:
56:        return 0;
57:    }
58:
59:    // Templatized Quicksort Function
60:    template <class T>
61:    void QuickSort(T* Input, int left, int right)
62:    {
63:        if (right > left)
64:        {
65:            T target = Input[right-1];
66:            int i = left-1;
67:            int x = right-1;
68:            for (;;)
69:            {
70:                while (*Input[++i] < *target)
71:                    ;
72:                while (*Input[--x] > *target)
73:                    ;
74:
75:                if (i >= x)
76:                    break;
77:                Swap(Input[i], Input[x]);
78:            }
79:
80:            Swap(Input[i], Input[right-1]);
81:            QuickSort(Input,left,i);
82:            QuickSort(Input,i+1,right);
83:
84:        }
85:    }
86:
87:    template <class T>
88:    inline void Swap(T& i, T& j)
89:    {
90:        T temp;
91:        temp = j;
92:        j = i;
93:        i = temp;
94:    }
```

```
Enter the string: eternal
Enter the string: vigalence
Enter the string: is the
Enter the string: price of
Enter the string: liberty

Unsorted:
eternal, vigalence, is the, price of, liberty

Sorted:
eternal, is the, liberty, price of, vigalence

Unsorted:
346, 130, 10982, 1090, 11656, 7117, 17595, 6415, 22948, 31126

Sorted:
130, 346, 1090, 6415, 7117, 10982, 11656, 17595, 22948, 31126
```

Listing 4.10 is similar to listing 4.9, except that the type of the object to be sorted has been parameterized in the declarations of both `QuickSort()` in line 9 and `Swap()` in line 10.

Invocation of `QuickSort()` on objects of type `String` is shown in line 30, and invocation of `QuickSort()` on integers is shown in line 49. Note, again, that no special declaration of these instances is required; function overloading does the job of telling the compiler to create an instance of these functions based on the template.

The integers for the unsorted array are created in line 41 by invocation of the standard library `rand()` function. This is not a great way to generate true random numbers, but it suffices for the purpose of demonstrating the sort.

Limitations of the *QuickSort()* Routine

`QuickSort()` is a good general-purpose sort, but its efficiency depends very much on what object you use as the target. In the versions shown earlier, the final member of the array always was chosen as the target. This method can introduce inefficiencies if the last member of the target happens to be the largest (or smallest) member of the array.

Many programmers work around this problem by using the *Median of Three* rule. To use this rule, choose the first, last, and middle elements in the array. Sort them and choose the middle value. Use that value as the target. Listing 4.11 illustrates `QuickSort()` using the Median of Three rule.

Listing 4.11 Using `QuickSort()` with Median of Three

```
1:    // Listing 4.11 Using QuickSort() with Median of Three
2:
3:    #include <iostream.h>
4:    #include <string.h>
```

continues

Listing 4.11 continued

```
5:      #include "string.hpp"
6:
7:      // function prototypes
8:      void QuickSort(String**, int, int);
9:      void Swap(String*& i, String*& j);
10:     int Median(String**,int,int,int);
11:
12:     int main()
13:     {
14:         // prompt for five strings
15:         // sort them using QuickSort and Median of Three
16:         char buffer[100];
17:         String *pArray[5];
18:         for (int i = 0; i<5; i++)
19:         {
20:             cout << "Enter the string: ";
21:             cin.getline(buffer,100);
22:             pArray[i] = new String(buffer);
23:         }
24:
25:         cout << "\nUnsorted: "<< endl;
26:         for (i = 0; i < 4; i++)
27:             cout << *pArray[i] << ", ";
28:         cout << *pArray[4] << endl;
29:
30:         QuickSort(pArray,0,5);
31:
32:         cout << "\nSorted: "<< endl;
33:         for (i = 0; i < 4; i++)
34:             cout << *pArray[i] << ", ";
35:         cout << *pArray[4] << endl;
36:
37:         return 0;
38:     }
39:
40:     // given three positions, return the middle value
41:     int Median(String** array,int left,int right,int middle)
42:     {
43:         if (array[left] < array[right])
44:             return array[left] > array[middle] ? left : middle;
45:         else
46:             return array[right] < array[middle] ? middle : right;
47:     }
48:
49:     // QuickSort implemented with Median of Three
50:     void QuickSort(String** Input, int left, int right)
51:     {
52:         if (right > left)
53:         {
54:             int med = Median(Input,left,right-1, (left + right) /2);
55:             String* target = Input[med];
56:             int i = left-1;
57:             int x = right;
58:             for (;;)
```

```
59:             {
60:                 while (*Input[++i] < *target)
61:                     ;
62:                 while (*Input[--x] > *target)
63:                     ;
64:
65:                 if (i >= x)
66:                     break;
67:                 Swap(Input[i], Input[x]);
68:             }
69:             Swap(Input[i], Input[med]);
70:             QuickSort(Input,left,i);
71:             QuickSort(Input,i+1,right);
72:         }
73:     }
74:
75:     void Swap(String*& i, String*& j)
76:     {
77:         String* temp;
78:         temp = j;
79:         j = i;
80:         i = temp;
81:     }
```

```
Enter the string: eternal
Enter the string: vigalence
Enter the string: is the
Enter the string: price of
Enter the string: liberty

Unsorted:
eternal, vigalence, is the, price of, liberty

Sorted:
eternal, is the, liberty, price of, vigalence

Unsorted:
346, 130, 10982, 1090, 11656, 7117, 17595, 6415, 22948, 31126

Sorted:
130, 346, 1090, 6415, 7117, 10982, 11656, 17595, 22948, 31126
```

Listing 4.11 is exactly like listing 4.9, except in how the target value is chosen. In the previous examples, the target value was always the last value in the array. This method works well for an unsorted list, but does not work well for a list that is fully or nearly fully sorted.

In line 54, the target position is chosen by calling Median() and passing in the leftmost value, the rightmost value, and a value from the middle of the array. Median() returns the position of the middle of these three values, and that position is used as the target or pivot point for the current round of the QuickSort(). With a sorted or nearly sorted array, this dramatically reduces the number of compares and swaps required.

Summary

Today you learned a number of techniques for sorting. Although academic books on sorts spend a great deal of time on the mathematics of sorts, proving why this one or that one is optimal in a particular situation, real-world programmers generally stick with a few tried-and-true sort algorithms.

You saw how insertion and selection sorts work, how the bubble sort works, and what it can do for your program. Then you saw how to use QuickSort(). You learned how to sort pointers when sorting large objects, and how to make a template of your sort algorithm so that you can sort differing *types* of objects. Finally, you learned how to set the target value for QuickSort() using the *Median of Three* rule.

Q&A

Q What are the important things to look for when evaluating the performance of a sorting algorithm?

A The most important issue is the number of times it must do its basic comparison, as a function of the number of items being sorted. Usually this is proportional to n squared (the number of items, squared), but some, like QuickSort(), are better. This should be evaluated for the common case, and for some special cases.

Q What are the special cases?

A The special cases are when the data already is sorted—both in the order you want and in the opposite order. Because data often will arrive in these orders, a good sorting algorithm will have good behavior on these cases.

Q How do the sorts in this chapter stack up, according to these criteria?

A SelectionSort() is pretty bad, doing n squared operations in all cases. (For every slot in the final, sorted list, it checks every one of the remaining values in order to find the lowest. Although this is not exactly n squared, it is proportional to it, which is what matters.)

InsertionSort() still is considered to be an n-squared algorithm, even though it short-circuits many of the operations when items are found to be sorted already. Given a completely sorted list, InsertionSort() performance is proportional to n, which is the best possible.

BubbleSort() has similar behavior to InsertionSort(). Both BubbleSort() and InsertionSort() have their best performance on an already sorted list, and their worst on a reverse-sorted list.

`QuickSort()` is the only algorithm seen so far with *n log n* performance. This means that the number of operations needed is proportional to n times the logarithm of n. For very long lists, this method is significantly better than n squared.

Q When should you sort pointers to items instead of the items themselves?

A Whenever swapping the items is noticeably more costly than swapping pointers. If the items are strings, this is clearly the case. If the items are floats, for example, it is close or the same. (Compare `sizeof(float)` with `sizeof(float *)` on your system.) If the items are doubles, pointers probably are better, although it's still pretty close.

Workshop

The Workshop provides quiz questions to help you solidify your understanding of the material covered, and exercises to provide you with experience in using what you have learned. Try to answer the quiz and exercise questions before checking the answers in Appendix A, and make sure that you understand the answers before continuing to the next chapter.

Quiz

1. Describe in words the algorithm of `SelectionSort()`.
2. Describe the optimization added in listing 4.2.
3. Describe in words the algorithm of `InsertionSort()`.
4. Describe in words the algorithm of `BubbleSort()`.
5. Describe in words the algorithm of `QuickSort()`.

Exercises

1. Modify the `SelectionSort()` function to sort highest to lowest instead of lowest to highest. Use the test program to test your results.
2. Use the parameterized `QuickSort()` to sort an array of ULONGs.
3. Parameterize the `InsertionSort()` algorithm.
4. Test the parameterized `InsertionSort()` from exercise 3 with an array of doubles.

Design

Traditionally, programmers sketched out a quick design on a scrap of paper and then started writing code. For small C programs, this method worked fairly well and, in truth, many useful programs were produced with only the flimsiest of preliminary designs.

C++ tends to be somewhat less tolerant of this approach. Countless hours of programming experience have shown that good C++ programs are designed well before coding begins. The reward for this diligence is programs that are flexible, extensible, and rock-solid.

The Personal Information Manager you will be writing over the course of this book is a nontrivial, real-world program and, as such, it deserves and demands an appropriate investment in design.

Today you will learn

☐ How to approach designing the PIM

☐ How to build the program in stages

☐ How to plan for data storage, persistence, and high performance

☐ How to plan for specification changes and extensions

The Specification

Specifications can usefully be divided into functional specifications and technical specifications. *Functional specifications* tell you what the user's experience will be like, and *technical specifications* tell you how the program actually will work.

Technical specifications then can be divided into class interfaces, database designs, inheritance diagrams, and so on.

The Functional Specification

ROBIN is, from a functional viewpoint, a Personal Information Manager (PIM) with which the user can store and quickly retrieve notes and other text-based information.

It is designed to provide quick access to the kinds of notes one usually writes in a notebook. The quick access, however, invites the user to use ROBIN as a phone book or a database of personal contacts. One can imagine storing away recipes, inventories of videotapes, and creating other general-purpose, simple databases.

What sets ROBIN apart from other database products is that the data is entered without regard to keywords, titles, subject headings, or other classifications. All the text in all the notes is indexed, and it later can be retrieved with a very simple interface.

Version 1 is designed to be a text-based product, with only a rudimentary command-line interface. Output is streamed to the console or screen and can be redirected to a file. Version 1 does not envision menus, dialog boxes, windows, buttons, or any of the other interface objects characteristic of graphical user interfaces—these are reserved for a subsequent release.

The command-line interface works with flags. A *flag* is a dash followed by a letter or word indicating a command. Every command can be abbreviated to a single letter. For example, -Index can be abbreviated as -I, and -Search can be abbreviated as -S.

Storing Data

The user stores data in ROBIN by one of three methods:

☐ Direct entry
☐ Providing a file as a note
☐ Providing a file, each line of which is to be made into a note

To provide direct entry, the user enters

```
ROBIN -I (Index)
```

followed by the text to index. All the text entered until the user presses Enter will be indexed on a new note.

Suppose that the user enters the following:

```
ROBIN -Index Remember to put out the recycling on the second Tuesday of every
month.
```

A new note will be created and time stamped with the following text:

```
Remember to put out the recycling on the second Tuesday of every month.
```

The user can open any word processor or editor that saves flat-text files and enter as much text as wanted, without regard to new lines and paragraphs. The user then would save the file (for example, with the name **NOTE1.TXT**) and then feed that file to ROBIN by writing the following:

```
ROBIN -File Note1.txt
```

ROBIN then would read the entire file and create a new, time-stamped note with the contents of that file.

Alternatively, the user can point to a file and ask ROBIN to incorporate a note that just references that file. In this case, the user might enter the following:

```
ROBIN -Reference Note2.txt How to make chicken soup
```

This line would create a note with the text *How to make chicken soup* and a reference to the file NOTE2.TXT.

5

Finally, the user also can provide a file with records separated by a new line. Such a file might have phone book entries, with one entry on each line. If the file were called PHONE.TXT, the user would enter the following:

```
ROBIN -Lines phone.txt
```

ROBIN would read the file and make a new time-stamped note for each line in the file.

A potential extension to this capability, not implemented in version 1, would be to let the users provide their own record delimiters, rather than using the new line character. Perhaps ROBIN could support the syntax -L";", where whatever appears between the quotation marks (in this case, a semicolon) would become the delimiter for new records. Thus, if the user wrote

```
ROBIN -L";" myRecords.txt
```

ROBIN would open a new time-stamped note for each record, where a record is all the text between semicolons.

Searching for Data

The user searches for data by entering ROBIN followed by the command -Search and then a list of target words. The user might write the following line, for example:

```
ROBIN -Search computer disk
```

This line will find any note with *either* the word *computer or* the word *disk*. Note that -? functions as a synonym for Search, so the user can enter the following:

```
ROBIN -? computer disk
```

One issue to consider is whether to support wild cards. You may want to use **comput***, for example, to match *computer, compute, computing,* and so on. A more advanced version of this capability would allow the user to enter **p*y**, which would match *party, parity, pinkey,* and so on. Some systems use the question mark (?) to match any single letter, so **p??y** would match *pony* and *play,* but not *party*. Version 1 will support only the wild card *, used at the end of a word to indicate any number of additional letters.

Future releases of ROBIN could be extended to include more powerful wild cards and perhaps Boolean search terms such as AND, OR, and NOT. You even may want to consider adding *general regular expression parsing* (GREP), which supports very powerful text searching.

Displaying Found Data

If the search returns no notes, the message Nothing found is displayed. If a single note is found, that note is displayed. If multiple notes are found, a menu of choices is provided.

In version 1, the user interface will be rudimentary. The menu of results will be numbered, with each entry displaying the first 30 characters of the note and its date. If the note is longer than 30 characters, the display will end with an ellipsis (...). At the bottom of the message, a menu is displayed.

If the user chooses a note, it is displayed, and then the user is returned to the menu of notes.

Database Management

ROBIN should be fairly easy to maintain by the user. Periodically, however, the user will want to be able to delete notes and to pack the database. The user is provided with three tools for database management: Delete, Undelete, and Pack.

Every message has a message number, which is displayed along with the message itself. The user can enter

```
ROBIN -Delete 123
```

to delete message 123. The system will display the first few lines of the message and the following prompt:

```
Delete this message (y/N)?
```

The user can press Y and then Enter to confirm the deletion. Pressing any other letter or just pressing Enter cancels the deletion.

The user can request to see all deleted messages that have not yet been packed (removed from the database) by entering the following:

```
ROBIN -Morgue
```

This provides a list of all notes marked as deleted, much like the list displayed after a search. A message can be undeleted by using the -Undelete flag. For example, ROBIN -U 123 will undelete message 123.

The deleted messages can be fully removed by packing the database with the -Pack flag. If the user enters

```
ROBIN  -Pack
```

the system confirms with the following message:

```
Really pack the database (y/N)
```

The user presses Y and Enter to confirm; pressing any other letter cancels the operation.

The system needs to know where to find its database of existing notes. It first searches for an environment variable, ROBIN. If this is set to a path, the system looks at that location for a file named `ROBIN.DB`. If the environment variable is not set, the system searches the user's path for the file. If `ROBIN.DB` is not found, the system displays the following message:

```
No database found, create one (y/N)
```

Confirmation works in the usual way; if the user presses Y, a new ROBIN.DB file is created.

Getting Help

Entering **ROBIN** with no parameters prints the preliminary Help message:

```
ROBIN (c) copyright 1994 Jesse Liberty Version 1.0
Usage:  -Index ¦ -File ¦ -Reference -Lines ¦ -Search (-?) ¦ -Delete ¦ -Morgue
 -Undelete ¦ -Pack  ¦ -Help
```

Entering **ROBIN** with **-Help** provides the Help prompt:

```
Help is available on a number of subjects. Enter Help Help for a full explanation
of Help, or enter Help followed by one of the following keywords: Index, File,
Lines, Search, Delete, Morgue, Undelete, Pack, for help on that subject.
```

Help itself is just a set of notes provided with the software, which uses a special search to find the designated topics.

A Moving Target

Developers always want a solid, immovable specification coupled with the flexibility to change their own designs as needed. Reality is quite different; your clients will, no doubt, reserve the right to change their specifications at will. Other developers working on your project, on the other hand, will complain long and loud if you change the interface to classes on which they depend!

It would be nice if we were all smart enough to get our designs right the first time and to write code that compiles, links, and runs without bugs on the first attempt; none of that is likely any time soon, however. Design, like coding, is *iterative*; this is programmer talk for the need to keep trying after the first attempt fails miserably.

The Technical Specification

Supporting the functional specification with an object-oriented design takes a great deal of thought and effort. There is no one, clear, true, and perfect way to design anything, and the world is full of other designers who might do whatever you do differently.

That doesn't mean that there aren't good designs and bad designs, however, or that it is impossible to tell the difference between them. A good design is flexible and extensible, but not

at the expense of being so general as to be insupportably complex. A good design adjusts to a changing specification, but still exhibits high performance and good reliability.

Iterative Design

I could cheat and write the whole program, debug it, release it, and then come back and write this chapter. It would be easy to do, and no one would be any the wiser. "What a genius," you would think, "his very first design worked perfectly." You would look inward with despair and lament "How come I can't get my design right the first time?"

Such an approach would leave you with that overwhelming feeling of inadequacy that technical writers delight in instilling in new programmers. But it would be a lie. No design of a complex program is 100 percent correct the first time you write it down. Let me rephrase that: No design of a complex program is 100 percent correct the first time *I* write it down.

What I will do, however, is present my unedited initial design, blemishes and all. I'll try to think out loud (okay, I'll try to think into my word processor, but let's not quibble). This will, I hope, give some insight into the design process.

Where Do I Start?

When creating a design from scratch, it is common to become overwhelmed by the complexity of the design. A good way to get grounded is to make a list of what you already know, and what you don't know.

In this case, you might write down that you know you will need notes, menus, and so on; but that you don't know whether there are derived types of notes, who will manage the display, how you will manage switching on the command line, and so on.

The second rule of good design is to concentrate on what 90 percent of the people will do 90 percent of the time. This rule was taught to me by Jay Leve at Citibank, and his point was that techies tend to get over-focused on boundary conditions (*yes, but what if the user does this weird thing...*). We lose sight of the 90-percent case.

Once your design handles the 90-percent case well, you always can work on the exceptions to the rule. You cannot stop at the 90-percent case, of course. Truly professional code is bulletproof and handles anything the user might possibly do, but that can be worried about fairly late in the design phase.

The third rule is not to confuse analysis with design. Although you will iterate over all of analysis, design, and programming, it is important to know when you are doing each. *Analysis* is the assessment of the problem domain, and *design* is exploration of the solution space. This goes back to differentiating between what you know and what you don't know.

5

It also is possible to become immobilized by conflicting designs. You finally decide on one approach, only later to realize that you should have gone with the earlier approach. You rip up your work, start over, and then halfway through decide you were right the first time.

This is called *analysis paralysis* (and a few other choice words). The only cure is, at some point, to make a decision and press onward. After you ship version 1, you may want to go back and redesign, but sooner or later it comes down to getting a product out the door. I would wager that more products have been destroyed by failing to ship than by poor design.

What Are the Initial Classes?

Certainly ROBIN will require a Note class. It is useful to append all the classes with a letter indicating that they belong to the same collection of classes, so I'll create an rNote class (pronounced *are-note*).

Because I'll be working with many rNotes, I'll need a Collection class, although it isn't immediately obvious what kinds of collections I'll need. A likely candidate is a sparse array. Sparse arrays are discussed in detail on day 9, but for now think of them as arrays with missing elements. The idea is to enable the user to delete rNotes without incurring any penalty, and to be able to recover the saved disk space.

I'll need a way to quickly find all the indexed words, both for when I'm adding new words and for when I'm conducting a search. Clearly, the words will have to be indexed with a tight and efficient structure, as described on day 7.

Regardless of what structure the words are stored in, clearly an rWord class will be required. Each rWord object will have the text of the term, and then a list of the rNotes associated with that rWord.

Assembling the menu will require yet another collection—this time of rHit objects. An rHit object will point to an rNote and will keep count of the number of hits on that rNote. This count will allow ROBIN to display the notes in order of how well they match the terms.

Event-Driven Programming

When the user starts ROBIN with a flag, a series of actions follows. Typically, these actions end with the presentation of a menu. From that time until the program is exited, ROBIN must respond to the user's requests, known as *events*.

NEW TERM An *event* is anything that causes a response in your program. Typical events include the user pressing a key or clicking the mouse button, but also may include timer events and other interrupts provided by the system.

Event-driven programming is discussed in depth on day 13, but essentially the idea is to create a program that responds to the user's requests instead of imposing a sequence of actions on the user.

Object Orientation

The hallmarks of object-oriented design are encapsulation, inheritance, and polymorphism. The central idea of *encapsulation* is to ensure that implementation details of the program are hidden in the objects most likely to need to know those details. Rather than your program maintaining an omniscient overview of every detail, it delegates responsibility for much of the action to the various classes.

There is no reason for any part of your program other than the rWord class itself, for example, to know how rWord objects are kept in memory. The memory management is an implementation detail that the clients (users) of rWord don't need or want to know. It may be that rWord objects are kept in a linked list or a binary tree (see Day 7), but this is a detail wholly encapsulated by the rWord class itself.

Inheritance refers to the capability for new types to be built up out of existing types. When setting out to create an object-oriented design, you want to look for is-a and has-a relationships. An *is-a* relationship implies public inheritance, and a *has-a* relationship probably implies containment or perhaps private inheritance.

In the case of ROBIN, few such relationships are obvious immediately. The rWord object is not a kind of rNote, nor is the rNote a kind of rHit. Both rWord and rNote seem to be at the top of the inheritance chain. Over time, however, different kinds of rNotes may emerge. Perhaps, for example, the Help notes really are a different but related type. Perhaps Help notes need additional data or behavior, even though they are rNotes at heart. This would imply that rHelp objects are a kind of rNote and should inherit publicly from rNote. It is too early to be certain, however, so I'll just file that away as a possibility.

Polymorphism refers to the capability to treat objects in a common way and to trust the individual objects to "do the right thing." Therefore, if you do create an rHelp object and derive it from rNote, you can tell either object to display(), and each will respond according to the semantics of its own type.

Getting Started

When the user enters the following, a new note is created, indexed, and stored:

```
ROBIN -I the quick brown fox
```

Now, stop right there. Who creates the note?

It would be nice to have a command-line parser that takes the flags and other terms entered on the command line and assumes responsibility to process them and create the right objects. Command-line processing is discussed in detail on day 6, but for now it will suffice to say that it is possible to read in these options as they are entered by the user, and to switch on the flags provided.

This implies that an rCommandLine object is needed, whose job it is to process the command line and create the right kinds of command objects. The command family might include the indexer, the searcher, and the database manager.

Presumably, the CommandLine object instantiates the right kind of command object, and that object in turn begins a process of fulfilling the request. In the case under discussion, an Indexer object would be created and would take, as the parameters to its constructor, the text of the message.

This constructor might be overloaded to take a file name, allowing for the -F flag as well as the -L flag. It may prove true that the indexer needs to be subclassed into two or three subclasses; such as CommandLineIndexer, FileIndexer, and LineIndexer; but that will become clearer as the design evolves.

The indexer will be responsible for creating the rNote, but not for storing the rNote in its collection, or for writing the rNote to disk; these functions will be the responsibility of the rNote constructor.

Additionally, the indexer will need to create rWord objects for every word in the rNote's text. These rWord objects will, likewise, be responsible for storing themselves in the index, as well as for writing themselves to disk.

It isn't clear whether the indexer has much to do that isn't covered in these other classes, so I'll consider having the CommandLine object just create an rNote object, bypassing the rIndexer altogether. The rNote then could index itself and then store itself, without any other help at all.

If the user enters an -S flag, the rCommandLine object will not create an rIndexer; instead, it will create an rMenu object. The rMenu will need to know how to get the index of words, and how to interact with that index to create a menu of rHits.

Likewise, if the user enters one of the database commands (such as Pack or Undelete), the rCommandLine object probably will create an rDataBaseManager object, which will take over responsibility for managing the database.

In summary, and after reflection, here's the plan: main() will pass the command line to the CommandLine object, which will read and switch on the flag. When it reads -i, -l, or -f, it will create a new rNote, calling the appropriate constructor and passing in the flag and the rest of the command line.

When the rNote is constructed, it will instantiate rWord objects for every word in the note; then it will time-stamp itself and store itself away.

If the `rCommandLine` object receives `-S` or `-?`, it will create an `rSearcher` object; and if it receives a database switch, it will create an `rDataBaseManager` object. The `rCommandLine` object also will be responsible for managing errors on the command line, and possibly for working with the environment variables to find the appropriate files.

Abstract Data Types

The program allows for the creation of two types of notes: with and without file references. Most of the objects don't really care which type of `rNote` is being used, but the two types must be distinguished in their behaviors.

The need to distinguish between notes with and without file references indicates that the two types of notes are related, but in what way? Call the type of note with a file an `rFileNote`, and call the type with all its data kept as text an `rInternalNote`. Does one inherit from the other?

An `rFileNote` might at first appear to be a type of `rNote`, indicating that it is derived from `rNote`, but there are methods in `rNote` that `rFileNote` doesn't need or care about. On the other hand, `rFileNote` has data and methods relating to the referred to file that `rNote` certainly doesn't need.

The answer is to create a common base class, `rNote`, and inherit both `rFileNotes` and `rNote` from that base. Because you never will create a pure `rNote`, you can make the `rNote` an abstract data type. Most of the clients of your code will deal with references or pointers to `rNotes`, but the actual objects will be of one of the derived types.

Searching

When the `CommandLine` object switches on an -S flag, it will instantiate an `rMenu` object, passing in the terms on which to search. The `rMenu` object will ask the collection of `rWords` to find each term in turn. It then will ask each `rWord` for its list of `rNotes`, adding `rHit` objects to its own collection for each `rNote` as it is found. The `rMenu` will add only one `rHit` object for each `rNote`; multiple hits on the same note will be tracked by a counter in the `rHit` object.

Note that each object does only those things that make sense for it to know how to do. The collection knows how to find each matching `rWord`. The `rWord` itself knows which notes it is associated with. The `rHit` object knows how many hits have been registered on each `rNote`.

The Collections

Although it is too early to describe the various collections in detail, some aspects now are well understood.

Make note of the fact that all our `Collectable` classes (`rWord`, `rNote`, and `rHit`) probably will need nodes as well. This is a good indication that a template may be required, even if these node objects may be stored in different types of collections.

Getting Started

It is impossible to write the program all at once, and it isn't wise to try to do so. My preference is to write a small part, get it working, and then write some more.

That said, I do find it useful to write a preliminary version of the *interface* to the principal classes even before getting any of it working. This provides a reference point, although very often the initial interface to the class is barely recognizable in the final product. Listing 5.1 provides a first cut at an rNote class.

Type

Listing 5.1 Using the rNote Class

```
1:      // Listing 5.1 - Using the rNote Class
2: #include "string.hpp"
3:
4:      class rNote
5:      {
6:      public:
7:
8:          // constructors
9:          rNote(char Flag, const String * const text);
10:         rNote(const DeSerializer&); // for reading from disk
11:         rNote(const rNote&);   // copy constructor
12:         ~rNote();
13:
14:         // accessors
15:         const String& GetText() const { return *myText; }
16:         ULONG GetNoteNumber() const { return myNoteNumber; }
17:         ULONG GetCreationDate() const { return myCreationDate; }
18:         ULONG GetModificationDate() const { return myModificationDate; }
19:         BOOL IsDeleted() const { return myIsDeleted; }
20:
21:         void SetText(const String& rhs)   { *myText = rhs; }
22:         void SetNoteNumber(ULONG num)   { myNoteNumber = num; }
23:         void SetCreationDate(ULONG newDate) { myCreationDate = newDate; }
24:         void SetModificationDate(ULONG newDate) { myModificationDate = newDate; }
25:         void SetDeleted(BOOL flag) { myIsDeleted = flag; }
26:
27:         // operators
28:         const rNote& operator=(const rNote&);
29:         DeSerializer operator>>(DeSerializer &);
30:
31:         // Display
32:         void Display();
33:
34:         //
35:
36:     private:
37:         String* myText;
38:         ULONG myNoteNumber;
39:         ULONG myCreationDate;
40:         ULONG myModificationDate;
41:         BOOL  myIsDeleted;
42:
43:     };
```

None. This is a class declaration.

The rNote object takes three constructors. The first, shown in line 9, is called by the CommandLine object, and takes a flag (I, F, or L) and a block of text. There is no convenient way to overload this function based on whether the text actually is to be indexed or is the name of a file; it is simpler to just have the constructor switch on the flag.

The second constructor, in line 10, takes a DeSerializer reference. Although the design has not yet specified *how* objects will be created from disk, it is clear that a constructor will be required that will take some sort of object from which the rNote will be created. Persistence is covered in depth on day 8, "Writing Objects To Disk", and at that time the nature of this DeSerializer can be determined.

A copy constructor (line 11) and an operator= (line 29) are provided, because this class controls dynamic memory in its myText pointer.

Various accessor functions (lines 15 through 25) allow the client to obtain and to set the various member data, which itself is in lines 37 through 41. The operator>>() function, shown in line 29, is a stand-in for whatever function will be used to serialize the object's data to disk.

The rWord Class

Although rNotes consist of strings, the user actually will search on words, as described earlier. The preliminary rWord class is shown in listing 5.2.

Listing 5.2 Using the Preliminary rWord Class

```
1:    // Listing 5.2 - Using the Preliminary rWord Class
2:
3:    class rWord
4:    {
5:
6:    public:
7:
8:        // constructors
9:        rWord(const String&);
10:       rWord(const char * const);
11:       rWord(const DeSerializer&); // for reading from disk
12:       rWord(const rWord&);  // copy constructor
13:       ~rWord();
14:
15:       // accessors
16:       const String& GetText() const { return *myText; }
17:       void SetText(const String& rhs)  { *myText = rhs; }
18:       const rNoteNode& GetHeadNode();
19:       void SetHeadNode(const rNoteNode&);
20:
```

continues

Listing 5.2 continued

```
21:       // operators
22:       const rWord& operator=(const rWord&);
23:       DeSerializer operator>>(DeSerializer &);
24:
25:       // data manipulation
26:       long AddToIndex();
27:
28:       // Display
29:       void Display();
30:
31:       //
32:
33:    private:
34:       String* myText;
35:       rNoteNode myFirstNode;
36:
37:    };
```

None. This is a class declaration.

Listing 5.2 represents a preliminary first take at the rWord class declaration. There are four constructors that provide the capability to create an rWord object from a String object (line 9) or from a C-style string (line 10). The constructor in line 11 creates rWord objects from disk, and line 12 includes the copy constructor.

The rWord object contains a pointer to the word itself, along with an array of nodes, each of which point to an rNote object.

Each rNoteNode will contain the offset of the word in the text, as well as the ordinal position of the word in the text. This data will be unused in version 1, but is reserved for future use. The offset will be used to highlight the word in the text after ROBIN is ported to a GUI. The ordinal position will be used for more sophisticated searching, so that the user can request matches of this word in proximity to another word (*computer* within five words of *screen*, for example). Listing 5.3 provides the preliminary interface of the rNoteNode object.

Type **Listing 5.3 Using rNoteNode**

```
1:       // Listing 5.3 - Using rNoteNode
2:
3:       class rNoteNode
4:       {
5:
6:       public:
7:
8:          // constructors
9:          rNoteNode(const rNote&);
```

```
10:         rNoteNode(const rNote&, ULONG offset, ULONG position);
11:         rNoteNode(const DeSerializer&); // for reading from disk
12:         rNoteNode(const rNoteNode&);  // copy constructor
13:         ~rNoteNode();
14:
15:         // accessors
16:         ULONG getNoteNumber() const { return myNoteNumber; }
17:         void setNoteNumber(ULONG number) { myNoteNumber = number; }
18:
19:         ULONG getOffset() const { return myOffset; }
20:         void setOffset(ULONG number) { myOffset = number; }
21:
22:         ULONG getPosition() const { return myPosition; }
23:         void setPosition(ULONG number) { myPosition = number; }
24:
25:         rNoteNode* GetNext() { return myNextNode; }
26:          void SetNext(rNoteNode* next) { myNextNode = next ; }
27:
28:         // operators
29:         const rNoteNode& operator=(const rNoteNode&);
30:         DeSerializer operator>>(DeSerializer &);
31:
32:     private:
33:         ULONG myNoteNumber;
34:         ULONG myOffset;
35:         ULONG myPosition;
36:         rNoteNode *myNextNode;
37:     };
```

None. This is a class declaration.

Listing 5.3 provides the preliminary interface to the rNoteNode class. When a word is added to the index, the rNote in which it appears must be registered, along with its position and offset in that rNote. To manage this relationship, an rNoteNode is created and added to the rWord's list.

The constructor for rNoteNode can take an rNote object, either with the offset and position of the matching word (line 10) or without (line 9). rNoteNodes can be stored to and retrieved from disk (lines 11 and 30), and a copy constructor (line 12) and operator=() (line 29) are provided as well.

Reviewing a Technical Specification

With the preliminary class interfaces and decisions made earlier in this chapter, you are ready to outline your technical specification sufficient to start writing the program.

The classes will be arranged in a number of data structures, all of which can be written to and read from disk. rWord objects will be indexed for quick retrieval in a tree structure to be determined later. Each node in that tree, however, will consist of an rWordNode object.

The rWord also will maintain a list of rNoteNode objects, each of which will provide access to the rNote in which the word appears, along with its offset and ordinal position.

When a menu of choices is created, it will consist of a list of rHit object nodes. Each rHit object will maintain a link to the particular rNote, and will provide a count of the number of matches in the current search. This method allows the menu to be sorted by how well each rNote matches the search.

Next Steps

To get started, you first will want to explore how the command flags will be read and processed. This process is covered on day 6 in an in-depth study of command-line processing, environment, and configuration files.

Next, you will want to create the set of indexed words, so on day 7 you learn about trees and complex data structures.

After you can read the command line and index the words, you need to be able to save that index to disk so that you don't have to re-create it each time you rerun the program. On day 8, you learn about object persistence.

The rMenu will be a collection, but probably not an indexed tree as the list of rWords will be, so on day 9 you learn about Collection classes. On day 10, you learn about providing iterators to your collections.

With these skills, you will be able to build a solid preliminary version of ROBIN. On day 11, you learn how to manage the growing database and keep the data free of corruption.

Up until day 11, you will be working with single words, but ROBIN needs to be able to parse all the words from a string. Therefore, on day 12, you learn more about text parsing. At that point, it will be time to turn to the user interface, building the menu of choices and responding to the user's choices. Day 13 includes an in-depth discussion of event-driven programming.

The second week ends with a review of object database issues, and here you learn how to delete and pack records, as well as how to provide the Undelete facility.

The third week takes a detour to talk about manipulating bits, which can be an important skill in working with databases. On day 16, you learn some advanced memory-management techniques.

On day 17, you look at providing synonyms for search terms and on reducing the size of your index through the use of *stop words*.

On day 18, you examine the performance characteristics of your program; on day 19, you explore advanced exception handling and error management. Day 20 reviews techniques for debugging your application, and the three weeks end with a discussion of marketing your program and enhancing it.

Other Designs: CLiDE

Although this book focuses on the Personal Information Manager, it can be beneficial to take a look at other products and designs from time to time. Doing so can help bring out other approaches and algorithms, and these then can be contrasted with the design of ROBIN to help build a more rounded picture of what professional programming is all about.

With this goal in mind, I will describe a second project—a *command-line directory enhancer* named *CLiDE*. As shown in the coming chapters, CLiDE provides all the normal directory capabilities (listing the files, showing their attributes, sorting them, and so on), along with some additional features that you will not see implemented but which I leave, as they say, as an exercise for the reader.

CLiDE's Functional Specifications

As stated previously, all good programs begin with a specification and a design. From a functional viewpoint, CLiDE is a powerful command-line utility that enables you to list files, combine directories, filter and sort the output, and call on DOS commands and internal commands to take action.

In version 1, CLiDE implements the capability to sort the directory based on file name, extension, size, and date. It also enables you to filter based on the usual DOS and UNIX wild cards. Internal commands such as Copy, Move, View, and others will be planned for, but not implemented, in version 1.

Portability Issues

One of the first issues facing such a utility is that it is, by its nature, operating-system specific. Although UNIX and DOS directories seem similar, they are quite different in some critical ways (for example, DOS doesn't use INODES). The MAC System 7 is so different that even the functional specification will not match.

If you don't have a DOS machine, don't worry; you will not spend much time implementing CLiDE in any case. I'm using it just to illustrate some of the other issues that might arise in object-oriented design.

The User Interface

To continue with the functional specification, you use CLiDE by typing **CLIDE** at the DOS prompt, followed by one or more switches and one or more file specifications. The switches are each a single letter, and they can be combined (you can write `CLIDE -i -a -o` or you can write `CLIDE -iao`, for example). The switches can appear in any order, and can follow or precede the file specifications.

Some switches require an argument; these always are followed by a colon and then the argument, with no spaces. In future versions, CLiDE will allow advanced wild cards in the file specifications, including general regular expressions. For version 1.0, however, only the standard DOS wild cards will be supported.

The result of a CLiDE search will be a set, and sets can be named or unnamed. Sets can be mixed and matched with each other, using set operators such as Union and Intersection. Named sets can be saved in CLiDE configuration files, and recalled as needed. A *set* is *not* a group of files—it is more like a stored query against the file system. A set is a specification for a sorted, filtered group of files.

The Technical Specification

CLiDE will attempt as much as possible to isolate the platform-specific code from the platform-independent code. It is anticipated, for example, that the DOS version of CLiDE might be migrated to Windows and then to Windows 95.

What Are the Objects?

Even a preliminary design of CLiDE is likely to include directory objects, file objects, sets, collections, filters, and sorters. One can imagine that the CommandLine object from ROBIN might work with CLiDE as well; parsing the flags here is a superset of what is required for ROBIN.

You immediately confront this question: Are *directories* collections of files, are they types of files, or are they something altogether different? At first glance, a directory might seem to be a collection, because the contents of the directory are files and other directories. DOS, however, considers directories and files as being very much the same when it comes to locating and displaying their names.

It is possible to combine both concepts into one hierarchy of objects by saying that directories inherit publicly from files and therefore are a kind of file, but that directories add the capability to contain files and other directories. A directory therefore would inherit much of the display and other characteristics of the file, but would add its own methods to manage its collections.

A second immediate design question is this: Do *sets* know how to filter their contents, or are there filter objects that know how to act on sets and directories? Similarly, do sets know how to order their collections, or are there sorters that know how to do this?

Prototyping

One way to test your tentative answers to these design questions is to build a prototype. Because CLiDE is a large, complex utility, there is great risk inherent in plowing ahead with a design before you have done any testing.

Building a prototype provides a safer alternative—one that enables you to prove your early design assumptions and explore which areas of implementation are likely to be most difficult.

Carefully deciding which methods to implement first is more important than it might sound at first. It might be tempting to get all the sorting working before worrying about the filtering, but that would undermine the point of the early prototype version. The idea is to get *one* sort and *one* filter criterion working, to display one type of directory listing, and to implement other representative methods.

Sorting, Filtering, and Displaying

The essence of CLiDE is this: Read the command-line switches, find the requested files, filter based on the switches, sort based on the switches, and then display 20 lines at a time.

CLiDE is, at least at first glance, quite procedural. The actual work of assembling the files is likely to be a large `for` loop that iterates through the different files in the requested directories and applies the filters. After the list is assembled, it will need to be sorted and then displayed.

Version 1 of CLiDE probably isn't even event driven; after the files are displayed, the program exits. This will change when CLiDE is ported to a windowing environment, where the user might ask for files to be moved or copied by dragging-and-dropping within the GUI or by choosing menu commands.

Object-oriented design and programming does have a role to play in the creation of CLiDE, however. The relationship between the files and the directories and sets cries out for inheritance. The discrete jobs of sorting, filtering, and displaying call for encapsulation. Finally, the capability to treat directories and files as a single type, asking each to display itself or otherwise be manipulated, looks very much like a candidate for polymorphism.

CLiDE's First Steps

Over the next few days, you will see many of the component requirements for CLiDE: sorting, filtering, parsing the command line, and so on. Even as you work on ROBIN, keep an eye out for how the lessons apply to CLiDE and to other projects of your own that you might have in mind. Think of CLiDE as ROBIN's dopey younger brother—along for the design ride and taking the hand-me-down algorithms.

Q&A

Q Why do C++ programs require more analysis and design than C programs?

A The purpose of C++ is to make it possible to write much larger and more complex programs than were practical in C. The cost, however, is more time spent thinking before you start to code.

Q Is analysis and design in C++ different than in C?

A Yes. You think in a very different way. In C, or in any procedural language (BASIC or Pascal, for example), you start the analysis by asking yourself "What is going to happen? What are the significant operations?" In C++, or in any object-oriented language (Smalltalk or Eiffel, for example), you start by asking yourself "What are the important things in this problem domain? What are the responsibilities of each thing? What does it need to know?"

Q Why are inheritance and polymorphism treated as different things? Isn't polymorphism just one of the uses for inheritance?

A In C++, polymorphism is implemented via the inheritance hierarchy: You define an abstract type with some virtual functions, and then you override the functions in your subclasses. In other object-oriented languages, however, polymorphism has nothing to do with inheritance. In Smalltalk, for example, any object can be sent any message (the equivalent of calling a method), as long as the class has declared an operation for that message. There is no need for two classes to share a common base class in order for them to be able to respond to the same message.

The term *inheritance* (when talking about encapsulation, polymorphism, and inheritance) refers to the idea of subclassing existing, working classes; modifying only a small part of their functionality; and very quickly producing other working classes. Although C++ uses the inheritance relationship to implement polymorphism, these two terms are not intrinsically related.

Q How detailed should the technical specification be? What is its purpose?

A The technical specification should be detailed enough that you understand the types of data that will be important, and the range of operations that you will want to do with the data. You should be able to comprehend the breadth and borders of the problem domain. There isn't much point to specifying the user interface in minute detail, because it probably will change three or four times before you ship the product anyway.

In ROBIN, for example, the basic functionality has been set down, and a very simple command-line user interface has been proposed for invoking the different operations. This is good enough to know what operations are needed, and the user interface will be fine for testing those operations, but it probably will change to something more user friendly before we "ship."

Q How detailed should my analysis and design be before I start implementing?

A This depends on the scope of the project. For a small, one-person project, you probably can get away with just a few notes scribbled on a sheet of paper. For a large, 40-person effort, you will need much more. Remember that the goal of the initial design is to implement something that works. The sooner you get something working, the sooner you will locate the inevitable design bugs. With this goal, you should identify the classes that are needed for minimal functionality and design those, considering (but not designing in detail) the immediate clients of these classes. Then get started on the code.

Q How do I know when to use an abstract data type?

A Whenever you are designing the public interface for a class, you should be thinking about the clients (the other classes or code) that will use this class. You need an ADT when your clients want to use more than one class as if they were all of the same type, but each class needs its own mutually exclusive data or behavior.

In ROBIN, for example, two types of notes exist: the regular notes that are stored in the file ROBIN.DB, and the notes that have the body stored in another file. For the latter type, only the file name is stored in ROBIN.DB.

Think about the clients of these two types of notes: They are whatever classes display notes, and whatever indexes notes. You may not know much (right now) about how the notes will be displayed, and less about how they will be indexed, but you know that the job of writing the displayer and the indexer will be much simpler if they just have to deal with the abstract concept of an rNote. It's true that the process of getting the text for one type of note is much harder than getting it for the other, but that is the problem of the specific types of notes. The displayer and the indexer don't care, and shouldn't have to care.

Workshop

The Workshop provides quiz questions to help you solidify your understanding of the material covered, and exercises to provide you with experience in using what you have learned. Try to answer the quiz and exercise questions before checking the answers in Appendix A, and make sure that you understand the answers before continuing to the next chapter.

Quiz

1. What are the hallmarks of a good design?
2. What are the major steps involved in creating a piece of software?
3. What is the first step of the analysis and design of a program, after you have figured out more or less what the program is going to do?
4. In ROBIN, what is the purpose of the rNote class?
5. In ROBIN, what is the purpose of the rWord class?
6. In ROBIN, what is the purpose of the rHit class?

Exercises

1. Suppose that you are designing an e-mail system. What will it need to do (the functional specification)? You don't need to detail how the user will invoke these operations the way you did for ROBIN—just identify the operations.

2. What are the major classes in the problem domain? (Remember, skip the storage and transport issues.)

3. Flesh out what is contained in each of your four major classes. Identify the type of the data members, if it isn't obvious.

4. The To field in both MailMessage and MailingList seems awkward. Any ideas? (Hint: What should you think about when two things are used in the same way by some clients?)

5. Redo exercise 3, in light of your clever design decision in exercise 4. Be sure to show the inheritance relationships.

Command-Line Processing and the Environment

The user wants to be able to invoke ROBIN with various command-line switches to control its initial state. The user also wants to be able to dictate how ROBIN generally responds, and where it creates and maintains its files. Today you will learn

- ☐ How to pass arguments in on the command line
- ☐ How to read environment variables
- ☐ How to create and use configuration files
- ☐ How to build alias programs

Command-Line Processing

Many operating systems, such as DOS and UNIX, enable the user to pass parameters to your program when the program starts. These are called command-line arguments, and typically are separated by spaces on the command line, as in the following example:

```
SomeProgram Param1 Param2 Param3
```

These parameters are not passed to main() directly. Instead, every program's main() function is passed three parameters. The first parameter is an integer count of the number of arguments on the command line. The program name itself is counted, so every program has at least one parameter. The example command line shown here has four parameters. (The name SomeProgram plus the three parameters makes a total of four command-line arguments.)

The second parameter passed to main() is an array of pointers to character strings. Because an array name is a constant pointer to the first element of the array, you can declare this argument to be a pointer to a pointer to char, or a pointer to an array of char.

The third argument also is an array of pointers to char, but this contains the system's *environment*. In DOS and UNIX, the environment typically includes the PATH statement and a variety of other defined values. Every environment variable, however, is a string. If you write SET MYVAR = 5 in your AUTOEXEC.BAT (in DOS), you define a variable named MYVAR and assign to it the string "5".

Typically, the first argument is called argc (argument count), but you can call it anything you want. The second argument often is called argv (argument vector) but, again, this is just a convention. The third argument often is called env.

It is legal to define main() to take any number of arguments from zero through three. If you declare main() to take no arguments, of course, none of these values will be legal. As you declare each of these arguments, their values become available, but they must include all the arguments to the left. The legal declarations of main's arguments follow:

```
int main()
int main(int argc)
int main(int argc, char** argv)
int main(int argc, char** argv, char** env)
```

You *cannot* try to declare the char** without also declaring the int, for example.

It is common to test argc to ensure that you have received the expected number of arguments, and to use argv to access the arguments themselves. Note that argv[0] is the name of the program, and argv[1] is the first parameter to the program, represented as a string. If your program takes two numbers as arguments, you will need to translate these numbers to strings. Listing 6.1 illustrates how to use the command-line arguments.

Listing 6.1 Using Command-Line Arguments

```
1:    #include <iostream.h>
2:      void main(int argc, char **argv, char ** env)
3:      {
4:         cout << "Received " << argc << " arguments...\n";
5:         for (int i=0; i<argc; i++)
6:            cout << "argument " << i << ": " << argv[i] << endl;
7:         for (int j = 0; env[j]!=0; j++)
8:           cout << "env var: " << env[j] << endl;
9:      }
```

```
d:\bc4\book2\exe>0601 Teach Yourself More C++ In 21 Days
Received 8 arguments...
argument 0: D:0601.EXE
argument 1: Teach
argument 2: Yourself
argument 3: More
argument 4: C++
argument 5: In
argument 6: 21
argument 7: Days
env var: CONFIG=Normal
env var: PROMPT=$p$g
env var: TEMP=c:\temp
env var: TMP=c:\temp
```

The function main() declares three arguments: argc is an integer that contains the count of command-line arguments; argv is a pointer to the array of strings; and env is also a pointer to an array of strings, each of which holds an environmental variable.

Each string in the array pointed to by argv is a command-line argument. Note that argv just as easily could have been declared as char *argv[]. It is a matter of programming style how you declare argv and env; even though this program declared it as a pointer to a pointer, array offsets still were used to access the individual strings. Even the names argc, argv, and env are arbitrary; the program will work just as well if you call them Sleepy, Sneezy, and Doc.

In line 4, argc is used to print the number of command-line arguments: eight in all, counting the program name itself.

In lines 5 and 6, each of the command-line arguments is printed, passing the NULL-terminated strings to cout by indexing into the array of strings. Similarly, in lines 7 and 8, the environment variables are accessed. Note that the output has been modified to remove a number of environment variables on my computer. Run the program and print your own environment; you might be surprised at what you find.

DO	DON'T

DO use the names argc, argv, and env.

DON'T forget that argv is indexed from 0 to argc-1.

DO remember that argv[0] is the name of the program.

DO treat argv as an array of pointers to C-style strings.

Command-Line Flags

ROBIN expects the first argument other than the name of the program (argv[1]) to contain a flag. You can process that flag with a switch statement. Because the protocol for ROBIN dictates that only the first letter of the flag is significant, the code for switching on the flag is straightforward, as shown in listing 6.2.

Type

Listing 6.2 Switching on Command-Line Flags

```
1:    // Listing 6.2 - Switching on Command-Line Flags
2:
3:    #include <iostream.h>
4:
5:    // function prototypes
6:    void Process(int argc, char ** argv);
7:    int main(int argc, char **argv, char ** env);
8:
9:    // driver program
10:   int main(int argc, char **argv, char ** env)
11:   {
12:       // rudimentary usage testing
13:       if (argc < 3 || argv[1][0] != '-')
14:       {
15:           cout << "Usage: " << argv[0] << " -Flag [arguments]" << endl;
16:           return 1;
17:       }
```

```
18:        Process (argc, argv);
19:        return 0;
20:    }
21:
22:    // switch on command line arguments
23:    void Process(int argc, char ** argv)
24:    {
25:        switch (argv[1][1])
26:        {
27:           case 'I':
28:           case 'i':
29:              cout << "Index following text" << endl;
30:              break;
31:
32:           case 'F':
33:           case 'f':
34:              cout << "Index from a File" << endl;
35:              break;
36:
37:           case 'L':
38:           case 'l':
39:              cout << "Make a note for each line in a file" << endl;
40:              break;
41:
42:           case 'S':
43:           case 's':
44:           case '?':
45:              cout << "Search for following text" << endl;
46:              break;
47:        }
48:    }
```

```
d:\>0602 -I this and that
Index following text

d:\>0602 -S this and that
Search for following text

d:\>0602 F this and that
Usage: d:\>0602.EXE -Flag [arguments]
```

In line 13, the number of arguments is checked. This program expects at least two (the name of the program and the flags, and at least one more). If there are fewer than three arguments, or if the first character of the second argument (the flag) isn't a dash, a usage statement is printed in line 15, and the program exits in line 16.

Assuming that the program passes this rudimentary usage testing, control is passed to the Process() function, and argc and argv are passed along.

The tests and actions illustrated in this function are a skeleton of what the actual program will do. Note that the text of the full word is not checked; the user might have entered 0602 -Fail and this program would have treated it exactly as if the user had written 0602 -File.

An Alternative to Flags

This program switches on one of a very limited set of flags. Exactly the same effect could be accomplished by copying the executable to a set of new names and then switching on argv[0]. In DOS, this is wasteful of disk space. In UNIX, however, links can be used (ln), thereby providing the same functionality with virtually no wasted disk space. Listing 6.3 illustrates this idea.

Listing 6.3 Using the Name of the File

```
1:  // Listing 6.3 - Using the Name of the File
2:
3:  #include <iostream.h>
4:  #include <string.h>
5:
6:  // function prototypes
7:  void Process(char **argv);
8:  int main(int argc, char **argv, char ** env);
9:
10: // driver program
11: int main(int argc, char **argv, char ** env)
12: {
13:     // rudimentary usage testing
14:     if (argc < 2 )
15:     {
16:         cout << "Usage: " << argv[0] << " [arguments]" << endl;
17:         return 1;
18:     }
19:     Process (argv);
20:     return 0;
21: }
22:
23: // switch on command line arguments
24: void Process(char ** argv)
25: {
26:     // find the name without the path
27:     int len = strlen(argv[0]);
28:     for (char *ptr = &argv[0][len-1]; *(ptr-1) != '\\';ptr-- );
29:
30:     if (strcmp(ptr,"INDEX.EXE") == 0)
31:         cout << "Index following text" << endl;
32:
33:     if (strcmp(ptr,"FILE.EXE") == 0)
34:         cout << "Index from a File" << endl;
35:
36:     if (strcmp(ptr,"LIST.EXE") == 0)
37:         cout << "Make a note for each line in a file" << endl;
38:
39:     if (strcmp(ptr,"FIND.EXE") == 0)
40:         cout << "Search for following text" << endl;
41: }
```

```
d:\>copy 0603.exe index.exe
d:\>copy 0603.exe find.exe

d:\>Index don't forget to rename the file
Index following text

d:\>find the text you saved
Search for following text
```

Note: Your compiler may warn you that the `env` parameter to `main()` is never used in this program and many of the subsequent listings.

Listing 6.3 is similar to listing 6.2. This time, however, `process()` is sent only the value of `argv`. In fact, you might want to send in only `argv[0]`, because that is the only argument that `Process()` really needs to consider.

In line 28, a pointer is set to the end of the string held in `argv[0]`. The pointer ticks backward, searching for the backslash character that DOS puts at the beginning of each directory. This takes a string such as `D:\PROGRAMS\TYMCPP\DAY6\FIND.EXE` and turns it into `FIND.EXE`. In lines 30, 33, 36, and 39, this string then is compared with the expected names for the program; when a match is found, the correct function will be called.

Although ROBIN does not take advantage of this technique, many other utilities do. There are a set of UNIX utilities that really are one program with a number of different names. The program "does the right thing," depending on how you call it.

Note: The specific processing of the file name as shown in line 28 is appropriate for DOS programs. If you are programming in a different environment, you may need to modify this line slightly. In UNIX, for example, the slash goes the other way (/).

6

Sorting Command-Line Arguments

It is convenient that DOS (and other operating systems) present the command line as an array of pointers to C-style strings. It therefore is easy to adapt the `QuickSort()` routine from day 4 to sort the command-line arguments. Listing 6.4 extends listing 6.2 to include the capability to sort the command line (except the file name and the flag) when the `-I` flag is used.

> **Note:** This program requires inclusion of string.hpp that you wrote earlier, and that you compile in string.cpp as a module of this program.

Listing 6.4 Sorting the Arguments

```
1:    // Listing 6.4 - Sorting the Arguments
2:
3:    #include <iostream.h>
4:    #include <string.h>
5:    #include "string.hpp"
6:
7:    // function prototypes
8:    void QuickSort(String**, int, int);
9:    void Swap(String*& i, String*& j);
10:   int main(int argc, char **argv, char ** env);
11:   void Process(int argc, char ** argv);
12:
13:   // driver program
14:   int main(int argc, char **argv, char ** env)
15:   {
16:       // rudimentary usage testing
17:       if (argc < 3 || argv[1][0] != '-')
18:       {
19:          cout << "Usage: " << argv[0] << " -Flag [arguments]" << endl;
20:          return 1;
21:       }
22:       Process (argc, argv);
23:       return 0;
24:   }
25:
26:   // switch on command line arguments
27:   void Process(int argc, char ** argv)
28:   {
29:       String *buffer[100];
30:       int i;
31:       switch (argv[1][1])
32:       {
33:
34:          case 'I':
35:          case 'i':
36:                  for (i=0; i<100 && i < argc-2; i++)
37:                      buffer[i] = new String(argv[i+2]);
38:                  QuickSort(buffer,0,argc-2);
39:                  for (i = 0; i < argc-3; i++)
40:                      cout << *buffer[i] << ", ";
41:                  cout << *buffer[argc-3] << endl;
42:              break;
43:
44:          case 'F':
```

```
45:            case 'f':
46:                cout << "Index from a File" << endl;
47:                break;
48:
49:            case 'L':
50:            case 'l':
51:                cout << "Make a note for each line in a file" << endl;
52:                break;
53:
54:            case 'S':
55:            case 's':
56:            case '?':
57:                cout << "Search for following text" << endl;
58:                break;
59:        }
60:    }
61:
62:    // QuickSort implemented with Median of Three
63:    void QuickSort(String** Input, int left, int right)
64:    {
65:        if (right > left)
66:        {
67:            int i = left-1;
68:            int x = right;
69:            for (;;)
70:            {
71:                while (*Input[++i] < *Input[right-1])
72:                    ;
73:                while (*Input[--x] > *Input[right-1])
74:                    ;
75:
76:                if (i >= x)
77:                    break;
78:                Swap(Input[i], Input[x]);
79:            }
80:            Swap(Input[i], Input[right-1]);
81:            QuickSort(Input,left,i);
82:            QuickSort(Input,i+1,right);
83:        }
84:    }
85:
86:    void Swap(String*& i, String*& j)
87:    {
88:        String* temp;
89:        temp = j;
90:        j = i;
91:        i = temp;
92:    }
```

```
d:\>0604 -I Eternal Vigilance Is The Price Of Liberty
Eternal, Is, Liberty, Of, Price, The, Vigilance
```

Listing 6.4 sorts the command-line arguments. It does so by creating an array of strings— one for each command-line argument other than the name of the program and the -I switch, and then passing the array of strings to QuickSort().

In line 37, the array is created; in line 38, it is passed to QuickSort(). One terrible flaw in this approach is that the array must be of fixed size, as shown in line 29. This is wasteful of memory and limits your program to the number of parameters specified as the upper limit of the array.

Note, by the way, that the buffer and int must be declared in lines 29 and 30—outside of the switch statement itself. It is tempting to declare them in line 36, but a case statement does not have scope and it is an error to declare variables there *unless* you use braces to create a scope. Lines 29 through 42 could be rewritten:

```
29:          switch (argv[1][1])
30:          {
31:
32:              case 'I':
33:              case 'i':
34:                  {
25:                  String *buffer[100];
36:                      for (int i=0; i<100 && i < argc-2; i++)
37:                          buffer[i] = new String(argv[i+2]);
38:                      QuickSort(buffer,0,argc-2);
39:                      for (i = 0; i < argc-3; i++)
40:                          cout << *buffer[i] << ", ";
41:                      cout << *buffer[argc-3] << endl;
42:                  }
43:              break;
```

This code would have worked just as well.

Command-Line Arguments and Linked Lists

As noted in the preceding section, listing 6.4 suffers the fatal flaw that it must declare a fixed-size buffer of String pointers. This problem is rectified easily by creating a dynamic array of strings, implemented using an unsorted linked list, as shown in listing 6.5. Note that even this program should be modified to flesh out the Array class and to parameterize it.

Type

Listing 6.5 Sorting a List of Command-Line Arguments

```
1:    // Listing 6.5 - Sorting a List of Command-Line Arguments
2:
3:    #include <iostream.h>
4:    #include <string.h>
5:    #include "string.hpp"
6:    typedef unsigned long ULONG;
7:
8:    // *************** String Node class ************
9:    class Node
10:   {
11:   public:
```

```
12:         Node (String*);
13:         Node ();
14:         ~Node();
15:         void InsertAfter(Node*);
16:         Node * GetNext() { return itsNext; }
17:         const Node *  GetNext() const { return itsNext; }
17:         void SetNext(Node * next) { itsNext = next; }
18:         String* GetString() const;
19:         String*& GetString();
20:
21:     private:
22:         String *itsString;
23:         Node * itsNext;
24:     };
25:
26:
27:     // **************** String List ************
28:     class StringList
29:     {
30:     public:
31:         StringList();
32:         ~StringList();
33:         ULONG   GetCount() const { return itsCount; }
34:         void    Insert(String *);
35:         void    Iterate(void (String::*f)()const) ;
36:         String*   operator[](ULONG) const ;
37:         String*&   operator[](ULONG) ;
38:
39:     private:
40:         Node   itsHead;
41:         ULONG itsCount;
42:     };
43:
44:     // *** node implementations ****
45:
46:       Node::Node(String* pString):
47:       itsString(pString),
48:       itsNext(0)
49:       {}
50:
51:       Node::Node():
52:       itsString(0),
53:       itsNext(0)
54:       {}
55:
56:
57:       Node::~Node()
58:       {
59:          delete itsString;
60:          itsString = 0;
61:          delete itsNext;
62:          itsNext = 0;
63:       }
64:
65:       void Node::InsertAfter(Node* newNode)
66:       {
```

6

continues

Listing 6.5 continued

```
67:          newNode->SetNext(itsNext);
68:          itsNext=newNode;
69:        }
70:
71:        String * Node::GetString() const
72:        {
73:          if (itsString)
74:              return itsString;
75:          else
76:              return NULL; //error
77:        }
78:
79:         String*& Node::GetString()
80:        {
81:              return itsString;
82:        }
83:
84:         // Implementations for Lists...
85:
86:        StringList::StringList():
87:          itsCount(0),
88:          itsHead(0)   // initialize head node to have no String
89:          {}
90:
91:        StringList::~StringList()
92:        {
93:        }
94:
95:        String *  StringList::operator[](ULONG offSet) const
96:        {
97:          const Node* pNode = itsHead.GetNext();
98:
99:          if (offSet+1 > itsCount)
100:             return NULL; // error
101:
102:          for (ULONG i=0;i<offSet; i++)
103:             pNode = pNode->GetNext();
104:
105:         return    pNode->GetString();
106:        }
107:
108:      String*&  StringList::operator[](ULONG offSet)
109:        {
110:
111:          if (offSet+1 > itsCount)
112:          {
113:              Node* NewNode = new Node;
114:              for (Node *pNode = &itsHead;;pNode = pNode->GetNext())
115:              {
116:                  if (pNode->GetNext() == NULL ) //¦¦ *(pNode->GetNext()) <
                      *NewNode)
```

```
117:                    {
118:                        pNode->InsertAfter(NewNode);
119:                        itsCount++;
120:                        return NewNode->GetString();
121:                    }
122:                }
123:            }
124:         Node *pNode   = itsHead.GetNext();
125:         for (ULONG i=0;i<offSet; i++)
126:            pNode = pNode->GetNext();
127:        return    pNode->GetString();
128:       }
129:
130:    void StringList::Insert(String* pString)
131:    {
132:        Node * NewNode = new Node(pString);
133:        itsCount++;
134:        for (Node * pNode = &itsHead;;pNode = pNode->GetNext())
135:        {
136:            if (pNode->GetNext() == NULL ) //¦¦ *(pNode->GetNext()) < *NewNode)
137:            {
138:                pNode->InsertAfter(NewNode);
139:                break;
140:            }
141:        }
142:    }
143:
144:    void StringList::Iterate(void (String::*func)()const)
145:    {
146:       for (Node* pNode = itsHead.GetNext();
147:            pNode;
148:            pNode=pNode->GetNext()
149:            )
150:            (pNode->GetString()->*func)();
151:
152:    }
153:
154:    // function prototypes
155:    void QuickSort(StringList&, int, int);
156:    void Swap(String*& i, String*& j);
157:    int main(int argc, char **argv, char ** env);
158:    void Process(int argc, char ** argv);
159:
160:    // driver program
161:    int main(int argc, char **argv, char ** env)
162:    {
163:        // rudimentary usage testing
164:        if (argc < 3 ¦¦ argv[1][0] != '-')
165:        {
166:            cout << "Usage: " << argv[0] << " -Flag [arguments]" << endl;
167:            return 1;
168:        }
169:        Process (argc, argv);
170:        return 0;
```

continues

Listing 6.5 continued

```
171:    }
172:
173:    // switch on command line arguments
174:    void Process(int argc, char ** argv)
175:    {
176:        StringList buffer;
177:        int i;
178:        switch (argv[1][1])
179:        {
180:
181:            case 'I':
182:            case 'i':
183:                    for (i=0; i<100 && i < argc-2; i++)
184:                        buffer[i] = new String(argv[i+2]);
185:                    QuickSort(buffer,0,argc-2);
186:                    for (i = 0; i < argc-3; i++)
187:                        cout << *buffer[i] << ", ";
188:                    cout << *buffer[argc-3] << endl;
189:                break;
190:
191:            case 'F':
192:            case 'f':
193:                cout << "Index from a File" << endl;
194:                break;
195:
196:            case 'L':
197:            case 'l':
198:                cout << "Make a String for each line in a file" << endl;
199:                break;
200:
201:            case 'S':
202:            case 's':
203:            case '?':
204:                cout << "Search for following text" << endl;
205:                break;
206:        }
207:    }
208:
209:    // QuickSort implemented with Median of Three
210:    void QuickSort(StringList& Input, int left, int right)
211:    {
212:        if (right > left)
213:        {
214:            int i = left-1;
215:            int x = right;
216:            for (;;)
217:            {
218:                    while (*Input[++i] < *Input[right-1])
219:                        ;
220:                    while (*Input[--x] > *Input[right-1])
221:                        ;
222:
223:                if (i >= x)
224:                    break;
225:                Swap(Input[i], Input[x]);
```

```
226:            }
227:            Swap(Input[i], Input[right-1]);
228:            QuickSort(Input,left,i);
229:            QuickSort(Input,i+1,right);
230:        }
231:    }
232:
233:    void Swap(String*& i, String*& j)
234:    {
235:        String* temp;
236:        temp = j;
237:        j = i;
238:        i = temp;
239:    }
```

```
d:\>0605 -I Eternal Vigilance Is The Price Of Liberty
Eternal, Is, Liberty, Of, Price, The, Vigilance
```

In lines 8 through 24, a string node class is declared. Two constructors are offered—one takes a pointer to a string, and the other is the default constructor, which takes no parameters.

In lines 15 through 19, simple accessor and manipulation functions are provided; and in lines 22 and 23, the member variables are declared.

In lines 27 through 42, the StringList class is declared. A StringList is an unsorted linked list of String objects. The critical method is declared in line 37: the non-constant offset operator[] is declared to return a reference to a pointer to a string. This is what enables you to swap strings in QuickSort().

The implementations for the StringList are much like what you saw on day 3, except for the implementation of the non-constant offset operator[]. If the user requests access to an element that does not yet exist, a new node is created in line 118, and the count of nodes is incremented in line 119. In line 120, the new node's string pointer is returned by reference. This allows the user to write the line of code that appears in line 184:

```
buffer[i] = new String(argv[i+2]);
```

This is a critical line of code, so examine it closely. A new String object is being created, initialized with a command-line argument. The pointer returned by new() is passed into the StringList using the offset operator[], but the offset requested does not yet exist in the array. A new node is created, which returns a reference to its pointer to String. That pointer then is set to point to the new string just created, so the command-line argument is put into the array.

The array is passed to QuickSort() in line 185, and then the results are printed in lines 186 through 188. QuickSort() operates as in previous examples, except that the array is in fact a StringList, passed into QuickSort() by reference to save memory. This cannot be a constant reference, of course, because QuickSort() changes the array.

6

Using the Environment Variables

The DOS operating system (and others as well) utilizes what is known as the *environment*. The environment consists of values stored by the operating system and available to your program. You can access these variables as an array of strings from your command line, much like the command arguments themselves. Listing 6.6 reworks listing 6.5 to present a sorted list of the environment variables.

 Listing 6.6 Sorting the Environment Variables

```
1:    //Listing 6.6 - Sorting the Environment Variables
2:
3:    #include <iostream.h>
4:    #include <string.h>
5:    #include "string.hpp"
6:
7:    typedef unsigned long ULONG;
8:
9:    // *************** String Node class ************
10:    class Node
11:    {
12:    public:
13:       Node (String*);
14:       Node ();
15:       ~Node();
16:       void InsertAfter(Node*);
17:       Node * GetNext() { return itsNext; }
18:       const Node *  GetNext() const { return itsNext; }
19:       void SetNext(Node * next) { itsNext = next; }
20:       String* GetString() const;
21:       String*& GetString();
22:
23:    private:
24:       String *itsString;
25:       Node * itsNext;
26:    };
27:
28:    // *************** String List ************
29:    class StringList
30:    {
31:    public:
32:       StringList();
33:       ~StringList();
34:       ULONG   GetCount() const { return itsCount; }
35:       void    Insert(String *);
36:       void    Iterate(void (String::*f)()const) ;
37:       String*   operator[](ULONG) const ;
38:       String*&  operator[](ULONG) ;
39:
40:    private:
41:       Node  itsHead;
42:       ULONG itsCount;
43:    };
44:
```

```
45:    // *** node implementations ****
46:
47:      Node::Node(String* pString):
48:      itsString(pString),
49:      itsNext(0)
50:      {}
51:
52:      Node::Node():
53:      itsString(0),
54:      itsNext(0)
55:      {}
56:
57:
58:      Node::~Node()
59:      {
60:         delete itsString;
61:         itsString = 0;
62:         delete itsNext;
63:         itsNext = 0;
64:      }
65:
66:      void Node::InsertAfter(Node* newNode)
67:      {
68:       newNode->SetNext(itsNext);
69:       itsNext=newNode;
70:      }
71:
72:      String * Node::GetString() const
73:      {
74:         if (itsString)
75:            return itsString;
76:         else
77:            return NULL; //error
78:      }
79:
80:       String*& Node::GetString()
81:      {
82:            return itsString;
83:      }
84:
85:       // Implementations for Lists...
86:
87:      StringList::StringList():
88:         itsCount(0),
89:         itsHead(0)  // initialize head node to have no String
90:         {}
91:
92:      StringList::~StringList()
93:      {
94:      }
95:
96:      String *  StringList::operator[](ULONG offSet) const
97:      {
98:         const Node* pNode = itsHead.GetNext();
99:
100:        if (offSet+1 > itsCount)
```

6

continues

Listing 6.6 continued

```
101:               return NULL; // error
102:
103:          for (ULONG i=0;i<offSet; i++)
104:              pNode = pNode->GetNext();
105:
106:        return    pNode->GetString();
107:      }
108:
109:     String*&  StringList::operator[](ULONG offSet)
110:      {
111:
112:          if (offSet+1 > itsCount)
113:          {
114:              Node* NewNode = new Node;
115:              for (Node *pNode = &itsHead;;pNode = pNode->GetNext())
116:              {
117:                  if (pNode->GetNext() == NULL ) //¦¦ *(pNode->GetNext()) <
                      *NewNode)
118:                  {
119:                      pNode->InsertAfter(NewNode);
120:                      itsCount++;
121:                      return NewNode->GetString();
122:                  }
123:              }
124:          }
125:          Node *pNode   = itsHead.GetNext();
126:          for (ULONG i=0;i<offSet; i++)
127:              pNode = pNode->GetNext();
128:        return    pNode->GetString();
129:      }
130:
131:     void StringList::Insert(String* pString)
132:      {
133:          Node * NewNode = new Node(pString);
134:          itsCount++;
135:          for (Node * pNode = &itsHead;;pNode = pNode->GetNext())
136:          {
137:              if (pNode->GetNext() == NULL ) //¦¦ *(pNode->GetNext()) < *NewNode)
138:              {
139:                  pNode->InsertAfter(NewNode);
140:                  break;
141:              }
142:          }
143:      }
144:
145:     void StringList::Iterate(void (String::*func)()const)
146:      {
147:        for (Node* pNode = itsHead.GetNext();
148:              pNode;
149:              pNode=pNode->GetNext()
150:              )
151:                (pNode->GetString()->*func)();
152:
```

```
153:    }
154:
155:    // function prototypes
156:    void QuickSort(StringList&, int, int);
157:    void Swap(String*& i, String*& j);
158:    int main(int argc, char **argv, char ** env);
159:
160:
161:    // driver program
162:    int main(int argc, char **argv, char ** env)
163:    {
164:        StringList buffer;
165:        for (int i = 0; env[i] != NULL; i++)
166:            buffer[i] = new String(env[i]);
167:        int NumEnv = i;
168:
169:        QuickSort(buffer,0,NumEnv);
170:
171:        for (i = 0; i < NumEnv-1; i++)
172:            cout << *buffer[i] << "\n";
173:        cout << *buffer[NumEnv-1] << endl;
174:
175:        return 0;
176:    }
177:
178:    void QuickSort(StringList& Input, int left, int right)
179:    {
180:        if (right > left)
181:        {
182:            int i = left-1;
183:            int x = right;
184:            for (;;)
185:            {
186:                while (*Input[++i] < *Input[right-1])
187:                    ;
188:                while (*Input[--x] > *Input[right-1])
189:                    ;
190:
191:                if (i >= x)
192:                    break;
193:                Swap(Input[i], Input[x]);
194:            }
195:            Swap(Input[i], Input[right-1]);
196:            QuickSort(Input,left,i);
197:            QuickSort(Input,i+1,right);
198:        }
199:    }
200:
201:    void Swap(String*& i, String*& j)
202:    {
203:        String* temp;
204:        temp = j;
205:        j = i;
206:        i = temp;
207:    }
```

6

```
d:\>Set
CONFIG=Normal
CFG_COMPILER=MSC8
COMSPEC=C:\NDOS.COM
CMDLINE=C:\AUTOEXEC.BAT
PROMPT=$p$g
PATH=C:\BIN
NU=d:\nu
PROCOMM=\comm\pro\
MOUSE=C:\MSMOUSE
TEMP=c:\temp
TMP=c:\temp
EPSPATH=d:\eps65
ESESSION=d:\eps65\EPSILON.SES

d:\>0606
CFG_COMPILER=MSC8
CMDLINE=proj0004
COMSPEC=C:\NDOS.COM
CONFIG=Normal
EPSPATH=d:\eps65
ESESSION=d:\eps65\EPSILON.SES
MOUSE=C:\MSMOUSE
NU=d:\nu
PATH=C:\BIN
PROCOMM=\comm\pro\
PROMPT=$p$g
TEMP=c:\temp
TMP=c:\temp
```

Listing 6.6 is similar to listing 6.5; however, this time it is the environment variables that are sorted. The output reflects an abridged environment set, first printed as it is output by DOS, and then reprinted using the program listed in listing 6.6.

In line 164, a `StringList` object is created, and it is filled by iterating through all the strings provided by the third parameter to `main()`. Because there is no equivalent to `argc` for the environment parameters, the `for` loop terminates when a `Null` string is found. The number of strings is recorded in the local variable `NumEnv`, and this number is passed into `QuickSort()` in line 169, and then used again when printing the list in lines 171 through 173.

Using *getenv*

It is possible to search the environment for a single variable. DOS, UNIX, and the ANSI-proposed standard all call for the `getenv()` function, which returns a pointer to the environment variable or NULL if the variable doesn't exist.

Listing 6.7 Using `getenv()`

```
1:    // Listing 6.7 - Using getenv()
2:
3:    #include <ctype.h>
```

```
4:      #include <stdio.h>
5:      #include <stdlib.h>
6:      #include <string.h>
7:      #include "string.hpp"
8:      #include <dos.h>
9:
10:
11:     typedef unsigned long ULONG;
12:
13:       int main()
14:     {
15:       char *ptr;
16:       char buffer[100];
17:
18:       cout << "What do you want to search for? ";
19:       cin.getline(buffer,100);
20:
21:       for (int i=0; i<strlen(buffer); i++)
22:          buffer[i] = toupper(buffer[i]);
23:
24:       ptr = getenv(buffer);
25:
26:       if (ptr)
27:       {
28:          String found(ptr);
29:          cout << "found: " << found << endl;
30:       }
31:       else
32:          cout << "Not found. Try again. \n" << endl;
33:
34:       return 0;
35:     }
```

```
What do you want to search for? include
found: y:\h;y:\rsrc;d:\bc4\include

What do you want to search for? abc
Not found. Try again.
```

6

The user is prompted for a string in line 18. The string is forced to all uppercase letters in lines 21 and 22 to match the environment variables on my machine. In line 24, the string is passed to getenv() and the result is assigned to the pointer ptr.

In line 26, the results are tested. If they are not null, a String object is created and displayed; otherwise, a message is printed.

Using *putenv*

It is possible to change the value of an environment variable once you have a pointer to it. Listing 6.8 demonstrates getting, changing, and displaying an environment variable.

Type **Listing 6.8 Using `putenv`**

```
1:   #include <ctype.h>
2:   #include <stdio.h>
3:   #include <stdlib.h>
4:   #include <string.h>
5:   #include <dos.h>
6:   #include <iostreams.h>
7:     int main()
8:     {
9:       char *ptr;
10:      char buffer[100];
11:      char buff2[100];
12:
13:      cout << "What do you want to search for? ";
14:      cin.getline(buffer,100);
15:      for (int i=0; i<strlen(buffer); i++)
16:         buffer[i] = toupper(buffer[i]);
17:      ptr = getenv(buffer);
18:      if (ptr)
19:      {
20:         cout << "found: " << ptr << endl;
21:         cout << "What do you want to set it to? " ;
22:         cin.getline(buff2,100);
23:         for (int i=0; i<strlen(buff2); i++)
24:            buff2[i] = toupper(buff2[i]);
25:         strcat(buffer,"=");
26:         strcat(buffer,buff2);
27:         putenv(buffer);
28:         cout << "Displaying..." << endl;
29:         while (_environ[i])
30:          cout << _environ[i++] << endl;
31:      }
32:      else
33:         cout << "Not found. Try again. \n" << endl;
34:
35:      return 0;
36:    }
```

```
SET FUN=programming
What do you want to search for? fun
found: programming
What do you want to set it to? sleeping
Displaying...
FUN=SLEEPING
```

This version dispenses with the String class altogether and uses old-fashioned, C-style strings. In line 13, the user is prompted for a string to search the environment for. If it is found, it is displayed in line 20 and the user is prompted for a replacement in line 21.

The original string, with the name of the environment variables, has an equal sign added to it in line 25 and the new value added in line 26, and that is inserted into the environment in line 27. The result is displayed in line 28.

Summary

Today you learned how to access the command-line parameters to your program in DOS and UNIX, and how to access the environment variables. These parameters and variables are text strings, and can be sorted, combined, and tested using normal text-manipulation functions.

There are two ways to access the environment variables in DOS: from the array of C-style strings passed to main(), and from the global array of C-style strings accessed using getenv().

Q&A

Q Why is the argument list presented as two variables, the count (argc) and the vector (argv), but the environment is presented as only the vector (env), which is terminated with a null pointer?

A The C programming language originally used just argc and argv, with no concept of the environment. The environment vector was added years later, after the C programming community had much more experience with vectors in general. By this time, it was known that a null-terminated list is easier to deal with than a count and a list. However, it was too late to go back and change all the existing programs, so argc and argv weren't changed. C++ inherits this behavior from C.

Q Why is it easier to use the name of the program rather than flags in UNIX than it is in DOS?

A It is easier for the user, because there is one less thing to type. In UNIX, there is no real cost to using this approach, because you can create "links" to the file. These make it appear as if the executable file appears several times, under different names, but in reality it is stored only once.

Q If I pass in a sentence as an argument, how can I prevent each word in the sentence from being considered to be a separate argument? I just want the whole sentence to be a single argument.

A Surround the sentence in quotation marks.

Q Are there command-line arguments in Windows?

A There are, but it is awkward to access them, so most Windows programs don't require their use. If you invoke a program using File Run, you have an opportunity to add parameters, and you can add parameters to the command line associated with an icon via File Properties. Finally, if you run something that is not executable, but its extension is listed in the [Extensions] portion of your WIN.INI file, the executable that is associated with that extension is run, and the file name you originally selected is passed in as an argument.

Workshop

The Workshop provides quiz questions to help you solidify your understanding of the material covered and exercises to provide you with experience in using what you have learned. Try to answer the quiz and exercise questions before checking the answers in Appendix A, and make sure that you understand the answers before continuing to the next chapter.

Quiz

1. What are the four legal ways to declare the function `main()`?
2. What are the two ways to access the environment variables?
3. If you invoke a program with two parameters, what value will `argc` have?
4. What string is at `argv[0]`?

Exercises

1. Write a program in which `main()` takes no parameters, and in which you obtain and sort the environment variables.
2. Write a program that inserts its own full path name into an environment variable called *self*.
3. BUG BUSTERS: What is wrong with this code?

```
1:      #include <ctype.h>
2:      #include <stdio.h>
3:      #include <stdlib.h>
4:      #include <string.h>
5:      #include <dos.h>
6:      #include <iostream.h>
7:        int main()
8:        {
9:         char *ptr;
10:        char buffer[100];
11:        char buff2[100];
12:
13:        cout << "What do you want to search for? ";
14:        cin.getline(buffer,100);
15:        for (int i=0; i<strlen(buffer); i++)
16:           buffer[i] = toupper(buffer[i]);
17:        ptr = getenv(buffer);
18:        if (ptr)
19:        {
20:           cout << "found: " << ptr << endl;
21:           cout << "What do you want to set it to? " ;
22:           cin.getline(buff2,100);
23:           for (int i=0; i<strlen(buff2); i++)
24:              buff2[i] = toupper(buff2[i]);
25:           strcat(ptr,"=");
```

```
26:          strcat(ptr,buff2);
27:          putenv(ptr);
28:          cout << "Displaying..." << endl;
29:          while (_environ[i])
30:            cout << _environ[i++] << endl;
31:        }
32:      else
33:          cout << "Not found. Try again. \n" << endl;
34:
35:      return 0;
36:    }
```

Complex Data
Structures

In previous days, you saw how to create sorted lists and how to sort lists of data. ROBIN and many other programs require the capability to quickly *find* data based on a requested value. Although sorting the data is a good start, there are efficient ways to store your records so that retrieval time is optimized. Today you will learn

☐ What hash tables are and how to use them

☐ What binary trees are and how to use them

☐ What the issues are with binary trees

Laying the Groundwork

This chapter explores a number of lists and other complex data structures. To avoid retyping the same code repeatedly, and to provide a good example of how professional programs are laid out, I'll start by defining some header files that will be used for the entire chapter.

Note: The programs in this book were designed with *portability* in mind. Nonetheless, your compiler may be a bit more of a stickler than mine, and you may get warnings (or perhaps errors!) when you compile some of the code in this book.

There are a few things to try if you encounter errors or warnings in this case. First, if your compiler complains about the use of the BOOL type, comment out the enumerated BOOL shown in the standard definition file that follows, and replace it with these lines:

```
1:      typedef int BOOL;
2:      const int FALSE = 0;
3:      const int TRUE = 1;
```

Be sure to contact me on Interchange or CompuServe if the code simply doesn't work for you. It may be that a typo slipped in despite our careful scrutiny, and we may be able to straighten it out for you. With this code, and every other line of code you read or create, don't assume that it is 100 percent correct as it stands.

Standard Definitions

Listing 7.1 shows stdef.hpp, the file in which some common definitions will be kept, along with a few #include statements that will be used by all subsequent programs. Virtually every listing will include stdef.hpp (*st*andard *def*inition).

Listing 7.1 Using Stdef.hpp to Store Standard Definitions

```
1:    // *************************************************
2:    // PROGRAM:  Standard Definitions
3:    // FILE:     stdef.hpp
4:    // PURPOSE:  provide standard inclusions and definitions
5:    // NOTES:
6:    // AUTHOR:   Jesse Liberty (jl)
7:    // REVISIONS: 10/23/94 1.0 jl  initial release
8:    // *************************************************
9:
10:
11:   #ifndef STDDEF_HPP                   // inclusion guards
12:   #define STDDEF_HPP
13:
14:   enum BOOL { FALSE, TRUE };
15:
16:   #include <iostream.h>
17:
18:   #endif
```

None.

Stdef.hpp provides the standard definitions and inclusions that will be used in various other programs. Note the inclusions guards in lines 11 and 12 and ending in line 18. This is a standard way to prevent header files from being included twice in your program. On line 11, the definition STDEF_HPP is tested. If this file has not yet been included, this line will test *true* and the rest of the file will be included. If the file has not already been included, this line will test false and nothing until the *endif* in line 18 will be included; the file therefore will be skipped.

In line 12, STDEF_HPP is defined so that the next time through, this check will fail and the file will not be included a second time.

The List Class

Much of this chapter will use the sorted list template developed on day 3 and reproduced in listing 7.2. This template will be stored in a file named linklist.hpp.

Listing 7.2 The Sorted Linked List Template

```
1:    // *************************************************
2:    // PROGRAM:  Linked List Header
3:    // FILE:     linklist.hpp
4:    // PURPOSE:  provide sorted linked list template
5:    // NOTES:
```

continues

Listing 7.2 continued

```
6:     // AUTHOR:    Jesse Liberty (jl)
7:     // REVISIONS: 10/23/94 1.0 jl  initial release
8:     // **************************************************
9:
10:
11:    #ifndef LINKLIST_HPP
12:    #define LINKLIST_HPP
13:
14:     // *************** Node class ************
15:      template <class T>
16:      class Node
17:      {
18:      public:
19:         Node (T*);
20:         ~Node();
21:         void InsertAfter(Node *);
22:         Node * GetNext() const           { return itsNext; }
23:         void SetNext(Node * next)          { itsNext = next; }
24:         T & GetObject() const            { return *itsObject; }
25:         int operator<(const Node &rhs) const;
26:         BOOL operator==(const T& rhs) const;
27:
28:      private:
29:         T * itsObject;
30:         Node * itsNext;
31:      };
32:
33:      // *************** Object List ************
34:      template <class T>
35:      class List
36:      {
37:      public:
38:         List();
39:         ~List();
40:         long     GetCount() const { return itsCount; }
41:         void     Insert(T &);
42:         void     Iterate(void (T::*f)()const);
43:         T &       operator[](long);
44:         T *       FindObject(const T& target );
45:
46:      private:
47:         Node<T>  itsHead;
48:         long itsCount;
49:      };
50:
51:      // *** node implementations ****
52:
53:       template <class T>
54:       Node<T>::Node(T * pObject):
55:       itsObject(pObject),
56:       itsNext(0)
57:       {}
58:
59:       template <class T>
60:       Node<T>::~Node()
```

```
61:        {
62:           delete itsObject;
63:           itsObject = 0;
64:           delete itsNext;
65:           itsNext = 0;
66:        }
67:
68:        template <class T>
69:        void Node<T>::InsertAfter(Node* newNode)
70:        {
71:         newNode->SetNext(itsNext);
72:         itsNext=newNode;
73:        }
74:
75:        template <class T>
76:        int Node<T>::operator<(const Node &rhs) const
77:        {
78:        return (*itsObject < rhs.GetObject());
79:        }
80:
81:        template <class T>
82:        BOOL Node<T>::operator==(const T& target) const
83:        {
84:           return (*itsObject == target);
85:        }
86:
87:         // Implementations for Lists...
88:
89:        template<class T>
90:        List <T>::List():
91:           itsCount(0),
92:           itsHead(0)   // initialize head node to have no Object
93:           {}
94:
95:        template<class T>
96:        List <T>::~List()
97:        {
98:        }
99:
100:        template<class T>
101:        T &  List<T>::operator[](long offSet)
102:        {
103:           if (offSet+1 > itsCount)
104:              return itsHead.GetObject(); // error
105:
106:           Node<T>* pNode = itsHead.GetNext();
107:
108:           for (long i=0;i<offSet; i++)
109:              pNode = pNode->GetNext();
110:
111:          return    pNode->GetObject();
112:        }
113:
114:        template<class T>
115:        T*  List<T>::FindObject(const T& target )
```

7

continues

155

Listing 7.2 continued

```
116:        {
117:            for (Node<T> * pNode = itsHead.GetNext();
118:                  pNode!=NULL;
119:                  pNode = pNode->GetNext()
120:                )
121:            {
122:                if ( *pNode == target)
123:                    break;
124:            }
125:            if (pNode == NULL)
126:                return 0;
127:            else
128:                return &(pNode->GetObject());
129:        }
130:
131:        template<class T>
132:        void List<T>::Insert(T & Object)
133:        {
134:            Node<T> * NewNode = new Node<T>(&Object);
135:
136:            for (Node<T> * pNode = &itsHead;;pNode = pNode->GetNext())
137:            {
138:                if (pNode->GetNext() == NULL ¦¦ *NewNode < *(pNode->GetNext() ))
139:                {
140:                    pNode->InsertAfter(NewNode);
141:                    itsCount++;
142:                    break;
143:                }
144:            }
145:        }
146:
147:        template<class T>
148:        void List<T>::Iterate(void (T::*func)()const)
149:        {
150:            for (Node<T>* pNode = itsHead.GetNext();
151:                  pNode;
152:                  pNode=pNode->GetNext()
153:                )
154:                (pNode->GetObject().*func)();
155:        }
156:
157:    #endif
```

Output   None.

Analysis   This code is very similar to the code used on day 3. The significant change is that it has been made into a header file, complete with a heading of its own and inclusion guards. Save this file to your disk as linklist.hpp.

Strings and Notes

The minimal rNote object as described on day 3 also will be used, along with the String class previously described. The rNote declaration is provided in note.hpp, and the String declaration is provided in string.hpp. The String implementation is provided in string.cpp. Listing 7.3 illustrates note.hpp, listing 7.4 shows string.hpp, and listing 7.5 has string.cpp.

Listing 7.3 Note.hpp

```
1:     // ****************************************************
2:     // PROGRAM:   Basic Note object
3:     // FILE:      note.hpp
4:     // PURPOSE:   provide simple note object
5:     // NOTES:
6:     // AUTHOR:    Jesse Liberty (jl)
7:     // REVISIONS: 10/23/94 1.0 jl  initial release
8:     // ****************************************************
9:
10:    #ifndef NOTE_HPP
11:    #define NOTE_HPP
12:
13:    #include "stdef.hpp"
14:
15:     class rNote
16:     {
17:     public:
18:        rNote(const String& text):
19:        itsText(text), itsDate(0L)
20:           {itsNoteNumber = theNoteNumber++;}
21:        ~rNote(){}
22:
23:        const String& GetText()const { return itsText; }
24:        long GetDate() const { return itsDate; }
25:        long GetNoteNumber() const { return itsNoteNumber; }
26:
27:        int operator<(const rNote& rhs)
28:         { return itsNoteNumber < rhs.GetNoteNumber(); }
29:        BOOL operator==(const rNote& rhs)
30:         { return itsText == rhs.GetText(); }
31:
32:        operator long() { return itsNoteNumber; }
33:
34:        void Display() const
35:           { cout << "Note #: " << itsNoteNumber;
36:           cout <<    " Text: " << itsText << endl; }
37:
38:        static long theNoteNumber;
39:     private:
40:        String itsText;
41:        long itsDate;
42:        long itsNoteNumber;
43:     };
44:
45:    #endif
```

None

This rNote object will be used in subsequent chapters as the basis for exploring complex data-manipulation objects. Store this listing in the file note.hpp.

Listing 7.4 String.hpp

```
1:    // ****************************************************
2:    // PROGRAM:   String declaration
3:    // FILE:      string.hpp
4:    // PURPOSE:   provide fundamental string functionality
5:    // NOTES:
6:    // AUTHOR:    Jesse Liberty (jl)
7:    // REVISIONS: 10/23/94 1.0 jl   initial release
8:    // ****************************************************
9:
10:   #ifndef STRING_HPP
11:   #define STRING_HPP
12:   #include <string.h>
13:   #include "stdef.hpp"
14:
15:
16:   class xOutOfBounds {};
17:
18:   class String
19:   {
20:   public:
21:
22:           // constructors
23:           String();
24:           String(const char *);
25:           String (const char *, int length);
26:           String (const String&);
27:           ~String();
28:
29:           // helpers and manipulators
30:           int  GetLength() const { return itsLen; }
31:           BOOL IsEmpty() const { return (BOOL) (itsLen == 0); }
32:           void Clear();                  // set string to 0 length
33:
34:           // accessors
35:           char operator[](int offset) const;
36:           char& operator[](int offset);
37:           const char * GetString()const  { return itsCString; }
38:
39:           // casting operators
40:            operator const char* () const { return itsCString; }
41:            operator char* () { return itsCString;}
42:
43:           // operators
44:           const String& operator=(const String&);
45:           const String& operator=(const char *);
46:
```

```
47:                void operator+=(const String&);
48:                void operator+=(char);
49:                void operator+=(const char*);
50:
51:                int operator<(const String& rhs)const;
52:                int operator>(const String& rhs)const;
53:                BOOL operator<=(const String& rhs)const;
54:                BOOL operator>=(const String& rhs)const;
55:                BOOL operator==(const String& rhs)const;
56:                BOOL operator!=(const String& rhs)const;
57:
58:
59:                // friend functions
60:                String operator+(const String&);
61:                String operator+(const char*);
62:                String operator+(char);
63:
64:                void Display()const { cout << *this << " "; }
65:                friend ostream& operator<< (ostream&, const String&);
66:
67:        private:
68:                // returns 0 if same, -1 if this is less than argument,
69:                // 1 if this is greater than argument
70:                int StringCompare(const String&) const;   // used by Boolean
                   operators
71:
72:                char * itsCString;
73:                int itsLen;
74:        };
75:
76:        #endif // end inclusion guard
```

Type Listing 7.5 String.cpp

```
1:     // **************************************************
2:     // PROGRAM:   String definition
3:     // FILE:      string.cpp
4:     // PURPOSE:   provide fundamental string functionality
5:     // NOTES:
6:     // AUTHOR:    Jesse Liberty (jl)
7:     // REVISIONS: 10/23/94 1.0 jl   initial release
8:     // **************************************************
9:
10:
11:     #include "string.hpp"
12:
13:     // default constructor creates string of 0 bytes
14:     String::String()
15:     {
16:         itsCString = new char[1];
17:         itsCString[0] = '\0';
18:         itsLen=0;
19:     }
```

7

continues

Listing 7.5 continued

```
20:
21:      String::String(const char *rhs)
22:      {
23:          itsLen = strlen(rhs);
24:          itsCString = new char[itsLen+1];
25:          strcpy(itsCString,rhs);
26:      }
27:
28:      String::String (const char *rhs, int length)
29:      {
30:          itsLen = strlen(rhs);
31:          if (length < itsLen)
32:              itsLen = length;   // max size = length
33:          itsCString = new char[itsLen+1];
34:          memcpy(itsCString,rhs,itsLen);
35:          itsCString[itsLen] = '\0';
36:      }
37:
38:      // copy constructor
39:      String::String (const String & rhs)
40:      {
41:          itsLen=rhs.GetLength();
42:          itsCString = new char[itsLen+1];
43:          memcpy(itsCString,rhs.GetString(),itsLen);
44:          itsCString[rhs.itsLen]='\0';
45:      }
46:
47:      String::~String ()
48:      {
49:          Clear();
50:      }
51:
52:      void String::Clear()
53:      {
54:          delete [] itsCString;
55:          itsLen = 0;
56:      }
57:
58:      //non constant offset operator
59:      char & String::operator[](int offset)
60:      {
61:          if (offset > itsLen)
62:          {
63:              throw xOutOfBounds();
64:              return itsCString[itsLen-1];
65:          }
66:          else
67:              return itsCString[offset];
68:      }
69:
70:      // constant offset operator
71:      char String::operator[](int offset) const
72:      {
73:          if (offset > itsLen)
74:          {
```

```
75:              throw xOutOfBounds();
76:              return itsCString[itsLen-1];
77:         }
78:       else
79:           return itsCString[offset];
80:    }
81:
82:    // operator equals
83:    const String& String::operator=(const String & rhs)
84:    {
85:       if (this == &rhs)
86:           return *this;
87:       delete [] itsCString;
88:       itsLen=rhs.GetLength();
89:       itsCString = new char[itsLen+1];
90:       memcpy(itsCString,rhs.GetString(),itsLen);
91:       itsCString[rhs.itsLen]='\0';
92:       return *this;
93:    }
94:
95:    const String& String::operator=(const char * rhs)
96:    {
97:       delete [] itsCString;
98:       itsLen=strlen(rhs);
99:       itsCString = new char[itsLen+1];
100:       memcpy(itsCString,rhs,itsLen);
101:       itsCString[itsLen]='\0';
102:       return *this;
103:    }
104:
105:
106:    // changes current string, returns nothing
107:    void String::operator+=(const String& rhs)
108:    {
109:       unsigned short rhsLen = rhs.GetLength();
110:       unsigned short totalLen = itsLen + rhsLen;
111:       char *temp = new char[totalLen+1];
112:       for (int i = 0; i<itsLen; i++)
113:           temp[i] = itsCString[i];
114:       for (int j = 0; j<rhsLen; j++, i++)
115:           temp[i] = rhs[j];
116:       temp[totalLen]='\0';
117:       *this = temp;
118:    }
119:
120:    int String::StringCompare(const String& rhs) const
121:    {
122:           return strcmp(itsCString, rhs.GetString());
123:    }
124:
125:    String String::operator+(const String& rhs)
126:    {
127:
128:       char * newCString = new char[GetLength() + rhs.GetLength() + 1];
129:       strcpy(newCString,GetString());
```

continues

Listing 7.5 continued

```
130:        strcat(newCString,rhs.GetString());
131:        String newString(newCString);
132:        return newString;
133:    }
134:
135:
136:    String String::operator+(const char* rhs)
137:    {
138:
139:        char * newCString = new char[GetLength() + strlen(rhs)+ 1];
140:        strcpy(newCString,GetString());
141:        strcat(newCString,rhs);
142:        String newString(newCString);
143:        return newString;
144:    }
145:
146:
147:    String String::operator+(char rhs)
148:    {
149:        int oldLen = GetLength();
150:        char * newCString = new char[oldLen + 2];
151:        strcpy(newCString,GetString());
152:        newCString[oldLen] = rhs;
153:        newCString[oldLen+1] = '\0';
154:        String newString(newCString);
155:        return newString;
156:    }
157:
158:
159:
160:    BOOL String::operator==(const String& rhs) const
161:    { return (BOOL) (StringCompare(rhs) == 0); }
162:    BOOL String::operator!=(const String& rhs)const
163:        { return (BOOL) (StringCompare(rhs) != 0); }
164:    int String::operator<(const String& rhs)const
165:        { return (BOOL) (StringCompare(rhs) < 0); }
166:    int String::operator>(const String& rhs)const
167:        { return (BOOL) (StringCompare(rhs) > 0); }
168:    BOOL String::operator<=(const String& rhs)const
169:        { return (BOOL) (StringCompare(rhs) <= 0); }
170:    BOOL String::operator>=(const String& rhs)const
171:        { return (BOOL) (StringCompare(rhs) >= 0); }
172:
173:    ostream& operator<< (ostream& ostr, const String& str)
174:    {
175:        ostr << str.itsCString;
176:        return ostr;
177:    }
```

None.

162

The string implementation provided here is the same as seen previously, except that it has been changed to work with the other included files. Save this as string.cpp.

String.hpp, string.cpp, note.hpp, linklist.hpp, and stdef.hpp now provide a set of functionalities with which you can explore the complex data structures seen in the rest of this chapter. Save these all in one directory, because you will be using them and extending them over the coming days.

Testing the Building Blocks

Before moving on, examine listing 7.6, which provides a small test program that exercises the listings provided earlier in this chapter.

 Listing 7.6 Testing the Building Blocks

```
1:     // ****************************************************
2:     // PROGRAM:   Test driver
3:     // FILE:      0706.cpp
4:     // PURPOSE:   Test String, Note and Linked List
5:     // NOTES:     Same functionality as 0307.cpps
6:     // AUTHOR:    Jesse Liberty (jl)
7:     // REVISIONS: 10/23/94 1.0 jl  initial release
8:     // ****************************************************
9:
10:      #include "String.hpp"  // string class
11:      #include "Note.hpp"    // notes
12:      #include "LinkList.hpp" // linked lists
13:      #include "Note.hpp"
14:      #include "stdef.hpp"   // standard definitions
15:
16:    long rNote::theNoteNumber = 0;
17:    void main()
18:    {
19:        List<rNote> pl;
20:        rNote * pNote = 0;
21:        long choice;
22:        char buffer[256];
23:
24:        while (1)
25:        {
26:           cout << "\n(0)Quit (1)Add Note ";
27:           cin >> choice;
28:           if (!choice)
29:              break;
30:
31:           cin.ignore(255,'\n');
32:           cout << "\nText: ";
33:           cin.getline(buffer,255);
34:           pNote = new rNote(buffer);
35:           pl.Insert(*pNote);
36:        }
37:
```

continues

Listing 7.6 continued

```
38:        cout << "\n\nResults: \n" << endl;
39:        void (rNote::*pFunc)()const = rNote::Display;
40:        pl.Iterate(pFunc);
41:
42:        cin.ignore(255,'\n');
43:        cout << "\nFind Note with text: ";
44:        cin.getline(buffer,255);
45:        rNote target(buffer);
46:        pNote=0;
47:        pNote =  pl.FindObject(target);
48:        if (pNote)
49:        {
50:         cout << "\nFound! " << endl;
51:         pNote->Display();
52:        }
53:        else
54:            cout << "Note not found." << endl;
55:    }
```

```
(0)Quit (1)Add Note 1
Text: Walk the walk
(0)Quit (1)Add Note 1
Text: Talk the talk
(0)Quit (1)Add Note 0

Results:

Note #: 0  Text: Walk the walk
Note #: 1  Text: Talk the talk

Find Note with text: Talk the talk
Found!
Note #: 1  Text: Talk the talk
```

Listing 7.6 reproduces the functionality of listing 3.7, "Using a Parameterized List Class," using the new .hpp files shown in the previous listings. This confirms that these listings are correct and will compile and link. Although it took a few pages to get here, you now know that you have solid, reusable code.

Using Hash Tables

A *hash table* is a convenient way to manage large amounts of data using a small number of storage locations. You can imagine a series of "buckets" with data in each. Each bucket is numbered, and all the data you want to store must go in one or another of the buckets. You create a *hashing algorithm* to take all your data and reduce it to one of the available bucket values.

A simple (and simplistic!) approach to storing terms for ROBIN might be to hash the data based on the first letter of each word. Words beginning with *A* would be in bucket 0, words beginning with *B* would be in bucket 1, and so on. This method would enable you to create an array of 26 words, and each word would have its specific and easily identified location.

The problem with this approach, of course, is that more than one word might evaluate to the same bucket. Both *boy* and *bottle* begin with *b*, for example. You could disallow this condition, but then ROBIN would become pretty unusable, pretty quickly.

A modest alternative would be for each array location to hold a linked list of words. Thus, when two words evaluate to the same bucket (such as *boy* and *bottle*), they would each be put in the same list. Listing 7.7 illustrates this approach.

NEW☞ A *bucket* is a numbered location for your data.
TERM

NEW☞ A *hashing algorithm* is a formula applied to the data that renders a hash
TERM bucket number.

Type

Listing 7.7 Hashing the Words in ROBIN

```
1:    // **************************************************
2:    // PROGRAM:  Hash Table
3:    // FILE:     0707.cpp
4:    // PURPOSE:  Provide simple hash table for words
5:    // NOTES:
6:    // AUTHOR:   Jesse Liberty (jl)
7:    // REVISIONS: 10/23/94 1.0 jl  initial release
8:    // **************************************************
9:
10:   #include "String.hpp"  // string class
11:   #include "LinkList.hpp" // linked lists
12:   #include "stdef.hpp"   // standard definitions
13:   #include <ctype.h>     //  toupper()
14:
15:   void main(int argc, char ** argv)
16:   {
17:       List<String> myArray[26];
18:
19:       for (int i=1; i<argc; i++)
20:       {
21:         int offset = toupper(argv[i][0]) - 'A';
22:         String* ps = new String(argv[i]);
23:         myArray[offset].Insert(*ps);
24:       }
```

continues

Listing 7.7 continued

```
25:
26:        for (i=0; i<26; i++)
27:          myArray[i].Iterate(String::Display);
28:
29:    }
```

```
d:\>0707 Eternal Vigilance Is The Price Of Liberty
Eternal Is Liberty Of Price The Vigilance
```

This small program develops a very complicated and interesting hash table. In line 17, myArray is declared to be an array of 26 String lists. In lines 19 through 24, each of the arguments to the program is analyzed, looking for the first letter. The letters are forced to uppercase and then the value of 'A' is subtracted, leaving a number between 0 and 25. That *hashed* value is the offset into the array of lists of strings at which this word will be kept.

A string is created in line 22 from the argument at argv[i], and that string is passed by reference into the array of lists, calling the Insert function.

In line 26, the entire array is canvassed, with Iterate() called on each list. The address of the String member function Display is passed into Iterate(), and each String of each member of each list is called.

Deciding When To Use Hash Tables

In truth, you almost never would use a hash table as was done here. The hallmark usage of a hash table is when you have a small number of items, which you need to access wicked fast. Typically, you would hope to have more buckets than items, keeping data collisions down to a very small number.

You still would implement the linked list to handle the occasional collision, but almost all these lists would have at most one item in them.

Using Trees and Other Powerful Data Structures

For a first version of ROBIN, the hash algorithm shown in this chapter might be sufficient. It is a fundamental design principle to get something working, and then to worry about optimizing it. Who knows? You might find that accessing the words is not the slow part of your program.

It is true, however, that there are more efficient ways to get at a great deal of data, and that when you have tens of thousands of words you can expect this approach to bog down. After all,

accessing the word *Thunder* means finding the bucket of *T* words, and then walking the linked list until you find *Thunder*. There must be a better way, and there is.

Using Trees

A tree is a linked list in which each node points to two or more next nodes. Figure 7.1 illustrates a basic tree structure.

Figure 7.1.
Basic tree structure.

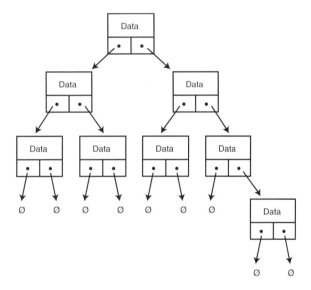

The topmost node in a tree is called the *root node*, and nodes that don't point to any other nodes are called *leaf nodes*.

> **NEW☞ TERM** The *root node* is the top of a tree.
>
> **NEW☞ TERM** A leaf node is a node that points to no other nodes.

Note that in a tree, nodes point only to other nodes farther "down" the tree. The nodes they point to are called *child nodes*, and thus the pointing node is called the *parent node*. In figure 7.1, the root node is parent to two children, each of which is a parent to two more children.

Using Binary Trees

The simplest form of tree is a *binary tree*, in which each node has no more than two child nodes. In a binary tree, each node is associated with a value. The left child node has values less than the current value, and the right child has values greater than the current value. Figure 7.2 illustrates this idea.

Figure 7.2.
A simple binary tree.

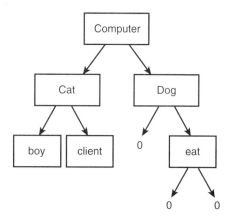

Note that each node either points to more nodes, or points to a null pointer.

Finding a Node

You search for a node by beginning at the root, and then moving down to the left for lesser values, and down to the right for greater values. In figure 7.3, the word *client* is searched for. The root is *Computer*, and *client* comes earlier in the alphabet, so the node to the left is examined. The word *client* comes later than the word *cat*, so the node to the right is searched, and the target word, *client*, is found.

Figure 7.3.
Searching for client.

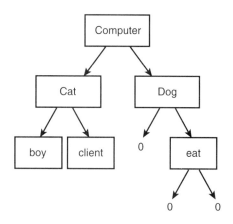

In figure 7.4, the word *drugs* is searched for. Again, you start at the root, *computer*. Because *drugs* comes later in the alphabet, the node to the right is examined. *Drugs* is larger than *dog*, so again the node to the right is examined, obtaining *eat*. Because *drugs* is less than *eat*, the node to the left would be examined, but it is null. The word is not found.

Figure 7.4.
Searching for drugs.

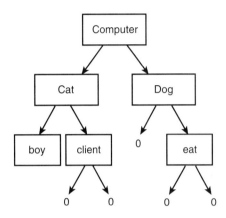

Inserting Nodes

If you wanted to insert a word into the list, you would search for it, and add it when you hit the first null. In the example in figure 7.4, *drugs* would be added as the left node of *eat*. Adding the word *drag* would work as shown in figure 7.5.

Figure 7.5.
Adding drag.

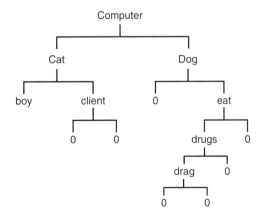

You start your search for *drag* at *computer*, go right to *dog*, go right to *eat*, go left to *drugs*, and then go left and get back null.

Deleting a Node

When you delete a node from the tree, it has child nodes or it is a leaf. Deleting a leaf is simple; deleting a node with child nodes, however, is a bit more complex.

Deleting a Leaf

To delete a leaf node from the tree, just tell its parent node not to point to it anymore, setting the parent node's pointer to null. Then delete the node, returning its memory to the free store, and removing whatever data it holds. This process is illustrated in figure 7.6, in which the leaf node *boy* is removed. The parent, *Cat*, now has its left pointer point to null; and the node, *boy*, is deleted.

Figure 7.6.
Deleting boy—*a leaf node.*

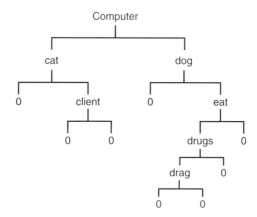

Deleting a Node with One Child

To delete a node with one child node, have the parent point to the child and then delete the node. Figure 7.7 illustrates this process by deleting *drugs*. To do this, the parent, *eat*, now points to *drag*, and *drugs* is deleted.

Figure 7.7.
Deleting drugs—*a node with one child.*

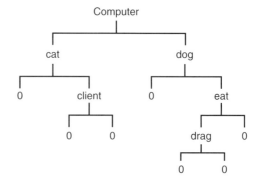

Deleting a Node with Two Children

Deleting a node with two children is somewhat more complicated. Examine figure 7.8, which has a different set of nodes; these are assembled from the words *four score and seven years ago our fore fathers brought forth on this continent a new nation.*

Figure 7.8.
A different set of nodes.

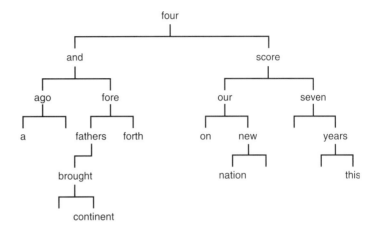

Notice that the word *and* has two child nodes. It is imperative that when *and* is removed, the tree remains in the right order, with each left child node having a lower value than the current node, and each right child node having a greater value. Here's how it is done:

1. Find the node with the next higher value (the *successor*). In this case, the successor is *brought.* Note that the successor will *never* have a left node, because that then would be the successor to the target.

2. Put the successor into the current position, maintaining the original links. Therefore, *brought* now points to *ago* and *fore.*

3. Promote the right child of the successor if there is one. In this case, *brought* points to *continent*, which becomes the right child of *ago.*

Deleting *and* in figure 7.8 leaves the binary tree, as shown in figure 7.9.

Creating an rWord Object

The binary tree will sort rWord objects in alphabetical order based on their strings. The rWord object shown in listing 7.8 is only a first approximation of the final rWord object—it will be used in ROBIN and is used here only for demonstration purposes.

7

Figure 7.9.
Deleting and.

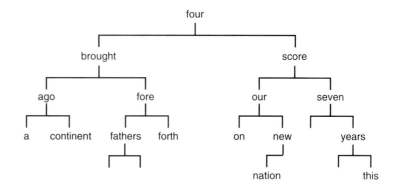

Listing 7.8 Using an rWord Declaration

```
1:     // ****************************************************
2:     // PROGRAM:   Basic word object
3:     // FILE:      word.hpp
4:     // PURPOSE:   provide simple word object
5:     // NOTES:
6:     // AUTHOR:    Jesse Liberty (jl)
7:     // REVISIONS: 10/23/94 1.0 jl  initial release
8:     // ****************************************************
9:
10:    #ifndef WORD_HPP
11:    #define WORD_HPP
12:
13:    #include "stdef.hpp"
14:    #include "string.hpp"
15:
16:    class rWord
17:    {
18:     public:
19:        rWord(const String& text):
20:        itsText(text), reserved1(0L), reserved2(0L) {}
21:        ~rWord(){}
22:
23:        const String& GetText()const { return itsText; }
24:
25:        int operator<(const rWord& rhs)
26:         { return itsText < rhs.GetText(); }
27:
28:        int operator>(const rWord& rhs)
29:         { return itsText > rhs.GetText(); }
30:
31:        int operator<=(const rWord& rhs)
32:         { return itsText <= rhs.GetText(); }
33:
34:        int operator=>(const rWord& rhs)
35:         { return itsText => rhs.GetText(); }
36:
31:        BOOL operator==(const rWord& rhs)
37:         { return itsText == rhs.GetText(); }
38:
```

```
39:        void Display() const
40:          { cout <<   "  Text: " << itsText << endl; }
41:
42:    private:
43:        String itsText;
44:        long reserved1;
45:        long reserved2;
46:    };
47:
48:    #endif
```

 None.

 The rWord object holds a string and reserves space for two long values. These may hold record numbers or other information later, when rWord is fleshed out. For now, rWord objects serve as string holders that can be placed in the binary tree.

Using the Demonstration Program

The demonstration program will read the command line and create an rWord object for each word in the command line. The rWord then will be added to the tree. When all the command-line words have been read, the tree will be printed. Indentation is used to show the relationship among the words, using a very simple display function provided by most compilers. Listing 7.9 provides the driver program to illustrate the binary tree.

Note: Most compilers support the ANSI function gotoxy(). If your compiler does not, however, you will need to modify this program so that the words are printed to the screen one after another.

Listing 7.9 Using the Driver Program

```
1:    // Using the Driver Program
2:
3:    #include "word.hpp"
4:    #include <conio.h>
5:
6:    class BinaryNode;       // forward declaration
7:
8:    class BinaryTree
9:    {
10:   public:
```

continues

173

Listing 7.9 continued

```
11:         BinaryTree():myHead(0),myCount(0){}
12:         ~BinaryTree(){}
13:         long GetCount() const { return myCount; }
14:         void Insert (rWord &);
15:         void Delete (rWord &);
16:         void Iterate(void (rWord::*f)() const);
17:         BinaryNode* FindObject(rWord& target);
18:         void PrintTree(int, char**);
19:         static long x;
20:         static long y;
21:
22:     private:
23:         BinaryNode* myHead;
24:         long myCount;
25:     };
26:
27:     class BinaryNode
28:     {
29:     public:
30:         BinaryNode(rWord* word);
31:         BinaryNode(rWord& word);
32:         BinaryNode(const BinaryNode&);
33:         ~BinaryNode() {}
34:         rWord* GetWord()const{ return myWord; }
35:         void SetWord(rWord* target) { myWord = target;}
36:
37:         void InsertSmaller(BinaryNode* NewNode);
38:         void InsertBigger(BinaryNode* NewNode);
39:
40:         BinaryNode* GetSmaller() const; // { return mySmaller;  }
41:         BinaryNode* GetBigger() const; // { return myBigger; }
42:         BinaryNode* GetParent() const; //{ return myParent; }
43:
44:         void SetSmaller(BinaryNode* target)   {mySmaller = target; }
45:         void SetBigger(BinaryNode* target)   {myBigger = target; }
46:         void SetParent(BinaryNode* target)   {myParent = target; }
47:
48:         int operator<(const BinaryNode &rhs) const
49:             {return *myWord < *(rhs.GetWord());}
50:         int operator>(const BinaryNode &rhs) const
51:             {return *myWord > *(rhs.GetWord());}
52:         BOOL operator==(const BinaryNode &rhs) const
53:             { return *myWord ==*(rhs.GetWord());}
54:         BOOL operator==(const rWord& target) const
55:             {return *myWord == target.GetText();} //
56:
57:     private:
58:
59:         BinaryNode * mySmaller;
60:         BinaryNode * myBigger;
61:         BinaryNode * myParent;
62:         rWord * myWord;
63:     };
64:
65:     BinaryNode* BinaryNode::GetSmaller() const
```

```
66:     {
67:         BinaryTree::y++;
68:         BinaryTree::x-= 14-BinaryTree::y*2;
69:         return mySmaller;
70:     }
71:
72:     BinaryNode* BinaryNode::GetBigger() const
73:     {
74:         BinaryTree::y++;
75:         BinaryTree::x+= 14-BinaryTree::y*2;
76:         return myBigger;
77:     }
78:
79:     BinaryNode* BinaryNode::GetParent() const
80:     {
81:         BinaryTree::y--;
82:         return myParent;
83:     }
84:
85:
86:     BinaryNode::BinaryNode(rWord* word):
87:         mySmaller(0),
88:         myBigger(0),
89:         myParent(0),
90:         myWord(word)
91:     {   }
92:
93:     BinaryNode::BinaryNode(rWord &word):
94:         mySmaller(0),
95:         myBigger(0),
96:         myParent(0),
97:         myWord(&word)
98:     {   }
99:
100:    BinaryNode::BinaryNode(const BinaryNode& rhs)
101:    {
102:        mySmaller=rhs.GetSmaller();
103:        myBigger=rhs.GetBigger();
104:        myParent=rhs.GetParent();
105:        myWord = rhs.GetWord();
106:    }
107:
108:
109:    void BinaryNode::InsertSmaller(BinaryNode* newNode)
110:    {
111:        newNode->SetSmaller(mySmaller);
112:        newNode->SetParent(this);
113:        mySmaller=newNode;
114:    }
115:
116:
117:    void BinaryNode::InsertBigger(BinaryNode* newNode)
118:    {
119:        newNode->SetBigger(myBigger);
120:        newNode->SetParent(this);
```

continues

175

Listing 7.9 continued

```
121:           myBigger=newNode;
122:      }
123:
124:
125:    void BinaryTree::Insert(rWord& rhs)
126:    {
127:       BinaryNode* newNode = new BinaryNode(&rhs);
128:
129:       if (myHead == 0)
130:       {
131:          myHead = newNode;
132:          return;
133:       }
134:
135:       BinaryNode* node = myHead;
136:       while (node)
137:       {
138:          // duplicate? replace
139:          if (newNode == node)
140:          {
141:             newNode->SetSmaller(node->GetSmaller());
142:             newNode->SetBigger(node->GetBigger());
143:             newNode->SetParent(node->GetParent());
144:             if (node == myHead)
145:                myHead = newNode;
146:             else
147:             {
148:                if ( node->GetParent()->GetSmaller() == node)
149:                   node->GetParent()->SetSmaller(newNode);
150:                else
151:                   node->GetParent()->SetBigger(newNode);
152:             }
153:             delete node;
154:             break;
155:          }
156:          if (*newNode < *node)
157:          {
158:             if (!node->GetSmaller())
159:             {
160:                node->SetSmaller(newNode);
161:                newNode->SetParent(node);
162:                break;
163:             }
164:             else
165:                node = node->GetSmaller();
166:          }
167:          else
168:          {
169:             if (!node->GetBigger())
170:             {
171:                node->SetBigger(newNode);
172:                newNode->SetParent(node);
173:                break;
174:             }
175:             else
```

```
176:                        node = node->GetBigger();
177:                }
178:           }    // end while
179:    }             // end function
180:
181:
182:    BinaryNode* BinaryTree::FindObject(rWord& rhs)
183:    {
184:        BinaryNode* node = myHead;
185:        x = 40;
186:        y = 1;
187:
188:        while (node)
189:        {
190:            if (*node == rhs)
191:                break;
192:
193:            if (*node < rhs)
194:                node = node->GetBigger();
195:            else
196:                node = node->GetSmaller();
197:        }
198:        return node;
199:    }
200:
201:    void BinaryTree::Delete (rWord & target)
202:    {
203:        BinaryNode* node = FindObject(target);
204:
205:        if (node)
206:        {
207:            if (!node->GetBigger())
208:            {
209:                if (!node->GetSmaller())
210:                {
211:                    if (node == myHead)
212:                        myHead = 0;
213:                    else
214:                    {
215:                        if (node->GetParent()->GetSmaller() == node)
216:                            node->GetParent()->SetSmaller(0);
217:                        else
218:                            node->GetParent()->SetBigger(0);
219:                    }
220:                }
221:                else // has a smaller
222:                {
223:                    if (node == myHead)
224:                        myHead = node->GetSmaller();
225:                    else
226:                    {
227:                        if (node->GetParent()->GetSmaller() == node)
228:                            node->GetParent()->SetSmaller(node->GetSmaller());
229:                        else
230:                            node->GetParent()->SetBigger(node->GetSmaller());
```

continues

Listing 7.9 continued

```
231:                    }
232:                }
233:            }
234:            else // node does have a bigger
235:            {
236:                if (!node->GetSmaller())
237:                {
238:                    if (node == myHead)
239:                        myHead = node->GetBigger();
240:                    else
241:                    {
242:                     if (node->GetParent()->GetSmaller() == node)
243:                        node->GetParent()->SetSmaller(node->GetBigger());
244:                    else
245:                        node->GetParent()->SetBigger(node->GetBigger());
246:                    }
247:                }
248:                else // node has both!!
249:                {
250:                    BinaryNode * next = node->GetBigger();
251:
252:                    while (next->GetSmaller())
253:                        next=next->GetSmaller();
254:
255:                    if (next->GetParent()->GetSmaller() == next)
256:                        next->GetParent()->SetSmaller(next->GetBigger());
257:                    else
258:                        next->GetParent()->SetBigger(next->GetBigger());
259:
260:                    node->SetWord(next->GetWord());
261:
262:                    if (next->GetBigger())
263:                        next->GetBigger()->SetParent(node);
264:
265:                    node = next;
266:                }
267:            } // end else does have bigger
268:        } // end if node
269:        delete node;
270:    } // end function
271:
272:    void BinaryTree::PrintTree(int argc, char **argv)
273:    {
274:        for (int i = 1; i<argc; i++)
275:        {
276:            rWord* word = new rWord(argv[i]);
277:            BinaryNode* pbn = FindObject(*word);
278:            delete word;
279:            // BinaryTree::x*=3; // 3 spaces per unit
280:            BinaryTree::x = BinaryTree::x < 0 ? 0 : BinaryTree::x;
281:            BinaryTree::x = BinaryTree::x > 80 ? 80 : BinaryTree::x;
282:            BinaryTree::y = BinaryTree::y < 0 ? 0 : BinaryTree::y;
283:            BinaryTree::y = BinaryTree::y > 25 ? 25 :BinaryTree::y;
284:
285:            gotoxy(BinaryTree::x, BinaryTree::y+10);
```

```
286:        cout << pbn->GetWord()->GetText();
287:      }
288:  }
289:
290:  long BinaryTree::x
291:  long BinaryTree::y;
292:  int main(int argc, char **argv)
293:  {
294:      BinaryTree tree;
295:      for (int i = 1; i< argc; i++)
296:      {
297:          rWord* word = new rWord(argv[i]);
298:          tree.Insert(*word);
299:      }
300:
301:      tree.PrintTree(argc,argv);
302:      cout << "\n\n\n" << endl;
303:
304:      return 0;
305:  }
```

Output

```
d:\>0708 now is the time for all good men to come to the aid


                                    now
                     is                        the
            for              men                     time
     all          good                                     to
 aid       come
```

Analysis

In line 3, the new word.hpp file is included, along with conio.h in line 4, which is the header file that Borland C++ 4.0 requires for the gotoxy() function. In line 6, the BinaryNode class is forward declared because BinaryTree will make reference to BinaryNode pointers, and the compiler must know that a BinaryNode is a type.

Note that in a real program, these declarations (of both BinaryNode and BinaryTree) would be moved off to a header file. The BinaryTree declares a constructor and destructor and a GetCount() method that returns the number of nodes in the tree (and that is not used in the demonstration program).

The Insert() and Delete() member functions will work as described earlier. The Iterate() function is a carryover from the linked List class, and again is not used in the demonstration program.

In line 18, PrintTree() is declared, and below it two public, static variables, x and y. These are used for demonstration purposes only, in order to print out a graph of the tree. This mechanism is rather crude and is included only to prove that the binary tree is working.

In lines 23 and 24, the private member variables are declared. Note that binary tree (unlike linked list) includes a pointer to the first link in the tree.

7

In lines 27 through 63, the `BinaryNode` class is declared. As described earlier, each node has four pointers, shown in lines 59 through 62. The node points to each of its two children (`mySmaller` and `mybigger`) as well as its parent and the `rword` object for which it is the node.

In addition to the usual constructors (lines 30 through 32), a variety of accessor functions is provided (lines 40 through 46) and comparison operators (lines 48 through 55). Note that the comparisons are immediately passed on to the `rWord`, which in turn does a comparison of its strings. Thus, comparing two nodes is the same as comparing the strings of their `rWord` objects.

The implementations of the accessors `GetSmaller()` and `GetBigger()` are made somewhat more complex because they keep track of the relative x and y coordinates of the node. That is, each time you go down a level, the static member `BinaryTree::y` is incremented, and each time you go right or left, the static member `BinaryTree::x` is incremented or decremented. Note that a simple but effective algorithm is used to decide how much to move right or left. As you go farther down the tree, you want to shift fewer spaces right or left before writing the word. This still does not prevent all overlaps, so it is possible for two words to print to the same space, overwriting each other. Keep this in mind as you experiment with different command-line arguments.

`BinaryNode::InsertSmaller()` in lines 109 through 114 and `BinaryNode::InsertBigger()` in lines 117 through 122 are fairly straightforward. When a node is inserted into the smaller position, it is told to set *its* smaller pointer to the current node's smaller pointer, and to set its parent node pointer to the current node. Then the current node sets its own smaller pointer to the new node.

The more interesting method, `BinaryTree::Insert()`, is shown in lines 125 through 179. Here, a word object is provided to the tree. The first thing the tree does is to create a new node for the word, in line 127. It then checks to see whether the root of the tree, `myHead`, already is occupied. If not, the new node is made the head and the insertion is complete.

Assuming that the head already exists, the trick now is to find the right position for the new node. A node pointer, `node`, is declared in line 135, and set to point to the head.

Each time through the `while` loop, the new node is compared to `node`. In the first case, this looks for a duplicate of the head node. Assuming that it fails the test in line 139, the new node is compared to the node to see whether it is larger or smaller. Assuming that it is smaller, it will pass the test in line 156; otherwise, it will fall through to the `else` statement in line 167.

If the new node is smaller, the next question is whether the current node already has a smaller pointer. If so, that becomes the current node, and the `while` loop starts again. If the current node does not have a smaller node, however, the new node is inserted as the current node's smaller node.

If the new node is a *bigger* node than the current node, the same test is applied: Does the current node have a bigger node? If not, the new node becomes the current node's bigger node; if there is already a bigger node, *it* becomes the current node and the `while` loop continues.

`FindObject()` also takes a word object. It initializes the x and y coordinates for display and then searches for the node in the tree.

`Delete()` follows the logic described earlier. Take the time to compare the code with the description and make sure that you follow how this works.

`PrintTree()`, shown in lines 272 through 277, is a quick hack to display the words in a simple graphical manner. It iterates through the command line and asks the binary tree to find each word in turn. The act of finding the word sets the x and y coordinates, which then are checked to make sure they are in range. Then `gotoxy()` is called, which moves the cursor to the appropriate screen coordinate, where the word is written.

In lines 290 and 291, the static member variables `BinaryNode::x` and `BinaryNode::y` are defined. Remember that declaring these in the class does *not* set aside memory; you must define them at global scope.

Rewriting the Binary Tree

The version of the binary tree shown in listing 7.9 works quite well but brings with it some unnecessary complexity. The printing algorithm is inefficient and not guaranteed to produce good results, and the insertion method is complex and potentially confusing.

The next example rewrites the binary tree to take advantage of the inherent recursion in trees: each node can be conceived, in some sense, as the top of its own tree. This makes insertion and deletion simpler.

It is important to be able to walk the tree when you need to print or search through the tree, although the particular order in which you walk the tree depends on what you are trying to accomplish.

The next program walks the tree in the following order: looking at the smaller value, looking at the current value, and then looking at the larger value. Recursing into this routine enables you to print the entire tree sideways. I'll discuss this in detail on day 8, but for now it enables the tree to show its contents quickly and easily. Listing 7.10 demonstrates these approaches.

 Listing 7.10 Another Way to Write a Binary Tree

```
1:  // *************************************************
2:  // PROGRAM:  Binary tree - Second version
3:  // FILE:     bintree.hpp
4:  // PURPOSE:  btree with recursive insertion
5:  // NOTES:    Special thanks to Stephen Zagieboylo
6:  // AUTHOR:   Jesse Liberty (jl)
7:  // REVISIONS: 11/3/94 1.0 jl  initial release
8:  // *************************************************
```

continues

Listing 7.10 continued

```
9:
10:     #include "stdef.hpp"
11:     #include "string.hpp"
12:     #include "word.hpp"
13:
14:     class BinaryNode;   // Forward reference
15:
16:     class BinaryTree
17:     {
18:     public:
19:         BinaryTree():myHead(0),myCount(0){}
20:         ~BinaryTree(){}
21:         long GetCount() const { return myCount; }
22:
23:         void Insert (const rWord& );
24:         BOOL Delete (const rWord& );       // Returns TRUE if found and deleted.
25:         void Iterate(void (*f)(const rWord&, int depth));
26:
27:     private:
28:         BinaryNode * myHead;
29:         long myCount;
30:     };
31:
32:     class BinaryNode
33:     {
34:     public:
35:         BinaryNode(const rWord &);
36:         ~BinaryNode() {}
37:         const rWord & GetValue()  { return myValue; }
38:         void SetValue(const rWord& val) { myValue = val;}
39:
40:         BinaryNode* GetSmaller() const   { return mySmaller;  }
41:         BinaryNode* GetBigger() const     { return myBigger; }
42:
43:         BinaryNode * Insert(const rWord&);
44:         static void ProcessDuplicateValue(const rWord& newValue, rWord&
            existingValue);
45:
46:         // Returns the new top of this subtree.
47:         // Sets the BOOL if it really deleted anything.
48:         BinaryNode * Delete(const rWord&, BOOL & DidDelete);
49:
50:         void SetSmaller(BinaryNode* target) { mySmaller = target; }
51:         void SetBigger(BinaryNode* target)  { myBigger = target; }
52:
53:         BOOL operator>(const rWord& rhs) const;
54:         BOOL operator==(const rWord& rhs) const;
55:
56:         void Iterate(void (*f)(const rWord&, int depth), int depth);
57:
58:     private:
59:         BinaryNode * mySmaller;
60:         BinaryNode * myBigger;
61:         rWord myValue;
62:     };
```

```
63:
64:    BinaryNode::BinaryNode(const rWord& word):
65:       mySmaller(0),
66:       myBigger(0),
67:       myValue(word)
68:    {  }
69:
70:
71:    BinaryNode * BinaryNode::Insert(const rWord& word)
72:    {
73:        if (*this == word)
74:            ProcessDuplicateValue(word, myValue);
75:        else if (*this > word)
76:        {
77:            if (mySmaller != 0)
78:                mySmaller = mySmaller->Insert(word);
79:            else
80:                mySmaller = new BinaryNode(word);
81:        }
82:        else
83:        {
84:            if (myBigger != 0)
85:                myBigger = myBigger->Insert(word);
86:            else
87:                myBigger = new BinaryNode(word);
88:        }
89:
90:        return this;
91:    }
92:
93:    void BinaryNode::ProcessDuplicateValue(const rWord& word , rWord&
       otherWord )
94:    {
95:        cout << otherWord.GetText() << " is a duplicate of ";
96:        cout << word.GetText() << endl;
97:    }
98:
99:    BinaryNode * BinaryNode::Delete(const rWord& word, BOOL & DidDelete)
100:   {
101:       if (*this == word)
102:       {
103:           // This is the one to remove.  It might be a leaf,
104:           // a single parent, or a double parent.
105:           if (mySmaller == 0)       // leaf or one type of single parent
106:           {
107:               // if myBigger == 0, return 0 anyway.
108:               BinaryNode * retval = myBigger;
109:               DidDelete = TRUE;
110:               delete this;   // Dangerous!  Must return immediately.
111:               return retval;
112:           }
113:           else if (myBigger == 0)        // other type of single parent
114:           {
115:               BinaryNode * retval = mySmaller;
116:               DidDelete = TRUE;
```

continues

Listing 7.10 continued

```
117:              delete this;   // Dangerous!  Must return immediately.
118:              return retval;
119:          }
120:          else        // Double parent
121:          {
122:              // Find the Node with the lowest value on
123:              // my Bigger subtree.  Remove him and put him in my place
124:              BinaryNode * smallest = myBigger;
125:              BinaryNode * hisparent = 0;
126:              while (smallest->GetSmaller() != 0)
127:              {
128:                  hisparent = smallest;
129:                  smallest = smallest->GetSmaller();
130:              }
131:
132:              // Remove him gracefully and put him in our place.
133:              // Watch out for the case where he is our child.
134:              if (hisparent != 0)   // not our immediate child.
135:              {
136:                  hisparent->SetSmaller(smallest->GetBigger());
137:                  smallest->SetBigger(myBigger);
138:              }
139:
140:              smallest->SetSmaller(mySmaller);
141:
142:              DidDelete = TRUE;
143:              delete this;   // Dangerous!  Must return immediately.
144:              return smallest;
145:          }
146:      }
147:      else if (*this > word)
148:      {
149:          if (mySmaller != 0)
150:              mySmaller = mySmaller->Delete(word, DidDelete);
151:          return this;
152:      }
153:      else
154:      {
155:          if (myBigger != 0)
156:              myBigger = myBigger->Delete(word, DidDelete);
157:          return this;
158:      }
159:  }
160:
161:
162:  BOOL BinaryNode::operator>(const rWord &rhs) const
163:  {
164:      return BOOL(myValue.GetText() > rhs.GetText());
165:  }
166:
167:
168:  BOOL BinaryNode::operator==(const rWord &rhs) const
169:  {
170:      return BOOL(myValue.GetText = rhs.GetText());
171:  }
```

```
172:
173:
174:
175:    void BinaryNode::Iterate(void (*f)(const rWord&, int depth), int depth)
176:    {
177:        if (mySmaller != 0)
178:            mySmaller->Iterate(f, depth+1);
179:
180:        f(myValue, depth);
181:
182:        if (myBigger != 0)
183:            myBigger->Iterate(f, depth+1);
184:    }
185:
186:
187:    void BinaryTree::Insert(const rWord& word)
188:    {
189:        if (myHead == 0)
190:            myHead = new BinaryNode(word);
191:        else
192:            myHead = myHead->Insert(word);
193:
194:        myCount++;
195:    }
196:
197:
198:    BOOL BinaryTree::Delete(const rWord& word)
199:    {
200:        BOOL DidDelete = FALSE;
201:
202:        if (myHead != 0)
203:            myHead = myHead->Delete(word, DidDelete);
204:
205:        if (DidDelete)
206:            myCount--;
207:
208:        return DidDelete;
209:    }
210:
211:    void BinaryTree::Iterate(void (*f)(const rWord&, int depth))
212:    {
213:        if (myHead != 0)
214:            myHead->Iterate(f, 1);
215:    }
216:
217:
218:    void Display(const rWord & word, int depth)
219:    {
220:        for ( ;depth > 0; depth--)
221:            cout << "    ";
222:        cout << word.GetText() << endl;
223:    }
224:
225:
226:    // Utility function used below.
```

7

continues

Listing 7.10 continued

```
227:    void ShowTree( BinaryTree & tree )
228:    {
229:        cout << "\n\nResults: \n" << endl;
230:        cout << "Count is: " << tree.GetCount() << endl;
231:        tree.Iterate(Display);
232:        cout << "\n\n" ;
233:    }
```

 ## Listing 7.11 Using the Driver Program

```
1:      // 7.11 - Using the Driver Program
2:      // second version
3:
4:      #include "btree.hpp"
5:
6:        int main()
7:      {
8:          char buffer[256];
9:          BinaryTree tree;
10:         static String ShowString("show");
11:
12:         while (1)
13:         {
14:             cout << "New String: ";
15:             cin.getline(buffer,255);
16:             rWord* word = new rWord(buffer);
17:
18:             if (buffer[0] == '\0')
19:                 break;
20:
21:             if (*word == ShowString)
22:                 {
23:                 ShowTree(tree);
24:                 continue;
25:                 }
26:
27:             tree.Insert(*word);
28:         }
29:
30:         ShowTree(tree);
31:
32:         while (1)
33:         {
34:             cout << "Word to Delete: ";
35:             cin.getline(buffer,255);
36:             rWord* word = new rWord(buffer);
37:
38:             if (buffer[0] == '\0')
39:                 break;
40:
```

```
41:            if (*word == ShowString)
42:                {
43:                ShowTree(tree);
44:                continue;
45:                }
46:
47:            if (!tree.Delete(*word))
48:                cout << "Not Found\n\n";
49:            }
50:
51:        tree.Iterate(Display);
52:    }
```

```
d:\112\day7>0711
New String: now
New String: is
New String: the
New String: time
New String: for
New String: all
New String: good
New String: men
New String: to
New String: come
New String: to
to is a duplicate of to
New String: the
the is a duplicate of the
New String: aid
New String: of
New String: the
the is a duplicate of the
New String: party

Results:

Count is: 16
                    aid
                all
                    come
            for
                good
        is
                men
    now
            of
                party
            the
                time
                    to

Word to Delete: good
Word to Delete: time
```

```
Word to Delete:
                        aid
                all
                        come
            for
        is
            men
    now
            of
                party
        the
            to
```

The `BinaryNode` and `BinaryTree` classes declared in listing 7.10 store the same rWord objects as the previous examples and utilize the same `stdef` inclusion file.

One addition to this tree is that it detects and reports on duplicates, without adding them to the tree. The `BinaryNode` class assumes much more of the work in this approach.

`BinaryTree::Insert()` is in line 187. It takes an rWord reference and passes it to its topmost node. The tree's only other job is to increment its count.

The real work is done in `BinaryNode::Insert()`, which is shown in lines 71 through 91. The word is examined to see whether it is a duplicate of the current node, and processed accordingly if it is. If it is not a duplicate, the word is either smaller or larger than the current node.

If the word is smaller and if there is no pointer to a smaller node, this new node becomes the smaller node. If there is already a smaller node, the new node is passed recursively to the insert method of the smaller node.

If the new node is larger than the current node, the same process occurs: If there is no larger node, the new node becomes the larger; if there already is a larger node, the new node is passed recursively down to the larger.

In this way, the new node is passed down the tree until its appropriate insertion point is found.

`Delete` works in much the same way. The problem facing the tree's `Delete()` function is that it must get back two values: the new head pointer (in case the current one is deleted) and a Boolean as to whether the deletion was completed. Deletion can fail if the item is not found in the tree.

This problem is solved by passing a Boolean to the `BinaryNode::Delete()` function by reference. The node then can set the value of `Delete`, while returning the new head pointer.

`BinaryNode::Delete()` is shown in lines 99 through 159. If the target node is the current node, the current node must be examined to see whether it has children. If it has no smaller child, `Delete()` returns its bigger child after deleting itself.

If it has a smaller child, but no bigger child, it returns the smaller child after deleting itself. The only other alternative is that it has two children. In that case, the logic in lines 120 through 145 is used, in which the "next value" is placed into the position of the removed node.

Summary

Today you saw how to create a hash table, which depends on a hashing algorithm to put values into discrete buckets. You saw how to resolve collisions when two objects hash to the same value, and you learned what the trade-offs are in using a hash table. You also learned two ways to implement a binary tree, and how to print the contents of the tree.

Q&A

Q When would you use a hash table in the real world?

A Although it is fairly memory-expensive, a hash table is the fastest way to retrieve data, as long as your table is big enough. You would use this technique only in times when speed is of the essence, typically because the access to the data is needed many times a second.

One example where a hash table often is used is for a software virtual memory system. You would keep in a hash table the records of which blocks of data are paged in. In a virtual memory system, the most important point of optimization is the speed of locating a block that is already in memory. If you have these in a hash table, this will be very fast, and the number of pages that can be in memory at one time is relatively low (compared to the number that might be out on disk).

Q What are the characteristics of a good hashing algorithm?

A The hashing algorithm determines the right bucket for a particular key. First, it should be very fast, because the whole point of using a hash table is speed. Second, given a typical set of keys, it should spread them out fairly evenly over the range, so that the buckets are equally full.

Q Give an example of a good hashing algorithm.

A For alphanumeric strings, XORing the first byte with the last one shifted left three bits is pretty good. Follow this by ANDing the number with an appropriate bit mask to cut it down to the right number of buckets (which has to be a power of two). This example will give you a number from 0 to 63, which you would use to index to a bucket:

```
inline int HashingAlgorithm(const char * s)
    {return (s[0] ^ (s[strlen(s)] << 3)) & 0x3f;}
```

Q In a binary tree, how many compares will it take to reach any one node in the tree? What is the average for all nodes as a function of the number of nodes in the tree?

A The number of compares it will take to reach any node is the depth or level of the tree. This will average less than $\log_2 N$, where N is the total number of nodes in the tree.

Q How much of a risk is it that binary trees will be badly unbalanced?

A If the data being inserted truly is random, then the binary tree will stay reasonably well balanced. However, real data sometimes already is sorted, depending on the source of the data. If sorted data is inserted into a binary tree, it creates the very worst case—a long chain of only right (or only left) branches. A solution to this problem is provided on day 8.

Workshop

The Workshop provides quiz questions to help you solidify your understanding of the material covered, and exercises to provide you with experience in using what you have learned. Try to answer the quiz and exercise questions before checking the answers in Appendix A, and make sure that you understand the answers before continuing to the next chapter.

Quiz

1. What is the hashing algorithm?
2. In a binary tree, what is a leaf node?
3. In a fully filled-out, four-level deep binary tree, what is the maximum number of nodes? Five levels deep? All values from 1 to 10?
4. In your fully filled-out binary trees, how many nodes are leaf nodes?
5. In a binary tree, if you delete a node with two children, what node ends up in the place the deleted node is vacating?

Exercises

1. What is wrong with this hashing algorithm?

```
inline int HashingAlgorithm(const char * s)
return (s[0] ^ (s[1] << 3) ^ (s[2] >> 3)) & 0x3f;}
```

2. Suppose that you are writing part of a virtual memory system. Your part of the system is a hash table that will keep track of data pages swapped in from disk. The pages are identified by a `long`, which is their position in the file. The important information about each swapped-in page is its address in memory, which is a `void *`.

   What classes would be involved in a hash table in order to maintain this information?

3. Suppose that you expect to be able to hold approximately 100 pages in memory at any one time, and so you decide to use a hash with 128 buckets. Write a good hashing algorithm that will distribute typical values evenly across this range. (The important thing here is to identify the expected values and show that your algorithm will end up with the values well distributed across the range.)

4. Parameterize the binary tree template shown in listing 7.10.

5. Write a test program that will exercise your binary tree template by making a tree of strings.

Advanced Data
Structure

On day 7, you learned how to create a binary tree and how to print its class members. Limitations exist in binary trees; you can use other structures to help solve some of these restrictions. Today you will learn:

☐ Other approaches to printing the tree

☐ How to create a FIFO queue

☐ What AVL trees are and how to use them

Printing a Tree

On day 7, you learned two ways to print a tree. The first way was rather awkward. The second way treated printing as a special case of walking the tree, which can be done in any number of sequences. You can imagine walking the tree in key-sequence order—alphabetical, in most cases. You also can imagine *depth-first* (go down the tree before you go across any levels) or *width-first* (go across a level before you go down.)

Today you will see two printing methods in more detail. The first method uses a first-in-first-out (FIFO) queue, and the second method revisits day 7's approach.

Using FIFO Queues

A *queue* is a structure in which objects enter one side, and leave the same or the other side. A *last-in-first-out* (LIFO) queue works so that the last thing added to the queue is the first thing to come out. A stack is a LIFO queue.

A first-in-first-out (FIFO) queue is like a line at a theater, as in figure 8.1 (and the British, in fact, talk about *queuing* up at a theater). The first person on line should be the first person through the door.

The easiest way to implement a FIFO queue is with an unsorted linked list. Listing 8.1 illustrates the interface to a simple FIFO queue. Listing 8.2 shows the implementation of the queue's methods, and listing 8.3 shows a driver program for the queue.

Figure 8.1

A FIFO queue.

8

Listing 8.1 FIFO Queue Header

```
1:    // ****************************************************
2:    // PROGRAM:  FIFO queue header
3:    // FILE:     queue.hpp
4:    // PURPOSE:  provide first in first out queue
5:    // NOTES:
6:    // AUTHOR:   Jesse Liberty (jl)
7:    // REVISIONS: 10/24/94 1.0 jl  initial release
8:    // ****************************************************
9:
10:      template <class T>
11:      class Node
12:      {
13:      public:
14:         Node (T*);
15:         ~Node();
16:         void InsertAfter(Node *);
17:         Node * GetNext() const           { return itsNext; }
18:         void SetNext(Node * next)         { itsNext = next; }
19:         T* GetObject() const           { return itsObject; }
20:
21:      private:
22:         T * itsObject;
23:         Node * itsNext;
24:      };
25:
26:      template <class T>
27:      class Queue
```

continues

Listing 8.1 continued

```
28:    {
29:      public:
30:        Queue();
31:        ~Queue();
32:        void        Push(T &);
33:        T*          Pop();
34:
35:      private:
36:        Node<T>  itsHead;
37:    };
```

Type   Listing 8.2 FIFO—Implementation

```
1:   // **************************************************
2:   // PROGRAM:   FIFO queue implementation
3:   // FILE:      queue.cpp
4:   // PURPOSE:   provide first in first out queue
5:   // NOTES:
6:   // AUTHOR:    Jesse Liberty (jl)
7:   // REVISIONS: 10/24/94 1.0 jl  initial release
8:   // **************************************************
9:
10:      #include "queue.hpp"
11:      template <class T>
12:      Node<T>::Node(T * pObject):
13:      itsObject(pObject),
14:      itsNext(0)
15:      {}
16:
17:       template <class T>
18:      Node<T>::~Node()
19:      {
20:         itsObject = 0;
21:         itsNext = 0;
22:      }
23:
24:       template <class T>
25:       void Node<T>::InsertAfter(Node* newNode)
26:      {
27:       newNode->SetNext(itsNext);
28:       itsNext=newNode;
29:      }
30:
31:      template<class T>
32:      Queue <T>::Queue():
33:         itsHead(0)  // initialize head node to have no Object
34:         {}
35:
36:      template<class T>
37:      Queue <T>::~Queue()
38:      {
39:      }
40:
```

```
41:        template<class T>
42:        void Queue<T>::Push(T & Object)
43:        {
44:            Node<T> * NewNode = new Node<T>(&Object);
45:
46:            for (Node<T> * pNode = &itsHead;;pNode = pNode->GetNext())
47:            {
48:                if (pNode->GetNext() == NULL)
49:                {
50:                    pNode->InsertAfter(NewNode);
51:                    break;
52:                }
53:            }
54:        }
55:
56:        template<class T>
57:        T* Queue<T>::Pop()
58:        {
59:            Node<T> * first = itsHead.GetNext();
60:            Node<T> * second = first->GetNext();
61:            if (first)
62:            {
63:                T* object = first->GetObject();
64:                if (second)
65:                    itsHead.SetNext(second);
66:                else
67:                    itsHead.SetNext(0);
68:                delete first;
69:                return object;
70:            }
71:            else
72:                return 0;
73:        }
```

Type Listing 8.3 Queue Driver Program

```
1:      #include "word.hpp"
2:      #include "queue.cpp"
3:
4:      int main(int argc, char **argv)
5:      {
6:          Queue<rWord> myQueue;
7:
8:          for (int i = 1; i< argc; i++)
9:          {
10:             rWord* word = new rWord(argv[i]);
11:             myQueue.Push(*word);
12:         }
13:
14:         for (i = 1; i< argc; i++)
15:             cout << myQueue.Pop()->GetText()<< "\n";
16:
17:         return 0;
18:     }
```

```
d:\>0803 eternal vigilance is the price of liberty
eternal
vigilance
is
the
price
of
liberty
```

Listing 8.1 provides a template-based FIFO queue. The Node class is very close to the Node class for the sorted linked list, and you could well make this new one a base class of that more complex node.

The Queue class itself is far simpler than the linked list: it offers Push(), which adds the entry to the end of the queue, and Pop(), which removes and returns the first item on the queue.

Using the Queue Class to Print

On day 7, you saw how to print the binary tree, using static members to keep track of indentation. The FIFO queue enables you to walk the tree horizontally. With this capability, you can print the tree, spacing out the words appropriately, or you can print it sideways by using gotoxy() to position each word in turn. Because the sideways approach provides space for a deeper tree, it is the one I'll use here. I'll leave as an exercise at the end of the chapter the job of printing this tree vertically, using the FIFO queue.

Listing 8.4 provides the interface to a Binary Tree class, where each node holds an rWord. A third class, BinaryNodeWrapper, also is provided, which will be the object placed into the FIFO queue. The BinaryNodeWrapper has a wordNode pointer, along with information about the indentation and level of the entry in the tree.

Listing 8.5 provides the implementation of these three classes, and listing 8.6 provides a driver program that walks the tree and prints the chart.

Listing 8.4 The Interfaces for a Binary Tree of Words

```
1:        #include "word.hpp"
2:        #include <conio.h>
3:
4:        class WordNode;      // forward declaration
5:
6:        class BinaryTree
7:        {
8:        public:
9:          BinaryTree():myHead(0),myCount(0){}
10:         ~BinaryTree(){}
11:         long GetCount() const { return myCount; }
12:         void Insert (rWord &);
13:         void Delete (rWord &);
14:         void Iterate(void (rWord::*f)() const);
15:         WordNode* FindObject( rWord& target);
```

16:        void PrintTree();
17:
18:    private:
19:        WordNode* myHead;
20:        long myCount;
21:    };
22:
23:    class WordNode
24:    {
25:    public:
26:        WordNode(rWord* word);
27:        WordNode(rWord& word);
28:        WordNode(WordNode&);
29:        ~WordNode() {}
30:        rWord* GetWord() { return myWord; }
31:        const rWord* const GetWord() const { return myWord; }
32:        void SetWord(rWord* target) { myWord = target;}
33:
34:        void InsertSmaller(WordNode* NewNode);
35:        void InsertBigger(WordNode* NewNode);
36:
37:        const WordNode* const GetSmaller() const { return mySmaller; }
38:        const WordNode* const GetBigger() const { return myBigger; }
39:        const WordNode* const GetParent() const { return myParent; }
40:
41:         WordNode*   GetSmaller()   { return mySmaller; }
42:         WordNode* GetBigger()   { return myBigger; }
43:         WordNode* GetParent() { return myParent; }
44:
45:
46:        void SetSmaller(WordNode* target)   {mySmaller = target; }
47:        void SetBigger(WordNode* target)   {myBigger = target; }
48:        void SetParent(WordNode* target)   {myParent = target; }
49:
50:        int operator<(const WordNode &rhs) const
51:           {return *myWord < *(rhs.GetWord());}
52:        int operator>(const WordNode &rhs) const
53:           {return *myWord > *(rhs.GetWord());}
54:        BOOL operator==(const WordNode &rhs) const
55:           { return *myWord ==*(rhs.GetWord());}
56:        BOOL operator==(const rWord& target) const
57:           {return *myWord == target.GetText();}
58:
59:    private:
60:
61:        WordNode * mySmaller;
62:        WordNode * myBigger;
63:        WordNode * myParent;
64:        rWord * myWord;
65:    };
66:
67:    class WNWrapper
68:    {
69:    public:
70:        WNWrapper(WordNode* wn):myWordNode(wn){}
71:        ~WNWrapper(){}
```

*continues*
```

Listing 8.4 continued

```
72:        //   WordNode& GetMyWordNode() { return myWordNode; }
73:        int GetLevel() { return myLevel; }
74:        void SetLevel (int level) {myLevel = level; }
75:        int GetIndent() { return myIndent; }
76:        void SetIndent (int Indent) {myIndent = Indent; }
77:        WordNode* GetSmaller() { return myWordNode->GetSmaller(); }
78:        WordNode* GetBigger() { return myWordNode->GetBigger(); }
79:        WordNode* GetWordNode() { return myWordNode; }
80:
81:    private:
82:        WordNode* myWordNode;
83:        int myLevel;
84:        int myIndent;
85:    };
```

Type

Listing 8.5 The Implementation of the Binary Tree of Words

```
1:    #include "btree.hpp"
2:    #include "queue.cpp"
3:
4:
5:    WordNode::WordNode(rWord* word):
6:        mySmaller(0),
7:        myBigger(0),
8:        myParent(0),
9:        myWord(word)
10:   {  }
11:
12:   WordNode::WordNode(rWord &word):
13:        mySmaller(0),
14:        myBigger(0),
15:        myParent(0),
16:        myWord(&word)
17:   {  }
18:
19:   WordNode::WordNode(  WordNode& rhs)
20:   {
21:        mySmaller=rhs.GetSmaller();
22:        myBigger=rhs.GetBigger();
23:        myParent=rhs.GetParent();
24:        myWord = rhs.GetWord();
25:   }
26:
27:
28:   void WordNode::InsertSmaller(WordNode* newNode)
29:   {
30:        newNode->SetSmaller(mySmaller);
31:        newNode->SetParent(this);
32:        mySmaller=newNode;
33:   }
34:
35:
36:   void WordNode::InsertBigger(WordNode* newNode)
```

```
37:    {
38:        newNode->SetBigger(myBigger);
39:        newNode->SetParent(this);
40:        myBigger=newNode;
41:    }
42:
43:
44:    void BinaryTree::Insert(rWord& rhs)
45:    {
46:        WordNode* newNode = new WordNode(&rhs);
47:
48:        if (myHead == 0)
49:        {
50:            myHead = newNode;
51:            return;
52:        }
53:
54:        WordNode* node = myHead;
55:        while (node)
56:        {
57:            // duplicate? replace
58:            if (newNode == node)
59:            {
60:                newNode->SetSmaller(node->GetSmaller());
61:                newNode->SetBigger(node->GetBigger());
62:                newNode->SetParent(node->GetParent());
63:                if (node == myHead)
64:                    myHead = newNode;
65:                else
66:                {
67:                    if ( node->GetParent()->GetSmaller() == node)
68:                        node->GetParent()->SetSmaller(newNode);
69:                    else
70:                        node->GetParent()->SetBigger(newNode);
71:                }
72:                delete node;
73:                break;
74:            }
75:            if (*newNode < *node)
76:            {
77:                if (!node->GetSmaller())
78:                {
79:                    node->SetSmaller(newNode);
80:                    newNode->SetParent(node);
81:                    break;
82:                }
83:                else
84:                    node = node->GetSmaller();
85:            }
86:            else
87:            {
88:                if (!node->GetBigger())
89:                {
90:                    node->SetBigger(newNode);
91:                    newNode->SetParent(node);
92:                    break;
```

continues

Listing 8.5 continued

```
93:                    }
94:                 else
95:                    node = node->GetBigger();
96:             }
97:         }   // end while
98:     }          // end function
99:
100:
101:    WordNode* BinaryTree::FindObject(rWord& rhs)
102:    {
103:       WordNode* node = myHead;
104:
105:
106:       while (node)
107:       {
108:          if (*node == rhs)
109:             break;
110:
111:          if (*node < rhs)
112:             node = node->GetBigger();
113:          else
114:             node = node->GetSmaller();
115:       }
116:       return node;
117:    }
118:
119:    void BinaryTree::Delete (rWord & target)
120:    {
121:       WordNode* node = FindObject(target);
122:
123:       if (node)
124:       {
125:          if (!node->GetBigger())
126:          {
127:             if (!node->GetSmaller())
128:             {
129:                if (node == myHead)
130:                   myHead = 0;
131:                else
132:                {
133:                   if (node->GetParent()->GetSmaller() == node)
134:                      node->GetParent()->SetSmaller(0);
135:                   else
136:                      node->GetParent()->SetBigger(0);
137:                }
138:             }
139:             else // has a smaller
140:             {
141:                if (node == myHead)
142:                   myHead = node->GetSmaller();
143:                else
144:                {
145:                   if (node->GetParent()->GetSmaller() == node)
146:                      node->GetParent()->SetSmaller(node->GetSmaller());
```

```
147:                else
148:                    node->GetParent()->SetBigger(node->GetSmaller());
149:            }
150:        }
151:    }
152:    else // node does have a bigger
153:    {
154:        if (!node->GetSmaller())
155:        {
156:            if (node == myHead)
157:                myHead = node->GetBigger();
158:            else
159:            {
160:                if (node->GetParent()->GetSmaller() == node)
161:                    node->GetParent()->SetSmaller(node->GetBigger());
162:                else
163:                    node->GetParent()->SetBigger(node->GetBigger());
164:            }
165:        }
166:        else // node has both!!
167:        {
168:            WordNode * next = node->GetBigger();
169:
170:            while (next->GetSmaller())
171:                next=next->GetSmaller();
172:
173:            if (next->GetParent()->GetSmaller() == next)
174:                next->GetParent()->SetSmaller(next->GetBigger());
175:            else
176:                next->GetParent()->SetBigger(next->GetBigger());
177:
178:            node->SetWord(next->GetWord());
179:
180:            if (next->GetBigger())
181:                next->GetBigger()->SetParent(node);
182:
183:            node = next;
184:        }
185:    } // end else does have bigger
186: } // end if node
187:    delete node;
188: } // end function
189:
190: // walk the tree horizontally and create wrappers in FIFO
191: void BinaryTree::PrintTree()
192: {
193:    Queue<WNWrapper> FIFO;
194:    if (!myHead)
195:    {
196:        cout << "Nothing in tree.\n" << endl;
197:        return;
198:    }
199:
200:    WNWrapper* theWrapper = new WNWrapper(myHead);
201:    int level = 1;
202:    theWrapper->SetLevel(level);
```

continues

203

Listing 8.5 continued

```
203:       int indent = level;
204:       theWrapper->SetIndent(indent);
205:       FIFO.Push(*theWrapper);
206:
207:       WNWrapper* wnr;
208:
209:       // ignore warning here!
210:       while (wnr = FIFO.Pop())
211:       {
212:          WordNode* pWN = wnr->GetSmaller();
213:          level = wnr->GetLevel();
214:          indent = wnr->GetIndent();
215:          if (pWN)
216:          {
217:             theWrapper = new WNWrapper(pWN);
218:             theWrapper->SetLevel(level+1);
219:             theWrapper->SetIndent(indent+1);
220:             FIFO.Push(*theWrapper);
221:          }
222:          pWN = wnr->GetBigger();
223:          if (pWN)
224:          {
225:             theWrapper = new WNWrapper(pWN);
226:             theWrapper->SetLevel(level+1);
227:             theWrapper->SetIndent(indent-1);
228:             FIFO.Push(*theWrapper);
229:          }
230:          int indent = wnr->GetIndent();
231:          gotoxy(5*level,indent+10);
232:          cout << wnr->GetWordNode()->GetWord()->GetText();
233:          delete wnr;
234:       }
235:       gotoxy(1,24);
236:   }
```

Listing 8.6 A Driver Program to Print a Binary Tree of Words

```
1:     // A Driver Program to Print a Binary Tree of Words
2:       int main(int argc, char **argv)
3:       {
4:          BinaryTree tree;
5:          for (int i = 1; i< argc; i++)
6:          {
7:             rWord* word = new rWord(argv[i]);
8:             tree.Insert(*word);
9:          }
10:
11:          tree.PrintTree();
12:
13:          return 0;
14:       }
```

```
d:\>0806 now is the time for all good men to

                        to
                time
        the
  now           men
        is              good
                for
                        all


d:\>0806 now is the time for all good men to come to the aid of
                        to
                to
                time
        the             the
  now           ofn
        is              good
                for             come
                        all
                                aid
```

The first printout demonstrates the use of the program.

In line 5 of listing 8.6, each word of the command line is used to create an rWord pointer, which then is inserted into the tree. The Insert() method works as discussed on day 7, and the word is moved into the right position in the tree.

After all the words are in the tree, the function PrintTree() is called in line 11. The implementation of this method is in lines 191 through 236 of listing 8.5.

A FIFO queue is instantiated in line 193, and the tree is checked to see whether it has any members. If not, a message is printed and the program ends.

Assuming that there is a head of the tree, a WNWrapper pointer is created based on the head word node in the tree. A number of local counting variables are initialized, and the wrapper is set to level 1 and indentation 1. Finally, in line 205, the wrapper is put into the queue.

The first WNWrapper is popped out of the queue and is assigned to the pointer to wrapper. Note that this assignment generates a warning with many compilers. The compiler is concerned that you might have confused the assignment operator (=) with the equal operator (==), but in this case, you *do* want the assignment operator.

If there is a smaller member, a new wrapper is created and its level and indentation are set based on the current wrapper, and the new (child) wrapper is pushed into the FIFO list.

In line 222, the bigger child is extracted in the same way. Now that the children have been wrapped up and put in the queue, the current word can be printed.

If you wanted to avoid using gotoxy(), you would rewrite this to indent according to the indentation level, and use new lines when the level variable changes.

This program is somewhat complex. You may want to run it a few times and then study the output, trying to understand line by line how the items are put on and then taken off the tree, and how they are pushed into and popped off of the queue.

Problems with This Approach

The second run of the program includes a larger set of text and reveals a bug in this approach. When the child of *the* is extracted (*men*), its level is 3 and its indentation is 0. This makes sense: the parent had a level of 2 and an indentation of 1—as the left child 1 is reduced from the parent's indentation, it returns to 0.

When the bigger child of *is* (*of*) is extracted, it too has a level of 3 and an indentation of 0. Its parent had a level of 2 and an indentation of –1, so the bigger child adds 1 to the indentation. Unfortunately, this position—level 3, indentation 0—already is taken, and the word *of* overwrites the first two letters of *men*.

Because symmetrical actions are taken on each level of the program, collisions are inevitable. It is possible to overcome this problem using complex algorithms, but the next set of programs uses a simpler solution.

Using Recursion to Print

Listing 8.7 provides a simple solution to printing the tree. The premise is to walk all the way down the left leg of the tree, print the last entry, then its parent, and then its sibling, working back up the tree.

Examine this tree from the previous listing:

```
d:\>0807 now is the time for all
        all
      for
    is
  now
    the
      time
```

One way to print this is to get to the top of the tree (*now*) and to pass it to the `PrintNode()` function. In `PrintNode()`, get the smaller child (*is*) and call `PrintNode()` on that; then call `DoPrint()` (which actually prints) and then call `PrintNode()` on the larger child.

When the first node, *now*, calls `PrintNode()` on the child, *is*, it in turn calls `PrintNode()` on *its* smaller child, *for*, which calls `PrintNode()` on *its* smaller child, *all*. Because *all* has no children, it prints itself, and then returns. The word *for* prints, has no larger child, and so returns, and so on up the recursion tree. Here's the listing. Note that only the declaration of the `PrintTree` and its implementation need to change.

Listing 8.7 Using Regression To Print the Tree

```
1:    // Listing 8.7 - Using Regression To Print the Tree
2:
3:    #include "word.hpp"
4:    #include "queue.cpp"
5:    #include <conio.h>
6:
7:    class WordNode;      // forward declaration
8:
9:    class BinaryTree
10:   {
11:   public:
12:      BinaryTree():myHead(0),myCount(0){}
13:      ~BinaryTree(){}
14:      long GetCount() const { return myCount; }
15:      void Insert (rWord &);
16:      void Delete (rWord &);
17:      void Iterate(void (rWord::*f)() const);
18:      WordNode* FindObject( rWord& target);
19:
20:                            // the changes are the next three!
21:      void PrintTree();
22:      static void PrintNode(WordNode* pNode, int indent);
23:      static void DoPrint(WordNode* pNode, int indent);
24:
25:   private:
26:      WordNode* myHead;
27:      long myCount;
28:   };
29:
30:   class WordNode
31:   {
32:   public:
33:      WordNode(rWord* word);
34:      WordNode(rWord& word);
35:      WordNode( WordNode&);
36:      ~WordNode() {}
37:      rWord* GetWord()  { return myWord; }
38:      const rWord* const GetWord() const { return myWord; }
39:
40:      void SetWord(rWord* target) { myWord = target;}
41:
42:      void InsertSmaller(WordNode* NewNode);
43:      void InsertBigger(WordNode* NewNode);
44:
45:      WordNode* GetSmaller() const  { return mySmaller;  }
46:      WordNode* GetBigger() const   { return myBigger; }
47:      WordNode* GetParent() const { return myParent; }
48:
49:      void SetSmaller(WordNode* target)   {mySmaller = target; }
50:      void SetBigger(WordNode* target)    {myBigger = target; }
51:      void SetParent(WordNode* target)    {myParent = target; }
52:
```

continues

Listing 8.7 continued

```
53:             int operator<(const WordNode &rhs) const
54:                 {return *myWord < *(rhs.GetWord());}
55:             int operator>(const WordNode &rhs) const
56:                 {return *myWord > *(rhs.GetWord());}
57:           BOOL operator==(const WordNode &rhs) const
58:               { return *myWord ==*(rhs.GetWord());}
59:           BOOL operator==(const rWord& target) const
60:               {return *myWord == target.GetText();}
61:       private:
62:          WordNode * mySmaller;
63:          WordNode * myBigger;
64:          WordNode * myParent;
65:          rWord * myWord;
66:        };
67:
68:       WordNode::WordNode(rWord* word):
69:          mySmaller(0),
70:          myBigger(0),
71:          myParent(0),
72:          myWord(word)
73:        {  }
74:
75:       WordNode::WordNode(rWord &word):
76:          mySmaller(0),
77:          myBigger(0),
78:          myParent(0),
79:          myWord(&word)
80:        {  }
81:
82:       WordNode::WordNode( WordNode& rhs)
83:        {
84:           mySmaller=rhs.GetSmaller();
85:           myBigger=rhs.GetBigger();
86:           myParent=rhs.GetParent();
87:           myWord = rhs.GetWord();
88:        }
89:
90:       void WordNode::InsertSmaller(WordNode* newNode)
91:        {
92:            newNode->SetSmaller(mySmaller);
93:            newNode->SetParent(this);
94:            mySmaller=newNode;
95:        }
96:
97:       void WordNode::InsertBigger(WordNode* newNode)
98:        {
99:            newNode->SetBigger(myBigger);
100:           newNode->SetParent(this);
101:           myBigger=newNode;
102:        }
103:
104:
105:      void BinaryTree::Insert(rWord& rhs)
106:       {
```

```
107:          WordNode* newNode = new WordNode(&rhs);
108:
109:        if (myHead == 0)
110:        {
111:            myHead = newNode;
112:            myHead->SetBigger(0);
113:            myHead->SetSmaller(0);
114:            return;
115:        }
116:
117:        WordNode* node = myHead;
118:        while (node)
119:        {
120:            // duplicate? replace
121:            if (newNode == node)
122:            {
123:                newNode->SetSmaller(node->GetSmaller());
124:                newNode->SetBigger(node->GetBigger());
125:                newNode->SetParent(node->GetParent());
126:                if (node == myHead)
127:                    myHead = newNode;
128:                else
129:                {
130:                    if ( node->GetParent()->GetSmaller() == node)
131:                        node->GetParent()->SetSmaller(newNode);
132:                    else
133:                        node->GetParent()->SetBigger(newNode);
134:                }
135:                delete node;
136:                break;
137:            }
138:            if (*newNode < *node)
139:            {
140:                if (!node->GetSmaller())
141:                {
142:                    node->SetSmaller(newNode);
143:                    newNode->SetParent(node);
144:                    break;
145:                }
146:                else
147:                    node = node->GetSmaller();
148:            }
149:            else
150:            {
151:                if (!node->GetBigger())
152:                {
153:                    node->SetBigger(newNode);
154:                    newNode->SetParent(node);
155:                    break;
156:                }
157:                else
158:                    node = node->GetBigger();
159:            }
160:        }   // end while
161:    }           // end function
```

continues

Listing 8.7 continued

```
162:
163:
164:      WordNode* BinaryTree::FindObject( rWord& rhs)
165:      {
166:          WordNode* node = myHead;
167:
168:
169:          while (node)
170:          {
171:              if (*node == rhs)
172:                  break;
173:
174:              if (*node < rhs)
175:                  node = node->GetBigger();
176:              else
177:                  node = node->GetSmaller();
178:          }
179:          return node;
180:      }
181:
182:      void BinaryTree::Delete (rWord & target)
183:      {
184:          WordNode* node = FindObject(target);
185:
186:          if (node)
187:          {
188:              if (!node->GetBigger())
189:              {
190:                  if (!node->GetSmaller())
191:                  {
192:                      if (node == myHead)
193:                          myHead = 0;
194:                      else
195:                      {
196:                          if (node->GetParent()->GetSmaller() == node)
197:                              node->GetParent()->SetSmaller(0);
198:                          else
199:                              node->GetParent()->SetBigger(0);
200:                      }
201:                  }
202:                  else // has a smaller
203:                  {
204:                      if (node == myHead)
205:                          myHead = node->GetSmaller();
206:                      else
207:                      {
208:                          if (node->GetParent()->GetSmaller() == node)
209:                              node->GetParent()->SetSmaller(node->GetSmaller());
210:                          else
211:                              node->GetParent()->SetBigger(node->GetSmaller());
212:                      }
213:                  }
214:              }
215:              else // node does have a bigger
```

```
216:                {
217:                    if (!node->GetSmaller())
218:                    {
219:                        if (node == myHead)
220:                            myHead = node->GetBigger();
221:                        else
222:                        {
223:                          if (node->GetParent()->GetSmaller() == node)
224:                            node->GetParent()->SetSmaller(node->GetBigger());
225:                        else
226:                            node->GetParent()->SetBigger(node->GetBigger());
227:                        }
228:                    }
229:                    else // node has both!!
230:                    {
231:                        WordNode * next = node->GetBigger();
232:
233:                        while (next->GetSmaller())
234:                            next=next->GetSmaller();
235:
236:                        if (next->GetParent()->GetSmaller() == next)
237:                            next->GetParent()->SetSmaller(next->GetBigger());
238:                        else
239:                            next->GetParent()->SetBigger(next->GetBigger());
240:
241:                        node->SetWord(next->GetWord());
242:
243:                        if (next->GetBigger())
244:                            next->GetBigger()->SetParent(node);
245:
246:                        node = next;
247:                    }
248:                } // end else does have bigger
249:            } // end if node
250:          delete node;
251:        } // end function
252:
253:
254:        void BinaryTree::PrintTree()
255:        {
256:            PrintNode(myHead,1);
257:        }
258:        void BinaryTree::PrintNode(WordNode* pNode, int indent)
259:        {
260:            WordNode* pWN = pNode->GetSmaller();
261:            if (pWN)
262:                PrintNode(pWN, indent+1);
263:            DoPrint(pNode, indent);
264:            pWN = pNode->GetBigger();
265:            if (pWN)
266:                PrintNode(pWN, indent+1);
267:
268:        }
269:        void BinaryTree::DoPrint(WordNode* pNode, int indent)
270:        {
271:            for (int i = 0; i<2*indent; i++)
```

continues

Listing 8.7 continued

```
272:            cout << " ";
273:          cout << pNode->GetWord()->GetText() << "\n";
274:      }
275:
276:
277:    int main(int argc, char **argv)
278:    {
279:       BinaryTree tree;
280:       for (int i = 1; i< argc; i++)
281:       {
282:          rWord* word = new rWord(argv[i]);
283:          tree.Insert(*word);
284:          tree.PrintTree();
285:
286:       }
287:       tree.PrintTree();
288:       return 0;
289:    }
290:
```

```
d:\>0807 now is the time for all good men to come to the aid of their party
              aid
              all
                come
          for
            good
      is
        men
    now
          of
            party
        the
            the
              their
          time
            to
              to
```

This listing is much like the previous, except that the WNwrapper class no longer is needed, and the print methods have changed.

In line 254, the single line of PrintTree() calls PrintNode(), with the pointer to the first node in the tree, and the indentation level of 1.

In line 258 of PrintNode(), the current node provides its smaller pointer, and PrintNode() is called recursively in line 260. DoPrint() is called right after the recursive call returns, and then the larger child is obtained and PrintNode() is again called, on the larger child.

The DoPrint() mechanism is simple: it counts off two spaces for each level of indentation and then prints the word.

Using Balanced Binary Trees

The biggest single problem with binary trees is that they can become badly out of balance. Suppose that you need to add the words *is hurry the how dog cat* to a binary tree. The tree would look like this:

```
cat
        dog
      how
    hurry
  is
    the
```

Finding *the* or *hurry* would be fairly quick, but finding *cat* would take many more searches than it should. It would be nice to be able to rebalance this tree so that there were fewer levels, like this:

```
cat
      dog
        how
  hurry
    is
        the
```

This provides three levels overall, rather than five. With larger trees, of course, the results can be even more dramatic.

Using AVL Trees

AVL trees promise that they will be no more than one level out of balance. That is, while the left node may have a child when the right does not, it will never be true, *at any point in the tree*, that one side has two levels of descendants when the other side has none.

Writing the AVL Tree

The trick with writing the AVL tree is that after each insert and each deletion, the tree must be in balance, or must be rebalanced. Recursion makes this possible, although it is by no means easy.

In order to write the AVL tree, the Node class must be modified to account for the imbalance in the tree. Listing 8.8 includes the declarations for the new node and the AVL tree itself. Note that this first attempt has not yet been parameterized; again, it is easier to develop and debug a class like this using actual types, rather than templates. Later, when you are confident the class is working well, you always can parameterize it.

Listing 8.9 provides the implementation, and listing 8.10 shows a short driver program. The analysis following listing 8.10 explains how the AVL tree works.

Listing 8.8 Declaring the AVL Tree

```
1:      // Listing 8.8 - Declaring the AVL Tree
2:
3:      #include "word.hpp"
4:      enum Tilt { tNone, tLeft, tRight};
5:
6:      class WordNode;      // forward declaration
7:
8:      class AVLTree
9:      {
10:     public:
11:         AVLTree():myHead(0),myCount(0),insertedOK(FALSE){}
12:         ~AVLTree(){}
13:
14:         long GetCount() const { return myCount; }
15:         void Insert (rWord &);
16:         void Delete (rWord &);
17:         void PrintTree();
18:
19:     protected:
20:         void InsertNode(WordNode*, WordNode*&);
21:         void DeleteBothChildren(WordNode*& target, WordNode* ptr, BOOL
                &deleteok);
22:         void RemoveNode(WordNode*& target, WordNode* doomed, BOOL &deleteok);
23:
24:         void leftBalance(WordNode*& target, BOOL &deleteok);
25:         void rightBalance(WordNode*& target,BOOL &deleteok);
26:         void RightRotate(WordNode *&);
27:         void LeftRotate(WordNode *&);
28:
29:         void PrintNode(WordNode* pNode, int indent);
30:         void DoPrint(WordNode* pNode, int indent);
31:
32:     private:
33:         WordNode* myHead;
34:         long myCount;
35:         BOOL insertedOK;
36:     };
37:
38:     class WordNode
39:     {
40:     public:
41:         // Constructors
42:         WordNode(rWord* word);
43:         WordNode(rWord& word);
44:         WordNode( WordNode&);
45:         ~WordNode() {}
46:
47:         // Accessors
48:         rWord* GetWord()  { return myWord; }
49:         const rWord* const GetWord() const  { return myWord; }
50:         void SetWord(rWord* target) { myWord = target;}
51:         WordNode*& GetSmaller()   { return mySmaller;  }
52:         WordNode*& GetBigger()    { return myBigger; }
```

```
53:          WordNode* GetParent() const { return myParent; }
54:
55:          void SetSmaller(WordNode* target)   {mySmaller = target; }
56:          void SetBigger(WordNode* target)   {myBigger = target; }
57:          void SetParent(WordNode* target)   {myParent = target; }
58:
59:          Tilt GetTilt() { return myTilt; }
60:          void SetTilt (Tilt theTilt) { myTilt = theTilt; }
61:
62:          // Insertion
63:          void InsertSmaller(WordNode* NewNode);
64:          void InsertBigger(WordNode* NewNode);
65:
66:          // overloaded operators
67:          int operator<(const WordNode &rhs) const
68:              {return *myWord < *(rhs.GetWord());}
69:          int operator<=(const WordNode &rhs) const
70:              {return *myWord <= *(rhs.GetWord());}
71:
72:
73:
74:          int operator>=(const WordNode &rhs) const
75:              {return *myWord >= *(rhs.GetWord());}
76:          int operator>(const WordNode &rhs) const
77:              {return *myWord > *(rhs.GetWord());}
78:          BOOL operator==(const WordNode &rhs) const
79:              { return *myWord ==*(rhs.GetWord());}
80:          BOOL operator==(const rWord& target) const
81:              {return *myWord == target.GetText();}
82:
83:      private:
84:          WordNode * mySmaller;
85:          WordNode * myBigger;
86:          WordNode * myParent;
87:          Tilt myTilt;
88:          rWord * myWord;
89:      };
90:
```

Type Listing 8.9 Implementing the AVL Tree

```
 1:      // Implementing the AVL tree
 2:      #include "avl.hpp"
 3:
 4:      WordNode::WordNode(rWord* word):
 5:          mySmaller(0),
 6:          myBigger(0),
 7:          myParent(0),
 8:          myTilt(tNone),
 9:          myWord(word)
10:      {  }
11:
12:      WordNode::WordNode(rWord &word):
13:          mySmaller(0),
```

continues

Listing 8.9 continued

```
14:          myBigger(0),
15:          myParent(0),
16:          myWord(&word)
17:     {  }
18:
19:     WordNode::WordNode(WordNode& rhs)
20:     {
21:        mySmaller=rhs.GetSmaller();
22:        myBigger=rhs.GetBigger();
23:        myParent=rhs.GetParent();
24:        myWord = rhs.GetWord();
25:     }
26:
27:     void WordNode::InsertSmaller(WordNode* newNode)
28:     {
29:         newNode->SetSmaller(mySmaller);
30:         newNode->SetParent(this);
31:         mySmaller=newNode;
32:     }
33:
34:     void WordNode::InsertBigger(WordNode* newNode)
35:     {
36:         newNode->SetBigger(myBigger);
37:         newNode->SetParent(this);
38:         myBigger=newNode;
39:     }
40:
41:
42:     void AVLTree::RightRotate(WordNode*& target)
43:     {
44:        WordNode *p2, *p3;
45:        p2 = target->GetBigger();
46:        if(p2->GetTilt()==tRight)   // single rotation
47:        {
48:           target->SetBigger(p2->GetSmaller());
49:           p2->SetSmaller(target);
50:           target->SetTilt(tNone);
51:           target = p2;
52:        }
53:        else      // double rotation
54:        {
55:           p3 = p2->GetSmaller();
56:           p2->SetSmaller(p3->GetBigger());
57:           p3->SetBigger(p2);
58:           target->SetBigger(p3->GetSmaller());
59:           p3->SetSmaller(target);
60:           p2->SetTilt(p3->GetTilt() == tLeft? tRight : tNone);
61:           target->SetTilt(p3->GetTilt() == tRight? tLeft: tNone);
62:           target = p3;
63:        }
64:        target->SetTilt(tNone);
65:     }
66:
67:     void AVLTree::LeftRotate(WordNode*& target)
```

```
68:     {
69:        WordNode *p2, *p3;
70:        p2 = target->GetSmaller();
71:        if(p2->GetTilt()==tLeft)          // single rotation
72:        {
73:           target->SetSmaller(p2->GetBigger());
74:           p2->SetBigger(target);
75:           target->SetTilt(tNone);
76:           target = p2;
77:        }
78:        else                             // double rotation
79:        {
80:           p3 = p2->GetBigger();
81:           p2->SetBigger(p3->GetSmaller());
82:           p3->SetSmaller(p2);
83:           target->SetSmaller(p3->GetBigger());
84:           p3->SetBigger(target);
85:           p2->SetTilt(p3->GetTilt() == tRight? tLeft : tNone);
86:           target->SetTilt(p3->GetTilt() == tLeft? tRight: tNone);
87:           target = p3;
88:        }
89:        target->SetTilt(tNone);
90:     }
91:
92:     void AVLTree::Delete(rWord& rhs)
93:     {
94:        BOOL deleteok = FALSE;
95:        WordNode* doomed = new WordNode(&rhs);
96:        RemoveNode(myHead,doomed,deleteok);
97:     }
98:
99:     void AVLTree::RemoveNode(WordNode*& target, WordNode* doomed, BOOL
        &deleteok)
100:    {
101:       WordNode* p;
102:       if (!target)
103:          deleteok = FALSE;
104:       else
105:       {
106:          if (*target == *doomed)
107:          {
108:             p = target;
109:             if (!target->GetBigger())
110:             {
111:                target = target->GetSmaller();
112:                deleteok = TRUE;
113:                delete p;
114:                p = 0;
115:             }
116:             else if (!target->GetSmaller())
117:             {
118:                target = target->GetBigger();
119:                deleteok = TRUE;
120:                delete p;
121:                p = 0;
122:             }
```

continues

Listing 8.9 continued

```
123:              else
124:              {
125:                  DeleteBothChildren(target, target->GetSmaller(), deleteok);
126:                  if (deleteok)
127:                      rightBalance(target,deleteok);
128:              }
129:          }
130:          else if (*doomed < *target)
131:          {
132:              RemoveNode(target->GetSmaller(), doomed, deleteok);
133:              if (deleteok)
134:                  rightBalance(target,deleteok);
135:          }
136:          else if (*doomed > *target)
137:          {
138:              RemoveNode(target->GetBigger(),doomed, deleteok);
139:              if (deleteok)
140:                  leftBalance(target,deleteok);
141:          }
142:      }
143:  }
144:
145:  void AVLTree::DeleteBothChildren(WordNode*& target, WordNode* ptr, BOOL
      &deleteok)
146:  {
147:      if (!ptr->GetBigger())
148:      {
149:          target->SetWord(ptr->GetWord());
150:          ptr=ptr->GetSmaller();
151:          deleteok = TRUE;
152:      }
153:      else
154:      {
155:          DeleteBothChildren(target, ptr->GetBigger(),deleteok);
156:          if (deleteok)
157:              leftBalance(ptr,deleteok);
158:      }
159:  }
160:
161:
162:  void AVLTree::leftBalance(WordNode*& target,BOOL &deleteok)
163:  {
164:      WordNode *p2, *p3;
165:      Tilt tilt2, tilt3;
166:
167:      switch (target->GetTilt())
168:      {
169:          case tRight:
170:              target->SetTilt(tNone);
171:              break;
172:          case tNone:
173:              target->SetTilt(tLeft);
174:              deleteok = FALSE;
175:              break;
```

```
176:           case tLeft:
177:               p2 = target->GetSmaller();
178:               tilt2 = p2->GetTilt();
179:               if (tilt2 != tRight)
180:               {
181:                   target->SetSmaller(p2->GetBigger());
182:                   p2->SetBigger(target);
183:                   if (tilt2 == tNone)
184:                   {
185:                       target->SetTilt(tLeft);
186:                       p2->SetTilt(tRight);
187:                       deleteok = FALSE;
188:                   }
189:                   else
190:                   {
191:                       target->SetTilt(tNone);
192:                       p2->SetTilt(tNone);
193:                   }
194:                   target = p2;
195:               }
196:               else
197:               {
198:                   p3=p2->GetBigger();
199:                   tilt3=p3->GetTilt();
200:                   p2->SetBigger(p3->GetSmaller());
201:                   p3->SetSmaller(p2);
202:                   target->SetSmaller(p3->GetBigger());
203:                   p3->SetBigger(target);
204:                   p2->SetTilt(tilt3 == tRight? tLeft : tNone);
205:                   target->SetTilt(tilt3 == tLeft?tRight:tNone);
206:                   target=p3;
207:                   p3->SetTilt(tNone);
208:               }
209:               break;
210:          }
211:     }
212:
213:     void AVLTree::rightBalance(WordNode*& target,BOOL &deleteok)
214:     {
215:         WordNode *p2, *p3;
216:         Tilt tilt2, tilt3;
217:
218:         switch (target->GetTilt())
219:         {
220:            case tLeft:
221:                target->SetTilt(tNone);
222:                break;
223:            case tNone:
224:                target->SetTilt(tRight);
225:                deleteok = FALSE;
226:                break;
227:            case tRight:
228:                p2 = target->GetBigger();
229:                tilt2 = p2->GetTilt();
230:                if (tilt2 != tLeft)
231:                {
```

continues

Listing 8.9 continued

```
232:                     target->SetBigger(p2->GetSmaller());
233:                     p2->SetSmaller(target);
234:                     if (tilt2 == tNone)
235:                     {
236:                         target->SetTilt(tRight);
237:                         p2->SetTilt(tLeft);
238:                         deleteok = FALSE;
239:                     }
240:                     else
241:                     {
242:                         target->SetTilt(tNone);
243:                         p2->SetTilt(tNone);
244:                     }
245:                     target = p2;
246:                 }
247:                 else
248:                 {
249:                     p3=p2->GetSmaller();
250:                     tilt3=p3->GetTilt();
251:                     p2->SetSmaller(p3->GetBigger());
252:                     p3->SetBigger(p2);
253:                     target->SetBigger(p3->GetSmaller());
254:                     p3->SetSmaller(target);
255:                     p2->SetTilt(tilt3 == tLeft?tRight:tNone);
256:                     target->SetTilt(tilt3 == tRight?tLeft:tNone);
257:                     target=p3;
258:                     p3->SetTilt(tNone);
259:                 }
260:                 break;
261:         }
262:     }
263:
264:
265:     void AVLTree::Insert(rWord& rhs)
266:     {
267:         WordNode* newNode = new WordNode(&rhs);
268:         InsertNode(newNode, myHead);
269:     }
270:
271:     void AVLTree::InsertNode(WordNode* newNode, WordNode*& target)
272:     {
273:         if (!target)
274:         {
275:             target = newNode;
276:             target->SetSmaller(0);
277:             target->SetBigger(0);
278:             target->SetTilt(tNone);
279:             insertedOK=TRUE;
280:             myCount++;
281:         }
282:         else if ((*newNode) <= (*target))
283:         {
284:             InsertNode(newNode,target->GetSmaller());
285:             switch(target->GetTilt())
```

```
286:            {
287:              case tLeft:
288:                 LeftRotate(target);
289:                 insertedOK=FALSE;
290:                 break;
291:              case tRight:
292:                 target->SetTilt(tNone);
293:                 insertedOK=FALSE;
294:                 break;
295:              case tNone:
296:                 target->SetTilt(tLeft);
297:            }
298:         }
299:         else
300:         {
301:            InsertNode(newNode,target->GetBigger());
302:            switch(target->GetTilt())
303:            {
304:              case tRight:
305:                 RightRotate(target);
306:                 insertedOK=FALSE;
307:                 break;
308:              case tLeft:
309:                 target->SetTilt(tNone);
310:                 insertedOK=FALSE;
311:                 break;
312:              case tNone:
313:                 target->SetTilt(tRight);
314:            }
315:         }
316:      }
317:
318:      void AVLTree::PrintTree()
319:      {
320:         PrintNode(myHead,1);
321:      }
322:      void AVLTree::PrintNode(WordNode* pNode, int indent)
323:      {
324:           WordNode* pWN = pNode->GetSmaller();
325:           if (pWN)
326:              PrintNode(pWN, indent+1);
327:           DoPrint(pNode, indent);
328:           pWN = pNode->GetBigger();
329:           if (pWN)
330:              PrintNode(pWN, indent+1);
331:
332:      }
333:
334:      void AVLTree::DoPrint(WordNode* pNode, int indent)
335:      {
336:         for (int i = 0; i<2*indent; i++)
337:            cout << " ";
338:         cout << pNode->GetWord()->GetText() << "\n";
339:      }
340:
```

Listing 8.10 Driver Program for the AVL Tree

```
 1:    // Listing 8.10 - Driver Program for the AVL Tree
 2:
 3:    int main(int argc, char **argv)
 4:    {
 5:       AVLTree tree;
 6:
 7:       // populate the tree
 8:       for (int i = 1; i< argc; i++)
 9:       {
10:          rWord* word = new rWord(argv[i]);
11:          tree.Insert(*word);
12:       }
13:
14:       tree.PrintTree();
15:
16:       // decimate the tree
17:       for (i = argc-1; i>=1; i-=3)
18:       {
19:          cout << "!! deleting " << argv[i] << endl;
20:          rWord *word = new rWord(argv[i]);
21:          tree.Delete(*word);
22:       }
23:
24:       tree.PrintTree();
25:       return 0;
26:    }
```

```
d:\>0810 now is the time for all good men to

           all
         for
            good
      is
         men
   now
            the
      time
            to

!! deleting to
!! deleting good
!! deleting for
!! deleting the

         for
            good
      is
   now
            the
         the
            to
```

In line 4 of listing 8.8, an enumerated constant Tilt is created, with three potential values: tNone, tLeft, and tRight. Every node tilts to the left or to the right, or has no tilt. Tilting to the left means that the left node has one depth greater than the right node.

The WordNode is declared in lines 42 through 89. In line 87, a new data member, myTilt, is declared to hold the individual node's tilt. Two new comparison operators are added: greater-than-or-equals in lines 74 and 75, and less-than-or-equals in lines 69 and 71.

Accessors for the Tilt are provided in lines 62 and 63; and GetSmaller() and GetBigger(), in lines 51 and 52, are modified to return a reference to the WordNode pointers, thus allowing the pointer to be changed by the calling program.

The AVL tree itself is declared in lines 8 through 40. A local variable, insertedOK, is created to keep track of when the tree needs balancing.

There is a simple set of public accessors, such as Insert() and Delete(), that call a suite of protected implementation methods. leftRotate() and rightRotate() are used by the insertion methods, and leftBalance() and rightBalance() are used by the deletion methods.

Take careful note that the left... and right... methods are complementary mirror images of each other.

Examine the Insert() method in lines 264 through 268. The object, in this case an rWord, is passed in and a node is created. InsertNode() is called with the new node and the pointer to the head of the list.

InsertNode() repeatedly tries to find a place for the new object, recursing into itself each time it descends a level. When objects are added, the parent object has its tilt set appropriately, and when the tilt becomes too great, the node is *rotated*.

In line 287, for example, if the node already has a left tilt, and another node is added to the left, then LeftRotate() is called.

Examine LeftRotate() in lines 66 through 89. The node is passed in, and its left node is examined. If the left node also has a left tilt, a single rotation is performed; otherwise a double rotation is performed.

Tip: When examining AVL trees and related binary trees, it is best to write down the structure on paper and manually walk through how nodes will be added and deleted.

Looking At Other Binary Trees

There are a host of other binary trees, but the truth is the only important remaining structure is the one you almost always will use when creating a program for storing items on disk: the B-tree. This structure is explained in detail on day 10 when `Collection` classes are covered.

Summary

Today you learned what a FIFO queue is and how to use it to print a binary tree. You also learned how to print a binary tree recursively, and what the primary limitations are in using binary trees. You learned what balanced trees are, and how to build one of the most powerful balanced trees: the AVL tree.

Q&A

Q Why is an unsorted linked list the easiest way to implement a FIFO queue?

A The alternative is to use an array, either of the objects or of pointers. Either you have to shuffle the array forward for each element removed from the list (or for each one added to the list, depending on which side you considered to be the front), or you have to use two pointers that represent the front and back, and they rotate around the list as if it were circular. Neither of these methods is terribly hard to implement, but the first one is inefficient and they both have the problem of the list filling up. Using a linked list is efficient and it never is full, because you always can add another node.

Q Is there any way to traverse a binary tree breadth-first without using a FIFO queue?

A Well, anything is possible, but it is very hard. You end up doing partial depth-first traversals many times, always keeping track of what depth you are supposed to be "traversing" in a breadth-first manner.

Q Why are there only three values in the enum `Tilt`, used in an AVL tree? Don't we need to know how much it tilts?

A Because an AVL tree is going to be kept nearly balanced, no one node will ever be left tilting by more than one in either direction.

Q How does the AVL tree perform in the case that is the nemesis of the regular binary tree—that is, where the elements being inserted already are sorted (or reverse sorted)?

A The AVL tree has no problem. Work it out (on paper, or using the program from the chapter) for inserting the letters A through O, in order. Although it does a fair bit of rebalancing, it ends up with a perfectly bushy tree.

Q When would an AVL tree be a good choice?

A An AVL tree is a great choice when the data structure is small enough to remain all in memory, but big enough and accessed commonly enough that performance is still an issue. If the data structure is too big for all of it to be in memory at once, then it is better to use a technique that is optimized for disk access (which you see on day 10). If the data structure will never get very big, or if it is not accessed frequently, then you shouldn't bother with the extra code and extra complication of a AVL tree over a binary tree.

Workshop

The Workshop provides quiz questions to help you solidify your understanding of the material covered, and exercises to provide you with experience in using what you have learned. Try to answer the quiz and exercise questions before checking the answers in Appendix A, and make sure that you understand the answers before continuing to the next chapter.

Quiz

1. What do FIFO and LIFO stand for? What is the more common name for a LIFO queue?
2. Describe the algorithm to traverse a binary tree in breadth-first order (using a FIFO queue).
3. How does an AVL tree avoid the worst cases that plague the binary tree?

Exercises

1. Modify the FIFO queue template so that it keeps track of the tail of the queue, rather than hunting down the list for it. Test it using the test program.
2. Make a generic queue template, which offers the methods `InsertFront`, `InsertBack`, `RemoveFront`, and `RemoveBack`.
3. Write a test program that makes a queue of strings, using the queue you created in exercise 2. Be sure that you test all the forms of insert and remove on empty and nonempty queues.
4. Write a test program that makes a queue of floats, using the queue template from exercise 2. If the queue template needed to be modified so that it could accept floats, then go back and redo exercise 3 to make sure that you didn't break it for strings.
5. Write a template for a stack, using the queue template you created in exercises 2 and 4 as its parent class. Use *private* inheritance, so the interface of queue is not visible to the clients of stack.

Writing to Disk

So far, you have created a number of complex data structures, but they all have been stored in memory. When your program ends, all the information is lost. Although saving data to disk is fairly straightforward, saving *objects* to disk can be a bit more complicated. Today you will learn

☐ How to save objects to disk

☐ How to create savable objects

☐ How to manipulate files

Writing Objects to Disk

Before you can focus on saving such complex structures as a binary tree to disk, you first must understand how to save individual objects, and how to read them back into memory. Your compiler vendor provides `ofstream` objects that provide basic file manipulation.

Your program can create an `ofstream` object, and then use it to open your files and to read data in and out. However, `ofstream` objects know nothing about your data. They are terrific for reading in a stream of characters, but your objects are more complex than that.

As you can imagine, it is your job to teach your classes how to be streamed to disk. There are a number of ways to do this.

The first question you must answer is whether your files will store mixed types of objects. If it is possible that you will need to read a record without knowing what type of object it is, then you will need to store more information in the file than if every record in that file were of the same type.

The second question is whether you are storing data of a fixed length. If you know that the next object to be read is 20 bytes, for example, you have an easier task than if you don't know how big the object is; in the latter case, the length must be stored with the object.

Listing 9.1 demonstrates a very simple program that opens a file, stores some text to it, closes the file, and then reopens it and reads the text.

Listing 9.1 Demonstrating fin and fout

```
1:      // Listing 9.1 - Demonstrating fin and fout
2:
3:      #include <fstream.h>
4:      void main()
5:      {
6:         char fileName[80];
7:         char buffer[255];     // for user input
8:         cout << "File name: ";
9:         cin >> fileName;
10:
11:        ofstream fout(fileName);  // open for writing
12:        fout << "This line written directly to the file...\n";
```

```
13:         cout << "Enter text for the file: ";
14:         cin.ignore(1,'\n');  // eat the new line after the file name
15:         cin.getline(buffer,255);  // get the user's input
16:         fout << buffer << "\n";   // and write it to the file
17:         fout.close();             // close the file, ready for reopen
18:
19:         ifstream fin(fileName);    // reopen for reading
20:         cout << "Here's the contents of the file:\n";
21:         char ch;
22:         while (fin.get(ch))
23:             cout << ch;
24:
25:         cout << "\n***End of file contents.***\n";
26:
27:         fin.close();              // always pays to be tidy
28:     }
```

```
d:\>0901
File name: mytest
Enter text for the file: Eternal vigilance is the price of liberty.
Here's the contents of the file:
This line written directly to the file...
Eternal vigilance is the price of liberty.

***End of file contents.***

d:\>dir

 Volume in drive D is unlabeled      Serial number is 1A46:13EA
 Directory of  d:\*.*

 .              <DIR>      10-29-94 12:24p
 ..             <DIR>      10-29-94 12:24p
 0901.cpp           868   10-29-94 12:38p
 0901.exe         78969   10-29-94 12:39p
 mytest              87   10-29-94 12:40p
        79,924 bytes in 3 file(s)
 131,727,360 bytes free

d:\>type mytest
This line written directly to the file...
Eternal vigilance is the price of liberty.
```

In line 11, an ofstream object, fout, is declared, and the file name is passed in. The default state of this file is to create the file if it doesn't yet exist, and to truncate the file (to delete all its contents) if it does exist.

The user is prompted for text that is written to the file in line 16. Note that ofstream already overloads the insertion operator (<<), so you don't have to.

In line 19, the file is opened for input, and the ofstream member function get() is called repeatedly in line 22.

Writing Data from an Object

Writing the contents of an rWord object would be fairly straightforward if all you wanted to do was to save the data and get it back. Listing 9.2 provides an illustration of this idea.

Listing 9.2 Writing Object Contents to Disk

```
1:      #include "word.hpp"
2:      #include <fstream.h>
3:
4:      int main()
5:      {
6:          char fileName[80];
7:          char buffer[255];      // for user input
8:          cout << "File name: ";
9:          cin >> fileName;
10:
11:         rWord* myArray[5];
12:         ofstream fout(fileName);  // open for writing
13:         cin.ignore(1,'\n');  // eat the new line after the file name
14:
15:         for (int i = 0; i<5; i++)
16:         {
17:             cout << "Please enter a word: " ;
18:             cin.getline(buffer,255);
19:             myArray[i] = new rWord(buffer);
20:             fout << myArray[i]->GetText() << "\n";   // and write it to the
                    file
21:         }
22:
23:         fout.close();              // close the file, ready for reopen
24:         ifstream fin(fileName);    // reopen for reading
25:
26:         cout << "Here's the contents of the file:\n";
27:         char ch;
28:         while (fin.get(ch))
29:            cout << ch;
30:
31:         cout << "\n***End of file contents.***\n";
32:
33:         fin.close();               // always pays to be tidy
34:         return 0;
35:     }
```

```
d:\>0902
File name: test2
Please enter a word: one
Please enter a word: two
Please enter a word: three
Please enter a word: four
Please enter a word: five
Here are the contents of the file:
one
```

```
two
three
four
five

***End of file contents.***

d:\>type test2
one
two
three
four
five
```

In line 11, an array of five pointers to rWord objects is created, and the user is prompted for five words, each of which is added to the array. In line 30, the contents of that word are written to disk, and that is played back to the user in lines 28 and 29.

Object Persistence versus Data Persistence

Listing 9.2 demonstrates data persistence, not object persistence. The text of the word objects is stored, but the object itself is lost. If reserved1 or reserved2 had important information, that would be lost. Also, other information within the contained String object is lost as well.

To save the object itself, *all* the data members must be stored. Clearly, all the work needed to store the object should be encapsulated in the object itself.

The rWord object consists of two longs and a string. The string, in turn, consists of a C-style, null-terminated string and a long. The right encapsulation is for the program to tell the rWord to save itself to disk. The rWord object should know how to store its longs and how to tell the string to store itself, but it should not know the details of string storage.

Storing Objects to Disk

To achieve this level of encapsulation, you need to provide a method in all your storables that takes an ofstream object and writes its contents into that object.

Instead of creating a method such as Serialize() or WriteToDisk(), I've overloaded the parentheses operator(). The operator() method writes the contents of the object to the disk by way of its ostream parameter. To get the object off the disk, you call a constructor that is overloaded to take an ifstream object.

Stddef.hpp has been modified to accommodate these changes and is shown in listing 9.3. Listing 9.4 is the interface to an improved String object, which knows how to store itself to disk and how to recover String objects from disk. Listing 9.5 shows its implementation.

Listing 9.6 has the interface and implementation for the new rWord object. Finally, listing 9.7 provides a driver program that uses these objects.

Type **Listing 9.3 stddef.hpp**

```
1:    // ****************************************************
2:    // PROGRAM:  Standard Definitions
3:    // FILE:     stdef.hpp
4:    // PURPOSE:  provide standard inclusions and definitions
5:    // NOTES:
6:    // AUTHOR:   Jesse Liberty (jl)
7:    // REVISIONS: 10/23/94 1.0 jl  initial release
8:    //            10/31/94 1.1 jl persistence
9:    // ****************************************************
10:
11:
12:   #ifndef STDDEF_HPP                  // inclusion guards
13:   #define STDDEF_HPP
14:
15:   const int szLong = sizeof (long int);
16:   const int szShort = sizeof (short int);
17:   const int szInt = sizeof (int);
18:
19:   enum BOOL { FALSE, TRUE };
20:
21:   #include <iostream.h>
22:
23:   #endif
```

Type **Listing 9.4 String.hpp**

```
1:    // ****************************************************
2:    // PROGRAM:  String declaration
3:    // FILE:     string.hpp
4:    // PURPOSE:  provide fundamental string functionality
5:    // NOTES:
6:    // AUTHOR:   Jesse Liberty (jl)
7:    // REVISIONS: 10/23/94 1.0 jl  initial release
8:    // ****************************************************
9:
10:   #ifndef STRING_HPP
11:   #define STRING_HPP
12:   #include <string.h>
13:   #include "stdef.hpp"
14:   #include "storable.hpp"
15:
16:   class xOutOfBounds {};
17:
18:   class String : public Storable
19:   {
20:   public:
21:
22:           // constructors
23:           String();
24:           String(const char *);
25:           String (const char *, int length);
26:           String (const String&);
```

```
27:                String(istream& iff);
28:                String(Reader&);
29:                ~String();
30:
31:                // helpers and manipulators
32:                int   GetLength() const { return itsLen; }
33:                BOOL IsEmpty() const { return (BOOL) (itsLen == 0); }
34:                void Clear();                    // set string to 0 length
35:
36:                // accessors
37:                char operator[](int offset) const;
38:                char& operator[](int offset);
39:                const char * GetString()const  { return itsCString; }
40:
41:                // casting operators
42:                 operator const char* () const { return itsCString; }
43:                 operator char* () { return itsCString;}
44:
45:                // operators
46:                const String& operator=(const String&);
47:                const String& operator=(const char *);
48:
49:                void operator+=(const String&);
50:                void operator+=(char);
51:                void operator+=(const char*);
52:
53:                BOOL operator<(const String& rhs)const;
54:                BOOL operator>(const String& rhs)const;
55:                BOOL operator<=(const String& rhs)const;
56:                BOOL operator>=(const String& rhs)const;
57:                BOOL operator==(const String& rhs)const;
58:                BOOL operator!=(const String& rhs)const;
59:
60:
61:                // friend functions
62:                String operator+(const String&);
63:                String operator+(const char*);
64:                String operator+(char);
65:
66:                void Display()const { cout << itsCString << " "; }
67:                friend ostream& operator<< (ostream&, const String&);
68:                ostream& operator() (ostream&);
69:                   void Write(Writer&);
70:
71:
72:    private:
73:                // returns 0 if same, -1 if this is less than argument,
74:                // 1 if this is greater than argument
75:                int StringCompare(const String&) const;  // used by Boolean
                   operators
76:                char * itsCString;
77:                int itsLen;
78:    };
79:
80:
81:    #endif // end inclusion guard
```

Listing 9.5 String.cpp

```cpp
1:     #include "string.hpp"
2:      // default constructor creates string of 0 bytes
3:     String::String()
4:     {
5:         itsCString = new char[1];
6:         itsCString[0] = '\0';
7:         itsLen=0;
8:     }
9:
10:
11:     String::String(istream& iff)
12:     {
13:         iff.read((char*) &itsLen,szLong);
14:
15:         itsCString = new char[itsLen+1];
16:         iff.read(itsCString,itsLen);
17:         itsCString[itsLen]='\0';
18:     }
19:
20:
21:     String::String(Reader& rdr)
22:     {
23:         rdr>>itsLen;
24:         rdr>>itsCString;
25:     }
26:
27:     String::String(const char *rhs)
28:     {
29:         itsLen = strlen(rhs);
30:         itsCString = new char[itsLen+1];
31:         strcpy(itsCString,rhs);
32:     }
33:
34:     String::String (const char *rhs, int length)
35:     {
36:         itsLen = strlen(rhs);
37:         if (length < itsLen)
38:            itsLen = length;   // max size = length
39:         itsCString = new char[itsLen+1];
40:         memcpy(itsCString,rhs,itsLen);
41:         itsCString[itsLen] = '\0';
42:     }
43:
44:     // copy constructor
45:     String::String (const String & rhs)
46:     {
47:         itsLen=rhs.GetLength();
48:         itsCString = new char[itsLen+1];
49:         memcpy(itsCString,rhs.GetString(),itsLen);
50:         itsCString[rhs.itsLen]='\0';
51:     }
52:
53:     String::~String ()
54:     {
```

```
55:        Clear();
56:    }
57:
58:    void String::Clear()
59:    {
60:        delete [] itsCString;
61:        itsLen = 0;
62:    }
63:
64:    //non constant offset operator
65:    char & String::operator[](int offset)
66:    {
67:        if (offset > itsLen)
68:        {
69:            throw xOutOfBounds();
70:            return itsCString[itsLen-1];
71:        }
72:        else
73:            return itsCString[offset];
74:    }
75:
76:    // constant offset operator
77:    char String::operator[](int offset) const
78:    {
79:        if (offset > itsLen)
80:        {
81:            throw xOutOfBounds();
82:            return itsCString[itsLen-1];
83:        }
84:        else
85:            return itsCString[offset];
86:    }
87:
88:    // operator equals
89:    const String& String::operator=(const String & rhs)
90:    {
91:        if (this == &rhs)
92:            return *this;
93:        delete [] itsCString;
94:        itsLen=rhs.GetLength();
95:        itsCString = new char[itsLen+1];
96:        memcpy(itsCString,rhs.GetString(),itsLen);
97:        itsCString[rhs.itsLen]='\0';
98:        return *this;
99:    }
100:
101:    const String& String::operator=(const char * rhs)
102:    {
103:        delete [] itsCString;
104:        itsLen=strlen(rhs);
105:        itsCString = new char[itsLen+1];
106:        memcpy(itsCString,rhs,itsLen);
107:        itsCString[itsLen]='\0';
108:        return *this;
109:    }
110:
```

continues

Listing 9.5 continued

```cpp
111:
112:    // changes current string, returns nothing
113:    void String::operator+=(const String& rhs)
114:    {
115:        unsigned short rhsLen = rhs.GetLength();
116:        unsigned short totalLen = itsLen + rhsLen;
117:        char *temp = new char[totalLen+1];
118:        for (int i = 0; i<itsLen; i++)
119:            temp[i] = itsCString[i];
120:        for (int j = 0; j<rhsLen; j++, i++)
121:            temp[i] = rhs[j];
122:        temp[totalLen]='\0';
123:        *this = temp;
124:    }
125:
126:    int String::StringCompare(const String& rhs) const
127:    {
128:            return strcmp(itsCString, rhs.GetString());
129:    }
130:
131:    String String::operator+(const String& rhs)
132:    {
133:
134:        char * newCString = new char[GetLength() + rhs.GetLength() + 1];
135:        strcpy(newCString,GetString());
136:        strcat(newCString,rhs.GetString());
137:        String newString(newCString);
138:        return newString;
139:    }
140:
141:
142:    String String::operator+(const char* rhs)
143:    {
144:
145:        char * newCString = new char[GetLength() + strlen(rhs)+ 1];
146:        strcpy(newCString,GetString());
147:        strcat(newCString,rhs);
148:        String newString(newCString);
149:        return newString;
150:    }
151:
152:
153:    String String::operator+(char rhs)
154:    {
155:        int oldLen = GetLength();
156:        char * newCString = new char[oldLen + 2];
157:        strcpy(newCString,GetString());
158:        newCString[oldLen] = rhs;
159:        newCString[oldLen+1] = '\0';
160:        String newString(newCString);
161:        return newString;
162:    }
163:
164:
165:
```

```
166:    BOOL String::operator==(const String& rhs) const
167:    { return (BOOL) (StringCompare(rhs) == 0); }
168:    BOOL String::operator!=(const String& rhs)const
169:       { return (BOOL) (StringCompare(rhs) != 0); }
170:    BOOL String::operator<(const String& rhs)const
171:       { return (BOOL) (StringCompare(rhs) < 0); }
172:    BOOL String::operator>(const String& rhs)const
173:       { return (BOOL) (StringCompare(rhs) > 0); }
174:    BOOL String::operator<=(const String& rhs)const
175:       { return (BOOL) (StringCompare(rhs) <= 0); }
176:    BOOL String::operator>=(const String& rhs)const
177:       { return (BOOL) (StringCompare(rhs) >= 0); }
178:
179:    ostream& operator<< (ostream& ostr, const String& str)
180:    {
181:        ostr << str.itsCString;
182:        return ostr;
183:    }
184:
185:    ostream& String::operator() (ostream& of)
186:    {
187:          of.write( (char*) & itsLen,szLong);
188:          of.write(itsCString,itsLen);
189:          return of;
190:    }
191:
192:    void String::Write(Writer& wrtr)
193:    {
194:        wrtr<<itsLen;
195:        wrtr<<itsCString;
196:    }
```

Type

Listing 9.6 Implementation for the New rWord Object

```
1:       // **************************************************
2:       // PROGRAM:   Basic word object
3:       // FILE:      word.hpp
4:       // PURPOSE:   provide simple word object
5:       // NOTES:
6:       // AUTHOR:    Jesse Liberty (jl)
7:       // REVISIONS: 10/23/94 1.0 jl  initial release
8:       //                    10/31/94 1.1 jl persistence
9:       // **************************************************
10:
11:      #ifndef WORD_HPP
12:      #define WORD_HPP
13:
14:      #include "stdef.hpp"
15:      #include "string.hpp"
16:      #include <fstream.h>
17:
18:
19:      class rWord
20:      {
```

continues

Listing 9.6 continued

```
21:        public:
22:          rWord(const String& text):
23:          itsText(text), reserved1(0L), reserved2(0L)
24:            {itsTextLength=itsText.GetLength();}
25:
26:         //rWord(istream& iff);
27:          rWord(istream& iff) :itsText(iff)
28:          {
29:              iff.read((char*) &reserved1,szLong);
30:              iff.read((char*) &reserved2,szLong);
31:          }
32:
33:          ~rWord(){}
34:
35:          const String& GetText()const { return itsText; }
36:
37:          long GetReserved1() const { return  reserved1; }
38:          long GetReserved2() const { return  reserved2; }
39:
40:          void SetReserved1(long val) { reserved1 = val; }
41:          void SetReserved2(long val) { reserved2 = val; }
42:
43:          int operator<(const rWord& rhs)
44:           { return itsText < rhs.GetText(); }
45:
46:          int operator>(const rWord& rhs)
47:           { return itsText > rhs.GetText(); }
48:
49:          BOOL operator<=(const rWord& rhs)
50:           { return itsText <= rhs.GetText(); }
51:
52:          BOOL operator>= (const rWord& rhs)
53:           { return itsText >= rhs.GetText(); }
54:
55:          BOOL operator==(const rWord& rhs)
56:           { return itsText == rhs.GetText(); }
57:
58:          void Display() const
59:             { cout <<   " Text: " << itsText << endl; }
60:
61:            ostream& rWord::operator() (ostream& of)
62:            {
63:               itsText(of);
64:               of.write((char*)&reserved1,szLong);
65:               of.write((char*)&reserved2,szLong);
66:               return of;
67:            }
68:
69:        private:
70:           long itsTextLength;
71:           String itsText;
72:           long reserved1;
73:           long reserved2;
74:        };
75:
76:        #endif
```

Type **Listing 9.7 Using the Driver Program for Writing to Disk**

```
1:    // Listing 9.7 - Using the Driver Program for Writing to Disk
2:
3:    #include "word.hpp"
4:    #include <fstream.h>
5:
6:    int main()
7:    {
8:        char fileName[80];
9:        char buffer[255];    // for user input
10:       cout << "File name: ";
11:       cin >> fileName;
12:
13:       rWord* theWord;
14:       ofstream fout(fileName,ios::binary);  // open for writing
15:       cin.ignore(1,'\n');  // eat the new line after the file name
16:
17:       for (int i = 0; i<5; i++)
18:       {
19:           cout << "Please enter a word: " ;
20:           cin.getline(buffer,255);
21:           theWord = new rWord(buffer);
22:           (*theWord)(fout);   // and write it to the file
23:       }
24:
25:       fout.close();               // close the file, ready for reopen
26:       ifstream fin(fileName,ios::binary);   // reopen for reading
27:
28:       cout << "Here's the contents of the file:\n";
29:
30:       for (i = 0; i<5; i++)
31:       {
32:           theWord = new rWord(fin);
33:           cout << theWord->GetText()<< endl;
34:       }
35:
36:        cout << "\n***End of file contents.***\n";
37:
38:       fin.close();               // always pays to be tidy
39:       return 0;
40:    }
```

Output

```
d:\>0903
File name: test3
Please enter a word: teacher
Please enter a word: leave
Please enter a word: them
Please enter a word: kids
Please enter a word: alone
Here are the contents of the file:
teacher
leave
them
```

```
kids
alone

***End of file contents.***
```

Analysis
In listing 9.3, stdef.hpp is updated to include szLong, szShort, and szInt; all of which declare constant names for the size of various types.

The entire string.hpp file is shown in listing 9.4 to reduce confusion. The big change is in line 27, with the declaration of a constructor that takes an istream reference, and in line 67, with the overloaded operator().

Listing 9.5 provides the implementation for these methods, along with the rest of the class implementation. Lines 10 through 17 show how a String object is created from a disk stream. In line 12, the length of the string is read; in line 14, a pointer is declared and memory is allocated; and in line 15, the data from the disk is read into that memory location.

Lines 177 through 182 provide the implementation for operator(). This enables the String to write itself to disk. It writes its length and then the contents of itsCString. This is *exactly* the order in which this data is read in the constructor, and that is not a coincidence. You *must* write the data out in the order it will be read back in.

Listing 9.6 shows the declaration for the rWord object, including its constructor taking an istream (lines 27 through 31) and its overload of operator() (lines 64 through 68).

The first thing operator() does, in line 64, is to tell itsText, which is a String, to write itself to disk. The remaining members then are written in lines 65 and 66.

In the constructor, itsText is initialized, calling the proper constructor for a String.

The driver program that brings all this together is shown in listing 9.7. The program creates an ostream object and then creates five rWord objects. Each rWord object is told to write itself to disk by calling its operator(), passing in the ofstream object in line 22.

After the words are stored, the file is closed in line 25 and an ifstream object is opened in line 26. This, of course, is the same file opened for reading. Each word is constructed by passing in the ifstream object in line 32.

Creating Classes to Handle Storage

Although the program listed earlier does the job, it has some glaring problems. The program must manage the file operators and each class must independently override operator() and the constructor taking an ifstream object. More problematic, each class must know how to stream every primitive type. That is, both rWord and String, as well as any other class you want to store, must know how to write a long to disk.

The essence of object-oriented programming is to encapsulate this kind of knowledge into a single set of classes that all your other classes can use. The solution is, first, to derive all your storable classes from a common base class; and second, to encapsulate all the disk reading and writing into a pair of reader and writer classes. The next set of listings provides exactly that functionality.

To create the new String class, follow these steps:

1. Replace line 18 of listing 9.4 with this line:

   ```
   class String : public Storable
   ```

2. Replace line 28 in listing 9.4 with this line:

   ```
                   string(Reader&);
   ```

3. Replace line 69 of listing 9.4 with this line:

   ```
                   void Write(Writer&);
   ```

4. Replace lines 21 through 25 of listing 9.5 with these lines:

   ```
       String::String(Reader& rdr)
       {
           rdr>>itsLen;
           rdr>>itsCString;
       }
   ```

5. Replace lines 192 through 196 of listing 9.5 with these lines:

   ```
       void String::Write(Writer& wrtr)
       {
           wrtr<<itsLen;
           wrtr<<itsCString;
       }
   ```

These changes cause String to derive from the abstract data type (ADT) Storable, shown in listing 9.8. The implementation for Storable is in listing 9.9. Listing 9.10 provides the new interface to rWord, and listing 9.11 shows the driver program that brings all this together.

 Listing 9.8 The Storable Interface

```
1:     // ***************************************************
2:     // PROGRAM:  ADT for storage
3:     // FILE:     storable.hpp
4:     // PURPOSE:  Object persistence
5:     // NOTES:
6:     // AUTHOR:   Jesse Liberty (jl)
7:     // REVISIONS: 11/1/94 1.0 jl  initial release
8:     // ***************************************************
9:
10:    #include <fstream.h>
11:    #include "stdef.hpp"
12:
```

continues

Listing 9.8 continued

```
13:    class Writer
14:    {
15:    public:
16:       Writer(char *fileName):fout(fileName,ios::binary){};
17:       ~Writer() {fout.close();}
18:       virtual Writer& operator<<(int&);
19:       virtual Writer& operator<<(long&);
20:       virtual Writer& operator<<(short&);
21:       virtual Writer& operator<<(char*);
22:
23:    private:
24:          ofstream fout;
25:    };
26:
27:    class Reader
28:    {
29:    public:
30:       virtual Reader& operator>>(int&);
31:       virtual Reader& operator>>(long&);
32:       virtual Reader& operator>>(short&);
33:       virtual Reader& operator>>(char*&);
34:
35:       Reader(char *fileName):fin(fileName,ios::binary){}
36:       ~Reader(){fin.close();}
37:
38:    private:
39:       ifstream fin;
40:    };
41:
42:    class Storable
43:    {
44:    public:
45:       Storable() {}
46:       Storable(Reader&){}
47:       virtual void Write(Writer&)=0;
48:
49:    private:
50:
51:    };
52:
53:
```

Listing 9.9 The Storable Implementation

```
1:    // ************************************************
2:    // PROGRAM:  ADT for storage
3:    // FILE:     storable.cpp
4:    // PURPOSE:  Object persistence
5:    // NOTES:
6:    // AUTHOR:   Jesse Liberty (jl)
7:    // REVISIONS: 11/1/94 1.0 jl  initial release
8:    // ************************************************
```

```
9:
10:      #include "storable.hpp"
11:      #include <string.h>
12:
13:      Writer& Writer::operator<<(int& data)
14:      {
15:         fout.write((char*)&data,szInt);
16:         return *this;
17:      }
18:
19:      Writer& Writer::operator<<(long& data)
20:      {
21:         fout.write((char*)&data,szLong);
22:         return *this;
23:      }
24:
25:      Writer& Writer::operator<<(short& data)
26:      {
27:         fout.write((char*)&data,szShort);
28:         return *this;
29:      }
30:
31:      Writer& Writer::operator<<(char * data)
32:      {
33:         int len = strlen(data);
34:         fout.write((char*)&len,szLong);
35:         fout.write(data,len);
36:         return *this;
37:      }
38:
39:      Reader& Reader::operator>>(int& data)
40:      {
41:         fin.read((char*)&data,szInt);
42:         return *this;
43:      }
44:      Reader& Reader::operator>>(long& data)
45:      {
46:         fin.read((char*)&data,szLong);
47:         return *this;
48:      }
49:      Reader& Reader::operator>>(short& data)
50:      {
51:         fin.read((char*)&data,szShort);
52:         return *this;
53:      }
54:      Reader& Reader::operator>>(char *& data)
55:      {
56:         int len;
57:         fin.read((char*) &len,szLong);
58:         data = new char[len+1];
59:         fin.read(data,len);
60:         data[len]='\0';
61:         return *this;
62:      }
63:
```

Type **Listing 9.10 The New Interface to rWord**

```
1:    // *************************************************
2:    // PROGRAM:   Basic word object
3:    // FILE:      word.hpp
4:    // PURPOSE:   provide simple word object
5:    // NOTES:
6:    // AUTHOR:    Jesse Liberty (jl)
7:    // REVISIONS: 10/23/94 1.0 jl  initial release
8:    //            10/31/94 1.1 jl  persistence
9:    //            11/1/94  1.2 jl  derives from storable
10:   // *************************************************
11:
12:   #ifndef WORD_HPP
13:   #define WORD_HPP
14:
15:   #include "stdef.hpp"
16:   #include "string.hpp"
17:   #include <fstream.h>
18:
19:
20:   class rWord : public Storable
21:   {
22:    public:
23:       rWord(const String& text):
24:       itsText(text), reserved1(0L), reserved2(0L)
25:         {itsTextLength=itsText.GetLength();}
26:
27:       rWord(const char* text):
28:       itsText(text), reserved1(0L), reserved2(0L)
29:         {itsTextLength=itsText.GetLength();}
30:
31:       rWord::rWord(Reader& rdr) :itsText(rdr)
32:       {
33:         rdr >> reserved1;
34:         rdr >> reserved2;
35:       }
36:
37:
38:
39:       ~rWord(){}
40:
41:
42:       const String& GetText()const { return itsText; }
43:
44:       long GetReserved1() const { return  reserved1; }
45:       long GetReserved2() const { return  reserved2; }
46:
47:       void SetReserved1(long val) { reserved1 = val; }
48:       void SetReserved2(long val) { reserved2 = val; }
49:
50:
51:       BOOL operator<(const rWord& rhs)
52:        { return itsText < rhs.GetText(); }
53:
```

```
54:          BOOL operator>(const rWord& rhs)
55:           { return itsText > rhs.GetText(); }
56:
57:
58:          BOOL operator<=(const rWord& rhs)
59:           { return itsText <= rhs.GetText(); }
60:
61:          BOOL operator>= (const rWord& rhs)
62:           { return itsText >= rhs.GetText(); }
63:
64:
65:          BOOL operator==(const rWord& rhs)
66:           { return itsText == rhs.GetText(); }
67:
68:          void Display() const
69:             { cout <<   " Text: " << itsText << endl; }
70:
71:        ostream& operator() (ostream&);
72:
73:        void Write(Writer& wrtr)
74:        {
75:           itsText.Write(wrtr);
76:           wrtr << reserved1;
77:           wrtr << reserved2;
78:        }
79:
80:
81:     private:
82:         long itsTextLength;
83:         String itsText;
84:         long reserved1;
85:         long reserved2;
86:      };
87:
88:
89:    #endif
```

Type Listing 9.11 Using the Driver Program

```
1:      // Listing 9.11 - Using the Driver Program
2:
3:      #include "word.hpp"
4:
5:      // NOT a member function!
6:      void operator<<(Writer& wrtr, rWord& rw)
7:      {
8:         rw.Write(wrtr);
9:      }
10:
11:     const int howMany = 5;
12:
13:     int main()
14:     {
```

continues

Listing 9.11 continued

```
15:          char fileName[80];
16:          char buffer[255];    // for user input
17:          cout << "File name: ";
18:          cin >> fileName;
19:          cin.ignore(1,'\n');  // eat the new line after the file name
20:          Writer* writer = new Writer(fileName);
21:          rWord* theWord;
22:
23:          for (long i = 0; i<howMany; i++)
24:          {
25:              cout << "Please enter a word: " ;
26:              cin.getline(buffer,255);
27:              theWord = new rWord(buffer);
28:              (*writer)<< *theWord;   // and write it to the file
29:          }
30:           delete writer;
31:
32:           Reader * reader = new Reader(fileName);
33:
34:          cout << "Here are the contents of the file:\n";
35:
36:          for (i = 0; i<howMany; i++)
37:          {
38:              theWord = new rWord(*reader);
39:              cout << theWord->GetText()<< endl;
40:          }
41:
42:           cout << "\n***End of file contents.***\n";
43:
44:           delete reader;
45:          return 0;
46:      }
```

Output

```
d:\>0911
File name: test3
Please enter a word: teacher
Please enter a word: leave
Please enter a word: them
Please enter a word: kids
Please enter a word: alone
Here are the contents of the file:
teacher
leave
them
kids
alone

***End of file contents.***
```

Analysis

The changes to String described in this section cause the String class to inherit from Storable, which is declared in listing 9.8. Note in line 47 of listing 9.8 that Write() is declared to be *pure virtual*. This ensures that every derived class *must* override this method.

9

Also note that Storable has a constructor that takes a reference to a Reader object. Both Reader and Writer are declared in listing 9.8. In line 16, Writer is declared to take a C-style string; and in the initialization of the Writer object, its member, an ofstream object, is initialized and thus opened.

Writer overloads the insertion operator for many of the built-in types. In a fully developed version of this class, *all* the built-in types would be represented. It is the job of Writer to provide storage services for all the built-in types.

Classes derived from Storable can store their members by use of these overridden insertion operators. If they have members that are *not* built-in types, those classes must provide for this.

In listing 9.11, you see that the program wants to write out an rWord object. Because rWord objects are not built-in types, the Writer will not know what to do with this unless you tell it. In lines 6 through 9 of listing 9.11, a *global* operator<< function is declared that takes both a Writer reference and a reference to an rWord. This method calls the Write() method in rWord, which knows how to write out all the members of an rWord object.

Because Write() is pure virtual in the base class, the compiler will check to make sure that you have overridden this in your derived class. It is the job of the author of the rWord class to override this method to do the right thing.

Listing 9.10 shows the declaration of the rWord class, and in lines 73 through 78, the rWord object writes its contents to the Writer object provided.

Be sure to note that the first thing that rWord does is call the Write() method on its contained String object. In the changes you made to listing 9.8, you saw that String has its own Write method that writes out first the length of itsCString and then itsCString itself.

The constructor for rWord, which takes a Reader reference (shown in lines 31 through 35), initializes itsString by calling the constructor of String, which reads the number of bytes, and then reads that many bytes into itsCString.

This symmetry is essential to the workings of this process. To make this explicit, I'll walk through listing 9.11 in precise detail.

In line 17, the user is prompted for a file name. In a real program, you probably would check your configuration file for this. The file name is stashed in a local variable, fileName. In line 20, a Writer object is created, with the fileName passed in as a parameter.

Listing 9.8, line 16 shows that this constructor initializes an ofstream object—fout—with the file name passed in as a parameter, and opens the file in binary mode.

In line 21 of listing 9.11, a pointer to an rWord is declared. In the loop beginning in line 23, the user is prompted for words, each of which is used to generate rWord objects. Each time an rWord object is created in line 27, it is written to disk in line 28 by calling operator<< on the Writer object, which was created in line 20.

This call to `operator<<` causes the program to jump to line 6 of listing 9.11. In line 8, the `rWord`'s `Write()` method is called. You could have called this directly in line 28, but it is more convenient to be able to use the `operator<<` overload.

This call to `Write()` causes the program to jump to line 73 of listing 9.10. In line 75, `Write()` is called on the member data `itsText`, which is of type `String`. You just as easily could have written `wrtr << itsText`; but then you would need a global function taking a `Writer` reference as its first parameter and a `String` object as its second parameter. In a real program, you would want to provide such an operator so that classes—such as `rWord`—that contain a `String` object can use the overloaded `operator<<`.

This call to `Write()` in `String` causes the program to jump to the implementation of `Write()` provided before listing 9.8. As you can see, `Writer`'s `operator<<` is called twice: once for `itsLen` and then again for `itsCstring`. The first causes the program to jump to line 18 of listing 9.9, and the second causes the program to jump to line 28 of listing 9.8.

The write of the `long` simply writes the 4 bytes to the `ofstream` object. The write of the `char*` writes the first 4 bytes of length, and then the data itself.

After the string is written, control returns to line 76 of listing 9.10, where `reserved1` and `reserved2` are written. This again causes the program twice to jump to line 18 of listing 9.9, where the `long`s are written.

After the entire `rWord` is written, control returns to line 29 of listing 9.11. After all the `rWord`s are written, the `writer` object is deleted in line 30. This closes the file. In line 32, a `Reader` object is created, again passing in the file name.

This calls the constructor shown in line 35 of listing 9.8, where the `ifstream` object is opened in binary mode using the `fileName` parameter.

In lines 36 through 40, each of the stored words is returned to memory. The constructor for `rWord` is called, passing in the `Reader` object. This causes control to jump to line 31 of listing 9.10. The first thing done is that `itsText` is initialized, passing in the `Reader` reference. This then passes control to the constructor of the `String` object, shown in listing 9.8.

The constructor calls the overloaded `operator>>`, first passing in the long `itsLen` and then the character pointer `itsCString`. The first passes control to line 39 of listing 9.9, and the second passes control to line 47 of listing 9.9.

Reading the `long` is straightforward: reading in the character string requires reading in the length, allocating the memory (line 51), reading in the data in line 52, and finally null-terminating the string in line 53.

After the string exists, control returns to line 33 of listing 9.10, where the two `long`s are created—again by calling the overloaded `operator>>` of the `reader` class.

In line 39 of listing 9.11, each rWord object calls its GetText() method, which returns a String object, which is in turn passed to the overloaded operator<< of the ostream, where it is printed to the screen.

Finally, in line 44, the reader object is deleted.

What Have We Gained?

Although this tour of the inner workings of Storable, Reader, and Writer may not have convinced you that this approach is any *simpler*, it does nicely encapsulate much of this work in a small number of classes. After Reader and Writer are working properly, you can use them and not worry again about how the primitive types are written to disk.

In fact, because user-defined types are composed of other user-defined types or of primitive types, every class ultimately needs to know only how to call operator<< on each of its members.

From Here to an Object Store

A number of capabilities still are missing in order to generalize the capabilities explored so far into a true object store. For one, each object needs to be identified uniquely in some way that enables objects to refer to one another.

In a true object store, an object should be able to ask the store for "object #12" and get back a valid pointer to a storable object. Also, the object store must be able to handle various *types* of storable objects, extracting enough information from the stored representation to invoke the correct constructor. You will see more detail on these issues on day 15.

Summary

Today you learned how to write data from an object to a disk file, and more important, how to serialize or stream an object to a file. You learned how to create reader and writer objects to encapsulate disk reads and writes, and you learned about object streaming and instantiating, which together make up the fundamental building blocks of an object store.

Q&A

Q Why is saving objects to disk so much trouble? Why can't you just take the sizeof() the object and write it out?

A Because the object itself may contain pointers, which are, of course, just references to things in memory. The next time your program is run, it may not get loaded into the same place in memory, or it may allocate space differently, so those pointers will not point to the correct things.

Q How about if I am careful not to declare any pointers in my object. Am I safe?

A This is still not enough, because there may be some pointers that you don't know about. If any contained classes have pointers, the same problem exists. Furthermore, if your class—or any of its parent classes, or any contained class, or their parents—declared any virtual functions, then there is a hidden pointer buried in the object: the virtual function table pointer.

Q If I am writing an application for which I want the data to be persistent, do I have to declare all my objects to be subclasses of Storable?

A Yes, if you want to write it yourself, and you want to use the technique that uses a Reader and a Writer. The *right* answer, however, is to buy one of the commercially available persistent store libraries. Developing one for yourself, as you did in this chapter, is a great way to understand how these libraries work, but in reality it is incredibly complex to get it right, and you would make better use of your time to buy a good library and use it.

Q Is this an object-oriented database?

A No. This is not quite a persistent store for C++, which still is less than an OODB. (You will create a full-featured persistent store before the book is over.) Full-blown OODBs include indexes, class and object versioning, multiuser access, transaction protocols, and other features that are well outside the ambitions of this book.

Workshop

The Workshop provides quiz questions to help you solidify your understanding of the material covered, and exercises to provide you with experience in using what you have learned. Try to answer the quiz and exercise questions before checking the answers in Appendix A, and make sure that you understand the answers before continuing to the next chapter.

Quiz

1. What is the significance of fixed-size versus variable-size records?
2. What is the difference between object persistence and data persistence?
3. What is the purpose of the `Writer` class?
4. What is the purpose of the `Storable` class?
5. What is required of a class if it is to be storable?

Exercises

1. Create a `Person` class that can be persistent. It should contain three strings for Name, Title, and Address, and a long for DateOfBirth. Be careful with the special constructor taking a Reader and with the Write method.

2. Add an enum position to your `Person` class created in exercise 1. The values are posPresident, posVicePresident, posDirector, posManager, posSoftwareEngineer, posAccountant, and so on. The question here is how you make an enum persistent. Try to keep this code portable.

3. Modify the `Writer` class to save the data in a buffer rather than writing it directly to the file. The class should have methods for getting the current size of the buffer and the buffer itself. The constructor should be changed to accept the size of the buffer the writer should allocate.

4. What is wrong with this class (besides the lack of accessors to its private members and the lack of any real functionality)?

```
class Foo : public Storable
{
public:
    Foo() : c('\0'), i(0), l(0L) { }
    Foo(Reader & rdr) : itsText(rdr) {rdr >> c >> i >> l;}

    void Write(Writer & wrtr)
        {wrtr << c << i << l;  itsText.Write(wrtr);}

private:
    char c;
    int I;
    long l;

    String itsText;
};
```

5. Does this class work as intended? Is the order of reading and writing correctly matched up?

```
class Foo : public Storable
{
public:
    Foo() : c('\0'), i(0), l(0L) { }
    Foo(Reader & rdr) : itsName(rdr), itsAddress(rdr)
                    {rdr  >> I;}

    void Write(Writer & wrtr)
        {itsName.Write(wrtr); itsAddress.Write(wrtr);
            wrtr << i;   }

private:
    String itsAddress;
    int I;
    String itsName;
};
```

10

Collection Classes
and B-Trees

You have created a number of powerful lists, including sorted and unsorted linked lists and AVL trees. By using these lists, you can create a wide variety of custom `Collection` classes.

Each of these lists is optimized for different things: some for ease of creation, some for speed of insertion, and some for quick searching. Each has a limitation as well, and for a program like ROBIN, which will store its data on disk, none of these programs is quite right. Today you will learn

- What dynamic and sparse arrays are
- What dictionaries and sets are
- How to create lists optimized for disk storage

Collection Classes

C++ provides one built-in collection type: the array. Most C++ primers show how to create a dynamic `Array` class, which enables you to combine the flexibility of linked lists with the ease of use of arrays.

The linked list shown in day 7, "Complex Data Structures," provides all you need to build a dynamic `Array` class. You will want to privatize the `FindObject()` method, and flesh out the offset operator ([]), but otherwise it is pretty much all there.

Sets

A set is a collection, often implemented with a list, where every data item is represented exactly once. Once an item is already in the set, a duplicate cannot be added.

Sets typically provide methods that implement the mathematical set operations, so that if you have two sets of data you can ask for the *intersection* of the sets, and get back only those items that appear in both sets. Similarly, you can ask for the *union* of the sets, and get those items that exist in either set. The returned object from these methods would be another set.

Dictionaries

Dictionaries are a special case of sets, in which each record has a *key* as well as its data. The key *may* be related to the data, but need not be. You might have a set of definitions, for example, whose keys are the words being defined. Or, alternatively, you might have a set of payment records, where the key is the social security number of the recipient.

A special case is the double-keyed dictionary, with which you can look up based on either value. A typical use of this is a name and address database, where records can be retrieved by either name or address.

Creating the Sparse Array Class

A *sparse array* is a special case of a dictionary in which the key is a numerical index into a virtual array. The sparse array uses the semantics of an `Array` class, but not all the elements exist. The array might allow you to enter the 12th, 85th, and 102nd members, for example. Rather than storing 102 elements, each entry is stored in a dictionary, keyed to the offset. When you request `myArray[85]`, the sparse array looks up the value 85 in its dictionary and returns the associated value.

Making your sparse array raises a number of design issues. Assuming that you have no previous `Collection` classes on which to build your new `SparseArray` class, here's how you might begin.

Like all programs, you need to start with a specification:

☐ Your sparse array will look and feel like an array.

☐ You add and retrieve items using the offset operator.

☐ Management of the array's internal lists will be invisible.

☐ The array will allocate room only for those items actually stored on the list.

10

Implementation Issues

As far as your user is concerned, the array will hold whatever type of item (string, word, numbers, and so on) the user chooses. As far as the program is concerned, the actual stored item will be a node with a pointer to the stored item and a key. The key will be the value on which the list will be sorted and searched.

When the user asks for a key that is not already in the list, a node will be created with that key, and an item of the appropriate type will be created as well. This will enable the user to write

```
SparseArray[5] = <some value>
```

and thereby assign that position to a new value. Listing 10.1 shows a modified rWord header file, listing 10.2 shows the sparse array template, and listing 10.3 shows a driver program that exercises the sparse array.

Note: In a real-world situation, you would not repeatedly re-create these `Collection` classes. You would, instead, design a suite of related `Collection` classes, and derive some of the more specific types from the more general types.

I have chosen to re-create many of these `Collection` classes to show a variety of approaches to creating such lists. This approach provides a number of design perspectives at the cost of undermining the fundamental lesson that you should strive for reusability in your designs.

Type **Listing 10.1 A Modified rWord Header File**

```
1:      // *****************************************************
2:      // PROGRAM:  Basic word object
3:      // FILE:     word.hpp
4:      // PURPOSE:  provide simple word object
5:      // NOTES:
6:      // AUTHOR:   Jesse Liberty (jl)
7:      // REVISIONS: 10/23/94 1.0 jl  initial release
8:      //           11/3/94  1.1 jl added constructor char *
9:      // *****************************************************
10:
11:     #ifndef WORD_HPP
12:     #define WORD_HPP
13:
14:     #include "stdef.hpp"
15:     #include "string.hpp"
16:
17:     class rWord
18:     {
19:      public:
20:         rWord(const String& text):
21:         itsText(text), reserved1(0L), reserved2(0L) {}
22:
23:         rWord(const char* txt):
24:            itsText(txt),reserved1(0L), reserved2(0L) {}
25:
26:         rWord(): itsText(), reserved1(0L), reserved2(0L) {}
27:
28:         ~rWord(){}
29:
30:         const String& GetText()const { return itsText; }
31:         void SetText(const String& rhs) { itsText = rhs; }
32:
33:         BOOL operator<(const rWord& rhs)
34:           { return itsText < rhs.GetText(); }
35:
36:         BOOL operator>(const rWord& rhs)
37:           { return itsText > rhs.GetText(); }
38:
39:         BOOL operator==(const rWord& rhs)
40:           { return itsText == rhs.GetText(); }
41:
42:         void Display() const
43:            { cout <<   " Text: " << itsText << endl; }
44:
45:
46:      private:
47:         String itsText;
48:         long reserved1;
49:         long reserved2;
50:     };
51:
52:     #endif
```

Listing 10.2 The Sparse Array Template

```
1:    // ****************************************************
2:    // PROGRAM:  SparseArray Header
3:    // FILE:     sparse array
4:    // PURPOSE:  provide sparse array
5:    // NOTES:
6:    // AUTHOR:   Jesse Liberty (jl)
7:    // REVISIONS: 11/3/94 1.0 jl  initial release
8:    // ****************************************************
9:
10:   #include "stdef.hpp"
11:
12:   #ifndef SPARSE_ARRAY_HPP
13:   #define SPARSE_ARRAY_HPP
14:
15:    // *************** Node class ***********
16:     template <class T>
17:     class Node
18:     {
19:     public:
20:        Node (T* Obj, long key):itsObject(Obj),itsNext(0),itsKey(key){}
21:        ~Node() { delete itsObject; itsNext=0;}
22:        Node (const Node& rhs);
23:        void InsertAfter(Node * newNode)
24:         { newNode->SetNext(itsNext); itsNext=newNode;}
25:        Node * GetNext() const    { return itsNext; }
26:        void SetNext(Node * next) { itsNext = next; }
27:        T & GetObject() const { return *itsObject; }
28:        long GetKey() const { return itsKey; }
29:        int operator<(const Node<T>& rhs) { return itsKey < rhs.GetKey();}
30:        int operator==(long rhs) const { return itsKey == rhs; }
31:        int operator<(long rhs) const { return itsKey < rhs; }
32:        int operator>(long rhs) const { return itsKey > rhs; }
33:        int operator<=(long rhs) const { return itsKey <= rhs; }
34:        int operator>=(long rhs) const { return itsKey >= rhs; }
35:
36:       const Node& operator=(T* rhs){ delete itsObject; itsObject = rhs; return
          *this;}
37:     private:
38:        T * itsObject;
39:        Node * itsNext;
40:        long itsKey;
41:     };
42:
43:     template <class T>
44:     Node<T>::Node(const Node& rhs)
45:     {
46:        itsObject = new T(rhs.GetObject());
47:        itsNext = rhs.GetNext();
48:        itsKey = rhs.GetKey();
49:     }
50:
51:
```

continues

Listing 10.2 continued

```
52:
53:      // *************** Object SparseArray ************
54:      template <class T>
55:      class SparseArray
56:      {
57:      public:
58:          SparseArray();
59:          ~SparseArray();
60:          long      GetCount() const { return itsCount; }
61:          void      Insert(T &, long);
62:          void      Iterate(void (T::*f)()const);
63:          T &        operator[](long);
64:
65:       private:
66:          Node<T>  itsHead;
67:          long itsCount;
68:      };
69:
70:          // Implementations for SparseArrays...
71:
72:          template<class T>
73:          SparseArray <T>::SparseArray():
74:             itsCount(0),
75:             itsHead(0,0)  // initialize head node to have no Object
76:             {}
77:
78:          template<class T>
79:          SparseArray <T>::~SparseArray()
80:          {
81:          }
82:
83:          template<class T>
84:          T&  SparseArray<T>::operator[](long key)
85:          {
86:             for (Node<T> * pNode = itsHead.GetNext();
87:                   pNode!=NULL;
88:                   pNode = pNode->GetNext()
89:                )
90:             {
91:                if ( *pNode >= key)
92:                    break;
93:             }
94:             if (pNode && *pNode == key)
95:               return pNode->GetObject();
96:
97:             else      // not found
98:             {
99:               T* pNew = new T;
100:              Insert (*pNew, key);
101:              return *pNew;
102:             }
103:
104:         }
105:
106:         template<class T>
107:         void SparseArray<T>::Insert(T & Object, long key)
```

```
108:        {
109:            Node<T> * NewNode = new Node<T>(&Object,key);
110:
111:            for (Node<T> * pNode = &itsHead;;pNode = pNode->GetNext())
112:            {
113:              int IsLess = FALSE;
114:              if (pNode->GetNext())
115:                IsLess = *NewNode < *(pNode->GetNext());
116:
117:              if ( (pNode->GetNext() == NULL) || IsLess)
118:              {
119:                    pNode->InsertAfter(NewNode);
120:                    itsCount++;
121:                    break;
122:              }
123:            }
124:        }
125:
126:     template<class T>
127:     void SparseArray<T>::Iterate(void (T::*func)()const)
128:     {
129:        for (Node<T>* pNode = itsHead.GetNext();
130:              pNode;
131:              pNode=pNode->GetNext()
132:            )
133:        {
134:              cout << "[" << pNode->GetKey() << "] ";
135:              (pNode->GetObject().*func)();
136:              // cout << "\n";
137:        }
138:     }
139:
140:   #endif
```

Type

Listing 10.3 A Driver Program for the Sparse Array

```
1:      // Listing 10.3 - A Driver Program for the Sparse Array
2:
3:      #include "sparse.hpp"
4:      #include "word.hpp"
5:
6:      int main    (int argc, char **argv)
7:      {
8:         SparseArray<rWord> array;
9:         rWord * pWord = 0;
10:
11:         for (int i = 0; i<argc; i++)
12:         {
13:            pWord = new rWord(argv[i]);
14:            array[i] = *pWord;
15:            array[5*(i+10)] = array[i];
16:         }
17:         array.Iterate(rWord::Display);
18:         return 0;
19:      }
```

```
d:\day10>1003 Imagination is more important than knowledge
[0]    Text: D:\DAY10\1003.EXE
[1]    Text: Imagination
[2]    Text: is
[3]    Text: more
[4]    Text: important
[5]    Text: than
[6]    Text: knowledge
[50]   Text: D:\DAY10\1003.EXE
[55]   Text: Imagination
[60]   Text: is
[65]   Text: more
[70]   Text: important
[75]   Text: than
[80]   Text: knowledge
```

In lines 23 and 24 of listing 10.1, the rWord class is extended to include a constructor that takes a C-style string.

The SparseArray class itself is declared in listing 10.2, along with its associated Node class. The Node class provides comparison operators to compare one node to another (line 29), as well as comparing the key value of a node with a provided long (lines 30 through 34).

The node itself stores a pointer to the object stored in the array (line 46), and a pointer to the next node in the array (line 47). In line 48, it also stores its key value, which is used as the offset in the array offset operator ([]), shown on line 63.

The SparseArray itself is straightforward. When a request is made for an object at a given offset, operator[] is called. The array is searched until the key is found, or until the key value is exceeded, and thus it is known that the key is not currently stored in the array.

If the key is found, the associated object is returned. If the key is not found, a default version of the object is created and inserted into the array, and the default object is returned.

Listing 10.3 provides a simple driver, which reads all the words on the command line and inserts them into the array. The first insertion, in line 14, is at the value of the argument; thus, the first argument is at array offset 0, the second at array offset 1, and so on. The second insertion, in line 15, demonstrates the capability to insert into the array at somewhat arbitrary intervals.

Note that when array[55] is created, the intervening (empty) array items are *not* created. The array is sparsely populated, as the specification requires.

Tip: There are a number of ways to optimize this and the other arrays you have seen. The sparse array, for example, would be quicker if a more sophisticated search algorithm were used to find the key or to decide where to insert the key. This optimization is left for day 17, "Profiling and Optimization."

Tree Structures and Object Persistence

Over the past few days, I've reviewed a number of powerful data structures. The single most significant drawback to *all* of them, however, is that they are not optimized for storage on disk.

In the real world, computers have limited memory, and users exit your program sooner or later. ROBIN will be quite useless if it cannot store its data, and the data structures seen so far are not good at quick retrieval from disk.

The binary trees and AVL trees seen yesterday and on days 7 and 8 have the nasty habit of becoming quite deep when they get large. Each layer of the tree represents at least one additional disk read, and the single most expensive thing you can do in your program, from the standpoint of performance, is to read the disk.

10

B-Trees

As you might have suspected, I have a solution to this problem: the B-tree. The B-tree was invented in 1972 by R. Bayer and E. McCreight, and was designed from the start to create shallow trees for fast disk access.

B-trees were recognized immediately as a powerful solution to the problem of disk-based storage, and virtually every commercial database system now uses B-trees or a variant as their storage mechanism.

A B-tree consists of *pages*. Each page has an *index*, which consists of a *key value* and a *pointer*. The pointer in an index can point to another page or to the data you are storing in the tree.

Every page has indexes that point to other pages or to data. In the former case, the page is called a *node page*; in the latter case, the page is called a *leaf page*. The number of indexes on a page is the page's order.

Every page therefore has a maximum of *order* child pages. It is a rule of B-trees that no pages, other than the top page and the node pages, ever have fewer than *order/2* indexes. A leaf page can have one fewer than that (*order/2–1*).

New indexes are added only to leaf pages. This fact is critical: you never add an index to a node page. Node pages are created when an existing page "splits."

Here's how it works. Assume that you are creating a B-tree of order 4, to store words. To simplify the example, I'll ignore the actual data, and have the index's key be the word itself. For this example, I'll build up a tree with the words *Four score and seven years ago, our fathers brought forth on this continent...*

When the tree is created, its root pointer, myRoot, points to nothing, as shown in figure 10.1.

The first word, *Four*, is added to a new page, as shown in figure 10.2. This new page is a leaf page, and the index, four, would point to the actual data.

Words are added to the page until order words, in this case four words, at which time the page is full, as shown in figure 10.3.

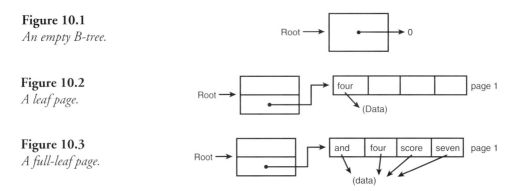

Figure 10.1
An empty B-tree.

Figure 10.2
A leaf page.

Figure 10.3
A full-leaf page.

When it is time to enter the word *for*, the page must split to make room. The algorithm follows:

1. Split the page in half.
2. Add the new word.
3. If the new word is smaller than the first word, adjust the pointer.
4. Return a pointer to the new page.
5. If the root detects that a new top page is required, create it.
6. Add an entry in the new top page to point to what the root points to.
7. Add an entry in the new top page for the return value from step 4.
8. Point the root to the new top page.

In the case shown in figure 10.4, the word *years* is to be added. To do this, the page must split. The new page is returned, and the root pointer recognizes that a new top page is needed. The new page is populated with an index pointing to the entry myRoot used to point to (And), and a second entry is made pointing to the new page. myRoot then is pointed to this new node page.

Figure 10.4
Splitting the page.

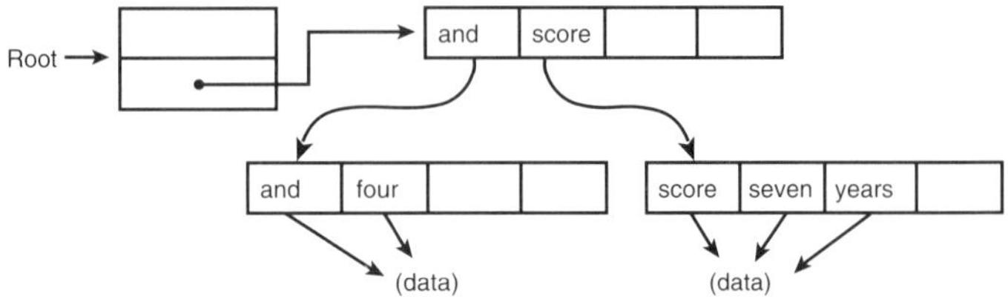

The next word to be added is *ago*. Because this is earlier than *and*, it is added before *and* on the leaf page, and the node page is "fixed up" to point to this earlier index, as shown in figure 10.5.

When a page node is filled, as shown in figure 10.6, it splits, as shown in figure 10.7, and the new pointer is added to the node pointer. This continues until the node page is full, as shown in figure 10.8.

Figure 10.5
Fixing up the node.

Figure 10.6
Getting ready to split.

10

Figure 10.7
After the split.

Figure 10.8
The tree when the node page is full.

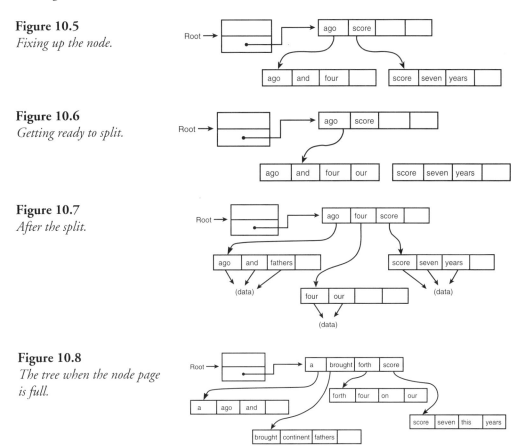

Adding the next word, *new*, to this tree presents a problem. The first page will have to split, and when it does, it will pass an entry to its parent node. That node, however, is full, so it too will have to split. When it does, the root pointer must recognize that a new node is required. This is shown in figure 10.9.

Figure 10.9
A third tier.

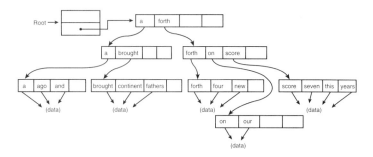

Deleting a Node

Although it is possible to delete nodes in a B-tree, you usually don't bother. ROBIN will take the expedient course of marking nodes as deleted and then rebuilding the tree when it is packed.

This method saves building the complex deletion algorithm into the class, and is the right way to handle this in any case. You will note, however, in the following section, that mark-for-deletion is not yet implemented. That detail is put off until day 11, when database management is discussed.

Implementing the B-Tree

Once the algorithms are fully understood, the implementation of the B-tree is straightforward. Listing 10.4 provides a slightly modified standard definition file (stdef.hpp). Listing 10.5 has the B-tree header file saved as btree.hpp. This provides the declarations for the B-tree, the page, and the Index classes.

Listing 10.6 is the implementation of the B-tree, listing 10.7 is the implementation of the page, and listing 10.8 is the implementation of the index. Finally, listing 10.9 is a simple driver program that creates a B-tree and prompts the user for entries.

Listing 10.4 Using stdef.hpp—the Standard Definition File

```
1:    // ************************************************
2:    // PROGRAM:  Standard Definitions
3:    // FILE:      stdef.hpp
4:    // PURPOSE:   provide standard inclusions and definitions
5:    // NOTES:
6:    // AUTHOR:    Jesse Liberty (jl)
7:    // REVISIONS: 10/23/94 1.0 jl  initial release
8:    // ************************************************
9:
10:
11:   #ifndef STDDEF_HPP                    // inclusion guards
12:   #define STDDEF_HPP
13:   #include <iostream.h>
```

```
14:
15:     const int szLong = sizeof (long int);
16:     const int szShort = sizeof (short int);
17:     const int szInt = sizeof (int);
18:
19:     enum BOOL { FALSE, TRUE };
20:
21:     #endif
```

Listing 10.5 Using btree.hpp—the B-Tree Header File

```
1:     // ****************************************************
2:     // PROGRAM:   Btree, Page and Index declarations
3:     // FILE:      btree.hpp
4:     // PURPOSE:   provide fundamental btree functionality
5:     // NOTES:
6:     // AUTHOR:    Jesse Liberty (jl)
7:     // REVISIONS: 11/1/94 1.0 jl  initial release
8:     // ****************************************************
9:     #ifndef BTREE_HPP                  // inclusion guards
10:    #define BTREE_HPP
11:
12:    #include <string.h>
13:    #include "stdef.hpp"
14:    const int Order = 4;
15:    const int dataLen = 11;
16:
17:    // forward declarations
18:    class Btree;
19:    class Index;
20:
21:    class Page
22:    {
23:    public:
24:       Page();
25:       Page(Index*,BOOL);
26:       Page(Index**, int, BOOL);
27:       ~Page(){}
28:       Page* Insert(Index*);
29:       Page* InsertLeaf(Index*);
30:       Page* InsertNode(Index*);
31:       Index* GetFirstIndex() { return myKeys[0]; }
32:       BOOL GetIsLeaf() const { return IsLeaf; }
33:       void Push(Index*,int offset=0);
34:       void Nullify(int offset);
35:       void Print();
36:       void ReCount();
37:    private:
38:       Index* myKeys[Order];
39:       int myCount;
40:       BOOL IsLeaf;
41:
42:    };
```

continues

Listing 10.5 continued

```
43:
44:    class Index
45:    {
46:    public:
47:        Index(char *);
48:        Index();
49:        Index(const Index&);
50:        char * GetData() const { return myData; }
51:        void SetData(const Index& rhs)
52:            { strcpy(myData,rhs.GetData()); }
53:        Page * GetPointer()const { return myPointer; }
54:        void SetPointer (Page* pg) { myPointer = pg; }
55:        void PrintKey();
56:        void PrintPage();
57:
58:        int operator==(const Index& rhs)
59:        {return strcmp(myData,rhs.GetData()) == 0; }
60:
61:        int operator < (const Index& rhs)
62:         {return strcmp(myData,rhs.GetData())<0;}
63:
64:        int operator <= (const Index& rhs)
65:         {return strcmp(myData,rhs.GetData())<=0;}
66:
67:        int operator > (const Index& rhs)
68:         {return strcmp(myData,rhs.GetData())>0;}
69:
70:        Page * Insert(Index* ptr)
71:            { return myPointer->Insert(ptr);}
72:
73:    public:
74:        Page* myPointer;
75:        char * myData;
76:    };
77:
78:
79:    class BTree
80:    {
81:    public:
82:        BTree():myRoot(0){}
83:        BTree(char* data);
84:        ~BTree();
85:        void AddKey(char* data);
86:        void PrintTree();
87:
88:    private:
89:        Page * myRoot;
90:    };
91:
92:    #endif
```

Listing 10.6 B-Tree Implementation

```
1:     // ****************************************************
2:     // PROGRAM:   Btree
3:     // FILE:      btree.cpp
4:     // PURPOSE:   provide fundamental btree functionality
5:     // NOTES:
6:     // AUTHOR:    Jesse Liberty (jl)
7:     // REVISIONS: 11/1/94 1.0 jl   initial release
8:     // ****************************************************
9:
10:    #include "btree.hpp"
11:    #include "stdef.hpp"
12:
13:    BTree::BTree(char *  data):myRoot(0)
14:    {
15:       Index * pIndex = new Index(data);
16:       myRoot = new Page (pIndex,TRUE);
17:    }
18:
19:    BTree::~BTree() {}
20:
21:    void BTree::AddKey(char * str)
22:    {
23:       Page * retVal =0;
24:       Index* pIndex = new Index(str);
25:       if (!myRoot)
26:          myRoot = new Page (pIndex,TRUE);
27:       else
28:       {
29:          retVal = myRoot->Insert(pIndex);
30:          if (retVal) // new top node
31:          {
32:             // create a new topmost node page
33:             Index * pIndex = new Index(*myRoot->GetFirstIndex());
34:             pIndex->SetPointer(myRoot);
35:             Page * pg = new Page(pIndex,FALSE);
36:             Index * pSib = new Index (*retVal->GetFirstIndex());
37:             pSib->SetPointer(retVal);
38:             pg->InsertLeaf(pSib);
39:             myRoot = pg;
40:          }
41:       }
42:    }
43:
44:    void BTree::PrintTree()
45:    {
46:       myRoot->Print();
47:    }
```

10

Listing 10.7 Page Implementation

```cpp
1:    // ***************************************************
2:    // PROGRAM:   Page
3:    // FILE:      Page.cpp
4:    // PURPOSE:   provide fundamental btree functionality
5:    // NOTES:
6:    // AUTHOR:    Jesse Liberty (jl)
7:    // REVISIONS: 11/1/94 1.0 jl  initial release
8:    // ***************************************************
9:
10:   #include "btree.hpp"
11:
12:   Page::Page()
13:   {
14:   }
15:
16:   Page::Page(Index* index, BOOL bLeaf):myCount(1),IsLeaf(bLeaf)
17:   {
18:      for (int i = 1; i<Order; i++)
19:         myKeys[i]=0;
20:      myKeys[0]=index;
21:      myCount = 1;
22:
23:   }
24:
25:   Page::Page(Index **array, int offset, BOOL leaf):IsLeaf(leaf)
26:   {
27:      myCount = 0;
28:      int i, j;
29:      for (i = 1; i<Order; i++)
30:         myKeys[i]=0;
31:      for (i=0, j = offset; j<Order; i++, j++)
32:      {
33:         myKeys[i]= new Index(*(array[j]));
34:         myCount++;
35:      }
36:   }
37:
38:   void Page::ReCount()
39:   {
40:      myCount = 0;
41:      for (int i = 0; i<Order; i++)
42:         if (myKeys[i])
43:            myCount++;
44:
45:   }
46:
47:   void Page::Nullify(int offset)
48:   {
49:      for (int i = offset; i<Order; i++)
50:      {
51:         if (myKeys[i])
52:         {
53:            delete myKeys[i];
```

```
54:                myKeys[i]= 0;
55:            }
56:        }
57:    }
58:
59:    Page * Page::Insert(Index* pIndex)
60:    {
61:        if (IsLeaf)
62:          return   InsertLeaf(pIndex);
63:        else
64:          return InsertNode(pIndex);
65:    }
66:
67:    Page * Page::InsertNode(Index* pIndex)
68:    {
69:        Page * retVal =0;
70:        BOOL inserted = FALSE;
71:        int i,j;
72:
73:        if (myKeys[0] && *pIndex < *(myKeys[0]))
74:        {
75:            myKeys[0]->SetData(*pIndex);
76:            retVal=myKeys[0]->Insert(pIndex);
77:            inserted = TRUE;
78:        }
79:        if (!inserted)
80:            for (i = Order-1; i>=0; i--)
81:            {
82:                if (myKeys[i])
83:                {
84:                    if (*pIndex > *(myKeys[i]))
85:                    {
86:                     retVal=myKeys[i]->Insert(pIndex);
87:                     inserted = TRUE;
88:                    }
89:                  break;
90:                }
91:            }
92:        if (!inserted)
93:            for (j = 0; j<i; j++)
94:            {
95:                if (myKeys[j+1] && *pIndex < *(myKeys[j+1]))
96:                {
97:                    retVal=myKeys[j]->Insert(pIndex);
98:                    break;
99:                }
100:           }
101:
102:        if (retVal) // got back a pointer to a new page
103:        {
104:            Index * pIndex = new Index(*retVal->GetFirstIndex());
105:            pIndex->SetPointer(retVal);
106:            retVal = InsertLeaf(pIndex);
107:        }
108:
109:        return retVal;
```

continues

Listing 10.7 continued

```
110:    }
111:
112:    Page * Page::InsertLeaf(Index* pIndex)
113:    {
114:        if (myCount < Order)
115:        {
116:            Push(pIndex);
117:            myCount++;
118:            return 0;
119:        }
120:        else        // overflow the page
121:        {
122:            Page* sibling = new Page(myKeys,Order/2,IsLeaf); // make sibling
123:            Nullify(Order/2);                        // nullify my right half
124:
125:            // does it fit in this side?
126:            if (myKeys[Order/2-1] && *pIndex <= *(myKeys[Order/2-1]))
127:                Push(pIndex);
128:            else
129:                sibling->Push(pIndex);
130:
131:            ReCount();
132:            return sibling;
133:        }
134:    }
135:
136:    void Page::Push(Index *pIndex,int offset)
137:    {
138:      for (int i=offset; i<Order; i++)
139:      {
140:          if (!myKeys[i]) // empty
141:          {
142:              myKeys[i]=pIndex;
143:              break;
144:          }
145:          else
146:          {
147:              if (myKeys[i] && *pIndex <= *myKeys[i])
148:              {
149:                  Push(myKeys[i],offset+1);
150:                  myKeys[i]=pIndex;
151:                  break;
152:              }
153:          }
154:      }
155:    }
156:
157:
158:    void Page::Print()
159:    {
160:        for (int i = 0; i<Order; i++)
161:        {
162:            if (myKeys[i])
163:            {
```

```
164:                if (IsLeaf)
165:                    myKeys[i]->PrintKey();
166:                else
167:                    myKeys[i]->PrintPage();
168:            }
169:            else
170:                break;
171:        }
172:    }
```

Type Listing 10.8 Index Implementation

```
1:      // **************************************************
2:      // PROGRAM:   index
3:      // FILE:      index.cpp
4:      // PURPOSE:   provide fundamental btree functionality
5:      // NOTES:
6:      // AUTHOR:    Jesse Liberty (jl)
7:      // REVISIONS: 11/1/94 1.0 jl  initial release
8:      // **************************************************
9:
10:     #include "btree.hpp"
11:
12:     Index::Index(char* str)
13:     {
14:
15:         myData = new char[dataLen+1];
16:         strncpy(myData,str,dataLen);
17:         myData[dataLen]='\0';
18:         myPointer=0;
19:     }
20:
21:     Index::Index(const Index& rhs)
22:     {
23:          myData = new char[dataLen+1];
24:         strcpy(myData, rhs.GetData());
25:         myPointer=rhs.GetPointer();
26:     }
27:
28:     Index::Index():myPointer(0)
29:     {
30:         myData = new char[dataLen+1];
31:         myData[0]='\0';
32:     }
33:
34:     void Index::PrintKey()
35:     {
36:         cout << "   " << myData;
37:     }
38:
39:     void Index::PrintPage()
40:     {
41:         cout << "\n" << myData << ": " ;
42:         myPointer->Print();
43:     }
```

Listing 10.9 The B-Tree Driver Program

```
1:     // Listing 10.9 - The B-Tree Driver Program
2:
3:     #include "String.hpp"
4:     #include "stdef.hpp"
5:     #include "btree.hpp"
6:
7:     int main()
8:     {
9:         BTree myTree;
10:        char buffer[255];
11:        for (;;)
12:        {
13:
14:            cout << "word: ";
15:            cin.getline(buffer,255);
16:            if (buffer[0])
17:                myTree.AddKey(buffer);
18:            else
19:                break;
20:        }
21:        myTree.PrintTree();
22:        return 0;
23:    }
```

```
d:\day10>1004
word: four
word: score
word: and
word: seven
word: years
word: ago
word: our
word: fathers
word: brought
word: forth
word: on
word: this
word: continent
word: a
word: new
word: nation
word:

a:
a:    a   ago   and
brought:   brought   continent
fathers:
fathers:   fathers   forth
four:   four   nation   new   on
score:   score   seven   this   years
```

Listing 10.5 is the interface to the B-tree, its constituent pages, and indexes. In line 14, the *order* of the tree is set—for this demonstration, to 4. This indicates that there will be at most 4 indexes on each page, and that node leaves that are not the top always will have at least 1.

Lines 18 and 19 are forward declarations of the Btree and Index classes, which are used by the Page class, which begins in line 21.

Page has three constructors, shown in lines 24 through 26. The last, in line 26, takes a pointer to an array of Index objects, and is used when splitting a Page. The Insert() method determines which of the following methods, InsertNode() or InsertLeaf(), is appropriate.

The Push() method is a quick approach to inserting a node into a page. This is a good method to target for optimization, however, as is discussed shortly.

The Page has an array of Index objects of size Order, a count of how many Index objects currently are in the array, and a Boolean indicating whether the current page is a leaf or a node page.

The Index class begins in line 44, and includes three constructors, including a copy constructor. There are accessors for the Index's data in lines 50 through 52, and for the Pointer, which points to the next node in the tree or to the data stored.

In lines 58 through 68, various comparison operators are provided to simplify comparing the data stored in Index objects. The operators act as *wrappers* on the data, enabling you to write

```
if *myNode < *otherNode
```

rather than

```
if myNode->GetData() < otherNode->GetData()
```

The Btree itself begins in line 79 and is a very simple class. It contains only a pointer to the topmost page. There are two constructors and a destructor, and two methods—one to add a new item to the tree and the other to print the tree.

The implementation of the Btree constructor that takes a pointer to data is in lines 13 through 17. An Index object is created and placed into a new Page object; the myRoot pointer then is set to point to that new page.

The AddKey() method is in lines 21 through 42. A pointer to a new Page object is created and initialized to NULL in line 23. A new Index object is created from the provided character string in line 24.

There are two cases considered: the first in which there is no root page, and the second in which the root page already exists. The former is simpler: a new Page object is created and the new Index is inserted.

If the myRoot pointer already points to a tree, the Insert() method is called and its return value is assigned to the retVal pointer, in line 29. If this pointer is non-null, then a new topmost page is needed, because the previous topmost page had to split and the new page was returned. In this case, the new page is created and an Index that points to the old topmost page is inserted. A second Index object also is created to point to the new sibling page. Finally, in line 39, the myRoot pointer is reassigned to point to the new topmost page.

The PrintTree() method simply passes along the command to print the tree to the topmost page.

Listing 10.7 has the implementation for the Page methods, including the constructor for new pages (lines 16 through 23) and for split-off pages (lines 25 through 36).

In the former case, myCount is initialized to 1 and IsLeaf is initialized to the value provided by whoever is creating the Page. The Index objects then are initialized to null pointers in lines 18 and 19, and the first Index pointer is set to the value passed in. Finally the myCount variable is set to 1.

The latter constructor, called when a Page is splitting, is similar, except that the myKeys array is initialized to the values passed in from the original Page, in lines 31 through 35.

The two utility methods, Recount() and Nullify(), are fairly straightforward. Recount() resets the counter, and Nullify() deletes all the Index objects starting at the provided offset.

The Insert() method examines the Page's IsLeaf Boolean and dispatches to the appropriate Insert... method. If the current Page is a node page, InsertNode, starting in line 67, is called.

In line 73, the value of the new index is compared to the value of the first index. Note the peculiar construction of

```
if (myKeys[0] && *pIndex < *(myKeys[0]))
```

This is used repeatedly throughout the program. First check to make sure that the pointer is not null, and then access it to call its comparison operator. Remember that if myKeys[0] evaluates to 0 (false), the second part of the && clause never will be evaluated.

The inserted flag is used to simplify the complex logic of when to continue evaluating and when to stop. The node has been inserted if the new value is less than the first member of the array. In this case, in line 75, the first member of the array is set to the value in the new index and then, in line 76, the new Index item is inserted into the tree. This call to the Index's Insert() method invokes the Insert() method of the page that the first member of the array points to, as shown in lines 70 and 71 of listing 10.5.

The situation you have just seen is this: a *node page* has a first value that is larger than the new value. The new value must be inserted into the node pointed to by that first Index, but that first index must be set to reflect this new smaller value. This is the situation as shown in figure 10.5.

If the test in line 73 fails, the next test is performed in line 82. This bit of code looks for the last entry in the array (counting back from the last entry in the index until one is found). If the new value is greater than that entry, the new value is inserted into the page pointed to by that entry.

If no value is found, the index is searched for the first instance where the *next* item is greater than the new Index object, and the new Index is inserted there.

Thus, if the page has *boy dog fence*, the word *angle* would be inserted into the page pointed to by *boy*, and the word *boy* would be changed to *angle*.

If the word *grape* were the new value, it would be inserted into the page pointed to by *fence* via the logic in the second test.

If the word *cat* were the new value, it would be inserted into the page pointed to by *boy*, because it is smaller than the entry to the right of *boy*.

In line 102, retVal is examined. This will be non-null if the child node was forced to split. In that case, the tree is adjusted. If the *current* page is forced to split as well, retVal will be set to point to the new sibling page, and the logic will recurse to the calling object.

The logic for InsertLeaf begins in line 112. If there is room in the array, the test in line 114 will evaluate TRUE; Push() will be called, the count will be incremented, and a null pointer will be returned to the calling function.

Push() is implemented in lines 136 through 155. This is not a very efficient algorithm, but it is fairly simple. It forces a sort of the array, recursively inserting objects into their appropriate slots in the array. It relies on the fact that the array always is packed to the left; there are never slots open unless there are no greater values. Thus, the first open slot may be used. If the slot is not open, a comparison is done; and if the new value is smaller, it is inserted and the old value is pushed.

Returning to InsertLeaf(), if the page is full, the else condition starting in line 120 is evaluated. A new Page object is created, passing in a pointer to the current array of Index objects, the offset of the middle of the array, and the *current* page's IsLeaf Boolean. The sibling page will be a node page if the current page is one, and it will be a leaf page if the current page is a leaf.

In lines 126 through 129, the new value is evaluated and pushed into the appropriate page. Because the array now has been sliced down, ReCount() is called and the new sibling Page is returned.

The PrintKey() method calls PrintKey() or PrintPage() on each of its Index objects, depending on whether the page itself is a leaf or a node.

Listing 10.8 shows the constructors for the Index objects, as well as the two rather simple Print methods. Listing 10.9 shows the driver program that exercises this B-tree by prompting the user for words and adding the words to the tree, which then is printed.

Writing Pages To Disk (Not Yet)

The entire purpose of a B-tree is to store data on a disk. The current implementation is not quite ready to do so, however. Rather than using pointers, it will need to store the offset of the Page objects in a disk file.

To facilitate getting pages off the disk and writing them back out, and to provide a cache to speed this up, you will need to create a PageManager object, as seen on day 11. You also will need the capability to read and write Page objects to disk, although this can be done as blocks of data rather than as persistent objects. All these details are considered in depth on day 11.

Summary

Today you learned what various Collection classes are and how to create them. You saw the implementation of a sparse array, and how to create a B-tree. You also explored some of the trade-offs in using each of these complex data structures.

Q&A

Q What is the prime determining characteristic of a set?

A The thing that makes a set special is that no value may appear more than once in the set.

Q What is the difference between a sparse array and a dictionary?

A A sparse array is a dictionary where the key value is an integral type (an integer or long, for example). It uses the offset operator ([ ]) to mimic the functionality of an array.

Q What is the difference between a sparse array and a regular array?

A A sparse array uses no memory for those values that are not held in the array.

Workshop

The Workshop provides quiz questions to help you solidify your understanding of the material covered, and exercises to provide you with experience in using what you have learned. Try to answer the quiz and exercise questions before checking the answers in Appendix A, and make sure that you understand the answers before continuing to the next chapter.

Quiz

1. What is a set?
2. What is a dictionary?
3. What is a sparse array?
4. What is a B-tree?
5. How is a B-tree different from a binary tree?

Exercises

1. Declare a `Dictionary` class.
2. Implement the `Dictionary` class.
3. Create a driver program to run the `Dictionary` class created in the first two exercises.
4. Modify the B-tree to not take duplicates.

11

Building Indexes
on Disk

You have learned how to create a variety of advanced data structures, including balanced trees and B-trees. As discussed on day 10, the entire purpose of B-trees is to make access to disk-based indexes quick and easy. Today you will learn

☐ How to design a disk-based B-tree

☐ How to add and search for records on disk

☐ How the B-tree will interact with your data records

Keeping It in Perspective

The goal, you will remember, is quick access to the records that match the keys your user will enter. In the case of ROBIN, that means finding the rNote objects that match the words the user types, but the more important general idea is to be able to find a *record* based on an *indexed* value.

This chapter continues to focus on the specific requirements of ROBIN: adding and removing rNote objects and rWord-based Index objects. Everything shown here, however, is directly applicable to any disk-based database.

The primary goal with all software development is to ship a product. The closer your program comes to meeting the specifications, budget, timeline, and other requirements of your employer or market demands, the more successful you will be. But remember, *the goal is to ship the product.*

The game you are playing is *pinball.* Do a good job, ship the product, score lots of points, and you get to play again.

Real-World Considerations

Let's take a short digression to talk about building a database in the real world. In all likelihood, here's how you will program your next database: you will pick up the phone, dial an 800 number to a mail-order house with a name like Programmer Credit-Card Heaven, and ask for the fastest, most reliable ISAM-based database system they have that meets your specifications. You then will plunk down a few hundred dollars and save yourself a few hundred hours of programming time.

Only in the most rare of circumstances will you actually "roll your own" database from scratch, as I am doing here. Even so, it is imperative that you understand how all this works, because whatever you buy, you will need to tweak it, extend it, and ultimately take ownership of it for your product.

Knowing What You Are Building

With ROBIN, the overall goal is to have a database of rNotes and an index file of words that enables you to quickly find all the note records that match the offered words.

The rNotes database (ROBIN.DB) consists of variable-length records. Each record, or rNote, will consist of a date (4 bytes), a length (4 bytes), and a variable-length string of characters. rNotes will be stored sequentially, with each note beginning right after the preceding note in the file. You will use the techniques you learned on day 9 for object persistence to store the notes.

The word index file (WORD.IDX) will consist of pages of indexes, leading ultimately to a leaf page with the index for the word found. This record will *not* point to ROBIN.DB directly; after all, each word probably will point to many different rNote records. Instead, each index will point to the first record in the Node index file (ROBIN.IDX), which will have a linked list of pointers to records in ROBIN.DB.

Here's how it works: The user requests a search on the word *THE*. Word.IDX, which is a disk-based B-tree, is searched. Node-page index entries lead to other node-page entries until a leaf page is found. The number recorded there is an offset into ROBIN.IDX. Each record in ROBIN.IDX points to a record in ROBIN.DB, and also points to the next entry in ROBIN.IDX (or to null when there are no more entries).

Using Disk-Based B-Trees

The B-tree you built on day 10 was memory-based; at no time were the records written to disk. The goal of a B-tree, however, is precisely that—to store the index on disk.

In the examples you saw on day 10, the index stored a pointer. Pointers are memory-based entities, however. Instead, you want not to store a *pointer*, but to store the appropriate *page*. Node-page index entries will store the page number they point to; leaf-page index entries will store the offset of the data to which they refer.

Caching

Rather than reading each page into memory each time it is needed and then tossing it away, it is far faster and more efficient if you can keep a few pages in memory. The index, however, doesn't want to keep track of whether the page it is pointing to is in memory (in which case a pointer is needed) or is on disk.

This capability would require the index to understand far too much about how pages are stored to disk. All the index should know is that it points to page number 5, for example.

A disk manager is needed. The node-page index hands the disk manager an offset and gets back a pointer to the requested page. It is the disk manager's job to decide whether the page already is in memory or must be picked up off the disk.

In the simplest case, the disk manager would keep an array of pages. When the array was full, it would toss out a page and bring in another. But which page should be tossed? It would be far more efficient to toss out a page that rarely is used than a page that is used all the time. After all, tossing out a page that is used all the time just means that the page will be loaded back in soon, and this defeats your purpose of trying to minimize disk reads.

The answer is a *least recently used* (LRU) queue. A *recently used* queue is the queue that was used most recently; a *least recently used* queue is the page you have gone the longest without needing. The idea is that if you haven't needed it for a while, you probably will not need it any time soon.

Every database can keep only a limited number of pages in memory at any one time. The amount is determined by the amount of memory the user has available, and truly sophisticated programs will increase or decrease that number dynamically. ROBIN will take a middle course, and allow the user to set the number of pages to be kept in memory (along with the order of the pages) from a configuration file.

Swapping Out

The problem with setting a very small number of pages to be held in memory at any one time is that the disk manager may swap out a page while it still is needed. One solution to this problem is to use *lockers* to lock down the page when it is in use; this is discussed on day 15 when memory management is covered.

B-trees reduce this problem somewhat by keeping a relatively shallow tree in memory. Depending on how many indexes you have on each page, you may be able to severely limit the number of pages you ever need in memory at the same time.

Determining How Big Each Page Should Be

The goal, again, is quick reads and writes. It turns out that most personal computers are fastest if they can read a block of data that is a multiple of 2. The ideal size is determined by the sector size of your disk. Because this size varies, you will want the program to get this size from a configuration file, but for now I'll use 512—the size for most PC disks.

Each index record needs to be a divisor of the order, so that an even number fit on each page. The index you have seen so far is 16 bytes: 4 bytes of pointer (now offset) and 11 bytes of data, with a final null byte terminating the string. There are 32 16-bytes in a 512-byte page, so each page will hold 32 index objects. The order of the B-tree therefore will be 32. A 32-order tree can hold 1,024 words in two levels, 32,768 words in three levels, and 33,554,432 words in five levels. Most searches probably can be accomplished in just a few disk reads, which is ideal.

Determining How Many Pages Can Be in Memory at Once

The algorithm you will use will be recursive, starting at the top node and working your way down, as seen in previous examples. Because each page has room for 32 indexes, the average case is that at any time, half of these will be in use—16 indexes per page.

Ten levels of pages with 16 indexes per page provide access to a trillion keys, which will be more than enough. Ten pages, however, will take up only 16 bytes per index: 16 indexes per page times 10 pages equals 2,560 bytes or 2K.

This is the power of B-trees in a nutshell: By having the capability to hold 2K of pages in memory at any time, B-trees give you access to a trillion keys.

Swapping to Disk

The fastest way to swap to disk is to do a single memcpy. C++ gains from its lineage in C the capability to hack memory when required so that all the indexes on a page can be loaded from disk in a single memory move. This capability is discussed in detail when the Page object is covered later in this section. Listing 11.1 is the header file for the disk-based, B-tree system.

Type

Listing 11.1 A Disk-Based, B-Tree Interface

```
1:    // ****************************************************
2:    // PROGRAM:  Btree, Page and Index declarations
3:    // FILE:      btree.hpp
4:    // PURPOSE:  provide fundamental btree functionality
5:    // NOTES:
6:    // AUTHOR:   Jesse Liberty (jl)
7:    // REVISIONS: 11/1/94 1.0 jl  initial release
8:    // ****************************************************
9:    #ifndef BTREE_HPP                    // inclusion guards
10:   #define BTREE_HPP
11:
12:   #include <time.h>
13:   #include <string.h>
14:   #include <fstream.h>
15:   #include "stdef.hpp"
16:
17:   const int Order =      31;  // 31 indexes and 1 header
18:   const int dataLen =    11;  // length of a key
19:   const int MaxPages =   20;  // more than we need
20:   const int SizeItem =   16;   // key + offset
21:   const int SizePointer = 4;  // size of offset
22:   const int PageSize = (Order+1) * SizeItem;
23:
24:   // forward declarations
25:   class Page;
26:   class Index;
```

continues

Listing 11.1 continued

```
27:
28:    // DiskManager - in memory keeps track of what pages are
29:    // already in memory and swaps to disk as required
30:    class DiskManager
31:    {
32:    public:
33:        // constructors & destructor
34:        DiskManager();
35:        ~DiskManager(){}
36:
37:        // management of files
38:        void Close(int);
39:        int Create();
40:        int Open();
41:
42:        // Page manipulation
43:        Page* GetPage(int);
44:        void SetPage(Page*);
45:        void Insert(Page * newPage);
46:        void Save(Page* pg);
47:        int NewPage(const Index&, BOOL);
48:        int NewPage(Index *array, int offset, BOOL leaf, int count);
49:
50:    private:
51:    Page* myPages[MaxPages];
52:    fstream myFile;
53:    int myCount;
54:    };
55:
56:    // the btree itself - has a pointer to first page
57:    class BTree
58:    {
59:    public:
60:        // constructors and destructor
61:        BTree();
62:        ~BTree();
63:
64:        // utility functions
65:        void AddKey(char* data);
66:        void PrintTree();
67:        int Find(char* data);
68:
69:        // page methods
70:        Page* GetPage(int page)
71:            { return theDiskManager.GetPage(page); }
72:        int NewPage(const Index& pIndex, BOOL IsLeaf)
73:            { return theDiskManager.NewPage(pIndex,FALSE); }
74:
75:        // public static member!
76:        static  DiskManager theDiskManager;
77:    private:
78:        int myRoot;
79:    };
80:
81:    // index objects point to pages or real data
82:    class Index
```

```
83:     {
84:     public:
85:         // constructors & destructor
86:         Index();
87:         Index(char *);
88:         Index (char*, int);
89:         Index(const Index&);
90:         ~Index(){}
91:
92:         // accessors
93:         const char * GetData() const  { return myData; }
94:         void SetData(const Index& rhs)
95:            { strcpy(myData,rhs.GetData()); }
96:         void SetData(const char * rhs)
97:             { strcpy(myData,rhs); }
98:         int GetPointer()const { return myPointer; }
99:         void SetPointer (int pg) { myPointer = pg; }
100:
101:         // utility functions
102:         void PrintKey();
103:         void PrintPage();
104:         int Insert(const Index& ref,BOOL findOnly = FALSE);
105:
106:         // overloaded operators
107:         int operator==(const Index& rhs) const
108:         {return strcmp(myData,rhs.GetData()) == 0; }
109:
110:         int operator < (const Index& rhs) const
111:          {return strcmp(myData,rhs.GetData())<0;}
112:
113:         int operator <= (const Index& rhs) const
114:          {return strcmp(myData,rhs.GetData())<=0;}
115:
116:         int operator > (const Index& rhs) const
117:          {return strcmp(myData,rhs.GetData())>0;}
118:
119:         int operator >= (const Index& rhs) const
120:          {return strcmp(myData,rhs.GetData())>=0;}
121:
122:     public:
123:         int myPointer;
124:         char myData[SizeItem - SizePointer];
125:     };
126:
127:
128:     // pages - consist of header and array of indexes
129:     class Page
130:     {
131:     public:
132:         // constructors and destructor
133:         Page();
134:         Page(char*);
135:         Page(const Index&,BOOL);
136:         Page(Index*, int, BOOL, int);
137:         ~Page(){}
138:
```

11

continues

Listing 11.1 continued

```
139:        // insertion and searchoperations
140:        int Insert(const Index&, BOOL findOnly = FALSE);
141:        int Find(const Index& idx) { return Insert(idx,TRUE); }
142:        int InsertLeaf(const Index&,BOOL findOnly = FALSE);
143:        int InsertNode(const Index&,BOOL findOnly = FALSE);
144:        void Push(const Index&,int offset=0, BOOL=TRUE);
145:
146:        // accessors
147:        Index GetFirstIndex() { return myKeys[0]; }
148:        BOOL GetIsLeaf() const { return myVars.IsLeaf; }
149:        int GetCount() const { return myVars.myCount; }
150:        void SetCount(int cnt) { myVars.myCount=cnt; }
151:        time_t GetTime() { return myTime; }
152:
153:        // page manipulation
154:        int GetPageNumber() const { return myVars.myPageNumber; }
155:        Page* GetPage(int page)
156:            { return BTree::theDiskManager.GetPage(page); }
157:        int NewPage(const Index& rIndex, BOOL IsLeaf)
158:            { return BTree::theDiskManager.NewPage(rIndex,FALSE); }
159:
160:        int NewPage(Index* arr, int off,BOOL isL, int cnt)
161:            { return   BTree::theDiskManager.NewPage(arr,off,isL, cnt); }
162:
163:        // utility functions
164:        void Nullify(int offset);
165:        void Print();
166:        fstream& Write(fstream&);
167:        void ReCount();
168:
169:        static int GetgPageNumber(){ return gPage; }
170:        static void SetgPageNumber(int pg) { gPage = pg; }
171:
172:    private:
173:        Index * const myKeys; // will point to myVars.mk
174:        union
175:        {
176:            char myBlock[PageSize];   // a page from disk
177:            struct
178:            {
179:                int myCount;
180:                BOOL IsLeaf;
181:                int myPageNumber;
182:                int lastKey;
183:                char mk[Order*sizeof(Index)];  // array of indexes
184:            }myVars;
185:        };
186:
187:        // memory only
188:        static int gPage;
189:        time_t myTime; // for lifo queue
190:    };
191:
192:    #endif
193:
```

 None.

 Lines 17 through 22 declare a number of constants used throughout the program. Many of these would be read out of a configuration file in a commercial version of ROBIN. Order determines how many indexes are held on each page, for example. When experimenting with this program, you may want to temporarily reduce this number, but don't forget to *increase* the number of pages if you do. A good rule of thumb is that their product should be greater than 600. If you reduce Order to 4, for example, be sure to increase MaxPages to at least 150.

DataLen is used when creating the key; the total length of the index's data is dataLen plus 1 for the terminating NULL. The SizeItem is the sum of the dataLen, plus the null, plus the SizePointer. Finally, each page's size is computed by assuming Order indexes plus an additional 16 bytes of header. Thus, 32 times 16, or 512 bytes.

Lines 25 and 26 provide forward declarations. The DiskManager class declaration begins in line 31 and ends in line 56. The purpose of this class is to provide transparent virtual memory—to swap pages in and out of memory as needed.

Clients of this class call GetPage() (line 43), providing a page number and getting back a pointer to a Page. The Insert() method (line 45) puts a page into the DiskManager's array of Pages. Save() instructs the Page to write itself out to disk.

The BTree class is declared in lines 57 through 79. This class remains quite simple; it has only a pointer to the first page and methods to add and obtain pages. Note, in line 76, that BTree contains a public static DiskManager object. This provides controlled global access to the single DiskManager for the Btree.

The Index class is declared in lines 82 through 125. There are no significant changes here from previous versions; the Index object needs virtually no awareness of whether the Index objects will be stored in memory or on disk.

The Page class is declared in lines 129 through 190. There are four constructors provided, and they will be discussed in detail as the implementation is described.

The most important thing to notice is the union shown in lines 178 through 189. The goal here is to allow the disk manager to read 512 bytes in one gulp and then to move it into a Page in a single call to memcpy().

MyBlock is declared to be a character array of 512 bytes, and that is a union with the four members and the arrays of indexes. You then can read in the 512 bytes treating the unnamed union as a character array, and read out the member variables using the members of the structure.

The problem is that the array of indexes cannot be put into a union, because the Index objects have a constructor. Therefore, a character array, mk, is declared of the same size as the array of indexes. An Index pointer then is declared, in line 177. This pointer is *not* stored on disk, but when the page is created in memory, this pointer is set to point to the mk array. You then can treat myKeys as if it were the array, indexing into it as you would index into the heap using a pointer to allocated memory.

In line 188, a static unsigned int, gPage, is declared to allow each page to be awarded a unique, sequential page number. In line 189, a time stamp is declared. Note that neither of these variables is stored on disk; they are memory only, and are created and manipulated only after the class is instantiated in memory.

Implementing the Tree

Listing 11.2 shows the B-Tree implementation, listing 11.3 shows the Page implementation, listing 11.4 shows the Index implementation, and listing 11.5 shows the DiskManager implementation.

Listing 11.2 The B-Tree Implementation

```
1:   // ***************************************************
2:   // PROGRAM:   Btree
3:   // FILE:      btree.cpp
4:   // PURPOSE:   provide fundamental btree functionality
5:   // NOTES:
6:   // AUTHOR:    Jesse Liberty (jl)
7:   // REVISIONS: 11/1/94 1.0 jl  initial release
8:   // ***************************************************
9:
10:  #include "btree.hpp"
11:  #include "stdef.hpp"
12:
13:  // construct the tree
14:  // initialize myRoot pointer to nothing
15:  // either create or read the index file
16:  BTree::BTree():myRoot(0)
17:  {
18:      myRoot = theDiskManager.Create();
19:  }
20:
21:  // write out the index file
22:  BTree::~BTree()
23:  {
24:      theDiskManager.Close(myRoot);
25:  }
26:
27:  // find an existing record
28:  int BTree::Find(char * str)
29:  {
30:      Index index(str);
31:      if (!myRoot)
32:          return 0L;
33:      else
```

```
34:            return GetPage(myRoot)->Find(index);
35:     }
36:
37:
38:
39:    void BTree::AddKey(char * str)
40:    {
41:
42:        int retVal =0;
43:        Index index(str);
44:        if (!myRoot)
45:        {
46:            myRoot = theDiskManager.NewPage (index,TRUE);
47:        }
48:        else
49:        {
50:            retVal = GetPage(myRoot)->Insert(index);
51:            if (retVal) // our root split
52:            {
53:                // create a pointer to the old top
54:                Index index(GetPage(myRoot)->GetFirstIndex());
55:                index.SetPointer(myRoot);
56:                // make the new page & insert the index
57:                int PageNumber = NewPage(index,FALSE);
58:
59:                Page* pg = GetPage(PageNumber);
60:
61:                //get a pointer to the new (sibling) page
62:                Index Sib(GetPage(retVal)->GetFirstIndex());
63:                Sib.SetPointer(retVal);
64:                // put it into the page
65:                pg->InsertLeaf(Sib);
66:
67:                // reset myRoot to point to the new top
68:                myRoot = PageNumber;
69:            }
70:        }
71:    }
72:
73:    void BTree::PrintTree()
74:    {
75:        GetPage(myRoot)->Print();
76:    }
```

Type   **Listing 11.3 The Page Implementation**

```
1:    // ***************************************************
2:    // PROGRAM:   Page
3:    // FILE:      Page.cpp
4:    // PURPOSE:   provide fundamental btree functionality
5:    // NOTES:
6:    // AUTHOR:    Jesse Liberty (jl)
7:    // REVISIONS: 11/1/94 1.0 jl  initial release
8:    // ***************************************************
```

continues

Listing 11.3 continued

```
9:
10:     #include "btree.hpp"
11:     #include <assert.h>
12:
13:     // constructors
14:
15:     // default constructor
16:     Page::Page()
17:     {
18:     }
19:
20:     // create a page from a buffer read in from disk
21:     Page::Page(char *buffer):
22:         myKeys((Index*)myVars.mk)
23:     {
24:         assert(sizeof(myBlock) == PageSize);
25:         assert(sizeof(myVars) == PageSize);
26:         memcpy(&myBlock,buffer,PageSize);
27:         myTime = time(NULL);
28:     }
29:
30:     // create a Page from the first index
31:     Page::Page(const Index& index, BOOL bLeaf):
32:         myKeys((Index*)myVars.mk)
33:     {
34:
35:         myVars.myCount=1;
36:         myVars.IsLeaf = bLeaf;
37:         myKeys[0]=index;
38:         myVars.myPageNumber = gPage++;
39:         myTime = time(NULL);
40:     }
41:
42:     // create a page by splitting another page
43:     Page::Page(Index *array, int offset, BOOL bLeaf,int count):
44:         myKeys((Index*)myVars.mk)
45:     {
46:         myVars.IsLeaf = bLeaf;
47:         myVars.myCount = 0;
48:         for (int i=0, j = offset; j<Order && i < count; i++, j++)
49:         {
50:             myKeys[i]= array[j];
51:             myVars.myCount++;
52:         }
53:         myVars.myPageNumber = gPage++;
54:         myTime = time(NULL);
55:     }
56:
57:     void Page::Nullify(int offset)
58:     {
59:         for (int i = offset; i<Order; i++)
60:         {
61:             myKeys[i].SetPointer(0);
62:             myVars.myCount--;
63:         }
```

```
64:     }
65:
66:     // decide whether I'm a leaf or a node
67:     // and pass this index to the right
68:     // function. If findOnly is true, don't insert
69:     // just return the page number (for now)
70:     int Page::Insert(const Index& rIndex, BOOL findOnly)
71:     {
72:        if (myVars.IsLeaf)
73:          return   InsertLeaf(rIndex,findOnly);
74:        else
75:          return InsertNode(rIndex,findOnly);
76:     }
77:
78:
79:     // find the right page for this index
80:     int Page::InsertNode(const Index& rIndex, BOOL findOnly)
81:     {
82:        int retVal =0;
83:        BOOL inserted = FALSE;
84:        int i,j;
85:
86:        assert(myVars.myCount>0); // nodes have at least 1
87:        assert(myKeys[0].GetPointer()); // must be valid
88:
89:        // does it go before my first entry?
90:        if (rIndex < myKeys[0])
91:        {
92:           if (findOnly)
93:              return 0L; // not found
94:
95:           myKeys[0].SetData(rIndex);
96:           retVal=myKeys[0].Insert(rIndex);
97:           inserted = TRUE;
98:        }
99:
100:       // does it go after my last?
101:       if (!inserted)
102:          for (i = myVars.myCount-1; i>=0; i--)
103:          {
104:             assert(myKeys[i].GetPointer());
105:             if (rIndex >= myKeys[i])
106:             {
107:                retVal=myKeys[i].Insert(rIndex,findOnly);
108:                inserted = TRUE;
109:                break;
110:             }
111:          }
112:
113:       // find where it does go
114:       if (!inserted)
115:          for (j = 0; j<i && j+1 < myVars.myCount; j++)
116:          {
117:             assert(myKeys[j+1].GetPointer());
118:             if (rIndex < myKeys[j+1])
119:             {
```

continues

Listing 11.3 continued

```
120:                        retVal=myKeys[j].Insert(rIndex,findOnly);
121:                        inserted = TRUE;
122:                        break;
123:                    }
124:            }
125:
126:        assert(inserted);   // change to exception if not!
127:
128:        // if you had to split
129:        if (retVal && !findOnly) // got back a pointer to a new page
130:        {
131:            Index * pIndex = new Index(GetPage(retVal)->GetFirstIndex());
132:            pIndex->SetPointer(retVal);
133:            retVal = InsertLeaf(*pIndex);
134:        }
135:        return retVal;
136:    }
137:
138:    // called if current page is a leaf
139:    int Page::InsertLeaf(const Index& rIndex, BOOL findOnly)
140:    {
141:        int result = 0;
142:
143:        // no duplicates!
144:        for (int i=0; i < myVars.myCount; i++)
145:            if (rIndex == myKeys[i])
146:            {
147:                if (findOnly)
148:                    return GetPageNumber();
149:                else
150:                    return result;
151:            }
152:
153:        if (findOnly)          // not found
154:            return result;
155:
156:        if (myVars.myCount < Order)
157:            Push(rIndex);
158:        else        // overflow the page
159:        {
160:            // make sibling
161:            int NewPg =
162:                NewPage(myKeys,Order/2,myVars.IsLeaf,myVars.myCount);
163:            Page* Sibling = GetPage(NewPg);
164:            Nullify(Order/2);                          // nullify my right half
165:
166:            // does it fit in this side?
167:            if (myVars.myCount>Order/2-1 && rIndex <= myKeys[Order/2-1])
168:                Push(rIndex);
169:            else  // push it into the new sibling
170:                Sibling->Push(rIndex);
171:
172:            result = NewPg; // we split, pass it up
173:        }
```

```
174:     return result;
175:   }
176:
177:   // put the new index into this page (in order)
178:   void Page::Push(const Index& rIndex,int offset,BOOL first)
179:   {
180:     BOOL inserted = FALSE;
181:     assert(myVars.myCount < Order);
182:     for (int i=offset; i<Order && i<myVars.myCount; i++)
183:     {
184:       assert(myKeys[i].GetPointer());
185:       if (rIndex <= myKeys[i])
186:       {
187:           Push(myKeys[i],offset+1,FALSE);
188:           myKeys[i]=rIndex;
189:           inserted = TRUE;
190:           break;
191:       }
192:     }
193:     if (!inserted)
194:       myKeys[myVars.myCount] = rIndex;
195:
196:     if (first)
197:       myVars.myCount++;
198:   }
199:
200:   void Page::Print()
201:   {
202:       for (int i = 0; i<Order && i < myVars.myCount; i++)
203:       {
204:         if (!myKeys[i].GetPointer())
205:         {
206:           cout << "error!! myKeys[" << i << "]";
207:           cout << "data: " << myKeys[i].GetData();
208:           assert(myKeys[i].GetPointer());
209:         }
210:
211:         if (myVars.IsLeaf)
212:           myKeys[i].PrintKey();
213:         else
214:           myKeys[i].PrintPage();
215:       }
216:   }
217:
218:   // write out the entire page as a block
219:   fstream& Page::Write(fstream& file)
220:   {
221:     char buffer[PageSize];
222:     memcpy(buffer,&myBlock,PageSize);
223:     file.seekp(myVars.myPageNumber*PageSize);
224:     file.write(buffer,PageSize);
225:     return file;
226:   }
```

11

Listing 11.4 The Index Implementation

```cpp
1:    // *************************************************
2:    // PROGRAM:   index
3:    // FILE:      index.cpp
4:    // PURPOSE:   provide fundamental btree functionality
5:    // NOTES:
6:    // AUTHOR:    Jesse Liberty (jl)
7:    // REVISIONS: 11/1/94 1.0 jl  initial release
8:    // *************************************************
9:
10:   #include "btree.hpp"
11:
12:   Index::Index(char* str):myPointer(1)
13:   {
14:      strncpy(myData,str,dataLen);
15:      myData[dataLen]='\0';
16:   }
17:
18:   Index::Index(char* str, int ptr):myPointer(ptr)
19:   {
20:
21:      strncpy(myData,str,dataLen);
22:      myData[dataLen]='\0';
23:   }
24:
25:   Index::Index(const Index& rhs):
26:      myPointer(rhs.GetPointer())
27:   {
28:      strcpy(myData, rhs.GetData());
29:   }
30:
31:   Index::Index():myPointer(0)
32:   {
33:      myData[0]='\0';
34:   }
35:
36:   void Index::PrintKey()
37:   {
38:      cout << "   " << myData;
39:   }
40:
41:   void Index::PrintPage()
42:   {
43:      cout << "\n" << myData << ": " ;
44:      BTree::theDiskManager.GetPage(myPointer)->Print();
45:   }
46:
47:   int Index::Insert(const Index& ref, BOOL findOnly)
48:   {
49:      return BTree::theDiskManager.GetPage(myPointer)->Insert(ref,findOnly);
50:   }
```

Listing 11.5 The DiskManager Implementation

```
1:    // **************************************************
2:    // PROGRAM:   diskmgr
3:    // FILE:      diskmgr.cpp
4:    // PURPOSE:   provide i/o for btree
5:    // NOTES:
6:    // AUTHOR:    Jesse Liberty (jl)
7:    // REVISIONS: 11/5/94 1.0 jl  initial release
8:    // **************************************************
9:
10:   #include "btree.hpp"
11:   #include <assert.h>
12:
13:   // on construction, try to open the file if it exists
14:   DiskManager::DiskManager():
15:      myFile("ROBIN.IDX",ios::binary ¦ ios::in ¦ ios::out ¦ ios::nocreate)
16:   {
17:      // initialize the pointers to null
18:      for (int i = 0; i< MaxPages; i++)
19:         myPages[i] = 0;
20:      myCount = 0;
21:
22:   }
23:
24:   // called by btree constructor
25:   // if we opened the file, read in the numbers we need
26:   // otherwise create the file
27:   int DiskManager::Create()
28:   {
29:      if (!myFile) // nocreate failed, first creation
30:      {
31:         // open the file, create it this time
32:         myFile.open("ROBIN.IDX",ios::binary ¦ ios::in ¦ ios::out);
33:
34:         char Header[PageSize];
35:         int MagicNumber = 1234; // a number we can check for
36:         memcpy(Header,&MagicNumber,4);
37:         int NextPage = 1;
38:         memcpy(Header+4,&NextPage,4);
39:         memcpy(Header+8,&NextPage,4);
40:         Page::SetgPageNumber(NextPage);
41:         char title[]="ROBIN.IDX. Ver 1.00";
42:         memcpy(Header+12,title,strlen(title));
43:         myFile.seekp(0);
44:         myFile.write(Header,PageSize);
45:         return 0;
46:      }
47:
48:
49:      // we did open the file, it already existed
50:      // get the numbers we need
51:      int MagicNumber;
52:      myFile.seekg(0);
53:      myFile.read((char *) &MagicNumber,4);
54:
```

continues

Listing 11.5 continued

```
55:        // check the magic number. If it is wrong the file is
56:        // corrupt or this isn't the index file
57:        if (MagicNumber != 1234)
58:        {
59:              // change to an exception!!
60:              cout << "Magic number failed!";
61:              return 0;
62:        }
63:
64:        int NextPage;
65:        myFile.seekg(4);
66:        myFile.read((char*) &NextPage,4);
67:        Page::SetgPageNumber(NextPage);
68:        int FirstPage;
69:        myFile.seekg(8);
70:        myFile.read((char*) &FirstPage,4);
71:        const int room =  PageSize - 12;
72:        char buffer[room];
73:        myFile.read(buffer,room);
74:        cout << buffer << endl;
75:        // read in all the pages
76:        for (int i = 1; i < NextPage; i++)
77:        {
78:              myFile.seekg(i * PageSize);
79:              char buffer[PageSize];
80:              myFile.read( buffer, PageSize);
81:              Page * pg = new Page(buffer);
82:              Insert(pg);
83:        }
84:
85:        return FirstPage;
86:    }
87:
88:    // write out the numbers we'll need next time
89:    void DiskManager::Close(int theRoot)
90:    {
91:
92:        for (int i = 0; i< MaxPages; i++)
93:            if (myPages[i])
94:                Save(myPages[i]);
95:        int NextPage = Page::GetgPageNumber();
96:        if (!myFile)
97:            cout << "Error opening myFile!" << endl;
98:        myFile.seekp(4);
99:        myFile.write ( (char *) &NextPage,4);
100:        myFile.seekp(8);
101:        myFile.write((char*) &theRoot,4);
102:        myFile.close();
103:    }
104:
105:    // wrapper function
106:    int DiskManager::NewPage(const Index& index, BOOL bLeaf)
107:    {
108:        Page * newPage = new Page(index, bLeaf);
```

```
109:        Insert(newPage);
110:        Save(newPage);
111:        return newPage->GetPageNumber();
112:    }
113:
114:    int DiskManager::NewPage(
115:        Index *array,
116:        int offset,
117:        BOOL leaf,
118:        int count)
119:    {
120:        Page * newPage = new Page(array, offset, leaf,count);
121:        Insert(newPage);
122:        Save(newPage);
123:        return newPage->GetPageNumber();
124:    }
125:
126:    void DiskManager::Insert(Page * newPage)
127:    {
128:    // add new page into array of page managers
129:
130:
131:        if (myCount < MaxPages)
132:        {
133:            assert(!myPages[myCount]);
134:            myPages[myCount++] = newPage;
135:        }
136:        else  // no room, time to page out to disk
137:        {
138:            int lowest = 0;
139:            for (int i = 0; i< MaxPages; i++)
140:                if (myPages[i]->GetTime() < myPages[lowest]->GetTime())
141:                    lowest = i;
142:            Save(myPages[lowest]);
143:            delete myPages[lowest];
144:            myPages[lowest] = newPage;
145:        }
146:    }
147:
148:    // tell the page to write itself out
149:    void DiskManager::Save(Page* pg)
150:    {
151:      pg->Write(myFile);
152:    }
153:
154:    // see if the page is in memory, if so return it
155:    // otherwise get it from disk
156:    // note: this won't scale, with lots of page managers
157:    // you'd need a more efficient search. 10 levels of page
158:    // managers, with 31 indexes per page gives you room for
159:    // 800 trillion words. Even if each page is only 1/2 full
160:    // on average, 10 levels of depth would represent 64 million
161:    // keys alone, not to mention the actual records.
162:
163:    Page * DiskManager::GetPage(int target)
164:    {
```

11

continues

Listing 11.5 continued

```
165:
166:        for (int i = 0; i< MaxPages; i++)
167:        {
168:           if (myPages[i]->GetPageNumber() == target)
169:              return  myPages[i];
170:        }
171:        myFile.seekg(target * PageSize);
172:        char buffer[PageSize];
173:        myFile.read( buffer, PageSize);
174:        Page * pg = new Page(buffer);
175:        Insert(pg);
176:        return pg;
177:    }
```

 Listing 11.6 The Driver Program

```
1:     #include "String.hpp"
2:     #include "stdef.hpp"
3:     #include "btree.hpp"
4:     DiskManager BTree::theDiskManager;
5:     int Page::gPage=1;
6:     int main()
7:     {
8:        BTree myTree;
9:        char buffer[255];
10:       for (;;)
11:       {
12:          cout << "word: ";
13:          cin.getline(buffer,255);
14:          if (buffer[0])
15:             if (buffer[0]=='?')
16:             {
17:                int found = myTree.Find(buffer+1);
18:                cout << "Found record: " << found << endl;
19:             }
20:             else
21:                myTree.AddKey(buffer);
22:          else
23:             break;
24:       }
25:       myTree.PrintTree();
26:       return 0;
27:    }
```

 This is a complicated collection of code, although you saw much of the fundamental logic on day 10. The best way to review this code is probably to walk through bringing the program up, entering some data, closing down, restarting, adding more, and then closing down again.

The driver program begins in line 4 with the definition of the two static class members: BTree's DiskManager and Page's gPage, which is initialized to 1.

The initialization of the DiskManager object calls its constructor, shown in lines 6 through 14 of listing 11.5. The initialization of myFile fails, because of the nocreate flag, which says not to open the file if it doesn't already exist. In the body of the constructor, the array of PageManager object pointers is initialized so that all the pointers have the value 0. The failure of the open call is expected and planned for (and desired). It is a signal that the index file does not already exist, and will be handled in the Create() method.

The driver program declares a BTree object that invokes the BTree constructor, which is seen in line 16 of listing 11.2. The root pointer is initialized to 0 and the static member, the DiskManager's Create() method, is called.

The first time you run the program, the opening of myFile, shown in the constructor for the disk manager, fails. Now that failure is detected in line 21, so the program knows that it is dealing with a new file. In line 24, the file is opened in binary mode, allowing both input and output.

A *magic number* is written as the first 4 bytes of the file. This number can be checked on subsequent opens, to ensure that the file you are reading is valid.

In line 29, the variable NextPage is initialized to 1 and written to the file, mostly as a place holder. This number is used to initialize the global variable gPage, using the static member function SetgPageNumber. Finally, in line 35, a title is written to the file. All of this is written into the first 512 bytes of the file in line 37.

On subsequent builds, the if statement would fail, and this function would begin in line 43. The MagicNumber is read in line 45 and checked in line 49. If it fails, an exception should be thrown.

The NextPage variable is read from the file, and that number is used to set the gPage variable. The FirstPage variable is read and will be returned when the function returns, allowing the BTree to set its root pointer.

In lines 68 through 75, the pages are read 512 bytes at a time. Each page is provided as a parameter to the Page constructor in line 73.

The Page constructor is shown in lines 20 through 27 of listing 11.3. The index pointer, myKeys, is initialized with the address of myVars.mk cast to an Index pointer. Note that this enables you to deal with myKeys *as if* it were the array of Index objects, but still load the array in the union with the buffer.

How the Union Works

When the Page object is in memory, you want to deal with it as if it consisted of four int objects and an array of Index objects. When getting the Page object off the disk, you want to deal with it as a block of 512 bytes. To do this, you make a union between a character array of 512 bytes with the other variables. Because you cannot put an array of objects that have constructors into a union, you instead create an array of characters of the size of your array of Index objects. You then use the pointer myKeys much like you use a pointer to dynamically created memory.

In the body of the constructor, there are two asserts that fall out in the final code. The one meaningful statement, in line 26, is the block move of the buffer loaded off the disk into the union of data members.

Control then returns to line 74 of listing 11.5. The newly created page is inserted into the DiskManager's array. When this function ends, control returns to the constructor of the BTree, which in turn returns to the driver program.

The user is prompted repeatedly for words that are added to the BTree in line 19. After the user presses Enter, the tree is printed in line 23.

Each call to AddKey transfers control to line 27 of listing 11.2. If the root does not yet point to a page, a new page is created in line 34. This transfers control to line 109 of listing 11.5. A new Page object is created, and it is inserted into the array of Pages and saved to disk. The *number* of that page is returned, and that number is saved in the myRoot pointer.

When AddKey is called subsequently, the myRoot pointer has a value, and control goes to line 38 of listing 11.2. Here, the logic of inserting a page and then checking the return value begins. The return value, if non-zero, indicates that the page already pointed to split. In this case, in line 39 of listing 11.2, this indicates that the top node split and a new top node is required.

The call for inserting into a page is shown in line 38. The GetPage() function call takes a page number and returns a pointer. That pointer then is used to invoke Insert() on the page returned from the DiskManager.

This moves control to line 66 of listing 11.3. The current page knows whether it is a leaf page or a node page. The first 31 times this is called, the root node will be a leaf. This invokes the InsertLeaf method, beginning in line 133.

The current value is checked to see whether it is a duplicate of an existing key. If so, for now it is just discarded. In ROBIN, of course, the actual data—the word record—will be updated for all the notes that reference that word, but there will be only one key per word.

In line 143, the page is checked to see whether there is room. If so, the Index is Pushed into the page. Otherwise, the page must split. *Splitting* involves creating a new page and dividing the contents of the original page with the sibling. The new value then is pushed into whichever of the two pages (original and sibling) it belongs to.

When a page splits, the page number of the new page is passed back to the calling function. If the calling function is a node, the new value is put into that page, which in turn may have to split. If the calling function is the AddKey() function of the BTree itself, then a new topmost node is created.

Note that if the user prepends a question mark to his new word, the driver program interprets this as a call to Find(). Page's Find() method calls its insert method and overrides the default value of FALSE for its second parameter, passing in TRUE instead, indicating find, not insert.

The Find() logic closely parallels the Insert() logic, so instead of creating duplicate code paths, I use a flag value (findOnly) to choose the right behavior in a unified method.

Currently, Find() just returns the page where the Index is stored; in the real program, this will return an array of notes on which this word was found.

Connecting Nodes to Data

Leaf-node index items in the examples provided point nowhere. In a real program, of course, they would point to the actual data. The specification for ROBIN, like for most B-trees, specifically designates that words will not be duplicated in the tree, but that each word may point to zero, one, or many individual notes.

Each leaf-node index item will point to a disk-based, linked list of pointers to notes. When the program searches for an entry (for example, the word *America*), the correct leaf node will be found. The index will have the offset of the first of the linked note pointers. Each note pointer will, in fact, have two pointers: one to a note object and the other to the next note pointer.

As more notes are added, each word will be parsed and submitted to the WORD.IDX. If the word already exists in the WORD.IDX, the linked list will be traced and a new entry will be placed on the tail.

Deleting Notes

In version 1 of ROBIN, notes never will be deleted. The database will grow forever. Future versions will, however, allow for the deletion of NOTES.

When notes are deleted from the database, each word will be traced and the appropriate entry will be removed from the linked list of note pointers. When a word has no entries, it is ready for deletion from the linked list.

This begs the question, "How are Index objects deleted from a B-tree?" It certainly is possible to delete an index from a B-tree, but it is a lot of work, it usually isn't needed, and it often isn't desirable.

The simpler and more common solution is to mark the index for deletion, and then remove it when the entire B-tree is packed. When an Index item is marked as deleted, it is treated by the tree as if it were removed.

When the B-tree is packed, it is rebuilt, entry by entry, with those Index objects marked for deletion simply not included in the new version. Typically, the entire tree is rebuilt in a new file and then copied over the old file.

Implementing Performance Enhancements

The B-tree shown in listing 11.2 is very fast. Disk reads are held to an absolute minimum, and the techniques shown for reading data into memory are among the fastest available. The one inefficiency is the technique for searching the disk manager's array.

If the Disk Manager were going to hold a large number of entries, the current implementation of reading through each and looking for the oldest entry would be entirely unacceptable. Because you can be certain, however, that no more than 10 entries will ever be needed, there is little point in optimizing Disk Manager. If you were going to optimize, the easiest way to do so would be to keep the array sorted. Then finding the earliest entry would be trivial and instant.

Similarly, in lines 144 through 146 of listing 11.3, you see a brute force search for a matching Index item. A *binary search* would significantly speed this search. The idea of a binary search is to check the middle value in the array of Index objects. If the target is smaller than the middle, you then search the left half; if it is larger, you search the right half. That second search is accomplished by comparing the middle value of the chosen half. Each half is halved again until the object is found or proven not to exist.

These and similar optimization approaches are discussed in more detail on day 17, "Profiling and Performance."

Summary

Today you learned how to write a B-tree to disk. The primary design concern with writing such a B-tree is to minimize the number of disk accesses and to make the reads as efficient and fast as possible.

Q&A

Q Why do you want to reduce the number of disk accesses?

A Reading and writing to disk is typically the slowest part of any program other than waiting for input from a modem.

Q Building this B-tree wasn't so hard. Why do you advise buying B-tree products rather than building them as needed?

A Building a first version is not terribly difficult, although we are not done yet. Getting it right and rock-solid reliable is much harder, though.

Q Why are the pages cached in memory?

A The goal is to reduce the number of times you must go to the disk. Because the node pages will be used frequently, keeping them in memory can greatly enhance the efficiency of your program.

Workshop

The Workshop provides quiz questions to help you solidify your understanding of the material covered, and exercises to provide you with experience in using what you have learned. Try to answer the quiz and exercise questions before checking the answers in Appendix A, and make sure that you understand the answers before continuing to the next chapter.

Quiz

1. Why do B-trees reduce disk accesses?

2. How is page size determined?

3. What does it mean to say a page is order 32?

4. Why was a union used?

5. Why was a pointer to `char` used as a member variable?

Exercises

1. Modify the index manager to print out whether it gets its page from memory or from disk.

2. Start with clean data files. Enter this text:

    Silent night, holy night, all is calm, all is right, round young virgin mother and child, sleep in heavenly bliss.

    Examine the output. How many pages are required to hold these 20 words? How many times are the pages accessed?

3. Change the header to set the order to 4. Delete the data and index files and run them again with the string from exercise 2. Examine the output. How many pages are required to hold these 20 words? How many times are the pages accessed? How often is the disk accessed?

4. Cut down the disk manager size to 5 pages, and run exercise 3 again, after clearing out the data and index files. Examine the output. How many pages are required to hold these 20 words? How many times are the pages accessed? How often is the disk accessed?

Records and
Parsing

You have seen how to create the B-tree for the data file, but not how to write the data itself to disk. Today you will learn

- How to create the data file
- How to connect a stored key to more than one note
- What some of the trade-offs are in building this database
- How to parse each word and combine command-line arguments into a single record

Putting the Notes into a Data File

You are closing in on the final version of your database, but you still have not saved the actual *notes*. Remember that until now all you have been saving is the index, with the key value. The note itself must, of course, be saved in your data file. After all, the machinations and manipulations to index and store the keys are for the purpose of storing and retrieving the notes. It is easy to lose sight of this goal as you focus on the B-tree algorithms, but to the end user, the notes are the entire *point* of the exercise.

Storing the Notes

How should the note be stored? Although it is possible to create a complex binary structure around these notes, there really is no reason to do so. The text can be written out to the file, and the offset of the text can be recorded and stored in the index.

The first iteration need not worry about the fact that each key may point to multiple notes. First, get the data-storage fundamentals working, and then you can worry about the intermediate index as described on day 11.

Improving the Code

After this is done, all the fundamental database features will be in place except one. You need to be able to associate more than one note to each key. You have eliminated duplicate index entries, but you cannot yet store the fact that a given key is used by more than one note.

One solution is to create an intermediary index file; I'll call this a *Word-Node-Join* or *WNJ* record. Rather than each index pointing directly to the note in the data file, it will point to a WNJ index entry. Each WNJ index entry will point both to a note and to the next WNJ index object.

The problem with this approach, however, is that some key values will have dozens of associated data files, and you now have introduced a terrible inefficiency into your program. You went to all the work of creating a very advanced B-tree structure to avoid multiple disk reads, and here you are back to reading this index repeatedly as you track down the offsets into the data file.

There are a few potential solutions to this problem. You could create yet another B-tree, but that would bring its own inefficiencies: Most keys will associate with only one, or a very small number, of notes. You could create an array of offsets, but that has two problems: The empty slots in the array take up disk space, and when you fill all the slots you are stuck—what do you do with the next note that matches that key?

The solution is to pick a reasonable but small number of slots, and reserve the last slot as a pointer to the next array. I'll use five slots as a starting point; if you have one to four notes that match a given key, their offsets will all fit in the array. When you get a fifth note, you will create a new array and put *its* offset into the fifth slot.

I believe this creates a reasonable trade-off between disk usage and speed of access, but in a commercial program you would want to make this a configurable number. There are a number of approaches to doing so: You might let the user set this number in a configuration file or, in a very advanced system, the program might adjust itself based on usage patterns.

In any case, changing this value can occur only when the database is repacked. You see more about packing the database when deletion of records is covered.

Recording Length and Data

As mentioned earlier, you will want to record the length of each data record so that displaying the complete record will be easier. You also need to record the date the note was created; according to the specification, the date of each note is displayed in the list of found notes.

Why record the length of the note? Remember that you are not writing the terminating null to disk—you are writing only the contents of the string. Having the length enables you to read in and display the correct number of characters when the user asks to see the complete note. One could argue that this is inefficient; saving the null costs 1 byte per string, and the length costs 4 bytes per string; but you will find it convenient to be able to read the length and then use that figure for formatting the string. If this becomes a real-world cost over time, it is easy to change in a later version.

Case Insensitivity

When searching for a value, the user probably would prefer to match without case sensitivity. Thus, when searching for *computer*, the user would like to match notes that include *Computer* and *COMPUTER*. There are a number of ways to accomplish this, but the easiest and most straightforward is to save all the indexed keys in uppercase.

Very Small Words

In a few days, you will see how to add *stop words*—those terms you do not want to search on and for which you don't want to allocate storage. There are some assumptions that you can make right now to reduce disk storage, however, and one is that one- and two-letter words almost never will have significance. There is little reason to index words such as *is, if, or, we, on, in,* and so on. You therefore can set the index to ignore words of fewer than three letters.

Again, in a commercial program, you might want to make this a configurable number, allowing the user to decide the minimum length of words suitable for indexing. For now, you will hard-wire in a minimum length of three letters.

Statistics

As the database grows, you will need statistics on its usage; the next version keeps track of how many pages (node and leaf) are created, and how many indexes are used in each page. This version displays these statistics at the end of each run, along with a display of all the indexed terms.

The Final Preliminary Version

There is much more to do for ROBIN V.1, which you will see on day 13. For now, however, you have a number of significant improvements, and the following listings display the changes described earlier in this chapter:

Listing 12.1	Btree.hpp	308
Listing 12.2	Datafile.cpp	313
Listing 12.3	BTree.cpp	317
Listing 12.4	DiskMgr.cpp	319
Listing 12.5	Index.cpp	322
Listing 12.6	Page.cpp	323
Listing 12.7	WNJFile.cpp	328
Listing 12.8	The new driver program	331

Listing 12.1 Btree.hpp

```
1:      // ***************************************************
2:      // PROGRAM:  Btree, Page and Index declarations
3:      // FILE:     btree.hpp
4:      // PURPOSE:  provide fundamental btree functionality
5:      // NOTES:
6:      // AUTHOR:   Jesse Liberty (jl)
```

```
7:          // REVISIONS: 11/1/94 1.0 jl  initial release
8:          // ************************************************
9:          #ifndef BTREE_HPP                   // inclusion guards
10:         #define BTREE_HPP
11:
12:         #include <time.h>
13:         #include <string.h>
14:         #include <fstream.h>
15:         #include "stdef.hpp"
16:
17:         const int Order =        31;  // 31 indexes and 1 header
18:         const int dataLen =      11;  // length of a key
19:         const int MaxPages =     20;  // more than we need
20:         const int SizeItem =     16;  // key + offset
21:         const int SizePointer = 2;  // size of offset
22:         const int PageSize = (Order+1) * SizeItem;
23:         const int WNJSize =       5;  // entries per wnj array
24:
25:         // forward declarations
26:         class Page;
27:         class Index;
28:
29:         class DataFile
30:         {
31:         public:
32:             // constructors & destructor
33:             DataFile();
34:             ~DataFile(){}
35:
36:             // management of files
37:             void Close();
38:             void Create();
39:             void GetRecord(long offset, char * buffer);
40:
41:             long Insert(char *);
42:
43:         private:
44:         fstream myFile;
45:         };
46:
47:         class WNJFile
48:         {
49:         public:
50:             // constructors & destructor
51:             WNJFile();
52:             ~WNJFile(){}
53:
54:             // management of files
55:             void Close();
56:             void Create();
57:             int* Find(int NextWNJ);
58:             int Insert(int, int);
59:             int Append(int);
60:
61:         private:
```

continues

Listing 12.1 continued

```
62:         static int myCount;
63:         fstream myFile;
64:         union
65:         {
66:            int myInts[5];
67:            char  myArray[5*4];
68:         };
69:         };
70:
71:         // DiskManager - in memory keeps track of what pages are
72:         // already in memory and swaps to disk as required
73:         class DiskManager
74:         {
75:         public:
76:            // constructors & destructor
77:            DiskManager();
78:            ~DiskManager(){}
79:
80:            // management of files
81:            void Close(int);
82:            int Create();
83:
84:            // Page manipulation
85:            Page* GetPage(int);
86:            void SetPage(Page*);
87:            void Insert(Page * newPage);
88:            void Save(Page* pg);
89:            int NewPage(Index&, int);
90:            int NewPage(Index *array, long offset, int leaf, int count);
91:
92:         private:
93:         Page* myPages[MaxPages];
94:         fstream myFile;
95:         int myCount;
96:         };
97:
98:         // the btree itself - has a pointer to first page
99:         class BTree
100:        {
101:        public:
102:           // constructors and destructor
103:           BTree();
104:           ~BTree();
105:
106:           // utility functions
107:           void AddKey(char* data, long offset);
108:           void Insert(char* buffer, int, char**);
109:           void Insert(char*);
110:           void PrintTree();
111:           int Find(char* data);
112:
113:           // page methods
114:           Page* GetPage(int page)
115:              { return theDiskManager.GetPage(page); }
116:           int NewPage(Index& pIndex, int IsLeaf)
```

```
117:                    { return theDiskManager.NewPage(pIndex,FALSE); }
118:
119:
120:            // public static member!
121:          static int myAlNum(char ch);
122:          static  DiskManager theDiskManager;
123:          static WNJFile    theWNJFile;
124:          static DataFile theDataFile;
125:          static int GetWord(char*, char*, int&);
126:          static void GetStats();
127:          static int NodeIndexCtr;
128:          static int LeafIndexCtr;
129:          static int NodePageCtr;
130:          static int LeafPageCtr;
131:          static int NodeIndexPerPage[Order+1];
132:          static int LeafIndexPerPage[Order+1];
133:
134:      private:
135:          int myRoot;
136:      };
137:
138:      // index objects point to pages or real data
139:      class Index
140:      {
141:      public:
142:          // constructors & destructor
143:          Index();
144:          Index(char *);
145:          Index (char*, int);
146:          Index(Index&);
147:          ~Index(){}
148:
149:          // accessors
150:          const char * GetData() const  { return myData; }
151:          void SetData(const Index& rhs)
152:              { strcpy(myData,rhs.GetData()); }
153:          void SetData(const char * rhs)
154:              { strcpy(myData,rhs); }
155:          int GetPointer()const { return myPointer; }
156:          void SetPointer (int pg) { myPointer = pg; }
157:
158:          // utility functions
159:          void PrintKey();
160:          void PrintPage();
161:          int Insert(Index& ref,int findOnly = FALSE);
162:
163:          // overloaded operators
164:          int operator==(const Index& rhs) const;
165:      //    {return strcmp(myData,rhs.GetData()) == 0; }
166:
167:          int operator < (const Index& rhs) const
168:            {return strcmp(myData,rhs.GetData())<0;}
169:
170:          int operator <= (const Index& rhs) const
171:            {return strcmp(myData,rhs.GetData())<=0;}
```

continues

311

Listing 12.1 continued

```
172:
173:            int operator > (const Index& rhs) const
174:             {return strcmp(myData,rhs.GetData())>0;}
175:
176:            int operator >= (const Index& rhs) const
177:             {return strcmp(myData,rhs.GetData())>=0;}
178:
179:        public:
180:            int myPointer;
181:            char myData[SizeItem - SizePointer];
182:        };
183:
184:
185:        // pages - consist of header and array of indexes
186:        class Page
187:        {
188:        public:
189:            // constructors and destructor
190:            Page();
191:            Page(char*);
192:            Page(Index&,int);
193:            Page(Index*, long, int, int);
194:            ~Page(){}
195:
196:            // insertion and searchoperations
197:            int Insert(Index&, int findOnly = FALSE);
198:            int Find(Index& idx) { return Insert(idx,TRUE); }
199:            int InsertLeaf(Index&);
200:            int FindLeaf(Index&,int findOnly);
201:            int InsertNode(Index&,int findOnly = FALSE);
202:            void Push(Index&,long offset=0L, int=TRUE);
203:
204:            // accessors
205:            Index GetFirstIndex() { return myKeys[0]; }
206:            int GetIsLeaf() const { return myVars.IsLeaf; }
207:            int GetCount() const { return myVars.myCount; }
208:            void SetCount(int cnt) { myVars.myCount=cnt; }
209:            time_t GetTime() { return myTime; }
210:
211:            // page manipulation
212:            int GetPageNumber() const { return myVars.myPageNumber; }
213:            Page* GetPage(int page)
214:                { return BTree::theDiskManager.GetPage(page); }
215:            int NewPage(Index& rIndex, int IsLeaf)
216:                { return BTree::theDiskManager.NewPage(rIndex,FALSE); }
217:
218:            int NewPage(Index* arr, int off,int isL, int cnt)
219:                { return   BTree::theDiskManager.NewPage(arr,off,isL, cnt); }
220:
221:            // utility functions
222:            void Nullify(long offset);
223:            void Print();
224:            fstream& Write(fstream&);
225:            void ReCount();
226:
```

```
227:          static int GetgPageNumber(){ return gPage; }
228:          static void SetgPageNumber(int pg) { gPage = pg; }
229:
230:      private:
231:         Index * const myKeys; // will point to myVars.mk
232:         union
233:         {
234:            char myBlock[PageSize];    // a page from disk
235:            struct
236:            {
237:               int myCount;
238:               int IsLeaf;
239:               int myPageNumber;
240:               int lastKey;
241:               char overhead[8];
242:               char mk[Order*sizeof(Index)];  // array of indexes
243:            }myVars;
244:         };
245:
246:         // memory only
247:         static int gPage;
248:         time_t myTime; // for lifo queue
249:      };
250:
251:      #endif
```

Type

Listing 12.2 Btree.cpp

```
1:      // ****************************************************
2:      // PROGRAM:  Btree
3:      // FILE:     btree.cpp
4:      // PURPOSE:  provide fundamental btree functionality
5:      // NOTES:
6:      // AUTHOR:   Jesse Liberty (jl)
7:      // REVISIONS: 11/1/94 1.0 jl  initial release
8:      // ****************************************************
9:
10:     #include "btree.hpp"
11:     #include "stdef.hpp"
12:     #include <assert.h>
13:     #include <ctype.h>
14:     #include <stdlib.h>
15: #if defined(_BC_16BIT) || defined(_BC32_BIT)
    #include <values.h>
    #endif
    #ifdef _MSVC_16BIT
    #define MAXINT 0x7FFF //(16 bit)
    #endif
    #ifdef _MSVC_32BIT
    #define 0x7FFFFFFF //(32 bit)
    #endif
16:
17:      // construct the tree
```

continues

Listing 12.2 continued

```
18:        // initialize myRoot pointer to nothing
19:        // either create or read the index file
20:        BTree::BTree():myRoot(0)
21:        {
22:            myRoot = theDiskManager.Create();
23:            theDataFile.Create();
24:            theWNJFile.Create();
25:
26:        }
27:
28:        // write out the index file
29:        BTree::~BTree()
30:        {
31:            theDiskManager.Close(myRoot);
32:            theDataFile.Close();
33:            theWNJFile.Close();
34:        }
35:
36:        // find an existing record
37:        int BTree::Find(char * str)
38:        {
39:            Index index(str);
40:            if (!myRoot)
41:                return 0L;
42:            else
43:                return GetPage(myRoot)->Find(index);
44:        }
45:
46:        void BTree::Insert(char * buffer, int argc, char** argv)
47:        {
48:            // get each word,
49:            long offset = theDataFile.Insert(buffer);
50:            for (int i = 1; i<argc; i++)
51:            {
52:                AddKey(argv[i],offset);
53:            }
54:
55:        }
56:
57:        void BTree::Insert(char* buffer)
58:        {
59:
60:            if (strlen(buffer) < 3)
61:                return;
62:
63:            char *buff = buffer;
64:            char word[PageSize];
65:            int wordOffset = 0;
66:            long offset;
67:
68:            if (GetWord(buff,word,wordOffset))
69:            {
70:                offset = theDataFile.Insert(buffer);
71:                AddKey(word,offset);
72:            }
```

```
73:
74:
75:          while (GetWord(buff,word,wordOffset))
76:          {
77:              AddKey(word,offset);
78:          }
79:
80:      }
81:
82:      void BTree::AddKey(char * str, long offset )
83:      {
84:
85:          if (strlen(str) < 3)
86:              return;
87:
88:          int retVal =0;
89:          assert (offset < MAXINT);
90:          Index index(str,(int)offset);
91:          if (!myRoot)
92:          {
93:              myRoot = theDiskManager.NewPage (index,TRUE);
94:          }
95:          else
96:          {
97:              retVal = GetPage(myRoot)->Insert(index);
98:              if (retVal) // our root split
99:              {
100:                 // create a pointer to the old top
101:                 Index index(GetPage(myRoot)->GetFirstIndex());
102:                 index.SetPointer(myRoot);
103:                 // make the new page & insert the index
104:                 int PageNumber = NewPage(index,FALSE);
105:
106:                 Page* pg = GetPage(PageNumber);
107:
108:                 //get a pointer to the new (sibling) page
109:                 Index Sib(GetPage(retVal)->GetFirstIndex());
110:                 Sib.SetPointer(retVal);
111:                 // put it into the page
112:                 pg->InsertLeaf(Sib);
113:
114:                 // reset myRoot to point to the new top
115:                 myRoot = PageNumber;
116:              }
117:          }
118:      }
119:
120:      void BTree::PrintTree()
121:      {
122:          GetPage(myRoot)->Print();
123:
124:          cout << "\n\nStats:" << endl;
125:          cout << "Node pages:   " << NodePageCtr << endl;
126:          cout << "Leaf pages:   " << LeafPageCtr << endl;
127:          cout << "Node indexes: " << NodeIndexCtr << endl;
```

12

continues

315

Listing 12.2 continued

```
128:          cout << "Leaf indexes: " << LeafIndexCtr << endl;
129:          for (int i = 0; i < Order +2; i++)
130:          {
131:              if (NodeIndexPerPage[i])
132:              {
133:                  cout << "Pages with " << i << " nodes:   ";
134:                  cout << NodeIndexPerPage[i] << endl;
135:              }
136:              if (LeafIndexPerPage[i])
137:              {
138:                  cout << "Pages with " << i << " leaves: ";
139:                  cout << LeafIndexPerPage[i] << endl;
140:              }
141:          }
142:
143:      }
144:
145:      int BTree::GetWord(char* string, char* word, int& wordOffset)
146:      {
147:
148:          if (!string[wordOffset])
149:              return FALSE;
150:
151:          char *p1, *p2;
152:          p1 = p2 = string+wordOffset;
153:
154:          // eat leading spaces
155:          for (int i = 0; i<(int)strlen(p1) && !(BTree::myAlNum(p1[0])); i++)
156:              p1++;
157:
158:          // see if you have a word
159:          if (!BTree::myAlNum(p1[0]))
160:              return FALSE;
161:
162:           p2 = p1; // point to start of word
163:
164:          // march p2 to end of word
165:          while (BTree::myAlNum(p2[0]))
166:              p2++;
167:
168:          int len = int(p2-p1);
169: #if defined(_MSVC_16BIT) || defined(_MSVC_32BIT)
   : {
   :    len = __min(len,(int)PageSize);
   : }
   : #else
   : {
   :    len = min(len,(int)PageSize);
   : }
   : #endif
170:
171:          strncpy (word,p1,len);
172:          word[len]='\0';
173:
```

```
174:            for (i = int (p2-string); i<(int)strlen(string) &&
                 !BTree::myAlNum(p2[0]); i++)
175:                p2++;
176:
177:            wordOffset = int (p2-string);
178:
179:            return TRUE;
180:        }
181:
182:        int BTree::myAlNum(char ch)
183:        {
184:            return isalnum(ch) ¦¦
185:                ch == '-' ¦¦
186:                ch == '\'' ¦¦
187:                ch == '(' ¦¦
188:                ch == ')';
189:        }
```

Type   Listing 12.3 Datafile.cpp

```
1:      // ***************************************************
2:      // PROGRAM:   Data file
3:      // FILE:      datafile.cpp
4:      // PURPOSE:
5:      // NOTES:
6:      // AUTHOR:    Jesse Liberty (jl)
7:      // REVISIONS: 11/5/94 1.0 jl  initial release
8:      // ***************************************************
9:
10:     #include "btree.hpp"
11:     #include <assert.h>
12:
13:     // on construction, try to open the file if it exists
14:     DataFile::DataFile():
15:         myFile("ROBIN.DAT",
16:         ios::binary ¦ ios::in ¦ ios::out ¦ ios::nocreate ¦ ios::app)
17:     {
18:     }
19:
20:     void DataFile::Create()
21:     {
22:         if (!myFile) // nocreate failed, first creation
23:         {
24:
25:             // open the file, create it this time
26:             myFile.clear();
27:
28:             myFile.open
29:                 ("ROBIN.DAT",ios::binary ¦ ios::in ¦ ios::out ¦ ios::app);
30:
31:             char Header[2];
32:             int MagicNumber = 1234; // a number we can check for
33:             memcpy(Header,&MagicNumber,2);
34:             myFile.clear();
```

continues

Listing 12.3 continued

```
35:            myFile.flush();
36:            myFile.seekp(0);
37:            myFile.write(Header,2);
38:            return;
39:        }
40:
41:        // we did open the file, it already existed
42:        // get the numbers we need
43:        int MagicNumber;
44:        myFile.seekg(0);
45:        myFile.read((char *) &MagicNumber,2);
46:
47:        // check the magic number. If it is wrong the file is
48:        // corrupt or this isn't the index file
49:        if (MagicNumber != 1234)
50:        {
51:            // change to an exception!!
52:            cout << "DataFile Magic number failed!";
53:        }
54:        return;
55:    }
56:
57:    // write out the numbers we'll need next time
58:    void DataFile::Close()
59:    {
60:        myFile.close();
61:    }
62:
63:
64:    long DataFile::Insert(char * newNote)
65:    {
66:        int len = strlen(newNote);
67:        int fullLen = len + 2;
68:        char buffer[PageSize];
69:        memcpy(buffer,&len,2);
70:        memcpy(buffer+2,newNote,len);
71:        myFile.clear();
72:        myFile.flush();
73:        myFile.seekp(0,ios::end);
74:        long offset = myFile.tellp();
75:        myFile.write(buffer,fullLen);
76:        myFile.flush();
77:        return offset;
78:    }
79:
80:    void DataFile::GetRecord(long offset, char* buffer)
81:    {
82:        int len;
83:        char tmpBuff[PageSize];
84:        myFile.flush();
85:        myFile.clear();
86:        myFile.seekg(offset);
87:        myFile.read(tmpBuff,PageSize);
88:        memcpy(&len,tmpBuff,2);
89:        strncpy(buffer,tmpBuff+2,len);
```

```
90:        buffer[len] = '\0';
91:    }
```

Listing 12.4 Idxmgr.cpp

```
1:    // **************************************************
2:    // PROGRAM:   diskmgr
3:    // FILE:      diskmgr.cpp
4:    // PURPOSE:   provide i/o for btree
5:    // NOTES:
6:    // AUTHOR:    Jesse Liberty (jl)
7:    // REVISIONS: 11/5/94 1.0 jl   initial release
8:    // **************************************************
9:
10:       #include "btree.hpp"
11:       #include <assert.h>
12:
13:       // on construction, try to open the file if it exists
14:       DiskManager::DiskManager():
15:          myFile("ROBIN.IDX",ios::binary ¦ ios::in ¦ ios::out ¦ ios::nocreate)
16:       {
17:          // initialize the pointers to null
18:          for (int i = 0; i< MaxPages; i++)
19:             myPages[i] = 0;
20:          myCount = 0;
21:
22:       }
23:
24:       // called by btree constructor
25:       // if we opened the file, read in the numbers we need
26:       // otherwise create the file
27:       int DiskManager::Create()
28:       {
29:          if (!myFile) // nocreate failed, first creation
30:          {
31:             // open the file, create it this time
32:             myFile.open("ROBIN.IDX",ios::binary ¦ ios::in ¦ ios::out);
33:
34:             char Header[PageSize];
35:             int MagicNumber = 1234; // a number we can check for
36:             memcpy(Header,&MagicNumber,2);
37:             int NextPage = 1;
38:             memcpy(Header+2,&NextPage,2);
39:             memcpy(Header+4,&NextPage,2);
40:             Page::SetgPageNumber(NextPage);
41:             char title[]="ROBIN.IDX. Ver 1.00";
42:             memcpy(Header+6,title,strlen(title));
43:             myFile.flush();
44:             myFile.clear();
45:             myFile.seekp(0);
46:             myFile.write(Header,PageSize);
47:             return 0;
48:          }
```

continues

319

Listing 12.4 continued

```
49:
50:          // we did open the file, it already existed
51:          // get the numbers we need
52:          int MagicNumber;
53:          myFile.seekg(0);
54:          myFile.read((char *) &MagicNumber,2);
55:
56:          // check the magic number. If it is wrong the file is
57:          // corrupt or this isn't the index file
58:          if (MagicNumber != 1234)
59:          {
60:              // change to an exception!!
61:              cout << "Index Magic number failed!";
62:              return 0;
63:          }
64:
65:          int NextPage;
66:          myFile.seekg(2);
67:          myFile.read((char*) &NextPage,2);
68:          Page::SetgPageNumber(NextPage);
69:          int FirstPage;
70:          myFile.seekg(4);
71:          myFile.read((char*) &FirstPage,2);
72:          const int room =  PageSize — 6;
73:          char buffer[room];
74:          myFile.read(buffer,room);
75:          buffer[room]='\0';
76:          cout << buffer << endl;
77:          // read in all the pages
78:          for (int i = 1; i < NextPage; i++)
79:          {
80:              myFile.seekg(i * PageSize);
81:              char buffer[PageSize];
82:              myFile.read( buffer, PageSize);
83:              Page * pg = new Page(buffer);
84:              Insert(pg);
85:          }
86:
87:          return FirstPage;
88:      }
89:
90:      // write out the numbers we'll need next time
91:      void DiskManager::Close(int theRoot)
92:      {
93:
94:          for (int i = 0; i< MaxPages; i++)
95:              if (myPages[i])
96:                  Save(myPages[i]);
97:          int NextPage = Page::GetgPageNumber();
98:          if (!myFile)
99:              cout << "Error opening myFile!" << endl;
100:          myFile.flush();
101:          myFile.clear();
102:          myFile.seekp(2);
103:          myFile.write ( (char *) &NextPage,2);
```

```
104:          myFile.seekp(4);
105:          myFile.write((char*) &theRoot,2);
106:          myFile.close();
107:      }
108:
109:      // wrapper function
110:      int DiskManager::NewPage(Index& index, int bLeaf)
111:      {
112:          Page * newPage = new Page(index, bLeaf);
113:          Insert(newPage);
114:          Save(newPage);
115:          return newPage->GetPageNumber();
116:      }
117:
118:      int DiskManager::NewPage(
119:          Index *array,
120:          long offset,
121:          int leaf,
122:          int count)
123:      {
124:          Page * newPage = new Page(array, offset, leaf,count);
125:          Insert(newPage);
126:          Save(newPage);
127:          return newPage->GetPageNumber();
128:      }
129:
130:      void DiskManager::Insert(Page * newPage)
131:      {
132:
133:          // add new page into array of page managers
134:          if (myCount < MaxPages)
135:          {
136:              assert(!myPages[myCount]);
137:              myPages[myCount++] = newPage;
138:          }
139:          else  // no room, time to page out to disk
140:          {
141:              int lowest = 0;
142:              for (int i = 0; i< MaxPages; i++)
143:                  if (myPages[i]->GetTime() < myPages[lowest]->GetTime())
144:                      lowest = i;
145:              Save(myPages[lowest]);
146:              delete myPages[lowest];
147:              myPages[lowest] = newPage;
148:          }
149:      }
150:
151:      // tell the page to write itself out
152:      void DiskManager::Save(Page* pg)
153:      {
154:        pg->Write(myFile);
155:      }
156:
157:      // see if the page is in memory, if so return it
158:      // otherwise get it from disk
```

12

continues

Listing 12.4 continued

```
159:
160:     Page * DiskManager::GetPage(int target)
161:     {
162:
163:         for (int i = 0; i< MaxPages; i++)
164:         {
165:             if (myPages[i]->GetPageNumber() == target)
166:                 return  myPages[i];
167:         }
168:         myFile.seekg(target * PageSize);
169:         char buffer[PageSize];
170:         myFile.read( buffer, PageSize);
171:         Page * pg = new Page(buffer);
172:         Insert(pg);
173:         return pg;
174:     }
```

Type

Listing 12.5 Index.cpp

```
1:      // ***************************************************
2:      // PROGRAM:   index
3:      // FILE:      index.cpp
4:      // PURPOSE:   provide fundamental btree functionality
5:      // NOTES:
6:      // AUTHOR:    Jesse Liberty (jl)
7:      // REVISIONS: 11/1/94 1.0 jl  initial release
8:      // ***************************************************
9:
10:     #include "btree.hpp"
11:     #include <ctype.h>
12:
13:     Index::Index(char* str):myPointer(1)
14:     {
15:         strncpy(myData,str,dataLen);
16:         myData[dataLen]='\0';
17:     }
18:
19:     Index::Index(char* str, int ptr):myPointer(ptr)
20:     {
21:
22:         strncpy(myData,str,dataLen);
23:         myData[dataLen]='\0';
24:     }
25:
26:     Index::Index(Index& rhs):
27:         myPointer(rhs.GetPointer())
28:     {
29:         strcpy(myData, rhs.GetData());
30:     }
31:
32:     Index::Index():myPointer(0)
33:     {
34:         myData[0]='\0';
```

```
35:    }
36:
37:    void Index::PrintKey()
38:    {
39:        cout << "  " << myData;
40:    }
41:
42:    void Index::PrintPage()
43:    {
44:        cout << "\n" << myData << ": " ;
45:        BTree::theDiskManager.GetPage(myPointer)->Print();
46:    }
47:
48:    int Index::Insert(Index& ref, int findOnly)
49:    {
50:        return BTree::theDiskManager.GetPage(myPointer)->Insert(ref,findOnly);
51:    }
52:
53:    int Index::operator==(const Index& rhs) const
54:    {
55:        int len1 = strlen(myData);
56:        int len2 = strlen(rhs.GetData());
57:        char w1[PageSize];
58:        char w2[PageSize];
59:        for (int i = 0; i<len1; i++)
60:            w1[i] = toupper(myData[i]);
61:        for (i = 0; i<len2; i++)
62:            w2[i] = toupper(rhs.GetData()[i]);
63:        w1[len1] = '\0';
64:        w2[len2]='\0';
65:        return (strcmp(w1,w2) == 0);
66:    }
```

12

Type **Listing 12.6 Page.cpp**

```
1:    // ****************************************************
2:    // PROGRAM:   Page
3:    // FILE:      Page.cpp
4:    // PURPOSE:   provide fundamental btree functionality
5:    // NOTES:
6:    // AUTHOR:    Jesse Liberty (jl)
7:    // REVISIONS: 11/1/94 1.0 jl  initial release
8:    // ****************************************************
9:
10:    #include "btree.hpp"
11:    #include <assert.h>
12:    #include <values.h>
13:
14:    // constructors
15:
16:    // default constructor
17:    Page::Page()
18:    {
```

continues

Listing 12.6 continued

```
19:      }
20:
21:      // create a page from a buffer read in from disk
22:      Page::Page(char *buffer):
23:          myKeys((Index*)myVars.mk)
24:      {
25:          assert(sizeof(myBlock) == PageSize);
26:          assert(sizeof(myVars) == PageSize);
27:          memcpy(&myBlock,buffer,PageSize);
28:          myTime = time(NULL);
29:      }
30:
31:      // create a Page from the first index
32:      Page::Page(Index& index, int bLeaf):
33:          myKeys((Index*)myVars.mk)
34:      {
35:
36:          myVars.myCount=1;
37:          myVars.IsLeaf = bLeaf;
38:          // if this is a leaf, this is the first
39:          // index on the first page, set its pointer
40:          // based on creating a new wnj. otherwise
41:          // you are here creating a new node, do not
42:          // set the pointer, it is already set.
43:          if (bLeaf)
44:              index.SetPointer(BTree::theWNJFile.Append(index.GetPointer()));
45:          myKeys[0]=index;
46:          myVars.myPageNumber = gPage++;
47:          myTime = time(NULL);
48:      }
49:
50:      // create a page by splitting another page
51:      Page::Page(Index *array, long offset, int bLeaf,int count):
52:          myKeys((Index*)myVars.mk)
53:      {
54:          myVars.IsLeaf = bLeaf;
55:          myVars.myCount = 0;
56:          assert (offset < MAXINT);
57:          int i = 0;
58:          int j = (int) offset;
59:          for (; j<Order && i < count; i++, j++)
60:          {
61:              myKeys[i]= array[j];
62:              myVars.myCount++;
63:          }
64:          myVars.myPageNumber = gPage++;
65:          myTime = time(NULL);
66:      }
67:
68:      void Page::Nullify(long offset)
69:      {
70:           assert (offset < MAXINT);
71:          for (int i = (int)offset; i<Order; i++)
72:          {
73:                  myKeys[i].SetPointer(0);
```

```
74:                   myVars.myCount--;
75:            }
76:      }
77:
78:      // decide whether I'm a leaf or a node
79:      // and pass this index to the right
80:      // function. If findOnly is true, don't insert
81:      // just return the page number (for now)
82:      int Page::Insert(Index& rIndex, int findOnly)
83:      {
84:         if (myVars.IsLeaf)
85:            return   FindLeaf(rIndex,findOnly);
86:         else
87:            return InsertNode(rIndex,findOnly);
88:      }
89:
90:
91:      // find the right page for this index
92:      int Page::InsertNode(Index& rIndex, int findOnly)
93:      {
94:         int retVal =0;
95:         int inserted = FALSE;
96:         int i,j;
97:
98:         assert(myVars.myCount>0); // nodes have at least 1
99:         assert(myKeys[0].GetPointer()); // must be valid
100:
101:        // does it go before my first entry?
102:        if (rIndex < myKeys[0])
103:        {
104:           if (findOnly)
105:              return 0L; // not found
106:
107:           myKeys[0].SetData(rIndex);
108:           retVal=myKeys[0].Insert(rIndex);
109:           inserted = TRUE;
110:        }
111:
112:        // does it go after my last?
113:        if (!inserted)
114:           for (i = myVars.myCount-1; i>=0; i--)
115:           {
116:              assert(myKeys[i].GetPointer());
117:              if (rIndex >= myKeys[i])
118:              {
119:                 retVal=myKeys[i].Insert(rIndex,findOnly);
120:                 inserted = TRUE;
121:                 break;
122:              }
123:           }
124:
125:        // find where it does go
126:        if (!inserted)
127:           for (j = 0; j<i && j+1 < myVars.myCount; j++)
128:              {
```

continues

Listing 12.6 continued

```
129:                assert(myKeys[j+1].GetPointer());
130:                if (rIndex < myKeys[j+1])
131:                {
132:                    retVal=myKeys[j].Insert(rIndex,findOnly);
133:                    inserted = TRUE;
134:                    break;
135:                }
136:            }
137:
138:        assert(inserted);   // change to exception if not!
139:
140:        // if you had to split
141:        if (retVal && !findOnly) // got back a pointer to a new page
142:        {
143:            Index * pIndex = new Index(GetPage(retVal)->GetFirstIndex());
144:            pIndex->SetPointer(retVal);
145:            retVal = InsertLeaf(*pIndex);
146:        }
147:        return retVal;
148:    }
149:
150:    // called if current page is a leaf
151:    int Page::FindLeaf(Index& rIndex, int findOnly)
152:    {
153:        int result = 0;
154:
155:        // no duplicates!
156:        for (int i=0; i < myVars.myCount; i++)
157:            if (rIndex == myKeys[i])
158:            {
159:                if (findOnly)              // return first WNJ
160:                    //return BTree::theWNJFile.Find(myKeys[i].GetPointer());
161:                    return myKeys[i].GetPointer();
162:                else
163:                    return BTree::theWNJFile.Insert(
164:                            rIndex.GetPointer(),
165:                                myKeys[i].GetPointer());
166:            }
167:
168:        if (findOnly)           // not found
169:            return result;
170:
171:        // this index item does not yet exist
172:        // before you push it into the index
173:        // push an entry into the wnj.idx
174:        // and set the index to point to that entry
175:        rIndex.SetPointer(BTree::theWNJFile.Append(rIndex.GetPointer())); //
            new!
176:        return InsertLeaf(rIndex);
177:    }
178:
179:    int Page::InsertLeaf(Index& rIndex)
180:    {
181:        int result = 0;
182:        if (myVars.myCount < Order)
```

```
183:            Push(rIndex);
184:        else        // overflow the page
185:        {
186:            // make sibling
187:            int NewPg =
188:                NewPage(myKeys,Order/2,myVars.IsLeaf,myVars.myCount);
189:            Page* Sibling = GetPage(NewPg);
190:            Nullify(Order/2);                          // nullify my right half
191:
192:            // does it fit in this side?
193:            if (myVars.myCount>Order/2-1 && rIndex <= myKeys[Order/2-1])
194:                Push(rIndex);
195:            else   // push it into the new sibling
196:                Sibling->Push(rIndex);
197:
198:            result = NewPg; // we split, pass it up
199:        }
200:      return result;
201:    }
202:
203:    // put the new index into this page (in order)
204:    void Page::Push(Index& rIndex,long offset,int first)
205:    {
206:        int inserted = FALSE;
207:        assert(myVars.myCount < Order);
208:        assert (offset < MAXINT);
209:
210:        for (int i=(int)offset; i<Order && i<myVars.myCount; i++)
211:        {
212:            assert(myKeys[i].GetPointer());
213:            if (rIndex <= myKeys[i])
214:            {
215:                Push(myKeys[i],offset+1,FALSE);
216:                myKeys[i]=rIndex;
217:                inserted = TRUE;
218:                break;
219:            }
220:        }
221:        if (!inserted)
222:            myKeys[myVars.myCount] = rIndex;
223:
224:        if (first)
225:            myVars.myCount++;
226:    }
227:
228:
229:    void Page::Print()
230:    {
231:        if (!myVars.IsLeaf)
232:        {
233:            BTree::NodePageCtr++;
234:            BTree::NodeIndexPerPage[myVars.myCount]++;
235:            BTree::NodeIndexCtr+=myVars.myCount;
236:        }
237:        else
```

continues

Listing 12.6 continued

```
238:          {
239:              BTree::LeafPageCtr++;
240:              BTree::LeafIndexPerPage[myVars.myCount]++;
241:              BTree::LeafIndexCtr+=myVars.myCount;
242:          }
243:
244:          for (int i = 0; i<Order && i < myVars.myCount; i++)
245:          {
246:              assert(myKeys[i].GetPointer());
247:              if (myVars.IsLeaf)
248:                  myKeys[i].PrintKey();
249:              else
250:                  myKeys[i].PrintPage();
251:          }
252:      }
253:
254:      // write out the entire page as a block
255:      fstream& Page::Write(fstream& file)
256:      {
257:          char buffer[PageSize];
258:          memcpy(buffer,&myBlock,PageSize);
259:          file.flush();
260:          file.clear();
261:          file.seekp(myVars.myPageNumber*PageSize);
262:          file.write(buffer,PageSize);
263:          return file;
264:      }
```

Type **Listing 12.7 WNJFile.cpp**

```
1:       // **************************************************
2:       // PROGRAM:   WNJ file
3:       // FILE:      WNJfile.cpp
4:       // PURPOSE:   Cross index from key to datafile
5:       // NOTES:
6:       // AUTHOR:    Jesse Liberty (jl)
7:       // REVISIONS: 11/5/94 1.0 jl  initial release
8:       // **************************************************
9:
10:      #include "btree.hpp"
11:      #include <assert.h>
12:
13:      // on construction, try to open the file if it exists
14:      WNJFile::WNJFile():
15:          myFile("ROBINWNJ.IDX",
16:          ios::binary | ios::in | ios::out | ios::nocreate)
17:      {
18:          for (int i = 0; i<WNJSize; i++)
19:              myInts[i]=0L;
20:      }
21:
22:      void WNJFile::Create()
23:      {
```

```
24:         char Header[8];
25:         int MagicNumber=0; // a number we can check for
26:         int zero = 0;
27:
28:         if (!myFile) // nocreate failed, first creation
29:         {
30:             // open the file, create it this time
31:             myFile.clear();
32:             myFile.open("ROBINWNJ.IDX",
33:                 ios::binary ¦ ios::in ¦ ios::out);
34:
35:             MagicNumber = 1234;
36:             memcpy(Header,&MagicNumber,2);
37:             memcpy(Header+2,&zero,2);
38:             myFile.seekp(0);
39:             myFile.write(Header,4);
40:             myFile.flush();
41:             return;
42:         }
43:
44:         // we did open the file, it already existed
45:         // get the numbers we need
46:
47:
48:         myFile.seekg(0);
49:         myFile.read(Header,4);
50:         memcpy(&MagicNumber,Header,2);
51:         memcpy(&myCount,Header+2,2);
52:
53:         // check the magic number. If it is wrong the file is
54:         // corrupt or this isn't the index file
55:         if (MagicNumber != 1234)
56:         {
57:                 // change to an exception!!
58:                 cout << "WNJ Magic number failed!";
59:                 cout << "Magic number: " << MagicNumber;
60:                 cout << "\nmyCount: " << myCount << endl;
61:         }
62:         return;
63:     }
64:
65:     // write out the numbers we'll need next time
66:     void WNJFile::Close()
67:     {
68:         myFile.seekg(2);
69:         myFile.write((char*)&myCount,2);
70:         myFile.close();
71:     }
72:
73:     int WNJFile::Append(int DataOffset)
74:     {
75:
76:         int newPos = 4 + myCount++ * (WNJSize*SizePointer);
77:         int offsets[WNJSize];
78:         offsets[0] = DataOffset;
```

continues

Listing 12.7 continued

```
79:            for (int i = 1; i<WNJSize; i++)
80:                offsets[i]=0;
81:            myFile.seekg(newPos);
82:            myFile.write((char*)offsets,WNJSize*SizePointer);
83:
84:            return newPos;
85:        }
86:
87:
88:        int WNJFile::Insert(int DataOffset,int WNJOffset)
89:        {
90:            int ints[WNJSize];
91:            myFile.seekg(WNJOffset);
92:            myFile.read((char*)ints,WNJSize*SizePointer);
93:
94:            int offset=WNJOffset;
95:
96:            while (ints[WNJSize-1])
97:            {
98:                offset = ints[WNJSize-1];
99:                myFile.clear();
100:                myFile.flush();
101:                myFile.seekg(ints[WNJSize-1]);
102:                myFile.read((char*)ints,WNJSize*SizePointer);
103:            }
104:            if (ints[WNJSize-2]) // full!
105:            {
106:                ints[WNJSize-1] = Append(DataOffset);
107:                myFile.clear();
108:                myFile.flush();
109:                myFile.seekg(offset);
110:                myFile.write((char*)ints,WNJSize*SizePointer);
111:            }
112:            else
113:            {
114:                for (int i = 0; i<WNJSize-1; i++)
115:                {
116:                    if (ints[i] == 0)
117:                    {
118:                        ints[i] = DataOffset;
119:                        myFile.clear();
120:                        myFile.flush();
121:                        myFile.seekg(offset);
122:                        myFile.write((char*)ints,WNJSize*SizePointer);
123:                        break;
124:                    }
125:                }
126:            }
127:            return 0;
128:        }
129:
130:
131:        int* WNJFile::Find(int NextWNJ)
132:        {
133:            int ints[WNJSize];
```

```
134:            int * results = new int[PageSize];
135:
136:            int i = 0, j=0;
137:
138:            while (j<PageSize)
139:                results[j++] = 0;
140:
141:            j = 0;
142:
143:            myFile.seekg(NextWNJ);
144:            myFile.read((char*)ints, WNJSize*SizePointer);
145:            while (j < PageSize)
146:            {
147:                if (ints[i])
148:                {
149:                    if (i == WNJSize-1)
150:                    {
151:                        myFile.seekg(ints[WNJSize-1]);
152:                        myFile.read((char*)ints,WNJSize*2);
153:                        i = 0;
154:                        continue;
155:                    }
156:                results[j++] = ints[i++];
157:                }
158:                else
159:                    break;
160:            }
161:        return results;
162:    }
```

Type Listing 12.8 Driver.cpp

12

```
1:    #include "String.hpp"
2:    #include "stdef.hpp"
3:    #include "btree.hpp"
4:    DiskManager BTree::theDiskManager;
5:    DataFile BTree::theDataFile;
6:    WNJFile BTree::theWNJFile;
7:
8:    int WNJFile::myCount=0L;
9:    int Page::gPage=1;
10:    int BTree::NodeIndexCtr=0;
11:    int BTree::LeafIndexCtr=0;
12:    int BTree::NodePageCtr=0;
13:    int BTree::LeafPageCtr=0;
14:    int BTree::NodeIndexPerPage[Order+1];
15:    int BTree::LeafIndexPerPage[Order+1];
16:
17:    int main(int argc, char ** argv)
18:    {
19:        BTree myTree;
20:
21:        for (int i = 0; i < Order +2; i++)
```

continues

Listing 12.8 continued

```
22:        {
23:            BTree::NodeIndexPerPage[i] =0;
24:            BTree::LeafIndexPerPage[i] = 0;
25:        }
26:
27:        char buffer[PageSize+1];
28:
29:        for (;;)
30:        {
31:            cout << "Enter a string (blank to stop): ";
32:            cin.getline(buffer,PageSize);
33:            // cin.ignore(PageSize,'\n');
34:            if (buffer[0])
35:                myTree.Insert(buffer);
36:            else
37:                break;
38:        }
39:
40:        for (;;)
41:        {
42:            cout << "Find: ";
43:            cin.getline(buffer,255);
44:            if (buffer[0])
45:            {
46:                    int offset = myTree.Find(buffer);
47:                    if (offset)
48:                    {
49:                        int* found  =  BTree::theWNJFile.Find(offset);
50:                        int i=0;
51:                        int len;
52:                        time_t theTime;
53:                        char buffer[512];
54:                        while (found[i])
55:                        {
56:                            BTree::theDataFile.GetRecord(found[i],buffer);
57:                            struct tm * ts = localtime(&theTime);
58:                            cout << "Found: ";
59:                            cout << ts->tm_mon << "/";
60:                            cout << ts->tm_mday << "/";
61:                            cout << ts->tm_year << " ";
62:                            cout <<  buffer << endl;
63:                            i++;
64:                        }
65:                        delete [] found;
66:                    }
67:            }
68:            else
69:                break;
70:        }
71:
72:        myTree.PrintTree();
73:
74:
75:        return 0;
76:    }
```

```
d:\day12>ROBIN
Enter a string (blank to stop): Computer: 486 33MHZ 16MB RAM
Enter a string (blank to stop): Remember to buy more RAM
Enter a string (blank to stop): The show is at noon.
Enter a string (blank to stop): Once more into the breach
Enter a string (blank to stop):
Find: more
Found: 10/25/94 Remember to buy more RAM
Found: 10/25/94 Once more into the breach
Find:
  16MB   33MHZ   486   Computer   Once   RAM   Remember   The   breach   buy   into
  more
 noon   show

Stats:
Node pages:    0
Leaf pages:    1
Node indexes: 0
Leaf indexes: 14
Pages with 14 leaves: 1

d:\day12>type ROBIN.DAT
-:·  ·   /°+.Computer: 486 33MHZ 16MB RAM·   3°+.Remember to buy more RAM·
                                             6°+.
The show is at noon·   ;°+.Once more into the breach
```

The first and most significant change is the addition of a data file and a WNJFile. The data file is named ROBIN.DAT and is opened much as the other files have been. However, this time the `ios:app` flag is used to indicate that the file should be opened in *append* mode. When a file is opened in append mode, all writes are to the end of the file, regardless of where the `tellp()` and `tellg()` flags are positioned.

The `Insert()` method, shown in line 64 of listing 12.2, could have been as simple as the `write()` shown in line 75, were it not that you need to know the offset in the file at which the text is written. Because the `write()` does not move the `tellp()` pointer, you must do so explicitly. The goal is to move to the end of the file *before* doing the write, so that you can note where the write starts (which becomes the offset of the string in the file).

The call to `seekp()` in line 73 takes two parameters. The second parameter is `ios::end`, which indicates that the pointer is to move to the end and then move back as many bytes as indicated by the first parameter. Because the first parameter is 0, this moves no bytes from the end of the file, and that value is stashed away in the local variable, `offset`.

It is this value, the offset of the string written to the DAT file, that is stored in the WNJFile index array.

To test the changes to the database, a new, temporary interface has been put into place. Instead of reading the command line, the driver program prompts repeatedly for new notes. Four notes are entered, and when a blank note is entered, the program prompts for a string for which to search.

Note that the word more appears only once in the index, but refers to two notes. The statistics show that no nodes have been created yet, because this is an order 31 B-tree and only 14 indexed values have been found. Note also that each note is prefaced by 8 bytes of binary information—the length of the note and the date.

The driver program, shown in listing 12.8, begins by defining the three static members: BTree::theDiskManager, BTree::theDataFile, and BTree::theWNJFile. It initializes the static counter variables: BTree::NodeIndexCtr, BTree::LeafIndexCtr, BTree::NodePageCtr, BTree::LeafPageCtr, BTree::NodeIndexPerPage, and BTree::LeafIndexPerPage.

The user is prompted repeatedly for notes in lines 31 through 38, and each note is inserted into the tree in line 35. In line 42, the user is prompted for a string to find, and that string is passed to the tree in line 46. If an index into the WNJ (Word-Node-Join) file is returned, that index is used in line 49 to access the WNJ array of records. For each record, the actual note is retrieved from the data file in line 56. The 4-byte time value is passed to the standard library's localtime() function, and a pointer to a time structure is returned, which is used to print the time in lines 58 through 61.

The most significant change in this version of the program is the addition of the Word-Node-Join index, as shown in listing 12.7. Note that in this preliminary version, the value 5 is hard coded for WNJSize, but in a release version, you would want to make this configurable.

The logic of the Insert() operation is to check whether the current array has a value in its last entry (WNJSize-1). If so, that is a pointer to the next array of WNJ entries. You chase these linked arrays until you find one where WNJSize-1 is empty. At that point, it is time to insert a new value.

If the next to last (WNJSize-2) already is occupied, you must create a new array and link it into place, as shown in lines 105 through 112. Otherwise, you can add the new data offset right into the first available slot, as shown in lines 113 through 126.

Finding a WNJFile record is the inverse operation, as shown in lines 132 through 162. You chase each record, adding it to the results array, and then return that array to the calling function.

Note that the *calling* function will delete the array after it finishes displaying the results (line 65 of the driver program). Note also that because this is an *array* of pointers, you must use the bracket operator with delete.

Summary

Today you learned how to create data files and to connect keys to multiple notes. You created a word-node-join record, which provided the necessary level of abstraction to allow a single key to point to multiple notes. Rather than attempting to create fixed-length records, which would

have been overly restrictive and wasteful of disk space, you recorded the length of each record in the index.

You then added a number of small but important features, including eliminating case sensitivity. This chapter represents the final code for the first version of the ROBIN Personal Information Management Utility.

Q&A

Q **The entire text of each key is stored in the index file. Why doesn't it just point to an instance of the word in the data file?**

A It is true that there is a data size cost to storing a copy of the key in the index file, but with today's computers, it is almost always the right choice. First of all, hard disk space currently is very cheap. You easily could store a copy of every English word that exists on most hard disks. Second, disk speeds still are relatively slow, as compared to processor speeds. If you were to put just a pointer to the word on the disk in the index rather than the word itself, this would mean that every comparison of a key would cost one more disk access. This is far too expensive. Finally, the version of the word in the data file has not been normalized to all uppercase for easy comparison. You would have to convert it each time it is used.

Q **Why bother with a Word-Node-Join? Why not just search for multiple-index entries?**

A Once again, the goal is to reduce the number of disk reads, because reading data from the disk is typically the slowest part of a database program.

Q **Why not create a WNJ node with 100 slots and save the bother of having the last slot point to the next record?**

A Most nodes will point only to a small number of records; 100 slots would waste a lot of disk space. Some words, however, will point to literally hundreds of notes, and it would be too restrictive to simply "run out" of nodes. The short answer is that any number large enough to avoid overrunning the limit would be very wasteful for most records.

Workshop

The Workshop provides quiz questions to help you solidify your understanding of the material covered, and exercises to provide you with experience in using what you have learned. Try to answer the quiz and exercise questions before checking the answers in Appendix A, and make sure that you understand the answers before continuing to the next chapter.

Quiz

1. What is the most expensive operation in a database?

2. What is the purpose of the Word-Node-Join?

3. Why did we eliminate case sensitivity?

4. Why not store the records all in uppercase?

Exercises

In ROBIN, we do some very simple parsing. In this set of exercises, you tackle a harder parsing challenge—mathematical expressions. For example, look at the following expression:

```
Expression:=
    Number ¦
    UnaryOperator Expression ¦
    ( Expression BinaryOperator Expression )
```

This is a Bacchus-Naur form of the sort of mathematical expressions that we are going to be able to parse. To read this, you need to know that the symbol := means *is defined as*, and | means *or*.

The statement shown here means *Expression is defined as a number, or a UnaryOperator followed by an Expression, or an open parenthesis followed by an Expression followed by a BinaryOperator followed by another Expression followed by a close parenthesis.* (We're going to require the parentheses in order to simplify our task.) The entire Bacchus-Naur definition follows.

Although it seems crazy to use the term *Expression* in its own definition, this actually makes sense when you think about mathematical expressions. After you make appropriate definitions of Number, UnaryOperation, and BinaryOperation, you can treat all of these as legal Expressions:

```
        2
        (7 + 8)
        (-1 * (((15 + 3) / (9 * -2)) - 1))

Expression:=
    Number ¦
    UnaryOperator Expression ¦
    ( Expression BinaryOperator Expression )

Digit :=
    0 ¦ 1 ¦ 2 ¦ 3 ¦ 4 ¦ 5 ¦ 6 ¦ 7 ¦ 8 ¦ 9

Number :=
    Digit ¦
    Number<adjoining>Digit
        where the resulting number is assigned
        the value of Number * 10 + Digit

UnaryOperator :=
    - ¦ ~
        which mean, respectively:  negate, complement
```

```
BinaryOperator :=
   + | - | * | / | & | | | ^
       where these mean, respectively:  add, subtract,
       multiply, divide, Boolean and, Boolean or,
       Boolean exclusive or
```

1. Create two of the classes: `Expression` and `UnaryOperation`. The class `Expression` should be the parent of the other three classes. (Note that a unary operation IS-A expression.) The class `Expression` should define a pure virtual function `GetValue`, which its child classes will override. Of course, also fill out the classes with the other methods and data members they need in order to be complete.

2. Before trying question 2, be sure to review the answer to question 1 and make sure that you fully understand it. Then, have your program add the classes `Number` and `BinaryOperation`.

3. Write a test program to test these classes. It should just create some instances of the classes manually. Think about the tree that you are building with the binary and unary operations.

4. Write a class `Tokenizer`, which accepts an input stream and an output stream. It should provide an interface to enable its callers to read tokens out of the input stream, skipping over white space. (Note that we have defined our expressions so that all tokens are single characters. This is why we broke `Number` down into individual digits.) All characters from the input stream should be echoed to the output stream (including white space) when they are accepted by the caller or skipped over.

   The class also should provide the capability for a caller to peek at the next token without removing it from the stream. Peeking at a token should not cause it to be echoed (although any white space skipped over to get to the token should cause that space to be echoed).

   The tokenizer also should have a flag to turn off echoing.

5. Write a set of Parse functions: `Parse`, `ParseNumber`, `ParseUnaryOperation`, and `ParseBinaryOperation`. Each of these should accept a Tokenizer and return an Expression *. Parse should peek only at the first token to figure out which of the other functions it should call. The other functions should extract the appropriate pieces from the tokenizer and return the appropriate subclass of expression. For the sub-expressions of the unary and binary operations, you should just call Parse! (These functions sound much harder than they really are.)

Write a test program to make sure that your functions work. Your program should accept legal expressions from cin, echo them back out, and output " = " and the expression's value. The test program should repeat this process until it reaches the end of the file.

13

ROBIN, V.1

The program is almost ready for your first release. You are, by now, eager to get an early version of the program into the hands of some "friendly users" who will help you test not only the robustness of the code, but the concept itself. There are just a few changes left to make to ensure that the program is usable. Today you will learn

- ☐ Testing your program for commercial release
- ☐ What alpha and beta testing are and why they are important
- ☐ What the final touches are on ROBIN and how to add them

Testing Your Program

In a real commercial release, there are a number of very important steps between finishing your program and shipping it to your customers. Typically, you would want the program extensively tested: first by yourself, then by a quality assurance team, and finally by friendly users.

After you have thoroughly tested the program, you will pass it to a professional quality assurance engineer, whose job it is to find those bugs you simply cannot find. This is a profession unto itself, with a specific intellectual discipline. If you don't have access to a QA engineer, however, you can get at least some of the benefits of QA testing by having someone *other than you* use the program for a while. You will want someone who will be forgiving of your bugs, but who also will be thorough at testing the product and detailed in writing down the specific steps that re-create the bug.

After you pass quality assurance, your program is ready for use by friendly users. Friendly users are, typically, divided first into co-workers and friends, and then into people outside your firm who would like a look at a preliminary release. The first group—family, friends, and folks with whom you work—usually are called *alpha testers*, because they see the *alpha*, or first, version of your program.

After your alpha users have had the product for a while, you may want to enter *beta* testing— the second round of testing. In this round, you give your program to people you know less well. They will put up with a few obscure bugs, and report faithfully on what they find, in exchange for an early (and usually free) copy of the program.

You can consider a commercial release only after your program has passed all these hurdles. The usual rule of thumb is that a week or two of QA testing, a month or so of alpha, and a few months of beta will suffice for *most* programs. A particularly simple utility might need less time, and a very complex program might need considerably more time. Programmers call the first release version of their program *gold*, or *shrink-wrap*. Some especially complex programs may go to an extended test of many potential users just before going gold; this often is called *gamma testing*.

Note: The code for ROBIN has been subjected to scrutiny and extensive testing, but nothing like the level of testing that would be appropriate for a commercial program. Remember that the code provided is for illustration purposes only, and treat this program like a beta release; do not assume that it is 100 percent bug free.

Finishing ROBIN, V.1

The program, as you left it on day 12, has almost all the functionality promised for your first release. You just need to add a driver program that reads the command line and takes the appropriate action. In the version shown today, the user may type **ROBIN**, followed by text to enter or by one of three flags:

☐ –? Search for text

☐ –! Display statistics

☐ –F Read a file and parse each line

In this version of the program, none of this functionality—reading the command line, parsing the commands, reading in an input file, and so on—is part of the class structure. All this is done in v1.cpp, a collection of small functions wrapped around the classes created in previous days.

Locking the Pages

One nasty bug waiting to happen for all these days has been the possibility that a page will be swapped out of memory by the index manager while still in use due to the recursion in the insertion methods. This has not been a problem when adding small records, but now that you will have the capability to add hundreds of records from a file, you will need to protect against this problem.

A careful examination of the code as it currently exists shows that the only time a page is deleted from memory is when the index manager is inserting a new page. New pages are inserted only during the recursive `Insert()` call. Thus, if you can lock a page when you call `Insert()` and unlock it when you finish that call, you should be safe.

A simple approach to this is to create a flag in `Page` and check that flag before removing the page from memory. Until now, I have not used the `lastKey` member variable, so I have renamed it `IsLocked` and I'll use that as the flag. Because this is private member data, accessor methods have been created to set and obtain the status of this lock.

13

Note carefully that in most applications a simple Boolean flag such as this will *not* be sufficient. If more than one function could lock or unlock the same page, you would be in danger of item 1 locking page 5, item 2 locking it as well, and then item 1 unlocking it and thereby losing the lock from item 2! Because there is only one source of a lock in the current case, a Boolean is quite safe, however.

Displaying Results

The specification calls for displaying a list of all notes that match the search criteria. I truncate the display so that the list stays orderly and neat. What is displayed is a menu of numbered choices and the first few letters from each note.

After the user presses the number next to the note, the entire note is displayed and the menu of choices is redisplayed. In a graphical environment, you might put the menu of choices into a list box and have a viewer display the contents of the highlighted note.

For purposes of keeping the code simple and the results readable, I restrict the set of matches to the first 20 found, but this is entirely arbitrary. In a later version of ROBIN, you may want to allow the user to page through these results.

Exercising the Program

After you use the program for a while, create a large text file and feed it to ROBIN using the – F flag. This will load in hundreds of keys and dozens of notes and give you a chance to examine the performance and reliability of the program under "load." I read in the entire text for day 12, and produced the output shown after the following listings, along with the ancillary functions as described earlier.

Listing 13.1   Btree.hpp

Listing 13.2   Btree.cpp

Listing 13.3   Datafile.cpp

Listing 13.4   IDXMgr.cpp

Listing 13.5   Index.cpp

Listing 13.6   Page.cpp

Listing 13.7   WNJFile.cpp

Listing 13.8   The driver program, R1.cpp

Listing 13.1 Btree.hpp

```
1:    // ****************************************************
2:    // PROGRAM:  Btree, Page and Index declarations
```

```
3:        // FILE:     btree.hpp
4:        // PURPOSE:   provide fundamental btree functionality
5:        // NOTES:
6:        // AUTHOR:    Jesse Liberty (jl)
7:        // REVISIONS: 11/1/94 1.0 jl  initial release
8:        // ****************************************************
9:        #ifndef BTREE_HPP                      // inclusion guards
10:       #define BTREE_HPP
11:
12:       #include <time.h>
13:       #include <string.h>
14:       #include <fstream.h>
15:
16:       #include "stdef.hpp"
17:
18:       const int Order =        31;  // 31 indexes and 1 header
19:       const int dataLen =      11; // length of a key
20:       const int MaxPages =     10; // more than we need
21:       const int SizeItem =     16;  // key + offset
22:       const int SizePointer = 2; // size of offset
23:       const int PageSize = (Order+1) * SizeItem;
24:
25:       // forward declarations
26:       class Page;
27:       class Index;
28:
29:       class DataFile
30:       {
31:       public:
32:          // constructors & destructor
33:          DataFile();
34:          ~DataFile(){}
35:
36:          // management of files
37:          void Close();
38:          void Create();
39:          void GetRecord(int, char*, int&, time_t&);
40:
41:          int Insert(char *);
42:
43:       private:
44:       fstream myFile;
45:       };
46:
47:       class WNJFile
48:       {
49:       public:
50:          // constructors & destructor
51:          WNJFile();
52:          ~WNJFile(){}
53:
54:          // management of files
55:          void Close();
56:          void Create();
57:          int* Find(int NextWNJ);
```

continues

343

Listing 13.1 continued

```
58:            int Insert(int, int);
59:            int Append(int);
60:
61:        private:
62:        static int myCount;
63:        fstream myFile;
64:        union
65:        {
66:            int myints[5];
67:            char  myArray[5*4];
68:        };
69:     };
70:
71:        // IDXManager - in memory keeps track of what pages are
72:        // already in memory and swaps to disk as required
73:        class IDXManager
74:        {
75:        public:
76:            // constructors & destructor
77:            IDXManager();
78:            ~IDXManager(){}
79:
80:            // management of files
81:            void Close(int);
82:            int Create();
83:
84:            // Page manipulation
85:            Page* GetPage(int);
86:            void SetPage(Page*);
87:            void Insert(Page * newPage);
88:            void Save(Page* pg);
89:            int NewPage(Index&, BOOL);
90:            int NewPage(Index *array, int offset, BOOL leaf, int count);
91:
92:        private:
93:        Page* myPages[MaxPages];
94:        fstream myFile;
95:        int myCount;
96:     };
97:
98:        // the btree itself - has a pointer to first page
99:        class BTree
100:        {
101:        public:
102:            // constructors and destructor
103:            BTree();
104:            ~BTree();
105:
106:            // utility functions
107:            void AddKey(char* data, int offset);
108:            void Insert(char* buffer, int, char**);
109:            void Insert(char*);
110:            void PrintTree();
111:            int Find(char* data);
112:
```

```
113:        // page methods
114:        Page* GetPage(int page)
115:            { return theDiskManager.GetPage(page); }
116:        int NewPage(Index& pIndex, BOOL IsLeaf)
117:            { return theDiskManager.NewPage(pIndex,FALSE); }
118:
119:        static int myAlNum(char ch);
120:        // public static member!
121:        static  IDXManager theDiskManager;
122:        static WNJFile    theWNJFile;
123:        static DataFile theDataFile;
124:        static BOOL GetWord(char*, char*, int&);
125:        static void GetStats();
126:        static int NodeIndexCtr;
127:        static int LeafIndexCtr;
128:        static int NodePageCtr;
129:        static int LeafPageCtr;
130:        static int NodeIndexPerPage[Order+1];
131:        static int LeafIndexPerPage[Order+1];
132:
133:    private:
134:        int myRoot;
135:    };
136:
137:    // index objects point to pages or real data
138:    class Index
139:    {
140:    public:
141:        // constructors & destructor
142:        Index();
143:        Index(char *);
144:        Index (char*, int);
145:        Index(Index&);
146:        ~Index(){}
147:
148:        // accessors
149:        const char * GetData() const  { return myData; }
150:        void SetData(const Index& rhs)
151:            { strcpy(myData,rhs.GetData()); }
152:        void SetData(const char * rhs)
153:            { strcpy(myData,rhs); }
154:        int GetPointer()const { return myPointer; }
155:        void SetPointer (int pg) { myPointer = pg; }
156:
157:        // utility functions
158:        void PrintKey();
159:        void PrintPage();
160:        int Insert(Index& ref,BOOL findOnly = FALSE);
161:
162:        // overloaded operators
163:        int operator==(const Index& rhs);
164:
165:        int operator < (const Index& rhs)
166:         {return strcmp(myData,rhs.GetData())<0;}
167:
```

continues

345

Listing 13.1 continued

```
168:            int operator <= (const Index& rhs)
169:             {return strcmp(myData,rhs.GetData())<=0;}
170:
171:            int operator > (const Index& rhs)
172:             {return strcmp(myData,rhs.GetData())>0;}
173:
174:            int operator >= (const Index& rhs)
175:             {return strcmp(myData,rhs.GetData())>=0;}
176:
177:        public:
178:            int myPointer;
179:            char myData[SizeItem — SizePointer];
180:        };
181:
182:
183:        // pages - consist of header and array of indexes
184:        class Page
185:        {
186:        public:
187:            // constructors and destructor
188:            Page();
189:            Page(char*);
190:            Page(Index&,BOOL);
191:            Page(Index*, int, BOOL, int);
192:            ~Page(){}
193:
194:            // insertion and searchoperations
195:            int Insert(Index&, BOOL findOnly = FALSE);
196:            int Find(Index& idx) { return Insert(idx,TRUE); }
197:            int InsertLeaf(Index&);
198:            int FindLeaf(Index&,BOOL findOnly);
199:            int InsertNode(Index&,BOOL findOnly = FALSE);
200:            void Push(Index&,int offset=0, BOOL=TRUE);
201:
202:            // accessors
203:            Index GetFirstIndex() { return myKeys[0]; }
204:            BOOL GetIsLeaf() const { return myVars.IsLeaf; }
205:            int GetCount() const { return myVars.myCount; }
206:            void SetCount(int cnt) { myVars.myCount=cnt; }
207:            time_t GetTime() { return myTime; }
208:            BOOL GetLocked() { return myVars.IsLocked; }
209:            void SetLocked (BOOL state) { myVars.IsLocked = state; }
210:
211:            // page manipulation
212:            int GetPageNumber() const { return myVars.myPageNumber; }
213:            Page* GetPage(int page)
214:               { return BTree::theDiskManager.GetPage(page); }
215:            int NewPage(Index& rIndex, BOOL IsLeaf)
216:               { return BTree::theDiskManager.NewPage(rIndex,FALSE); }
217:
218:            int NewPage(Index* arr, int off,BOOL isL, int cnt)
219:               { return    BTree::theDiskManager.NewPage(arr,off,isL, cnt); }
220:
221:            // utility functions
222:            void Nullify(int offset);
```

```
223:          void Print();
224:          fstream& Write(fstream&);
225:          void ReCount();
226:
227:          static int GetgPageNumber(){ return gPage; }
228:          static void SetgPageNumber(int pg) { gPage = pg; }
229:
230:     private:
231:          Index * const myKeys; // will point to myVars.mk
232:          union
233:          {
234:              char myBlock[PageSize];    // a page from disk
235:              struct
236:              {
237:                  int myCount;
238:                  BOOL IsLeaf;
239:                  int myPageNumber;
240:                  BOOL IsLocked;
241:                  char overhead[8];
242:                  char mk[Order*sizeof(Index)];  // array of indexes
243:              }myVars;
244:          };
245:
246:          // memory only
247:          static int gPage;
248:          time_t myTime; // for lifo queue
249:     };
250:
251:     #endif
252:
253:
254:
```

Type

Listing 13.2 Btree.cpp

```
1:      // ***************************************************
2:      // PROGRAM:   BTree
3:      // FILE:      btree.cpp
4:      // PURPOSE:   provide fundamental btree functionality
5:      // NOTES:
6:      // AUTHOR:    Jesse Liberty (jl)
7:      // REVISIONS: 11/1/94 1.0 jl  initial release
8:      // ***************************************************
9:
10:     #include "btree.hpp"
11:     #include "stdef.hpp"
12:     #include <ctype.h>
13:     #include <stdlib.h>
14:
15:     // construct the tree
16:     // initialize myRoot pointer to nothing
17:     // either create or read the index file
18:     BTree::BTree():myRoot(0)
```

continues

Listing 13.2 continued

```
19:         {
20:             myRoot = theDiskManager.Create();
21:             theDataFile.Create();
22:             theWNJFile.Create();
23:
24:         }
25:
26:         // write out the index file
27:         BTree::~BTree()
28:         {
29:             theDiskManager.Close(myRoot);
30:             theDataFile.Close();
31:             theWNJFile.Close();
32:         }
33:
34:         // find an existing record
35:         int BTree::Find(char * str)
36:         {
37:             Index index(str);
38:             if (!myRoot)
39:                 return 0L;
40:             else
41:                 return GetPage(myRoot)->Find(index);
42:         }
43:
44:         void BTree::Insert(char * buffer, int argc, char** argv)
45:         {
46:             // get each word,
47:             int offset = theDataFile.Insert(buffer);
48:             for (int i = 1; i<argc; i++)
49:             {
50:                 AddKey(argv[i],offset);
51:             }
52:
53:         }
54:
55:         void BTree::Insert(char* buffer)
56:         {
57:
58:             if (strlen(buffer) < 3)
59:                 return;
60:
61:             char *buff = buffer;
62:             char word[PageSize];
63:             int wordOffset = 0;
64:             int offset;
65:
66:             if (GetWord(buff,word,wordOffset))
67:             {
68:                 offset = theDataFile.Insert(buffer);
69:                 AddKey(word,offset);
70:             }
71:
72:
73:             while (GetWord(buff,word,wordOffset))
```

```
74:           {
75:               AddKey(word,offset);
76:           }
77:
78:       }
79:
80:
81:
82:
83:       void BTree::AddKey(char * str, int offset )
84:       {
85:
86:           if (strlen(str) < 3)
87:               return;
88:
89:           int retVal =0;
90:           Index index(str,offset);
91:           if (!myRoot)
92:           {
93:               myRoot = theDiskManager.NewPage (index,TRUE);
94:           }
95:           else
96:           {
97:               retVal = GetPage(myRoot)->Insert(index);
98:               if (retVal) // our root split
99:               {
100:                   // create a pointer to the old top
101:                   Index index(GetPage(myRoot)->GetFirstIndex());
102:                   index.SetPointer(myRoot);
103:                   // make the new page & insert the index
104:                   int PageNumber = NewPage(index,FALSE);
105:
106:                   Page* pg = GetPage(PageNumber);
107:
108:                   //get a pointer to the new (sibling) page
109:                   Index Sib(GetPage(retVal)->GetFirstIndex());
110:                   Sib.SetPointer(retVal);
111:                   // put it into the page
112:                   pg->InsertLeaf(Sib);
113:
114:                   // reset myRoot to point to the new top
115:                   myRoot = PageNumber;
116:               }
117:           }
118:       }
119:
120:       void BTree::PrintTree()
121:       {
122:           GetPage(myRoot)->Print();
123:
124:           cout << "\n\nStats:" << endl;
125:           cout << "Node pages:    " << NodePageCtr << endl;
126:           cout << "Leaf pages:    " << LeafPageCtr << endl;
127:           cout << "Node indexes: " << NodeIndexCtr << endl;
128:           cout << "Leaf indexes: " << LeafIndexCtr << endl;
```

continues

Listing 13.2 continued

```
129:        for (int i = 0; i < Order +2; i++)
130:        {
131:            if (NodeIndexPerPage[i])
132:            {
133:                cout << "Pages with " << i << " nodes:   ";
134:                cout << NodeIndexPerPage[i] << endl;
135:            }
136:            if (LeafIndexPerPage[i])
137:            {
138:                cout << "Pages with " << i << " leaves: ";
139:                cout << LeafIndexPerPage[i] << endl;
140:            }
141:        }
142:
143:    }
144:
145:
146:
147:    BOOL BTree::GetWord(char* string, char* word, int& wordOffset)
148:    {
149:
150:        if (!string[wordOffset])
151:            return FALSE;
152:
153:        char *p1, *p2;
154:        p1 = p2 = string+wordOffset;
155:
156:        // eat leading spaces
157:        for (int i = 0; i<(int)strlen(p1) && !BTree::myAlNum(p1[0]); i++)
158:            p1++;
159:
160:        // see if you have a word
161:        if (!BTree::myAlNum(p1[0]))
162:            return FALSE;
163:
164:         p2 = p1; // point to start of word
165:
166:        // march p2 to end of word
167:        while (BTree::myAlNum(p2[0]))
168:            p2++;
169:
170:        int len = int (p2 - p1);
171:        int pgSize = PageSize;
172:    #if defined(_MSVC_16BIT) || defined(_MSVC_32BIT)
   :        {
   :            len = __min(len,(int)PageSize);
   :        }
   :        #else
   :        {
   :            len = min(len,(int)PageSize);
   :        }
   :        #endif
173:
174:        strncpy (word,p1,len);
175:        word[len]='\0';
```

```
176:
177:        for (i = int(p2-string); i<(int)strlen(string) &&
!BTree::myAlNum(p2[0]); i++)
178:            p2++;
179:
180:        wordOffset = int(p2-string);
181:
182:        return TRUE;
183:    }
184:
185:    int BTree::myAlNum(char ch)
186:    {
187:        return isalnum(ch) ¦¦
188:            ch == '-' ¦¦
189:            ch == '\'' ¦¦
190:            ch == '(' ¦¦
191:            ch == ')';
192:    }
193:
```

Listing 13.3 Datafile.cpp

```
1:        // ****************************************************
2:        // PROGRAM:   Data file
3:        // FILE:      datafile.cpp
4:        // PURPOSE:
5:        // NOTES:
6:        // AUTHOR:    Jesse Liberty (jl)
7:        // REVISIONS: 11/5/94 1.0 jl  initial release
8:        // ****************************************************
9:
10:       #include "btree.hpp"
11:       #include <assert.h>
12:
13:       // on construction, try to open the file if it exists
14:       DataFile::DataFile():
15:          myFile("ROBIN.DAT",
16:          ios::binary ¦ ios::in ¦ ios::out ¦ ios::nocreate ¦ ios::app)
17:       {
18:       }
19:
20:       void DataFile::Create()
21:       {
22:           if (!myFile) // nocreate failed, first creation
23:           {
24:
25:               // open the file, create it this time
26:               myFile.clear();
27:
28:               myFile.open
29:                   ("ROBIN.DAT",ios::binary ¦ ios::in ¦ ios::out ¦ ios::app);
30:
31:               char Header[2];
```

continues

351

Listing 13.3 continued

```
32:                 int MagicNumber = 1234; // a number we can check for
33:                 memcpy(Header,&MagicNumber,2);
34:                 myFile.clear();
35:                 myFile.flush();
36:                 myFile.seekp(0);
37:                 myFile.write(Header,2);
38:                 return;
39:             }
40:
41:         // we did open the file, it already existed
42:         // get the numbers we need
43:         int MagicNumber;
44:         myFile.seekg(0);
45:         myFile.read((char *) &MagicNumber,2);
46:
47:         // check the magic number. If it is wrong the file is
48:         // corrupt or this isn't the index file
49:         if (MagicNumber != 1234)
50:         {
51:             // change to an exception!!
52:             cout << "DataFile Magic number failed!";
53:         }
54:         return;
55:     }
56:
57:     // write out the numbers we'll need next time
58:     void DataFile::Close()
59:     {
60:         myFile.close();
61:     }
62:
63:
64:     int DataFile::Insert(char * newNote)
65:     {
66:         int len = strlen(newNote);
67:         int fullLen = len + 6;
68:
69:         time_t theTime;
70:         theTime = time(NULL);
71:
72:         char buffer[PageSize];
73:         memcpy(buffer,&len,2);
74:         memcpy(buffer+2,&theTime,4);
75:         memcpy(buffer+6,newNote,len);
76:
77:         myFile.clear();
78:         myFile.flush();
79:         myFile.seekp(0,ios::end);
80:         int offset = (int) myFile.tellp();
81:         myFile.write(buffer,fullLen);
82:         myFile.flush();
83:         return offset;
84:     }
85:
```

```
86:         void DataFile::GetRecord(int offset, char* buffer, int& len, time_t&
            theTime)
87:         {
88:             char tmpBuff[PageSize];
89:             myFile.flush();
90:             myFile.clear();
91:             myFile.seekg(offset);
92:             myFile.read(tmpBuff,PageSize);
93:             memcpy(&len,tmpBuff,2);
94:             memcpy(&theTime,tmpBuff+2,4);
95:             strncpy(buffer,tmpBuff+6,len);
96:             buffer[len] = '\0';
97:         }
```

Type
Listing 13.4 IDXMgr.cpp

```
1:       // ****************************************************
2:       // PROGRAM:   Idxmr
3:       // FILE:      Idxmgr.cpp
4:       // PURPOSE:   provide i/o for btree
5:       // NOTES:
6:       // AUTHOR:    Jesse Liberty (jl)
7:       // REVISIONS: 11/5/94 1.0 jl  initial release
8:       // ****************************************************
9:
10:      #include "btree.hpp"
11:      #include <assert.h>
12:
13:      // on construction, try to open the file if it exists
14:      IDXManager::IDXManager():
15:         myFile("ROBIN.IDX",ios::binary | ios::in | ios::out | ios::nocreate)
16:      {
17:         // initialize the pointers to null
18:         for (int i = 0; i< MaxPages; i++)
19:            myPages[i] = 0;
20:         myCount = 0;
21:
22:      }
23:
24:      // called by btree constructor
25:      // if we opened the file, read in the numbers we need
26:      // otherwise create the file
27:      int IDXManager::Create()
28:      {
29:         if (!myFile) // nocreate failed, first creation
30:         {
31:            // open the file, create it this time
32:            myFile.open("ROBIN.IDX",ios::binary | ios::in | ios::out);
33:
34:            char Header[PageSize];
35:            int MagicNumber = 1234; // a number we can check for
36:            memcpy(Header,&MagicNumber,2);
37:            int NextPage = 1;
38:            memcpy(Header+2,&NextPage,2);
```

continues

Listing 13.4 continued

```
39:                memcpy(Header+4,&NextPage,2);
40:                Page::SetgPageNumber(NextPage);
41:                char title[]="ROBIN.IDX. Ver 1.00";
42:                memcpy(Header+6,title,strlen(title));
43:                myFile.flush();
44:                myFile.clear();
45:                myFile.seekp(0);
46:                myFile.write(Header,PageSize);
47:                return 0;
48:            }
49:
50:         // we did open the file, it already existed
51:         // get the numbers we need
52:         int MagicNumber;
53:         myFile.seekg(0);
54:         myFile.read((char *) &MagicNumber,2);
55:
56:         // check the magic number. If it is wrong the file is
57:         // corrupt or this isn't the index file
58:         if (MagicNumber != 1234)
59:         {
60:                // change to an exception!!
61:                cout << "Index Magic number failed!";
62:                return 0;
63:         }
64:
65:         int NextPage;
66:         myFile.seekg(2);
67:         myFile.read((char*) &NextPage,2);
68:         Page::SetgPageNumber(NextPage);
69:         int FirstPage;
70:         myFile.seekg(4);
71:         myFile.read((char*) &FirstPage,2);
72:         const int room =  PageSize - 6;
73:         char buffer[room];
74:         myFile.read(buffer,room);
75:         buffer[20]='\0';
76:         // cout << buffer << endl;
77:         // read in all the pages
78:         for (int i = 1; i < NextPage; i++)
79:         {
80:                myFile.seekg(i * PageSize);
81:                char buffer[PageSize];
82:                myFile.read( buffer, PageSize);
83:                Page * pg = new Page(buffer);
84:                Insert(pg);
85:         }
86:
87:         return FirstPage;
88:        }
89:
90:     // write out the numbers we'll need next time
91:     void IDXManager::Close(int theRoot)
92:        {
93:
```

```
94:            for (int i = 0; i< MaxPages; i++)
95:                if (myPages[i])
96:                    Save(myPages[i]);
97:            int NextPage = Page::GetgPageNumber();
98:            if (!myFile)
99:                cout << "Error opening myFile!" << endl;
100:           myFile.flush();
101:           myFile.clear();
102:           myFile.seekp(2);
103:           myFile.write ( (char *) &NextPage,2);
104:           myFile.seekp(4);
105:           myFile.write((char*) &theRoot,2);
106:           myFile.close();
107:       }
108:
109:       // wrapper function
110:       int IDXManager::NewPage(Index& index, BOOL bLeaf)
111:       {
112:           Page * newPage = new Page(index, bLeaf);
113:           Insert(newPage);
114:           Save(newPage);
115:           return newPage->GetPageNumber();
116:       }
117:
118:       int IDXManager::NewPage(
119:           Index *array,
120:           int offset,
121:           BOOL leaf,
122:           int count)
123:       {
124:           Page * newPage = new Page(array, offset, leaf,count);
125:           Insert(newPage);
126:           Save(newPage);
127:           return newPage->GetPageNumber();
128:       }
129:
130:       void IDXManager::Insert(Page * newPage)
131:       {
132:
133:           // add new page into array of page managers
134:           if (myCount < MaxPages)
135:           {
136:               assert(!myPages[myCount]);
137:               myPages[myCount++] = newPage;
138:           }
139:           else  // no room, time to page out to disk
140:           {
141:               int lowest = -1;
142:
143:               for (int i = 0; i< MaxPages; i++)
144:               {
145:                   if (myPages[i]->GetLocked() == FALSE )
146:                       lowest = i;
147:               }
148:               if (lowest == -1)
```

continues

13

Listing 13.4 continued

```
149:                    assert(lowest != -1); // change to exception if -1 (no page to
                    kill)
150:
151:            for (i = 0; i< MaxPages; i++)
152:                if (myPages[i]->GetTime() < myPages[lowest]->GetTime() &&
                    myPages[i]->GetLocked() == FALSE)
153:
154:
155:                    lowest = i;
156:
157:            assert(myPages[lowest]);
158:            Save(myPages[lowest]);
159:            delete myPages[lowest];
160:            myPages[lowest] = newPage;
161:
162:        }
163:    }
164:
165:    // tell the page to write itself out
166:    void IDXManager::Save(Page* pg)
167:    {
168:      pg->Write(myFile);
169:    }
170:
171:    // see if the page is in memory, if so return it
172:    // otherwise get it from disk
173:    // note: this won't scale, with lots of page managers
174:    // you'd need a more efficient search. 10 levels of page
175:    // managers, with 31 indexes per page gives you room for
176:    // 800 trillion words. Even if each page is only 1/2 full
177:    // on average, 10 levels of depth would represent 64 million
178:    // keys alone, not to mention the actual records.
179:
180:    Page * IDXManager::GetPage(int target)
181:    {
182:
183:        for (int i = 0; i< MaxPages; i++)
184:        {
185:           if (myPages[i]->GetPageNumber() == target)
186:               return  myPages[i];
187:        }
188:        myFile.seekg(target * PageSize);
189:        char buffer[PageSize];
190:        myFile.read( buffer, PageSize);
191:        Page * pg = new Page(buffer);
192:        Insert(pg);
193:        return pg;
194:    }
```

Type

Listing 13.5 Index.cpp

```
1:    // ****************************************************
2:    // PROGRAM:  index
```

```
3:     // FILE:      index.cpp
4:     // PURPOSE:   provide fundamental btree functionality
5:     // NOTES:
6:     // AUTHOR:    Jesse Liberty (jl)
7:     // REVISIONS: 11/1/94 1.0 jl  initial release
8:     // ****************************************************
9:
10:    #include "btree.hpp"
11:    #include <ctype.h>
12:
13:    Index::Index(char* str):myPointer(1)
14:    {
15:       strncpy(myData,str,dataLen);
16:       myData[dataLen]='\0';
17:       for (int i = 0; i< strlen(myData); i++)
18:          myData[i] = toupper(myData[i]);
19:    }
20:
21:    Index::Index(char* str, int ptr):myPointer(ptr)
22:    {
23:
24:       strncpy(myData,str,dataLen);
25:       myData[dataLen]='\0';
26:       for (int i = 0; i< strlen(myData); i++)
27:          myData[i] = toupper(myData[i]);
28:
29:    }
30:
31:    Index::Index(Index& rhs):
32:       myPointer(rhs.GetPointer())
33:    {
34:       strcpy(myData, rhs.GetData());
35:       for (int i = 0; i< strlen(myData); i++)
36:          myData[i] = toupper(myData[i]);
37:
38:    }
39:
40:    Index::Index():myPointer(0)
41:    {
42:       myData[0]='\0';
43:    }
44:
45:    void Index::PrintKey()
46:    {
47:       cout << "   " << myData;
48:    }
49:
50:    void Index::PrintPage()
51:    {
52:       cout << "\n" << myData << ": " ;
53:       BTree::theDiskManager.GetPage(myPointer)->Print();
54:    }
55:
56:    int Index::Insert(Index& ref, BOOL findOnly)
57:    {
```

continues

Listing 13.5 continued

```
58:           return BTree::theDiskManager.GetPage(myPointer)->Insert(ref,findOnly);
59:      }
60:
61:      int Index::operator==(const Index& rhs)
62:      {
63:          return (strcmp(myData,rhs.GetData()) == 0); // case insensitive
64:      }
```

Type

Listing 13.6 Page.cpp

```
1:       // **************************************************
2:       // PROGRAM:   Page
3:       // FILE:      Page.cpp
4:       // PURPOSE:   provide fundamental btree functionality
5:       // NOTES:
6:       // AUTHOR:    Jesse Liberty (jl)
7:       // REVISIONS: 11/1/94 1.0 jl   initial release
8:       // **************************************************
9:
10:      #include "btree.hpp"
11:      #include <assert.h>
12:
13:      // constructors
14:
15:      // default constructor
16:      Page::Page()
17:      {
18:      }
19:
20:      // create a page from a buffer read in from disk
21:      Page::Page(char *buffer):
22:          myKeys((Index*)myVars.mk)
23:      {
24:          assert(sizeof(myBlock) == PageSize);
25:          assert(sizeof(myVars) == PageSize);
26:          memcpy(&myBlock,buffer,PageSize);
27:          SetLocked(FALSE);
28:          myTime = time(NULL);
29:      }
30:
31:      // create a Page from the first index
32:      Page::Page(Index& index, BOOL bLeaf):
33:          myKeys((Index*)myVars.mk)
34:      {
35:
36:          myVars.myCount=1;
37:          myVars.IsLeaf = bLeaf;
38:          SetLocked(FALSE);
39:          // if this is a leaf, this is the first
40:          // index on the first page, set its pointer
41:          // based on creating a new wnj. otherwise
42:          // you are here creating a new node, do not
43:          // set the pointer, it is already set.
```

```
44:           if (bLeaf)
45:               index.SetPointer(BTree::theWNJFile.Append(index.GetPointer()));
46:           myKeys[0]=index;
47:           myVars.myPageNumber = gPage++;
48:           myTime = time(NULL);
49:       }
50:
51:       // create a page by splitting another page
52:       Page::Page(Index *array, int offset, BOOL bLeaf,int count):
53:           myKeys((Index*)myVars.mk)
54:       {
55:           myVars.IsLeaf = bLeaf;
56:           myVars.myCount = 0;
57:           for (int i=0, j = offset; j<Order && i < count; i++, j++)
58:           {
59:               myKeys[i]= array[j];
60:               myVars.myCount++;
61:           }
62:           myVars.myPageNumber = gPage++;
63:           SetLocked(FALSE);
64:           myTime = time(NULL);
65:       }
66:
67:       void Page::Nullify(int offset)
68:       {
69:           for (int i = offset; i<Order; i++)
70:           {
71:                   myKeys[i].SetPointer(0);
72:                   myVars.myCount--;
73:           }
74:       }
75:
76:       // decide whether I'm a leaf or a node
77:       // and pass this index to the right
78:       // function. If findOnly is true, don't insert
79:       // just return the page number (for now)
80:       int Page::Insert(Index& rIndex, BOOL findOnly)
81:       {
82:           int result;
83:           if (myVars.IsLeaf)
84:           {
85:               SetLocked(TRUE);
86:               result = FindLeaf(rIndex,findOnly);
87:               SetLocked(FALSE);
88:               return result;
89:           }
90:           else
91:           {
92:               SetLocked(TRUE);
93:               result = InsertNode(rIndex,findOnly);
94:               SetLocked(FALSE);
95:               return result;
96:           }
97:       }
98:
```

13

continues

Listing 13.6 continued

```
99:
100:      // find the right page for this index
101:      int Page::InsertNode(Index& rIndex, BOOL findOnly)
102:      {
103:          int retVal =0;
104:          BOOL inserted = FALSE;
105:          int i,j;
106:
107:          assert(myVars.myCount>0); // nodes have at least 1
108:          assert(myKeys[0].GetPointer()); // must be valid
109:
110:          // does it go before my first entry?
111:          if (rIndex < myKeys[0])
112:          {
113:              if (findOnly)
114:                  return 0L; // not found
115:
116:              myKeys[0].SetData(rIndex);
117:              retVal=myKeys[0].Insert(rIndex);
118:              inserted = TRUE;
119:          }
120:
121:          // does it go after my last?
122:          if (!inserted)
123:              for (i = myVars.myCount-1; i>=0; i--)
124:              {
125:                  assert(myKeys[i].GetPointer());
126:                  if (rIndex >= myKeys[i])
127:                  {
128:                      retVal=myKeys[i].Insert(rIndex,findOnly);
129:                      inserted = TRUE;
130:                      break;
131:                  }
132:               }
133:
134:          // find where it does go
135:          if (!inserted)
136:              for (j = 0; j<i && j+1 < myVars.myCount; j++)
137:              {
138:                  assert(myKeys[j+1].GetPointer());
139:                  if (rIndex < myKeys[j+1])
140:                  {
141:                      retVal=myKeys[j].Insert(rIndex,findOnly);
142:                      inserted = TRUE;
143:                      break;
144:                  }
145:              }
146:
147:          assert(inserted);  // change to exception if not!
148:
149:          // if you had to split
150:          if (retVal && !findOnly) // got back a pointer to a new page
151:          {
152:              Index * pIndex = new Index(GetPage(retVal)->GetFirstIndex());
153:              pIndex->SetPointer(retVal);
```

```
154:            retVal = InsertLeaf(*pIndex);
155:        }
156:        return retVal;
157:    }
158:
159:    // called if current page is a leaf
160:    int Page::FindLeaf(Index& rIndex, BOOL findOnly)
161:    {
162:        int result = 0;
163:
164:        // no duplicates!
165:        for (int i=0; i < myVars.myCount; i++)
166:            if (rIndex == myKeys[i])
167:            {
168:                if (findOnly)                  // return first WNJ
169:                    //return BTree::theWNJFile.Find(myKeys[i].GetPointer());
170:                    return myKeys[i].GetPointer();
171:                else
172:                    return BTree::theWNJFile.Insert(
173:                            rIndex.GetPointer(),
174:                                myKeys[i].GetPointer());
175:            }
176:
177:        if (findOnly)            // not found
178:            return result;
179:
180:        // this index item does not yet exist
181:        // before you push it into the index
182:        // push an entry into the wnj.idx
183:        // and set the index to point to that entry
184:        rIndex.SetPointer(BTree::theWNJFile.Append(rIndex.GetPointer())); //
            new!
185:        return InsertLeaf(rIndex);
186:    }
187:
188:    int Page::InsertLeaf(Index& rIndex)
189:    {
190:        int result = 0;
191:        if (myVars.myCount < Order)
192:            Push(rIndex);
193:        else      // overflow the page
194:        {
195:            // make sibling
196:            int NewPg =
197:                NewPage(myKeys,Order/2,myVars.IsLeaf,myVars.myCount);
198:            Page* Sibling = GetPage(NewPg);
199:            Nullify(Order/2);                       // nullify my right half
200:
201:            // does it fit in this side?
202:            if (myVars.myCount>Order/2-1 && rIndex <= myKeys[Order/2-1])
203:                Push(rIndex);
204:            else  // push it into the new sibling
205:                Sibling->Push(rIndex);
206:
207:            result = NewPg; // we split, pass it up
```

continues

Listing 13.6 continued

```
208:              }
209:          return result;
210:      }
211:
212:      // put the new index into this page (in order)
213:      void Page::Push(Index& rIndex,int offset,BOOL first)
214:      {
215:          BOOL inserted = FALSE;
216:          assert(myVars.myCount < Order);
217:          for (int i=offset; i<Order && i<myVars.myCount; i++)
218:          {
219:              assert(myKeys[i].GetPointer());
220:              if (rIndex <= myKeys[i])
221:              {
222:                  Push(myKeys[i],offset+1,FALSE);
223:                  myKeys[i]=rIndex;
224:                  inserted = TRUE;
225:                  break;
226:              }
227:          }
228:          if (!inserted)
229:              myKeys[myVars.myCount] = rIndex;
230:
231:          if (first)
232:              myVars.myCount++;
233:      }
234:
235:
236:      void Page::Print()
237:      {
238:              if (!myVars.IsLeaf)
239:              {
240:                  BTree::NodePageCtr++;
241:                  BTree::NodeIndexPerPage[myVars.myCount]++;
242:                  BTree::NodeIndexCtr+=myVars.myCount;
243:              }
244:              else
245:              {
246:                  BTree::LeafPageCtr++;
247:                  BTree::LeafIndexPerPage[myVars.myCount]++;
248:                  BTree::LeafIndexCtr+=myVars.myCount;
249:              }
250:
251:              for (int i = 0; i<Order && i < myVars.myCount; i++)
252:              {
253:                  assert(myKeys[i].GetPointer());
254:                  if (myVars.IsLeaf)
255:                      myKeys[i].PrintKey();
256:                  else
257:                      myKeys[i].PrintPage();
258:              }
259:      }
260:
261:      // write out the entire page as a block
```

```
262:      fstream& Page::Write(fstream& file)
263:      {
264:         char buffer[PageSize];
265:         memcpy(buffer,&myBlock,PageSize);
266:         file.flush();
267:         file.clear();
268:         file.seekp(myVars.myPageNumber*PageSize);
269:         file.write(buffer,PageSize);
270:         return file;
271:      }
```

Type   Listing 13.7 WNJFile.cpp

```
1:        // ***************************************************
2:        // PROGRAM:  WNJ file
3:        // FILE:       WNJfile.cpp
4:        // PURPOSE:
5:        // NOTES:
6:        // AUTHOR:   Jesse Liberty (jl)
7:        // REVISIONS: 11/5/94 1.0 jl  initial release
8:        // ***************************************************
9:
10:       #include "btree.hpp"
11:       #include <assert.h>
12:
13:       // on construction, try to open the file if it exists
14:       WNJFile::WNJFile():
15:          myFile("ROBINWNJ.IDX",
16:          ios::binary ¦ ios::in ¦ ios::out ¦ ios::nocreate)
17:       {
18:          for (int i = 0; i<5; i++)
19:             myints[i]=0L;
20:       }
21:
22:       void WNJFile::Create()
23:       {
24:          char Header[4];
25:          int MagicNumber=0; // a number we can check for
26:          int zero = 0;
27:
28:          if (!myFile) // nocreate failed, first creation
29:          {
30:             // open the file, create it this time
31:             myFile.clear();
32:             myFile.open("ROBINWNJ.IDX",
33:                ios::binary ¦ ios::in ¦ ios::out);
34:
35:             MagicNumber = 1234;
36:             memcpy(Header,&MagicNumber,4);
37:             memcpy(Header+2,&zero,2);
38:             myFile.seekp(0);
39:             myFile.write(Header,4);
40:             myFile.flush();
```

13

continues

Listing 13.7 continued

```
41:              return;
42:          }
43:
44:          // we did open the file, it already existed
45:          // get the numbers we need
46:
47:
48:          myFile.seekg(0);
49:          myFile.read(Header,4);
50:          memcpy(&MagicNumber,Header,2);
51:          memcpy(&myCount,Header+2,2);
52:
53:          // check the magic number. If it is wrong the file is
54:          // corrupt or this isn't the index file
55:          if (MagicNumber != 1234)
56:          {
57:              // change to an exception!!
58:              cout << "WNJ Magic number failed!";
59:              cout << "Magic number: " << MagicNumber;
60:              cout << "\nmyCount: " << myCount << endl;
61:          }
62:          return;
63:      }
64:
65:      // write out the numbers we'll need next time
66:      void WNJFile::Close()
67:      {
68:          myFile.seekg(2);
69:          myFile.write((char*)&myCount,2);
70:          myFile.close();
71:      }
72:
73:      int WNJFile::Append(int DataOffset)
74:      {
75:
76:          int newPos = 4 + myCount++ * (5*2);
77:          int offsets[5];
78:          offsets[0] = DataOffset;
79:          for (int i = 1; i<5; i++)
80:              offsets[i]=0;
81:          myFile.seekg(newPos);
82:          myFile.write((char*)offsets,5*2);
83:
84:          return newPos;
85:      }
86:
87:
88:      int WNJFile::Insert(int DataOffset,int WNJOffset)
89:      {
90:          int ints[5];
91:          myFile.seekg(WNJOffset);
92:          myFile.read((char*)ints,5*2);
93:
94:          int offset=WNJOffset;
95:
```

```
96:            while (ints[4])
97:            {
98:                offset = ints[4];
99:                myFile.clear();
100:               myFile.flush();
101:               myFile.seekg(ints[4]);
102:               myFile.read((char*)ints,5*2);
103:           }
104:           if (ints[3]) // full!
105:           {
106:               ints[4] = Append(DataOffset);
107:               myFile.clear();
108:               myFile.flush();
109:               myFile.seekg(offset);
110:               myFile.write((char*)ints,5*2);
111:           }
112:           else
113:           {
114:               for (int i = 0; i<4; i++)
115:               {
116:                   if (ints[i] == 0)
117:                   {
118:                       ints[i] = DataOffset;
119:                       myFile.clear();
120:                       myFile.flush();
121:                       myFile.seekg(offset);
122:                       myFile.write((char*)ints,5*2);
123:                       break;
124:                   }
125:               }
126:           }
127:           return 0;
128:       }
129:
130:
131:       int* WNJFile::Find(int NextWNJ)
132:       {
133:           int ints[5];
134:           int * results = new int[256];
135:
136:           int i = 0, j=0;
137:
138:           while (j<256)
139:               results[j++] = 0;
140:
141:           j = 0;
142:
143:           myFile.seekg(NextWNJ);
144:           myFile.read((char*)ints,5*2);
145:
146:           while (j < 256)
147:           {
148:               if (ints[i])
149:               {
150:                   if (i == 4)
```

Listing 13.7 continued

```
151:                    {
152:                        myFile.seekg(ints[4]);
153:                        myFile.read((char*)ints,5*2);
154:                        i = 0;
155:                        continue;
156:                    }
157:                    results[j++] = ints[i++];
158:                }
159:                else
160:                    break;
161:            }
162:            return results;
163:        }
```

Type Listing 13.8 R1.cpp

```
1:      // ****************************************************
2:      // PROGRAM:   R1
3:      // FILE:      r1.cpp
4:      // PURPOSE:   Fundamental functionality for ROBIN v1.
5:      // NOTES:
6:      // AUTHOR:    Jesse Liberty (jl)
7:      // REVISIONS: 11/1/94 1.0 jl  ALPHA release
8:      // ****************************************************
9:
10:     #include "String.hpp"
11:     #include "stdef.hpp"
12:     #include "btree.hpp"
13:     #include <stdlib.h>
14:
15:     // static definitions
16:     IDXManager BTree::theDiskManager;
17:     DataFile BTree::theDataFile;
18:     WNJFile BTree::theWNJFile;
19:
20:     int WNJFile::myCount=0L;
21:     int Page::gPage=1;
22:     int BTree::NodeIndexCtr=0;
23:     int BTree::LeafIndexCtr=0;
24:     int BTree::NodePageCtr=0;
25:     int BTree::LeafPageCtr=0;
26:     int BTree::NodeIndexPerPage[Order+1];
27:     int BTree::LeafIndexPerPage[Order+1];
28:
29:
30:     // prototypes
31:     void parseCommandLines(char *buffer,int argc,char **argv);
32:     void ShowMenu(long*);
33:     void DoFind(int, char**, BTree&);
34:     void ParseFile(int, char**, BTree&);
35:
36:     // driver program
37:     int main(int argc, char ** argv)
```

```
38:     {
39:         BTree myTree;
40:
41:         for (int i = 0; i < Order +2; i++)
42:         {
43:             BTree::NodeIndexPerPage[i] =0;
44:             BTree::LeafIndexPerPage[i] = 0;
45:         }
46:
47:         char buffer[PageSize+1];
48:
49:         if (argc == 1)
50:         {
51:             cout << "Please provide command line arguments";
52:             return 1;
53:         }
54:
55:         // check for flags, if none add text to data file
56:         if (argv[1][0] == '-')
57:         {
58:
59:             switch (argv[1][1])
60:             {
61:                 case '?':
62:                     DoFind(argc,argv,myTree);
63:                     break;
64:
65:                 case '!':
66:                         myTree.PrintTree();
67:                         break;
68:
69:                 case 'F':
70:                 case 'f':
71:                         ParseFile(argc,argv,myTree);
72:                         break;
73:             }
74:         }
75:         else
76:         {
77:             parseCommandLines(buffer,argc,argv);
78:             myTree.Insert(buffer,argc,argv);
79:             cout << "Inserted.\n";
80:         }
81:         return 0;
82:     }
83:
84:     // concatenate remaining command line arguments
85:     void parseCommandLines(char *buffer,int argc,char **argv)
86:     {
87:         size_t len = 0;
88:         size_t argLen=0;
89:         for (int i = 1; i< argc; i++)
90:         {
91:             argLen = strlen(argv[i]);
92:             if (len + argLen +2 < PageSize)
```

continues

Listing 13.8 continued

```
93:             {
94:                 strncpy(buffer+len,argv[i],argLen);
95:                 strncpy(buffer+len+argLen," ",1);
96:                 len += argLen+1;
97:             }
98:         }
99:         buffer[len] = '\0';
100:    }
101:
102:    // having found matches, show the menu of choices
103:    // each entry is numbered and dated
104:    void ShowMenu(int *list)
105:    {
106:        int j=0;
107:        char buffer[PageSize+1];
108:        time_t theTime;
109:        int len;
110:        char listBuff[256];
111:        struct tm * ts;
112:        int dispSize;
113:
114:        while (list[j] && j < 20)
115:            {
116:            BTree::theDataFile.GetRecord(list[j],buffer,len, theTime);
117:    #if defined(_MSVC_16BIT) || defined(_MSVC_32BIT)
   :        {
   :            dispSize = __min(len,32); // THIS is a DOUBLE UNDERSCORE
   :        }
   :    #else
   :        {
   :            dispSize = min(len,32);
   :        }
   :    #endif
118:            strncpy(listBuff,buffer,dispSize);
119:            if (dispSize == 32)
120:                {
121:                listBuff[29] = '.';
122:                listBuff[30] = '.';
123:                listBuff[31] = '.';
124:                }
125:            listBuff[dispSize]='\0';
126:            ts = localtime(&theTime);
127:            cout << "[" << (j+1) << "] ";
128:            cout << ts->tm_mon << "/";
129:            cout << ts->tm_mday << "/";
130:            cout << ts->tm_year << " ";
131:            cout <<  listBuff << endl;
132:            j++;
133:            }
134:    }
135:
136:    // handle -? command
137:    // find matches, show the menu, request choice
138:    // display record and redisplay menu
139:    void DoFind(int argc, char ** argv, BTree& myTree)
```

```
140:    {
141:
142:        // create an array of total set of WNJ
143:        // offsets. This will be used to display
144:        // choices and to find actual text
145:        int  list[PageSize];
146:
147:        // initialize the array to all zeros
148:        for (int i = 0; i<PageSize; i++)
149:            list[i] = 0;
150:
151:        int k = 0;
152:
153:        // for each word in the command line
154:        // search for the matching set of records
155:        for (i = 2; i< argc; i++)
156:        {
157:            int offset = myTree.Find(argv[i]);
158:            if (offset)
159:            {
160:                // get the array of offsets from WNJfile
161:                int *found  =  BTree::theWNJFile.Find(offset);
162:                int j = 0;
163:
164:                // add any you don't already have
165:                for (;k < PageSize && found[j];j++,k++)
166:                {
167:                    for (int l = 0; l < k; l++)
168:                    {
169:                        if (list[l] == found[j])
170:                            continue;
171:                    }
172:                    list[k] = found [j];
173:                }
174:                    delete [] found;
175:            }
176:        }
177:
178:        cout << "\n";
179:
180:        if (!list[0])
181:        {
182:            cout << "Nothing found.\n";
183:            return;
184:        }
185:
186:        ShowMenu(list);
187:
188:        int choice;
189:        char buffer[PageSize];
190:        int len;
191:        time_t theTime;
192:
193:        for (;;)
194:        {
```

13

continues

Listing 13.8 continued

```
195:                cout << "Choice (0 to stop): " ;
196:                cin >> choice;
197:                if (!choice)
198:                    break;
199:                BTree::theDataFile.GetRecord(list[choice-1],buffer,len, theTime);
200:                cout << "\n>> ";
201:                cout << buffer;
202:                cout << "\n\n";
203:                ShowMenu(list);
204:            }
205:    }
206:
207:    // open a file and create a new note for each line
208:    // index every word in the line
209:    void ParseFile(int argc,char **argv, BTree& myTree)
210:    {
211:
212:        char buffer[PageSize];
213:        char theString[PageSize];
214:
215:        ifstream theFile(argv[2],ios::in );
216:        if (!theFile)
217:        {
218:            cout << "Error opening input file!\n";
219:            return;
220:        }
221:        int offset = 0;
222:        for (;;)
223:        {
224:                theFile.read(theString,PageSize);
225:                int len = theFile.gcount();
226:                if (!len)
227:                    break;
228:                theString[len]='\0';
229:                char *p1, *p2, *p0;
230:                p0 = p1 = p2 = theString;
231:
232:                while (p1[0] && (p1[0] == '\n' || p1[0] == '\r'))
233:                    p1++;
234:
235:                p2 = p1;
236:
237:                while (p2[0] && p2[0] != '\n' && p2[0] != '\r')
238:                    p2++;
239:
240:                int bufferLen = p2 - p1;
241:                int totalLen = p2 - p0;
242:
243:                if (!bufferLen)
244:                    continue;
245:
246:                // lstrcpyn(buffer,p1,bufferLen);
247:                strncpy(buffer,p1,bufferLen);
248:                buffer[bufferLen]='\0';
249:
```

```
250:              // for (int i = 0; i< PageSize; i++)
251:                 cout << "\r";
252:              cout << "Parsing " << buffer;
253:              myTree.Insert(buffer);
254:              offset += totalLen;
255:              theFile.clear();
256:              theFile.seekg(offset,ios::beg);
257:         }
258:     }
```

```
d:\day13>-f day12.txt
d:\day13>r1 -? file
[1]  10/25/94 You have seen how to create t...
[2]  10/25/94    [bl] How to create the data ...
[3]  10/25/94 (c)Putting the notes into a d...
[4]  10/25/94 The next iteration of the pro...
[5]  10/25/94 and write the entire text of ...
[6]  10/25/94 out to the file, and the offs...
[7]  10/25/94 3:     // FILE:     stdef.hpp
[8]  10/25/94 3:     // FILE:     btree.hpp
[9]  10/25/94 2:     // PROGRAM:  Data file
[10] 10/25/94 3:     // FILE:      datafile....
[11] 10/25/94 13:    // on construction, tr...
[12] 10/25/94 24:         // open the file...
[13] 10/25/94 36:      // we did open the
[14] 10/25/94 42:      // check the magic ...
[15] 10/25/94 43:      // corrupt or this ...
[16] 10/25/94 The file is opened much as th...
[17] 10/25/94 the file should be opened in ...
[18] 10/25/94 the file should be opened in ...
[19] 10/25/94 opened in append mode all wri...
[20] 10/25/94 that you need to know the off...
Choice (0 to stop): 16

>> The file is opened much as the other files have been,

[1]  10/25/94 You have seen how to create t...
[2]  10/25/94    [lb] How to create the data ...
[3]  10/25/94 (c)Putting the notes into a d...
[4]  10/25/94 The next iteration of the pro...
[5]  10/25/94 and write the entire text of ...
[6]  10/25/94 out to the file, and the offs...
[7]  10/25/94 3:     // FILE:     stdef.hpp
[8]  10/25/94 3:     // FILE:     btree.hpp
[9]  10/25/94 2:     // PROGRAM:  Data file
[10] 10/25/94 3:     // FILE:      datafile....
[11] 10/25/94 13:    // on construction, tr...
[12] 10/25/94 24:          // open the file...
[13] 10/25/94 36:      // we did open the ...
[14] 10/25/94 42:      // check the magic ...
[15] 10/25/94 43:      // corrupt or this ...
[16] 10/25/94 The file is opened much as th...
[17] 10/25/94 the file should be opened in ...
[18] 10/25/94 the file should be opened in ...
[19] 10/25/94 opened in append mode all wri...
```

13

```
[20] 10/25/94 that you need to know the off...
Choice (0 to stop):-!

        // NOTE: list of words left out of this listing

Stats:
Node pages:    2
Leaf pages:    18
Node indexes: 20
Leaf indexes: 343
Pages with 2 nodes:   1
Pages with 15 leaves: 6
Pages with 16 leaves: 2
Pages with 18 nodes:  1
Pages with 18 leaves: 1
Pages with 19 leaves: 3
Pages with 20 leaves: 2
Pages with 21 leaves: 1
Pages with 25 leaves: 1
Pages with 29 leaves: 1
Pages with 31 leaves: 1
```

All the changes discussed at the beginning of this chapter are implemented in this set of code. The page-locking mechanism is implemented by the `IsLocked` member variable of `Page`, declared in line 239 of listing 13.1. The accessors are in lines 207 and 208 of the same listing.

The lock actually is set and cleared in the `Insert()` method of `Page`, shown in lines 80 through 97 of listing 13.6. The check for the lock is implemented in the `IDXManager` code, shown in lines 131 through 165 of listing 13.4. This ensures that no page currently in use by the `Insert()` method will be swapped out of memory.

The code to elicit user input is shown in listing 13.8. The command line is examined, and if the first character is not a dash, indicating a flag, the entire command line other than the program name itself is turned into a note and added to the database.

If the first character is a dash, the flag is examined for the legal values of ?, !, and F or f. If the command is ?, the `DoFind()` method is called, which searches for a match and then displays a menu of matching titles. Each title is prepended with a menu number and the date of the entry. The user can choose from the menu and see the entire text of that note.

If the flag is -F, the next word must be a legitimate file name, in which case the file is read line by line, and each line is made into a note. This is shown in the output when a text file from day 12 is read and parsed. The result of this is reflected in the statistics, which are shown by entering the -! flag.

Note: Note that the output displayed here does not include the complete list of all of the indexed words (there are 343).

The logic for reading the contents of a file and creating a note from each line is in the method ParseFile(), shown in lines 210 through 259 of listing 13.6. The only tricky part is this: Each line is read, and the length of the line is after the new line character is found (in lines 233 through 239). After a buffer is created with all the characters up to the first new line character, it is passed to the B-tree's Insert() method, and the next line is obtained by seeking to the offset of the new line character and reading from there.

The ShowMenu() method, listed in lines 104 through 134 of listing 13.8, is a rudimentary display of the first 20 matches returned from the database. One of the first things you want to do before releasing this as a commercial program is to enhance the user's capability to page through *all* the matching records.

Getting It Out the Door

You now have enough of a program to show it to co-workers and others who might be interested, in an attempt to "sanity-check" the idea behind the program. Yes, it is crude, and there are a thousand things you would like to change, fix, enhance, redesign, and so on.

It is my considered opinion, after 10 years in this industry, that a heck of a lot more programs never make it to market because they are kept too long in the lab than because they are released too early. Get it out there, and then *listen* to the feedback. Your users may not even notice many of the things you hate, and don't be surprised if they come back and complain long and loud about the few things you thought you had *right*!

The *point* of an alpha release is to get enough out there to get feedback—*not* to prove that your program is nearly done. It isn't nearly done—it has only just started—but it is time to hear what real people think of it.

Looking At What You Didn't Fix

The list of things that remain to be fixed for ROBIN is long and intimidating. You haven't even *started* to performance tune it, and you will not do this for a few more days. You still need to put a nice front end on it; remember that users react much more to the look and feel than to the neat B-tree you implemented, and ROBIN's look and feel are, to say the least, rudimentary.

You need to add stop words, not to mention the capability to delete, if not edit, entries in the database. The single biggest weakness in the current version of ROBIN is that it is not nearly robust enough. You have put in almost no error-checking, and there is much to do to make this a professional, well-crafted, hearty program. All of that will come in the next few days, however; for now, you have created a program that demonstrates the fundamental functionality, and it is time to start using it.

Even though ROBIN is a learning tool and not a commercial enterprise, and therefore you will not, in fact, give it to anyone else, you still can use it yourself. Try keeping notes with it. Put your phone numbers in, play with it on a daily basis, and keep a list of all the ways you would like to enhance it, change it, and fix it. Note where it is slow, and most important, note where it breaks!

What's Ahead

On day 14, you will take a break from ROBIN and look at some advanced bit-twiddling techniques. After the break for the second week in review, I'll review memory-management techniques. Then you will return to ROBIN and add synonyms and stop words. The remaining days look at building robust, excellent code and enhancing performance. Finally, I'll walk you through an advanced debugging session and you will add the finishing touches to this program.

Summary

Today you learned what role alpha and beta testing play in the preparation of a commercial release. You also saw how to add robustness to your program with simple page-locking, and a little bit about the reality of shipping high-quality, but "good enough" commercial products.

Q&A

Q What is QA testing?

A Quality assurance (QA) testing is a rigorous test of your program by trained professionals who understand how to force a program through virtually every code path. A good QA engineer can automate many of these tests, and is on the lookout not only for obvious bugs but for whether the product complies with the specification.

Q At what point should your program go to QA?

A There is a trade-off in this decision, as in most aspects of programming. If you send a program too early to QA, you will only get it back with a stack of bugs and everyone involved will be frustrated. If you spend too much time testing your own code, however, you will miss the opportunity to move on and do further development. My rule of thumb is this: When you cannot find a bug for hours at a time of testing, give it to QA and move on to the next problem.

Q What is an alpha test?

A The alpha phase is when you distribute the program only to a very small group of very friendly users. The purpose of it is more to gain feedback on the functionality of the program rather than to weed out bugs. Alpha test programs are *not* feature complete; you are looking for high-level feedback early in the process.

Q What is a beta test?

A The beta phase is distributed to more users, who are perhaps somewhat less tolerant of bugs. The purpose is more to weed out the bugs than to provide feedback. If there is significant negative feedback during the beta phase of a program (more than cosmetic changes), perhaps it is time to go back to the drawing board.

Workshop

The Workshop provides quiz questions to help you solidify your understanding of the material covered, and exercises to provide you with experience in using what you have learned. Try to answer the quiz and exercise questions before checking the answers in Appendix A, and make sure that you understand the answers before continuing to the next chapter.

Quiz

1. What is the difference between alpha and beta testing?
2. What kinds of things should QA test for?
3. Why shouldn't developers test their own code?

Exercises

1. How would you modify the Page class so that the locking mechanism could be re-entrant? In other words, if a page is locked twice, it should need to be unlocked twice before it is considered to be not locked. You should change only the class Page, and you should not change its public interface at all.
2. Recompile and rerun the program with your changes from exercise 1, to prove that it still works correctly.
3. Modify the function ParseFile to count the number of lines that are in the file, and to output a message when the file is complete, telling the user the number of lines that were added to the database.

Advanced Data
Manipulation

It is time to step back from the project at hand and go over some of the more advanced data-manipulation techniques that C++ inherits from C. Today you will learn

- ☐ How to create and use bit fields
- ☐ How to manipulate individual bits in a byte
- ☐ How memory is used
- ☐ How to convert between decimal, binary, and hexadecimal

Bit Twiddling

Often, you will want to set flags in your objects to keep track of the states of your objects. (Has the object been initialized yet? Is this the first usage? Are you coming or going?)

You can set flags with user-defined Booleans, but when you have many flags, and when storage size is an issue, it is convenient to be able to use the individual bits as flags.

Each byte has 8 bits, so in a 4-byte long code snippet, you can hold 32 separate flags. A bit is *set* if its value is 1, and it is *clear* if its value is 0. When you set a bit, you make its value 1, and when you clear it, you make its value 0. You can set and clear bits by changing the value of the long, but that can be tedious and confusing.

C++ provides bitwise operators that act on the individual bits. These are presented in table 14.1.

Table 14.1 The Bitwise Operators

Symbol	Operator
&	AND
|	OR
^	exclusive OR
~	complement

Operator AND

The AND operator (&) is a single ampersand, as opposed to the logical AND, which is two ampersands. When you AND 2 bits, the result is 1 if both bits are 1, but 0 if either bit is 0 or both bits are 0. The way to think of this is *the result is 1 if bit 1 is set **and** if bit 2 is set.*

Operator OR

The second bitwise operator is OR (|). Again, this is a single vertical bar, as opposed to the logical OR, which is two vertical bars. When you OR 2 bits, the result is 1 if either bit is set, or if both bits are set.

Operator Exclusive OR

The third bitwise operator is exclusive OR (^). When you exclusive OR 2 bits, the result is 1 if the two bits are different. The way to think of this is *the result is 1 if bit 1 is set and bit 2 is clear, or if bit 1 is clear and bit 2 is set.*

The Complement Operator

The complement operator (~) clears every bit in a number that is set and sets every bit that is clear. If the current value of the number is 1010 0011, the complement of that number is 0101 1100.

Setting Bits

When you want to set or clear a particular bit, you use masking operations. If you have a 4-byte flag and you want to set bit 8 TRUE, you need to OR the flag with the value 128; 128 is 1000 0000 in binary, so the value of the eighth bit is 128. Whatever the current value of that bit (set or clear), if you OR it with the value 128, you will set that bit and not change any of the other bits. Assume that the current value of the 8 bits is 1010 0110 0010 0110. ORing 128 to it looks like this:

```
           9 8765 4321
    1010 0110 0010 0110    // bit 8 is clear
|   0000 0000 1000 0000    // 128
------------------
    1010 0110 1010 0110    // bit 8 is set
```

You should note a few things. First, as usual, bits are counted from right to left. Second, the value 128 is all zeros except for bit 8, the bit you want to set. Third, the starting number 1010 0110 0010 0110 is left unchanged by the OR operation, except that bit 8 was set. Had bit 8 already been set, it would have remained set, which is what you want.

Clearing Bits

If you want to clear bit 8, you can AND the bit with the complement of 128. The complement of 128 is the number you get when you take the bit pattern of 128 (1000 0000), set every bit that is clear, and clear every bit that is set (0111 1111). When you AND these numbers, the original number is unchanged, except for the eighth bit, which is forced to zero:

```
  1010 0110 1010 0110   // bit 8 is set
& 1111 1111 0111 1111   // ~128
_____
  1010 0110 0010 0110   // bit 8 cleared
```

To fully understand this solution, do the math yourself. Each time both bits are 1, write 1 in the answer. If either bit is 0, write 0 in the answer. Compare the answer with the original number. It should be the same except that bit 8 was cleared.

Flipping Bits

Finally, if you want to flip bit 8, no matter what its state, you exclusive OR the number with 128:

```
  1010 0110 1010 0110   // number
^ 0000 0000 1000 0000   // 128
_____
  1010 0110 0010 0110   // bit flipped
^ 0000 0000 1000 0000   // 128
_____
  1010 0110 1010 0110   // flipped back
```

DO	**DON'T**

Working with Bits

DO set bits by using masks and the OR operator.

DO clear bits by using masks and the AND operator.

DO flip bits using masks and the exclusive OR operator.

Bit Fields

There are circumstances under which every byte counts, and saving six or eight bytes in a class can make all the difference. If your class or structure has a series of Boolean variables, or variables that can have only a very small number of possible values, you may save some room by using bit fields.

Using the standard C++ data types, the smallest type you can use in your class is a type char, which is 1 byte. More often, you will end up using an int, which is 2 or, more often, 4 bytes. By using bit fields, you can store eight binary values in a char and 32 binary values in a long.

Here's how bit fields work: Bit fields are named and accessed like any class member. Their type always is declared to be unsigned int. After the bit field name, write a colon followed by a

number. The number is an instruction to the compiler as to how many bits to assign to this variable. If you write 1, the bit will represent either the value 0 or 1. If you write 2, the bit can represent 0, 1, 2, or 3—a total of four values. A 3-bit field can represent eight values, and so on. Appendix C reviews binary numbers. Listing 14.1 illustrates the use of bit fields.

Type **Listing 14.1 Using Bit Fields**

```
1:      #include <iostream.h>
2:      #include <string.h>
3:
4:      enum STATUS { FullTime, PartTime } ;
5:      enum GRADLEVEL { UnderGrad, Grad } ;
6:      enum HOUSING { Dorm, OffCampus };
7:      enum FOODPLAN { OneMeal, AllMeals, WeekEnds, NoMeals };
8:
9:      class student
10:     {
11:     public:
12:         student():myStatus(FullTime),myGradLevel(UnderGrad),myHousing(Dorm),
                myFoodPlan(NoMeals){}
13:         ~student(){}
14:         STATUS GetStatus();
15:         void SetStatus(STATUS);
16:         FOODPLAN GetPlan() { return myFoodPlan; }
17:
18:     private:
19:         unsigned myStatus : 1;
20:         unsigned myGradLevel: 1;
21:         unsigned myHousing : 1;
22:         unsigned myFoodPlan : 2;
23:     };
24:
25:     STATUS student::GetStatus()
26:     {
27:         if (myStatus)
28:             return FullTime;
29:         else
30:             return PartTime;
31:     }
32:     void student::SetStatus(STATUS theStatus)
33:     {
34:         myStatus = theStatus;
35:     }
36:
37:
38:     void main()
39:     {
40:         student Jim;
41:
42:         if (Jim.GetStatus()== PartTime)
43:             cout << "Jim is part time" << endl;
44:         else
45:             cout << "Jim is full time" << endl;
```

continues

381

Listing 14.1 continued

```
46:
47:        Jim.SetStatus(PartTime);
48:
49:        if (Jim.GetStatus())
50:            cout << "Jim is part time" << endl;
51:        else
52:            cout << "Jim is full time" << endl;
53:
54:        cout << "Jim is on the " ;
55:
56:        char Plan[80];
57:        switch (Jim.GetPlan())
58:        {
59:           case  OneMeal: strcpy(Plan,"One meal"); break;
60:           case  AllMeals: strcpy(Plan,"All meals"); break;
61:           case WeekEnds: strcpy(Plan,"Weekend meals"); break;
62:           case NoMeals: strcpy(Plan,"No Meals");break;
63:           default : cout << "Something bad went wrong!\n"; break;
64:        }
65:        cout << Plan << " food plan." << endl;
66:
67:    }
```

```
Jim is part time
Jim is full time
Jim is on the No Meals food plan.
```

In lines 4 through 7, a number of enumerated types are defined. These serve to define the possible values for the bit fields within the Student class.

Student itself is declared in lines 9 through 23. Although this is a trivial class, it is interesting in that all the data is packed into 5 bits. The first bit represents the student's status: full-time or part-time. The second bit represents whether the student is an undergraduate. The third bit represents whether the student lives in a dorm. The final two bits represent the four possible food plans.

The class methods are written as for any other class, and are in no way affected by the fact that these are bit fields and not integers or enumerated types.

The member function GetStatus() reads the Boolean bit and returns an enumerated type, but this is not necessary. It could just as easily have been written to return the value of the bit field directly. The compiler would have done the translation.

To prove that to yourself, replace the GetStatus() implementation with this code:

```
STATUS student::GetStatus()
{
    return myStatus;
}
```

There should be no change whatsoever to the functioning of the program. It is a matter of clarity when reading the code; the compiler isn't particular.

Note that the code in line 42 *must* check the status and then print the meaningful message. It is tempting to write this:

```
cout << "Jim is " << Jim.GetStatus() << endl;
```

That will simply print this:

```
Jim is 0
```

The compiler has no way to translate the enumerated constant PartTime into meaningful text.

In line 57, the program switches on the food plan. Then, for each possible value, it puts a reasonable message into the buffer, which then is printed in line 65. Note again that the switch statement could have been written as this:

```
case  0: strcpy(Plan,"One meal"); break;
case  1: strcpy(Plan,"All meals"); break;
case  2: strcpy(Plan,"Weekend meals"); break;
case  3: strcpy(Plan,"No Meals");break;
```

The most important thing about using bit fields is that the client of the class does not need to worry about the data-storage implementation. Because the bit fields are private, you can feel free to change them later, and the interface will not need to change.

Learning How Memory Works

When you call a function, the code branches to the called function, parameters are passed in, and the body of the function is executed. When the function completes, a value is returned (unless the function returns void), and control returns to the calling function.

How is this task accomplished? How does the code know where to branch to? Where are the variables kept when they are passed in? What happens to variables that are declared in the body of the function? How is the return value passed back out? How does the code know where to resume?

If you don't understand how this works, you will find that programming remains a fuzzy mystery and debugging (covered on day 20) is nearly impossible. The explanation requires a brief tangent into a discussion of computer memory.

Examining the Levels of Abstraction

One of the principal hurdles in programming is grappling with the many layers of intellectual abstraction. Computers, of course, are just electronic machines. They don't know about windows and menus, they don't know about programs or instructions, and they don't even know about 1s and 0s. All that is really going on is that voltage is being measured at various places on an integrated circuit. Even this is an abstraction; electricity itself is just an intellectual concept, representing the behavior of subatomic particles.

Few programmers bother much with any level of detail below the idea of values in RAM. After all, you don't need to understand particle physics to drive a car, make toast, or hit a baseball, and you don't need to understand the electronics of a computer to program one.

You do need to understand how memory is organized, however. Without a reasonably strong mental picture of where your variables are when they are created, and how values are passed among functions, it will all remain an unmanageable mystery.

Partitioning RAM

When you begin your program, your operating system (DOS, UNIX, OS/2, or Windows) sets up various areas of memory based on the requirements of your compiler. As a C++ programmer, you often will be concerned with the global name space, the free store, the registers, the code space, and the stack.

Global variables and their close cousins, static variables, are (surprise!) in global name space. Local variables are on the stack, and variables you create with operator new are on the heap. All this gets much more complex when you zero in on how memory is managed on specific platforms (the Intel x86 platform, for example) and by specific operating systems (Windows, for example) but the essence is the same: You have global name space, a stack, and a heap.

Using Registers and the Instruction Pointer

Registers are a special area of memory built right into the central processing unit (or CPU). Registers take care of internal housekeeping. Much of what goes on in the registers is beyond the scope of this book, but what you are concerned about is the set of registers responsible for pointing, at any given moment, to the next line of code. This book refers to those registers as the *instruction pointer*. It is the job of the instruction pointer to keep track of which line of code is to be executed next.

The code itself is in code space, which is that part of memory set aside to hold the binary form of the instructions you created in your program. Each line of source code is translated into a series of instructions, and each of these instructions is at a particular address in memory. The instruction pointer has the address of the next instruction to execute.

Using the Stack

The *stack* is a special area of memory allocated for your program to hold the data required by each of the functions in your program. It is called a *stack* because it is a last-in-first-out queue, much like a stack of dishes at a cafeteria.

Last-in-first-out means that whatever is added to the stack last will be the first thing taken off. Most queues are like a line at a theater: The first one in line is the first one off. A stack is more like a stack of coins: If you stack 10 pennies on a tabletop and then take some back, the last three you put on will be the first three you take off.

When data is "pushed" onto the stack, the stack grows; as data is "popped" off the stack, the stack shrinks. It isn't possible to pop a dish off of the stack without first popping off all the dishes placed after that dish.

A stack of dishes is the common analogy. It is fine as far as it goes, but it is wrong in a fundamental way. A more accurate mental picture is of a series of cubbyholes aligned top to bottom. The top of the stack is whatever cubby the stack pointer (which is another register) happens to be pointing to.

Each of the cubbies has a sequential address, and one of those addresses is kept in the stack pointer register. Everything below that magic address, known as the top of the stack, is considered to be on the stack. Everything above the top of the stack is considered to be off the stack and invalid.

When data is put on the stack, it is placed into a cubby above the stack pointer, and then the stack pointer is moved to the new data. When data is popped off the stack, all that really happens is that the address of the stack pointer is changed by moving it down the stack.

Understanding How the Stack Works with Functions

When a program running on a PC under DOS branches to a function, the following things happen:

1. The address in the instruction pointer is incremented to the next instruction past the function call. That address then is placed on the stack, and it will be the return address when the function returns.

2. Room is made on the stack for the return type you have declared. On a system with 2-byte integers, if the return type is declared to be int, another 2 bytes are added to the stack, but no value is placed in these bytes.

3. The address of the called function, which is kept in a special area of memory set aside for that purpose, is loaded into the instruction pointer, so the next instruction executed will be in the called function.

4. The current top of the stack now is noted and is held in a special pointer called the *stack frame*. Everything added to the stack from now until the function returns will be considered "local" to the function.

5. All the arguments to the function are placed on the stack.

6. The instruction now in the instruction pointer is executed, thus executing the first instruction in the function.

7. Local variables are pushed onto the stack as they are defined.

When the function is ready to return, the return value is placed in the area of the stack reserved in step 2. The stack then is popped all the way up to the stack frame pointer, which effectively throws away all the local variables and the arguments to the function.

The return value is popped off the stack and assigned as the value of the function call itself, and the address stashed away in step 1 is retrieved and put into the instruction pointer. The program thus resumes immediately after the function call, with the value of the function retrieved.

Some of the details of this process change from compiler to compiler, or between computers, but the essential ideas are consistent across environments. In general, when you call a function, the return address and the parameters are put on the stack. During the life of the function, local variables are added to the stack. When the function returns, these are all removed by popping the stack.

Using the Heap

Free memory dedicated to your program but not assigned to the stack is available for your use and is referred to as the *heap*. On some computers and in some memory models, the stack and the heap actually can run into one another if you put more on the stack than it can hold. It therefore is important to tell your linker how much room to allocate for your stack so that this doesn't happen.

Most often you will use the built-in, compiler-provided operators `new` and `delete` for managing the heap, although on day 15 you will see how to override these operators as required.

The best way to think of the heap is as a pile of memory in no particular order and with no particular organization. This is absurd, of course, because it is exactly the same type of memory as the stack (and the code segment, for that matter) uses. You have no orderly access to this memory, however, except through the pointers returned by operator `new`.

The fact that two allocated variables abut each other in the heap is totally invisible to you. Even if you do become aware of the fact, you cannot count on it not changing over time unless you create a union of the two values. The best approach therefore is not to worry about the physical organization of the heap and, instead, to hang onto that pointer and use it to access your variables on the heap.

Working with Binary and Hexadecimal Values

When you examine memory in a debugger, you often will be confronted with values listed in hexadecimal or binary. Binary is the closest representation of the "real" value, as it corresponds to the bit values that underlie, at least at one level, all your programs and data.

Hexadecimal is simply a convenient way to aggregate binary data so that it is more easily "grokked" by humans. (For those few of you who are not Robert L. Heinlein fans, to *grok* something is to attain a deep and full understanding of it.) You soon will see that there is a trick for quickly and easily converting between binary and hexadecimal.

What Are These Strange Numbers?

You learned the fundamentals of arithmetic so long ago, it is hard to imagine what it would be like without that knowledge. When you look at the number 145, you instantly see *one-hundred forty-five* without much reflection.

Understanding binary and hexadecimal requires that you reexamine the number 145 and see it not as a number, but as a code for a number.

Start small: Examine the relationship between the number three and "3." The *numeral* 3 is a squiggle on a piece of paper, but the number three is an idea. The numeral is used to represent the number.

The distinction can be made clear by realizing that *three*, *3*, *III*, *III*, *and* *** all can be used to represent the same idea of three.

In base 10 (decimal) math, you use the numerals 0,1,2,3,4,5,6,7,8,9 to represent all numbers. How is the number ten represented?

One can imagine that we would have evolved a strategy of using the letter A to represent ten; or we might have used IIIIIIIIII to represent that idea. The Romans used X. The Arabic system, which we use, makes use of *position* with numerals to represent values. The first (far right) column is used for "ones," and the next column is used for tens. Thus, the number fifteen is represented as 15 (read that one-five); that is 1 ten and 5 ones.

14

Certain rules emerge, from which some generalizations can be made:

1. Base 10 uses the digits 0 through 9
2. The columns are powers of ten: 1s, 10s, 100s, and so on.
3. If the third column is 100, the largest number you can make with two columns is 99. More generally, with n columns, you can represent 0 to (10^n-1). Thus, with three columns, you can represent 0 to (10^3-1) or 0–999.

Using Other Bases

It is not a coincidence that we use base 10; we have 10 fingers. One can imagine a different base, however. Using the rules found in base 10, you can describe base 8:

1. The digits used in base 8 are 0 through 7.
2. The columns are powers of 8: 1s, 8s, 72s, and so on.
3. With n columns, you can represent 0 to 8^{n-1}.

To distinguish numbers written in each base, write the base as a subscript next to the number. The number fifteen in base ten would be written as 15_{10} and read as "one-five, base ten."

Thus, to represent the number 15_{10} in base 8, you would write 17_8. This is read "one seven base eight." Note that it also can be read "fifteen," because that is the number it continues to represent.

Why 17? The 1 means 1 eight, and the 7 means 7 ones. One eight plus seven ones equals fifteen. Consider fifteen asterisks:

```
*****     *****
*****
```

The natural tendency is to make two groups: a group of ten asterisks and another group of five asterisks. This would be represented in decimal as 15 (1 ten and 5 ones). You also can group the asterisks as

```
*****        ******
****
```

That is, eight asterisks and seven. That would be represented in base nine as 17_8—one eight and seven ones.

You can represent the number fifteen in base 10 as 15, in base 9 as 16_9, in base 8 as 17_8, and in base 7 as 21_7. Why 21_7? In base 7, there is no numeral 8. In order to represent fifteen, you will need two sevens and one 1.

How do you generalize the process? To convert a base 10 number to base 7, think about the columns: in base 7 they are 1s, 7s, 49s, 343s, and so on. Why these columns? They represent 7^0, 7^1, 7^2, 7^3, and so on. Create a table for yourself:

4	3	2	1
7^3	7^2	7^1	7^0
343	49	7	1

The first row represents the column number. The second row represents the power of 7. The third row represents the binary value of each number in that row.

To convert from a decimal value to base 7, examine the number and decide which column to use first. If the number is 200, for example, you know that column 4 (343) is 0, and you don't have to worry about it.

To find out how many 49s there are, divide 200 by 49. The answer is 4, so put 4 in column 3 and examine the remainder: 4. There are no 7s in 4, so put a 0 in the 7s column. There are 4 1s in 4, so put a 4 in the 1s column. The answer is 404_7.

To convert the number 968 to base 6:

5	4	3	2	1
6^4	6^3	6^2	6^1	6^0
1296	216	36	6	1

There are no 1296s in 968, so column 5 has 0. Dividing 968 by 216 yields 4, with a remainder of 104. Column 4 has the value 4. Dividing 104 by 36 yields 2, with a remainder of 32. Column 3 has the value 2. Dividing 32 by 6 yields 5, with a remainder of 2. The answer therefore is 4252_6.

5	4	3	2	1
6^4	6^3	6^2	6^1	6^0
1296	216	36	6	1
0	4	2	5	2

There is a shortcut when converting from one base to another base (such as 6) to base 10. You can multiply:

```
4  *  216  =  864
2  *   36  =   72
5  *    6  =   30
2  *    1  =    2
              968
```

14

Working with Binary Values

Base 2 is the ultimate extension of this idea. There are only two digits: 0 and 1. The columns follow:

Column:	8	7	6	5	4	3	2	1
Power:	2^7	2^6	2^5	2^4	2^3	2^2	2^1	2^0
Value:	128	64	32	16	8	4	2	1

To convert the number 88 to base 2, you follow the same procedure: there are no 128s, so column 8 is 0.

There is one 64 in 88, so column 7 is 1 and 24 is the remainder. There are no 32s in 24, so column 6 is 0.

There is one sixteen in 24, so column 5 is 1. The remainder is 8. There is one 8 in 8, so column 4 is 1. There is no remainder, so the rest of the columns are 0:

```
0    1    0    1    1    0    0    0
```

To test this answer, convert it back:

```
1  *  64  =  64
0  *  32  =   0
1  *  16  =  16
1  *   8  =   8
0  *   4  =   0
0  *   2  =   0
0  *   1  =   0
                88
```

Why Base 2?

The power of base 2 is that it corresponds so cleanly to what a computer needs to represent. Computers do not really know anything at all about letters, numerals, instructions, or programs. At their core, they are just circuitry—at a given juncture, there is a great deal of power or there is very little.

To keep the logic clean, engineers do not treat this as a relative scale—"a little power, some power, more power, lots of power, tons of power." Instead, they treat it as a binary scale—"enough power or not enough power." Rather than saying even enough or not enough, they simplify it down to "yes or no." Yes or no, or TRUE or FALSE, can be represented as 1 or 0. By convention, 1 means TRUE or Yes, but that is just a convention; it just as easily could have meant FALSE or No.

After you make this great leap of intuition, the power of binary becomes clear. With 1s and 0s, you can represent the fundamental truth of every circuit: There is power or there isn't power. All a computer ever knows is "Is you is, or is you ain't?" Is you is = 1; is you ain't = 0.

Bits and Bytes

After the decision is made to represent TRUE and FALSE with 1s and 0s, binary digits (or bits) become very important. Because early computers could send 8 bits at a time, it was natural to start writing code using 8-bit numbers, called *bytes*.

With 8 binary digits, you can represent up to 256 different values. Examine the columns: If all 8 bits are set (1), the value is 255. If none is set (all the bits are clear or 0), the value is 0. 0 through 255 represents 256 possible states.

What Is a K?

It turns out that 2^{10} (1,024) is roughly equal to 10^3 (1,000). This coincidence was too good to pass up, so computer scientists started referring to 2^{10} bytes as 1K or 1 kilobyte, based on the scientific prefix of *kilo* for thousand.

Similarly, 1,024 times 1,024 (1,048,576) is close enough to 1 million to receive the designation 1M or 1 megabyte, and 1,024 megabytes is called 1 gigabyte (*giga* implies thousand-million or billion.)

Binary Numbers

Computers use patterns of 1s and 0s to encode everything they do. Machine instructions are encoded as a series of 1s and 0s, and are interpreted by the fundamental circuitry. Arbitrary sets of 1s and 0s can be translated back into numbers by computer scientists, but it would be a mistake to think that these numbers have intrinsic meaning.

The Intel 80x6 chip set, for example, interprets the bit pattern 1001 0101 as an instruction. You certainly can translate this into decimal (149), but that number has no meaning.

Sometimes the numbers are instructions, sometimes they are values, and sometimes they are codes. One important standardized code set is ASCII. In *ASCII*, every letter and punctuation is given a 7-digit binary representation. The lowercase letter *a*, for example, is represented by 0110 0001. This is *not* a number, although you can translate it to the number 97 (64 + 32 + 1). It is in this sense that people say that the letter *a* is represented by 97 in ASCII; but the truth is that the binary representation of 97, 0110 0001, is the encoding of the letter *a*, and the decimal value 97 is a human convenience.

14

Note: Note that the value for the uppercase *A* is different from the value for the lowercase *a*. This is because the real meaning of the bit pattern 01100001 is tied to the key pressed (in this case, the *a* key), and Shift+A is represented by 0100 0001 or 65.

Working with Hexadecimal Values

Because binary numbers are difficult to read, a simpler way to represent the same values is needed. Translating from binary to base 10 involves a fair bit of manipulation of numbers, but it turns out that translating from base 2 to base 16 is very simple because there is a very good shortcut.

To understand this, first you must understand base 16, which is known as hexadecimal. In base 16, there are 16 numerals: 0,1,2,3,4,5,6,7,8,9,A,B,C,D,E,F. The last six are arbitrary; the letters A through F were chosen because they are easy to represent on a keyboard. The columns in hexadecimal follow:

4	3	2	1
16^3	16^2	16^1	16^0
4096	256	16	1

To translate from hexadecimal to decimal, you can multiply. The number F8C represents the following:

```
F  *  256  =  15  *  256  =  3840
8  *   16  =            128
C  *    1  =  12  *    1  =    12
                            3980
```

Translating the number FC to binary is best done by translating first to base 10, and then to binary:

```
F  *  16  =  15  *  16  =  240
C  *   1  =  12  *   1  =   12
                          252
```

Converting 252_{10} to binary requires the chart:

Column:	9	8	7	6	5	4	3	2	1
Power:	2^8	2^7	2^6	2^5	2^4	2^3	2^2	2^1	2^0
Value:	256	128	64	32	16	8	4	2	1

```
There are no 256s.
                1 128 leaves 124
                    1 64 leaves 60
                        1 32 leaves 28
                            1 16 leaves 12
                                1 8 leaves 4
                                    1 4 leaves 0
                                        0
                                                    0
            1   1   1   1   1   1   0   0
```

The answer in binary therefore is 1111 1100.

It turns out that if you treat this binary number as two sets of four digits, you can do a magical transformation.

The right set is 1100. In decimal, that is 12; or in hexadecimal, it is C.

The left set is 1111, which in base 10 is 15, or in hexadecimal is F.

You therefore have the following:

```
1111  1100
F     C
```

Putting the two hexadecimal numbers together is FC, which is the real value of 1111 1100. This shortcut always works. You can take any binary number of any length and reduce it to sets of 4, translate each set of four to hexadecimal, and put the hexadecimal numbers together to get the result in hexadecimal. Here's a much larger number:

```
1011  0001  1101  0111
```

The columns are 1, 2, 4, 8, 16, 32, 64, 128, 256, 512, 1024, 2048, 4096, 8192, 16384, and 32768.

```
1 * 1   =           1
1 * 2   =           2
1 * 4   =           4
0 * 8   =           0

1 * 16  =          16
0 * 32  =           0
1 * 64  =          64
1 * 128 =         128

1 * 256 =         256
0 * 512 =           0
0 * 1024 =          0
0 * 2048 =          0

1 * 4096 =      4,096
1 * 8192 =      8,192
0 * 16384 =         0
1 * 32768 =    32,768
Total:         45,527
```

Converting this to hexadecimal requires a chart with the hexadecimal values:

```
65535      4096    256    16    1
```

There are no 65,535s in 45,527, so the first column is 4,096. There are 11 4096s (45,056), with a remainder of 471. There is 1 256 in 471, with a remainder of 215. There are 13 16s (208) in 215, with a remainder of 7. The hexadecimal number therefore is B1D7.

Check the math:

```
B  (11)  *   4096  =   45,056
1   *   256  =            256
D  (13)  *   16  =        208
7   *  1   =               7
Total                  45,527
```

The shortcut version would be to take the original binary number, 1011000111010111, and break it into groups of 4: 1011 0001 1101 0111. Each of the four then is evaluated as a hexadecimal number:

```
1011 =
1 * 1 =        1
1 * 2 =        2
0 * 4 =        0
1 * 8 =        8
Total         11
Hex:           B

0001 =
1 * 1 =        1
0 * 2 =        0
0 * 4 =        0
0 * 8 =        0
Total          1
Hex:           1

1101 =
1 * 1 =        1
0 * 2 =        0
1 * 4 =        4
1 * 8 =        8
Total         13
Hex =          D

0111 =
0 * 1 =        1
1 * 2 =        2
1 * 4 =        4
0 * 8 =        0
Total          7
Hex:           7

Total Hex:  B1D7
```

Summary

Today you learned a bit more about the layout of memory, including the stack, the heap, and code space. You also saw how to create and manipulate bit fields, and how to turn bits on and off using by bit masks. Finally, you saw in detail how binary and hexadecimal numbers can be manipulated and used.

Q&A

Q Why do I need to understand bit twiddling?

A Although new programs have done a good job of hiding much of the internal representation of data from the user, professional programmers simply *must* understand how the data is stored and manipulated in order to make efficient use of the available machinery.

Q When would you use a bit field?

A Use a bit field when you need to store a number of small bits of information and storage size matters to your program. Often it is easier to read a program that "wastes" the space of devoting 2 bytes to a Boolean operator, instead of stuffing more information into a bit field than a programmer easily can understand.

Q Why is hexadecimal used?

A There is a convenient mapping between 4 binary bits and one hexadecimal digit.

Workshop

The Workshop provides quiz questions to help you solidify your understanding of the material covered, and exercises to provide you with experience in using what you have learned. Try to answer the quiz and exercise questions before checking the answers in Appendix A, and make sure that you understand the answers before continuing to the next chapter.

Quiz

1. What is the difference between OR and Exclusive-Or?
2. How do you set a bit?
3. How do you clear a bit?
4. What is the difference between the heap and the stack?
5. What is the value 1011 1101 in hexadecimal? Explain two ways to compute the answer.

Exercises

1. Write a function that will accept an unsigned short and will return the value with the high and low bits swapped.

2. Write masks to access the different values in the specification that follows. (Don't worry yet what the different values mean.) The masks all should be const unsigned chars. In the nomenclature that follows, D0 is the lowest bit in the byte, and D7 is the highest.

   For the fields that are more than a single bit, also include a mask that will cover the entire field (all of the relevant bits set). These will be needed in exercise 3.

3. Exercise 2 shows the specifications for a serial communications chip. Design a class that will encapsulate its behavior. (Write the public part of the class declaration.)

   The chip is configured into your computer to appear at a fixed memory location, as if it were regular memory. The values in the status byte and the received character byte, however, are changed by the chip to reflect the events on the communications line, rather than those set by you. If you read the status byte, for example, the lowest bit (receive ready) would be 0 until some data is sent through the communication line (presumably from some other computer or a modem). When a full byte of data is received, the chip sets the data received bit to 1, and the received character byte to the value that was received. When the byte is read from the receive buffer, the bit is reset (set to 0).

   The four bytes defined later in this exercise will appear to your computer as if they are in three successive memory locations. Your class should accept, in its constructor, the address of byte 0, and it will find the next three bytes in the next three memory locations. In other words, it should treat the passed-in address as a pointer to an unsigned char array with a length of 4.

   Your class should provide the capability to read and write over the serial port. If Read is called and there are no characters available, it should return 00 (the NULL character). If a read error is detected, your serial port class always should return 00 until a special ResetError method is called. (The chip will reset the error bits when you read from the receive data location.) Your Write method should make sure that the chip is ready for the next character to be transmitted (by testing for transmit ready). If the chip isn't ready for another character to be transmitted (it's still working on the last character), your Write function should wait.

   Your class also should have methods to set the different configuration values. (One common error to watch out for: When setting one of the values in the configuration byte, don't wipe out the other values. Use the masks cleverly.)

**Note:** The parity error bit is set when the last received character has the incorrect parity, according to the parity setting in the configuration byte. An overrun error occurs when a character has been fully received before the preceding character has been read. This would cause the receiving computer to lose one of the characters.

4. Write the entire class discussed in exercise 3. Be sure to start the communication port with reasonable defaults for the configuration parameters, and be sure to clear any errors it might have pending.

14

Iterators

An *iterator* is an object that points into a list and can return the first, current, last, or next item on that list. Generic iterators are difficult to write and raise many interesting programming and database issues. Today you will learn

☐ How to create an iterator for the BTree class

☐ How to use that iterator to extend the search functionality

☐ What issues iterators present to the programmer

An iterator enables you to move through a list from a given starting point, examining each node in turn. General purpose iterators can be very flexible, enabling you to walk forward and backward in the list.

Most collections let the program ask for more than one iterator on the list, which means that the user can have iterators pointing to different parts of the same list. Additionally, some iterators are read/write, which enables the user to insert and delete items in the list.

Using an Iterator

The best way to study iterators is to use one to solve a real-world problem. ROBIN, as currently written, has a significant limitation: You can search only for an exact match on a given term. If there are notes with the words *computer*, *computing*, and *computerize*, there is no easy way to search for all these at the same time.

Presumably, the user would like to enter the string comput and see all the notes with words that begin with these six letters. Searching the list for each of these permutations is tricky, however, because the words *computing* and *computerize* might not be on the same page.

Getting from *computing* to *computerize* requires going up through two nodes and back down to a new leaf page. Putting the capability to do this into the list makes no sense; the list's primary mode of finding and adding indexes is the existing recursive routines.

Creating an iterator for the BTree class solves this problem. The program searches for the *first* word that matches the target string and returns that index. The search also initializes the iterator, so that calling GetNext() will return the *next* index that matches the string.

Because the list is sorted alphabetically, finding all the words that match the string is as simple as finding the first match, and then iterating through the list until you find the first word that does *not* match the target string, at which time you are done.

Understanding How the Iterator Works

To accomplish this goal, the B-tree must be extended to include an iterator object. The job of the iterator is to answer the question *What is the next entry in the list?*

To simplify this task, I've tailored the iterator to meet the specific needs of the existing B-tree. The iterator keeps track of every page that matches the target string until the leaf page is found. The *next* index is defined as the next index in the tree after the last find().

Usually, the next index is on the same page as the current index, but not always. When the iterator must find the next page, it walks up its node list, hunting for the first node that has another index in its list. After the iterator finds that node, it works its way back down the tree to the first index on the leaf page and returns that value.

It is a design goal of the Iterator class to hide all the details of finding the next index from its clients. The client calls GetNext(), which returns the offset of the next matching record, or 0 if there is none.

Illustrating an Iterator over a B-Tree

To keep the code simple, and to allow a full and in-depth exploration of how the iterator works, I'll implement only the most fundamental functionality in the iterator, as shown in the following listings. Listing 15.1 provides the header file BTree.hpp. Listing 15.2 is BTree.cpp, listing 15.3 is Page.cpp, listing 15.4 is Iterator.cpp, and listing 15.5 is Index.cpp. The data file and wnjfile listings have not changed, but are provided here for completeness as listings 15.6 and 15.7, respectively. Listing 15.9 is the driver program.

Type **Listing 15.1 BTree.hpp**

```
 1:    //***********************************************
 2:        // PROGRAM:   Btree, Page and Index declarations
 3:        // FILE:      btree.hpp
 4:        // PURPOSE:   provide fundamental btree functionality
 5:        // NOTES:
 6:        // AUTHOR:    Jesse Liberty (jl)
 7:        // REVISIONS: 11/1/94 1.0 jl  initial release
 8:        // ***********************************************
 9:        #ifndef BTREE_HPP              // inclusion guards
10:        #define BTREE_HPP
11:    #include <time.h>
12:        #include <string.h>
13:        #include <fstream.h>
14:    #include "stdef.hpp"
15:        const int Order =      4; //31;  // 31 indices and 1 header
16:        const int dataLen =   11; // length of a key
17:        const int MaxPages =  500; // more than we need
18:        const int SizeItem =   16;  // key + offset
19:        const int SizePointer = 2; // size of offset
20:        const int PageSize = (Order+1) * SizeItem;
21:        const int offInt = 2;
22:        // forward declarations
23:    class Page;
24:        class Index;
```

continues

Listing 15.1 continued

```
25:      // all members are public
26:      // used only by Iterator
27:     struct History
28:      {
29:         History(int, int,BOOL);
30:         int PageNo;
31:         int OffSet;
32:         BOOL IsNode;
33:      };
34:      // Iterator class keeps track
35:      // of current (and next) index
36:     class Iterator
37:      {
38:     public:
39:         Iterator();
40:         ~Iterator();
41:         void RecordNode(int, int);
42:         void RecordLeaf(int, int);
43:         History * GetLast();
44:         History * GetFirst();
45:         int GetNext(const Index&);
46:         void Reset();
47:      private:
48:       History* myHistory[MaxPages];
49:       int myNext;
50:      };
51:     class DataFile
52:      {
53:      public:
54:         // constructors & destructor
55:         DataFile();
56:         ~DataFile(){}
57:         // management of files
58:         void Close();
59:         void Create();
60:         void GetRecord(int, char*, int&, time_t&);
61:         int Insert(char *);
62:      private:
63:      fstream myFile;
64:      };
65:     class WNJFile
66:      {
67:      public:
68:         // constructors & destructor
69:         WNJFile();
70:         ~WNJFile(){}
71:         // management of files
72:         void Close();
73:         void Create();
74:         int* Find(int NextWNJ);
75:         int Insert(int, int);
76:       int Append(int);
77:      private:
78:      static int myCount;
```

```
79:      fstream myFile;
80:      union
81:      {
82:         int myints[5];
83:        char  myArray[5*4];
84:      };
85:      };
86:
87:      // IDXManager - in memory keeps track of what pages are
88:      // already in memory and swaps to disk as required
89:      class IDXManager
90:      {
91:      public:
92:         // constructors & destructor
93:         IDXManager();
94:         ~IDXManager(){}
95:
96:         // management of files
97:         void Close(int);
98:         int Create();
99:
100:        // Page manipulation
101:        Page* GetPage(int);
102:        void SetPage(Page*);
103:        void Insert(Page * newPage);
104:        void Save(Page* pg);
105:        int NewPage(Index&, BOOL);
106:        int NewPage(Index *array, int offset, BOOL leaf, int count);
107:
108:     private:
109:        Page* myPages[MaxPages];
110:        fstream myFile;
111:        int myCount;
112:        };
113:
114:        // the btree itself -has a pointer to first page
115:        class BTree
116:        {
117:        public:
118:           // constructors and destructor
119:           BTree();
120:           ~BTree();
121:
122:           // utility functions
123:           void AddKey(char* data, int offset);//,BOOL synonym = FALSE);
124:           void Insert(char* buffer, int, char**);
125:           void Insert(char*);
126:           void PrintTree();
127:           int Find(char* data);
128:           int FindExact(char* data);
129:           int GetNext(char* data);
130:
131:           // page methods
132:           Page* GetPage(int page)
133:              { return theIDXManager.GetPage(page); }
```

continues

Listing 15.1 continued

```
134:        int NewPage(Index& pIndex, BOOL IsLeaf)
135:            { return theIDXManager.NewPage(pIndex,FALSE); }
136:
137:        static int myAlNum(char ch);
138:        // public static member!
139:        static  IDXManager theIDXManager;
140:        static WNJFile    theWNJFile;
141:        static DataFile theDataFile;
142:        static Iterator theIter;
143:
144:        static BOOL GetWord(char*, char*, int&);
145:        static void GetStats();
146:        static int NodeIndexCtr;
147:        static int LeafIndexCtr;
148:        static int NodePageCtr;
149:        static int LeafPageCtr;
150:        static int NodeIndexPerPage[Order+1];
151:        static int LeafIndexPerPage[Order+1];
152:
153:    private:
154:        int myRoot;
155:    };
156:
157:    // index objects point to pages or real data
158:    class Index
159:    {
160:    public:
161:        // constructors & destructor
162:        Index();
163:        Index(char *);
164:        Index (char*, int);
165:        Index(Index&);
166:        ~Index(){}
167:
168:        // accessors
169:        const char * GetData() const  { return myData; }
170:        void SetData(const Index& rhs)
171:            { strcpy(myData,rhs.GetData()); }
172:        void SetData(const char * rhs)
173:            { strcpy(myData,rhs); }
174:        int GetPointer()const { return myPointer; }
175:        void SetPointer (int pg) { myPointer = pg; }
176:
177:        // utility functions
178:        void PrintKey();
179:        void PrintPage();
180:        int Insert(Index& ref,BOOL findOnly = FALSE);//, BOOL findExac = FALSE);
181:
182:        int Begins(const Index& rhs) const;
183:
184:        // overloaded operators
185:        int operator==(const Index& rhs);
186:
187:        int operator < (const Index& rhs)
```

```
188:          {return strcmp(myData,rhs.GetData())<0;}
189:
190:      int operator <= (const Index& rhs)
191:          {return strcmp(myData,rhs.GetData())<=0;}
192:
193:      int operator > (const Index& rhs)
194:          {return strcmp(myData,rhs.GetData())>0;}
195:
196:      int operator >= (const Index& rhs)
197:          {return strcmp(myData,rhs.GetData())>=0;}
198:
199:  public:
200:      int myPointer;
201:      char myData[SizeItem - SizePointer];
202:  };
203:
204:
205:  // pages - consist of header and array of indices
206:  class Page
207:  {
208:  public:
209:      // constructors and destructor
210:      Page();
211:      Page(char*);
212:      Page(Index&,BOOL);
213:      Page(Index*, int, BOOL, int);
214:      ~Page(){}
215:
216:      // insertion and searchoperations
217:      int Insert(Index&, BOOL findOnly = FALSE);//, BOOL synonym = FALSE);
218:      int Find(Index& idx) { return Insert(idx,TRUE); }
219:      int InsertLeaf(Index&);
220:      int FindLeaf(Index&,BOOL findOnly);//, BOOL synonym = FALSE);
221:      int InsertNode(Index&,BOOL findOnly = FALSE);//, BOOL synonym = FALSE);
222:      void Push(Index&,int offset=0, BOOL=TRUE);
223:
224:      // accessors
225:      Index GetFirstIndex() { return myKeys[0]; }
226:      Index GetIndex(int offset) { return myKeys[offset]; }
227:      BOOL GetIsLeaf() const { return myVars.IsLeaf; }
228:      int GetCount() const { return myVars.myCount; }
229:      void SetCount(int cnt) { myVars.myCount=cnt; }
230:      time_t GetTime() { return myTime; }
231:      BOOL GetLocked() { return myVars.IsLocked; }
232:      void SetLocked (BOOL state) { myVars.IsLocked = state; }
233:
234:      // page manipulation
235:      int GetPageNumber() const { return myVars.myPageNumber; }
236:      Page* GetPage(int page)
237:          { return BTree::theIDXManager.GetPage(page); }
238:      int NewPage(Index& rIndex, BOOL IsLeaf)
239:          { return BTree::theIDXManager.NewPage(rIndex,FALSE); }
240:
241:      int NewPage(Index* arr, int off,BOOL isL, int cnt)
242:          { return    BTree::theIDXManager.NewPage(arr,off,isL, cnt); }
```

continues

405

Listing 15.1 continued

```
243:
244:        // utility functions
245:        void Nullify(int offset);
246:        void Print();
247:        fstream& Write(fstream&);
248:        void ReCount();
249:
250:        static int GetgPageNumber(){ return gPage; }
251:        static void SetgPageNumber(int pg) { gPage = pg; }
252:
253:    private:
254:        Index * const myKeys; // will point to myVars.mk
255:        union
256:        {
257:            char myBlock[PageSize];   // a page from disk
258:            struct
259:            {
260:                int myCount;
261:                BOOL IsLeaf;
262:                int myPageNumber;
263:                BOOL IsLocked;
264:                char filler[8]; // we want 16 bytes of overhead
265:                char mk[Order*sizeof(Index)];   // array of indices
266:            }myVars;
267:        };
268:
269:        // memory only
270:        static int gPage;
271:        time_t myTime; // for lifo queue
272:    };
273:
274:    #endif
```

Type Listing 15.2 BTree.cpp

```
1:     // ************************************************
2:     // PROGRAM:  Btree
3:     // FILE:     btree.cpp
4:     // PURPOSE:  provide fundamental btree functionality
5:     // NOTES:
6:     // AUTHOR:   Jesse Liberty (jl)
7:     // REVISIONS: 11/1/94 1.0 jl  initial release
8:     // ************************************************
9:
10:    #include "btree.hpp"
11:    #include "stdef.hpp"
12:    #include <ctype.h>
13:    #include <stdlib.h>
14:
15:    // construct the tree
16:    // initialize myRoot pointer to nothing
17:    // either create or read the index file
```

```
18:      BTree::BTree():myRoot(0)
19:      {
20:         myRoot = theIDXManager.Create();
21:         theDataFile.Create();
22:         theWNJFile.Create();
23:
24:      }
25:
26:      // write out the index file
27:      BTree::~BTree()
28:      {
29:         theIDXManager.Close(myRoot);
30:         theDataFile.Close();
31:         theWNJFile.Close();
32:      }
33:
34:      // find an existing record
35:      int BTree::Find(char * str)
36:      {
37:         Index index(str);
38:         BTree::theIter.Reset();
39:         if (!myRoot)
40:            return 0L;
41:         else
42:            return GetPage(myRoot)->Find(index);
43:      }
44:
45:
46:      int BTree::GetNext(char * str)
47:      {
48:         Index index(str);
49:         return BTree::theIter.GetNext(index);
50:      }
51:
52:
53:      void BTree::Insert(char * buffer, int argc, char** argv)
54:      {
55:         // get each word,
56:         int offset = theDataFile.Insert(buffer);
57:         for (int i = 1; i<argc; i++)
58:         {
59:            AddKey(argv[i],offset);
60:         }
61:
62:      }
63:
64:      void BTree::Insert(char* buffer)
65:      {
66:
67:         if (strlen(buffer) < 3)
68:            return;
69:
70:          char *buff = buffer;
71:          char word[PageSize];
72:          int wordOffset = 0;
```

continues

407

Listing 15.2 continued

```
73:           int offset;
74:
75:       if (GetWord(buff,word,wordOffset))
76:       {
77:           offset = theDataFile.Insert(buffer);
78:           AddKey(word,offset);
79:       }
80:
81:
82:       while (GetWord(buff,word,wordOffset))
83:       {
84:           AddKey(word,offset);
85:       }
86:
87:    }
88:
89:    void BTree::AddKey(char * str, int offset )
90:    {
91:
92:       if (strlen(str) < 3)
93:           return;
94:
95:       int retVal =0;
96:       Index index(str,offset);
97:       if (!myRoot)
98:       {
99:           myRoot = theIDXManager.NewPage (index,TRUE);
100:      }
101:      else
102:      {
103:          retVal = GetPage(myRoot)->Insert(index);
104:          if (retVal) // our root split
105:          {
106:              // create a pointer to the old top
107:              Index index(GetPage(myRoot)->GetFirstIndex());
108:              index.SetPointer(myRoot);
109:              // make the new page & insert the index
110:              int PageNumber = NewPage(index,FALSE);
111:
112:              Page* pg = GetPage(PageNumber);
113:
114:              //get a pointer to the new (sibling) page
115:              Index Sib(GetPage(retVal)->GetFirstIndex());
116:              Sib.SetPointer(retVal);
117:              // put it into the page
118:              pg->InsertLeaf(Sib);
119:
120:              // reset myRoot to point to the new top
121:              myRoot = PageNumber;
122:          }
123:      }
124:    }
125:
126:    void BTree::PrintTree()
127:    {
```

```
128:        GetPage(myRoot)->Print();
129:
130:        cout << "\n\nStats:" << endl;
131:        cout << "Node pages:    " << NodePageCtr << endl;
132:        cout << "Leaf pages:    " << LeafPageCtr << endl;
133:        cout << "Node indexes: " << NodeIndexCtr << endl;
134:        cout << "Leaf indexes: " << LeafIndexCtr << endl;
135:        for (int i = 0; i < Order +1; I++)
136:        {
137:            if (NodeIndexPerPage[i])
138:            {
139:                cout << "Pages with " << i << " nodes:   ";
140:                cout << NodeIndexPerPage[i] << endl;
141:            }
142:            if (LeafIndexPerPage[i])
143:            {
144:                cout << "Pages with " << i << " leaves: ";
145:                cout << LeafIndexPerPage[i] << endl;
146:            }
147:        }
148:
149:    }
150:
151:    BOOL BTree::GetWord(char* string, char* word, int& wordOffset)
152:    {
153:
154:        if (!string[wordOffset])
155:            return FALSE;
156:
157:        char *p1, *p2;
158:        p1 = p2 = string+wordOffset;
159:
160:        // eat leading spaces
161:        for (int i = 0; i<(int)strlen(p1) && !BTree::myAlNum(p1[0]); i++)
162:            p1++;
163:
164:        // see if you have a word
165:        if (!BTree::myAlNum(p1[0]))
166:            return FALSE;
167:
168:         p2 = p1; // point to start of word
169:
170:        // march p2 to end of word
171:        while (BTree::myAlNum(p2[0]))
172:            p2++;
173:
174:        int len = int(p2-p1);
175:    #if defined(_MSVC_16BIT) || defined(_MSVC_32BIT)
    :    {
    :        len = __min(len,(int)PageSize);
    :    }
    :    #else
    :    {
    :        len = min(len,(int)PageSize);
    :    }
    :    #endif
```

continues

Listing 15.2 continued

```
176:
177:        strncpy (word,p1,len);
178:        word[len]='\0';
179:
180:        for (i = int (p2-string); i<(int)strlen(string) &&
               !BTree::myAlNum(p2[0]); i++)
181:           p2++;
182:
183:        wordOffset = int (p2-string);
184:
185:        return TRUE;
186:    }
187:
188:    int BTree::myAlNum(char ch)
189:    {
190:        return isalnum(ch) ||
191:           ch == '-' ||
192:           ch == '\'' ||
193:           ch == '(' ||
194:           ch == ')';
195:    }
```

Type

Listing 15.3 Page.cpp

```
1:    // **************************************************
2:    // PROGRAM:  Page
3:    // FILE:     Page.cpp
4:    // PURPOSE:  provide fundamental btree functionality
5:    // NOTES:
6:    // AUTHOR:   Jesse Liberty (jl)
7:    // REVISIONS: 11/1/94 1.0 jl  initial release
8:    // **************************************************
9:
10:   #include "btree.hpp"
11:   #include <assert.h>
12:
13:   // constructors
14:
15:   // default constructor
16:   Page::Page()
17:   {
18:   }
19:
20:   // create a page from a buffer read in from disk
21:   Page::Page(char *buffer):
22:      myKeys((Index*)myVars.mk)
23:   {
24:      assert(sizeof(myBlock) == PageSize);
25:      assert(sizeof(myVars) == PageSize);
26:      memcpy(&myBlock,buffer,PageSize);
27:      SetLocked(FALSE);
```

```
28:            myTime = time(NULL);
29:        }
30:
31:        // create a Page from the first index
32:        Page::Page(Index& index, BOOL bLeaf):
33:            myKeys((Index*)myVars.mk)
34:        {
35:
36:            myVars.myCount=1;
37:            myVars.IsLeaf = bLeaf;
38:            SetLocked(FALSE);
39:            // if this is a leaf, this is the first
40:            // index on the first page, set its pointer
41:            // based on creating a new wnj. otherwise
42:            // you are here creating a new node, do not
43:            // set the pointer, it is already set.
44:            if (bLeaf)
45:                index.SetPointer(BTree::theWNJFile.Append(index.GetPointer()));
46:            myKeys[0]=index;
47:            myVars.myPageNumber = gPage++;
48:            myTime = time(NULL);
49:        }
50:
51:        // create a page by splitting another page
52:        Page::Page(Index *array, int offset, BOOL bLeaf,int count):
53:            myKeys((Index*)myVars.mk)
54:        {
55:            myVars.IsLeaf = bLeaf;
56:            myVars.myCount = 0;
57:            for (int i=0, j = offset; j<Order && i < count; i++, j++)
58:            {
59:                myKeys[i]= array[j];
60:                myVars.myCount++;
61:            }
62:            myVars.myPageNumber = gPage++;
63:            SetLocked(FALSE);
64:            myTime = time(NULL);
65:        }
66:
67:        void Page::Nullify(int offset)
68:        {
69:            for (int i = offset; i<Order; i++)
70:            {
71:                    myKeys[i].SetPointer(0);
72:                    myVars.myCount—;
73:            }
74:        }
75:
76:        // decide whether I'm a leaf or a node
77:        // and pass this index to the right
78:        // function. If findOnly is true, don't insert
79:        // just return the page number (for now)
80:        int Page::Insert(Index& rIndex, BOOL findOnly)
81:        {
82:            int result;
```

continues

Listing 15.3 continued

```
83:            if (myVars.IsLeaf)
84:            {
85:                SetLocked(TRUE);
86:                result = FindLeaf(rIndex,findOnly);
87:                SetLocked(FALSE);
88:                return result;
89:            }
90:            else
91:            {
92:                SetLocked(TRUE);
93:                result = InsertNode(rIndex,findOnly);
94:                SetLocked(FALSE);
95:                return result;
96:            }
97:        }
98:
99:
100:       // find the right page for this index
101:       int Page::InsertNode(Index& rIndex, BOOL findOnly)
102:       {
103:           int retVal =0;
104:           BOOL inserted = FALSE;
105:           int i;
106:
107:           assert(myVars.myCount>0); // nodes have at least 1
108:           assert(myKeys[0].GetPointer()); // must be valid
109:
110:           if (findOnly)
111:           {
112:               for (i = 0; i< myVars.myCount; i++)
113:               {
114:                   if (rIndex.Begins(myKeys[i]))
115:                   {
116:                       BTree::theIter.RecordNode(myVars.myPageNumber,i);
117:                       return myKeys[i].Insert(rIndex,findOnly);
118:                   }
119:               }
120:           }
121:
122:
123:           // does it go before my first entry?
124:           if (!inserted && rIndex < myKeys[0])
125:           {
126:
127:               if (findOnly)
128:                   return 0L;
129:
130:               myKeys[0].SetData(rIndex);
131:               BTree::theIter.RecordNode(myVars.myPageNumber,0);
132:               retVal=myKeys[0].Insert(rIndex,findOnly);
133:               inserted = TRUE;
134:           }
135:
136:           // find insertion point
```

```
137:        if (!inserted)
138:        {
139:            for (i = myVars.myCount-1; i>=0; i—)
140:            {
141:                assert(myKeys[i].GetPointer());
142:                if ( (rIndex >= myKeys[i]))
143:                {
144:                    BTree::theIter.RecordNode(myVars.myPageNumber,i);
145:                    retVal=myKeys[i].Insert(rIndex,findOnly);
146:                    inserted = TRUE;
147:                    break;
148:                }
149:            }
150:        }
151:        assert(inserted);   // change to exception if not!
152:
153:        // if you had to split
154:        if (retVal && !findOnly) // got back a pointer to a new page
155:        {
156:            Index * pIndex = new Index(GetPage(retVal)->GetFirstIndex());
157:            pIndex->SetPointer(retVal);
158:            retVal = InsertLeaf(*pIndex);
159:        }
160:        return retVal;
161:    }
162:
163:    // called if current page is a leaf
164:    int Page::FindLeaf(Index& rIndex, BOOL findOnly)
165:    {
166:        int result = 0;
167:
168:        // no duplicates!
169:        for (int i=0; i < myVars.myCount; i++)
170:        {
171:            if (findOnly)
172:            {
173:                if (rIndex.Begins(myKeys[i]))
174:                {
175:                    BTree::theIter.RecordLeaf(myVars.myPageNumber,i);
176:                    return myKeys[i].GetPointer();
177:                }
178:            }
179:            else
180:                if (rIndex == myKeys[i])
181:                    return BTree::theWNJFile.Insert(
182:                            rIndex.GetPointer(),
183:                                myKeys[i].GetPointer());
184:        }
185:
186:        if (findOnly)              // not found
187:            return result;
188:
189:        // this index item does not yet exist
190:        // before you push it into the index
191:        // push an entry into the wnj.idx
```

continues

Listing 15.3 continued

```
192:        // and set the index to point to that entry
193:        rIndex.SetPointer(BTree::theWNJFile.Append(rIndex.GetPointer())); //
            new!
194:        return InsertLeaf(rIndex);
195:    }
196:
197:    int Page::InsertLeaf(Index& rIndex)
198:    {
199:        int result = 0;
200:        if (myVars.myCount < Order)
201:            Push(rIndex);
202:        else      // overflow the page
203:        {
204:            // make sibling
205:            int NewPg =
206:                NewPage(myKeys,Order/2,myVars.IsLeaf,myVars.myCount);
207:            Page* Sibling = GetPage(NewPg);
208:            Nullify(Order/2);                       // nullify my right half
209:
210:            // does it fit in this side?
211:            if (myVars.myCount>Order/2-1 && rIndex <= myKeys[Order/2-1])
212:                Push(rIndex);
213:            else  // push it into the new sibling
214:                Sibling->Push(rIndex);
215:
216:            result = NewPg; // we split, pass it up
217:        }
218:        return result;
219:    }
220:
221:    // put the new index into this page (in order)
222:    void Page::Push(Index& rIndex,int offset,BOOL first)
223:    {
224:        BOOL inserted = FALSE;
225:        assert(myVars.myCount < Order);
226:        for (int i=offset; i<Order && i<myVars.myCount; i++)
227:        {
228:            assert(myKeys[i].GetPointer());
229:            if (rIndex <= myKeys[i])
230:            {
231:                Push(myKeys[i],offset+1,FALSE);
232:                myKeys[i]=rIndex;
233:                inserted = TRUE;
234:                break;
235:            }
236:        }
237:        if (!inserted)
238:            myKeys[myVars.myCount] = rIndex;
239:
240:        if (first)
241:            myVars.myCount++;
242:    }
243:
244:
```

```
245:    void Page::Print()
246:    {
247:          if (!myVars.IsLeaf)
248:          {
249:              BTree::NodePageCtr++;
250:              BTree::NodeIndexPerPage[myVars.myCount]++;
251:              BTree::NodeIndexCtr+=myVars.myCount;
252:          }
253:          else
254:          {
255:              BTree::LeafPageCtr++;
256:              BTree::LeafIndexPerPage[myVars.myCount]++;
257:              BTree::LeafIndexCtr+=myVars.myCount;
258:          }
259:
260:          for (int i = 0; i<Order && i < myVars.myCount; i++)
261:          {
262:              assert(myKeys[i].GetPointer());
263:              if (myVars.IsLeaf)
264:                  myKeys[i].PrintKey();
265:              else
266:                  myKeys[i].PrintPage();
267:          }
268:    }
269:
270:    // write out the entire page as a block
271:    fstream& Page::Write(fstream& file)
272:    {
273:        char buffer[PageSize];
274:        memcpy(buffer,&myBlock,PageSize);
275:        file.flush();
276:        file.clear();
277:        file.seekp(myVars.myPageNumber*PageSize);
278:        file.write(buffer,PageSize);
279:        return file;
280:    }
```

Type   Listing 15.4 Iterator.cpp

```
1:      // *****************************************************
2:      // PROGRAM:  Iterator
3:      // FILE:     iter.cpp
4:      // PURPOSE:  iterator for BTree
5:      // NOTES:
6:      // AUTHOR:   Jesse Liberty (jl)
7:      // REVISIONS: 12/1/94 1.0 jl  initial release
8:      // *****************************************************
9:      #include "btree.hpp"
10:
11:     // history class implementations
12:     History::History(int pno, int off, BOOL node):
13:         PageNo(pno),
14:         OffSet(off),
```

continues

Listing 15.4 continued

```
15:          IsNode(node)
16:      {}
17:
18:      // Iterator implementations
19:
20:      // start off with blank iterator
21:      Iterator::Iterator()
22:      {
23:          Reset();
24:      }
25:
26:      Iterator::~Iterator()
27:      {
28:          for (int i = 0; i<MaxPages; i++)
29:              delete myHistory[i];
30:      }
31:
32:      void Iterator::RecordNode(int PageNo, int OffSet)
33:      {
34:          myHistory[myNext++] = new History(PageNo,OffSet,TRUE);
35:      }
36:
37:      void Iterator::RecordLeaf(int PageNo, int OffSet)
38:      {
39:          myHistory[myNext++] = new History(PageNo,OffSet,FALSE);
40:      }
41:
42:      History* Iterator::GetLast()
43:      {
44:          return myHistory[myNext-1];
45:      }
46:
47:      History* Iterator::GetFirst()
48:      {
49:          return myHistory[0];
50:      }
51:
52:      void Iterator::Reset()
53:      {
54:          for (int i = 0; i<MaxPages; i++)
55:              myHistory[i] = 0;
56:          myNext = 0;
57:      }
58:
59:
60:      int Iterator::GetNext(const Index& theIndex)
61:      {
62:
63:          for (;;)
64:          {
65:              History * pHist = GetLast();
66:              int pgNo = pHist-> PageNo;
67:              int newOffSet = pHist->OffSet+1;
68:              Page * pg = BTree::theIDXManager.GetPage(pgNo);
```

```
69:
70:            if (newOffSet < pg->GetCount())
71:            {
72:                Index Idx = pg->GetIndex(newOffSet);
73:                pHist->OffSet = newOffSet;
74:                for (;;)
75:                {
76:                    if (pg->GetIsLeaf())
77:                    {
78:                        // cout << "Key: " << Idx.GetData() << endl;
79:                        if (theIndex.Begins(Idx))
80:                            return Idx.GetPointer();
81:                        else
82:                            return 0;
83:                    }
84:                    else
85:                    {
86:                    pg = BTree::theIDXManager.GetPage(Idx.GetPointer());
87:                    Idx = pg->GetFirstIndex();
88:                    pHist = new History(pg->GetPageNumber(),0, (BOOL)
                        !pg->GetIsLeaf());
89:                    myHistory[myNext++] = pHist;
90:                    }
91:                }  // end inner for loop
92:            }
93:            else
94:            {
95:                delete myHistory[myNext-1];
96:                myHistory[myNext-1] = 0;
97:                myNext—;
98:                if (!myNext)
99:                    return 0;
100:           }
101:       }  // end outer for loop
102:   }
```

Listing 15.5 Index.cpp

```
1:      // **************************************************
2:      // PROGRAM:  index
3:      // FILE:     index.cpp
4:      // PURPOSE:  provide fundamental btree functionality
5:      // NOTES:
6:      // AUTHOR:   Jesse Liberty (jl)
7:      // REVISIONS: 11/1/94 1.0 jl  initial release
8:      // **************************************************
9:
10:     #include "btree.hpp"
11:     #include <ctype.h>
12:
13:     Index::Index(char* str):myPointer(1)
14:     {
15:         strncpy(myData,str,dataLen);
```

continues

417

Listing 15.5 continued

```
16:             myData[dataLen]='\0';
17:             for (int i = 0; i< strlen(myData); i++)
18:                 myData[i] = toupper(myData[i]);
19:         }
20:
21:        Index::Index(char* str, int ptr):myPointer(ptr)
22:        {
23:
24:            strncpy(myData,str,dataLen);
25:            myData[dataLen]='\0';
26:            for (int i = 0; i< strlen(myData); i++)
27:                myData[i] = toupper(myData[i]);
28:
29:        }
30:
31:        Index::Index(Index& rhs):
32:            myPointer(rhs.GetPointer())
33:        {
34:            strcpy(myData, rhs.GetData());
35:            for (int i = 0; i< strlen(myData); i++)
36:                myData[i] = toupper(myData[i]);
37:
38:        }
39:
40:        Index::Index():myPointer(0)
41:        {
42:            myData[0]='\0';
43:        }
44:
45:        void Index::PrintKey()
46:        {
47:            cout << "   " << myData;
48:        }
49:
50:        void Index::PrintPage()
51:        {
52:            cout << "\n" << myData << ": " ;
53:            BTree::theIDXManager.GetPage(myPointer)->Print();
54:        }
55:
56:        int Index::Insert(Index& ref, BOOL findOnly)
57:        {
58:            return BTree::theIDXManager.GetPage(myPointer)->Insert(ref,findOnly);
59:        }
60:
61:        int Index::operator==(const Index& rhs)
62:        {
63:            return (strcmp(myData,rhs.GetData()) == 0); // case insensitive
64:        }
65:
66:        int Index::Begins(const Index& rhs) const
67:        {
68:            int len = strlen(myData);
69:            if (!len)
```

```
70:              return TRUE;
71:          return (strncmp(myData,rhs.GetData(),len) == 0);
72:      }
```

 Listing 15.6 Datafile.cpp

```
1:      // ****************************************************
2:      // PROGRAM:  Data file
3:      // FILE:     datafile.cpp
4:      // PURPOSE:
5:      // NOTES:
6:      // AUTHOR:   Jesse Liberty (jl)
7:      // REVISIONS: 11/5/94 1.0 jl  initial release
8:      // ****************************************************
9:
10:     #include "btree.hpp"
11:     #include <assert.h>
12:
13:     // on construction, try to open the file if it exists
14:     DataFile::DataFile():
15:         myFile("ROBIN.DAT",
16:         ios::binary ¦ ios::in ¦ ios::out ¦ ios::nocreate ¦ ios::app)
17:     {
18:     }
19:
20:     void DataFile::Create()
21:     {
22:         if (!myFile) // nocreate failed, first creation
23:         {
24:
25:             // open the file, create it this time
26:             myFile.clear();
27:
28:             myFile.open
29:                 ("ROBIN.DAT",ios::binary ¦ ios::in ¦ ios::out ¦ ios::app);
30:
31:             char Header[2];
32:             int MagicNumber = 1234; // a number we can check for
33:             memcpy(Header,&MagicNumber,2);
34:             myFile.clear();
35:             myFile.flush();
36:             myFile.seekp(0);
37:             myFile.write(Header,2);
38:             return;
39:         }
40:
41:         // we did open file, it already existed
42:         // get the numbers we need
43:         int MagicNumber;
44:         myFile.seekg(0);
45:         myFile.read((char *) &MagicNumber,2);
46:
47:         // check the magic number. If it is wrong the file is
```

continues

Listing 15.6 continued

```
48:                // corrupt or this isn't the index file
49:                if (MagicNumber != 1234)
50:                {
51:                        // change to an exception!!
52:                        cout << "DataFile Magic number failed!";
53:                }
54:                return;
55:            }
56:
57:            // write out the numbers we'll need next time
58:            void DataFile::Close()
59:            {
60:                myFile.close();
61:            }
62:
63:
64:            int DataFile::Insert(char * newNote)
65:            {
66:                int len = strlen(newNote);
67:                int fullLen = len + 6;
68:
69:                time_t theTime;
70:                theTime = time(NULL);
71:
72:                char buffer[PageSize];
73:                memcpy(buffer,&len,2);
74:                memcpy(buffer+2,&theTime,4);
75:                memcpy(buffer+6,newNote,len);
76:
77:                myFile.clear();
78:                myFile.flush();
79:                myFile.seekp(0,ios::end);
80:                int offset = (int) myFile.tellp();
81:                myFile.write(buffer,fullLen);
82:                myFile.flush();
83:                return offset;
84:            }
85:
86:            void DataFile::GetRecord(int offset, char* buffer, int& len,
                   time_t&theTime)
87:            {
88:                char tmpBuff[PageSize];
89:                myFile.flush();
90:                myFile.clear();
91:                myFile.seekg(offset);
92:                myFile.read(tmpBuff,PageSize);
93:                memcpy(&len,tmpBuff,2);
94:                memcpy(&theTime,tmpBuff+2,4);
95:                strncpy(buffer,tmpBuff+6,len);
96:                buffer[len] = '\0';
97:            }
```

Type Listing 15.7 IdxMgr.cpp

```
1:    // *****************************************************
2:    // PROGRAM:  Idxmr
3:    // FILE:     Idxmgr.cpp
4:    // PURPOSE:  provide i/o for btree
5:    // NOTES:
6:    // AUTHOR:   Jesse Liberty (jl)
7:    // REVISIONS: 11/5/94 1.0 jl  initial release
8:    // *****************************************************
9:
10:   #include "btree.hpp"
11:   #include <assert.h>
12:
13:   // on construction, try to open the file if it exists
14:   IDXManager::IDXManager():
15:      myFile("ROBIN.IDX",ios::binary | ios::in | ios::out | ios::nocreate)
16:   {
17:      // initialize the pointers to null
18:      for (int i = 0; i< MaxPages; i++)
19:         myPages[i] = 0;
20:      myCount = 0;
21:
22:   }
23:
24:   // called by btree constructor
25:   // if we opened the file, read in the numbers we need
26:   // otherwise create the file
27:   int IDXManager::Create()
28:   {
29:      if (!myFile) // nocreate failed, first creation
30:      {
31:         // open the file, create it this time
32:         myFile.open("ROBIN.IDX",ios::binary | ios::in | ios::out);
33:
34:         char Header[PageSize];
35:         int MagicNumber = 1234; // a number we can check for
36:         memcpy(Header,&MagicNumber,2);
37:         int NextPage = 1;
38:         memcpy(Header+2,&NextPage,2);
39:         memcpy(Header+4,&NextPage,2);
40:         Page::SetgPageNumber(NextPage);
41:         char title[]="ROBIN.IDX. Ver 1.00";
42:         memcpy(Header+6,title,strlen(title));
43:         myFile.flush();
44:         myFile.clear();
45:         myFile.seekp(0);
46:         myFile.write(Header,PageSize);
47:         return 0;
48:      }
49:
50:      // we did open the file, it already existed
51:      // get the numbers we need
```

continues

421

Listing 15.7 continued

```
52:             int MagicNumber;
53:             myFile.seekg(0);
54:             myFile.read((char *) &MagicNumber,2);
55:
56:             // check the magic number. If it is wrong the file is
57:             // corrupt or this isn't the index file
58:             if (MagicNumber != 1234)
59:             {
60:                 // change to an exception!!
61:                 cout << "Index Magic number failed!";
62:                 return 0;
63:             }
64:
65:             int NextPage;
66:             myFile.seekg(2);
67:             myFile.read((char*) &NextPage,2);
68:             Page::SetgPageNumber(NextPage);
69:             int FirstPage;
70:             myFile.seekg(4);
71:             myFile.read((char*) &FirstPage,2);
72:             const int room =  PageSize - 6;
73:             char buffer[room];
74:             myFile.read(buffer,room);
75:             buffer[20]='\0';
76:             // cout << buffer << endl;
77:             // read in all the pages
78:             for (int i = 1; i < NextPage; i++)
79:             {
80:                 myFile.seekg(i * PageSize);
81:                 char buffer[PageSize];
82:                 myFile.read( buffer, PageSize);
83:                 Page * pg = new Page(buffer);
84:                 Insert(pg);
85:             }
86:
87:             return FirstPage;
88:         }
89:
90:         // write out the numbers we'll need next time
91:         void IDXManager::Close(int theRoot)
92:         {
93:
94:             for (int i = 0; i< MaxPages; i++)
95:                 if (myPages[i])
96:                     Save(myPages[i]);
97:             int NextPage = Page::GetgPageNumber();
98:             if (!myFile)
99:                 cout << "Error opening myFile!" << endl;
100:            myFile.flush();
101:            myFile.clear();
102:            myFile.seekp(2);
103:            myFile.write ( (char *) &NextPage,2);
104:            myFile.seekp(4);
105:            myFile.write((char*) &theRoot,2);
```

```
106:        myFile.close();
107:    }
108:
109:    // wrapper function
110:    int IDXManager::NewPage(Index& index, BOOL bLeaf)
111:    {
112:        Page * newPage = new Page(index, bLeaf);
113:        Insert(newPage);
114:        Save(newPage);
115:        return newPage->GetPageNumber();
116:    }
117:
118:    int IDXManager::NewPage(
119:        Index *array,
120:        int offset,
121:        BOOL leaf,
122:        int count)
123:    {
124:        Page * newPage = new Page(array, offset, leaf, count);
125:        Insert(newPage);
126:        Save(newPage);
127:        return newPage->GetPageNumber();
128:    }
129:
130:    void IDXManager::Insert(Page * newPage)
131:    {
132:
133:        // add new page into array of page managers
134:        if (myCount < MaxPages)
135:        {
136:            assert(!myPages[myCount]);
137:            myPages[myCount++] = newPage;
138:        }
139:        else   // no room, time to page out to disk
140:        {
141:            int lowest = -1;
142:
143:            for (int i = 0; i< MaxPages; i++)
144:            {
145:                if (myPages[i]->GetLocked() == FALSE )
146:                    lowest = i;
147:            }
148:            if (lowest == -1)
149:                assert(lowest != -1); // change to exception if -1 (no page to
                    kill)
150:
151:            for (i = 0; i< MaxPages; i++)
152:                if (myPages[i]->GetTime() < myPages[lowest]->GetTime() &&
                    myPages[i]->GetLocked() == FALSE)
153:
154:
155:                    lowest = i;
156:
157:            assert(myPages[lowest]);
158:            Save(myPages[lowest]);
```

continues

423

Listing 15.7 continued

```
159:            delete myPages[lowest];
160:            myPages[lowest] = newPage;
161:
162:        }
163:    }
164:
165:    // tell the page to write itself out
166:    void IDXManager::Save(Page* pg)
167:    {
168:      pg->Write(myFile);
169:    }
170:
171:    // see if the page is in memory, if so return it
172:    // otherwise get it from disk
173:    // note: this won't scale, with lots of page managers
174:    // you'd need a more efficient search. 10 levels of page
175:    // managers, with 31 indexes per page gives you room for
176:    // 800 trillion words. Even if each page is only 1/2 full
177:    // on average, 10 levels of depth would represent 64 million
178:    // keys alone, not to mention the actual records.
179:
180:    Page * IDXManager::GetPage(int target)
181:    {
182:
183:        for (int i = 0; i< MaxPages; i++)
184:        {
185:            if (myPages[i]->GetPageNumber() == target)
186:                return  myPages[i];
187:        }
188:        myFile.seekg(target * PageSize);
189:        char buffer[PageSize];
190:        myFile.read( buffer, PageSize);
191:        Page * pg = new Page(buffer);
192:        Insert(pg);
193:        return pg;
194:    }
```

Type

Listing 15.8 WNJFile.cpp

```
1:     // **************************************************
2:     // PROGRAM:   WNJ file
3:     // FILE:      WNJfile.cpp
4:     // PURPOSE:
5:     // NOTES:
6:     // AUTHOR:    Jesse Liberty (jl)
7:     // REVISIONS: 11/5/94 1.0 jl  initial release
8:     // **************************************************
9:
10:    #include "btree.hpp"
11:    #include <assert.h>
12:
13:    // on construction, try to open the file if it exists
```

```
14:        WNJFile::WNJFile():
15:           myFile("ROBINWNJ.IDX",
16:           ios::binary ¦ ios::in ¦ ios::out ¦ ios::nocreate)
17:        {
18:           for (int i = 0; i<5; i++)
19:               myints[i]=0L;
20:        }
21:
22:        void WNJFile::Create()
23:        {
24:           char Header[4];
25:           int MagicNumber=0; // a number we can check for
26:           int zero = 0;
27:
28:           if (!myFile) // nocreate failed, first creation
29:           {
30:               // open the file, create it this time
31:               myFile.clear();
32:               myFile.open("ROBINWNJ.IDX",
33:                   ios::binary ¦ ios::in ¦ ios::out);
34:
35:               MagicNumber = 1234;
36:               memcpy(Header,&MagicNumber,4);
37:               memcpy(Header+2,&zero,2);
38:               myFile.seekp(0);
39:               myFile.write(Header,4);
40:               myFile.flush();
41:               return;
42:           }
43:
44:           // we did open the file, it already existed
45:           // get the numbers we need
46:
47:
48:           myFile.seekg(0);
49:           myFile.read(Header,4);
50:           memcpy(&MagicNumber,Header,2);
51:           memcpy(&myCount,Header+2,2);
52:
53:           // check the magic number. If it is wrong the file is
54:           // corrupt or this isn't the index file
55:           if (MagicNumber != 1234)
56:           {
57:               // change to an exception!!
58:               cout << "WNJ Magic number failed!";
59:               cout << "Magic number: " << MagicNumber;
60:               cout << "\nmyCount: " << myCount << endl;
61:           }
62:           return;
63:        }
64:
65:        // write out the numbers we'll need next time
66:        void WNJFile::Close()
67:        {
68:           myFile.seekg(2);
```

continues

425

Listing 15.8 continued

```cpp
69:            myFile.write((char*)&myCount,2);
70:            myFile.close();
71:       }
72:
73:       int WNJFile::Append(int DataOffset)
74:       {
75:
76:          int newPos = 4 + myCount++ * (5*2);
77:          int offsets[5];
78:          offsets[0] = DataOffset;
79:          for (int i = 1; i<5; i++)
80:             offsets[i]=0;
81:          myFile.seekg(newPos);
82:          myFile.write((char*)offsets,5*2);
83:
84:          return newPos;
85:       }
86:
87:
88:       int WNJFile::Insert(int DataOffset,int WNJOffset)
89:       {
90:          int ints[5];
91:          myFile.seekg(WNJOffset);
92:          myFile.read((char*)ints,5*2);
93:
94:          int offset=WNJOffset;
95:
96:          while (ints[4])
97:          {
98:             offset = ints[4];
99:             myFile.clear();
100:            myFile.flush();
101:            myFile.seekg(ints[4]);
102:            myFile.read((char*)ints,5*2);
103:         }
104:         if (ints[3]) // full!
105:         {
106:            ints[4] = Append(DataOffset);
107:            myFile.clear();
108:            myFile.flush();
109:            myFile.seekg(offset);
110:            myFile.write((char*)ints,5*2);
111:         }
112:         else
113:         {
114:            for (int i = 0; i<4; i++)
115:            {
116:               if (ints[i] == 0)
117:               {
118:                  ints[i] = DataOffset;
119:                  myFile.clear();
120:                  myFile.flush();
121:                  myFile.seekg(offset);
122:                  myFile.write((char*)ints,5*2);
```

```
123:                    break;
124:                }
125:            }
126:        }
127:        return 0;
128:    }
129:
130:
131:    int* WNJFile::Find(int NextWNJ)
132:    {
133:        int ints[5];
134:        int * results = new int[256];
135:
136:        int i = 0, j=0;
137:
138:        while (j<256)
139:            results[j++] = 0;
140:
141:        j = 0;
142:
143:        myFile.seekg(NextWNJ);
144:        myFile.read((char*)ints,5*2);
145:
146:        while (j < 256)
147:        {
148:            if (ints[i])
149:            {
150:                if (i == 4)
151:                {
152:                    myFile.seekg(ints[4]);
153:                    myFile.read((char*)ints,5*2);
154:                    i = 0;
155:                    continue;
156:                }
157:            results[j++] = ints[i++];
158:            }
159:            else
160:                break;
161:        }
162:        return results;
163:    }
```

Type Listing 15.9 Driver.cpp

```
1:      // Listing 15.9 - Driver.cpp
2:
3:      #include "String.hpp"
4:      #include "stdef.hpp"
5:      #include "btree.hpp"
6:
7:      IDXManager BTree::theIDXManager;
8:      DataFile BTree::theDataFile;
9:      WNJFile BTree::theWNJFile;
```

continues

Listing 15.9 continued

```
10:      Iterator BTree::theIter;
11:
12:      int WNJFile::myCount=0L;
13:      int Page::gPage=1;
14:      int BTree::NodeIndexCtr=0;
15:      int BTree::LeafIndexCtr=0;
16:      int BTree::NodePageCtr=0;
17:      int BTree::LeafPageCtr=0;
18:      int BTree::NodeIndexPerPage[Order+1];
19:      int BTree::LeafIndexPerPage[Order+1];
20:
21:      int main()
22:      {
23:         BTree myTree;
24:
25:         for (int i = 0; i < Order +2; i++)
26:         {
27:            BTree::NodeIndexPerPage[i] =0;
28:            BTree::LeafIndexPerPage[i] = 0;
29:         }
30:
31:         char buffer[PageSize+1];
32:
33:         for (;;)
34:         {
35:            cout << "Enter a string (blank to stop): ";
36:            cin.getline(buffer,PageSize);
37:            // cin.ignore(PageSize,'\n');
38:            if (buffer[0])
39:               myTree.Insert(buffer);
40:            else
41:               break;
42:         }
43:         for (;;)
44:         {
45:            cout << "Find: ";
46:            cin.getline(buffer,255);
47:            if (buffer[0])
48:            {
49:                int offset = myTree.Find(buffer);
50:                while (offset)
51:                {
52:                   int* found  =  BTree::theWNJFile.Find(offset);
53:                   int i=0;
54:                   int len;
55:                   time_t theTime;
56:                   char buff[512];
57:                   while (found[i])
58:                   {
59:                      BTree::theDataFile.GetRecord(found[i],buff,len,
                         theTime);
60:                      struct tm * ts = localtime(&theTime);
61:                      cout << "Found: ";
62:                      cout << ts->tm_mon << "/";
```

63:                        cout << ts->tm_mday << "/";
64:                        cout << ts->tm_year << " ";
65:                        cout << buff << endl;
66:                        i++;
67:                    }
68:                    delete [] found;
69:                    offset = myTree.GetNext(buffer);
70:                }
71:            }
72:            else
73:                break;
74:        }
75:
76:        myTree.PrintTree();
77:
78:        return 0;
79:    }
```

d:\112\day16>r1
Enter a string (blank to stop): There is a place for us
Enter a string (blank to stop): The quick brown fox jumps
Enter a string (blank to stop): Is that a theater production?
Enter a string (blank to stop): Theirs is not to question
Enter a string (blank to stop): There's no place like home
Enter a string (blank to stop):
Find: home
Found: 11/2/94 There's no place like home
Find: the
Found: 11/2/94 The quick brown fox jumps
Found: 11/2/94 Is that a theater production?
Found: 11/2/94 Theirs is not to question
Found: 11/2/94 There is a place for us
Found: 11/2/94 There's no place like home
Find:

BROWN:
BROWN:   BROWN   FOR
FOX:    FOX   HOME   JUMPS   LIKE
NOT:
NOT:    NOT   PLACE   PRODUCTION   QUESTION
QUICK:   QUICK   THAT
THE:    THE   THEATER
THEIRS:   THEIRS   THERE   THERE'S

Stats:
Node pages:    3
Leaf pages:    6
Node indexes: 8
Leaf indexes: 17
Pages with 2 nodes:  2
Pages with 2 leaves: 3
Pages with 3 leaves: 1
Pages with 4 nodes:  1
Pages with 4 leaves: 2
```

In line 40 of BTree.hpp (refer to listing 15.1), the Iterator class is declared. It has an array of history structures, which are declared in lines 30 through 36 of the same file. Each history object knows which binary page it is on, and what its offset is. It also knows whether it is a node (or a page).

In line 155, a static iterator theIter is declared. In line 38 of listing 15.2, the iterator is reset. In line 49, you see that the BTree method, GetNext(), creates an index object and passes it in to the iterator's GetNext() method, which iterates over its list of objects.

In line 10 of the driver program (refer to listing 15.9), the iterator is defined (space is allocated). In line 45, the user is prompted to enter a string for which the program will search. The search is in line 52 and, once found, the record is displayed. In line 69, the iterator—which was created in the Find() method—is used to find the *next* matching record.

Extending the Iterator

A full-fledged iterator should support the *previous* operation, as well as the *next* operation. It also should let you start at the first or last node in the tree, and should tell you whether you have gone past the start or end of the tree.

If you were building an iterator for general use, you would want to add a method to BTree that returns a copy of its iterator. You also would want to add methods to Iterator itself (or to BTree as appropriate) to set the iterator to the first or last index in the first or last page.

Examining Issues with Iterators

As mentioned earlier, the trickiest problem when working with iterators is when you allow additions and deletions to the list through the iterator, and you also allow more than one iterator to point to the same list.

If you need to implement this functionality, you have to provide your tree with a list of all the iterators currently pointing into the tree. If the tree is changed for any reason (a node is added or deleted, for example), you need to update all the iterators so that they still are valid.

You didn't have this problem with the iterator shown in the preceding section, because the iterator never was provided as a stand-alone object; the tree maintained its own iterator and kept it up to date each time it did a search.

Summary

Today you learned what iterators are and how to create an iterator for the BTree class. You used the iterator to search the list, and you examined many of the programming trade-offs that iterators present.

15

Q&A

Q **Why bother with iterators?**

A An iterator enables you to walk a list that otherwise might not be presented in the desired order.

Q **Can you have more than one iterator on a list?**

A Yes—that is one of the great advantages of iterators. You can walk the list from different parts of the same set of data.

Q **What is a disadvantage of providing an iterator?**

A Writing a complete Iterator class is not easy. There are significant issues having to do with adding and deleting items in the list.

Workshop

The Workshop provides quiz questions to help you solidify your understanding of the material covered, and exercises to provide you with experience in using what you have learned. Try to answer the quiz and exercise questions before checking the answers in Appendix A, and make sure that you understand the answers before continuing to the next chapter.

Quiz

1. What is the difference between an iterator and an index?
2. Why does the delete operation present a challenge for the iterator?
3. What is the principal design goal of a good iterator?

Exercises

1. Design (write the public interface for) these two classes: IntList—a list of integers—and IntListIterator. The only public interface that IntList should provide (besides constructors and trivial accessors) is a method that returns a new IntListIterator. **Do not** use linked lists; instead, just provide a very simple, fixed-size array of ints. (The size should be passed in as an argument to the constructor. You do not need to provide resize capability.)

   The IntListIterator should provide methods to get and set the *current* value (the value in the list that the iterator is pointing to). It also should provide the capability to walk forward and backward through the list, and to jump to the beginning or the end. (Indexed access to the list is unnecessary.) All the methods that move the current position should return a Boolean that specifies whether the current position is valid.

2. Write the body of the `IntList` and `IntListIterator` classes.

3. Write a test program proving that your `IntList` works.

4. Convert the `IntList` and `IntListIterator` to use templates and to accept the type of elements in the list as a parameter.

5. Write a test program that proves `GenList<int>` works the same as `IntList` did. Also, you should create a `GenList<char *>` and demonstrate that your polymorphic list works in this case, as well.

16

Synonyms

ROBIN is now almost a full-fledged application. It is time to turn your attention to making the code more robust and ensuring that it is maintainable. In the next few chapters, I'll discuss profiling programs to enhance performance, using a debugger to track down serious problems, and building tough maintainable code. Today, however, I'll try to prove that ROBIN is *extensible*—that the architecture allows for growth and enhancements.

There are a number of features that you might want to add to ROBIN, even at this early date. The most pressing, in my opinion, is the capability to designate synonyms, so that when searching for *computer*, for example, ROBIN will match records with *PC* and *MAC* in the title. Today you will learn

☐ How to create synonyms in ROBIN

☐ How to examine your code for extensibility

☐ What trade-offs might be made between flexibility and maintainability

Maintainable and Extensible Code

One of the hallmarks of maintainable code is that you can explain how your program works to an intelligent programmer in a matter of hours. If your program is too complicated to explain, no matter how clever it is, it will not be maintainable over the long haul.

The second hallmark of maintainable code, however, is that it can be extended to incorporate new features. This *extensibility* is crucial. Many programmers spend much of their career building on *legacy* code—programs they didn't write, but that they must maintain. A good program allows for the addition of new features without breaking.

ROBIN was not originally designed to include synonyms, but the architecture is sufficiently nimble and the complexity is sufficiently isolated that adding this feature should not be an overwhelming task. A good programmer should be able to get the fundamental functionality in place in less than one day.

How Synonyms Work

ROBIN's current design works like this: When the user asks to find a term, the B-tree is passed the string for which to search. The B-tree starts at its first page and asks each page for the first index on that page that "begins with" the text passed in.

When the index is found, the page is examined to see whether it is a node or a leaf. If it is a node, the index points to the next page in the chain. After a leaf is found, the index points to a WNJ (Word-Node-Join) record. The WNJ record includes a list of offsets into the data file where the actual record resides.

When you insert a synonym (*PC*, for example) for a term (*Computer*, for example) you want the tree to find the same WNJFile record for the synonym (*PC*) as it does for the term (*COMPUTER*).

The algorithm for inserting the synonym is straightforward: Find the WNJ record for the original term and then create a new index for the new term pointing to that WNJ record.

Remember that when a new index is added, it originally points to the data in the file but then is adjusted to point to a new WNJ record. In this case, you want to fill the index with the WNJ record index of the original term, and not allow it to be adjusted.

Two significant changes must be made to the code, in addition to adding a function to handle the Add Synonym request. First, there must be logic to distinguish this special case so that the index is handled properly. In addition, there must be logic to ensure that only an exact match is found for the original term; if you are adding a synonym for *phone* (*telephone*, for example) you do not want to add that synonym to *phonetics*!

In both cases, a flag is required: *Are you adding a synonym?* There are two ways to handle this: I've chosen to pass these flags to every function that needs them, defaulting their value to FALSE (the more common case). An alternative would be to set a static Boolean variable in the tree, and to get this value each time the test needs to be tried.

In retrospect, I suspect the code would be cleaner if this and the related flags (FindOnly, for example) were moved into static variables in BTREE. This is left, as they say, as an exercise for the reader.

Listing 16.1 shows the modified BTree.hpp, including the new flags on the node insertion and find methods, as discussed in the analysis that follows. Listing 16.2 is Btree.cpp, with a modified AddKey() method. Listing 16.3 is Index.cpp, which changed to accommodate the new flags. Listing 16.4 is Page.cpp, where the bulk of the changes are located. Listing 16.5 (Datafile.cpp), listing 16.6 (IdxManager.cpp), listing 16.7 (Iter.cpp), and listing 16.8 (WNJFile.cpp) are included for completeness. Finally, listing 16.9 is the driver program, which enables you to enter synonyms using the syntax R2 -Synonym *OldTerm NewTerm*.

 Note: The listings in this chapter are for illustrative purposes only. Your compiler might issue a warning if you use the listings exactly as shown in this chapter.

Listing 16.1 BTree.hpp

```
1:      // ***************************************************
2:      // PROGRAM:   Btree, Page and Index declarations
3:      // FILE:      btree.hpp
4:      // PURPOSE:   provide fundamental btree functionality
5:      // NOTES:
6:      // AUTHOR:    Jesse Liberty (jl)
7:      // REVISIONS: 11/1/94 1.0 jl  initial release
8:      // ***************************************************
9:      #ifndef BTREE_HPP                    // inclusion guards
10:     #define BTREE_HPP
11:
12:     #include <time.h>
13:     #include <string.h>
14:     #include <fstream.h>
15:
16:     #include "stdef.hpp"
17:
18:     const int Order =       4; //31;  // 31 indexes and 1 header
19:     const int dataLen =    11; // length of a key
20:     const int MaxPages =  500; // more than we need
21:     const int SizeItem =   16;  // key + offset
22:     const int SizePointer = 2; // size of offset
23:     const int PageSize = (Order+1) * SizeItem;
24:     const int offInt = 2;
25:
26:     // forward declarations
27:     class Page;
28:     class Index;
29:
30:     // all members are public
31:     // used only by Iterator
32:     struct History
33:     {
34:        History(int, int,BOOL);
35:        int PageNo;
36:        int OffSet;
37:        BOOL IsNode;
38:     };
39:
40:
41:     // Iterator class keeps track
42:     // of current (and next) index
43:     class Iterator
44:     {
45:     public:
46:        Iterator();
47:        ~Iterator();
48:        void RecordNode(int, int);
49:        void RecordLeaf(int, int);
50:        History * GetLast();
51:        History * GetFirst();
52:        int GetNext(const Index&);
53:        void Reset();
54:
```

```
55:     private:
56:      History* myHistory[MaxPages];
57:      int myNext;
58:     };
59:
60:
61:     class DataFile
62:     {
63:     public:
64:         // constructors & destructor
65:         DataFile();
66:         ~DataFile(){}
67:
68:         // management of files
69:         void Close();
70:         void Create();
71:         void GetRecord(int, char*, int&, time_t&);
72:
73:         int Insert(char *);
74:
75:     private:
76:     fstream myFile;
77:     };
78:
79:     class WNJFile
80:     {
81:     public:
82:         // constructors & destructor
83:         WNJFile();
84:         ~WNJFile(){}
85:
86:         // management of files
87:         void Close();
88:         void Create();
89:         int* Find(int NextWNJ);
90:         int Insert(int, int);
91:         int Append(int);
92:
93:     private:
94:     static int myCount;
95:     fstream myFile;
96:     union
97:     {
98:         int myints[5];
99:         char  myArray[5*4];
100:    };
101:    };
102:
103:    // IDXManager - in memory keeps track of what pages are
104:    // already in memory and swaps to disk as required
105:    class IDXManager
106:    {
107:    public:
108:        // constructors & destructor
109:        IDXManager();
110:        ~IDXManager(){}
```

continues

437

Listing 16.1 continued

```
111:
112:        // management of files
113:        void Close(int);
114:        int Create();
115:
116:        // Page manipulation
117:        Page* GetPage(int);
118:        void SetPage(Page*);
119:        void Insert(Page * newPage);
120:        void Save(Page* pg);
121:        int NewPage(Index&, BOOL);
122:        int NewPage(Index *array, int offset, BOOL leaf, int count);
123:
124:    private:
125:    Page* myPages[MaxPages];
126:    fstream myFile;
127:    int myCount;
128:    };
129:
130:    // the btree itself - has a pointer to first page
131:    class BTree
132:    {
133:    public:
134:        // constructors and destructor
135:        BTree();
136:        ~BTree();
137:
138:        // utility functions
139:        void AddKey(char* data, int offset,BOOL synonym = FALSE);
140:        void Insert(char* buffer, int, char**);
141:        void Insert(char*);
142:        void PrintTree();
143:        int Find(char* data);
144:        int FindExact(char* data);
145:        int GetNext(char* data);
146:
147:        // page methods
148:        Page* GetPage(int page)
149:           { return theIDXManager.GetPage(page); }
150:        int NewPage(Index& pIndex, BOOL IsLeaf)
151:           { return theIDXManager.NewPage(pIndex,FALSE); }
152:
153:        static int myAlNum(char ch);
154:        // public static member!
155:        static  IDXManager theIDXManager;
156:        static WNJFile    theWNJFile;
157:        static DataFile theDataFile;
158:        static Iterator theIter;
159:
160:        static BOOL GetWord(char*, char*, int&);
161:        static void GetStats();
162:        static int NodeIndexCtr;
163:        static int LeafIndexCtr;
164:        static int NodePageCtr;
165:        static int LeafPageCtr;
```

```
166:        static int NodeIndexPerPage[Order+1];
167:        static int LeafIndexPerPage[Order+1];
168:
169:    private:
170:        int myRoot;
171:    };
172:
173:    // index objects point to pages or real data
174:    class Index
175:    {
176:    public:
177:        // constructors & destructor
178:        Index();
179:        Index(char *);
180:        Index (char*, int);
181:        Index(Index&);
182:        ~Index(){}
183:
184:        // accessors
185:        const char * GetData() const  { return myData; }
186:        void SetData(const Index& rhs)
187:           { strcpy(myData,rhs.GetData()); }
188:        void SetData(const char * rhs)
189:           { strcpy(myData,rhs); }
190:        int GetPointer()const { return myPointer; }
191:        void SetPointer (int pg) { myPointer = pg; }
192:
193:        // utility functions
194:        void PrintKey();
195:        void PrintPage();
196:        int Insert(Index& ref,BOOL findOnly = FALSE, BOOL findExac = FALSE);
197:
198:        int Begins(const Index& rhs) const;
199:
200:        // overloaded operators
201:        int operator==(const Index& rhs);
202:
203:        int operator < (const Index& rhs)
204:         {return strcmp(myData,rhs.GetData())<0;}
205:
206:        int operator <= (const Index& rhs)
207:         {return strcmp(myData,rhs.GetData())<=0;}
208:
209:        int operator > (const Index& rhs)
210:         {return strcmp(myData,rhs.GetData())>0;}
211:
212:        int operator >= (const Index& rhs)
213:         {return strcmp(myData,rhs.GetData())>=0;}
214:
215:    public:
216:        int myPointer;
217:        char myData[SizeItem - SizePointer];
218:    };
219:
220:
221:    // pages - consist of header and array of indexes
```

continues

Listing 16.1 continued

```
222:    class Page
223:    {
224:    public:
225:        // constructors and destructor
226:        Page();
227:        Page(char*);
228:        Page(Index&,BOOL);
229:        Page(Index*, int, BOOL, int);
230:        ~Page(){}
231:
232:        // insertion and searchoperations
233:        int Insert(Index&, BOOL findOnly = FALSE, BOOL synonym = FALSE);
234:        int Find(Index& idx) { return Insert(idx,TRUE); }
235:        int InsertLeaf(Index&);
236:        int FindLeaf(Index&,BOOL findOnly, BOOL synonym = FALSE);
237:        int InsertNode(Index&,BOOL findOnly = FALSE, BOOL synonym = FALSE);
238:        void Push(Index&,int offset=0, BOOL=TRUE);
239:
240:        // accessors
241:        Index GetFirstIndex() { return myKeys[0]; }
242:        Index GetIndex(int offset) { return myKeys[offset]; }
243:        BOOL GetIsLeaf() const { return myVars.IsLeaf; }
244:        int GetCount() const { return myVars.myCount; }
245:        void SetCount(int cnt) { myVars.myCount=cnt; }
246:        time_t GetTime() { return myTime; }
247:        BOOL GetLocked() { return myVars.IsLocked; }
248:        void SetLocked (BOOL state) { myVars.IsLocked = state; }
249:
250:        // page manipulation
251:        int GetPageNumber() const { return myVars.myPageNumber; }
252:        Page* GetPage(int page)
253:            { return BTree::theIDXManager.GetPage(page); }
254:        int NewPage(Index& rIndex, BOOL IsLeaf)
255:            { return BTree::theIDXManager.NewPage(rIndex,FALSE); }
256:
257:        int NewPage(Index* arr, int off,BOOL isL, int cnt)
258:            { return    BTree::theIDXManager.NewPage(arr,off,isL, cnt); }
259:
260:        // utility functions
261:        void Nullify(int offset);
262:        void Print();
263:        fstream& Write(fstream&);
264:        void ReCount();
265:
266:        static int GetgPageNumber(){ return gPage; }
267:        static void SetgPageNumber(int pg) { gPage = pg; }
268:
269:    private:
270:        Index * const myKeys; // will point to myVars.mk
271:        union
272:        {
273:            char myBlock[PageSize];   // a page from disk
274:            struct
275:            {
276:                int myCount;
```

```
277:          BOOL IsLeaf;
278:          int myPageNumber;
279:          BOOL IsLocked;
280:          char filler[8]; // we want 16 bytes of overhead
281:          char mk[Order*sizeof(Index)];  // array of indexes
282:       }myVars;
283:    };
284:
285:    // memory only
286:    static int gPage;
287:    time_t myTime; // for lifo queue
288: };
289:
290: #endif
```

Listing 16.2 BTree.cpp

```
1:    // ****************************************************
2:    // PROGRAM:  Btree
3:    // FILE:     btree.cpp
4:    // PURPOSE:  provide fundamental btree functionality
5:    // NOTES:
6:    // AUTHOR:   Jesse Liberty (jl)
7:    // REVISIONS: 11/1/94 1.0 jl  initial release
8:    // ****************************************************
9:
10:   #include "btree.hpp"
11:   #include "stdef.hpp"
12:   #include <ctype.h>
13:   #include <stdlib.h>
14:
15:   // construct the tree
16:   // initialize myRoot pointer to nothing
17:   // either create or read the index file
18:   BTree::BTree():myRoot(0)
19:   {
20:      myRoot = theIDXManager.Create();
21:      theDataFile.Create();
22:      theWNJFile.Create();
23:
24:   }
25:
26:   // write out the index file
27:   BTree::~BTree()
28:   {
29:      theIDXManager.Close(myRoot);
30:      theDataFile.Close();
31:      theWNJFile.Close();
32:   }
33:
34:   // find an existing record
35:   int BTree::Find(char * str)
36:   {
37:      Index index(str);
```

continues

Listing 16.2 continued

```
38:          BTree::theIter.Reset();
39:          if (!myRoot)
40:             return 0L;
41:          else
42:             return GetPage(myRoot)->Find(index);
43:       }
44:
45:    // find an existing record
46:     int BTree::FindExact(char * str)
47:     {
48:        Index index(str);
49:        BTree::theIter.Reset();
50:        if (!myRoot)
51:           return 0L;
52:        else
53:            return GetPage(myRoot)->Insert(index,TRUE, TRUE);
54:     }
55:
56:
57:     int BTree::GetNext(char * str)
58:     {
59:        Index index(str);
60:        return BTree::theIter.GetNext(index);
61:     }
62:
63:
64:     void BTree::Insert(char * buffer, int argc, char** argv)
65:     {
66:        // get each word,
67:        int offset = theDataFile.Insert(buffer);
68:        for (int i = 1; i<argc; i++)
69:        {
70:           AddKey(argv[i],offset);
71:        }
72:
73:     }
74:
75:     void BTree::Insert(char* buffer)
76:     {
77:
78:        if (strlen(buffer) < 3)
79:           return;
80:
81:         char *buff = buffer;
82:         char word[PageSize];
83:         int wordOffset = 0;
84:         int offset;
85:
86:        if (GetWord(buff,word,wordOffset))
87:        {
88:           offset = theDataFile.Insert(buffer);
89:           AddKey(word,offset);
90:        }
91:
92:
```

```
93:          while (GetWord(buff,word,wordOffset))
94:          {
95:              AddKey(word,offset);
96:          }
97:
98:      }
99:
100:     void BTree::AddKey(char * str, int offset, BOOL synonym )
101:     {
102:
103:         if (strlen(str) < 3)
104:             return;
105:
106:         int retVal =0;
107:         Index index(str,offset);
108:         if (!myRoot)
109:         {
110:             myRoot = theIDXManager.NewPage (index,TRUE);
111:         }
112:         else
113:         {
114:             retVal = GetPage(myRoot)->Insert(index,FALSE, synonym);
115:             if (retVal) // our root split
116:             {
117:                 // create a pointer to the old top
118:                 Index index(GetPage(myRoot)->GetFirstIndex());
119:                 index.SetPointer(myRoot);
120:                 // make the new page & insert the index
121:                 int PageNumber = NewPage(index,FALSE);
122:
123:                 Page* pg = GetPage(PageNumber);
124:
125:                 //get a pointer to the new (sibling) page
126:                 Index Sib(GetPage(retVal)->GetFirstIndex());
127:                 Sib.SetPointer(retVal);
128:                 // put it into the page
129:                 pg->InsertLeaf(Sib);
130:
131:                 // reset myRoot to point to the new top
132:                 myRoot = PageNumber;
133:             }
134:         }
135:     }
136:
137:     void BTree::PrintTree()
138:     {
139:         GetPage(myRoot)->Print();
140:
141:         cout << "\n\nStats:" << endl;
142:         cout << "Node pages:    " << NodePageCtr << endl;
143:         cout << "Leaf pages:    " << LeafPageCtr << endl;
144:         cout << "Node indexes: " << NodeIndexCtr << endl;
145:         cout << "Leaf indexes: " << LeafIndexCtr << endl;
146:         for (int i = 0; i < Order +2; i++)
147:         {
148:             if (NodeIndexPerPage[i])
```

continues

Listing 16.2 continued

```
149:            {
150:                cout << "Pages with " << i << " nodes:   ";
151:                cout << NodeIndexPerPage[i] << endl;
152:            }
153:            if (LeafIndexPerPage[i])
154:            {
155:                cout << "Pages with " << i << " leaves: ";
156:                cout << LeafIndexPerPage[i] << endl;
157:            }
158:        }
159:
160:    }
161:
162:    BOOL BTree::GetWord(char* string, char* word, int& wordOffset)
163:    {
164:
165:        if (!string[wordOffset])
166:            return FALSE;
167:
168:        char *p1, *p2;
169:        p1 = p2 = string+wordOffset;
170:
171:        // eat leading spaces
172:        for (int i = 0; i<(int)strlen(p1) && !BTree::myAlNum(p1[0]); i++)
173:            p1++;
174:
175:        // see if you have a word
176:        if (!BTree::myAlNum(p1[0]))
177:            return FALSE;
178:
179:         p2 = p1; // point to start of word
180:
181:        // march p2 to end of word
182:        while (BTree::myAlNum(p2[0]))
183:            p2++;
184:
185:        int len = int(p2-p1);
186: #if defined(_MSVC_16BIT) || defined(_MSVC_32BIT)
   : {
   :    len = __min(len,(int)PageSize);
   : }
   : #else
   : {
   :    len = min(len,(int)PageSize);
   : }
   : #endif
187:
188:        strncpy (word,p1,len);
189:        word[len]='\0';
190:
191:        for (i = int (p2-string); i<(int)strlen(string) &&
!BTree::myAlNum(p2[0]); i++)
192:            p2++;
193:
194:        wordOffset = int (p2-string);
```

```
195:
196:        return TRUE;
197:    }
198:
199:    int BTree::myAlNum(char ch)
200:    {
201:        return isalnum(ch) ||
202:            ch == '-' ||
203:            ch == '\'' ||
204:            ch == '(' ||
205:            ch == ')';
206:    }
```

Type   Listing 16.3 Index.cpp

```
1:      // **************************************************
2:      // PROGRAM:   index
3:      // FILE:      index.cpp
4:      // PURPOSE:   provide fundamental btree functionality
5:      // NOTES:
6:      // AUTHOR:    Jesse Liberty (jl)
7:      // REVISIONS: 11/1/94 1.0 jl  initial release
8:      // **************************************************
9:
10:     #include "btree.hpp"
11:     #include <ctype.h>
12:
13:     Index::Index(char* str):myPointer(1)
14:     {
15:         strncpy(myData,str,dataLen);
16:         myData[dataLen]='\0';
17:         for (int i = 0; i< (int)strlen(myData); i++)
18:             myData[i] = toupper(myData[i]);
19:     }
20:
21:     Index::Index(char* str, int ptr):myPointer(ptr)
22:     {
23:
24:         strncpy(myData,str,dataLen);
25:         myData[dataLen]='\0';
26: for (int i = 0; i< (int)strlen(myData); i++)
27:             myData[i] = toupper(myData[i]);
28:
29:     }
30:
31:     Index::Index(Index& rhs):
32:         myPointer(rhs.GetPointer())
33:     {
34:         strcpy(myData, rhs.GetData());
35:         for (int i = 0; i< (int)strlen(myData); i++)
36:             myData[i] = toupper(myData[i]);
37:
38:     }
39:
```

continues

Listing 16.3 continued

```
40:      Index::Index():myPointer(0)
41:      {
42:          myData[0]='\0';
43:      }
44:
45:      void Index::PrintKey()
46:      {
47:          cout << "   " << myData;
48:      }
49:
50:      void Index::PrintPage()
51:      {
52:          cout << "\n" << myData << ": " ;
53:          BTree::theIDXManager.GetPage(myPointer)->Print();
54:      }
55:
56:      int Index::Insert(Index& ref, BOOL findOnly, BOOL findExact)
57:      {
58:          return BTree::theIDXManager.GetPage(myPointer)-
                 >Insert(ref,findOnly,findExact);
59:      }
60:
61:      int Index::operator==(const Index& rhs)
62:      {
63:          return (strcmp(myData,rhs.GetData()) == 0); // case insensitive
64:      }
65:
66:      int Index::Begins(const Index& rhs) const
67:      {
68:          int len = strlen(myData);
69:          if (!len)
70:              return TRUE;
71:          return (strncmp(myData,rhs.GetData(),len) == 0);
72:      }
```

Type Listing 16.4 Page.cpp

```
1:       // **************************************************
2:       // PROGRAM:   Page
3:       // FILE:      Page.cpp
4:       // PURPOSE:   provide fundamental btree functionality
5:       // NOTES:
6:       // AUTHOR:    Jesse Liberty (jl)
7:       // REVISIONS: 11/1/94 1.0 jl  initial release
8:       // **************************************************
9:
10:      #include "btree.hpp"
11:      #include <assert.h>
12:
13:      // constructors
14:
15:      // default constructor
16:      Page::Page()
```

```
17:        {
18:        }
19:
20:        // create a page from a buffer read in from disk
21:        Page::Page(char *buffer):
22:            myKeys((Index*)myVars.mk)
23:        {
24:            assert(sizeof(myBlock) == PageSize);
25:            assert(sizeof(myVars) == PageSize);
26:            memcpy(&myBlock,buffer,PageSize);
27:            SetLocked(FALSE);
28:            myTime = time(NULL);
29:        }
30:
31:        // create a Page from the first index
32:        Page::Page(Index& index, BOOL bLeaf):
33:            myKeys((Index*)myVars.mk)
34:        {
35:
36:            myVars.myCount=1;
37:            myVars.IsLeaf = bLeaf;
38:            SetLocked(FALSE);
39:            // if this is a leaf, this is the first
40:            // index on the first page, set its pointer
41:            // based on creating a new wnj. otherwise
42:            // you are here creating a new node, do not
43:            // set the pointer, it is already set.
44:            if (bLeaf)
45:                index.SetPointer(BTree::theWNJFile.Append(index.GetPointer()));
46:            myKeys[0]=index;
47:            myVars.myPageNumber = gPage++;
48:            myTime = time(NULL);
49:        }
50:
51:        // create a page by splitting another page
52:        Page::Page(Index *array, int offset, BOOL bLeaf,int count):
53:            myKeys((Index*)myVars.mk)
54:        {
55:            myVars.IsLeaf = bLeaf;
56:            myVars.myCount = 0;
57:            for (int i=0, j = offset; j<Order && i < count; i++, j++)
58:            {
59:                myKeys[i]= array[j];
60:                myVars.myCount++;
61:            }
62:            myVars.myPageNumber = gPage++;
63:            SetLocked(FALSE);
64:            myTime = time(NULL);
65:        }
66:
67:        void Page::Nullify(int offset)
68:        {
69:            for (int i = offset; i<Order; i++)
70:            {
71:                    myKeys[i].SetPointer(0);
72:                    myVars.myCount--;
```

continues

Listing 16.4 continued

```
73:        }
74:    }
75:
76:    // decide whether I'm a leaf or a node
77:    // and pass this index to the right
78:    // function. If findOnly is true, don't insert
79:    // just return the page number (for now)
80:    int Page::Insert(Index& rIndex, BOOL findOnly, BOOL synonym)
81:    {
82:        int result;
83:        if (myVars.IsLeaf)
84:        {
85:            SetLocked(TRUE);
86:            result = FindLeaf(rIndex,findOnly,synonym);
87:            SetLocked(FALSE);
88:            return result;
89:        }
90:        else
91:        {
92:            SetLocked(TRUE);
93:            result = InsertNode(rIndex,findOnly,synonym);
94:            SetLocked(FALSE);
95:            return result;
96:        }
97:    }
98:
99:
100:   // find the right page for this index
101:   int Page::InsertNode(Index& rIndex, BOOL findOnly,BOOL synonym)
102:   {
103:       int retVal =0;
104:       BOOL inserted = FALSE;
105:       int i;
106:
107:       assert(myVars.myCount>0); // nodes have at least 1
108:       assert(myKeys[0].GetPointer()); // must be valid
109:
110:       if (findOnly)
111:       {
112:           for (i = 0; i< myVars.myCount; i++)
113:           {
114:             if (!synonym)
115:             {
116:                 if (rIndex.Begins(myKeys[i]))
117:                 {
118:                     BTree::theIter.RecordNode(myVars.myPageNumber,i);
119:                     return myKeys[i].Insert(rIndex,findOnly,synonym);
120:                 }
121:             }
122:             else
123:             {
124:                 if (rIndex == (myKeys[i]))
125:                 {
126:                     BTree::theIter.RecordNode(myVars.myPageNumber,i);
127:                     return myKeys[i].Insert(rIndex,findOnly,synonym);
```

```
128:                    }
129:
130:
131:                }
132:            }
133:        }
134:
135:
136:        // does it go before my first entry?
137:        if (!inserted && rIndex < myKeys[0])
138:        {
139:
140:            if (findOnly)
141:                return 0L;
142:
143:            myKeys[0].SetData(rIndex);
144:            BTree::theIter.RecordNode(myVars.myPageNumber,0);
145:            retVal=myKeys[0].Insert(rIndex,findOnly,synonym);
146:            inserted = TRUE;
147:        }
148:
149:        // find insertion point
150:        if (!inserted)
151:        {
152:            for (i = myVars.myCount-1; i>=0; i--)
153:            {
154:                assert(myKeys[i].GetPointer());
155:                if ( (rIndex >= myKeys[i]))
156:                {
157:                    BTree::theIter.RecordNode(myVars.myPageNumber,i);
158:                    retVal=myKeys[i].Insert(rIndex,findOnly,synonym);
159:                    inserted = TRUE;
160:                    break;
161:                }
162:            }
163:        }
164:        assert(inserted);   // change to exception if not!
165:
166:        // if you had to split
167:        if (retVal && !findOnly) // got back a pointer to a new page
168:        {
169:            Index * pIndex = new Index(GetPage(retVal)->GetFirstIndex());
170:            pIndex->SetPointer(retVal);
171:            retVal = InsertLeaf(*pIndex);
172:        }
173:        return retVal;
174:    }
175:
176:    // called if current page is a leaf
177:    int Page::FindLeaf(Index& rIndex, BOOL findOnly, BOOL synonym)
178:    {
179:        int result = 0;
180:
181:        // no duplicates!
182:        for (int i=0; i < myVars.myCount; i++)
183:        {
```

continues

449

Listing 16.4 continued

```
184:            if (findOnly)
185:            {
186:                if (!synonym)
187:                {
188:                    if (rIndex.Begins(myKeys[i]))
189:                    {
190:                        BTree::theIter.RecordLeaf(myVars.myPageNumber,i);
191:                        return myKeys[i].GetPointer();
192:                    }
193:                }
194:                else
195:                {
196:                    if (rIndex ==(myKeys[i]))
197:                    {
198:                        BTree::theIter.RecordLeaf(myVars.myPageNumber,i);
199:                        return myKeys[i].GetPointer();
200:                    }
201:
202:
203:                }
204:            }
205:            else
206:                if (rIndex == myKeys[i])
207:                    return BTree::theWNJFile.Insert(
208:                            rIndex.GetPointer(),
209:                                myKeys[i].GetPointer());
210:        }
211:
212:        if (findOnly)         // not found
213:            return result;
214:
215:        // this index item does not yet exist
216:        // before you push it into the index
217:        // push an entry into the wnj.idx
218:        // and set the index to point to that entry
219:        if (!synonym)
220:            rIndex.SetPointer(BTree::theWNJFile.Append(rIndex.GetPointer())); //
                new!
221:        return InsertLeaf(rIndex);
222:    }
223:
224:    int Page::InsertLeaf(Index& rIndex)
225:    {
226:        int result = 0;
227:        if (myVars.myCount < Order)
228:            Push(rIndex);
229:        else      // overflow the page
230:        {
231:            // make sibling
232:            int NewPg =
233:                NewPage(myKeys,Order/2,myVars.IsLeaf,myVars.myCount);
234:            Page* Sibling = GetPage(NewPg);
235:            Nullify(Order/2);                        // nullify my right half
236:
237:            // does it fit in this side?
```

```
238:                    if (myVars.myCount>Order/2-1 && rIndex <= myKeys[Order/2-1])
239:                        Push(rIndex);
240:                    else  // push it into the new sibling
241:                        Sibling->Push(rIndex);
242:
243:                    result = NewPg; // we split, pass it up
244:                }
245:            return result;
246:    }
247:
248:    // put the new index into this page (in order)
249:    void Page::Push(Index& rIndex,int offset,BOOL first)
250:    {
251:        BOOL inserted = FALSE;
252:        assert(myVars.myCount < Order);
253:        for (int i=offset; i<Order && i<myVars.myCount; i++)
254:        {
255:            assert(myKeys[i].GetPointer());
256:            if (rIndex <= myKeys[i])
257:            {
258:                    Push(myKeys[i],offset+1,FALSE);
259:                    myKeys[i]=rIndex;
260:                    inserted = TRUE;
261:                    break;
262:            }
263:        }
264:        if (!inserted)
265:            myKeys[myVars.myCount] = rIndex;
266:
267:        if (first)
268:            myVars.myCount++;
269:    }
270:
271:
272:    void Page::Print()
273:    {
274:            if (!myVars.IsLeaf)
275:            {
276:                BTree::NodePageCtr++;
277:                BTree::NodeIndexPerPage[myVars.myCount]++;
278:                BTree::NodeIndexCtr+=myVars.myCount;
279:            }
280:            else
281:            {
282:                BTree::LeafPageCtr++;
283:                BTree::LeafIndexPerPage[myVars.myCount]++;
284:                BTree::LeafIndexCtr+=myVars.myCount;
285:            }
286:
287:            for (int i = 0; i<Order && i < myVars.myCount; i++)
288:            {
289:                assert(myKeys[i].GetPointer());
290:                if (myVars.IsLeaf)
291:                    myKeys[i].PrintKey();
292:                else
293:                    myKeys[i].PrintPage();
```

continues

Listing 16.4 continued

```
294:              }
295:          }
296:
297:     // write out the entire page as a block
298:     fstream& Page::Write(fstream& file)
299:     {
300:         char buffer[PageSize];
301:         memcpy(buffer,&myBlock,PageSize);
302:         file.flush();
303:         file.clear();
304:         file.seekp(myVars.myPageNumber*PageSize);
305:         file.write(buffer,PageSize);
306:         return file;
307:     }
```

Type   **Listing 16.5 Datafile.cpp**

```
1:      // **************************************************
2:      // PROGRAM:   Data file
3:      // FILE:      datafile.cpp
4:      // PURPOSE:
5:      // NOTES:
6:      // AUTHOR:    Jesse Liberty (jl)
7:      // REVISIONS: 11/5/94 1.0 jl  initial release
8:      // **************************************************
9:
10:     #include "btree.hpp"
11:     #include <assert.h>
12:
13:     // on construction, try to open the file if it exists
14:     DataFile::DataFile():
15:        myFile("ROBIN.DAT",
16:        ios::binary | ios::in | ios::out | ios::nocreate | ios::app)
17:     {
18:     }
19:
20:     void DataFile::Create()
21:     {
22:         if (!myFile) // nocreate failed, first creation
23:         {
24:
25:             // open the file, create it this time
26:             myFile.clear();
27:             myFile.open
28:                ("ROBIN.DAT",ios::binary | ios::in | ios::out | ios::app);
29:
30:             char Header[offInt];
31:             int MagicNumber = 1234; // a number we can check for
32:             memcpy(Header,&MagicNumber,offInt);
33:             myFile.clear();
34:             myFile.flush();
35:             myFile.seekp(0);
36:             myFile.write(Header,offInt);
```

```
37:                    return;
38:              }
39:
40:          // we did open the file, it already existed
41:          // get the numbers we need
42:          int MagicNumber;
43:          myFile.seekg(0);
44:          myFile.read((char *) &MagicNumber,offInt);
45:
46:          // check the magic number. If it is wrong the file is
47:          // corrupt or this isn't the index file
48:          if (MagicNumber != 1234)
49:          {
50:                  // change to an exception!!
51:                  cout << "DataFile Magic number failed!";
52:          }
53:          return;
54:      }
55:
56:      // write out the numbers we'll need next time
57:      void DataFile::Close()
58:      {
59:          myFile.close();
60:      }
61:
62:
63:      int DataFile::Insert(char * newNote)
64:      {
65:          int len = strlen(newNote);
66:
67:
68:          time_t theTime;
69:          theTime = time(NULL);
70:
71:          int offTime = sizeof(time_t);
72:          int fullLen = len + offInt + offTime;
73:
74:          char buffer[PageSize];
75:          memcpy(buffer,&len,offInt);
76:          memcpy(buffer+sizeof(len),&theTime,offTime);
77:          memcpy(buffer+offInt+offTime,newNote,len);
78:
79:          myFile.clear();
80:          myFile.flush();
81:          myFile.seekp(0,ios::end);
82:          int offset = (int) myFile.tellp();
83:          myFile.write(buffer,fullLen);
84:          myFile.flush();
85:          return offset;
86:      }
87:
88:      void DataFile::GetRecord(int offset, char* buffer, int& len, time_t&
           theTime)
89:      {
90:
91:          int offLen = sizeof(int);
```

continues

Listing 16.5 continued

```
92:            int offTime = sizeof(time_t);
93:            char tmpBuff[PageSize];
94:            myFile.flush();
95:            myFile.clear();
96:            myFile.seekg(offset);
97:            myFile.read(tmpBuff,PageSize);
98:            memcpy(&len,tmpBuff,offLen);
99:            memcpy(&theTime,tmpBuff+offLen,offTime);
100:           strncpy(buffer,tmpBuff+offLen+offTime,len);
101:           buffer[len] = '\0';
102:       }
```

 Listing 16.6 IdxManager.cpp

```
1:     // ***************************************************
2:     // PROGRAM:  Idxmr
3:     // FILE:     Idxmgr.cpp
4:     // PURPOSE:  provide i/o for btree
5:     // NOTES:
6:     // AUTHOR:   Jesse Liberty (jl)
7:     // REVISIONS: 11/5/94 1.0 jl  initial release
8:     // ***************************************************
9:
10:    #include "btree.hpp"
11:    #include <assert.h>
12:
13:    // on construction, try to open the file if it exists
14:    IDXManager::IDXManager():
15:        myFile("ROBIN.IDX",ios::binary | ios::in | ios::out | ios::nocreate)
16:    {
17:        // initialize the pointers to null
18:        for (int i = 0; i< MaxPages; i++)
19:            myPages[i] = 0;
20:        myCount = 0;
21:
22:    }
23:
24:    // called by btree constructor
25:    // if we opened the file, read in the numbers we need
26:    // otherwise create the file
27:    int IDXManager::Create()
28:    {
29:        if (!myFile) // nocreate failed, first creation
30:        {
31:            // open the file, create it this time
32:            myFile.open("ROBIN.IDX",ios::binary | ios::in | ios::out);
33:            char Header[PageSize];
34:            int MagicNumber = 1234; // a number we can check for
35:            memcpy(Header,&MagicNumber,offInt);
36:            int NextPage = 1;
37:            memcpy(Header+offInt,&NextPage,offInt);
38:            memcpy(Header+2*offInt,&NextPage,offInt);
39:            Page::SetgPageNumber(NextPage);
```

```
40:                char title[]="ROBIN.IDX. Ver 1.00";
41:                memcpy(Header+3*offInt,title,strlen(title));
42:                myFile.flush();
43:                myFile.clear();
44:                myFile.seekp(0);
45:                myFile.write(Header,PageSize);
46:                return 0;
47:            }
48:
49:        // we did open the file, it already existed
50:        // get the numbers we need
51:        int MagicNumber;
52:        myFile.seekg(0);
53:        myFile.read((char *) &MagicNumber,offInt);
54:
55:        // check the magic number. If it is wrong the file is
56:        // corrupt or this isn't the index file
57:        if (MagicNumber != 1234)
58:        {
59:                // change to an exception!!
60:                cout << "Index Magic number failed!";
61:                return 0;
62:        }
63:
64:        int NextPage;
65:        myFile.seekg(offInt);
66:        myFile.read((char*) &NextPage,offInt);
67:        Page::SetgPageNumber(NextPage);
68:        int FirstPage;
69:        myFile.seekg(2*offInt);
70:        myFile.read((char*) &FirstPage,offInt);
71:        const int room =  PageSize - 3*offInt;
72:        char buffer[room];
73:        myFile.read(buffer,room);
74:        buffer[20]='\0';
75:        // cout << buffer << endl;
76:        // read in all the pages
77:        for (int i = 1; i < NextPage; i++)
78:        {
79:                myFile.seekg(i * PageSize);
80:                char buffer[PageSize];
81:                myFile.read( buffer, PageSize);
82:                Page * pg = new Page(buffer);
83:                Insert(pg);
84:        }
85:
86:        return FirstPage;
87:    }
88:
89:    // write out the numbers we'll need next time
90:    void IDXManager::Close(int theRoot)
91:    {
92:
93:        for (int i = 0; i< MaxPages; i++)
94:            if (myPages[i])
95:                Save(myPages[i]);
```

continues

Listing 16.6 continued

```
96:          int NextPage = Page::GetgPageNumber();
97:          if (!myFile)
98:             cout << "Error opening myFile!" << endl;
99:          myFile.flush();
100:         myFile.clear();
101:         myFile.seekp(offInt);
102:         myFile.write ( (char *) &NextPage,offInt);
103:         myFile.seekp(2*offInt);
104:         myFile.write((char*) &theRoot,offInt);
105:         myFile.close();
106:     }
107:
108:     // wrapper function
109:     int IDXManager::NewPage(Index& index, BOOL bLeaf)
110:     {
111:         Page * newPage = new Page(index, bLeaf);
112:         Insert(newPage);
113:         Save(newPage);
114:         return newPage->GetPageNumber();
115:     }
116:
117:     int IDXManager::NewPage(
118:         Index *array,
119:         int offset,
120:         BOOL leaf,
121:         int count)
122:     {
123:         Page * newPage = new Page(array, offset, leaf,count);
124:         Insert(newPage);
125:         Save(newPage);
126:         return newPage->GetPageNumber();
127:     }
128:
129:     void IDXManager::Insert(Page * newPage)
130:     {
131:
132:         // add new page into array of page managers
133:         if (myCount < MaxPages)
134:         {
135:             assert(!myPages[myCount]);
136:             myPages[myCount++] = newPage;
137:         }
138:         else  // no room, time to page out to disk
139:         {
140:             int lowest = -1;
141:
142:             for (int i = 0; i< MaxPages; i++)
143:             {
144:                 if (myPages[i]->GetLocked() == FALSE )
145:                     lowest = i;
146:             }
147:             if (lowest == -1)
148:                 assert(lowest != -1); // change to exception if -1 (no page to
                    kill)
149:
```

```
150:                 for (i = 0; i< MaxPages; i++)
151:                     if (myPages[i]->GetTime() < myPages[lowest]->GetTime() &&
152:                         myPages[i]->GetLocked() == FALSE)
152:                         lowest = i;
153:
154:                 assert(myPages[lowest]);
155:                 Save(myPages[lowest]);
156:                 delete myPages[lowest];
157:                 myPages[lowest] = newPage;
158:
159:             }
160:     }
161:
162:     // tell the page to write itself out
163:     void IDXManager::Save(Page* pg)
164:     {
165:       pg->Write(myFile);
166:     }
167:
168:     // see if the page is in memory, if so return it
169:     // otherwise get it from disk
170:     // note: this won't scale, with lots of page managers
171:     // you'd need a more efficient search. 10 levels of page
172:     // managers, with 31 indexes per page gives you room for
173:     // 800 trillion words. Even if each page is only 1/2 full
174:     // on average, 10 levels of depth would represent 64 million
175:     // keys alone, not to mention the actual records.
176:
177:     Page * IDXManager::GetPage(int target)
178:     {
179:
180:         for (int i = 0; i< MaxPages; i++)
181:         {
182:             if (myPages[i]->GetPageNumber() == target)
183:                 return  myPages[i];
184:         }
185:         myFile.seekg(target * PageSize);
186:         char buffer[PageSize];
187:         myFile.read( buffer, PageSize);
188:         Page * pg = new Page(buffer);
189:         Insert(pg);
190:         return pg;
191:     }
```

Type **Listing 16.7 Iter.cpp**

```
1:      // ***************************************************
2:      // PROGRAM:   Iterator
3:      // FILE:      iter.cpp
4:      // PURPOSE:   iterator for BTree
5:      // NOTES:
6:      // AUTHOR:    Jesse Liberty (jl)
7:      // REVISIONS: 12/1/94 1.0 jl  initial release
8:      // ***************************************************
```

continues

Listing 16.7 continued

```
9:        #include "btree.hpp"
10:
11:       // history class implementations
12:       History::History(int pno, int off, BOOL node):
13:          PageNo(pno),
14:          OffSet(off),
15:          IsNode(node)
16:       {}
17:
18:       // Iterator implementations
19:
20:       // start off with blank iterator
21:       Iterator::Iterator()
22:       {
23:          Reset();
24:       }
25:
26:       Iterator::~Iterator()
27:       {
28:          for (int i = 0; i<MaxPages; i++)
29:             delete myHistory[i];
30:       }
31:
32:       void Iterator::RecordNode(int PageNo, int OffSet)
33:       {
34:          myHistory[myNext++] = new History(PageNo,OffSet,TRUE);
35:       }
36:
37:       void Iterator::RecordLeaf(int PageNo, int OffSet)
38:       {
39:          myHistory[myNext++] = new History(PageNo,OffSet,FALSE);
40:       }
41:
42:       History* Iterator::GetLast()
43:       {
44:          return myHistory[myNext-1];
45:       }
46:
47:       History* Iterator::GetFirst()
48:       {
49:          return myHistory[0];
50:       }
51:
52:       void Iterator::Reset()
53:       {
54:          for (int i = 0; i<MaxPages; i++)
55:             myHistory[i] = 0;
56:          myNext = 0;
57:       }
58:
59:
60:       int Iterator::GetNext(const Index& theIndex)
61:       {
62:
63:          for (;;)
```

```
64:           {
65:               History * pHist = GetLast();
66:               int pgNo = pHist-> PageNo;
67:               int newOffSet = pHist->OffSet+1;
68:               Page * pg = BTree::theIDXManager.GetPage(pgNo);
69:
70:               if (newOffSet < pg->GetCount())
71:               {
72:                   Index Idx = pg->GetIndex(newOffSet);
73:                   pHist->OffSet = newOffSet;
74:                   for (;;)
75:                   {
76:                       if (pg->GetIsLeaf())
77:                       {
78:                           // cout << "Key: " << Idx.GetData() << endl;
79:                           if (theIndex.Begins(Idx))
80:                               return Idx.GetPointer();
81:                           else
82:                               return 0;
83:                       }
84:                       else
85:                       {
86:                       pg = BTree::theIDXManager.GetPage(Idx.GetPointer());
87:                       Idx = pg->GetFirstIndex();
88:                       pHist = new History(pg->GetPageNumber(),0, (BOOL)!pg-
                           >GetIsLeaf());
89:                       myHistory[myNext++] = pHist;
90:                       }
91:                   }  // end inner for loop
92:               }
93:               else
94:               {
95:                   delete myHistory[myNext-1];
96:                   myHistory[myNext-1] = 0;
97:                   myNext--;
98:                   if (!myNext)
99:                       return 0;
100:              }
101:          }  // end outer for loop
102:      }
```

Type   Listing 16.8 WNJFile.cpp

```
1:       // **************************************************
2:       // PROGRAM:   Word-Node-Join
3:       // FILE:      WNJFile.cpp
4:       // PURPOSE:
5:       // NOTES:
6:       // AUTHOR:    Jesse Liberty (jl)
7:       // REVISIONS: 11/5/94 1.0 jl  initial release
8:       // **************************************************
9:
10:      #include "btree.hpp"
11:      #include <assert.h>
```

continues

Listing 16.8 continued

```
12:
13:      // on construction, try to open the file if it exists
14:      WNJFile::WNJFile():
15:          myFile("ROBINWNJ.IDX",
16:          ios::binary | ios::in | ios::out | ios::nocreate)
17:      {
18:          for (int i = 0; i<5; i++)
19:              myints[i]=0L;
20:      }
21:
22:      void WNJFile::Create()
23:      {
24:
25:          char Header[2*offInt];
26:          int MagicNumber=0; // a number we can check for
27:          int zero = 0;
28:
29:          if (!myFile) // nocreate failed, first creation
30:          {
31:              // open the file, create it this time
32:              myFile.clear();
33:              myFile.open("ROBINWNJ.IDX",
34:                  ios::binary | ios::in | ios::out);
35:
36:              MagicNumber = 1234;
37:              memcpy(Header,&MagicNumber,offInt);
38:              memcpy(Header+offInt,&zero,offInt);
39:              myFile.seekp(0);
40:              myFile.write(Header,2*offInt);
41:              myFile.flush();
42:              return;
43:          }
44:
45:          // we did open the file, it already existed
46:          // get the numbers we need
47:
48:
49:          myFile.seekg(0);
50:          myFile.read(Header,2*offInt);
51:          memcpy(&MagicNumber,Header,offInt);
52:          memcpy(&myCount,Header+offInt,offInt);
53:
54:          // check the magic number. If it is wrong the file is
55:          // corrupt or this isn't the index file
56:          if (MagicNumber != 1234)
57:          {
58:              // change to an exception!!
59:              cout << "WNJ Magic number failed!";
60:              cout << "Magic number: " << MagicNumber;
61:              cout << "\nmyCount: " << myCount << endl;
62:          }
63:          return;
64:      }
65:
66:      // write out the numbers we'll need next time
67:      void WNJFile::Close()
```

```
68:        {
69:
70:            myFile.seekg(offInt);
71:            myFile.write((char*)&myCount,offInt);
72:            myFile.close();
73:        }
74:
75:        int WNJFile::Append(int DataOffset)
76:        {
77:
78:            int newPos = 2*offInt + myCount++ * (5*offInt);
79:            int offsets[5];
80:            offsets[0] = DataOffset;
81:            for (int i = 1; i<5; i++)
82:                offsets[i]=0;
83:            myFile.seekg(newPos);
84:            myFile.write((char*)offsets,5*offInt);
85:
86:            return newPos;
87:        }
88:
89:
90:        int WNJFile::Insert(int DataOffset,int WNJOffset)
91:        {
92:
93:            int ints[5];
94:            myFile.seekg(WNJOffset);
95:            myFile.read((char*)ints,5*offInt);
96:
97:            int offset=WNJOffset;
98:
99:            while (ints[4])
100:            {
101:                offset = ints[4];
102:                myFile.clear();
103:                myFile.flush();
104:                myFile.seekg(ints[4]);
105:                myFile.read((char*)ints,5*offInt);
106:            }
107:            if (ints[3]) // full!
108:            {
109:                ints[4] = Append(DataOffset);
110:                myFile.clear();
111:                myFile.flush();
112:                myFile.seekg(offset);
113:                myFile.write((char*)ints,5*offInt);
114:            }
115:            else
116:            {
117:                for (int i = 0; i<4; i++)
118:                {
119:                    if (ints[i] == 0)
120:                    {
121:                        ints[i] = DataOffset;
122:                        myFile.clear();
123:                        myFile.flush();
```

continues

Listing 16.8 continued

```
124:                        myFile.seekg(offset);
125:                        myFile.write((char*)ints,5*offInt);
126:                        break;
127:                    }
128:                }
129:            }
130:        return 0;
131:    }
132:
133:
134:    int* WNJFile::Find(int NextWNJ)
135:    {
136:        int ints[5];
137:
138:        int * results = new int[256];
139:
140:        int i = 0, j=0;
141:
142:        while (j<256)
143:            results[j++] = 0;
144:
145:        j = 0;
146:
147:        myFile.seekg(NextWNJ);
148:        myFile.read((char*)ints,5*offInt);
149:
150:        while (j < 256)
151:        {
152:            if (ints[i])
153:            {
154:                if (i == 4)
155:                {
156:                    myFile.seekg(ints[4]);
157:                    myFile.read((char*)ints,5*offInt);
158:                    i = 0;
159:                    continue;
160:                }
161:                results[j++] = ints[i++];
162:            }
163:            else
164:                break;
165:        }
166:        return results;
167:    }
```

Type **Listing 16.9 R2.cpp**

```
1:    // **************************************************
2:    // PROGRAM:   R2
3:    // FILE:      r2.cpp
4:    // PURPOSE:   Add synonyms to ROBIN.
5:    // NOTES:
6:    // AUTHOR:    Jesse Liberty (jl)
```

```
7:        // REVISIONS: 1/1/95 1.0 jl
8:        // ***************************************************
9:
10:
11:       #include "stdef.hpp"
12:       #include "btree.hpp"
13:       #include <stdlib.h>
14:
15:       // static definitions
16:       IDXManager BTree::theIDXManager;
17:       DataFile BTree::theDataFile;
18:       WNJFile BTree::theWNJFile;
19:       Iterator BTree::theIter;
20:
21:       int WNJFile::myCount=0L;
22:       int Page::gPage=1;
23:       int BTree::NodeIndexCtr=0;
24:       int BTree::LeafIndexCtr=0;
25:       int BTree::NodePageCtr=0;
26:       int BTree::LeafPageCtr=0;
27:       int BTree::NodeIndexPerPage[Order+1];
28:       int BTree::LeafIndexPerPage[Order+1];
29:
30:
31:       // prototypes
32:       void parseCommandLines(char *buffer,int argc,char **argv);
33:       void ShowMenu(long*);
34:       void DoFind(int, char**, BTree&);
35:       void ParseFile(int, char**, BTree&);
36:       void DoSyn(char *orig, char* syn, BTree& myTree);
37:
38:       // driver program
39:       int main(int argc, char ** argv)
40:       {
41:          BTree myTree;
42:
43:          for (int i = 0; i < Order +2; i++)
44:          {
45:             BTree::NodeIndexPerPage[i] =0;
46:             BTree::LeafIndexPerPage[i] = 0;
47:          }
48:
49:          char buffer[PageSize+1];
50:
51:          if (argc == 1)
52:          {
53:             cout << "Please provide command line arguments";
54:             return 1;
55:          }
56:
57:          // check for flags, if none add text to data file
58:          if (argv[1][0] == '-')
59:          {
60:
61:             switch (argv[1][1])
62:             {
```

continues

463

Listing 16.9 continued

```
63:              case '?':
64:                  DoFind(argc,argv,myTree);
65:                  break;
66:
67:              case '!':
68:                  myTree.PrintTree();
69:                  break;
70:
71:              case 'F':
72:              case 'f':
73:                  ParseFile(argc,argv,myTree);
74:                  break;
75:
76:              case 'S':
77:              case 's':
78:                  DoSyn(argv[2],argv[3],myTree);
79:                  break;
80:          }
81:      }
82:      else
83:      {
84:          parseCommandLines(buffer,argc,argv);
85:          myTree.Insert(buffer,argc,argv);
86:          cout << "Inserted.\n";
87:      }
88:      return 0;
89:  }
90:
91:  // concatenate remaining command line arguments
92:  void parseCommandLines(char *buffer,int argc,char **argv)
93:  {
94:      size_t len = 0;
95:      size_t argLen=0;
96:      for (int i = 1; i< argc; i++)
97:      {
98:          argLen = strlen(argv[i]);
99:          if (len + argLen +2 < PageSize)
100:         {
101:             strncpy(buffer+len,argv[i],argLen);
102:             strncpy(buffer+len+argLen," ",1);
103:             len += argLen+1;
104:         }
105:     }
106:     buffer[len] = '\0';
107: }
108:
109: // having found matches, show the menu of choices
110: // each entry is numbered and dated
111: void ShowMenu(int *list)
112: {
113:     int j=0;
114:     char buffer[PageSize+1];
115:     time_t theTime;
116:     int len;
```

```
117:        char listBuff[256];
118:        struct tm * ts;
119:        int dispSize;
120:
121:        while (list[j] && j < 20)
122:        {
123:            BTree::theDataFile.GetRecord(list[j],buffer,len, theTime);
124:        #if defined(_MSVC_16BIT) || defined(_MSVC_32BIT)
  :            {
  :                dispSize = __min(len,32); // THIS is a DOUBLE UNDERSCORE
  :            }
  :        #else
  :            {
  :                dispSize = min(len,32);
  :            }
  :        #endif
125:            strncpy(listBuff,buffer,dispSize);
126:            if (dispSize == 32)
127:                {
128:                listBuff[29] = '.';
129:                listBuff[30] = '.';
130:                listBuff[31] = '.';
131:                }
132:            listBuff[dispSize]='\0';
133:            ts = localtime(&theTime);
134:            cout << "[" << (j+1) << "] ";
135:            cout << ts->tm_mon << "/";
136:            cout << ts->tm_mday << "/";
137:            cout << ts->tm_year << " ";
138:            cout <<  listBuff << endl;
139:            j++;
140:        }
141:    }
142:
143:    // handle -? command
144:    // find matches, show the menu, request choice
145:    // display record and redisplay menu
146:    void DoFind(int argc, char ** argv, BTree& myTree)
147:    {
148:
149:        // create an array of total set of WNJ
150:        // offsets. This will be used to display
151:        // choices and to find actual text
152:        int  list[PageSize];
153:
154:        // initialize the array to all zeros
155:        for (int i = 0; i<PageSize; i++)
156:            list[i] = 0;
157:
158:        // for each word in the command line
159:        // search for the matching set of records
160:        for (i = 2; i< argc; i++)
161:        {
162:            int offset = myTree.Find(argv[i]);
163:            while (offset)
```

continues

Listing 16.9 continued

```
164:            {
165:               int* found  =  BTree::theWNJFile.Find(offset);
166:               int j=0;
167:               int len;
168:               time_t theTime;
169:               char buff[512];
170:               while (found[j])
171:               {
172:                   BTree::theDataFile.GetRecord(found[j],buff,len, theTime);
173:                   struct tm * ts = localtime(&theTime);
174:                   cout << "Found: ";
175:                   cout << ts->tm_mon << "/";
176:                   cout << ts->tm_mday << "/";
177:                   cout << ts->tm_year << " ";
178:                   cout <<  buff << endl;
179:                   j++;
180:               }
181:               delete [] found;
182:               offset = myTree.GetNext(argv[i]);
183:            }
184:         }
185:
186:         cout << "\n";
187:
188:         if (!list[0])
189:             return;
190:
191:
192:         ShowMenu(list);
193:
194:         int choice;
195:         char buffer[PageSize];
196:         int len;
197:         time_t theTime;
198:
199:         for (;;)
200:         {
201:             cout << "Choice (0 to stop): " ;
202:             cin >> choice;
203:             if (!choice)
204:                 break;
205:             BTree::theDataFile.GetRecord(list[choice-1],buffer,len, theTime);
206:             cout << "\n>> ";
207:             cout << buffer;
208:             cout << "\n\n";
209:             ShowMenu(list);
210:         }
211:     }
212:
213:     // open a file and create a new note for each line
214:     // index every word in the line
215:     void ParseFile(int argc,char **argv, BTree& myTree)
216:     {
217:
```

```
218:        char buffer[PageSize];
219:        char theString[PageSize];
220:
221:        ifstream theFile(argv[2],ios::in );
222:        if (!theFile)
223:        {
224:           cout << "Error opening input file!\n";
225:           return;
226:        }
227:        int offset = 0;
228:        for (;;)
229:        {
230:              theFile.read(theString,PageSize);
231:              int len = theFile.gcount();
232:              if (!len)
233:                 break;
234:              theString[len]='\0';
235:              char *p1, *p2, *p0;
236:              p0 = p1 = p2 = theString;
237:
238:              while (p1[0] && (p1[0] == '\n' || p1[0] == '\r'))
239:                 p1++;
240:
241:              p2 = p1;
242:
243:              while (p2[0] && p2[0] != '\n' && p2[0] != '\r')
244:                 p2++;
245:
246:              int bufferLen = int(p2 - p1);
247:              int totalLen = int (p2 - p0);
248:
249:              if (!bufferLen)
250:                 continue;
251:
252:              // lstrcpyn(buffer,p1,bufferLen);
253:              strncpy(buffer,p1,bufferLen);
254:              buffer[bufferLen]='\0';
255:
256:              // for (int i = 0; i< PageSize; i++)
257:                 cout << "\r";
258:              cout << "Parsing " << buffer;
259:              myTree.Insert(buffer);
260:              offset += totalLen;
261:              theFile.clear();
262:              theFile.seekg(offset,ios::beg);
263:           }
264:        }
265:
266:
267:    // add synonyms to the tree
268:     void DoSyn(char *orig, char* syn, BTree& myTree)
269:     {
270:        int offset = myTree.FindExact(syn);
271:        if (!offset)  // syn can't exist
272:        {
273:           int offset = myTree.FindExact(orig);
```

continues

Listing 16.9 continued

```
274:            if (offset) // orig must exist
275:                myTree.AddKey(syn,offset,TRUE);
276:        }
277:    }
```

Note: Numbering has been added to the output to make analysis easier. Your output will not include this numbering.

```
1:      d:\>r2 now is the time for all good men to
2:      Inserted.
3:
4:      d:\>r2 come to the aid of their party
5:      Inserted.
6:
7:      d:\>r2 what is the meaning of this
8:      Inserted.
9:
10:     d:\>r2 eternal vigilance is the price of liberty
11:     Inserted.
12:
13:     d:\>r2 when in Rome, do as the Romans
14:     Inserted.
15:
16:     d:\>r2 -!
17:
18:     AID:
19:     AID:    AID  ALL
20:     COME:   COME  ETERNAL  FOR
21:     GOOD:   GOOD  LIBERTY  MEANING  MEN
22:     NOW:
23:     NOW:    NOW  PARTY
24:     PRICE:  PRICE  ROMANS  ROME
25:     THE:    THE  THEIR
26:     THIS:
27:     THIS:   THIS  TIME
28:     VIGILANCE:   VIGILANCE  WHAT  WHEN
29:
30:     Stats:
31:     Node pages:    4
32:     Leaf pages:    8
33:     Node indexes: 11
34:     Leaf indexes: 21
35:     Pages with 2 nodes:   1
36:     Pages with 2 leaves: 4
37:     Pages with 3 nodes:   3
38:     Pages with 3 leaves: 3
39:     Pages with 4 leaves: 1
40:
```

```
41:    d:\>r2 -? liberty
42:    Found: 0/16/95 eternal vigilance is the price of liberty
43:
44:
45:    d:\>r2 -? jesse
46:
47:
48:    d:\>r2 -S liberty jesse
49:
50:    d:\>r2 -? liberty
51:    Found: 0/16/95 eternal vigilance is the price of liberty
52:
53:
54:    d:\>r2 -? jesse
55:    Found: 0/16/95 eternal vigilance is the price of liberty
```

16

 Let's start by examining the output. The data files and indexes were deleted before beginning this test of the program.

In lines 1, 4, 7, 10, and 13, data was added to the files. In line 16, a report was requested, which is shown in lines 18 through 39. You will note that this database is *order 4* (4 indexes on a page), which is not efficient, but is useful during debugging.

In line 41, the user searches for the term *liberty*; it is found, as shown in line 42. In line 45, the user searches for the term *jesse*, but this is not found. In line 48, the user establishes *jesse* as a *synonym* for *liberty*. There is no feedback, although it would be nice if the program came back and verified the addition of the synonym.

In line 50, the user again searches for *liberty* and receives the same results as the first attempt. In line 54, the user searches for *jesse* and this time receives a response: The same as if the term *liberty* had been searched for, which is consistent with the establishment of a synonym.

The easiest way to see how the synonym is established is to examine lines 76 through 79 of listing 16.9. When the user enters -S, a synonym is to be created. The next term and the word following are passed to the new DoSyn() method, as shown in lines 268 through 277 of the same listing.

In line 270, the tree is searched for the synonym. If it exists already as a term in the database, it will *not* be added as a synonym. Otherwise, the tree is searched for the original term.

Note that a new method has been added to BTree: FindExact. The implementation is shown in lines 46 through 54 of listing 16.2. The significant difference from Find is that the call to the page's Insert() method passes in TRUE to the last two parameters. These are declared in line 233 of listing 16.1, in the declaration of the Page object. The implementation is shown in lines 80 through 97 of listing 16.4.

Note that the Boolean value synonym is passed along to both FindLeaf() and InsertNode(). These values are passed from method to method until they are needed. The first use of the value is in line 114 of listing 16.4. It is imperative to match only on an exact match with the original term, so the value for synonym is examined and the correct method (Begins() or operator==) is called accordingly. This is repeated in lines 186 through 200.

If the original term is not found, the synonym will not be added. If the term is found, BTree::AddKey() is called, passing in the synonym, the offset, and the Boolean value TRUE.

Examination of the interface for the AddKey() method, as shown in line 139 of listing 16.1, shows that AddKey() has a third parameter, synonym, which defaults to FALSE.

Program execution jumps to line 100 of listing 16.2. An index object is created, using the new term as its str value, and the offset returned by the call to FindExact() as its offset value. This is *exactly* what you want: The index now points to the correct entry in the WNJFile. The trick will be to avoid adding this record to the data file and giving it its own WNJFile entry.

Once again, the synonym flag is used—this time in line 219 of listing 16.4. When this flag is set, the index object is *not* passed to the WNJFile for appending, and its pointer is *not* set to point to the new WNJFile record. Because the pointer already points to the correct WNJFile record, the index is left as it is before being added to the page.

Summary

Today you learned how to add synonyms to the utility, and in general how to create extensible programs. You examined the cost of developing a program that is maintainable and that can grow over time, and you learned a specific technique for adding synonyms to a database program.

Q&A

Q What does it take to make a program maintainable?

A The program must be designed with a clarity of vision, the modules must be discrete, the interfaces must be well-defined, and the code must be well-documented.

Q Are smaller programs more maintainable than larger programs?

A All things being equal, it is, of course, easier to understand a smaller program. A well-written large program, however, can be far easier to maintain than a small utility written without regard to documentation and maintainability.

Q If I'm the programmer and no one else is working on the program, why bother with comments?

A When you return to your program in a few months (to fix a bug, to extend its functionality, or simply to learn how you solved a problem that has returned in a new program), you will need the comments to help you remember how the program works in detail.

Workshop

The Workshop provides quiz questions to help you solidify your understanding of the material covered, and exercises to provide you with experience in using what you have learned. Try to answer the quiz and exercise questions before checking the answers in Appendix A, and make sure that you understand the answers before continuing to the next chapter.

Quiz

1. What makes a program maintainable?
2. Explain the difference between good comments and poor comments.
3. What is legacy code and why is it a challenge?
4. What is the purpose of a synonym in a database program?

Exercises

1. Rewrite the methods that currently take the synonym and findExact flags not to take these flags. Create static flags in Btree and use these instead.
2. Add functionality to the program to signal whether a synonym was added. If a synonym was not added, tell the user what went wrong.
3. Add a help message that is printed out if the user runs ROBIN with an unsupported switch.
4. Add a feature to accept multiple lines for input from cin.
5. Modify the feature added in exercise 4 so that after the user indicates that he is done adding lines, it shows how many new lines were added.

17

Profiling and Optimization

When your program is complete and runs well, it is time to make it smaller and faster. The compiler can help, but there are advanced professional techniques and tools that can do a far better job than any compiler.

Today you will learn

☐ What optimization is and how to do it

☐ What profiling is and how it can help

☐ What the trade-offs are and how to make your decisions

Optimizing Your Code

Programming is, to coin a phrase, *the art of compromise*. You constantly are trading off speed for size, memory for storage, development time for maintenance time, and so on. Most professional level C++ compilers do an excellent job optimizing your code for size or performance, but you must decide which to accentuate.

For some applications, size is critical. Your program must fit on one disk, or it must be transferred easily by modem when your customer is paying by the minute. For most applications, however, size is less important than performance. Most customers will put up with a slightly larger program in exchange for a slightly faster program.

Programming Optimization

There are a number of places you can optimize your own code even before your compiler lends a hand. Inline code can be seen as an optimization of performance for size. Each inline function is repeated every time it is called, thus bloating the size of the code. The overhead of a function call is avoided, however, which slightly speeds up your program. The rule of thumb I use is, if the function is one line, consider making it inline.

This and most other hand-optimizations, however, are best left to the compiler. Modern C++ compilers can optimize away inline code, the creation of unneeded temporaries, the creation of unreferenced variables, and so on. In order to go beyond what your compiler can give you, you need to use a profiler, as described in the next section.

Compiler Optimization

Don't underestimate the power of your compiler to optimize your code. Borland, Microsoft, Symantec, and all the major vendors offer optimizing compilers that can do a fantastic job of making your program smaller and faster. In fact, many programmers choose their compiler

principally on its success at optimization. Check the reviews of the various C++ compilers in the programming magazines to find out how they stack up against one another in speed and size optimization and flexibility.

One thing to keep in mind is that while you are creating and debugging your code, *turn optimization off!* An optimizing compiler is free to rearrange your code, to collapse variables, to stash away data in registers, and so on. Although these actions are highly desirable in your run-time commercial release, it can undermine your debugging efforts, as described on day 20.

Most professional compilers offer a variety of settings for optimization, but the three most important follow:

1. Turn off optimization.
2. Minimize space.
3. Optimize speed.

Using Profilers

To go beyond what your compiler can offer you in performance optimization, you need to examine your program in detail to find out where it is spending its time. This is called *profiling* your program—you generate a profile of what gets called, and how often and how long each function call or other event takes.

Studies have shown that most programmers don't profile their programs, and that most programmers guess *incorrectly* about where to optimize their code. The distinguishing characteristic of very fast programs is not the programmer's skill in writing tight, fast code, but instead the programmer's willingness to profile the final product and then to tweak the important areas.

Because profilers are programs, and because each compiler vendor offers a different profiler, most advanced programming books avoid discussing them. It is difficult to be precise about how a profiler works, because each profiling program works differently.

Nonetheless, profiling is a critical subject for a professional programmer, and there are many things that can be said here that will apply to all profilers. The overall approach is very similar across the various profilers, and the techniques you learn today will apply regardless of which product you end up using. Of course, you should carefully review the documentation of your specific profiler to find out what it offers and how to invoke it.

For purposes of illustration, I'll be using the profiler provided with Microsoft Visual C++ version 1.5. I will *not* be discussing the syntax of invoking this profiler, but I will examine those aspects of its reports that are universal to all profilers. Once again, your output might look slightly different, but the information should be essentially the same.

Profiling Your Program

To illustrate the points made in this chapter, reexamine the selection sort shown on day 4. Listing 17.1 is the code for the first version of this program.

Listing 17.1 Using a Selection Sort

```
1:    // Listing 4.1 - Using a Selection Sort
2:
3:    #include <iostream.h>
4:    #include <string.h>
5:
6:    void Swap( char *Array, int index1, int index2);
7:    void SelectionSort(char *Array);
8:
9:    int main()
10:   {
11:      char buffer[100];
12:      cout << "Enter up to 100 characters: ";
13:      cin.getline(buffer,100);
14:      cout << "Unsorted:\t" << buffer << endl;
15:      SelectionSort(buffer);
16:      cout << "Sorted:\t\t" << buffer << endl;
17:      return 0;
18:   }
19:
20:   // Read through each member of the array in turn
21:   // For every member, examine every remaining member and
22:   // swap with smallest
23:   void SelectionSort(char *Array)
24:   {
25:      int ArrayLen = strlen(Array);
26:      for (int i = 0; i<ArrayLen; i++)
27:      {
28:         int min = i;
29:         for (int j = i+1; j< ArrayLen; j++)
30:            if (Array[j] < Array[min])
31:               min = j;
32:         Swap(Array,min,i);
33:      }
34:   }
35:
36:   void Swap( char *Array, int left, int right)
37:   {
38:      char tmp = Array[left];
39:      Array[left]=Array[right];
40:      Array[right]=tmp;
41:   }
```

```
Enter up to 100 characters: Eternal vigilance is the price of liberty
Unsorted:       Eternal vigilance is the price of liberty
Sorted:         Eaabcceeeeefghiiiiilllnnoprrrstttvy
```

Profiling Function Count

The first and simplest statistic about this program is how many function calls it makes. An analysis of this simple question often can point out where a program is spending much of its time. Listing 17.2 shows the function count report for this program.

 Listing 17.2 Function Count Report

```
 1:   Microsoft PLIST Version 1.30.200
 2:
 3:   Profile: Function counting, sorted by counts.
 4:   Date:     Sat Jan 21 16:44:47 1995
 5:
 6:
 7:   Program Statistics
 8:   ------------------
 9:       Total functions: 8
10:       Total hits: 54
11:       Function coverage: 100.0%
12:
13:   Module Statistics for d:\112\day17\1701.exe
14:   -------------------------------------------
15:       Functions in module: 8
16:       Hits in module: 54
17:       Module function coverage: 100.0%
18:
19:    Hit
20:   count   %   Function
21:   -------------------
22:     41  75.9 Swap (1701.cpp:37)
23:      4   7.4 ostream::operator<< (ostream.h:85)
24:      2   3.7 ostream::operator<< (ostream.h:88)
25:      2   3.7 flush (ostream.h:118)
26:      2   3.7 endl (ostream.h:119)
27:      1   1.9 istream::getline (istream.h:118)
28:      1   1.9 main (1701.cpp:10)
29:      1   1.9 SelectionSort (1701.cpp:24)
30:
```

 The first few lines of this report and all profiler reports identify what you tested and when. Lines 9 and 10 indicate that the profiler found calls to eight different functions and that a total of 54 function calls were made.

Of the 54 function calls, nearly 76 percent (41 calls) were made to the Swap() function. The report indicates that this is shown in line 37 of 1701.cpp, the file that holds this program.

Note: The line numbers included in these reports will not always correspond to the line numbers shown in the listings in this book, due to special publishing considerations. In your own programs, these line numbers *should* correspond to the line numbers in your program.

Note that operator<< is reported on twice, due to operator overloading. The profiler reports on the different types of calls to cout operator <<.

Examining Time versus Occurrence

So far, all you know is that Swap() is being called a lot. Although it is tempting to examine whether you can reduce the number of calls, the first thing you must determine is how long each call takes. After all, if calling Swap() 66 times takes less time than calling operator << six times, then you may want to turn your attention to cout. The next report, shown in listing 17.3, is a report of where this program is spending its time.

Listing 17.3 Time Report

```
1:   Microsoft PLIST Version 1.30.200
2:
3:   Profile: Function timing, sorted by time.
4:   Date:    Sat Jan 21 16:47:51 1995
5:
6:   Program Statistics
7:   ------------------
8:      Total time: 6907.295 milliseconds
9:      Time outside of functions: 2.803 milliseconds
10:     Call depth: 5
11:     Total functions: 8
12:     Total hits: 54
13:     Function coverage: 100.0%
14:
15:   Module Statistics for d:\112\day17\1701.exe
16:   -------------------------------------------
17:     Time in module: 6904.491 milliseconds
18:     Percent of time in module: 100.0%
19:     Functions in module: 8
20:     Hits in module: 54
21:     Module function coverage: 100.0%
22:
23:        Func          Func+Child      Hit
24:        Time    %      Time    %     count Function
25:   -------------------------------------------------------
26:     6881.761  99.7   6881.761  99.7    1 istream::getline (istream.h:118)
27:       22.008   0.3     22.008   0.3    2 flush (ostream.h:118)
28:        0.361   0.0   6904.491 100.0    1 main (1701.cpp:10)
```

478

```
29:         0.144    0.0        0.144    0.0      41 Swap (1701.cpp:37)
30:         0.117    0.0       22.184    0.3       4 ostream::operator<< (ostream.h:85)
31:         0.058    0.0        0.058    0.0       2 ostream::operator<< (ostream.h:88)
32:         0.041    0.0        0.185    0.0       1 SelectionSort (1701.cpp:24)
33:         0.002    0.0       22.132    0.3       2 endl (ostream.h:119)
```

Analysis

This report indicates that the entire running time of the program was just less than seven seconds (there are 1,000 milliseconds in each second). The report goes on to tell you that it took 2.803 milliseconds (line 9) between the start of the program and the first function call.

Line 10 tells you that the deepest nesting of functions was five. This information can be vital when examining recursive functions.

The timing section reveals critical information. Although the Swap() method was called 41 times, and getline was called only once, 99.7 percent of the time spent in this program was spent in getline!

This would seem to be a significant datum indeed, until you realize that nearly all that time was spent waiting for the user to input data. Clearly this line has no significance, and if you run the program again and type slowly, this number will skyrocket!

An examination of the rest of the numbers is interesting, however; 22 milliseconds were spent on the two flush calls, but only .144 millisecond was spent in all 41 calls to Swap(). Eureka! If you do want to optimize this program, the calls to flush() are clearly candidates for reexamination.

But where is the call to flush()? Try as you might, you will not find it in listing 17.3. Remember, however, that endl does call flush(). There's the culprit. If speed were critical in this program, you might want to consider replacing the two endl calls with a simple line feed ("\n").

Profiling by Line

In addition to telling you how often your function is called and how long the program spends in each function, it is possible to break down your profile by line number. Listing 17.4 illustrates this by profiling every line in program 1701.cpp.

Listing 17.4 Profiling by Line

```
1:    Microsoft PLIST Version 1.30.200
2:
3:    Profile: Line timing, sorted by time.
4:    Date:     Sat Jan 21 17:03:15 1995
5:
6:
```

continues

479

Listing 17.4 continued

```
 7:    Program Statistics
 8:    ------------------
 9:        Total time: 5767.145 milliseconds
10:        Time before any line: 1.080 milliseconds
11:        Total lines: 28
12:        Total hits: 2077
13:        Line coverage: 100.0%
14:
15:    Module Statistics for d:\112\day17\1701.exe
16:    -------------------------------------------
17:        Time in module: 5766.065 milliseconds
18:        Percent of time in module: 100.0%
19:        Lines in module: 28
20:        Hits in module: 2077
21:        Module line coverage: 100.0%
22:
23:        Line          Hit
24:        Time    %   count Line
25:    ---------------------------
26:     5706.451  99.0     1 (istream.h:118)
27:       23.561   0.4   820 (1701.cpp:32)
28:       16.695   0.3   820 (1701.cpp:30)
29:        9.828   0.2     2 (ostream.h:118)
30:        3.164   0.1    41 (1701.cpp:39)
31:        1.793   0.0     1 (1701.cpp:18)
32:        1.162   0.0    86 (1701.cpp:31)
33:        0.660   0.0    41 (1701.cpp:40)
34:        0.532   0.0    41 (1701.cpp:29)
35:        0.377   0.0    41 (1701.cpp:37)
36:        0.320   0.0    41 (1701.cpp:41)
37:        0.289   0.0    41 (1701.cpp:38)
38:        0.254   0.0    41 (1701.cpp:33)
39:        0.234   0.0     1 (1701.cpp:14)
40:        0.218   0.0    41 (1701.cpp:28)
41:        0.135   0.0     1 (1701.cpp:12)
42:        0.125   0.0     1 (1701.cpp:16)
43:        0.082   0.0     2 (ostream.h:88)
44:        0.060   0.0     1 (1701.cpp:17)
45:        0.035   0.0     4 (ostream.h:85)
46:        0.022   0.0     1 (1701.cpp:15)
47:        0.018   0.0     1 (1701.cpp:10)
48:        0.016   0.0     2 (ostream.h:119)
49:        0.009   0.0     1 (1701.cpp:25)
50:        0.008   0.0     1 (1701.cpp:13)
51:        0.007   0.0     1 (1701.cpp:26)
52:        0.006   0.0     1 (1701.cpp:34)
53:        0.005   0.0     1 (1701.cpp:24)
```

Analysis In this particular case, listing 17.4 provides little new information. It is likely, however, that when you are examining larger, more complex functions, the capability to zero in on a particular line can be very useful.

Note that line-by-line profiling can take a very long time and produce a very large report. Most profilers will let you specify which range of lines and which functions you want to profile.

Using Coverage Profiling

For large programs, where profiling can take a very long time, a good first approximation can be achieved with a coverage analysis. This analysis tells you which lines have been executed without telling you how often they are called or how long they take. The idea is to tell you what parts of your program actually are being used, and which are laying dormant. Listing 17.5 shows the coverage report.

Listing 17.5 Coverage Report

```
 1:     Microsoft PLIST Version 1.30.200
 2:
 3:     Profile: Line coverage, sorted by line.
 4:     Date:    Sat Jan 21 17:10:38 1995
 5:
 6:
 7:     Program Statistics
 8:     ------------------
 9:         Total lines: 28
10:         Line coverage: 100.0%
11:
12:     Module Statistics for d:\112\day17\1701.exe
13:     -------------------------------------------
14:         Lines in module: 28
15:         Module line coverage: 100.0%
16:
17:     Source file: c:\msvc\include\ostream.h
18:
19:      >>> analysis here of header files!
20:
21:     Source file: d:\112\day17\1701.cpp
22:
23:       Line Covered Source
24:       --------------------
25:         1:          //Listing 4.1 - Demonstrates Selection Sort
26:         2:
27:         3:          #include <iostream.h>
28:         4:          #include <string.h>
29:         5:
30:         6:          void Swap( char *Array, int index1, int index2);
31:         7:          void SelectionSort(char *Array);
32:         8:
33:         9:          int main()
34:        10:   *      {
35:        11:              char buffer[100];
36:        12:   *          cout << "Enter up to 100 characters: ";
37:        13:   *          cin.getline(buffer,100);
```

continues

Listing 17.5 continued

```
38:   14:   *        cout << "Unsorted:\t" << buffer << endl;
39:   15:   *        SelectionSort(buffer);
40:   16:   *        cout << "Sorted:\t\t" << buffer << endl;
41:   17:   *        return 0;
42:   18:   *    }
43:   19:
44:   20:        // Read through each member of the array in turn
45:   21:        // For every member, examine every remaining member and
46:   22:        // swap with smallest
47:   23:        void SelectionSort(char *Array)
48:   24:   *    {
49:   25:   *        int ArrayLen = strlen(Array);
50:   26:   *        for (int i = 0; i<ArrayLen; i++)
51:   27:            {
52:   28:   *            int min = i;
53:   29:   *            for (int j = i+1; j< ArrayLen; j++)
54:   30:   *                if (Array[j] < Array[min])
55:   31:   *                    min = j;
56:   32:   *            Swap(Array,min,i);
57:   33:   *        }
58:   34:   *    }
59:   35:
60:   36:        void Swap( char *Array, int left, int right)
61:   37:   *    {
62:   38:   *        char tmp = Array[left];
63:   39:   *        Array[left]=Array[right];
64:   40:   *        Array[right]=tmp;
65:   41:   *    }
```

A complete coverage analysis of the included files normally would appear in lines 17 through 21. In this case, however, those files are copyright by Microsoft, and therefore are not reproduced here. This coverage report shows an asterisk (*) next to each line that actually is called. In listing 17.5, every line except the header file lines is called.

Typically, you can ask for coverage on a line-by-line or function-by-function basis, just as you can for time and count.

Putting the Profile to Use

On day 4, I illustrated two versions of the Bubble Sort. Listing 17.6 shows the earlier, nonoptimized version.

Listing 17.6 Bubble Sort

```
1:        #include <iostream.h>
2:        #include <string.h>
3:        void BubbleSort(char *Array);
4:        void swap(char& i, char& j);
```

```
5:
6:          // Ask for a buffer full of characters
7:          // Use the bubble sort to sort 'em
8:          int main()
9:          {
10:
11:            char * buffer = "Teach Yourself More C++ in 21 Days by Jesse
                 Liberty";
12:
13:            cout << "Unsorted:\t" << buffer << endl;
14:
15:            BubbleSort(buffer);
16:
17:            cout << "Sorted:\t\t" << buffer << endl;
18:
19:            return 0;
20:          }
21:
22:          enum BOOL {FALSE, TRUE};
23:
24:          // Examine each member in turn, bubbling into place
25:          // any smaller member
26:          void BubbleSort(char *Input)
27:          {
28:            int N = strlen(Input);
29:            for (int i = 0; i< N; i++)
30:            {
31:              cout << "i: " << i << " buffer: " << Input << endl;
32:              for (int j = N-1; j>0; j--)
33:                if (Input[j-1] > Input[j])
34:                   swap(Input[j-1],Input[j]);
35:            }
36:          }
37:
38:          void swap(char& i, char& j)
39:          {
40:            char temp;
41:            temp = j;
42:            j = i;
43:            i = temp;
44:          }
```

17

Listing 17.7 shows the count analysis of this program, and listing 17.8 shows the time analysis. Note that the program has been modified to use a preset string for sorting. This eliminates the variable of user input time.

Type **Listing 17.7 Count Analysis of Bubble Sort**

```
1:    Microsoft PLIST Version 1.30.200
2:
3:    Profile: Function counting, sorted by counts.
4:    Date:    Sat Jan 21 17:22:34 1995
```

continues

Listing 17.7 continued

```
5:
6:
7:      Program Statistics
8:      ------------------
9:         Total functions: 7
10:        Total hits: 822
11:        Function coverage: 100.0%
12:
13:     Module Statistics for d:\112\day17\1706.exe
14:     -------------------------------------------
15:        Functions in module: 7
16:        Hits in module: 822
17:        Module function coverage: 100.0%
18:
19:      Hit
20:     count   %   Function
21:     -------------------
22:      555  67.5 swap (1701.cpp:39)
23:      106  12.9 ostream::operator<< (ostream.h:85)
24:       53   6.4 ostream::operator<< (ostream.h:88)
25:       53   6.4 flush (ostream.h:118)
26:       53   6.4 endl (ostream.h:119)
27:        1   0.1 main (1701.cpp:9)
28:        1   0.1 BubbleSort (1701.cpp:27)
```

Note that the vast majority of hits are on the swap() function (67.5 percent). Examination of the time spent in the swap() function is shown in listing 17.8.

Listing 17.8 Time Analysis of Bubble Sort

```
1:     Microsoft PLIST Version 1.30.200
2:
3:     Profile: Function timing, sorted by time.
4:     Date:    Sat Jan 21 17:23:20 1995
5:
6:
7:     Program Statistics
8:     ------------------
9:        Total time: 648.279 milliseconds
10:       Time outside of functions: 2.441 milliseconds
11:       Call depth: 6
12:       Total functions: 7
13:       Total hits: 822
14:       Function coverage: 100.0%
15:
16:    Module Statistics for d:\112\day17\1706.exe
17:    -------------------------------------------
18:       Time in module: 645.838 milliseconds
19:       Percent of time in module: 100.0%
20:       Functions in module: 7
21:       Hits in module: 822
22:       Module function coverage: 100.0%
```

```
23:
24:         Func          Func+Child       Hit
25:         Time    %      Time     %     count Function
26:     -------------------------------------------------
27:      609.947  94.4   609.947   94.4     53 flush (ostream.h:118)
28:       11.671   1.8    11.671    1.8    555 swap (1701.cpp:39)
29:       10.744   1.7   617.940   95.7      1 BubbleSort (1701.cpp:27)
30:        5.844   0.9   623.206   96.5    106 ostream::operator<< (ostream.h:85)
31:        4.267   0.7     4.267    0.7     53 ostream::operator<< (ostream.h:88)
32:        3.149   0.5   620.073   96.0     53 endl (ostream.h:119)
33:        0.216   0.0   645.838  100.0      1 main (1701.cpp:9)
```

 Once again, flush is very expensive, as one would expect. The second most expensive activity in this program is the repeated calls to Swap(). Listing 17.9 provides a time analysis of every line in the Bubble Sort.

 Listing 17.9 Time Analysis of Each Line of Bubble Sort

```
1:      Microsoft PLIST Version 1.30.200
2:
3:      Profile: Line timing, sorted by line.
4:      Date:    Sat Jan 21 17:23:54 1995
5:
6:
7:      Program Statistics
8:      ------------------
9:         Total time: 897.300 milliseconds
10:        Time before any line: 1.037 milliseconds
11:        Total lines: 25
12:        Total hits: 8808
13:        Line coverage: 100.0%
14:
15:     Module Statistics for d:\112\day17\1706.exe
16:     -------------------------------------------
17:        Time in module: 896.263 milliseconds
18:        Percent of time in module: 100.0%
19:        Lines in module: 25
20:        Hits in module: 8808
21:        Module line coverage: 100.0%
22:
23:     Source file: c:\msvc\include\ostream.h
24:
25:
26:     Source file: d:\112\day17\1706.cpp
27:
28:                    Line       Hit
29:        Line        Time    %  count Source
30:     -------------------------------------------
31:        1:                           #include <iostream.h>
32:        2:                           #include <string.h>
33:        3:                           void BubbleSort(char *Array);
34:        4:                           void swap(char& i, char& j);
35:        5:
```

continues

485

Listing 17.9 continued

```
36:     6:                                  // Ask for a buffer full of characters
37:     7:                                  // Use the bubble sort to sort 'em
38:     8:                                  int main()
39:     9:      0.022   0.0    1            {
40:    10:
41:    11:      0.080   0.0    1                char * buffer = "Teach Yourself ...
42:    12:
43:    13:      0.180   0.0    1                cout << "Unsorted:\t" << buffer <<
                                              endl;
44:    14:
45:    15:      0.034   0.0    1                BubbleSort(buffer);
46:    16:
47:    17:      0.136   0.0    1                cout << "Sorted:\t\t" << buffer <<
                                              endl;
48:    18:
49:    19:      0.034   0.0    1                return 0;
50:    20:      1.471   0.2    1            }
51:    21:
52:    22:                                  enum BOOL {FALSE, TRUE};
53:    23:
54:    24:                                  // Examine each member in turn, bubbling
                                              into place
55:    25:                                  // any smaller member
56:    26:                                  void BubbleSort(char *Input)
57:    27:      0.018   0.0    1            {
58:    28:      0.022   0.0    1                int N = strlen(Input);
59:    29:      0.018   0.0    1                for (int i = 0; i< N; i++)
60:    30:                                      {
61:    31:     15.928   1.8    51                cout << "i: " << i << " buffer: "
                                                  << Input << endl;
62:    32:      3.014   0.3    51                for (int j = N-1; j>0; j--)
63:    33:    107.410  12.0  2550                  if (Input[j-1] > Input[j])
64:    34:     12.074   1.3   555                    swap(Input[j-1],Input[j]);
65:    35:     81.884   9.1  2550              }
66:    36:      0.018   0.0    1            }
67:    37:
68:    38:                                  void swap(char& i, char& j)
69:    39:     30.049   3.4   555           {
70:    40:                                      char temp;
71:    41:     19.049   2.1   555                temp = j;
72:    42:     14.348   1.6   555                j = i;
73:    43:     36.621   4.1   555                i = temp;
74:    44:     14.992   1.7   555           }
```

Analysis

In many ways, this is the most interesting report. It indicates that the conditional test in line 63, `if (Input[j-1] > Input[j]`, is very expensive, taking 12 percent of the time and being called 2,550 times. The 555 calls to `swap()` pales next to this call.

False Optimizations

Programmers often are called on to tighten up their code, making their programs smaller, faster, or both. Although it is tempting to dive in and make a few quick optimizations, it is imperative that you first profile your code, or you run the risk of optimizing the wrong thing. There is little benefit in optimizing a segment of code that is called only once, while ignoring a second section of code that is called thousands of times.

On day 4, I optimized the bubble sort as shown in listing 17.10.

 Listing 17.10 Optimized Bubble Sort

```
1:          #include <iostream.h>
2:          #include <string.h>
3:          void BubbleSort(char *);
4:          void BetterBubble(char *);
5:          void swap(char& i, char& j);
6:
7:          // Ask for a buffer full of characters
8:          // Use the bubble sort to sort 'em
9:          int main()
10:         {
11:
12:             char * buffer = "Teach Yourself More C++ in 21 Days by Jesse
                Liberty";
13:             char * buff2 = "Teach Yourself More C++ in 21 Days by Jesse Liberty";
14:
15:             cout << "Unsorted:\t" << buffer << endl;
16:
17:             BubbleSort(buffer);
18:
19:             cout << "Sorted:\t\t" << buffer << endl;
20:
21:             BetterBubble(buff2);
22:
23:             cout << "Sorted:\t\t" << buff2 << endl;
24:
25:             return 0;
26:         }
27:
28:         enum BOOL {FALSE, TRUE};
29:         // Examine each member in turn, bubbling into place
30:         // any smaller member
31:         void BubbleSort(char *Input)
32:         {
33:             int N = strlen(Input);
34:             int compare = 0;
35:             int didSwap = 0;
```

continues

Listing 17.10 continued

```
36:                 for (int i = 0; i< N; i++)
37:                 {
38:                     for (int j = N-1; j>0; j--)
39:                     {
40:                         compare++;
41:                         if (Input[j-1] > Input[j])
42:                         {
43:                             didSwap++;
44:                             swap(Input[j-1],Input[j]);
45:                         }
46:                     }
47:                 }
48:                 cout << compare << " compares; " << didSwap << " swaps" << endl;
49:             }
50:
51:         void BetterBubble(char *Input)
52:         {
53:             int n = strlen(Input);
54:             int compare = 0;
55:             int didSwap = 0;
56:             BOOL swapped = TRUE;
57:
58:             for (int i=0; swapped; i++)
59:             {
60:                 swapped = FALSE;
61:                 for (int j=n-1;j>i; j--)
62:                 {
63:                     compare++;
64:                     if (Input[j-1] > Input[j])
65:                     {
66:                         swap(Input[j-1], Input[j]);
67:                         swapped = TRUE;
68:                         didSwap++;
69:                     }
70:                 }
71:             }
72:             cout << compare << " compares; " << didSwap << " swaps" << endl;
73:         }
74:
75:         void swap(char& i, char& j)
76:         {
77:             char temp;
78:             temp = j;
79:             j = i;
80:             i = temp;
81:         }
```

Analysis This program took the basic bubble sort, and improved on it, producing BetterBubble().
The basis of the improvement was a pair of observations. The first is that if you are sorting
upward, after you move a value into position, there is no reason to compare other values
with that value ever again. That is, if you bubble the lowest number to the top of the array, there

is no reason to compare other numbers to see whether they are lower than that number; after all, that is what a bubble sort does—it moves the lowest number up into position, and then it moves the second lowest, and so on.

The second observation is that if you make no swaps in any comparison all the way through one iteration, you are done; no future iterations will create swaps either. The driver program runs both approaches to illustrate the performance improvement.

Profile analysis will show how much of an improvement actually was registered. Listing 17.11 shows the count profile.

 Listing 17.11 Count Analysis of the Improved Bubble Sort

```
 1:     Microsoft PLIST Version 1.30.200
 2:
 3:     Profile: Function counting, sorted by counts.
 4:     Date:    Sat Jan 21 17:40:13 1995
 5:
 6:
 7:     Program Statistics
 8:     ------------------
 9:         Total functions: 8
10:         Total hits: 1138
11:         Function coverage: 100.0%
12:
13:     Module Statistics for d:\112\day17\1701.exe
14:     -------------------------------------------
15:         Functions in module: 8
16:         Hits in module: 1138
17:         Module function coverage: 100.0%
18:
19:      Hit
20:     count   %   Function
21:     -------------------
22:     1110  97.5 swap (1701a.cpp:76)
23:       10   0.9 ostream::operator<< (ostream.h:85)
24:        5   0.4 ostream::operator<< (ostream.h:88)
25:        5   0.4 flush (ostream.h:118)
26:        5   0.4 endl (ostream.h:119)
27:        1   0.1 main (1701a.cpp:10)
28:        1   0.1 BubbleSort (1701a.cpp:32)
29:        1   0.1 BetterBubble (1701a.cpp:52)
```

 This report is not promising. There is no distinction made between the various calls to swap(), although you do note that swap is called 1,110 times. When only the original Bubble() program was run, it was called 555 times, so there seems to be no savings there. Listing 17.12 provides the timing analysis.

Listing 17.12 Timing Analysis

```
 1:     Microsoft PLIST Version 1.30.200
 2:
 3:     Profile: Function timing, sorted by time.
 4:     Date:    Sat Jan 21 17:40:32 1995
 5:
 6:
 7:     Program Statistics
 8:     ------------------
 9:         Total time: 129.902 milliseconds
10:         Time outside of functions: 2.398 milliseconds
11:         Call depth: 6
12:         Total functions: 8
13:         Total hits: 1138
14:         Function coverage: 100.0%
15:
16:     Module Statistics for d:\112\day17\1701.exe
17:     -------------------------------------------
18:         Time in module: 127.505 milliseconds
19:         Percent of time in module: 100.0%
20:         Functions in module: 8
21:         Hits in module: 1138
22:         Module function coverage: 100.0%
23:
24:         Func            Func+Child         Hit
25:         Time    %       Time      %     count Function
26:     ---------------------------------------------------
27:         59.561  46.7    59.561   46.7      5 flush (ostream.h:118)
28:         33.126  26.0    33.126   26.0   1110 swap (1701a.cpp:76)
29:         30.072  23.6    51.260   40.2      1 BubbleSort (1701a.cpp:32)
30:          3.818   3.0    19.460   15.3      1 BetterBubble (1701a.cpp:52)
31:          0.585   0.5    60.302   47.3     10 ostream::operator<< (ostream.h:85)
32:          0.187   0.1   127.505  100.0      1 main (1701a.cpp:10)
33:          0.115   0.1     0.115    0.1      5 ostream::operator<< (ostream.h:88)
34:          0.041   0.0    59.996   47.1      5 endl (ostream.h:119)
```

Analysis Here, you do see substantial improvement. The call to BubbleSort() took 30 milliseconds, and the call to BetterBubble() took only 3 milliseconds—a substantial savings.

Applying the Lessons

Although these sample programs show only trivial improvements in performance, the lesson is clear. Profiling can help you target those areas of your program where changes can make a big difference. The question now arises, "What kind of changes?"

Tightening code is rarely an answer. Although making a given function inline or using a particular construct might save you a minimal amount of time, the really *big* savings are in changing your algorithm.

If you have a function that is called hundreds or thousands of times, it only makes sense to make sure that it runs very, very fast.

If you have a slow function that is called only once or twice, in most large programs, fixing that function will not help very much. This is not so in the tiny programs examined so far, but in most real-world programs, the savings from changing an `endl()` call to a new line will not amount to a significant percentage of the actual program time.

Summary

Today you saw how to use a profiler to examine your code. You saw how to count the number of calls to a function and how often a line of code is used. Finally, you learned how to examine the amount of time each function or line of code takes to execute.

Modern compilers can offer tremendous optimization without any effort on your part, but targeted improvements to critical areas of the code can make a significant difference in the overall performance of the program. Profilers differ in the reports they generate and the syntax used to invoke them, but all provide a way to analyze how your program is running and where to put your efforts.

Q&A

Q Why bother profiling your code when the optimizing compiler already has done all it can?

A The point of profiling is to find those areas of the code where you can change an algorithm or otherwise manipulate your code to achieve significant savings.

Q What is the purpose of coverage analysis?

A Coverage analysis helps you focus on those areas of your code where the action is. There is little point in fine-tuning a function that is rarely called.

Q How big must a program be to warrant profiling?

A Any program larger than a single function can benefit from profiling. Larger programs, of course, get the most benefit because they have more corners in which inefficiencies can hide.

Workshop

The Workshop provides quiz questions to help you solidify your understanding of the material covered, and exercises to provide you with experience in using what you have learned. Try to answer the quiz and exercise questions before checking the answers in Appendix A, and make sure that you understand the answers before continuing to the next chapter.

Quiz

1. What is the difference between optimization and profiling?
2. If function A() is called 1,000 percent more often than function B(), which one is the better candidate for performance improvement?
3. In listing 17.3, the total time was reported as 6907.295 milliseconds. How many seconds is this?

Exercises

Note that the exercises for the profiler are dependent on the specific software provided by your compiler vendor, and the results will vary based on the speed of your computer and its disks. Answers are *not* provided for these exercises, but you are strongly encouraged to examine your results and to use your profiler sufficiently to become comfortable with its operation and results.

1. Read your documentation and determine how your profiler works. Run a profile of the QuickSort() example in listing 4.10, shown in day 4.
2. Examine the results, speculate on what changes might be made, and in which areas to focus.
3. Examine the improvement to QuickSort() in listing 4.11 of day 4. Run a profile and compare the results to those obtained from exercise 2.
4. Run a profile of the entire ROBIN program shown at the end of day 16. Are any of the timings surprising?

Advanced
Exceptions and
Error Handling

The code you have seen in this book has been created for illustration purposes. It has not dealt with errors so that you would not be distracted from the central issues being presented. Real-world programs must take into consideration error conditions, and professional programs must be bulletproof.

Today you will learn

- How exceptions are used in professional programs, and what issues they raise
- How to build exception hierarchies
- How exceptions fit into an overall error-handling approach

Reviewing Exceptions

Programmers use powerful compilers and sprinkle their code with asserts to catch programming errors. They use design reviews and exhaustive testing to find logic errors.

Exceptions are different, however. You cannot eliminate exceptional circumstances; you only can prepare for them. Your users *will* run out of memory from time to time, and the only question is what your program will do. The choices are limited to the following:

1. Crash or hang.
2. Inform the user and exit gracefully.
3. Inform the user and allow the user to try to recover and continue.
4. Take corrective action and continue without disturbing the user.

Although it is not necessary or even desirable for every program you write to automatically and silently recover from all exceptional circumstances, it is clear that you must do better than crashing.

C++ exception handling provides a type-safe, integrated method for coping with the predictable but unusual conditions that arise while running a program.

In C++, an exception is an object that is passed from the area of code where a problem occurs to the part of the code that is going to handle the problem. The type of the exception determines which area of code will handle the problem, and the contents of the object thrown, if any, may be used to provide feedback to the user.

The basic idea behind exceptions is fairly straightforward:

- The actual allocation of resources (for example, the allocation of memory or the locking of a file) usually is done at a very low level in the program.
- The logic of what to do when an operation fails, memory cannot be allocated, or a file cannot be locked is usually high in the program, located in the same set of modules as the User Interface.

☐ Exceptions provide an express path from the code that allocates resources to the code that can handle the error condition. If there are intervening layers of functions, they are given an opportunity to clean up memory allocations, but they are not required to include code in which the only purpose is to pass along the error condition.

Seeing How Exceptions Are Used

Try blocks are created to surround areas of code that may have a problem. For example:

```
try
{
    SomeDangerousFunction();
}
```

Catch blocks handle the exceptions thrown in the try block. For example:

```
try
{
    SomeDangerousFunction();
}
catch(OutOfMemory)
{
    // take some actions
}
catch(FileNotFound)
{
    // take other action
}
```

The basic steps in using exceptions follow:

1. Identify those areas of the program where you begin an operation that might raise an exception, and put them in try blocks.

2. Create catch blocks to catch the exceptions if they are thrown, and to clean up allocated memory and inform the user as appropriate. Listing 18.1 illustrates the use of try blocks and catch blocks.

 Exceptions are objects used to transmit information about a problem.

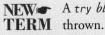 A *try block* is a block surrounded by braces in which an exception may be thrown.

 A *catch block* is the block immediately following a try block, in which exceptions are handled.

NEW☞ When an exception is *thrown* (or *raised*), control transfers to the catch
TERM block immediately following the current try block.

Note: Some older compilers do not support exceptions. Exceptions are part of the
emerging C++ standard, however. All major compiler vendors have committed to
supporting exceptions in their next release, if they have not done so already. If you
have an older compiler, you will not be able to compile and run the exercises in this
chapter. It's still a good idea to read through the entire chapter, however, and
return to this material when you upgrade your compiler.

Remember that the listings included in this chapter are for illustrative purposes
only. Your compiler might issue a warning if you use the code exactly as written.

 Listing 18.1 Raising an Exception

```
1:    #include <iostream.h>
2:
3:    const int DefaultSize = 10;
4:
5:    class Array
6:    {
7:    public:
8:        // constructors
9:        Array(int itsSize = DefaultSize);
10:       Array(const Array &rhs);
11:       ~Array() { delete [] pType;}
12:
13:       // operators
14:       Array& operator=(const Array&);
15:       int& operator[](int offSet);
16:       const int& operator[](int offSet) const;
17:
18:       // accessors
19:       int GetitsSize() const { return itsSize; }
20:
21:       // friend function
22:      friend ostream& operator<< (ostream&, const Array&);
23:
24:       class xBoundary {};  // define the exception class
25:    private:
26:       int *pType;
27:       int  itsSize;
28:    };
```

```
29:
30:
31:    Array::Array(int size):
32:    itsSize(size)
33:    {
34:       pType = new int[size];
35:       for (int i = 0; i<size; i++)
36:          pType[i] = 0;
37:    }
38:
39:
40:    Array& Array::operator=(const Array &rhs)
41:    {
42:       if (this == &rhs)
43:          return *this;
44:       delete [] pType;
45:       itsSize = rhs.GetitsSize();
46:       pType = new int[itsSize];
47:       for (int i = 0; i<itsSize; i++)
48:          pType[i] = rhs[i];
49:    }
50:
51:    Array::Array(const Array &rhs)
52:    {
53:       itsSize = rhs.GetitsSize();
54:       pType = new int[itsSize];
55:       for (int i = 0; i<itsSize; i++)
56:          pType[i] = rhs[i];
57:    }
58:
59:
60:    int& Array::operator[](int offSet)
61:    {
62:       int size = GetitsSize();
63:       if (offSet >= 0 && offSet < GetitsSize())
64:          return pType[offSet];
65:       throw xBoundary();
66:    }
67:
68:
69:    const int& Array::operator[](int offSet) const
70:    {
71:       int mysize = GetitsSize();
72:       if (offSet >= 0 && offSet < GetitsSize())
73:          return pType[offSet];
74:       throw xBoundary();
75:    }
76:
77:    ostream& operator<< (ostream& output, const Array& theArray)
78:    {
79:       for (int i = 0; i<theArray.GetitsSize(); i++)
80:          output << "[" << i << "] " << theArray[i] << endl;
81:       return output;
82:    }
```

continues

Listing 18.1 continued

```
83:
84:    void main()
85:    {
86:        Array intArray(20);
87:        try
88:        {
89:            for (int j = 0; j< 100; j++)
90:            {
91:                intArray[j] = j;
92:                cout << "intArray[" << j << "] okay..." << endl;
93:            }
94:        }
95:        catch (Array::xBoundary)
96:        {
97:            cout << "Unable to process your input!\n";
98:        }
99:        cout << "Done.\n";
99:    }
```

```
intArray[0] okay...
intArray[1] okay...
intArray[2] okay...
intArray[3] okay...
intArray[4] okay...
intArray[5] okay...
intArray[6] okay...
intArray[7] okay...
intArray[8] okay...
intArray[9] okay...
intArray[10] okay...
intArray[11] okay...
intArray[12] okay...
intArray[13] okay...
intArray[14] okay...
intArray[15] okay...
intArray[16] okay...
intArray[17] okay...
intArray[18] okay...
intArray[19] okay...
Unable to process your input!
Done.
```

Listing 18.1 presents a somewhat stripped-down Array class, based on the template developed on day 19. In line 24, a new class is contained within the declaration of the array: xBoundary.

This new class is not in any way distinguished as an exception class. xBoundary is just a class like any other. This particular class is incredibly simple: it has no data and no methods. Nonetheless, it is a valid class in every way.

In fact, it is incorrect to say that xBoundary has no methods, because the compiler automatically assigns it a default constructor, destructor, copy constructor, and copy operator (operator equals). xBoundary therefore actually has four class functions, but no data.

Note that declaring Boundary from within Array serves only to couple the two classes together. As discussed on day 15, Array has no special access to xBoundary, nor does xBoundary have preferential access to the members of Array.

In lines 60 through 66 and lines 69 through 75, the offset operators are modified to examine the offset requested and, if it is out of range, to throw the xBoundary class as an exception. The parentheses are required to distinguish between this call to the xBoundary constructor and the use of an enumerated constant.

In line 87, the keyword try begins a try block that ends in line 94. Within that try block, 100 integers are added to the array that was declared in line 86.

In line 95, the catch block to catch xBoundary exceptions is declared.

In the driver program in lines 84 through 89 a try block is created in which each member of the array is initialized. When j (line 89) is incremented to 20, the member at offset 20 is accessed. This causes the test in line 63 to fail, and operator[] raises an xBoundary exception in line 65.

Program control switches to the catch block in line 95, and the exception is caught or handled by the case on the same line, which prints an error message. Program flow drops through to the end of the catch block in line 98.

Try **Blocks**

Syntax

A try block is a set of statements that begin with the word try, are followed by an opening brace, and end with a closing brace.

Example:

```
try
{
    Function();
};
```

Catch **Blocks**

A catch block is a series of statements, each of which begins with the word catch, followed by an exception type in parentheses, followed by an opening brace, and ending with a closing brace.

Example:

```
Try
{
    Function();
};
Catch (OutOfMemory)
{
    // take action
}
```

Using *Try* Blocks and *Catch* Blocks

Figuring out where to put your try blocks is non-trivial; it is not always obvious which actions might raise an exception. The next question is where to catch the exception. You might want to throw all memory exceptions where the memory is allocated, but catch the exceptions high in the program where you deal with the user interface.

When determining try block locations, look to where you allocate memory or use resources. Other things to look for are out-of-bounds errors, illegal input, and so on.

Catching Exceptions

When an exception is thrown, the call stack is examined. The *call stack* is the list of function calls created when one part of the program invokes another function.

The call stack tracks the execution path. If main() calls the function Animal::GetFavoriteFood(), and GetFavoriteFood() calls Animal::LookupPreferences(), which in turn calls fstream::operator>>(), all these are on the call stack. A recursive function might be on the call stack many times.

The exception is passed up the call stack to each enclosing block. As the stack is "unwound," the destructors for local objects on the stack are invoked, and the objects are destroyed.

One or more catch statements are after each try block. If the exception matches one of the catch statements, it is considered to be handled by having that statement execute. If it doesn't match any catch statements, the unwinding of the stack continues.

If the exception reaches all the way to the beginning of the program (main()) and still is not caught, a built-in handler is called that terminates the program.

It is important to note that the exception unwinding of the stack is a one-way street. As it progresses, the stack is unwound and objects on the stack are destroyed. There is no going back; after the exception is handled, the program continues after the try block of the catch statement that handled the exception.

In listing 18.1, therefore, execution continues in line 99—the first line after the try block of the catch statement that handled the xBoundary exception. Remember that when an exception is raised, program flow continues after the catch block, and *not* after the point where the exception was thrown. In this case, because there is nothing after the catch block, the function returns.

Using More Than One Catch Specification

It is possible for more than one condition to cause an exception. In this case, the catch statements can be lined up one after another, much as the conditions in a switch statement. The equivalent to the default statement is the "catch everything" statement indicated by catch(...). Listing 18.2 illustrates multiple exception conditions.

Listing 18.2 Multiple Exceptions

```cpp
1:     #include <iostream.h>
2:
3:     const int DefaultSize = 10;
4:
5:     class Array
6:     {
7:     public:
8:         // constructors
9:         Array(int itsSize = DefaultSize);
10:        Array(const Array &rhs);
11:        ~Array() { delete [] pType;}
12:
13:        // operators
14:        Array& operator=(const Array&);
15:        int& operator[](int offSet);
16:        const int& operator[](int offSet) const;
17:
18:        // accessors
19:        int GetitsSize() const { return itsSize; }
20:
21:        // friend function
22:       friend ostream& operator<< (ostream&, const Array&);
23:
24:      // define the exception classes
25:        class xBoundary {};
26:        class xTooBig {};
27:        class xTooSmall{};
28:        class xZero {};
29:        class xNegative {};
30:    private:
31:        int *pType;
32:        int  itsSize;
33:    };
34:
35:
36:    Array::Array(int size):
37:    itsSize(size)
38:    {
39:       if (size == 0)
40:          throw xZero();
41:       if (size < 10)
42:          throw xTooSmall();
43:       if (size > 30000)
44:          throw xTooBig();
45:       if (size < 1)
46:          throw xNegative();
47:
48:       pType = new int[size];
49:       for (int i = 0; i<size; i++)
50:         pType[i] = 0;
51:    }
52:
53:
```

18

continues

501

Listing 18.2 continued

```
54:
55:     void main()
56:     {
57:
58:         try
59:         {
60:             Array intArray(0);
61:             for (int j = 0; j< 100; j++)
62:             {
63:                 intArray[j] = j;
64:                 cout << "intArray[" << j << "] okay..." << endl;
65:             }
66:         }
67:         catch (Array::xBoundary)
68:         {
69:             cout << "Unable to process your input!\n";
70:         }
71:         catch (Array::xTooBig)
72:         {
73:             cout << "This array is too big..." << endl;
74:         }
75:         catch (Array::xTooSmall)
76:         {
77:             cout << "This array is too small..." << endl;
78:         }
79:         catch (Array::xZero)
80:         {
81:             cout << "You asked for an array of zero objects!" << endl;
82:         }
83:         catch (...)
84:         {
85:             cout << "Something went wrong, but I've no idea what!" << endl;
86:         }
87:         cout << "Done.\n";
88:     }
```

```
You asked for an array of zero objects!
Done.
```

The implementations of all of Array's methods, except for its constructor, have been left out because they are unchanged from listing 18.1.

Four new classes are created in lines 26 through 29 of listing 18.2: xTooBig, xTooSmall, xZero, and xNegative. In the constructor, in lines 36 through 51, the size passed to the constructor is examined. If it is too big, too small, negative, or zero, an exception is thrown.

The try block is changed to include catch statements for each condition other than negative, which is caught by the "catch everything" statement catch(...) shown in line 83.

Try this with a number of values for the size of the array. Then try putting in –5. You might have expected xNegative to be called, but the order of the tests in the constructor prevented this:

size < 10 was evaluated before size < 1. To fix this, swap lines 41 and 42 with lines 45 and 46 and recompile.

Using Exception Hierarchies

Exceptions are classes and, as such, they can be derived from. It may be advantageous to create a class xSize, and to derive from it xZero, xTooSmall, xTooBig, and xNegative. Some functions therefore might just catch xSize errors, while other functions might catch the specific type of xSize error. Listing 18.3 illustrates this idea.

Listing 18.3 Class Hierarchies and Exceptions

```
1:      #include <iostream.h>
2:
3:      const int DefaultSize = 10;
4:
5:      class Array
6:      {
7:      public:
8:          // constructors
9:          Array(int itsSize = DefaultSize);
10:         Array(const Array &rhs);
11:         ~Array() { delete [] pType;}
12:
13:         // operators
14:         Array& operator=(const Array&);
15:         int& operator[](int offSet);
16:         const int& operator[](int offSet) const;
17:
18:         // accessors
19:         int GetitsSize() const { return itsSize; }
20:
21:         // friend function
22:        friend ostream& operator<< (ostream&, const Array&);
23:
24:       // define the exception classes
25:         class xBoundary {};
26:         class xSize {};
27:         class xTooBig : public xSize {};
28:         class xTooSmall : public xSize {};
29:         class xZero   : public xTooSmall {};
30:         class xNegative  : public xSize {};
31:      private:
32:         int *pType;
33:         int  itsSize;
34:      };
35:
36:
37:      Array::Array(int size):
38:      itsSize(size)
39:      {
40:          if (size == 0)
```

continues

503

Listing 18.3 continued

```
41:            throw xZero();
42:        if (size > 30000)
43:            throw xTooBig();
44:        if (size <1)
45:            throw xNegative();
46:        if (size < 10)
47:            throw xTooSmall();
48:
49:        pType = new int[size];
50:        for (int i = 0; i<size; i++)
51:          pType[i] = 0;
52:    }
```

```
This array is too small...
Done.
```

Listing 18.3 leaves out the implementation of the array functions because they are unchanged, and it leaves out main() because it is identical to that in listing 18.2.

The significant change is in lines 26 through 30, where the class hierarchy is established. Classes xTooBig, xTooSmall, and xNegative are derived from xSize; and xZero is derived from xTooSmall.

The Array is created with size zero, but what's this? The wrong exception appears to be caught! Examine the catch block carefully, however, and you will find that it looks for an exception of type xTooSmall *before* it looks for an exception of type xZero. Because an xZero object is thrown and an xZero object *is* an xTooSmall object, it is caught by the handler for xTooSmall. Once handled, the exception is *not* passed on to the other handlers, so the handler for xZero never is called.

The solution to this problem is to carefully order the handlers so that the most specific handlers come first and the less specific handlers come later. In this particular example, switching the placement of the two handlers xZero and xTooSmall will fix the problem.

Exception Objects

Often, you will want to know more than just what type of exception was thrown so that you can respond properly to the error. Exception classes are like any other class. You are free to provide data, initialize that data in the constructor, and read that data at any time. Listing 18.4 illustrates how to do this.

Listing 18.4 Getting Data Out of an Exception Object

```
1:    #include <iostream.h>
2:
3:    const int DefaultSize = 10;
4:
```

```
5:      class Array
6:      {
7:      public:
8:          // constructors
9:          Array(int itsSize = DefaultSize);
10:         Array(const Array &rhs);
11:         ~Array() { delete [] pType;}
12:
13:         // operators
14:         Array& operator=(const Array&);
15:         int& operator[](int offSet);
16:         const int& operator[](int offSet) const;
17:
18:         // accessors
19:         int GetitsSize() const { return itsSize; }
20:
21:          // friend function
22:       friend ostream& operator<< (ostream&, const Array&);
23:
24:      // define the exception classes
25:         class xBoundary {};
26:         class xSize
27:         {
28:         public:
29:             xSize(int size):itsSize(size) {}
30:             ~xSize(){}
31:             int GetSize() { return itsSize; }
32:         private:
33:             int itsSize;
34:         };
35:
36:         class xTooBig : public xSize
37:         {
38:         public:
39:             xTooBig(int size):xSize(size){}
40:         };
41:
42:         class xTooSmall : public xSize
43:         {
44:         public:
45:             xTooSmall(int size):xSize(size){}
46:         };
47:
48:         class xZero   : public xTooSmall
49:         {
50:         public:
51:             xZero(int size):xTooSmall(size){}
52:         };
53:
54:         class xNegative : public xSize
55:         {
56:         public:
57:             xNegative(int size):xSize(size){}
58:         };
59:
60:      private:
```

continues

18

Listing 18.4 continued

```
61:          int *pType;
62:          int  itsSize;
63:     };
64:
65:
66:     Array::Array(int size):
67:     itsSize(size)
68:     {
69:          if (size == 0)
70:               throw xZero(size);
71:          if (size > 30000)
72:               throw xTooBig(size);
73:          if (size <1)
74:               throw xNegative(size);
75:          if (size < 10)
76:               throw xTooSmall(size);
77:
78:          pType = new int[size];
79:          for (int i = 0; i<size; i++)
80:            pType[i] = 0;
81:     }
82:
83:
84:     void main()
85:     {
86:
87:          try
88:          {
89:               Array intArray(9);
90:               for (int j = 0; j< 100; j++)
91:               {
92:                    intArray[j] = j;
93:                    cout << "intArray[" << j << "] okay..." << endl;
94:               }
95:          }
96:          catch (Array::xBoundary)
97:          {
98:               cout << "Unable to process your input!\n";
99:          }
100:         catch (Array::xZero theException)
101:         {
102:              cout << "You asked for an array of zero objects!" << endl;
103:              cout << "Received " << theException.GetSize() << endl;
104:         }
105:         catch (Array::xTooBig theException)
106:         {
107:              cout << "This array is too big..." << endl;
108:              cout << "Received " << theException.GetSize() << endl;
109:         }
110:         catch (Array::xTooSmall theException)
111:         {
112:              cout << "This array is too small..." << endl;
113:              cout << "Received " << theException.GetSize() << endl;
114:         }
```

```
115:        catch (...)
116:        {
117:            cout << "Something went wrong, but I've no idea what!" << endl;
118:        }
119:        cout << "Done.\n";
120:    }
```

```
This array is too small...
Received 9
Done.
```

The declaration of xSize has been modified to include a member variable, itsSize, in line 33 and a member function, GetSize(), in line 31. Additionally, a constructor has been added that takes an integer and initializes the member variable, as shown in line 29.

The derived classes declare a constructor that does nothing but initialize the base class. No other functions were declared, partly to save space in the listing.

The catch statements in lines 100 through 118 are modified to name the exception they catch, theException, and to use this object to access the data stored in itsSize.

Note: Keep in mind that if you are constructing an exception, it is because an exception has been raised; something has gone wrong and your exception should be careful not to kick off the same problem. If you are creating an OutOfMemory exception, therefore, you probably don't want to allocate memory in its constructor.

It is a tedious and error-prone process to have each of these catch statements individually print the appropriate message. This job belongs to the object, which knows what type of object it is and what value it received. Listing 18.5 takes a more object-oriented approach to this problem, using virtual functions so that each exception does the right thing.

Listing 18.5 Passing by Reference and Using Virtual Functions in Exceptions

```
1:     #include <iostream.h>
2:
3:     const int DefaultSize = 10;
4:
5:     class Array
6:     {
7:     public:
8:         // constructors
9:         Array(int itsSize = DefaultSize);
10:        Array(const Array &rhs);
```

continues

Listing 18.5 continued

```
11:        ~Array() { delete [] pType;}
12:
13:        // operators
14:        Array& operator=(const Array&);
15:        int& operator[](int offSet);
16:        const int& operator[](int offSet) const;
17:
18:        // accessors
19:        int GetitsSize() const { return itsSize; }
20:
21:        // friend function
22:       friend ostream& operator<< (ostream&, const Array&);
23:
24:     // define the exception classes
25:       class xBoundary {};
26:       class xSize
27:       {
28:       public:
29:          xSize(int size):itsSize(size) {}
30:          ~xSize(){}
31:          virtual int GetSize() { return itsSize; }
32:          virtual void PrintError() { cout << "Size error. Received: " <<
           itsSize << endl; }
33:       protected:
34:          int itsSize;
35:       };
36:
37:       class xTooBig : public xSize
38:       {
39:       public:
40:          xTooBig(int size):xSize(size){}
41:          virtual void PrintError() { cout << "Too big! Received: " <<
            xSize::itsSize << endl; }
42:       };
43:
44:       class xTooSmall : public xSize
45:       {
46:       public:
47:          xTooSmall(int size):xSize(size){}
48:          virtual void PrintError() { cout << "Too small! Received: " <<
           xSize::itsSize << endl; }
49:       };
50:
51:       class xZero  : public xTooSmall
52:       {
53:       public:
54:          xZero(int size):xTooSmall(size){}
55:          virtual void PrintError() { cout << "Zero!!. Received: " <<
           xSize::itsSize << endl; }
56:       };
57:
58:       class xNegative : public xSize
59:       {
60:       public:
```

```
61:            xNegative(int size):xSize(size){}
62:            virtual void PrintError() { cout << "Negative! Received: " <<
               xSize::itsSize << endl; }
63:        };
64:
65:    private:
66:        int *pType;
67:        int  itsSize;
68:    };
69:
70:    Array::Array(int size):
71:    itsSize(size)
72:    {
73:        if (size == 0)
74:            throw xZero(size);
75:        if (size > 30000)
76:            throw xTooBig(size);
77:        if (size <1)
78:            throw xNegative(size);
79:        if (size < 10)
80:            throw xTooSmall(size);
81:
82:        pType = new int[size];
83:        for (int i = 0; i<size; i++)
84:          pType[i] = 0;
85:    }
86:
87:    void main()
88:    {
89:
90:        try
91:        {
92:            Array intArray(9);
93:            for (int j = 0; j< 100; j++)
94:            {
95:                intArray[j] = j;
96:                cout << "intArray[" << j << "] okay..." << endl;
97:            }
98:        }
99:        catch (Array::xBoundary)
100:        {
101:            cout << "Unable to process your input!\n";
102:        }
103:        catch (Array::xSize& theException)
104:        {
105:            theException.PrintError();
106:        }
107:        catch (...)
108:        {
109:            cout << "Something went wrong, but I've no idea what!" << endl;
110:        }
111:        cout << "Done.\n";
112:    }
```

18

```
Too small! Received 9
Done.
```

Listing 18.5 declares a virtual method in the xSize class, PrintError(), which prints an error message and the actual size of the class. This is overridden in each of the derived classes.

In line 103, the exception object is declared to be a reference. When PrintError() is called with a reference to an object, polymorphism causes the correct version of PrintError() to be invoked. The code is cleaner, easier to understand, and easier to maintain.

Using Exceptions with Templates

When creating exceptions to work with templates, you have a choice: you can create an exception for each instance of the template, or you can use Exception classes declared outside the template declaration. Listing 18.6 illustrates both approaches.

Listing 18.6 Using Exceptions with Templates

```
1:    #include <iostream.h>
2:
3:    const int DefaultSize = 10;
4:    class xBoundary {};
5:
6:    template <class T>
7:    class Array
8:    {
9:    public:
10:       // constructors
11:       Array(int itsSize = DefaultSize);
12:       Array(const Array &rhs);
13:       ~Array() { delete [] pType;}
14:
15:       // operators
16:       Array& operator=(const Array<T>&);
17:       T& operator[](int offSet);
18:       const T& operator[](int offSet) const;
19:
20:       // accessors
21:       int GetitsSize() const { return itsSize; }
22:
23:       // friend function
24:      friend ostream& operator<< (ostream&, const Array<T>&);
25:
26:     // define the exception classes
27:
28:       class xSize {};
29:
30:    private:
31:       int *pType;
```

```
32:        int  itsSize;
33:     };
34:
35:     template <class T>
36:     Array<T>::Array(int size):
37:     itsSize(size)
38:     {
39:        if (size <10 || size > 30000)
40:           throw xSize();
41:        pType = new T[size];
42:        for (int i = 0; i<size; i++)
43:          pType[i] = 0;
44:     }
45:
46:     template <class T>
47:     Array<T>& Array<T>::operator=(const Array<T> &rhs)
48:     {
49:        if (this == &rhs)
50:           return *this;
51:        delete [] pType;
52:        itsSize = rhs.GetitsSize();
53:        pType = new T[itsSize];
54:        for (int i = 0; i<itsSize; i++)
55:           pType[i] = rhs[i];
56:     }
57:     template <class T>
58:     Array<T>::Array(const Array<T> &rhs)
59:     {
60:        itsSize = rhs.GetitsSize();
61:        pType = new T[itsSize];
62:        for (int i = 0; i<itsSize; i++)
63:           pType[i] = rhs[i];
64:     }
65:
66:     template <class T>
67:     T& Array<T>::operator[](int offSet)
68:     {
69:        int size = GetitsSize();
70:        if (offSet >= 0 && offSet < GetitsSize())
71:           return pType[offSet];
72:        throw xBoundary();
73:     }
74:
75:     template <class T>
76:     const T& Array<T>::operator[](int offSet) const
77:     {
78:        int mysize = GetitsSize();
79:        if (offSet >= 0 && offSet < GetitsSize())
80:           return pType[offSet];
81:        throw xBoundary();
82:     }
83:
84:     template <class T>
85:     ostream& operator<< (ostream& output, const Array<T>& theArray)
86:     {
87:        for (int i = 0; i<theArray.GetitsSize(); i++)
```

continues

511

Listing 18.6 continued

```
88:            output << "[" << i << "] " << theArray[i] << endl;
89:        return output;
90:     }
91:
92:
93:     void main()
94:     {
95:
96:         try
97:         {
98:            Array<int> intArray(9);
99:            for (int j = 0; j< 100; j++)
100:           {
101:               intArray[j] = j;
102:               cout << "intArray[" << j << "] okay..." << endl;
103:           }
104:        }
105:        catch (xBoundary)
106:        {
107:           cout << "Unable to process your input!\n";
108:        }
109:        catch (Array<int>::xSize)
110:        {
111:           cout << "Bad Size!\n";
112:        }
113:
114:        cout << "Done.\n";
115:     }
```

```
Bad Size!
Done.
```

The first exception, xBoundary, is declared outside the template definition in line 4. The second exception, xSize, is declared from within the definition of the template.

The exception xBoundary is not tied to the Template class, but can be used like any other class. xSize is tied to the template, and must be called based on the instantiated array. You can see the difference in the syntax for the two catch statements. Line 105 shows catch (xBoundary), but line 109 shows catch (Array<int>::xSize). Line 109 is tied to the *instantiation* of an integer array.

Using Exceptions without Errors

When C++ programmers get together for a virtual beer in the cyberspace bar after work, talk often turns to whether exceptions should be used for routine conditions. Some programmers maintain that exceptions should be reserved for those predictable but exceptional circumstances (hence the name!) that a programmer must anticipate, but that are not part of the routine processing of the code.

Other programmers point out that exceptions offer a powerful and clean way to return through many layers of function calls without danger of memory leaks. A frequent example is this: The user requests an action in a GUI environment. The part of the code that catches the request must call a member function on a dialog manager, which calls code that processes the request, which calls code that decides which dialog box to use, which calls code to put up the dialog box, which finally calls code that processes the user's input. If the user chooses Cancel, the code must return to the very first calling method, where the original request was handled.

One approach to this problem is to put a try block around the original call and catch CancelDialog as an exception, which can be raised by the handler for the Cancel button. This approach is safe and effective, but choosing Cancel is a routine circumstance, not an exceptional one.

This frequently becomes something of a religious argument, but there is a reasonable way to decide the question: Does use of exceptions in this way make the code easier to understand or harder? Are there fewer or more risks of errors and memory leaks? Will it be harder to maintain this code or easier? These decisions, like so many others, will require an analysis of the trade-offs; there is no single, obvious, correct answer.

Q&A

Q Why bother with raising exceptions? Why not handle the error right where it happens?

A Often, the same error can be generated in a number of different parts of the code. Exceptions enable you to centralize the handling of errors. Additionally, the part of the code that generates the error may not be the best place to determine *how* to handle the error.

Q Why generate an object? Why not just pass an error code?

A Objects are more flexible and powerful than error codes. They can convey more information, and the constructor/destructor mechanisms can be used for the creation and removal of resources that may be required to properly handle the exceptional condition.

Q Why not use exceptions for nonerror conditions? Isn't it convenient to be able to express-train back to previous areas of the code, even when nonexceptional conditions exist?

A Yes, some C++ programmers use exceptions for just that purpose. The danger is that exceptions might create memory leaks as the stack is unwound and some objects are inadvertently left in the free store. With careful programming techniques and a good compiler, this problem usually can be avoided. Otherwise, it is a matter of personal aesthetics; some programmers feel that exceptions should not be used for routine conditions.

Q Does an exception have to be caught in the same place where the try block created the exception?

A No. It is possible to catch an exception anywhere in the call stack. As the stack is unwound, the exception is passed up the stack until it is handled.

Workshop

The Workshop contains quiz questions to help solidify your understanding of the material covered, and exercises to provide you with experience in using what you have learned. Try to answer the quiz and exercise questions before checking the answers in Appendix A, and make sure that you understand the answers before going to the next chapter.

Quiz

1. What is an exception?
2. What is a try block?
3. What is a catch statement?
4. What information can an exception contain?
5. When are exception objects created?
6. Should you pass exceptions by value or by reference?
7. Will a catch statement catch a derived exception if it is looking for the base class?
8. If there are two catch statements, one for base and one for derived, which should come first?
9. What does catch(...) mean?

Exercises

1. Create a try block, a catch statement, and a simple exception.
2. Modify the answer from exercise 1; put data into the exception, along with an accessor function; and use it in the catch block.
3. Modify the class from exercise 2 to be a hierarchy of exceptions. Modify the catch block to use the derived objects and the base objects.
4. Modify the program from exercise 3 to have three levels of function calls.

5. **BUG BUSTERS:** What is wrong with the following code?

```
class xOutOfMemory
{
public:
    xOutOfMemory( const String& message ) : itsMsg( message ){}
    ~xOutOfMemory(){}
    virtual const String& Message(){ return itsMsg};
private:
    String itsMsg;              // assume you are using the string class as
previously defined
}

main()
{
    try {
        char *var = new char;
        if ( var == 0 )
            throw xOutOfMemory();
    }
    catch( xOutOfMemory& theException )
    {
        cout <<  theException.Message() << "\n";
    }
}
```

18

19

Writing Solid Code

All non-trivial programs have bugs at some point in the development cycle. The bigger the program, the more bugs, and many of those bugs actually "get out the door" and into final, released software. The job of the professional programmer is to make sure that the bugs are stomped *before* they are released to an unsuspecting customer.

As you will see on day 20, the earlier in the development process that you can find and eliminate bugs, the less expensive those bugs are. Day 20 focuses on finding and removing bugs. Today focuses on the other aspects of building professional-quality code.

Today you will learn

☐ How to build robust code

☐ How to build extensible code

☐ How to build maintainable code

Writing It Isn't the Hard Part

It is possible—in fact, it often is quite easy—to write a program that behaves well when the customer does exactly what you expect him to do. Solid, professional-quality code, however, can handle even the most bizarre and unexpected customer behavior without crashing and burning.

If you are building a space shuttle or an F-111 fighter, it is reasonable to expect the pilot to get just about everything right. We are willing to spend tens of thousands of dollars in training so that the pilot doesn't eject when he means to lower the landing gear; we are less willing, however, to invest that much in training and practice to use a spreadsheet or a word processor.

This isn't to say that those who work on fighter-jet aircraft and nuclear power stations can be sloppy in their work. Although a nuclear engineer can be expected to understand how his equipment works, avoiding preventable errors certainly is a priority, as the citizens of Pennsylvania can assure you.

The $1,500-a-day consultant does not distinguish herself from the $25-per-hour novice by writing more impressive code, by producing code more quickly, or by shaving a few milliseconds of performance off a routine. Although these are important skills, there always will be someone else who is quicker or craftier.

The true professional brings a superset of these skills, and leaves the customer with a program that can grow and provide headache-free service for longer and at less cost than the cute hack thrown together by a novice. The hallmarks of a good program are robustness, extensibility, and maintainability.

Robustness

Robustness is the capability of your program to run and keep on running in the face of low memory, novice users, new hardware, unexpected conditions, and so on. Robustness does not arise spontaneously; it is cooked into the program from the beginning by the programmer who pays attention to it, and who values and invests in building bulletproof code.

This year, the Quality Assurance team at AT&T Interchange reported a bug in a routine I had written. I tried to reproduce the bug, but no matter what I did, I couldn't make it happen, so I marked the bug as *NR* (*Not Reproducible*). Two days later, the bug report was back on my desk, and Celia Fitzgerald, Manager of Quality Assurance, was at my desk.

"Open your dialog," she said. "Now, choose search by Date." I did, and an entry field opened. "Now enter −1."

Before I could stop myself, I said, "But no one would do that." She just smiled. Of course, a user had done exactly that, attempting to search for articles written the day before.

I dutifully entered −1 into the date field, chose Search, and watched my well-crafted and much-loved dialog box crash and burn. There were no survivors.

Defensive programming is the art of asking yourself, "What happens if the user..." and filling in every blank you can think of. If you ask for a string of 10 characters, consider what happens if users enter 11. What happens if they enter 100? What if they don't enter anything at all? What if they enter numbers?

The truth is that there is a cadre of sick, twisted, small-minded users who will spend hours trying to crash your code by putting in bizarre and unexpected data. In our company, these disturbed people are called *Quality Assurance Engineers*, and they are well paid and much respected, if not much loved, by the developers. We know, in our heart of hearts, that it is better for them to find our bugs than for our customers to find the bugs, but that doesn't mean we're necessarily happy to see them standing at our desks with triumphant smiles on their faces. When they are happy, you can bet we are miserable.

19

Extensibility

A program is *extensible* if you can add new features and behaviors without breaking the program or rearchitecting fundamental components. I'm not absolutely sure that you will find *extensible* in any dictionary, but every programmer I've ever met uses the word to mean that the program was written with growth and evolution in mind.

As an aside, the *architecture* of a program is the underlying structure—the set of metaphors and ideas that lend the program coherence. The architecture tells you which classes exist and how they interact with one another. When you *rearchitect* a program, you redesign its fundamental structure.

Extensibility is not an accident. A program must be designed from the start with extensibility in mind if you are not going to find yourself fighting the code every time you want to add a feature.

Extensibility also often brings a cost. A highly extensible program often is typified by a great deal of indirection and generality. Instead of hard coding behavior and values, a highly extensible program often is written so that new values and behaviors can be added to resource files or patched in using common, and thus general, interfaces.

Extensibility often is the litmus test of a well-crafted, object-oriented program. A program with many small and distinct objects that interact along narrow and well-defined interfaces is far more extensible than a jumble of interacting and mutually dependent objects whose interdependencies barely can be understood.

Maintainability

The software industry is changing rapidly, and a great deal of new code is being written every day. The truth is, however, that the vast majority of programmers are engaged in the difficult and often unrewarding task of maintaining legacy code. *Legacy code* is code written some years ago, usually by someone else.

Companies invest heavily in legacy code, and management is eager to amortize the investment over many years of use. Thus, legacy code often is patched and extended and cobbled together to solve new problems in a rapidly changing environment.

Highly maintainable code is easily read and understood by new programmers, and is marked by good documentation, meaningful comments, and a straightforward, portable coding style.

Often, an expert programmer will forgo a clever and efficient statement in order to make her intentions clearer.

Using Asserts

Although there is much wisdom shared among programmers in the creation of maintainable and extensible code, the first order of business is to ensure that what you do have is rock solid, bulletproof, and stable. That means testing your code at every opportunity.

Testing does not just involve running the program, or having others run it. It means putting tests *right into your program*, so that your program constantly monitors its own progress and reports on unexpected values or situations.

Because such tests can be expensive in performance degradation, programmers often create macros to run the tests in debug mode; these macros "disappear" when the program is compiled for release.

The simplest of these macros is the ASSERT macro. In its base form, the ASSERT macro evaluates the expression passed in and takes no action if it evaluates TRUE (0). If, on the other hand, the expression evaluates FALSE, the ASSERT macro takes action; the macro puts up an error message or throws an exception.

ASSERT macro definitions typically are surrounded by #ifdef DEBUG guards, which define ASSERT(x) to be nothing if DEBUG isn't defined. For those cases where you *want* the argument evaluated even in release mode, but you don't want the error action taken unless you are debugging, consider creating a second macro such as VERIFY.

ASSERT macros have one additional, side benefit. They serve as self-documentation to the code. If the programmer is ASSERTing that a value is non-zero, that tells you a great deal about what the programmer thinks is happening at that point in the program. Listing 19.1 shows this self-documenting effect.

 Listing 19.1 Using Asserts

```
1:    Page::Page(char *buffer):
2:        myKeys((Index*)myVars.mk)
3:    {
4:        assert(sizeof(myBlock) == PageSize);
5:        assert(sizeof(myVars) == PageSize);
6:        memcpy(&myBlock,buffer,PageSize);
7:        SetLocked(FALSE);
8:        myTime = time(NULL);
9:    }
```

 None.

 This excerpt from the implementation of the Page class seen in previous chapters has no comments or other documentation. Nonetheless, you can tell from the assert statements on lines 4 and 5 that the programmer believes that at this step of the program the PageSize must be equal to the size of the member variable myBlock *and* to the size of myVars. Note that line 6 takes advantage of this equality to copy myBlock bytes to buffer from PageSize.

Leave the Assert in There

Novice programmers often surround difficult areas of code with print statements or tests, and then strip them out when it is time to ship the code. The beauty of the assert statement is that there is no reason to remove it: it costs you nothing if debug isn't defined, and it comments your code. Leave in the assert statement, even long after the code is fully working. It's free, and you never know when you will need it.

Beware of Side Effects

Remember, however, that the assert statement will disappear when the release version is created. Don't be trapped by the common mistake of using an assert with a (desirable) side effect that then will disappear in the final version of your code. Listing 19.2 illustrates this problem.

Listing 19.2 Asserts with Side Effects

```
1: SomeFunction(char * buff, char * buff2)
2: {
3:     int x = strlen(buff);
4:     int y = strlen (buff2);
4:     assert (y++ = x);  // oops
6:     otherFunc(y);
7: }
```

None.

The programmer intended to assert that buff2 is one character shorter than buff. Unfortunately, as part of the assert, y is incremented before it is passed to otherFunc. When the run-time version is created, the assert will become inoperative and the increment will not be performed, potentially breaking otherFunc.

Class Invariants

Most classes have data that must be in a determinable state in order for the class to be valid. An Employee class, for example, might always require a name and a social security number in order for it to be a valid Employee class.

These invariant attributes can and should be tested for each time you manipulate an object of the class. Typically, C++ programmers will create a method of the class called Invariants() that tests each of these criteria and returns a Boolean value—TRUE if the class meets its requirements, and FALSE otherwise.

The programmer then can call invariants from within an assert statement: assert(Invariants());. If the class is in an unacceptable state and if debug is defined, this will display a helpful error dialog box, flagging the problem for the developer.

Many C++ programmers are scrupulous in their use of `Invariants()`, bracketing virtually every member function with calls to this important test.

Test the Return Value from *New*

Nearly all C++ programmers know that *operator new* returns NULL if it cannot allocate memory. Nonetheless, virtually no C++ programmers test the return value from operator new. It is rare to run out of memory, and it isn't always obvious what to do if you do get a NULL in return, but letting your program crash or hang probably is not the desired answer.

Make Destructors Virtual

If your class has one or more virtual functions, be sure to make the destructor virtual. If you create virtual functions, sooner or later you will subclass the object. At that point, it is possible to have a pointer to the base class, and to fill it with the address of a derived object. When you use the pointer, the "right thing" happens.

If, however, you then delete the pointer, and you have failed to create a virtual destructor, only a base class object will be deleted, and you will have created a memory leak.

There is little additional overhead to creating a virtual destructor once you already have a v-table, and the 4 bytes it typically costs will be well worth it when you delete the object.

Initialize Pointers to Zero

It is common to test a pointer to make sure that it is assigned a meaningful value before using it. It is imperative, however, that the pointer be initialized to zero at its creation, or the test will not work properly. When the pointer is deleted, it must be reset to zero for the same reason. Listing 19.3 illustrates the proper use of this technique.

Type **Listing 19.3 Setting Pointers to Zero**

```
1:  CAT::CAT():
2:      pMyOwner(0) // initialize to zero
3:  {
4:     if (!pMyOwner)
5:      pMyOwner= new Person;
6:      // other code
7:     delete pMyOwner;
8:      pMyOwner= 0;
9:     // other code
10:     if (pMyOwner)
11:        pMyOwner->BuyCatFood();
12: }
```

Between lines 7 and 10 in this example, there could be dozens of lines of code in which pMyOwner may or may not be assigned to a new Person object. In line 10, the program tests the pointer to make sure that it is valid before using it. If you did not assign 0 to that pointer in line 8, the test would be meaningless.

Similarly, without the initialization shown in line 2, the test in line 4 would not work properly. It is imperative that pointers be assigned 0 when the pointer is not valid.

Use *Const* Wherever You Can

The compiler is your friend. It will enforce the contracts and rules that you establish for your data and functions, reminding you when you use them in ways you had not intended originally.

To get the most help from your compiler, however, you must tell it when you don't expect to modify the data. The compiler then can warn you when you write over or modify that data.

Const can be used to signal many different requirements:

- ☐ A pointer will not point to other data.
- ☐ A pointer will not change the data to which it points.
- ☐ A member function's this pointer is constant.
- ☐ A member function will not change its object.

For example:

```
const * const Person CAT::myFunction(const Person&) const;
```

This declaration should not look unfamiliar or excessive to you if you are using const a great deal. It says that myFunction is a member of the CAT class, that it takes a reference to a constant person and returns a constant pointer to a constant person, and that the function itself is constant.

A reference to a constant person means that the variable passed into this function cannot be changed by this function even though it is, for the sake of efficiency, being passed by reference.

A constant pointer to a constant person is much like a constant reference. The pointer cannot be reassigned to point to anyone else (like a reference cannot) and the pointer cannot be used to change the person object (like a constant reference cannot).

The fact that the function itself is const means that the this pointer of the CAT object is const, and thus the CAT object itself cannot be modified by this function.

Managing Object Creation

Any time you create a class with one or more pointers, be sure to write your own constructor that initializes the pointer. You also must write a destructor that deletes the pointer.

Be sure to create a copy constructor and an operator equals, both of which must perform "deep" copies of the pointed-to memory, allocating necessary memory for the new object and managing the freed memory in the case of the operator equals.

Initialize in the Order You Declare Your Member Variables

The C++ compiler will ignore the initialization order you set in your constructor and will initialize your objects in the order in which they are declared in the interface to the class. You should make a point, however, of listing the initializations in the order in which you declare your member variables, so that your code accurately documents what really is happening.

This only matters when one member depends on the value of another, but it can make a great difference when you are debugging and trying to determine the current value of a given variable.

Never, Ever, Return a Reference to a Local Object. Ever.

Remember that references can never be NULL. If you declare an object in your function and then return a reference to that object, to what does it refer when the function has popped off the stack?

Similarly, avoid references to objects on the heap that might be deleted. Dereferenced pointers are dangerous candidates for references. If the pointer is deleted and the memory is freed, you will be left with an illegal reference to a nonexistent object.

19

Create a Consistent Style

It is important to adopt a consistent coding style, although in many ways it doesn't matter which style you adopt. A consistent style makes it easier to guess what you meant by a particular part of the code, and you avoid having to look up whether you spelled the function with an initial capital letter the last time you invoked it.

More important, consistency in your code makes it easier for another programmer to take over maintenance and development of your code. If you always declare your member variables to begin with my, your local variables with a lowercase letter, and your functions with an uppercase letter, then names such as myAge, ageOfBook, and AgeBook are easier to categorize.

The following guidelines are arbitrary; they are based on the guidelines used in projects I have worked on in the past, and they have worked well. You just as easily can make up your own guidelines, but these will get you started.

Braces

How to align braces can be the most controversial topic between C and C++ programmers. Here are the tips I suggest:

☐ Matching braces should be aligned vertically.

☐ The outermost set of braces in a definition or declaration should be at the left margin. Statements within should be indented. All other sets of braces should be in line with their leading statements.

☐ No code should appear on the same line as a brace, as shown in the following example:

```
if (condition==true)
{
    j = k;
    SomeFunction();
}
m++;
```

Long Lines

Keep lines to the width that can be displayed on a single screen. Code that is off to the right easily is overlooked, and scrolling horizontally is annoying. When a line is broken, indent the following lines. Try to break the line at a reasonable place, and try to leave the intervening operator at the end of the preceding line (as opposed to the beginning of the following line) so that it is clear that the line does not stand alone and that there is more coming.

In C++, functions tend to be far shorter than they were in C, but the old, sound advice still applies. Try to keep your functions short enough to print the entire function on one page.

Switch Statements

Indent switches to conserve horizontal space, as shown in the following code:

```
switch(variable)
{
case ValueOne:
    ActionOne();
    break;
case ValueTwo:
    ActionTwo();
    break;
default:
    assert("bad Action");
    break;
}
```

Program Text

You can use several tips to create code that is easy to read. Code that is easy to read is easy to maintain. Keep these tips in mind:

- ☐ Use white space to help readability.
- ☐ Objects and arrays really are referring to one thing. Don't use spaces within object references (., ->, [ ]).
- ☐ Unary operators are associated with their operand, so don't put a space between them. Do put a space on the side away from the operand. Unary operators include !, ~, ++, --, -, * (for pointers), & (casts), and sizeof.
- ☐ Binary operators should have spaces on both sides: +, =, *, /, %, >>, <<, <, >, ==, !=, &, ¦, &&, ¦¦, ?:, =, +=, and so on.
- ☐ Don't use lack of spaces to indicate precedence (4+ 3*2).
- ☐ Put a space *after* commas and semicolons—*not* before.
- ☐ A parenthesis should not have spaces on either side.
- ☐ Keywords, such as if, should be set off by a space. For example, if (a == b).
- ☐ The body of a comment should be set off from the // with a space.
- ☐ Place the pointer or reference indicator next to the type name—not the variable name:

```
char* foo;
int& theInt;
```

```
rather than
```

```
char *foo;
int &theInt;
```

- ☐ Do *not* declare more than one variable on the same line.

Identifier Names

Here are some guidelines for working with identifiers:

- ☐ Identifier names should be long enough to be descriptive.
- ☐ Avoid cryptic abbreviations.
- ☐ Take the time and energy to spell things out.
- ☐ Short names (i, p, x, and so on) should be used only where their brevity makes the code more readable *and* where the usage is so obvious that a descriptive name is not needed.

☐ The length of a variable's name should be proportional to its scope.

☐ Make sure that identifiers look and sound different from one another in order to minimize confusion.

☐ Function (or method) names usually are verbs or verb-noun phrases, such as `Search()`, `Reset()`, `FindParagraph()`, or `ShowCursor()`. Variable names usually are abstract nouns, possibly with an additional noun—for example, `count`, `state`, `windSpeed`, or `windowHeight`. Boolean variables should be named appropriately (`windowIconized` or `fileIsOpen`, for example).

Spelling and Capitalization of Names

Spelling and capitalization should not be overlooked when creating your own style. Some tips for these areas follow:

☐ Use all uppercase letters and underscores to separate the logical words of names, such as `SOURCE_FILE_TEMPLATE`. Note, however, that these are rare in C++. Consider using constants and templates in most cases.

☐ All other identifiers should use mixed case and no underscores. Function names, methods, classes, `typedef`, and `struct` names should begin with a capital letter. Elements like data members or locals should begin with a lowercase letter.

☐ Enumerated constants should begin with a few lowercase letters as an abbreviation for the `enum`, as shown in the following code:

```
enum TextStyle
{
    tsPlain,
    tsBold,
    tsItalic,
    tsUnderscore,
};
```

Comments

Comments can make it much easier to understand a program. Often, you will not work on a program for several days or even months, so you might forget what certain code does or why it has been included. Problems in understanding code also can occur when someone else reads your code. Comments that are applied in a consistent, well thought-out style can be well worth the effort. There are several tips to remember concerning comments:

☐ Wherever possible, use C++ `//` comments rather than the `/* */` style. Reserve C-style comments for blocking out sections of code.

☐ Higher level comments are infinitely more important than process details. Add value; do not merely restate the code. For example:

```
n++;    // n is incremented by one
```

This comment isn't worth the time it takes to type it in. Concentrate on the semantics of functions and blocks of code. Say what a function does. Indicate side effects, types of parameters, and return values. Describe all assumptions that are made (or not made), such as *assumes n is non-negative* or *will return −1 if x is invalid*. Within complex logic, use comments to indicate the conditions that exist at that point in the code.

☐ Use complete English sentences with appropriate punctuation and capitalization. The extra typing is worth it. Don't be overly cryptic and don't abbreviate. What seems exceedingly clear to you as you write code will be amazingly obtuse in a few months.

☐ Use blank lines freely to help the reader understand what is going on. Separate statements into logical groups.

Access

The way you access portions of your program also should be consistent. Some tips for accessing parts of your program follow:

☐ Always use `public:`, `private:`, and `protected:` labels. Don't rely on the defaults.

☐ List the public members first, followed by the protected members, followed by the private members. List the data members in a group after the methods.

☐ Put the constructor(s) first in the appropriate section, followed by the destructor. List overloaded methods with the same name adjacent to each other. Group accessor functions together when possible.

☐ Consider alphabetizing the method names within each group and alphabetizing the member variables. Be sure to alphabetize the file names in `include` statements.

☐ Even though the use of the `virtual` keyword is optional when overriding, use it anyway. It helps to remind you that it is virtual, and also keeps the declaration consistent.

☐ Reserve the keyword `struct` for those classes that contain only data and all of whose members should be public. An alternative is to avoid this term altogether.

Class Definitions

Try to keep the definitions of methods in the same order as the declarations. It makes things easier to find. Alternatively, consider alphabetizing the methods, both in the declaration and in the cpp file.

When defining a function, place the return type and all other modifiers on a previous line so that the class name and function name begin on the left margin. This makes it much easier to find functions.

Include Files

Try as hard as you can to keep from including files in header files. The ideal minimum is the header file for the class this one derives from. Other mandatory includes will be those for objects that are members of the class being declared. Classes that are merely pointed to or referenced only need forward references of the form.

Don't leave out an `include` file in a header just because you assume that whatever cpp file includes this one also will have the needed `include`.

Evolve Your Own Rules and Write Them Down

If you are working with other programmers, try to establish a set of style guidelines with which you can all work. This method will simplify greatly the job of exchanging code listings.

Reviewing Your Code

An essential component of writing good code is having your code, design, and documentation reviewed by others. A classic mistake in such reviews, however, is to mix design reviews and code reviews.

Design Reviews

A design review can be a very helpful experience, but it must be handled correctly. The first guideline is to review at the right time—late enough in the process to have thought through the major issues, but early enough that you can incorporate what you learn into the review.

A second essential for a successful review is that the design be summarized in a preliminary document circulated a few days before the review. The reviewers are obliged to read the document and to make notes; obviously, the document must be sufficiently complete that the reviewers are left with a correct impression of the overall design approach.

A danger in such review sessions is that the developer whose design is being reviewed can become very defensive. If your peers are reviewing your code, it is difficult to maintain your objectivity; if your boss is participating, it can be even more threatening.

One approach that has worked well is this: Don't try to *solve* any of the problems that arise during the review; just make a note and move on. The developer might want to talk about why she made one decision over another, but if a reviewer suggests an alternative approach, write it down and continue.

A delicate balance must be maintained between clarifying ideas on the one hand, and advocating and defending ideas on the other. The point of the review should be to clarify and articulate ideas, but evaluation of their merit should be left until after the meeting. If the developer is relatively senior, he might evaluate all the suggestions on his own, incorporating some and rejecting others based on his own judgment and experience. A more junior engineer might want to review the ideas with his manager, but the review meeting probably is not the right place.

Code Reviews

A code review is completely different from a design review. This time, code is circulated, and the reviewers assemble to discuss what they have found. The upfront investment by the reviewers is substantially greater; they must walk the code with a fine-tooth comb looking for syntax errors, memory leaks, logic flaws, and so on.

There is less room for judgment in a code review. The idea is not to question the overall approach, but to locate bugs and errors in the execution. The moderator, typically the developer whose code is being reviewed, must be careful to rule out of order comments on the design; the purpose must be a single-minded search for errors.

A good code review acts as a *core sample*, digging deep but with little breadth into the developer's product. The idea is *not* to find all the bugs in the program, but to uncover one or a few of each type of problem that might be represented in the rest of the program.

This is a good time to put emphasis on and get feedback about readability. Is the code well documented? Do the comments help? Are sections laid out in a clear and understandable fashion?

Knuth writes that good code can be read like a novel. Although C++ does not look like English to the uninitiated, the truth is that good code is easily understood.

Comments, of course, should be used to lay out the overall plot of the section of code and to clarify what might otherwise be a confusing section. The developer, however, should prefer that the code speak for itself whenever possible. As a simple example:

```
int x = myObject.GetValue();   // get the age and assign it to the minimum age variable
```

is far less clear or maintainable than

```
int MinAge = Employee.GetAge();
```

19

The second statement stands on its own, and because it needs no comment, there is no chance of the comment becoming obsolete and thus misleading.

Documentation Reviews

Documentation is like the weather—everyone complains when it is bad, but no one does anything about it. The truth is that investing the time and cost of writing good documentation is so difficult that few organizations get it right. Consider having the documentation for a set of code reviewed by someone other than the developer—preferably by the person who will be responsible for maintaining the code if the developer is not available.

Planning for Change

Developers often write their code like they always will be around to take care of it, to nurture it, and to clarify any confusion. The reality is that developers move on to other projects (or other jobs!) and someone else often is stuck trying to disentangle a particularly clever, read-obtuse, bit of code. The only antidote to this disease is to ensure that the code is maintainable while it is being developed, and especially at delivery.

Summary

Today you learned about writing robust, bulletproof, highly tested, extensible, maintainable code. You saw how to use ASSERT macros and Class Invariant() methods to add reliability to your code and how to *test your assumptions*.

Q&A

Q What is the good of an assert if it will not be in the release code?

A An assert is put into the code to alert you to problems during debugging. The point of an assert is to flag a bug. In theory, your release code will not have bugs, and thus will not need the assert. Then again, in theory, theory and practice are the same, but in practice they aren't.

Q What is the difference between an *assert* and an *exception*?

A An *assert* flags a bug in your code. An *exception* flags a predictable problem that must be handled properly. It is *not* a bug to run out of memory, but it is a bug to crash when you do run out of memory.

Q What is the difference between *maintainable* and *extensible* code?

A *Maintainable* code can be fixed. *Extensible* code can be extended—that is, new functionality easily can be added.

Workshop

The Workshop provides quiz questions to help you solidify your understanding of the material covered, and exercises to provide you with experience in using what you have learned. Try to answer the quiz and exercise questions before checking the answers in Appendix A, and make sure that you understand the answers before continuing to the next chapter.

Quiz

1. How do you ensure that the assert will not be in the release code?
2. What are *side effects*, and how do you prevent them?
3. What do you do if you want to assert if something isn't TRUE, but you *need* the evaluation done in the release code?
4. Where do you put the invariant() assertion?
5. Why should destructors be virtual?

Exercises

1. Write an ASSERT macro definition.
2. Write a VERIFY macro definition.
3. Write the class invariants for the String class shown in listings 3.1 and 3.2 in day 3.
4. Rewrite the methods shown in exercise 3.2 to use the ASSERT macro you wrote in exercise 1 with the invariant methods you wrote in exercise 3.

19

Debugging

No matter how well you design your program and how carefully you write the code, sooner or later you will find a bug. Something doesn't work as intended, the program is slower than it should be, data is corrupted, or the program crashes. The difference between a poor programmer and a good one is not whether there are bugs in the code, but how quickly the bugs are found and squashed, and whether any survive into the shipping product.

Today you will learn

- ☐ What the different types of bugs are and how to find them
- ☐ How to use a debugger to help find and squish bugs
- ☐ What tools can help you in your debugging

Examining Bugs, Errors, and Design Problems

There are many reasons why a program may not behave as intended. Not all these reasons are bugs; some are problems in the design, architecture, or logic of the program. Other reasons are misimplemented features. Some problems are, in fact, simply bugs: errors in syntax or the semantics of what you were trying to do.

Looking At the Cost of Bugs

Industry estimates are that the overwhelming cost of software development is in the testing, debugging, and maintenance stages—not in the design and development! More important, repeated studies have shown beyond any contention that the later in the development process a bug is detected, the more expensive it is to fix.

Bugs caught by Quality Assurance engineers are less expensive to fix than bugs caught by the customer. Bugs caught by the developer are less expensive to fix than those found by QA, and bugs found in the design phase are less expensive than those found during the coding phase.

Writing a Good Specification

Many bugs are really a disagreement or misunderstanding between the developer and the person providing the specification for the program. Informal specifications particularly are subject to this type of problem. The program does exactly what the developer intended; unfortunately, this is not what the client wants.

The best time to fix this bug is before you start your design. To the extent possible, get a complete specification. Most clients, and a surprising number of developers, have *no* idea how to create a good written specification.

The first and most important thing about a specification is that it is written. If you are designing a program for a graphical user interface (GUI), be sure to include screen shots.

Your specification should detail the entire user experience, including what the user will see and what the user can enter, as well as all the potential events and their effects. An *event* is any action to which the program must react, such as user input, mouse movements, modem detection, and so on.

The specification should detail any filtering or validation you must do on user input, and how the program is to react to normal—and abnormal!—user actions. The specification should explain the exact hardware requirements (the user will need an 80386 or more powerful computer with at least 16MB of RAM, and so on) and how the program should respond when the required hardware is not present.

The specification should go on to detail how the program responds to errors, exceptions, and other predictable (and not so predictable) problems. The specification should, in short, provide details on how the program works from the user's perspective.

Notice that this specification says *nothing* about how you will architect or implement the program. I work with a graphic artist named David Rollert, and he once told me that his clients will often say, "Use more red here..." He asks them to tell him what they are trying to accomplish. "Do you want it to look prettier, more soothing, more noticeable..." he asks them. The idea is that his client should specify what effect they want and leave the implementation to him. After all, that is the skill for which they hired him.

Similarly, ask your clients to tell you what behavior and characteristics they want (high performance, quick response, robustness, and so on) and let them leave the implementation to you; you are the C++ expert! Don't misunderstand a user who says "I want you to keep an array of employee IDs" to mean that he really wants you to use an array; he just wants you to be able to save and access the IDs when they are needed. How you manage the magic is your business.

Writing the Design Document

After you have a reasonably frozen specification, it is time to write the design document. This document should specify how you intend to organize your program—what the principal classes are, and how the data will be preserved. The size of the design document (and all the other documentation mentioned here) should correspond to the overall size of the program. It makes no sense to create a 30-page design for a 100-line program; but it also makes no sense to launch a 50-programmer effort based on notes sketched on a scrap of paper.

Considering Reality and Schedules

The reality of real-world programming is that the specification almost never is completed before the code (let alone the design document) is written. Further, in our rush to meet deadlines, the design document often is skimped on, and even when fleshed out reasonably well, it quickly becomes obsolete. That said, to the extent that you can get everyone working from a shared set of assumptions, you will be able to avoid many of the pitfalls that cause significant delays in so much of the industry.

Using Debuggers

My dad used to tell me the story of why the leaky roof was never fixed. When it was raining, you couldn't fix the roof because it was wet, and the shingles wouldn't set correctly. And on sunny days, he would explain, no one was motivated to go up on the roof when they could sit in the backyard and enjoy the weather!

Most of us treat debuggers like a leaky roof. When our code is working properly, we have little motivation to sit down and learn how to use the debugger. When the code is broken, we have no time to learn new skills because we have to fix that bug! The truth, however, is that even rudimentary skill with a real debugger can save you hours and hours of effort.

Before launching into an explanation of using a world-class debugger, let me take a brief tangent into the alternative techniques used by many programmers.

Use the Source, Luke

The simplest and often the most effective way to find bugs is—surprise!—to read the code. You would be surprised how often a bug can be found *on inspection*, just by carefully re-reading what you have written. One technique that works *very* well for me, especially when I'm completely stuck, is to explain to someone else why what I'm seeing makes no sense and why there cannot possibly be a bug in this particular section of code.

Invariably, one of two things happens: I prove the bug really *cannot* be here, and I go figure out where it is, or I smack myself on the head and say, "Oh! Now that I said it out loud, of course it is right here!"

Use TRACE Macros

The most popular method for finding bugs among old C hackers probably was to put `printf` statements into the code, which printed out the current value of variables so that the programmer could examine the values stored at various memory locations. Of course, C++ programmers never would be so crude as to use `printf`. We use `cout` instead, but the advantages and disadvantages remain: You see what is going on, but your code becomes bloated and unreadable.

The solution to this code bloat is to create a TRACE macro. Typically, a TRACE macro would take a string as a parameter. In debug mode, `trace` passes the string to `cout`; in the release version, however, it does nothing.

Using trace throughout your code is a crude way to manage debugging, and your debugger provides a better alternative, but trace does have an important role to play nonetheless. Many programmers use TRACE macros to report on run-time failures, and to provide a running commentary on which areas of their code have been entered and exited.

Use Logs

An effective adjunct to TRACE macros is to create a log file, and to write progress messages and other status messages to the log. You can create macros that write to the log only in debug mode, or only when certain flags are set. Often, reduced but vital information will be logged even in the release version of a product, enabling tech support to use the logs to diagnose problems encountered by customers.

If you are writing log-in macros, you may want to consider creating a variety of numbered logs. This method will enable you to turn on and off logging by section or by level, as your needs change.

Another important consideration in creating logs is *buffering*. Most operating systems allow for buffered and unbuffered output, and it is important to consider this when creating your logs. If all your logging uses a write-through, unbuffered mechanism, your program will slow as it writes to the disk. If, on the other hand, you make all your logging buffered, you run the risk that you will lose vital information when your program crashes.

Using the Debugger

Nearly all modern development environments include one or more high-powered debuggers. The essential idea behind these tools is this: You run the debugger, which loads your source code, and then you run your program from *within* the debugger. This method enables you to see each instruction in your program as it executes, and to examine each variable as it changes during the life of your program.

All compilers will enable you to compile with or without symbols. Compiling with symbols tells the compiler to create the necessary mapping between your source code and the generated program; the debugger uses this to point to the line of source code that corresponds to the next action in the program.

This point is critical and often misunderstood by programmers: Your source code has been translated into object code and then into machine language by the time you run your program. Each machine-language instruction corresponds to one assembler instruction, and early debuggers showed your source code only in assembler.

Modern compilers and debuggers work together to enable you to step through each line of your C++ code as if each line were one machine instruction. The reality, however, is that each line represents many assembler instructions, and most compilers will reveal this to you if you asked for mixed symbols and assembler.

Using Symbolic Debuggers

Full-screen symbolic debuggers make walking your code a delight. After you load your debugger, it reads through all your source code and shows the code in a window. You can step over function calls or direct the debugger to step into each function, line by line.

With most debuggers, you can switch between the source code and the output to see the results of each executed statement. You can examine the current state of each variable, look at complex data structures, examine the value of member data within classes, and look at the actual values in memory of various pointers and other memory locations.

You can switch to mixed source and step through each assembler instruction, and you usually can jump over instructions or manipulate the value of memory locations. You also can instruct your debugger to race through the code, stopping only when it reaches a particular location, when a memory variable has a certain value, or when it has iterated over a section of code a specified number of times.

Using Break Points

Break points are instructions to the debugger that when a particular line of code is ready to be executed, the program should stop. Break points enable you to run your program unimpeded until the line in question is reached. They also help you analyze the current condition of variables just before and after a critical line of code.

Using Watch Points

It is possible to tell the debugger to show you the value of a particular variable, or to break when a particular variable is written to or read. Watch points enable you to set these conditions, and at times to even modify the value of a variable *while the program is running.*

Examining Memory

At times, it is important to see the actual values held in memory. Modern debuggers can show values in the form of the actual variable—strings can be shown as characters, longs can be shown as numbers rather than as 4 bytes, and so on. Sophisticated C++ debuggers even can show complete classes, providing the current value of all the member variables, including the *this* pointer.

Using a Call Stack

At any break point in your program, you can examine the call stack. The *call stack* will display the series of function calls leading up to the current function. This can answer that age-honored question of so many programmers, "How the devil did we get *here?*"

It is important, however, to note that the call stack gives you less information than you might otherwise suspect. Remember that when a function is called and then returns, it falls off the call stack. It therefore is possible for main() to call Func1(), and for Func1() to call Func2(). Func2() can return, and then Func1() can call Func3(). The call stack at that point will *not* include Func2(), even though it is true that Func2() is called before Func3() is called.

If you are trying to prove that some field is initialized in Func2() before Func3() is called, the call stack may not be able to help you. The right way to track this down is to put a break point in Func2().

Turning Off Optimization

Modern compilers do a wonderful job of optimizing your code to be smaller and faster. They accomplish this by reorganizing your code at compile time. Although this is very desirable in your shipping code, it will undermine completely your efforts to step through and debug your code. When you create your debug versions, be sure to turn off all optimizations.

Zen Mind, Debugging Mind

It has been said in dozens of books and is no less true for being commonplace: Debugging is a state of mind. Moreover, the mind-set needed for debugging is quite different from that needed for programming.

Although leaps of intuition always are welcome in all creative fields, and no less so in programming, debugging is best accomplished as a methodical process of hypothesis, experimentation, and evaluation. The great dangers in debugging come from unexamined assumptions and sloppy evaluation. Often, a programmer will whiz right by the bug as he pursues a half-baked theory before all the evidence is evaluated.

Defining the Problem

The first step in successful debugging is to define the problem: What is the bug you are after? What are its manifestations? What might cause such a problem?

There are, I must confess, some shortcuts along the way. If your code crashes, for example, it is likely that you are writing into memory you don't own. This is a good indication that you may have your pointers wrong. Look for things like writing past the end of an array, deleting an already deleted pointer, using a deleted pointer, and so on.

If your bug appears suddenly when you change a different area of code, you might want to consider whether you have a pointer problem. Problems that come and go when memory changes often are pointer problems that only show up when different areas of memory are being corrupted. That is, the problem never really goes away, but it is masked when unimportant memory is corrupted, and it is manifest when critical memory is stepped on.

Locating, Isolating, and Destroying the Problem

The crucial trick in finding a bug is to isolate the problem, eliminate the extraneous and confounding variables, and zero in on the problem. If you are seeing a crash in a particular section of code, try commenting out much of the code until you find the responsible code.

Often, you can save time by conducting an impromptu binary search of your code. If you have narrowed the problem to a particular function, for example, comment out the bottom half of the function. If the problem goes away, uncomment the bottom and comment out the top. If you prove that the problem is in the bottom, leave the top commented and comment out half of the bottom half, and so on.

To the extent that you can eliminate areas of code, variables, and other factors, you can simplify the problem. A problem sufficiently simplified may offer up its own solution on inspection. Even if this doesn't happen, the fewer variables you are contending with, the likelier it is you will be able to quickly solve the problem.

Knowing What to Look For

After you narrow your problem to a specific area of code, what do you do next? The first thing to do is to open a watch window and examine the value of all your variables. Do the values make sense? Are your pointers pointing to reasonable areas of memory?

Does your bug occur each time or only after so many iterations? Examine your call stack; are you getting here along the path you expect? Open the assembler window; are you executing the code you think you are? Examine the registers; are you in the section of code and memory you think you are?

If data is getting unexpectedly trashed, examine the stack pointer. Are you overrunning the stack? Are you running with *stack trace* on? Most compilers will enable you to trace the stack and will issue a warning in your debugger if you run past the top of your stack.

Where are you storing your variables? In segmented memory (that is, in DOS-based applications), there are near and far memory, and you have much less near memory than far memory. Is it possible that you are running out of near memory?

Questioning Your Assumptions

One of the great benefits of interactive debugging is that you can question and reexamine your assumptions. "That variable must be greater than zero." Oh? A debugger can tell you whether you are right. "I initialized that pointer already." A debugger can show you the exact address stored in that pointer.

Looking At Logic Flaws

Often, a bug is not a mistake in syntax or an overwritten array, but instead a flaw in your algorithm. These flaws can be the hardest to find. You may be searching for a "mistake," for example, and thus not realize that the error is not a misplaced semicolon but instead a lapse in understanding.

Logic flaws can be found in complex sections of your code, and in very simple sections where unexpected starting or ending conditions can throw off your reasoning. These flaws often can be found by having someone else check your reasoning. Explain to another programmer what you are doing; even before she points out the error of your ways, you may realize it yourself.

Finding Bugs That Only Show Up in Release Code

Sometimes, your code will work perfectly in debug mode but will break in the release version. This can drive you crazy—just when you thought it was safe to go back into the water...

The first thing to look for when this happens is debug-mode macro side effects. As explained on day 19, for example, your ASSERT macro usually evaluates to nothing at run time. If you write

```
BigClassPtr * pBigClass = getBigClass();
ASSERT(pBigClass);
```

the assertion will disappear at run time, leaving behind absolutely no assembler instructions. This is just what you want and will have no bad effects on your program.

However, if you write

```
BigClassPtr * pBigClass = 0;
ASSERT ((pBigClass = getBigClass()) != NULL);
```

20

in debug mode, this code will have the same effect as the preceding code. In non-debug mode, however, the ASSERT macro will evaluate to nothing, and the assignment will not be made; this will leave the pointer, pBigClass, pointing to nothing and initialized to zero.

Watching for Some Common Bugs

Some bugs are so common, even in the code of experienced programmers, that it is worthwhile to keep them in mind every time you are debugging. The next few sections present a partial list. Over time, you will create your own dirty dozen of repeated nasty errors.

Making Fence-Post Errors

No matter how long we code, we still make this bush-league error. Declare an array of 100 items, and then try to access myArray[100]. Or, as an example of a somewhat more subtle error, declare a buffer to hold a C-style, null-terminated string of 100 bytes, and then copy 100 bytes into it, leaving no room for the terminating null.

Switching back and forth between C++ string objects and C-style character arrays can generate fence-post errors, as can passing pointers and then using pointer arithmetic to access members of a predefined array.

Deleting Memory Twice, or Not at All

Memory management can be confusing and enervating. It is imperative that you keep careful track of "who" is responsible for owning a block of memory, and for restoring that memory when the last pointer is destroyed (and *not* before).

Remember to zero initialize all pointers that you aren't using, and to set pointers to zero after they are deleted. Of course, all of that does you no good if you don't test the pointer before using it.

Wrapping around an Integer

Unsigned integers can hold any value from 0 through 65,535. When you declare an int variable, however, you actually declare a *signed* integer, and any value past 32,767 will "wrap around" to a very large negative number. This effect can cause surprisingly subtle bugs.

Returning a Reference to a Local Variable

References can simplify greatly the syntax of your function, but beware of returning a reference to an item on the stack. A variant on this is to return a reference to a deleted item. Remember, a reference can *never* refer to a null object.

Memory Checking

Although the debugger is certainly your first line of defense against programming bugs, there now are new and powerful methods that you can use. A whole class of special boundary- and memory-checking utilities exist, exemplified by NuMega Technology's Bounds Checker utility.

Like a debugger, Bounds Checker is run first, and Bounds Checker then runs your program. As your code executes, Bounds Checker is looking for fence-post errors, memory overwrites, memory leaks, and so on. This can be a *very* effective way to find problems in your code and can save you many hours of painful debugging.

I have nothing to do with Nu Mega Technologies, except that I'll never write another DOS or Windows programs without first checking it with Bounds Checker. It has saved me *hundreds* of hours of effort with its well-crafted tools.

A Word about Rest

If I had not experienced this more than once, and were it not for the fact that dozens of other programmers have reported the same thing, I wouldn't bother saying it here. *You cannot debug a complex program when you are exhausted.*

It happens to all of us: The deadline is imminent, it is 2 a.m., you have been at it for 16 hours straight, and the program will not work. You simply *know* that another hour's work will find the problem. Unfortunately, more often than not, what really happens is that the program begins to unravel as you make stupid and irreversible mistakes.

There is a tried and true technique for solving this problem, and it works surprisingly well. Save your file, get up, walk away, and get six hours of sleep. More often than not, you will come back and fix the problem in less than an hour.

This technique works for two reasons. First, you need to be rested. Second, you well may have been processing the problem for much of the time you were away. Learn the lesson from the experience of others: Sometimes a break and a good night's sleep is what is needed.

Looking At Some Debugging Examples

Finding example code to teach debugging techniques is particularly difficult. Trivial programs lend themselves to solutions on inspection, and complex problems mask the debugging techniques behind the obscurity of the program itself. Further, true debugging requires a full and visceral understanding of the program. Trying to debug someone else's code (or your own code after you have been away from it for a long time) particularly is difficult.

20

Nonetheless, the following listings provide a starting point for exploration. Listing 20.1 is the interface to a String class not unlike that used throughout this book. Listing 20.2 is the implementation, and listing 20.3 is a simple driver program.

Type

Listing 20.1 Interface to String Class

```
1:     #include <iostream.h>
2:     #include <string.h>
3:     #define UINT unsigned int
4:     enum BOOL { FALSE, TRUE };
5:
6:     class xOutOfBounds {};
7:
8:     class String
9:     {
10:    public:
11:
12:            // constructors
13:            String();
14:            String(const char *);
15:            String (const char *, UINT length);
16:            String (const String&);
17:            ~String();
18:
19:            // helpers and manipulators
20:            UINT   GetLength() const { return itsLen; }
21:            BOOL IsEmpty() const { return (BOOL) (itsLen == 0); }
22:            void Clear();                    // set string to 0 length
23:
24:            // accessors
25:            char operator[](UINT offset) const;
26:            char& operator[](UINT offset);
27:            const char * GetString()const   { return itsCString; }
28:
29:            // casting operators
30:             operator const char* () const { return itsCString; }
31:             operator char* () { return itsCString;}
32:
33:            void operator+=(const String&);
34:            void operator+=(char);
35:            void operator+=(const char*);
36:
37:            BOOL operator<(const String& rhs)const;
38:            BOOL operator>(const String& rhs)const;
39:            BOOL operator<=(const String& rhs)const;
40:            BOOL operator>=(const String& rhs)const;
41:            BOOL operator==(const String& rhs)const;
42:            BOOL operator!=(const String& rhs)const;
43:
44:
45:            // friend functions
46:            String operator+(const String&);
47:            String operator+(const char*);
48:            String operator+(char);
49:
```

```
50:             friend ostream& operator<< (ostream&, const String&);
51:
52:     private:
53:             // returns 0 if same, -1 if this is less than argument,
54:             // 1 if this is greater than argument
55:             int StringCompare(const String&) const;  // used by Boolean
                operator
56:
57:
58:             char * itsCString;
59:             UINT itsLen;
60:     };
```

Listing 20.2 Implementation of String

```
1:      #include "string.hpp"
2:       // default constructor creates string of 0 bytes
3:      String::String()
4:      {
5:         itsCString = new char[1];
6:         itsCString[0] = '\0';
7:         itsLen=0;
8:      }
9:
10:     String::String(const char *rhs)
11:     {
12:        itsLen = strlen(rhs);
13:        itsCString = new char[itsLen+1];
14:        strcpy(itsCString,rhs);
15:     }
16:
17:     String::String (const char *rhs, UINT length)
18:     {
19:        itsLen = strlen(rhs);
20:        if (length < itsLen)
21:           itsLen = length;   // max size = length
22:        itsCString = new char[itsLen+1];
23:        memcpy(itsCString,rhs,itsLen);
24:        itsCString[itsLen] = '\0';
25:     }
26:
27:     // copy constructor
28:     String::String (const String & rhs)
29:     {
30:        itsLen=rhs.GetLength();
31:        itsCString = new char[itsLen+1];
32:        memcpy(itsCString,rhs.GetString(),itsLen);
33:        itsCString[rhs.itsLen]='\0';
34:     }
35:
36:     String::~String ()
37:     {
38:        Clear();
```

continues

Listing 20.2 continued

```
39:    }
40:
41:    void String::Clear()
42:    {
43:       delete [] itsCString;
44:       itsLen = 0;
45:    }
46:
47:    //non constant offset operator
48:    char & String::operator[](UINT offset)
49:    {
50:       if (offset > itsLen)
51:       {
52:          //throw xOutOfBounds();
53:           return itsCString[itsLen-1];
54:       }
55:       else
56:          return itsCString[offset];
57:    }
58:
59:    // constant offset operator
60:    char String::operator[](UINT offset) const
61:    {
62:       if (offset > itsLen)
63:       {
64:          //throw xOutOfBounds();
65:          return itsCString[itsLen-1];
66:       }
67:       else
68:          return itsCString[offset];
69:    }
70:
71:
72:
73:    // changes current string, returns nothing
74:    void String::operator+=(const String& rhs)
75:    {
76:       unsigned short rhsLen = rhs.GetLength();
77:       unsigned short totalLen = itsLen + rhsLen;
78:       char *temp = new char[totalLen+1];
79:       for (UINT i = 0; i<itsLen; i++)
80:          temp[i] = itsCString[i];
81:       for (UINT j = 0; j<rhsLen; j++, i++)
82:          temp[(UINT)i] = rhs[(UINT)j];
83:       temp[totalLen]='\0';
84:       *this = temp;
85:    }
86:
87:    int String::StringCompare(const String& rhs) const
88:    {
89:          return strcmp(itsCString, rhs.GetString());
90:    }
91:
```

```
92:     String String::operator+(const String& rhs)
93:     {
94:
95:         char * newCString = new char[GetLength() + rhs.GetLength() + 1];
96:         strcpy(newCString,GetString());
97:         strcat(newCString,rhs.GetString());
98:         String newString(newCString);
99:         return newString;
100:    }
101:
102:
103:    String String::operator+(const char* rhs)
104:    {
105:
106:        char * newCString = new char[GetLength() + strlen(rhs)+ 1];
107:        strcpy(newCString,GetString());
108:        strcat(newCString,rhs);
109:        String newString(newCString);
110:        return newString;
111:    }
112:
113:
114:    String String::operator+(char rhs)
115:    {
116:        int oldLen = GetLength();
117:        char * newCString = new char[oldLen + 2];
118:        strcpy(newCString,GetString());
119:        newCString[oldLen] = rhs;
120:        newCString[oldLen+1] = '\0';
121:        String newString(newCString);
122:        return newString;
123:    }
124:
125:
126:
127:    BOOL String::operator==(const String& rhs) const
128:    { return (BOOL) (StringCompare(rhs) == 0); }
129:    BOOL String::operator!=(const String& rhs)const
130:        { return (BOOL) (StringCompare(rhs) != 0); }
131:    BOOL String::operator<(const String& rhs)const
132:        { return (BOOL) (StringCompare(rhs) < 0); }
133:    BOOL String::operator>(const String& rhs)const
134:        { return (BOOL) (StringCompare(rhs) > 0); }
135:    BOOL String::operator<=(const String& rhs)const
136:        { return (BOOL) (StringCompare(rhs) <= 0); }
137:    BOOL String::operator>=(const String& rhs)const
138:        { return (BOOL) (StringCompare(rhs) >= 0); }
139:
140:    ostream& operator<< (ostream& ostr, const String& str)
141:    {
142:        ostr << str.itsCString;
143:        return ostr;
144:    }
```

20

Listing 20.3 Driver Program

```
1:     #include <iostream.h>
2:     #include "string.hpp"
3:
4:     int main()
5:     {
6:
7:         String *CatName = new String("Fritz");
8:         char buffer[100];
9:         cout << "The cat name is " << *CatName;
10:        cout << "\nEnter a new name for the cat: ";
11:        cin.getline(buffer,100);
12:        String *NewName = new String(buffer);
13:        *CatName = *NewName;
14:        delete NewName;
15:
16:        // String * MyName = new String("Jesse Liberty");
17:
18:        cout << "The cat name is " << *CatName;
19:        return 0;
20:     }
```

```
The cat name is Fritz
Enter a new name for the cat: Fido
The cat name is Fido

The cat name is Fritz
Enter a new name for the cat: Fido
The cat name is Jesse Liberty
```

The interface to `String` *appears* to be okay. Inspection of the implementation reveals no obvious problems, and the driver program is straightforward. When I ran the program the first time, it worked perfectly. I then uncommented line 16 in listing 20.3, and suddenly the program stopped working.

As you learned earlier in this chapter, the first approach might be to review the program and to walk through how it works. If this reveals no obvious solution, you might fire up the debugger, or you might pause and think about the bug for a while, speculating on what might cause this behavior.

A first hypothesis might be that somehow `CatName` is being replaced by `MyName`, or that somehow `MyName` is trashing the pointer to `NewName`.

The debugger clarifies the problem virtually instantly. I opened a watch window and put in

```
*CatName
*NewName
*MyName
```

This put watch statements on all three strings. I also put a break point in line 9. After this line, `CatName` pointed to Fritz as expected. After line 12, `CatName` continued to point to Fritz and `NewName` pointed to `Fido` (also as expected). After line 13, both pointed to `Fido`.

After line 14 however, *both pointers* were trashed! And, even more surprising, after line 16, *all three* pointers pointed to `Jesse Liberty`! What was going on?

The answer, of course, is that the `String` class shown does not include an operator equals. Thus, the compiler-supplied shallow-copy operator is used. When line 13 executes, `CatName` and `NewName` are set to point to the same buffer in memory. When `NewName` then is deleted (properly), unfortunately the memory pointed to by `CatName` is deleted as well.

When the new string, in line 16, is allocated, the new data is assigned to the memory abandoned by `NewName`. This causes `CatName` to point to that area, and thus when `CatName` is printed, the contents of `MyName` are printed.

In the first run, when line 16 was commented out, nothing overwrote that area of memory, and so it was printed, but the pointer was a time bomb waiting to go off.

Note that even in the second run, the program didn't crash. If that area of memory was later used for something other than a string, however, the inadvertently deleted pointer could well bring the system to its knees.

The simple capability to set a watch on these three variables, and to step through the program seeing where and when the data was corrupted, was enough to make the cause of the bug and its solution immediately evident.

Summary

Today you learned the importance of developing professional debugging techniques. You learned the fundamentals of using a source-level debugger, and explored some of the powerful capabilities that such a system brings to your efforts to produce error-free code.

Q&A

20

Q **What is the difference between the debugger in my integrated development environment and the stand-alone debugger that came with my compiler?**

A Typically, development environments come with a somewhat simplified debugger that works with the editor and compiler in an integrated fashion, and a stand-alone debugger that provides extra features and capabilities.

Q **What is the difference between *hard-mode* and *soft-mode* debugging?**

A This answer may depend in detail on the system on which you are developing. Typically, however, this distinction refers to the memory model in which the debugging is accomplished. In hard-mode debugging, no other programs can run when the debugger runs—it takes over the machine.

Q What makes a debugger symbolic?

A In the early days of programming in "high level" languages such as C, the debugger could not show the symbolic names of variables (myAge, for example) but only the actual memory address. It was up to the programmer to figure out which variable was which, based on map files provided by the linker.

Workshop

The Workshop provides quiz questions to help you solidify your understanding of the material covered, and exercises to provide you with experience in using what you have learned. Try to answer the quiz and exercise questions before checking the answers in Appendix A, and make sure that you understand the answers before continuing to the next chapter.

Quiz

1. What is the difference between a *watch statement* and a *break point*?
2. What is the *call stack*?
3. What is a *TRACE macro*?
4. Why should you turn off optimization when debugging?

Exercises

1. Identify the fence-post bugs in the following code. (Assume that there is a String class available that supports the operations asked of it.)

```
char * CStrNewCopy(const char * src)
{
    int size = strlen(src);
    char * retCStr = new char[size];
    strcpy(retCStr, src);
    return retCStr;
}

const int MaxNameLength = 30;
const int NameCount = 10;
String GlobalNameArray[NameCount];

void FillGlobalNameArray()
{
    cout << "Enter names\n";
    for (int i = 0; i<=NameCount; I++)
    {
        char buffer[MaxNameLength];
        cin.getline(buffer, MaxNameLength);
        GlobalNameArray[i] = buffer;
    }
}
```

2. Find the common error, by inspection. (Assume that Test really tests something meaningful, and that there is a point to this whole thing.)

```
// Returns TRUE if test passes.
BOOL Test(int theValue, const String & theString);

void Foo()
{
    cout << "Enter a value ";

    int x;
    cin >> x;

    cout << "Enter a String ";
    char buffer[30];
    cin.getline(buffer, 29);
    String * str = new String(buffer);

    if (Test(x, str))
    {
        cout << "Passed\n";
    }
    else
    {
        cout << "Failed\n";
        if (x == 0)
            return;
    }
    delete str;
}
```

3. What follows is a piece of code and the log output from running it. Explain why the log shows one more constructor than destructor. (EX2003.CPP)

```
#include <iostream.h>
#include <math.h>

#define LOG(x) cout << x << "\n"

class Complex
{
public:
    Complex() : myReal(0.0), myImaginary(0.0)
        {LOG("Complex c-tor");}
    Complex(double real, double imaginary)
        : myReal(real), myImaginary(imaginary)
        {LOG("Complex c-tor 2");}
    ~Complex() {LOG("Complex d-tor");}

    double Absolute() const
        {return sqrt(myReal * myReal
                    + myImaginary * myImaginary);}

    int CompareAbsolute(Complex rhs) const;
```

```
private:
    double myReal, myImaginary;
};

int Complex::CompareAbsolute(Complex rhs) const
{
    double myAbs = Absolute();
    double rhsAbs = rhs.Absolute();

    if (myAbs < rhsAbs)
        return -1;
    else if (myAbs == rhsAbs)
        return 0;
    else
        return 1;
}

Complex glComplex(5.0,2.2);
void main()
{
    LOG("Starting main");
    Complex c1(2.1,5.5);

    int x = c1.CompareAbsolute(glComplex);

    LOG("Ending main");
}


// Log output
Complex c-tor 2
Starting main
Complex c-tor 2
Complex d-tor
Ending main
Complex d-tor
Complex d-tor
```

4. Find, by inspection, the bug in the following code used for an imaginary compression/ decompression tool. The implementation of CompressCStr is elsewhere and is assumed to work as advertised.

```
// This will compress src into target. It will write no
// more than len bytes.
// Returns the number of bytes actually written, or -1 if
// there was not enough space.
int CompressCStr(char * target, unsigned len, char * src);

int CompressCStrArray(char * target, unsigned len, char ** array)
{
    unsigned LenUsed = 0;
    unsigned TotalLenUsed = 0;

    // array is an array of pointers
    // Compress until array has a null pointer
    while(*array != 0)
```

```
    {
        LenUsed =
         CompressCStr(target, len - TotalLenUsed, *array);

        if (LenUsed < 0)
            return -1;

        TotalLenUsed+=LenUsed;
        target+=LenUsed;
        array++;
    }
    return TotalLenUsed;
}
```

5. The following function crashes under some unusual circumstances. (You don't know what those circumstances are, exactly. You only know that it is rare.) You have set break points in the debugger, but you never have been able to witness it crash. The most common symptom is that you get a protection fault on the last line (not counting the LOG).

Your first step in debugging this code is to add the LOGs. After filling up a file with logs, you find that in the error case it reaches the first LOG successfully and crashes before the second LOG. What is the bug?

```
void PrintMessage(int MessageID)
{
    char * msg;
    switch (MessageID)
    {
    case 1:
        msg = "The first message."
        break;
    case 2:
        msg = "The second message."
        break;
    case 3:
        msg = "The third message."
        break;
    case 4:
        msg = "The fourth message."
        break;
    case 5:
        msg = "The fifth message."
        break;
    case 6:
        msg = "The sixth message."
        break;
    }

    LOG("About to output message");
    cout << msg << "\n";
    LOG("Done outputting message");
}
```

20

WEEK 3

Next Steps

Congratulations! You have made it through three weeks of intense, advanced C++, and now are ready to take on professional-level assignments.

Today you will learn

☐ How to enhance your products to make them fully professional

☐ How to prepare, market, and ship your products

☐ How to manage version control in larger projects

☐ What is next in your education as a professional programmer

Using Version Control

Before you learn about putting the final touches on your software, you will learn about version control in this section. As you develop your software, you may find that you have taken a wrong turn and need to back up. If you have been working on the only copy of your program, you easily could put yourself in a position where it takes you days to recover.

At an absolute minimum, you will want to make daily backups of your code, but that often isn't enough to get you back in business. If you changed some classes on Monday, and others on Tuesday, putting together a working version from your backups can be murderously difficult.

Version control software, also called revision control software, solves this problem and other issues as well.

Learning How Version Control Works

In a good version control system, every file is checked into the system, and the first iteration of the file is given revision 1. When you want to revise the file, you check it out of the revision control system (RCS), edit it, and check it back in with a new revision number (myFile.cpp Rev 2, for example).

Files that are checked into the system are made read only on your local disk, so that you cannot inadvertently edit the files without checking them out again.

From time to time, you will want to create a named revision of your program (ROBIN v3, for example). You tell the RCS which version of each file to include in that name. ROBIN v3, for example, might include the following: String.cpp,5 (String.cpp revision number 5); String.hpp,4; Page,7; and so on.

Note that not all the revision numbers are the same. It is perfectly reasonable to revise one file many times between revisions while another file remains unchanged. The complete set of files for ROBIN v3 might look like this:

```
String.hpp, 2
String.cpp, 4
Page.cpp, 5
Page.hpp, 5
IdxMgr.cpp, 9
IdxMgr.hpp, 4
```

...and so on. If you make a wrong turn at some point, you always can check out of your RCS the entire set of ROBIN 3, and know that that complete set of files will create a buildable version of the program.

Managing More Than One Programmer

Once you have two or more programmers working on a product, revision control becomes an absolute necessity. It is impossible to keep track of who has a particular file without the capability to check files in and out.

If you didn't have this capability, here's what might happen. You open Idxmgr.cpp to make some revisions. At the same time, unknown to you, your partner starts making revisions to the same file. You save your changes, he saves his and overwrites yours, and all your work is lost.

You could solve this problem by never editing files that are shared on a network. You could decide, by convention, to copy those files to your local hard disk to edit them. The problem, of course, is that the overwriting just as easily could happen when the files are returned to the network.

Some developers solve this dilemma by *moving* the file to their local hard drive—not leaving a copy behind on the network. This solves the overwriting problem, but what if you both need to work on the file at the same time?

A good RCS will allow simultaneous edits, by letting one developer work on the trunk of the project, while the other works on a branch.

Understanding Branches and Trunks

A *branch* is simply a revision against a file that already is checked out by another developer. If you check out ROBIN.CPP version 4, and I also want to make edits to version 4, for example, I can take out a branch. Your file will be named ROBIN,5 when you return it to the RCS, but mine will be called ROBIN,4a1.

My file will not overwrite your changes; it will stand on its own as a separate departure point from version 4. At some point, probably fairly quickly after we're both done, we will want to merge the changes back into yet another version—for example, ROBIN,6. A good RCS makes that merger easy, often providing a script or side-by-side windows for comparing and merging the two versions.

21

Understanding Release Branches

With a large and complex project, you often will find that you need to be working on bug fixes for one released version of your program even as you are developing the next released version of the program. A powerful RCS lets you accomplish this by creating an entire branch release, consisting of branched versions of every file in the project.

You therefore can work on the branch to release 2 while continuing development on release 3. Because the entire set of files has a name, it is easy to check out all the files for the latest fixes to ROBIN v2, make your edits, check the name in, and then return to working on files for ROBIN v3.

Creating Dynamic Names

Professional level version control systems enable you to create dynamic names. You might create a name called ROBIN Latest, for example. Checking out the files in ROBIN Latest does *not* provide a static set of files (as checking out ROBIN v2 does) but instead provides the latest revision of every file in the ROBIN project. This feature can be enormously convenient, because most of the time you really do want the very latest version of everything.

Making Enhancements

A good product never really is finished. If you designed for extensibility and maintainability, your customers will tell you what features they would like to see added and for which features they would be willing to pay more.

The greatest single danger to V1 of your product is *creeping featurism*—that inevitable trend to put in just one more "essential" feature. The later your product is to market, the more market share you lose; yet, perversely, this very lateness leads some developers to feel they must add features to keep up with the competition.

I believe that you should release version 1 with the absolute minimum set of features. Early on in your development cycle, ask yourself, "What is the smallest set of features with which I can reasonably go to market?" Then cut that list!

During the development of V1, set a very high barrier to adding features, and consider eliminating those features that turn out to be expensive (in time, resources, or program size) to develop. Keep a version 2 list so that you don't forget all the cool stuff you left out of V1, but make your highest priority for V1 to get out there into the marketplace and compete.

It is my experience that far more products fail in the marketplace because of being late to market than because of being light on features. In fact, I'll go further and say that even relatively buggy code often succeeds if it is first in the market and the upgrade and bug fix are quickly available.

That latter point is dangerous, however. Many products never recover from the poor first impression they make on the market. What's more, there will be plenty of bugs left in your code if you do all you can to squash them; a tolerance of releasing buggy code is almost certain to sink you as you earn a reputation for shoddy work.

The bottom line is this: Draw up a list of the absolutely required features; develop a solid, reliable, and *extensible* product; and then get out there with it and start listening to your customers. They will be sure to tell you what you got wrong, and what you left out, if you listen. If you then respond and your program is seen to be good and getting better, you almost cannot help succeeding.

Using Shareware

Commercial, shrink-wrapped, on-the-shelf, at your local software discount store programs are not the only options available to software developers now. Shareware is a huge market presence in this industry.

In short, a shareware program is *free* to try, but the user is obliged to purchase it if he uses it past an initial trial time. The interesting thing about shareware is that it typically is delivered via electronic online services such as Interchange, ZiffNet, and so on; or on local bulletin board systems. This accessibility means that hundreds of thousands of people will have instant access to your software.

If you are interested in this unique distribution channel, be sure to contact the Shareware Products Association for information on their guidelines for producing, marketing, distributing, and being paid for your program.

Writing Commercial Software

Whether you distribute your program as shareware or as a shrink-wrapped product, your customers will expect more from a product for which they are paying. At a minimum, they will expect your program to do what it says it will, to be reasonably well documented, to be reliable and robust, and—if it is both expensive and complex—to be supported.

Support is a very expensive problem for the industry. Some companies have developed a very good reputation for providing excellent (and often free) telephone support. Other companies have aggravated their users with long waits to talk to misinformed and unfriendly support technicians.

Some companies still provide free, unlimited support via toll-free numbers, but in the past few years many have found this to be prohibitively expensive. Some of the larger companies have started charging for support, and many others have shunted some or all of their support to electronic services such as Interchange or CompuServe, or via fax or other indirect methods.

21

If your product is a simple utility, offered for free or at little expense, few will expect you to provide much support. (But don't be surprised by the occasional midnight call from an irate customer screaming, "Your program says press any key, but I don't have an AnyKey!")

Finding Help and Advice

The first thing you should do when you finish this book is to tap into a C++ conference on an online service. These groups supply immediate contact with hundreds or thousands of C++ programmers who can answer your questions, offer advice, and provide a sounding board for your ideas. As an advanced C++ programmer, you also can contribute to this community of ideas, which answers questions and provides advice to those just starting out.

I participate in the C++ discussions on Interchange (of course), as well as many C++ forums on Ziffnet, CompuServe, and other dial-in services. I'm also active in the C++ Internet news group (comp.lang.c++), and I recommend all of these as good sources of information and support.

Also, you might want to look for local user groups. Many cities have C++ interest groups where you can meet other programmers and exchange ideas.

Required Reading

The very next book I would run out and buy and read is

> Meyers, Scott. *Effective C++* (ISBN: 0-201-56364-9). Addison-Wesley Publishing, 1993.

This is by far the most useful book I've ever read, and I've read it three times.

At this point, however, you have a solid grounding in C++: both the syntax of the language and its more advanced capabilities. There are two obvious areas to explore from here: advanced object-oriented analysis and design; and development in a graphical user interface environment such as Windows, the Mac, or OS/2.

Getting More Information about Object-Oriented Analysis and Design

If you are serious about object-oriented programming and design, be sure to pick up an advanced book. Either of the following books will be a valuable addition to your library:

> Booch, Grady. *Object-Oriented Analysis and Design with Applications*, 2nd Edition (ISBN: 0-8053-5340-2). The Benjamin/Cummings Publishing Company, Inc., 1994.
>
> Rumbaugh, et al. *Object-Oriented Modeling and Design* (ISBN: 0-13-629841-9). Prentice Hall, Inc., 1991.

Writing for Windows or the Macintosh

There are dozens of books on developing Windows and Macintosh programs, but few from an object-oriented perspective. As the Microsoft foundation classes become more popular, there will be more and more books describing how to create Windows programs using this system. The Think C and Symantec C++ libraries have been very successful on the Mac, and there are a few books on that system as well.

If you are serious about learning Windows, there is one book you must consider, even though it was written for C programmers and not for C++. The absolute rock-solid bible on Windows development is

> Petzold, Charles. *Programming Windows 3.1*, Third Edition (ISBN: 1-55615-395-3). Microsoft Press, 1992.

Once you understand Windows, you immediately will want to look at a C++ perspective. I recommend these:

> Shammas, Namir. *Teach Yourself Visual C++ in 21 Days* (ISBN: 0-672-30372-8). Sams Publishing, 1993.
>
> Kruglinski, David. *Inside Visual C++* (ISBN: 1-55615-511-5). Microsoft Press, 1993.

Writing Solid Code

A number of books have been published lately about writing high-quality code. I highly recommend these three:

> McConnel, Steve. *Code Complete* (ISBN: 1-55615-484-4). Microsoft Press, 1993.
>
> Maguire, Steve. *Writing Solid Code* (ISBN: 1-55615-551-4). Microsoft Press, 1993.
>
> Thielen, David. *No Bugs! Delivering Error-Free Code in C and C++* (ISBN: 0-201-60890-1). Addison-Wesley Publishing, 1992.

Getting More Information from Magazines

Reading all these books and more is vitally important, and going online will give you day-to-day access to other C++ programmers. There is one more thing you can do to strengthen your skills: subscribe to a good magazine on C++ programming. The absolute best magazine of this kind, in my opinion, is *C++ Report* from SIGS Publishing (Sigs Publications, P.O. Box 2031, Langhorne, PA 19047-9700). Every issue is packed with useful articles. Save them; what you don't care about today will become critically important tomorrow. I have no affiliation with the magazine (I work for two other publishers!) but their magazine is the best, bar none.

21

Staying in Touch

If you have comments, suggestions, or ideas about this book or other books, I would love to hear them. Please write to me on Interchange, or on the Internet at jl@ichange.com. I look forward to hearing from you.

Summary

Today you learned what version control systems are and what they can do to help you keep your project organized and on track. You also learned a bit about shareware and some of the considerations in releasing commercial software. Finally, I told you about some of the online discussion groups, other books to read, and at least one very important industry journal.

Q&A

Q What is the difference between *shareware* and *public domain*?

A Software enters the *public domain* when the author relinquishes the copyright that inheres to software when it is created, or when the copyright expires. *Shareware* is copyrighted and owned by the author but is distributed on a "pay if you like it" basis.

Q What happens if you don't pay for shareware?

A Your soul is consigned to the darkest and foulest regions of hell, where you must spend all of eternity listening to Led Zeppelin orchestrated for 1,001 strings.

Q Is there any point in bothering with version control software if I work alone?

A Yes. Version control software can help you "roll back" to a previous working version when you take a wrong turn. More important, it can help you manage various releases of your software if you are supporting more than one platform, or if you are working on Version 2 while still fixing version 1.

Workshop

The Workshop provides quiz questions to help you solidify your understanding of the material covered, and exercises to provide you with experience in using what you have learned. Try to answer the quiz and exercise questions before checking the answers in Appendix A, and make sure that you understand the answers before continuing to the next chapter.

Quiz

1. What is the difference between checking out a file on the *trunk* of your version control system and checking it out on a *branch*?

2. What is a *named release*?

3. What is the next thing you're going to read?

4. How do you contact me on the Internet?

5. What is the meaning of life?

Exercises

School's out; no summer assignments. No exercises for today. Enjoy and congratulations!

21

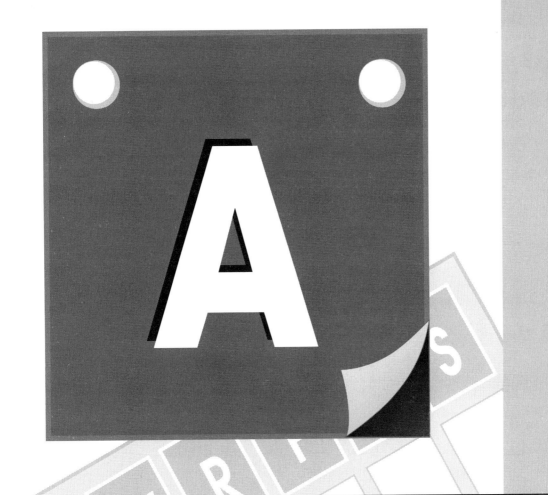

Answers

Answers for Day 1, "Getting Started"

Quiz

1. `const char const * String::getText() const`

2. The former declares that `ptrOne` is a pointer to a constant integer; the integer itself cannot be changed using this pointer. The latter declares that `ptrTwo` is a constant pointer to an integer. Once initialized, this pointer cannot be reassigned.

3. The assignment operator acts on an existing object, and the copy constructor creates a new one.

4. The `this` pointer is a hidden parameter in every member function that points to the object itself.

5. A v-table, or virtual function table, is a common way for compilers to manage virtual functions in C++. The table keeps a list of the addresses of all the virtual functions, and depending on the runtime type of the object pointed to, invokes the right function.

6. Both `Horse` and `Bird` initialize their base class, `Animal`, in their constructors. `Pegasus` does as well, and when a `Pegasus` is created, the `Horse` and `Bird` initializations of `Animal` are ignored.

7. *Containment* describes the idea of one class having a data member that is an object of another type. *Delegation* expresses the idea that one class uses another class to accomplish a task or goal. Delegation usually is accomplished by containment.

8. *Delegation* expresses the idea that one class uses another class to accomplish a task or goal. *Implemented in terms of* expresses the idea of inheriting implementation from another class.

9. *Public* inheritance declares an is-a relationship; all member functions and data maintain their accessibility in the derived class. *Private* inheritance declares an implemented in terms of relationship; all member data and functions in the base class are private in the derived class.

10. The first form of `get()` is without parameters. This returns the value of the character found, and will return EOF (end of file) if end of file is reached.

    The second form of `get()` takes a character reference as its parameter; that character is filled with the next character in the input stream. The return value is an iostream object.

    The third form of `get()` takes an array, a maximum number of characters to "get," and a terminating character. This form of `get()` fills the array with up to one fewer characters than the maximum (appending null) unless it reads the terminating

character, in which case it immediately writes a null and leaves the terminating character in the buffer.

11. `cin.read()` is used for reading binary data structures. `getline()` is used to read from the iostream's buffer.

Exercises

1. Here is the answer:

```
1:      // Demonstrates solving the Nth
2:      // Fibonnacci number using iteration
3:
4:      #include <iostreams.h>
5:
6:      typedef unsigned long int ULONG;
7:
8:      ULONG fib(ULONG position);
9:
10:     void main()
11:     {
12:        ULONG answer, position;
13:        cout << "Which position? ";
14:        cin >> position;
15:        cout << "\n";
16:
17:        answer = fib(position);
18:        cout << answer << " is the ";
19:        cout << position << "th Fibonnacci number.\n";
20:     }
21:
22:     ULONG fib(ULONG n)
23:     {
24:        ULONG minusTwo=1, minusOne=1, answer=2;
25:
26:        if (n < 3)
27:           return 1;
28:
29:        for (n -= 3; n; n--)
30:        {
31:           minusTwo=minusOne;
32:           minusOne=answer;
33:           answer = minusOne + minusTwo;
34:        }
35:
36:        return answer;
37:     }

1:      // Demonstrates solving the Nth
2:      // Fibonnacci number using recursion
3:
4:      #include <iostream.h>
5:
6:      int fib(int n);
```

```
 7:
 8:     void main()
 9:     {
10:
11:        int n, answer;
12:        cout << "Enter number to find: ";
13:        cin >> n;
14:
15:        cout << "\n\n";
16:
17:        answer = fib(n);
18:
19:        cout << answer << " is the " << answer << "th Fibonnacci number\n";
20:
21:     }
22:
23:     int fib (int n)
24:     {
25:        cout << "Processing fib(" << n << ")... ";
26:
27:        if (n == 1 || n == 2)
28:        {
29:           cout << "Return " << n << "!\n";
30:           return (n);
31:        }
32:        else
33:        {
34:           cout << "Call fib(" << (n-ms]2) << ") and fib(" << (n-1) <<
               ").\n";
35:           return( fib(n-2) + fib(n-1));
36:        }
37:     }
```

2. Here is the answer:

```
 1:     // A short program declaring a class with three
 2:     // member variables and one static member variable.
 3:     // The constructor initializes the member variables and
 4:     // increments the static member variable. The
 5:     // destructor decrements the static member variable.
 6:
 7:     #include <iostream.h>
 8:
 9:     class myClass
10:     {
11:        public:
12:              myClass(int, int, int);
13:              ~myClass();
14:              void ShowVals() const;
15:              static int valStatic;
16:        private:
17:              int valOne, valTwo, valThree;
18:
19:     };
20:
```

```
21:     int myClass::valStatic = 0;
22:
23:     myClass::myClass(int v1, int v2, int v3):
24:         valOne(v1),
25:         valTwo(v2),
26:         valThree(v3)
27:     {
28:         valStatic++;
29:     }
30:
31:     myClass::~myClass()
32:     {
33:         valStatic--;
34:     }
35:
36:     void myClass::ShowVals() const
37:     {
38:         cout << "valOne: " << valOne << endl;
39:         cout << "valTwo: " << valTwo << endl;
40:         cout << "valThree: " << valThree << endl;
41:         cout << "valStatic: " << valStatic << endl;
42:     }
43:
44:     void main()
45:     {
46:
47:         myClass *one = new myClass(1,2,3);
48:         one->ShowVals();
49:
50:         myClass two(3,5,7);
51:         two.ShowVals();
52:
53:         myClass *three = new myClass(2,4,6);
54:         three ->ShowVals();
55:
56:         delete one;
57:         three->ShowVals();
58:
59:         delete three;
60:         two.ShowVals();
61:     }
```

3. Here is the answer:

```
1:      #include <fstream.h>
2:      enum BOOL { FALSE, TRUE };
3:
4:      int main(int argc, char**argv)    // returns 1 on error
5:      {
6:
7:          if (argc != 2)
8:          {
9:              cout << "Usage: argv[0] <infile>\n";
10:             return(1);
11:         }
12:
```

```
13:     // open the input stream
14:         ifstream fin (argv[1],ios::binary);
15:         if (!fin)
16:         {
17:             cout << "Unable to open " << argv[1] << " for reading.\n";
18:             return(1);
19:         }
20:
21:         char ch;
22:         while ( fin.get(ch))
23:             if ((ch > 32 && ch < 127) || ch == '\n' || ch == '\t')
24:                 cout << ch;
25:         fin.close();
26:     }
```

4. Here is the answer:

```
1:      #include <iostreams.h>
2:
3:      // Abstract exception data type
4:      class Exception
5:      {
6:      public:
7:          Exception(){}
8:          virtual ~Exception(){}
9:          virtual void PrintError() = 0;
10:     };
11:
12:     // Derived class to handle memory problems.
13:     // Note no allocation of memory in this class!
14:     class OutOfMemory : public Exception
15:     {
16:     public:
17:         OutOfMemory(){}
18:         ~OutOfMemory(){}
19:         virtual void PrintError();
20:     private:
21:     };
22:
23:     void OutOfMemory::PrintError()
24:     {
25:         cout << "Out of Memory!!\n";
26:     }
27:
28:     // Derived class to handle bad numbers
29:     class RangeError : public Exception
30:     {
31:     public:
32:         RangeError(unsigned long number){badNumber = number;}
33:         ~RangeError(){}
34:         virtual void PrintError();
35:         virtual unsigned long GetNumber() { return badNumber; }
36:         virtual void SetNumber(unsigned long number) {badNumber = number;}
37:     private:
38:         unsigned long badNumber;
```

```
39:     };
40:
41:     void RangeError::PrintError()
42:     {
43:         cout << "Number out of range. You used " << GetNumber() << "!!\n";
44:     }
45:
46:     // func. prototypes
47:     void MyFunction();
48:     unsigned int * FunctionTwo();
49:     void FunctionThree(unsigned int *);
50:
51:     void main()
52:     {
53:         try
54:         {
55:             MyFunction();
56:         }
57:         // Only one catch required, use virtual functions to do the
58:         // right thing.
59:         catch (Exception& theException)
60:         {
61:             theException.PrintError();
62:         }
63:     }
64:
65:     unsigned int * FunctionTwo()
66:     {
67:         unsigned int *myInt = new unsigned int;
68:         if (myInt == 0)
69:             throw OutOfMemory();
70:         return myInt;
71:     }
72:
73:
74:     void MyFunction()
75:     {
76:         unsigned int *myInt = FunctionTwo();
77:
78:         FunctionThree(myInt);
79:         cout << "Ok. myInt: " << *myInt;
80:         delete myInt;
81:     }
82:
83:     void FunctionThree(unsigned int *ptr)
84:     {
85:         long testNumber;
86:         cout << "Enter an int: ";
87:         cin >> testNumber;
88:         // this weird test should be replaced by a series
89:         // of tests to complain about bad user input
90:         if (testNumber > 3768 || testNumber < 0)
91:             throw RangeError(testNumber);
92:         *ptr = testNumber;
93:     }
```

Answers for Day 2, "Templates"

Quiz

1. Templates are built into the C++ language, and are type-safe. Macros are implemented by the preprocessor, and are not type-safe.

2. The parameter to a template creates an instance of the template for each type. If you create six template instances, six different classes or functions are created. The parameters to the function change the behavior or data of the function, but only one function is created.

3. The general template friend function creates one function for every type of the `Parameterized` class; the type-specific function creates a type-specific instance for each instance of the `Parameterized` class.

4. Yes. Create a specialized function for the particular instance. In addition to creating `Array<t>::SomeFunction()`, create `Array<int>::SomeFunction()` to change the behavior for integer arrays.

5. One static variable for each instance of the *class* is created.

Exercises

1. Here is the answer:

```
template <class Type>
class List
{

public:
      List():head(0),tail(0),theCount(0) { }
      virtual ~List();

      void insert( Type value );
      void append( Type value );
      int is_present( Type value ) const;
      int is_empty() const { return head == 0; }
      int count() const { return theCount; }

private:
      class ListCell
      {
      public:
          ListCell(Type value, ListCell *cell = 0):val(value),next(cell){}
          Type val;
          ListCell *next;
      };

      ListCell *head;
      ListCell *tail;
      int theCount;
};
```

2. Here is the answer:

```cpp
void List::insert(int value)
{
    ListCell *pt = new ListCell( value, head );
    assert (pt != 0);

    // this line added to handle tail
    if ( head == 0 ) tail = pt;

    head = pt;
    theCount++;
}

void List::append( int value )
{
    ListCell *pt = new ListCell( value );
    if ( head == 0 )
        head = pt;
    else
        tail->next = pt;

    tail = pt;
    theCount++;
}

int List::is_present( int value ) const
{
    if ( head == 0 ) return 0;
    if ( head->val == value || tail->val == value )
        return 1;

    ListCell *pt = head->next;
    for (; pt != tail; pt = pt->next)
        if ( pt->val == value )
            return 1;

    return 0;
}
```

3. Here is the answer:

```cpp
template <class Type>
List<Type>::~List()
{
    ListCell *pt = head;

    while ( pt )
    {
        ListCell *tmp = pt;
        pt = pt->next;
        delete tmp;
    }
    head = tail = 0;
}

template <class Type>
void List<Type>::insert(Type value)
```

```
    {
        ListCell *pt = new ListCell( value, head );
        assert (pt != 0);

        // this line added to handle tail
        if ( head == 0 ) tail = pt;

        head = pt;
        theCount++;
    }

    template <class Type>
    void List<Type>::append( Type value )
    {
        ListCell *pt = new ListCell( value );
        if ( head == 0 )
            head = pt;
        else
            tail->next = pt;

        tail = pt;
        theCount++;
    }

    template <class Type>
    int List<Type>::is_present( Type value ) const
    {
        if ( head == 0 ) return 0;
        if ( head->val == value ¦¦ tail->val == value )
            return 1;

        ListCell *pt = head->next;
        for (; pt != tail; pt = pt->next)
            if ( pt->val == value )
                return 1;

        return 0;
    }
```

4. Here is the answer:

```
List<String> string_list;
List<Window> Window_List;
List<int> int_List;
```

5. Window doesn't have operator == defined; all operations that compare the values in the List cells, such as is_present, will result in compiler errors. To reduce the chance of this, place abundant comments before the template definition stating what operations must be defined in order for the instatiation to compile.

6. Here is the answer:

```
friend int operator==( const Type& lhs, const Type& rhs );
```

7. Here is the answer:

```
template <class Type>
int List<Type>::operator==( const Type& lhs, const Type& rhs )
{
    // compare lengths first
    if ( lhs.theCount != rhs.theCount )
        return 0;      // lengths differ

    ListCell *lh = lhs.head;
    ListCell *rh = rhs.head;

    for(; lh != 0; lh = lh.next, rh = rh.next )
        if ( lh.value != rh.value )
            return 0;

    return 1;          // if they don't differ, they must match
}
```

8. Yes; because comparing the array involves comparing the elements, operator!= must be defined for the elements as well.

9. Here is the answer:

```
// template swap:
// must have assignment and the copy constructor defined for the Type.
template <class Type>
void swap( Type& lhs, Type& rhs)
{
    Type temp( lhs );
    lhs = rhs;
    rhs = temp;
}
```

Answers to Day 3, "Strings and Lists"

Quiz

1. A C-style string is an array of characters, terminated by the null character, which can be represented as '\0'.

2. Yes. A character array or char* is an array of signed integers of size char. It might contain a 0 in the middle, or any other integer value within the limits of the number of bits in an int. A C-style string is restricted to printable characters, and the first null terminates it even if the array has more space allocated beyond the null.

3. The iterate function in the list accepts a pointer to a member function of the objects held in the list, and then calls that function on every member of the list.

4. The node held by the list must be of the same type as the list. A list of notes therefore must have a note-node, and a list of cars must have a car-node.

5. To use the template unaltered, a class for which you plan to make a list must have an operator == and an operator <. Note that you still can use the template for classes without these methods if you replace the templates for Node<YourClass>::operator == and Node<YourClass>::operator <.

Exercises

1. Here is the answer:

```
1:        #include "list.hpp"
    2:        #include "string.hpp"
3:
4:        void main()
5:        {
6:            ULONG choice;
7:            char buffer[256];
8:            List<String> StringList;
9:
10:           while (1)
11:           {
12:               cout << "\n(0)Quit (1)Add String ";
13:               cin >> choice;
14:               if (!choice)
15:                   break;
16:
17:               cin.ignore(255,'\n');
18:               cout << "\nNew String: ";
19:               cin.getline(buffer,255);
20:               String * pString = new String(buffer);
21:               StringList.Insert(*pString);
22:           }
23:
24:           cout << "\n\nResults: \n" << endl;
25:
26:           cout << "Count is: " << StringList.GetCount() << endl;
27:
28:           for (ULONG i = 0; i < StringList.GetCount(); i++)
29:               cout << StringList[i] << endl;
30:       }
```

2. Here is the answer:

```
1:        #include "list.hpp"
2:        #include "string.hpp"
3:
4:        void main()
5:        {
6:            ULONG choice;
7:            char buffer[256];
8:            List<String> StringList;
9:
```

```
10:            while (1)
11:            {
12:               cout << "\n(0)Quit (1)Add String ";
13:               cin >> choice;
14:               if (!choice)
15:                  break;
16:
17:               cin.ignore(255,'\n');
18:               cout << "\nNew String: ";
19:               cin.getline(buffer,255);
20:               String * pString = new String(buffer);
21:               StringList.Insert(*pString);
22:            }
23:
24:            cout << "\n\nResults: \n" << endl;
25:
26:            cout << "Count is: " << StringList.GetCount() << endl;
27:
28:            for (ULONG i = 0; i < StringList.GetCount(); i++)
29:               cout << StringList[i] << endl;
30:
31:            while (1)
32:            {
33:               LONG index;
34:               cout << "\nEnter an index.  (Enter -1 to quit.) ";
35:               cin >> index;
36:               if (index == -1)
37:                  break;
38:
39:               if (index >= StringList.GetCount())
40:                  cout << "Ooops.  Too high.\n\n";
41:               else
42:                  cout  << StringList[index] << endl;
43:            }
44:        }
```

3. Here is the answer:

```
1:       #include <iostream.h>
2:       #include "String.hpp"
3:       #include <stdlib.h>
4:       typedef unsigned long ULONG
5:       typedef unsigned short USHORT
6:
7:          // *************** Node class ***********
8:          template <class T>
9:          class Node
10:         {
11:         public:
12:            Node (T*);
13:            ~Node();
14:            void InsertAfter(Node *);
15:            Node * GetNext() const             { return itsNext; }
16:            void SetNext(Node * next)          { itsNext = next; }
17:            T & GetObject() const              { return *itsObject; }
18:            BOOL operator<(const Node &rhs) const;
```

579

```
19:              BOOL operator==(const T& target) const;
20:
21:          private:
22:              T * itsObject;
23:              Node * itsNext;
24:          };
25:
26:          // *************** Object List ***********
27:          template <class T>
28:          class List
29:          {
30:          public:
31:              List();
32:              ~List();
33:              ULONG      GetCount() const { return itsCount; }
34:              void       Insert(T &);
35:
36:          // ********************************** Here's change #1 of 3
37:              void       Iterate(void (*f)(const T&));
38:
39:              T &        operator[](ULONG);
40:              T *        FindObject(const T& target );
41:
42:          private:
43:              Node<T>  itsHead;
44:              ULONG itsCount;
45:          };
46:
47:          // *** node implementations ****
48:
49:            template <class T>
50:            Node<T>::Node(T * pObject):
51:            itsObject(pObject),
52:            itsNext(0)
53:            {}
54:
55:            template <class T>
56:            Node<T>::~Node()
57:            {
58:               delete itsObject;
59:               itsObject = 0;
60:               delete itsNext;
61:               itsNext = 0;
62:            }
63:
64:            template <class T>
65:            void Node<T>::InsertAfter(Node* newNode)
66:            {
67:             newNode->SetNext(itsNext);
68:             itsNext=newNode;
69:            }
70:
71:            template <class T>
72:            BOOL Node<T>::operator<(const Node &rhs) const
73:            {
74:             return (*itsObject < rhs.GetObject());
```

```
75:              }
76:
77:              template <class T>
78:              BOOL Node<T>::operator==(const T& target) const
79:              {
80:                  return (*itsObject == target);
81:              }
82:
83:               // Implementations for Lists...
84:
85:              template<class T>
86:              List <T>::List():
87:                  itsCount(0),
88:                  itsHead(0)  // initialize head node to have no Object
89:                  {}
90:
91:              template<class T>
92:              List <T>::~List()
93:              {
94:              }
95:
96:              template<class T>
97:              T &  List<T>::operator[](ULONG offSet)
98:              {
99:                  if (offSet+1 > itsCount)
100:                     return itsHead.GetObject(); // error
101:
102:                 Node<T>* pNode = itsHead.GetNext();
103:
104:                 for (ULONG i=0;i<offSet; i++)
105:                     pNode = pNode->GetNext();
106:
107:                return   pNode->GetObject();
108:             }
109:
110:             template<class T>
111:             T*  List<T>::FindObject(const T& target )
112:             {
113:                 for (Node<T> * pNode = itsHead.GetNext();
114:                      pNode!=NULL;
115:                      pNode = pNode->GetNext()
116:                     )
117:                 {
118:                     if ( *pNode == target)
119:                         break;
120:                 }
121:                 if (pNode == NULL)
122:                     return 0;
123:                 else
124:                     return &(pNode->GetObject());
125:             }
126:
127:             template<class T>
128:             void List<T>::Insert(T & Object)
129:             {
```

```
130:                 Node<T> * NewNode = new Node<T>(&Object);
131:
132:                 for (Node<T> * pNode = &itsHead;;pNode = pNode->GetNext())
133:                 {
134:                     if (pNode->GetNext() == NULL || *NewNode < *(pNode-
                         >GetNext()) )
135:                     {
136:                         pNode->InsertAfter(NewNode);
137:                         itsCount++;
138:                         break;
139:                     }
140:                 }
141:             }
142:
143:     // ************************************* Here's change #2 of 3
144:         template<class T>
145:         void List<T>::Iterate(void (*func)(const T&) )
146:         {
147:             for (Node<T>* pNode = itsHead.GetNext();
148:                     pNode;
149:                     pNode=pNode->GetNext()
150:                 )
151:     // ************************************* Here's change #3 of 3
152:                     func(pNode->GetObject());
153:         }
```

4. Here is the answer:

```
1:          #include "03x3.hpp"
2:          #include <iostream.h>
3:          #include <string.h>
4:
5:
6:          void DisplayDouble(const double &);
7:
8:          void main()
9:          {
10:             List<double> DoubleList;
11:
12:             while (1)
13:             {
14:                 double d;
15:                 cout << "\nEnter a number.  ( Enter -1 to quit.) ";
16:                 cin >> d;
17:                 if (d == -1)
18:                     break;
19:
20:                 double * pDouble = new double(d);
21:                 DoubleList.Insert(*pDouble);
22:             }
23:
24:             cout << "\n\nResults: \n" << endl;
25:
26:             cout << "Count is: " << DoubleList.GetCount() << endl;
27:
28:             DoubleList.Iterate(DisplayDouble);
```

```
29:        }
30:
31:
32:        void DisplayDouble(const double &d)
33:        {
34:            cout << d << endl;
35:        }
```

5. Here is the answer:

```
1:        #include "list.hpp"
2:        #include "string.hpp"
3:
4:        class Text
5:        {
6:        public:
7:            Text() { }
8:            Text(const String & str) : itsString(str) { }
9:
10:           const String & GetString() const  {return itsString;}
11:
12:           BOOL IsEqualTo(const Text& rhs) const
13:                   {return itsString == rhs.GetString();}
14:
15:           BOOL IsLessThan(const Text& rhs) const
16:                   {return itsString < rhs.GetString();}
17:
18:           void Display() const;
19:
20:       private:
21:           String itsString;
22:       };
23:
24:       void Text::Display() const
25:       {
26:          cout << itsString << endl;
27:       }
28:
29:       BOOL Node<Text>::operator==(const Text& rhs) const
30:       {
31:          return itsObject->IsEqualTo(rhs);
32:       }
33:
34:       BOOL Node<Text>::operator<(const Node & rhsNode) const
35:       {
36:          return itsObject->IsLessThan(rhsNode.GetObject());
37:       }
38:
39:
40:        void main()
41:        {
42:           ULONG choice;
43:           char buffer[256];
44:           List<Text> TextList;
45:
46:           while (1)
```

```
47:        {
48:            cout << "\n(0)Quit (1)Add String ";
49:            cin >> choice;
50:            if (!choice)
51:                break;
52:
53:            cin.ignore(255,'\n');
54:            cout << "\nNew String: ";
55:            cin.getline(buffer,255);
56:            String str(buffer);
57:
58:            Text * pText = new Text(str);
59:            TextList.Insert(*pText);
60:        }
61:
62:        cout << "\n\nResults: \n" << endl;
63:
64:        cout << "Count is: " << TextList.GetCount() << endl;
65:
66:        TextList.Iterate(Text::Display);
67:    }
```

Answers to Day 4, "Sorting"

Quiz

1. For every slot in order, select from the remaining items the right item to be in this slot. Swap it with the item that is there now.

2. After you have selected an item to belong in the next slot, if it is the item that already is there, don't bother swapping it (with itself).

3. Insert each item into the correct spot in the sorted list that is to the left of the item. Each time an item is processed, this causes the sorted list to grow by one and the unsorted list to diminish by one, until the unsorted portion disappears.

4. Starting at the back of the list, bubble lower values forward by comparing adjacent values and swapping whenever the lower value is behind a higher value. Quit when you have gone through the entire list and have no swaps to perform.

5. Pick one value that you hope is near the middle of the values. Put all values that are lower than that value to its left, and all values that are higher than it to its right. Repeat the process for the group on the left, and again for the group on the right.

Exercises

1. Here is the answer:

```
1:    #include <iostream.h>
2:    #include <string.h>
3:
```

```
 4:        void Swap( char *Array, int index1, int index2);
 5:        void SelectionSort(char *Array);
 6:
 7:        int main()
 8:        {
 9:           char buffer[100];
10:           cout << "Enter up to 100 characters: ";
11:           cin.getline(buffer,100);
12:           cout << "Unsorted:\t" << buffer << endl;
13:           SelectionSort(buffer);
14:           cout << "Sorted:\t\t" << buffer << endl;
15:           return 0;
16:        }
17:
18:        // Read through each member of the array in turn
19:        // For every member, examine every remaining member and
20:        // swap with largest
21:        void SelectionSort(char *Array)
22:        {
23:           int ArrayLen = strlen(Array);
24:           for (int i = 0; i<ArrayLen; i++)
25:           {
26:              int max = i;
27:              for (int j = i+1; j< ArrayLen; j++)
28:                 if (Array[j] > Array[max])
29:                    max = j;
30:              Swap(Array,max,i);
31:           }
32:        }
33:
34:        void Swap( char *Array, int left, int right)
35:        {
36:           char tmp = Array[left];
37:           Array[left]=Array[right];
38:           Array[right]=tmp;
39:        }
```

2. Here is the answer:

```
 1:        #include <iostream.h>
 2:        #include <string.h>
 3:        #include <stdlib.h>
 4:
 5:        #include "string.hpp"
 6:
 7:        template <class T> void QuickSort(T*, int, int);
 8:        template <class T> void Swap(T& i, T& j);
 9:
10:        typedef unsigned long ULONG;
11:        // Ask for a buffer full of characters
12:        // Use the insertion sort to sort 'em
13:        int main()
14:        {
15:           ULONG *array[10];
16:           for (int i = 0; i < 10; i++)
17:           {
18:              array[i] = new ULONG;
```

```
19:             *array[i] = rand();
20:         }
21:
22:         cout << "\nUnsorted: "<< endl;
23:         for (i = 0; i < 9; i++)
24:             cout << *array[i] << ", ";
25:         cout << *array[9] << endl;
26:
27:         QuickSort(array,0,10);
28:
29:         cout << "\nSorted: "<< endl;
30:         for (i = 0; i < 9; i++)
31:             cout << *array[i] << ", ";
32:         cout << *array[9] << endl;
33:
34:         return 0;
35:     }
36:
37:     // Templatized QuickSort Function
38:     template <class T>
39:     void QuickSort(T* Input, int left, int right)
40:     {
41:         if (right > left)
42:         {
43:             T target = Input[right-1];
44:             int i = left-1;
45:             int x = right-1;
46:             for (;;)
47:             {
48:                 while (*Input[++i] < *target)
49:                     ;
50:                 while (*Input[--x] > *target)
51:                     ;
52:
53:                 if (i >= x)
54:                     break;
55:                 Swap(Input[i], Input[x]);
56:             }
57:
58:             Swap(Input[i], Input[right-1]);
59:             QuickSort(Input,left,i);
60:             QuickSort(Input,i+1,right);
61:
62:         }
63:     }
64:
65:     template <class T>
66:     inline void Swap(T& i, T& j)
67:     {
68:         T temp;
69:         temp = j;
70:         j = i;
71:         i = temp;
72:     }
```

3. Here is the answer:

```
1:      #include <iostream.h>
2:      #include <string.h>
3:      #include <stdlib.h>
4:      #include "string.hpp"
5:
6:      template <class T> void  SelectionSort(T*, int);
7:      template <class T> void Swap(T& i, T& j);
8:
9:      // Templatized QuickSort Function
10:
11:      template <class T>
12:      void SelectionSort(T* array, int howMany)
13:      {
14:
15:         for (int i = 0; i<howMany; i++)
16:         {
17:            int min = i;
18:            for (int j = i+1; j< howMany; j++)
19:               if (*array[j] < *array[min])
20:                  min = j;
21:            Swap(array[min],array[i]);
22:         }
23:      }
24:
25:      template <class T>
26:      inline void Swap(T& i, T& j)
27:      {
28:         T temp;
29:         temp = j;
30:         j = i;
31:         i = temp;
32:      }
```

4. Here is the answer:

```
1:      #include "04x3.cpp" // include previous answer
2:
3:      // Ask for a buffer full of characters
4:      // Use the insertion sort to sort 'em
5:      int main()
6:      {
7:         char buffer[100];
8:         String *pArray[5];
9:         for (int i = 0; i<5; i++)
10:        {
11:           cout << "Enter the string: ";
12:           cin.getline(buffer,100);
13:           pArray[i] = new String(buffer);
14:        }
15:
16:        cout << "\nUnsorted: "<< endl;
17:        for (i = 0; i < 4; i++)
18:           cout << *pArray[i] << ", ";
19:        cout << *pArray[4] << endl;
20:
```

```
21:          SelectionSort(pArray,5);
22:
23:          cout << "\nSorted: "<< endl;
24:          for (i = 0; i < 4; i++)
25:             cout << *pArray[i] << ", ";
26:          cout << *pArray[4] << endl;
27:
28:          int *intArray[10];
29:          for (i = 0; i < 10; i++)
30:          {
31:             intArray[i] = new int;
32:             *intArray[i] = rand();
33:          }
34:
35:          cout << "\nUnsorted: "<< endl;
36:          for (i = 0; i < 9; i++)
37:             cout << *intArray[i] << ", ";
38:          cout << *intArray[9] << endl;
39:
40:         SelectionSort(intArray,10);
41:
42:          cout << "\nSorted: "<< endl;
43:          for (i = 0; i < 9; i++)
44:             cout << *intArray[i] << ", ";
45:          cout << *intArray[9] << endl;
46:
47:          return 0;
48:     }
```

Answers to Chapter 5, "Design"

Quiz

1. A good design is flexible and extensible, but not at the expense of being so general as to be insupportably complex. A good design adjusts to a changing specification, but still exhibits high performance and good reliability.

2. These are the major steps:

   ☐ Figure out what sort of program it is

   ☐ Write a functional specification—enough that you can understand the problem domain and the range of operations that will be applied to it

   ☐ Analysis and Design. Produce a technical specification

   ☐ Implementation

   ☐ Test

   The important thing to remember is that this process is not linear. At each step, you may find yourself backing up to the earlier steps. After testing your first, minimal

implementation, you will go back to analysis and design to redesign parts of it and to design more of it.

3. Start by identifying the initial core classes—the objects that will be needed for a minimally working implementation.

4. The rNote class is a note that the user writes. The entire purpose of ROBIN is to collect these notes and retrieve them as needed. The rNote actually is an abstract class; each actual instance of a note will be an rInternalNote or an rFileNote.

5. The rWord class is an entry in the index. It contains a word that appears in at least one note, as well as a list of all the rNotes in which that word appears. When you add a new note to the ROBIN database, you will add a new reference for all the words in the note that already were in the index (because they also appear in some other note), and you will add a new rWord object for every word that appears for the first time in this new note.

6. An rHit is the association between an rWord and an rNote. Every rWord object contains a list of rHit objects—one for every note that contains this word. The rHit object contains not only a reference to an rNote, but also the number of times the word appears in the note.

Exercises

Because this is an analysis and design chapter, the exercises are an attempt to give you some practice with these skills. Remember as you do these that there are many right answers (but many more wrong answers) to every design question. Your designs might not agree with these answers, but they still may be "right." If your design decisions differ from these decisions, you should ask yourself whether your result is as flexible and extensible as the answers provided, and try to understand why or why not.

Unlike the usual policy for quiz and exercise problems, you should look at the answer to each exercise before going on to the next exercise, because some of the exercises build from the provided solutions to the previous exercises. A successive question might not make sense at all when applied to your design.

1. Your system will need to allow users to create, delete, send, and receive mail messages. Your users will want to maintain lists of the messages they have sent and received. They may want to create their own lists, where they can categorize their mail messages.

   The users will need to address the mail messages, so they will need to be able to access a list of all the users that are available.

   The users also will want to have mailing lists, which they can create, edit, and delete. Of course, they will want to be able to address mail to mailing lists as well as to other

users. The mailing lists should be able to reference other mailing lists as well as users.

All this information needs to be stored somewhere, and the mail messages have to be transported from user to user (unless they are all on one big mainframe). In any case, for the rest of these exercises, ignore both the storage and transport issues. Pretend that it all just stays in memory on one computer that all users can access.

Finally, there are system administrator operations. Users must be added to and removed from the system, and system-wide mailing lists must be maintained.

Users also will need to log in and log out, which will require them to enter their passwords.

2. User, MailMessage, and MailingList are the three most important classes. You also might have SystemAdministrator, but there is a good case for just putting a SecurityLevel property in User. (Use the latter technique, at least for now.)

You also might have a class EmailSystem, which will contain the global information. This seems much cleaner than just having each bit of global information (like the list of users) hanging loose as a global variable, so do it. (This has another benefit beyond just seeming cleaner. If you were to start worrying about the storage of the information, you would need some object that is capable of being persistent to contain this global information.)

There also are lists of Users, lists of MailMessages, and lists of MailingLists, but you don't need to consider these lists to be separate classes (even though they are) because you have templates for these, making them seem more like primitive types.

3. User: Name, Password, SecurityLevel, Incoming (list of messages), Sent (list of messages), Drafts (list of messages), and a list of mailing lists.

MailMessage: Title, Body, the From field, and the To field. From might be a reference to a User object (User&), or it might just be the text of the User's name (the one sending the MailMessage). The To field might be a list of User&s and MailingList&s, or maybe it is just text of their names, which has to be parsed out when the message is sent.

MailingList: Name and a To field just like the one in MailMessage.

EmailSystem: The master list of Users and the master list of globally available MailingLists.

4. You could pull out of User and MailingList the abstract concept of being an addressee. It would have a name, and it would be able to accept a MailMessage sent to it. This would be a pure virtual function, which would have different implementations in the two subclasses (User and MailingList).

User::AcceptMail would stick the new MailMessage into the User's incoming mail list.

MailingList::AcceptMail would call AcceptMail with the message on all of the Addressee's that are contained inside the MailingList.

5. Addressee: Name. Virtual method AcceptMail defined.

   User (superclass Addressee): Password, SecurityLevel, Incoming (list of messages), Sent (list of messages), Drafts (list of messages), and a list of mailing lists.

   MailMessage: Title, Body, From (User&), and To (list of Addressee&s).

   MailingList (superclass Addressee): To (list of Addressee&s).

   EmailSystem: The master list of Users and the master list of globally available MailingLists.

   Note that User and MailingList no longer have the data member Name. This is because they both inherit the property from their common parent, Addressee.

Answers to Day 6, "Command-Line Processing and the Environment"

Quiz

1. Here are the four legal ways to declare the function `main()`:

   ```
   int main()
   int main(int argc)
   int main(int argc, char** argv)
   int main(int argc, char** argv, char** env)
   ```

   (Note that you could replace any of the `char **X` declarations with `char *X[]` without changing anything. The two are exactly the same type.)

2. You can declare `main()` with all three arguments, as in question 1, or you can use the function `getenv()`.

3. `argc` will contain the value 3.

4. The name of the program. On almost all operating systems, the name is expanded out to include the full pathname and extension.

Exercises

1. Write the smallest program you can in which `main()` takes no parameters, and in which you print the environment variables:

   ```
   1:     #include <stdlib.h>
   2:     #include <string.h>
   3:     #include <iostreams.h>
   4:
   5:      /* putenv example */
   6:
   7:     #include <stdio.h>
   ```

```
8:      #include <stdlib.h>
9:      #include <alloc.h>
10:     #include <string.h>
11:     #include <dos.h>
12:
13:     int main()
14:     {
15:       int i = 0;
16:       while (_environ[i])
17:             cout << _environ[i++] << endl;
18:        return 0;
19:     }
```

2. Here is the answer:

```
1:      #include <stdlib.h>
2:      #include <string.h>
3:      #include <iostreams.h>
4:
5:        int main(int argc, char **argv)
6:      {
7:         char buffer[100];
8:         int i=0;
9:
10:        strcpy(buffer,"SELF=");
11:        strcat(buffer,argv[0]);
12:        putenv(buffer);
13:        cout << "Displaying..." << endl;
14:        while (_environ[i])
15:          cout << _environ[i++] << endl;
16:
17:        return 0;
18:     }
```

3. The result of the call to getenv() is a pointer to the environment variable. You have not allocated space for this array of characters and therefore can not extend it using strcat, as is done in line 25. This almost certainly will crash your computer, because random memory will be written over with the new string.

Answers to Day 7, "Complex Data Structures"

Quiz

1. A hashing algorithm is the algorithm used to determine the appropriate bucket for a given key.

2. A leaf node is a node at the very end of the tree. Any node with no children is considered to be a leaf.

3. Here is the answer:

Level	Maximum Nodes
1	1
2	3
3	7
4	15
5	31
6	63
7	127
8	255
9	511
10	1023

4. Exactly half, rounded up.

5. The very next successor. It is the leftmost node of the right subtree. It always will be either a leaf or a node with only a right child, so it easily is removed from its current spot.

Exercises

1. If the string is 0 or 1 character long, then this algorithm XORs in an essentially random number (s[2]). If any given key doesn't evaluate to the same hash number, the algorithm is broken.

2. Hash Table: The first class would be the hash table itself. You should make this a class in order to encapsulate its operation and to provide a clean interface.

   PageReference: This class would contain the pair, long PageID, and void * PageAddress. It will need compare operators, which really compare the PageID values.

   List<PageReference>: One for each bucket.

   Node<PageReference>: Created automatically inside List<PageReference>.

3. You might have a different solution and still be correct, as long as you considered these two factors:

   ☐ The PageIDs are positions in the file. This probably will be used on complete disk pages, for efficiency, so the values for PageID will be evenly divisible by the size of a disk sector (typically 128, 256, 512, or 1024). This means that the low byte of the PageID usually will be all zeros, so you cannot count on variation in the low byte to cause your even distribution.

☐ On the other hand, your data files probably will not grow to be more than a couple of hundred megabytes or so. This means that the top 4 bits of your PageID usually will be 0.

The conclusion is that the second lowest byte varies well through the range, although with the larger disk sector sizes, its lowest couple of bits always might be 0. Because your target for the hash is 0 to 127, you can drop the lowest bit of this byte by shifting it right once. The next byte changes frequently as well, as the file size ranges from 1 to 16 megabytes. Because its low bits vary well, you don't want to lose them by shifting.

One algorithm is to XOR together the two middle bytes, shifting the lower of the two to the right first. Because you have to shift to get the bytes anyway, do it all at once. (Other techniques—tricks with pointers—are faster but generally are non-portable.)

UUUU UUUU   UXXX XXXX   YYYY YYYU   UUUU UUUU

If these are the bits of the long (most significant on the left), the algorithm ends up with the X bits XORed with the Y bits. The U bits are unused. This algorithm will spread out the expected values across the range, and it is lightning fast:

```
inline int HashingAlgorithm(long ul)
{return int (((ul >> 16) ^ (ul >> 9)) & 0x7F);}
```

4. Here is the answer:

```
1:      #include "stdef.hpp"
2:
3:      template <class T> class BinaryNode;    // Forward reference
4:
5:      template <class T>
6:      class BinaryTree
7:      {
8:      public:
9:          BinaryTree():myHead(0),myCount(0){}
10:         ~BinaryTree(){}
11:         long GetCount() const { return myCount; }
12:
13:         void Insert (const T& t);
14:
15:         // Returns TRUE if found and deleted.
16:         BOOL Delete (const T& t);
17:
18:         void Iterate(void (*f)(const T&, int depth));
19:
20:     private:
21:         BinaryNode<T> * myHead;
22:         long myCount;
23:     };
24:
25:     template <class T>
26:     class BinaryNode
27:     {
28:     public:
29:         BinaryNode(const T &);
30:         ~BinaryNode() {}
```

```
31:         const T & GetValue()  { return myValue; }
32:         void SetValue(const T& val) { myValue = val;}
33:
34:         BinaryNode<T>* GetSmaller() const   { return mySmaller;  }
35:         BinaryNode<T>* GetBigger() const       { return myBigger; }
36:
37:
38:         BinaryNode<T> * Insert(const T&);
39:         static void ProcessDuplicateValue(const T& newValue, T&
            existingValue);
40:         BinaryNode<T> * Delete(const T&, BOOL & DidDelete);
41:
42:         void SetSmaller(BinaryNode* target) { mySmaller = target; }
43:         void SetBigger(BinaryNode* target)  { myBigger = target; }
44:
45:         BOOL operator>(const T& rhs) const;
46:         BOOL operator==(const T& rhs) const;
47:
48:         void Iterate(void (*f)(const T&, int depth), int depth);
49:
50:     private:
51:         BinaryNode<T> * mySmaller;
52:         BinaryNode<T> * myBigger;
53:         T myValue;
54:     };
55:
56:
57:     template <class T>
58:     BinaryNode<T>::BinaryNode(const T& t):
59:         mySmaller(0),
60:         myBigger(0),
61:         myValue(t)
62:     {  }
63:
64:     template <class T>
65:     BinaryNode<T> * BinaryNode<T>::Insert(const T& t)
66:     {
67:         if (*this == t)
68:             ProcessDuplicateValue(t, myValue);
69:         else if (*this > t)
70:         {
71:             if (mySmaller != 0)
72:                 mySmaller = mySmaller->Insert(t);
73:             else
74:                 mySmaller = new BinaryNode<T>(t);
75:         }
76:         else
77:         {
78:             if (myBigger != 0)
79:                 myBigger = myBigger->Insert(t);
80:             else
81:                 myBigger = new BinaryNode<T>(t);
82:         }
83:
84:         return this;
85:     }
86:
```

595

```
87:     // The default duplicate processing is not to do anything.
88:     // The client can override this method to do whatever is
89:     // appropriate for the type.
90:     template <class T>
91:     void BinaryNode<T>::ProcessDuplicateValue(const T& , T& )
92:     {
93:     }
94:
95:     template <class T>
96:     BinaryNode<T> * BinaryNode<T>::Delete(const T& t, BOOL & DidDelete)
97:     {
98:        if (*this == t)
99:        {
100:           // This is the one to remove.  It might be a leaf,
101:           // a single parent, or a double parent.
102:           if (mySmaller == 0)        // leaf or one type of single parent
103:           {
104:              // if myBigger == 0, return 0 anyway.
105:              BinaryNode<T> * retval = myBigger;
106:              DidDelete = TRUE;
107:              delete this;   // Dangerous!  Must return immediately.
108:              return retval;
109:           }
110:           else if (myBigger == 0)        // other type of single parent
111:           {
112:              BinaryNode<T> * retval = mySmaller;
113:              DidDelete = TRUE;
114:              delete this;   // Dangerous!  Must return immediately.
115:              return retval;
116:           }
117:           else           // Double parent
118:           {
119:              // Find the Node with the lowest value on
120:              // my Bigger subtree.  Remove him and put him in my place
121:              BinaryNode<T> * smallest = myBigger;
122:              BinaryNode<T> * hisparent = 0;
123:              while (smallest->GetSmaller() != 0)
124:              {
125:                 hisparent = smallest;
126:                 smallest = smallest->GetSmaller();
127:              }
128:
129:              // Remove him gracefully and put him in our place.
130:              // Watch out for the case where he is our child.
131:              if (hisparent != 0)    // not our immediate child.
132:              {
133:                 hisparent->SetSmaller(smallest->GetBigger());
134:                 smallest->SetBigger(myBigger);
135:              }
136:
137:              smallest->SetSmaller(mySmaller);
138:
139:              DidDelete = TRUE;
140:              delete this;   // Dangerous!  Must return immediately.
141:              return smallest;
142:           }
```

```
143:        } // end if (*this == t)
144:        else if (*this > t)
145:        {
146:           if (mySmaller != 0)
147:              mySmaller = mySmaller->Delete(t, DidDelete);
148:           return this;
149:        }
150:        else
151:        {
152:           if (myBigger != 0)
153:              myBigger = myBigger->Delete(t, DidDelete);
154:           return this;
155:        }
156:     }
157:
158:     // Client can override comparison operators if he wants
159:     // to use some other technique for comparing.
160:     template <class T>
161:     BOOL BinaryNode<T>::operator>(const T &rhs) const
162:     {
163:        return BOOL(myValue > rhs);
164:     }
165:
166:     template <class T>
167:     BOOL BinaryNode<T>::operator==(const T &rhs) const
168:     {
169:        return BOOL(myValue == rhs);
170:     }
171:
172:
173:     template <class T>
174:     void BinaryNode<T>::Iterate(void (*f)(const T&, int depth), int depth)
175:     {
176:        if (mySmaller != 0)
177:           mySmaller->Iterate(f, depth+1);
178:
179:        f(myValue, depth);
180:
181:        if (myBigger != 0)
182:           myBigger->Iterate(f, depth+1);
183:     }
184:
185:     template <class T>
186:     void BinaryTree<T>::Insert(const T& t)
187:     {
188:        if (myHead == 0)
189:           myHead = new BinaryNode<T>(t);
190:        else
191:           myHead = myHead->Insert(t);
192:
193:        myCount++;
194:     }
195:
196:
197:     template <class T>
198:     BOOL BinaryTree<T>::Delete(const T& t)
```

```
199:    {
200:       BOOL DidDelete = FALSE;
201:
202:       if (myHead != 0)
203:           myHead = myHead->Delete(t, DidDelete);
204:
205:       if (DidDelete)
206:           myCount--;
207:
208:       return DidDelete;
209:    }
210:
211:    template <class T>
212:    void BinaryTree<T>::Iterate(void (*f)(const T&, int depth))
213:    {
214:       if (myHead != 0)
215:           myHead->Iterate(f, 1);
216:    }
217:
218:
219:     #include "string.hpp"
220:
221:    // Function to be passed to BinaryTree<String>::Iterate
222:    void Display(const String & s, int depth)
223:    {
224:       for ( ;depth > 0; depth--)
225:           cout << "      ";
226:       cout << s << endl;
227:    }
228:
229:    // For my BinaryTree<String>::Insert, I want a message displayed
230:    // anytime a duplicate is found when attempting to insert.
231:    // So I can override this template function.
232:    void BinaryNode<String>::ProcessDuplicateValue(const String& s,
        String&)
233:    {
234:       cout << "\nDuplicate: " << s << "\n\n";
235:    }
236:
237:
238:    // Utility function used below.
239:    void ShowTree( BinaryTree<String> & tree )
240:    {
241:        cout << "\n\nResults: \n" << endl;
242:        cout << "Count is: " << tree.GetCount() << endl;
243:        tree.Iterate(Display);
244:        cout << "\n\n" ;
245:    }
```

5. Here is the answer:

```
1:      void main()
2:       {
3:          char buffer[256];
4:          BinaryTree<String> StringList;
5:          static String ShowString("show");
6:
```

```
 7:            while (1)
 8:            {
 9:                cout << "New String: ";
10:                cin.getline(buffer,255);
11:                String str(buffer);
12:
13:                if (buffer[0] == '\0')
14:                    break;
15:
16:                if (str == ShowString)
17:                    {
18:                    ShowTree(StringList);
19:                    continue;
20:                    }
21:
22:                StringList.Insert(str);
23:            }
24:
25:            ShowTree(StringList);
26:
27:            while (1)
28:            {
29:                cout << "String to Delete: ";
30:                cin.getline(buffer,255);
31:                String str(buffer);
32:
33:                if (buffer[0] == '\0')
34:                    break;
35:
36:                if (str == ShowString)
37:                    {
38:                    ShowTree(StringList);
39:                    continue;
40:                    }
41:
42:                if (!StringList.Delete(str))
43:                    cout << "Not Found\n\n";
44:            }
45:
46:            StringList.Iterate(Display);
47:        }
```

Answers to Day 8, "Advanced Data Structures"

Quiz

1. FIFO stands for *First In, First Out.*

    LIFO stands for *Last In, First Out.*

    A LIFO queue usually is called a *stack.*

2. Put the head node in the FIFO. Until there are no more nodes in the FIFO, remove the first node from the FIFO, push its children (if it has any) onto the FIFO, and finally process the node (print it, for example).

3. By keeping every node balanced. At every node, you could measure the depth of its two subtrees (measuring to the deepest node in the subtree), and the depths would never differ by more than one. Rebalancing operations might happen after every insert and every delete.

Exercises

1. Here is the answer:

```
1:    // *************************************************
2:    // PROGRAM:   FIFO queue header
3:    // FILE:      08x01.hpp
4:    // PURPOSE:   provide first in first out queue
5:    // NOTES:
6:    // AUTHOR:    Jesse Liberty (jl)
7:    // REVISIONS: 10/24/94 1.0 jl   initial release
8:    //            11/09/94 1.1 jl   Keeps track of tail
9:    // *************************************************
10:
11:    template <class T>
12:    class Node
13:    {
14:    public:
15:        Node (T*);
16:        ~Node();
17:        void InsertAfter(Node *);
18:        Node * GetNext() const        { return itsNext; }
19:        void SetNext(Node * next)      { itsNext = next; }
20:        T* GetObject() const         { return itsObject; }
21:
22:    private:
23:        T * itsObject;
24:        Node * itsNext;
25:    };
26:
27:    template <class T>
28:    class Queue
29:    {
30:      public:
31:        Queue();
32:        ~Queue();
33:        void        Push(T &);
34:        T*          Pop();
35:
36:      private:
37:        Node<T>  itsHead;
38:        Node<T> * itsTailp;        // Added V1.1
39:    };
```

```
1:     // *****************************************************
2:     // PROGRAM:   FIFO queue implementation
3:     // FILE:      08x01.cpp
4:     // PURPOSE:   provide first in first out queue
5:     // NOTES:
6:     // AUTHOR:    Jesse Liberty (jl)
7:     // REVISIONS: 10/24/94 1.0 jl   initial release
8:     //            11/09/94 1.1 jl   Keeps track of tail
9:     // *****************************************************
10:
11:    #include "08x01.hpp"
12:    template <class T>
13:    Node<T>::Node(T * pObject):
14:    itsObject(pObject),
15:    itsNext(0)
16:    {}
17:
18:     template <class T>
19:     Node<T>::~Node()
20:    {
21:       itsObject = 0;
22:       itsNext = 0;
23:    }
24:
25:     template <class T>
26:     void Node<T>::InsertAfter(Node* newNode)
27:    {
28:     newNode->SetNext(itsNext);
29:     itsNext=newNode;
30:    }
31:
32:    template<class T>
33:    Queue <T>::Queue():
34:       itsHead(0),           // initialize head node to have no Object
35:       itsTailp(&itsHead)  // initial Tail is just the head    V1.1
36:       {}
37:
38:    template<class T>
39:    Queue <T>::~Queue()
40:    {
41:    }
42:
43:    template<class T>
44:    void Queue<T>::Push(T & Object)
45:    {
46:        Node<T> * oldTailp = itsTailp;
47:        itsTailp = new Node<T>(&Object);
48:
49:        oldTailp->InsertAfter(itsTailp);    // Changed, V1.1
50:    }
51:
52:    template<class T>
53:    T* Queue<T>::Pop()
54:    {
55:       Node<T> * first = itsHead.GetNext();
56:       Node<T> * second = first->GetNext();
57:       if (first)
```

```
58:              {
59:                  T* object = first->GetObject();
60:                  if (second)
61:                      itsHead.SetNext(second);
62:                  else
63:                      {
64:                      itsHead.SetNext(0);
65:                      itsTailp = &itsHead;        // If empty, point tail at head.
                                                         V1.1
66:                      }
67:                  delete first;
68:                  return object;
69:              }
70:              else
71:                  return 0;
72:          }
73:
74:
75:
76:     #include "word.hpp"
77:
78:
79:     int main(int argc, char **argv)
80:     {
81:         Queue<rWord> myQueue;
82:
83:         for (int i = 1; i< argc; i++)
84:         {
85:             rWord* word = new rWord(argv[i]);
86:             myQueue.Push(*word);
87:         }
88:
89:         for (i = 1; i< argc; i++)
90:             cout << myQueue.Pop()->GetText()<< "\n";
91:
92:         return 0;
93:     }
```

2. Here is the answer:

```
1:      // **************************************************
2:      // PROGRAM:   queue header
3:      // FILE:      queue.hpp
4:      // PURPOSE:   provide generic queue
5:      // NOTES:
6:      // AUTHOR:    Jesse Liberty (jl)
7:      // REVISIONS:    10/24/94 1.0 jl    initial release
8:      //               11/09/94 1.1 jl    keep track of tail
9:      //               11/09/94  1.2 jl   generic queue
10:     // **************************************************
11:
12:        template <class T>
13:        class Node
14:        {
15:        public:
16:           Node (T*);
17:           ~Node();
18:           void InsertAfter(Node *);
```

```
19:            Node * GetNext() const          { return itsNext; }
20:            void SetNext(Node * next)         { itsNext = next; }
21:            T* GetObject() const           { return itsObject; }
22:
23:        private:
24:           T * itsObject;
25:           Node * itsNext;
26:        };
27:
28:     template <class T>
29:     class Queue
30:     {
31:        public:
32:           Queue();
33:           ~Queue();
34:
35:           void       InsertFront(T &);
36:           void       InsertBack(T &);
37:           T*           RemoveFront();
38:           T*           RemoveBack();
39:
40:        private:
41:           Node<T>  itsHead;
42:           Node<T> * itsTailp;        // Added V1.1
43:        };
```

3. Here is the answer:

```
1:      #include "stdef.hpp"
2:      #include "08x02.hpp"
3:
4:         template <class T>
5:         Node<T>::Node(T * pObject):
6:         itsObject(pObject),
7:         itsNext(0)
8:         {}
9:
10:         template <class T>
11:         Node<T>::~Node()
12:         {
13:            itsObject = 0;
14:            itsNext = 0;
15:         }
16:
17:         template <class T>
18:         void Node<T>::InsertAfter(Node* newNode)
19:         {
20:          newNode->SetNext(itsNext);
21:          itsNext=newNode;
22:         }
23:
24:         template<class T>
25:         Queue <T>::Queue():
26:            itsHead(0),              // initialize head node to have no Object
27:            itsTailp(&itsHead)  // initial Tail is just the head    V1.1
28:            {}
29:
30:         template<class T>
```

603

```
31:         Queue <T>::~Queue()
32:         {
33:         }
34:
35:         template<class T>
36:         void Queue<T>::InsertFront(T & Object)
37:         {
38:             Node<T> * newNode = new Node<T>(&Object);
39:
40:             itsHead.InsertAfter(newNode);
41:
42:             if (itsTailp == &itsHead)
43:                 itsTailp = newNode;
44:         }
45:
46:         template<class T>
47:         void Queue<T>::InsertBack(T & Object)
48:         {
49:             Node<T> * oldTailp = itsTailp;
50:             itsTailp = new Node<T>(&Object);
51:
52:             oldTailp->InsertAfter(itsTailp);
53:         }
54:
55:         template<class T>
56:         T* Queue<T>::RemoveFront()
57:         {
58:            Node<T> * first = itsHead.GetNext();
59:            Node<T> * second = first->GetNext();
60:            if (first)
61:            {
62:                T* object = first->GetObject();
63:                if (second)
64:                    itsHead.SetNext(second);
65:                else
66:                    {
67:                    itsHead.SetNext(0);
68:                    itsTailp = &itsHead;          // If empty, point tail at head.
                                                     V1.1
69:                    }
70:                delete first;
71:                return object;
72:            }
73:            else
74:                return 0;
75:         }
76:
77:         template<class T>
78:         T* Queue<T>::RemoveBack()
79:         {
80:            if (itsHead.GetNext())
81:            {
82:                // Find the second to last one.
83:                for (Node<T> * penultimatep = &itsHead;
84:                     penultimatep->GetNext() != itsTailp;
85:                     penultimatep = penultimatep->GetNext())
86:                   ;
87:
```

```
88:                Node<T> * oldTailp = itsTailp;
89:                itsTailp = penultimatep;        // This might be itsHead, which
                                                    is OK
90:                itsTailp->SetNext(0);
91:
92:                T* object = itsTailp->GetObject();
93:                delete oldTailp;
94:                return object;
95:            }
96:          else
97:              return 0;
98:        }
99:
100:
101:
102:    #include "string.hpp"
103:
104:    int main()
105:    {
106:        long choice;
107:        char buffer[256];
108:        Queue<String> myQueue;
109:
110:        while (1)
111:        {
112:            cout << "\n(0)Quit (1)Add front  (2) Add back  (3) Remove
                Front  (4) Remove Back   ";
113:            cin >> choice;
114:            if (!choice)
115:                break;
116:
117:            switch (choice)
118:            {
119:                case 1:
120:                    {
121:                    cin.ignore(255,'\n');
122:                    cout << "New String: ";
123:                    cin.getline(buffer,255);
124:                    String *sp = new String(buffer);
125:
126:                    myQueue.InsertFront(*sp);
127:                    }
128:                    break;
129:                case 2:
130:                    {
131:                    cin.ignore(255,'\n');
132:                    cout << "New String: ";
133:                    cin.getline(buffer,255);
134:                    String *sp = new String(buffer);
135:
136:                    myQueue.InsertBack(*sp);
137:                    }
138:                    break;
139:                case 3:
140:                    {
141:                    String * sp = myQueue.RemoveFront();
```

```
142:                    if (sp)
143:                        {
144:                        cout <<  *sp << '\n';
145:                        delete sp;
146:                        }
147:                    else
148:                        cout << "Queue was empty\n";
149:                    }
150:                    break;
151:                case 4:
152:                    {
153:                    String * sp = myQueue.RemoveFront();
154:                    if (sp)
155:                        {
156:                        cout <<  *sp << '\n';
157:                        delete sp;
158:                        }
159:                    else
160:                        cout << "Queue was empty\n";
161:                    }
162:                    break;
163:                default:
164:                    break;
165:            }
166:        }
167:
168:
169:     return 0;
170:    }
```

4. Here is the answer:

```
1:    int main()
2:    {
3:        long choice;
4:        Queue<float> myQueue;
5:
6:        while (1)
7:        {
8:            cout << "\n(0)Quit (1)Add front  (2) Add back  3) Remove Front
             (4) Remove Back  ";
9:            cin >> choice;
10:           if (!choice)
11:               break;
12:
13:           switch (choice)
14:           {
15:               case 1:
16:                   {
17:                   cout << "New float: ";
18:                   float *sp = new float;
19:                   cin >> *sp;
20:
21:                   myQueue.InsertFront(*sp);
22:                   }
23:                   break;
24:               case 2:
```

```
25:                            {
26:                                cout << "New float: ";
27:                                float *sp = new float;
28:                                cin >> *sp;
29:
30:                                myQueue.InsertBack(*sp);
31:                            }
32:                            break;
33:                        case 3:
34:                            {
35:                                float * sp = myQueue.RemoveFront();
36:                                if (sp)
37:                                    {
38:                                        cout <<  *sp << '\n';
39:                                        delete sp;
40:                                    }
41:                                else
42:                                    cout << "Queue was empty\n";
43:                            }
44:                            break;
45:                        case 4:
46:                            {
47:                                float * sp = myQueue.RemoveFront();
48:                                if (sp)
49:                                    {
50:                                        cout <<  *sp << '\n';
51:                                        delete sp;
52:                                    }
53:                                else
54:                                    cout << "Queue was empty\n";
55:                            }
56:                            break;
57:                        default:
58:                            break;
59:                }
60:            }
61:
62:
63:        return 0;
64:    }
```

5. Here is the answer:

```
1:      #include "stdef.hpp"
2:      #include "08x02.cpp"
3:
4:      template <class T>
5:      class Stack : private Queue<T>
6:      {
7:        public:
8:          Stack() : Queue<T>() { }
9:          ~Stack() { }
10:
11:          void        Push(T & t)      {Queue<T>::InsertFront(t);}
12:          T*          Pop()            {return Queue<T>::RemoveFront();}
13:      };
```

Answers to Day 9, "Writing to Disk"

Quiz

1. Reading in fixed-size records is much easier, because you know how many bytes off the disk you are going to need. Also, the allocation, deallocation, and reallocation of the disk space is much easier, because you know that any record will fit into the space left empty by a deleted record.

   On the other hand, if your data has wide variations in size, then forcing it into a fixed size will be very wasteful. Consider the notes in ROBIN; one might be a couple of paragraphs, while most are just a short sentence. In order to use strictly fixed-size records, you would have to allocate a huge amount of space for every record, or you would have to limit the note size to something uncomfortably small.

2. Object persistence includes enough information to bring the objects back into existence, with all the interconnections that they used to have. Data persistence is something less, where the data can be retrieved but the objects cannot really be re-created.

3. The `Writer` class encapsulates the operations of writing the different data types to disk. With the process completely encapsulated, you will be free to change the way it works internally without having to change any of the classes that use it.

4. All the classes that will be capable of being written to disk must descend from the `Storable` class. So far, this class only defines the operations of reading and writing, but it will become more important when you are trying to write different types of records to the same file. It will define the techniques you can use to recognize the type of the record and re-create it. Also, it will enable you to be able to have one *storable* object (an object that is an instantiation of any subclass of storable) refer to another storable object.

5. First, the class must descend from the `Storable` class. Second, it must declare a constructor that accepts a reference to a reader, and it must declare a write method that accepts a reference to a writer. As you add more capabilities and features of storable, there may be more that you have to do.

Exercises

1. This answer requires a minor modification to the `String` class, whose header and implementation follow. The other classes are storable and person, followed by a `Driver` class.

```
1:     // **************************************************
2:     // PROGRAM:  String declaration
```

```
3:      // FILE:     string.hpp
4:      // PURPOSE:  provide fundamental string functionality
5:      // NOTES:
6:      // AUTHOR:   Jesse Liberty (jl)
7:      // REVISIONS: 10/23/94 1.0 jl  initial release
8:      // ***************************************************
9:
10:     #ifndef STRING_HPP
11:     #define STRING_HPP
12:     #include <string.h>
13:     #include "stdef.hpp"
14:     #include "storable.hpp"
15:
16:     class xOutOfBounds {};
17:
18:     class String : public Storable
19:     {
20:     public:
21:
22:             // constructors
23:             String();
24:             String(const char *);
25:             String (const char *, LONG length);
26:             String (const String&);
27:             String(istream& iff);
28:             String(Reader&);
29:             String(ScreenReader&);
30:
31:             ~String();
32:
33:             // helpers and manipulators
34:             LONG  GetLength() const { return itsLen; }
35:             BOOL IsEmpty() const { return (BOOL) (itsLen == 0); }
36:             void Clear();                    // set string to 0 length
37:
38:             // accessors
39:             char operator[](LONG offset) const;
40:             char& operator[](LONG offset);
41:             const char * GetString()const  { return itsCString; }
42:
43:             // casting operators
44:              operator const char* () const { return itsCString; }
45:              operator char* () { return itsCString;}
46:
47:             // operators
48:             const String& operator=(const String&);
49:             const String& operator=(const char *);
50:
51:             void operator+=(const String&);
52:             void operator+=(char);
53:             void operator+=(const char*);
54:
55:             BOOL operator<(const String& rhs)const;
56:             BOOL operator>(const String& rhs)const;
57:             BOOL operator<=(const String& rhs)const;
58:             BOOL operator>=(const String& rhs)const;
```

```
59:            BOOL operator==(const String& rhs)const;
60:            BOOL operator!=(const String& rhs)const;
61:
62:
63:            // friend functions
64:            String operator+(const String&);
65:            String operator+(const char*);
66:            String operator+(char);
67:
68:            void Display()const { cout << itsCString << " "; }
69:            friend ostream& operator<< (ostream&, const String&);
70:            ostream& operator() (ostream&);
71:            void Write(Writer&);
72:            void Write(ScreenWriter&);
73:
74:     private:
75:            // returns 0 if same, -1 if this is less than argument,
76:            // 1 if this is greater than argument
77:            LONG StringCompare(const String&) const;  // used by Boolean
                                                              operators
78:            char * itsCString;
79:            LONG itsLen;
80:     };
81:
82:
83:     #endif // end inclusion guard

1:     #include "string.hpp"
2:      // default constructor creates string of 0 bytes
3:     String::String()
4:     {
5:        itsCString = new char[1];
6:        itsCString[0] = '\0';
7:        itsLen=0;
8:     }
9:
10:    String::String(Reader& rdr)
11:    {
12:       rdr>>itsLen;
13:       rdr>>itsCString;
14:    }
15:
16:    String::String(ScreenReader& rdr)
17:    {
18:       rdr>>itsCString;
19:       itsLen = strlen(itsCString);
20:    }
21:
22:    String::String(const char *rhs)
23:    {
24:       itsLen = strlen(rhs);
25:       itsCString = new char[itsLen+1];
26:       strcpy(itsCString,rhs);
27:    }
28:
29:    String::String (const char *rhs, LONG length)
30:    {
```

```
31:        itsLen = strlen(rhs);
32:        if (length < itsLen)
33:           itsLen = length;   // max size = length
34:        itsCString = new char[itsLen+1];
35:        memcpy(itsCString,rhs,itsLen);
36:        itsCString[itsLen] = '\0';
37:     }
38:
39:     // copy constructor
40:     String::String (const String & rhs)
41:     {
42:        itsLen=rhs.GetLength();
43:        itsCString = new char[itsLen+1];
44:        memcpy(itsCString,rhs.GetString(),itsLen);
45:        itsCString[rhs.itsLen]='\0';
46:     }
47:
48:     String::~String ()
49:     {
50:        Clear();
51:     }
52:
53:     void String::Clear()
54:     {
55:        delete [] itsCString;
56:        itsLen = 0;
57:     }
58:
59:     //non constant offset operator
60:     char & String::operator[](LONG offset)
61:     {
62:        if (offset > itsLen)
63:        {
64:           throw xOutOfBounds();
65:           // return itsCString[itsLen-1];
66:        }
67:        else
68:           return itsCString[offset];
69:     }
70:
71:     // constant offset operator
72:     char String::operator[](LONG offset) const
73:     {
74:        if (offset > itsLen)
75:        {
76:           throw xOutOfBounds();
77:           // return itsCString[itsLen-1];
78:        }
79:        else
80:           return itsCString[offset];
81:     }
82:
83:     // operator equals
84:     const String& String::operator=(const String & rhs)
85:     {
86:        if (this == &rhs)
87:           return *this;
```

611

```
88:        delete [] itsCString;
89:        itsLen=rhs.GetLength();
90:        itsCString = new char[itsLen+1];
91:        memcpy(itsCString,rhs.GetString(),itsLen);
92:        itsCString[rhs.itsLen]='\0';
93:        return *this;
94:     }
95:
96:     const String& String::operator=(const char * rhs)
97:     {
98:        delete [] itsCString;
99:        itsLen=strlen(rhs);
100:       itsCString = new char[itsLen+1];
101:       memcpy(itsCString,rhs,itsLen);
102:       itsCString[itsLen]='\0';
103:       return *this;
104:    }
105:
106:
107:    // changes current string, returns nothing
108:    void String::operator+=(const String& rhs)
109:    {
110:       unsigned short rhsLen = rhs.GetLength();
111:       unsigned short totalLen = itsLen + rhsLen;
112:       char *temp = new char[totalLen+1];
113:       for (LONG i = 0; i<itsLen; i++)
114:           temp[i] = itsCString[i];
115:       for (LONG j = 0; j<rhsLen; j++, i++)
116:           temp[i] = rhs[j];
117:       temp[totalLen]='\0';
118:       *this = temp;
119:    }
120:
121:    LONG String::StringCompare(const String& rhs) const
122:    {
123:            return strcmp(itsCString, rhs.GetString());
124:    }
125:
126:    String String::operator+(const String& rhs)
127:    {
128:
129:       char * newCString = new char[GetLength() + rhs.GetLength() + 1];
130:       strcpy(newCString,GetString());
131:       strcat(newCString,rhs.GetString());
132:       String newString(newCString);
133:       return newString;
134:    }
135:
136:
137:    String String::operator+(const char* rhs)
138:    {
139:
140:       char * newCString = new char[GetLength() + strlen(rhs)+ 1];
141:       strcpy(newCString,GetString());
142:       strcat(newCString,rhs);
143:       String newString(newCString);
144:       return newString;
```

```
145:    }
146:
147:
148:    String String::operator+(char rhs)
149:    {
150:        LONG oldLen = GetLength();
151:        char * newCString = new char[oldLen + 2];
152:        strcpy(newCString,GetString());
153:        newCString[oldLen] = rhs;
154:        newCString[oldLen+1] = '\0';
155:        String newString(newCString);
156:        return newString;
157:    }
158:
159:
160:
161:    BOOL String::operator==(const String& rhs) const
162:    { return (BOOL) (StringCompare(rhs) == 0); }
163:    BOOL String::operator!=(const String& rhs)const
164:        { return (BOOL) (StringCompare(rhs) != 0); }
165:    BOOL String::operator<(const String& rhs)const
166:        { return (BOOL) (StringCompare(rhs) < 0); }
167:    BOOL String::operator>(const String& rhs)const
168:        { return (BOOL) (StringCompare(rhs) > 0); }
169:    BOOL String::operator<=(const String& rhs)const
170:        { return (BOOL) (StringCompare(rhs) <= 0); }
171:    BOOL String::operator>=(const String& rhs)const
172:        { return (BOOL) (StringCompare(rhs) >= 0); }
173:
174:    ostream& operator<< (ostream& ostr, const String& str)
175:    {
176:        ostr << str.itsCString;
177:        return ostr;
178:    }
179:
180:    ostream& String::operator() (ostream& of)
181:    {
182:            of.write( (char*) & itsLen,szLong);
183:            of.write(itsCString,itsLen);
184:            return of;
185:    }
186:
187:    void String::Write(Writer& wrtr)
188:    {
189:        wrtr<<itsLen;
190:        wrtr<<itsCString;
191:    }
192:
193:    void String::Write(ScreenWriter& wrtr)
194:    {
195:        wrtr<<itsCString;
196:    }
1:      // ****************************************************
2:      // PROGRAM:  Storable header
3:      // FILE:     storable.hpp
4:      // PURPOSE:  provide object permanence
```

```
5:      // NOTES:
6:      // AUTHOR:    Jesse Liberty (jl)
7:      // REVISIONS: 11/20/94 1.0 jl  initial release
8:      // *************************************************
9:
10:     #include <fstream.h>
11:     #include "stdef.hpp"
12:
13:     // forward declarations
14:     class String;
15:
16:     class Writer
17:     {
18:     public:
19:        Writer() {;}
20:        virtual ~Writer() {;}
21:
22:        virtual Writer& operator<<(int&) = 0;
23:        virtual Writer& operator<<(LONG&) = 0;
24:        virtual Writer& operator<<(SHORT&) = 0;
25:        virtual Writer& operator<<(LONG&) = 0;
26:        virtual Writer& operator<<(SHORT&) = 0;
27:        virtual Writer& operator<<(char*) = 0;
28:
29:     };
30:
31:     class FileWriter : public Writer
32:     {
33:     public:
34:        FileWriter(char *fileName):fout(fileName,ios::binary){};
35:        ~FileWriter() {fout.close();}
36:
37:        virtual Writer& operator<<(int&);
38:        virtual Writer& operator<<(LONG&);
39:        virtual Writer& operator<<(SHORT&);
40:        virtual Writer& operator<<(LONG& in)
41:                              { return this->operator<<((LONG&)in); }
42:        virtual Writer& operator<<(SHORT& in)
43:                              { return this->operator<<((SHORT&)in); }
44:        virtual Writer& operator<<(char*);
45:
46:     private:
47:         ofstream fout;
48:     };
49:
50:     class ScreenWriter : public Writer
51:     {
52:     public:
53:        ScreenWriter() {;}
54:        ~ScreenWriter() {;}
55:
56:        virtual Writer& operator<<(int&);
57:        virtual Writer& operator<<(LONG&);
58:        virtual Writer& operator<<(SHORT&);
59:        virtual Writer& operator<<(LONG& in)
60:                              { return this->operator<<((LONG&)in); }
```

```
 61:        virtual Writer& operator<<(SHORT& in)
 62:                             { return this->operator<<((SHORT&)in); }
 63:        virtual Writer& operator<<(char*);
 64:
 65:    private:
 66:        void    WriteBuffer();
 67:
 68:        char buffer[255];
 69:    };
 70:
 71:    class Reader
 72:    {
 73:    public:
 74:        virtual Reader& operator>>(int&) = 0;
 75:        virtual Reader& operator>>(LONG&) = 0;
 76:        virtual Reader& operator>>(SHORT&) = 0;
 77:        virtual Reader& operator>>(LONG&) = 0;
 78:        virtual Reader& operator>>(SHORT&) = 0;
 79:        virtual Reader& operator>>(char*&) = 0;
 80:
 81:        Reader() {;}
 82:        virtual ~Reader() {;}
 83:    private:
 84:    };
 85:
 86:    class FileReader : public Reader
 87:    {
 88:    public:
 89:        virtual Reader& operator>>(int&);
 90:        virtual Reader& operator>>(LONG&);
 91:        virtual Reader& operator>>(SHORT&);
 92:        virtual Reader& operator>>(LONG& in)
 93:                             { return this->operator>>((LONG&)in); }
 94:        virtual Reader& operator>>(SHORT& in)
 95:                             { return this->operator>>((SHORT&)in); }
 96:        virtual Reader& operator>>(char*&);
 97:
 98:        FileReader(char *fileName):fin(fileName,ios::binary){}
 99:        ~FileReader(){fin.close();}
100:    private:
101:        ifstream fin;
102:    };
103:
104:    class ScreenReader : public Reader
105:    {
106:    public:
107:        virtual Reader& operator>>(int&);
108:        virtual Reader& operator>>(LONG&);
109:        virtual Reader& operator>>(SHORT&);
110:        virtual Reader& operator>>(LONG& in)
111:                             { return this->operator>>((LONG&)in); }
112:        virtual Reader& operator>>(SHORT& in)
113:                             { return this->operator>>((SHORT&)in); }
114:        virtual Reader& operator>>(char*&);
115:
```

```
116:        ScreenReader() {;}
117:        ~ScreenReader() {;}
118:     private:
119:        char buffer[255];
120:     };
121:
122:     class Storable
123:     {
124:     public:
125:        Storable() {;}
126:        Storable(Reader&){;}
127:        virtual void Write(Writer&)=0;
128:
129:     private:
130:     //    Reader itsReader;
131:      //    Writer itsWriter;
132:     };

1:      // ************************************************
2:      // PROGRAM:   Storable implementation
3:      // FILE:      storable.cpp
4:      // PURPOSE:   provide object permanence
5:      // NOTES:
6:      // AUTHOR:    Jesse Liberty (jl)
7:      // REVISIONS: 11/20/94 1.0 jl  initial release
8:      // ************************************************
9:
10:     #include "storable.hpp"
11:     #include <string.h>
12:
13:     #include <stdlib.h>    // for atoi
14:
15:     // FILEWRITER Operators
16:     Writer& FileWriter::operator<<(int& data)
17:     {
18:        fout.write((char*)&data,szInt);
19:        return *this;
20:     }
21:
22:     Writer& FileWriter::operator<<(LONG& data)
23:     {
24:        fout.write((char*)&data,szLong);
25:        return *this;
26:     }
27:
28:     Writer& FileWriter::operator<<(SHORT& data)
29:     {
30:        fout.write((char*)&data,szShort);
31:        return *this;
32:     }
33:
34:     Writer& FileWriter::operator<<(char * data)
35:     {
36:        SHORT len = strlen(data);
37:        fout.write((char*)&len,szLong);
38:        fout.write(data,len);
39:        return *this;
```

```
40:     }
41:
42:     // SCREEN WRITER operators
43:     Writer& ScreenWriter::operator<<(int& data)
44:     {
45:         itoa(data, buffer, 10);
46:         WriteBuffer();
47:         return *this;
48:     }
49:
50:     Writer& ScreenWriter::operator<<(LONG& data)
51:     {
52:         ltoa(data, buffer, 10);
53:         WriteBuffer();
54:         return *this;
55:     }
56:
57:     Writer& ScreenWriter::operator<<(SHORT& data)
58:     {
59:         itoa(data, buffer, 10);
60:         WriteBuffer();
61:         return *this;
62:     }
63:
64:     Writer& ScreenWriter::operator<<(char * data)
65:     {
66:         strcpy(buffer, data);  // needed because WriteBuffer appends extra
                                       null
67:         WriteBuffer();
68:         return *this;
69:     }
70:
71:     void   ScreenWriter::WriteBuffer()
72:     {
73:         int len = strlen(buffer);
74:         buffer[len+1] = 0x00;   // needed to get correct formatting
75:         cout << buffer;
76:     }
77:
78:     // FILEREADER operators
79:     Reader& FileReader::operator>>(int& data)
80:     {
81:         fin.read((char*)&data,szInt);
82:         return *this;
83:     }
84:     Reader& FileReader::operator>>(LONG& data)
85:     {
86:         fin.read((char*)&data,szLong);
87:         return *this;
88:     }
89:     Reader& FileReader::operator>>(SHORT& data)
90:     {
91:         fin.read((char*)&data,szShort);
92:         return *this;
93:     }
94:     Reader& FileReader::operator>>(char *& data)
```

```
95:     {
96:         SHORT len;
97:         fin.read((char*) &len,szLong);
98:         data = new char[len+1];
99:         fin.read(data,len);
100:        data[len]='\0';
101:        return *this;
102:    }
103:
104:    // SCREENREADER operators
105:    Reader& ScreenReader::operator>>(int& data)
106:    {
107:        cin.getline(buffer,255);    /* 32765 is 5 digits, + sign */
108:        data = atoi(buffer);
109:        return *this;
110:    }
111:
112:    Reader& ScreenReader::operator>>(LONG& data)
113:    {
114:        cin.getline(buffer, 255);
115:        data = atol(buffer);
116:        return *this;
117:    }
118:
119:    Reader& ScreenReader::operator>>(SHORT& data)
120:    {
121:        cin.getline(buffer, 255);
122:        data = atoi(buffer);
123:        return *this;
124:    }
125:    Reader& ScreenReader::operator>>(char *& data)
126:    {
127:        cin.getline(buffer,255);
128:
129:        SHORT len = strlen(buffer);
130:        data = new char[len+1];
131:        strcpy(data, buffer);
132:        return *this;
133:    }

1:      // **************************************************
2:      // PROGRAM:  Person
3:      // FILE:     person.hpp
4:      // PURPOSE:  provide definition of the Person class
5:      // NOTES:
6:      // AUTHOR:   Jesse Liberty
7:      // REVISIONS: 11/19/94 1.0   initial release
8:      // **************************************************
9:      #ifndef PERSON_HPP                    // inclusion guards
10:     #define PERSON_HPP
11:
12:     #include "string.hpp"                 // also a Storable
13:
14:     class Person : public Storable
15:     {
16:     public:
17:         Person(Reader&);
```

```
18:        Person(ScreenReader&);
19:        ~Person();
20:
21:        void Write(Writer&);
22:        void Write(ScreenWriter&);
23:
24:     private:
25:        LONG      myDateOfBirth;
26:        String    myName;
27:        String    myTitle;
28:        String    myAddress;
29:
30:
31:     public:
32:     //    Accessors
33:        String& const    GetName()                        { return myName; }
34:        void             SetName(const String& in)        { myName = in; }
35:
36:        String& const    GetTitle()                       { return myTitle; }
37:        void             SetTitle(const String& in)       { myTitle = in; }
38:
39:        String& const    GetAddress()                     { return myAddress; }
40:        void             SetAddress(const String& in)     { myAddress = in; }
41:
42:        LONG             GetDateOfBirth()                 { return
                                                                 myDateOfBirth; }
43:        void             SetDateOfBirth(LONG in)          { myDateOfBirth = in; }
44:     };
45:
46:     #endif

1:     // ****************************************************
2:     // PROGRAM:  Person
3:     // FILE:     person.cpp
4:     // PURPOSE:  provide implementation of the person class
5:     // NOTES:
6:     // AUTHOR:   Jesse Liberty
7:     // REVISIONS: 11/19/94 1.0 jl
8:     // ****************************************************
9:     #include "person.hpp"
10:
11:     Person::Person(Reader& in)
12:     {
13:        String name(in);      // use temporaries for 2 reasons:
14:        myName = name;        // 1) String is a complex object not
15:                              //    known to Reader, so String must
16:        String title(in);     //    manage calls to Reader
17:        myTitle = title;      // 2) Cannot directly construct members
18:                              //    using the Reader by calling from
19:        String address(in);   //    the class initialization step, since
20:        myAddress = address;  //    order is not guaranteed.
21:                              //       Ie. Person::Person(Reader& in) :
                                           myName(in) {}
22:        in >> myDateOfBirth;
23:     }
24:
```

619

```
25:     Person::Person(ScreenReader& in)
26:     {
27:         cout << "Name: ";
28:         String name(in);
29:         myName = name;
30:
31:         cout << "Title: ";
32:         String title(in);
33:         myTitle = title;
34:
35:         cout << "Address: ";
36:         String address(in);
37:         myAddress = address;
38:
39:         cout << "DOB: ";
40:         in >> myDateOfBirth;
41:     }
42:
43:     Person::~Person()
44:     {
45:     }
46:
47:     void Person::Write(Writer& out)
48:     {
49:         myName.Write(out);
50:         myTitle.Write(out);
51:         myAddress.Write(out);
52:         out << myDateOfBirth;
53:     }
54:
55:     void Person::Write(ScreenWriter& out)
56:     {
57:         out << "\nName: ";
58:         myName.Write(out);
59:         out << "\nTitle: ";
60:         myTitle.Write(out);
61:         out << "\nAddress: ";
62:         myAddress.Write(out);
63:         out << "\nDBO: ";
64:         out << myDateOfBirth;
65:     }
```

```
1:      // Driver Program for Person Class
2:
3:      #include "person.hpp"
4:
5:      int main()
6:      {
7:          ScreenReader    in;
8:          Person someone(in);
9:
10:         char    fname[] = {"test"};
11:
12:         FileWriter* fileOut = new FileWriter(fname);      // open file
13:         someone.Write(*fileOut);                          // store the object
14:         delete fileOut;                                   // close the file
15:
16:         FileReader*    fileIn = new FileReader(fname);    // open the file
```

```
17:        Person   clone(*fileIn);                      // load an object
18:        delete fileIn;                                // close the file
19:
20:        ScreenWriter   out;
21:        clone.Write(out);
22:        return 0;
23:    }
```

2. Here is the answer:

```
1:     // **************************************************
2:     // PROGRAM:  Person
3:     // FILE:     person.hpp
4:     // PURPOSE:  provide definition of the Person class
5:     // NOTES:
6:     // AUTHOR:   Jesse Liberty
7:     // REVISIONS: 11/19/94 1.0   initial release
8:     // **************************************************
9:     #ifndef PERSON_HPP              // inclusion guards
10:    #define PERSON_HPP
11:
12:    #include "string.hpp"           // also a Storable
13:
14:    class Person : public Storable
15:    {
16:    public:
17:       Person(Reader&);
18:       Person(ScreenReader&);
19:       ~Person();
20:
21:       void Write(Writer&);
22:       void Write(ScreenWriter&);
23:
24:    private:
25:       LONG      myDateOfBirth;
26:       String    myName;
27:       String    myTitle;
28:       String    myAddress;
29:
30:
31:    public:
32:    //   Accessors
33:       String& const   GetName()                      { return myName; }
34:       void            SetName(const String& in)      { myName = in; }
35:
36:       String& const   GetTitle()                     { return myTitle; }
37:       void            SetTitle(const String& in)     { myTitle = in; }
38:
39:       String& const   GetAddress()                   { return myAddress; }
40:       void            SetAddress(const String& in)   { myAddress = in; }
41:
42:       LONG            GetDateOfBirth()               { return
                                                            myDateOfBirth; }
43:       void            SetDateOfBirth(LONG in)        { myDateOfBirth = in;
}
44:    };
45:
46:    #endif
```

621

Answers

```
1:      // **************************************************
2:      // PROGRAM:   Person
3:      // FILE:      person.cpp
4:      // PURPOSE:   provide implementation of the person class
5:      // NOTES:
6:      // AUTHOR:    Jesse Liberty
7:      // REVISIONS: 11/19/94 1.0 jl
8:      // **************************************************
9:      #include "person.hpp"
10:
11:     Person::Person(Reader& in)
12:     {
13:         String name(in);       // use temporaries for 2 reasons:
14:         myName = name;         // 1) String is a complex object not
15:                                //    known to Reader, so String must
16:         String title(in);      //    manage calls to Reader
17:         myTitle = title;       // 2) Cannot directly construct members
18:                                //    using the Reader by calling from
19:         String address(in);    //    the class initialization step, since
20:         myAddress = address;   //    order is not guaranteed.
21:                                //    Ie. Person::Person(Reader& in) :
                                          myName(in) {}
22:         in >> myDateOfBirth;
23:     }
24:
25:     Person::Person(ScreenReader& in)
26:     {
27:         cout << "Name: ";
28:         String name(in);
29:         myName = name;
30:
31:         cout << "Title: ";
32:         String title(in);
33:         myTitle = title;
34:
35:         cout << "Address: ";
36:         String address(in);
37:         myAddress = address;
38:
39:         cout << "DOB: ";
40:         in >> myDateOfBirth;
41:     }
42:
43:     Person::~Person()
44:     {
45:     }
46:
47:     void Person::Write(Writer& out)
48:     {
49:         myName.Write(out);
50:         myTitle.Write(out);
51:         myAddress.Write(out);
52:         out << myDateOfBirth;
53:     }
54:
55:     void Person::Write(ScreenWriter& out)
```

```
56:      {
57:          out << "\nName: ";
58:          myName.Write(out);
59:          out << "\nTitle: ";
60:          myTitle.Write(out);
61:          out << "\nAddress: ";
62:          myAddress.Write(out);
63:          out << "\nDBO: ";
64:          out << myDateOfBirth;
65:      }
```

3. Here is the answer:

```
1:    // **************************************************
2:    // PROGRAM:  Storable header
3:    // FILE:      storable.hpp
4:    // PURPOSE:  provide object permanence
5:    // NOTES:
6:    // AUTHOR:   Jesse Liberty (jl)
7:    // REVISIONS: 11/20/94 1.0 jl  initial release
8:    // **************************************************
9:
10:   #include <fstream.h>
11:   #include "stdef.hpp"
12:
13:   // forward declarations
14:   class String;
15:
16:   class Writer
17:   {
18:   public:
19:       Writer() {;}
20:       virtual ~Writer() {;}
21:
22:       virtual Writer& operator<<(int&) = 0;
23:       virtual Writer& operator<<(LONG&) = 0;
24:       virtual Writer& operator<<(SHORT&) = 0;
25:       virtual Writer& operator<<(LONG&) = 0;
26:       virtual Writer& operator<<(SHORT&) = 0;
27:       virtual Writer& operator<<(char*) = 0;
28:
29:   };
30:
31:   class FileWriter : public Writer
32:   {
33:   public:
34:       FileWriter(char *fileName):fout(fileName,ios::binary){};
35:       ~FileWriter() {fout.close();}
36:
37:       virtual Writer& operator<<(int&);
38:       virtual Writer& operator<<(LONG&);
39:       virtual Writer& operator<<(SHORT&);
40:       virtual Writer& operator<<(LONG& in)
41:                                 { return this->operator<<((LONG&)in); }
42:       virtual Writer& operator<<(SHORT& in)
43:                                 { return this->operator<<((SHORT&)in); }
44:       virtual Writer& operator<<(char*);
```

```
45:
46:    protected:
47:        ofstream fout;
48:    };
49:
50:    class BufferWriter : public FileWriter
51:    {
52:    public:
53:        BufferWriter(SHORT, char* fileName);
54:        ~BufferWriter();
55:
56:        virtual Writer& operator<<(int&);
57:        virtual Writer& operator<<(LONG&);
58:        virtual Writer& operator<<(SHORT&);
59:        virtual Writer& operator<<(LONG& in)
60:                                { return this->operator<<((LONG&)in); }
61:        virtual Writer& operator<<(SHORT& in)
62:                                { return this->operator<<((SHORT&)in); }
63:        virtual Writer& operator<<(char*);
64:
65:        // Accessors
66:        char * GetBuffer() const      { return myBuffer; }
67:        SHORT GetBufferSize() const   { return myBuffPos; }
68:
69:    private:
70:        void      ResizeBuffer(SHORT newsize);
71:        void      AddToBuffer(void *, SHORT);
72:
73:        SHORT   BufferLeft() const    { return myBuffLen - (myBuffPos+1); }
74:        char *  CurPos()   const          { return myBuffer + myBuffPos; }
75:
76:        char * myBuffer;
77:        SHORT myBuffLen;
78:        SHORT myBuffPos;
79:    };
80:
81:    class ScreenWriter : public Writer
82:    {
83:    public:
84:        ScreenWriter() {;}
85:        ~ScreenWriter() {;}
86:
87:        virtual Writer& operator<<(int&);
88:        virtual Writer& operator<<(LONG&);
89:        virtual Writer& operator<<(SHORT&);
90:        virtual Writer& operator<<(LONG& in)
91:                                { return this->operator<<((LONG&)in); }
92:        virtual Writer& operator<<(SHORT& in)
93:                                { return this->operator<<((SHORT&)in); }
94:        virtual Writer& operator<<(char*);
95:
96:    private:
97:        void   WriteBuffer();
98:
99:        char buffer[255];
100:   };
```

```
101:
102:    class Reader
103:    {
104:    public:
105:       virtual Reader& operator>>(int&) = 0;
106:       virtual Reader& operator>>(LONG&) = 0;
107:       virtual Reader& operator>>(SHORT&) = 0;
108:       virtual Reader& operator>>(LONG&) = 0;
109:       virtual Reader& operator>>(SHORT&) = 0;
110:       virtual Reader& operator>>(char*&) = 0;
111:
112:       Reader() {;}
113:       virtual ~Reader() {;}
114:    private:
115:    };
116:
117:    class FileReader : public Reader
118:    {
119:    public:
120:       virtual Reader& operator>>(int&);
121:       virtual Reader& operator>>(LONG&);
122:       virtual Reader& operator>>(SHORT&);
123:       virtual Reader& operator>>(LONG& in)
124:                                  { return this->operator>>((LONG&)in); }
125:       virtual Reader& operator>>(SHORT& in)
126:                                  { return this->operator>>((SHORT&)in); }
127:       virtual Reader& operator>>(char*&);
128:
129:       FileReader(char *fileName):fin(fileName,ios::binary){}
130:       ~FileReader(){fin.close();}
131:    private:
132:       ifstream fin;
133:    };
134:
135:    class ScreenReader : public Reader
136:    {
137:    public:
138:       virtual Reader& operator>>(int&);
139:       virtual Reader& operator>>(LONG&);
140:       virtual Reader& operator>>(SHORT&);
141:       virtual Reader& operator>>(LONG& in)
142:                                  { return this->operator>>((LONG&)in); }
143:       virtual Reader& operator>>(SHORT& in)
144:                                  { return this->operator>>((SHORT&
                                       in); }
145:       virtual Reader& operator>>(char*&);
146:
147:       ScreenReader() {;}
148:       ~ScreenReader() {;}
149:    private:
150:       char buffer[255];
151:    };
152:
153:    class Storable
154:    {
155:    public:
```

```
156:      Storable() {;}
157:      Storable(Reader&){;}
158:      virtual void Write(Writer&)=0;
159:
160:  private:
161:  //    Reader itsReader;
162:   //    Writer itsWriter;
163:  };

1:    // **************************************************
2:    // PROGRAM:   Storable implementation
3:    // FILE:      storable.cpp
4:    // PURPOSE:   provide object permanence
5:    // NOTES:
6:    // AUTHOR:    Jesse Liberty (jl)
7:    // REVISIONS: 11/20/94 1.0 jl  initial release
8:    // **************************************************
9:    #include "storable.hpp"
10:   #include <string.h>
11:
12:   #include <stdlib.h>    // for atoi
13:
14:   // FILEWRITER Operators
15:   Writer& FileWriter::operator<<(int& data)
16:   {
17:      fout.write((char*)&data,szInt);
18:      return *this;
19:   }
20:
21:   Writer& FileWriter::operator<<(LONG& data)
22:   {
23:      fout.write((char*)&data,szLong);
24:      return *this;
25:   }
26:
27:   Writer& FileWriter::operator<<(SHORT& data)
28:   {
29:      fout.write((char*)&data,szShort);
30:      return *this;
31:   }
32:
33:   Writer& FileWriter::operator<<(char * data)
34:   {
35:      SHORT len = strlen(data);
36:      fout.write((char*)&len,szShort);
37:      fout.write(data,len);
38:      return *this;
39:   }
40:
41:   // BUFFERWRITER Operators
42:   BufferWriter::BufferWriter(SHORT bufSize, char* fileName) :
43:      FileWriter(fileName)
44:   {
45:      if (bufSize == 0)
46:         myBuffLen = 1;
47:      else
48:         myBuffLen = bufSize;
49:      myBuffer = new char [myBuffLen];
```

A

```
50:       myBuffPos = 0;
51:    }
52:
53:    BufferWriter::~BufferWriter()
54:    {
55:       fout.write(myBuffer,myBuffPos);
56:       delete myBuffer;
57:    }
58:
59:    void BufferWriter::AddToBuffer(void * newstuff, SHORT len)
60:    {
61:       if (BufferLeft() < len)        // make sure there is room
62:       {
63:          ResizeBuffer(myBuffLen + len);
64:       }
65:       memcpy(CurPos(), newstuff, len);
66:       myBuffPos += len;
67:    }
68:
69:    void BufferWriter::ResizeBuffer(SHORT newsize)
70:    {
71:       if (newsize <= myBuffPos+1)    // do not call memcpy with more data
                                         than buffer
72:          return;rrrrr
73:       char * oldBuff = myBuffer;
74:       myBuffer = new char [newsize];
75:       memcpy(myBuffer, oldBuff, myBuffPos+1);
76:       myBuffLen = newsize;
77:       delete oldBuff;
78:    }
79:
80:    Writer& BufferWriter::operator<<(int& data)
81:    {
82:       AddToBuffer((void*)&data,szInt);
83:       return *this;
84:    }
85:
86:    Writer& BufferWriter::operator<<(LONG& data)
87:    {
88:       AddToBuffer((void*)&data,szLong);
89:       return *this;
90:    }
91:
92:    Writer& BufferWriter::operator<<(SHORT& data)
93:    {
94:       AddToBuffer((void*)&data,szShort);
95:       return *this;
96:    }
97:
98:    Writer& BufferWriter::operator<<(char * data)
99:    {
100:      SHORT len = strlen(data);
101:      AddToBuffer((void*)&len,szShort);
102:      AddToBuffer((void*)data,len);
103:      return *this;
104:   }
```

627

```
105:
106:    // SCREEN WRITER operators
107:    Writer& ScreenWriter::operator<<(int& data)
108:    {
109:       itoa(data, buffer, 10);
110:       WriteBuffer();
111:       return *this;
112:    }
113:
114:    Writer& ScreenWriter::operator<<(LONG& data)
115:    {
116:       ltoa(data, buffer, 10);
117:       WriteBuffer();
118:       return *this;
119:    }
120:
121:    Writer& ScreenWriter::operator<<(SHORT& data)
122:    {
123:       itoa(data, buffer, 10);
124:       WriteBuffer();
125:       return *this;
126:    }
127:
128:    Writer& ScreenWriter::operator<<(char * data)
129:    {
130:       strcpy(buffer, data);   // needed because WriteBuffer appends extra
                                   null
131:       WriteBuffer();
132:       return *this;
133:    }
134:
135:    void    ScreenWriter::WriteBuffer()
136:    {
137:       int len = strlen(buffer);
138:       buffer[len+1] = 0x00;   // needed to get correct formatting
139:       cout << buffer;
140:    }
141:
142:    // FILEREADER operators
143:    Reader& FileReader::operator>>(int& data)
144:    {
145:       fin.read((char*)&data,szInt);
146:       return *this;
147:    }
148:    Reader& FileReader::operator>>(LONG& data)
149:    {
150:       fin.read((char*)&data,szLong);
151:       return *this;
152:    }
153:    Reader& FileReader::operator>>(SHORT& data)
154:    {
155:       fin.read((char*)&data,szShort);
156:       return *this;
157:    }
158:    Reader& FileReader::operator>>(char *& data)
159:    {
```

```
160:        SHORT len;
161:        fin.read((char*) &len,szShort);
162:        data = new char[len+1];
163:        fin.read(data,len);
164:        data[len]='\0';
165:        return *this;
166:    }
167:
168:    // SCREENREADER operators
169:    Reader& ScreenReader::operator>>(int& data)
170:    {
171:       cin.getline(buffer,255);    /* 32765 is 5 digits, + sign */
172:       data = atoi(buffer);
173:       return *this;
174:    }
175:
176:    Reader& ScreenReader::operator>>(LONG& data)
177:    {
178:       cin.getline(buffer, 255);
179:       data = atol(buffer);
180:       return *this;
181:    }
182:
183:    Reader& ScreenReader::operator>>(SHORT& data)
184:    {
185:       cin.getline(buffer, 255);
186:       data = atoi(buffer);
187:       return *this;
188:    }
189:    Reader& ScreenReader::operator>>(char *& data)
190:    {
191:       cin.getline(buffer,255);
192:
193:       SHORT len = strlen(buffer);
194:       data = new char[len+1];
195:       strcpy(data, buffer);
196:       return *this;
197:    }
```

4. The problem is that the data members of class Foo are not read from the reader in the same order that they are written to the writer. itsText is read from the reader first, because it is done in the initialization stage, which is executed before the Foo constructor. In the write method, however, itsText is written out last. The order of reading and writing must match exactly.

5. It certainly looks as though the two strings are being read and written in the same order (itsName and then itsAddress). However, this isn't the case. The write method certainly writes the strings in that order, but the initialization phase of any constructor *ignores* the order in which data members are listed in the constructor. Instead, it constructs the data members in the order that they are *declared in the class*. In this case, itsAddress will be constructed before itsName. Consequently, when you read this object back from disk, it switches the two values.

Answers to Day 10, "Collection Classes and B-Trees"

Quiz

1. A *set* is a collection within which each value may appear only once.

2. A *dictionary* is a collection that ties a key to a value. A word may be tied to a definition, a part number to a record, and so on, for example.

3. A *sparse array* is a dictionary in which the key is an integral type, such as an integer. It appears to the user as an array, but no storage is set aside for values that are not in the array.

4. A *B-tree* is a linked list where each node may point to a large number of other nodes.

5. In a binary tree, each node points to two other nodes; in a B-tree, there are many more pointers per node.

Exercises

1. Declare a `Dictionary` class.

```
1:      // **************************************************
2:      // PROGRAM:   Basic word object
3:      // FILE:      word.hpp
4:      // PURPOSE:   provide simple word object
5:      // NOTES:
6:      // AUTHOR:    Jesse Liberty (jl)
7:      // REVISIONS: 10/23/94 1.0 jl  initial release
8:      // **************************************************
9:
10:     #ifndef WORD_HPP
11:     #define WORD_HPP
12:
13:     #include "stdef.hpp"
14:     #include "string.hpp"
15:
16:     class rWord
17:     {
18:       public:
19:         rWord(): itsText(), reserved1(0L), reserved2(0L) {}
20:         rWord(const String& text):
21:         itsText(text), reserved1(0L), reserved2(0L) {}
22:         ~rWord(){}
23:
24:         const String& GetText()const { return itsText; }
25:
26:         BOOL operator<(const rWord& rhs)
27:           { return itsText < rhs.GetText(); }
28:
```

```
29:        BOOL operator>(const rWord& rhs)
30:          { return itsText > rhs.GetText(); }
31:
32:        BOOL operator==(const rWord& rhs)
33:          { return itsText == rhs.GetText(); }
34:
35:        void Display() const
36:          { cout <<    "  Text: " << itsText << endl; }
37:
38:      private:
39:        String itsText;
40:        long reserved1;
41:        long reserved2;
42:      };
43:
44:    #endif

1:     // *************************************************
2:     // PROGRAM:    SparseArray Header
3:     // FILE:       sparse array
4:     // PURPOSE:    provide sparse array
5:     // NOTES:
6:     // AUTHOR:     Jesse Liberty (jl)
7:     // REVISIONS:  11/3/94 1.0 jl  initial release
8:     //                     Test function added
9:     // *************************************************
10:
11:    #include "stdef.hpp"
12:
13:    #ifndef SPARSE_ARRAY_HPP
14:    #define SPARSE_ARRAY_HPP
15:
16:     // *************** Node class ************
17:      template <class T>
18:      class Node
19:      {
20:      public:
21:        Node (T* Obj, long key):itsObject(Obj),itsNext(0),itsKey(key){}
22:        ~Node() { delete itsObject; itsNext=0;}
23:        Node (const Node& rhs);
24:        void InsertAfter(Node * newNode)
25:          { newNode->SetNext(itsNext); itsNext=newNode;}
26:        Node * GetNext() const    { return itsNext; }
27:        void SetNext(Node * next) { itsNext = next; }
28:        T & GetObject() const { return *itsObject; }
29:        long GetKey() const { return itsKey; }
30:        BOOL operator<(const Node<T> rhs) { return itsKey <
           rhs.GetKey();}
31:        BOOL operator==(long rhs) const { return itsKey == rhs; }
32:        BOOL operator<(long rhs) const { return itsKey < rhs; }
33:        BOOL operator>(long rhs) const { return itsKey > rhs; }
34:        BOOL operator<=(long rhs) const { return itsKey <= rhs; }
35:        BOOL operator>=(long rhs) const { return itsKey >= rhs; }
36:
37:        const Node& operator=(T* rhs){ delete itsObject; itsObject=rhs;
           return *this;}
38:      private:
```

```
39:          T * itsObject;
40:          Node * itsNext;
41:          long itsKey;
42:       };
43:
44:        template <class T>
45:        Node<T>::Node(const Node& rhs)
46:        {
47:          itsObject = new T(rhs.GetObject());
48:          itsNext = rhs.GetNext();
49:          itsKey = rhs.GetKey();
50:        }
51:
52:
53:
54:       // *************** Object SparseArray ***********
55:       template <class T>
56:       class SparseArray
57:       {
58:       public:
59:          SparseArray();
60:          ~SparseArray();
61:          long      GetCount() const { return itsCount; }
62:          void      Insert(T &, long);
63:          void      Iterate(void (T::*f)()const);
64:          T &       operator[](long);
65:          T*        Test(const rWord& rhs, BOOL (T::*func)(const
                        rWord&));
66:
67:       private:
68:          Node<T>  itsHead;
69:          long itsCount;
70:       };
71:
72:        template<class T>
73:        SparseArray <T>::SparseArray():
74:          itsCount(0),
75:          itsHead(0,0)  // initialize head node to have no Object
76:          {}
77:
78:        template<class T>
79:        SparseArray <T>::~SparseArray()
80:        {
81:        }
82:
83:        template<class T>
84:        T&  SparseArray<T>::operator[](long key)
85:        {
86:           for (Node<T> * pNode = itsHead.GetNext();
87:                 pNode!=NULL;
88:                 pNode = pNode->GetNext()
89:                )
90:           {
91:              if ( *pNode >= key)
92:                 break;
93:           }
94:           if (pNode && *pNode == key)
```

```
95:            return pNode->GetObject();
96:
97:        if (!pNode ¦¦ (pNode && *pNode > key)  ) // not found
98:        {
99:          T* pNew = new T;
100:          Insert (*pNew, key);
101:          return *pNew;
102:        }
103:    }
104:
105:    template<class T>
106:    void SparseArray<T>::Insert(T & Object, long key)
107:    {
108:        Node<T> * NewNode = new Node<T>(&Object,key);
109:
110:        for (Node<T> * pNode = &itsHead;;pNode = pNode->GetNext())
111:        {
112:         BOOL IsLess = FALSE;
113:         if (pNode->GetNext())
114:           IsLess = *NewNode < *(pNode->GetNext());
115:
116:         if ( (pNode->GetNext() == NULL) ¦¦ IsLess)
117:         {
118:             pNode->InsertAfter(NewNode);
119:             itsCount++;
120:             break;
121:         }
122:        }
123:    }
124:
125:    template<class T>
126:    void SparseArray<T>::Iterate(void (T::*func)()const)
127:    {
128:        for (Node<T>* pNode = itsHead.GetNext();
129:             pNode;
130:             pNode=pNode->GetNext()
131:            )
132:        {
133:            cout << "[" << pNode->GetKey() << "] ";
134:            (pNode->GetObject().*func)();
135:            // cout << "\n";
136:        }
137:    }
138:
139:    template<class T>
140:    T* SparseArray<T>::Test(const rWord& rhs, BOOL (T::*func)(const
       rWord&))
141:    {
142:        for (Node<T>* pNode = itsHead.GetNext();
143:             pNode;
144:             pNode=pNode->GetNext()
145:            )
146:        {
147:            if ((pNode->GetObject().*func)(rhs))
148:                return &(pNode->GetObject());
149:            // cout << "\n";
```

A

```
150:           }
151:          return 0;
152:       }
153:    #endif

1:     // ****************************************************
2:     // PROGRAM:   Dictionary Header
3:     // FILE:      dict.hpp
4:     // PURPOSE:   dictionary implemented in terms
5:     //               of a sparse array
6:     // NOTES:
7:     // AUTHOR:    Jesse Liberty (jl)
8:     // REVISIONS: 11/3/94 1.0 jl  initial release
9:     // ****************************************************
10:    #ifndef DICTIONARY_HPP
11:    #define DICTIONARY_HPP
12:
13:    #include "stdef.hpp"
14:    #include "word.hpp"
15:    #include "sparse.hpp"
16:
17:    class Dictionary
18:    {
19:    public:
20:       Dictionary()  {}
21:       ~Dictionary() {}
22:
23:       BOOL   Find(const rWord&);
24:       BOOL   Add(const rWord&);
25:       void   Iterate(void (rWord::*f)()const);
26:
27:    private:
28:       void   Add(const rWord&, short);
29:
30:       SparseArray<rWord>  myList;
31:    };
32:
33:    #endif
```

2. Implement the Dictionary class.

```
1:     // ****************************************************
2:     // PROGRAM:   Dictionary Implementation
3:     // FILE:      dict.cpp
4:     // PURPOSE:   dictionary implemented as a sparse array
5:     // NOTES:
6:     // AUTHOR:    Jesse Liberty (jl)
7:     // REVISIONS: 11/3/94 1.0 jl  initial release
8:     // ****************************************************
9:
10:    #include "dict.hpp"
11:
12:    BOOL Dictionary::Find(const rWord& target)
13:    {
14:       return (myList.Test(target, rWord::operator==) != 0);
15:    }
16:
```

```
17:     BOOL Dictionary::Add(const rWord& target)
18:     {
19:        if (! Find(target))
20:        {
21:           LONG key = *((LONG*)(target.GetText().GetString()));
22:           myList.Insert((rWord&)target, key);
23:           return TRUE;
24:        }
25:
26:        return FALSE;
27:     }
28:     void
29:     Dictionary::Iterate(void (rWord::*f)()const)
30:     {
31:        myList.Iterate(f);
32:     }
```

3. Create a driver program to run the Dictionary class created in exercises 1 and 2.

```
1:      // Driver Program for Sparse Array
2:
3:      #include "dict.hpp"
4:
5:      int main   (int argc, char **argv)
6:      {
7:         Dictionary dict;
8:         rWord * pWord = 0;
9:
10:        for (int i = 1; i<argc; i++)
11:        {
12:           pWord = new rWord(argv[i]);
13:           dict.Add(*pWord);
14:        }
15:        dict.Iterate(rWord::Display);
16:        return 0;
17:     }
```

4. Modify the B-tree to not take duplicates.

```
1:      // ***************************************************
2:      // PROGRAM:  Page
3:      // FILE:     Page.cpp
4:      // PURPOSE:  provide fundamental btree functionality
5:      // NOTES:
6:      // AUTHOR:   Jesse Liberty (jl)
7:      // REVISIONS: 11/1/94 1.0 jl  initial release
8:      //                   Revised for exercise 4, push changed
9:      //                      to eliminate duplicates
10:     // ***************************************************
11:
12:     #include "btree.hpp"
13:
14:     Page::Page()
15:     {
16:     }
17:
18:     Page::Page(Index* index, BOOL bLeaf):myCount(1),IsLeaf(bLeaf)
```

```
19:    {
20:        for (INT i = 1; i<Order; i++)
21:            myKeys[i]=0;
22:        myKeys[0]=index;
23:        myCount = 1;
24:
25:    }
26:
27:    Page::Page(Index **array, INT offset, BOOL leaf):IsLeaf(leaf)
28:    {
29:        myCount = 0;
30:        INT i, j;
31:        for (i = 1; i<Order; i++)
32:            myKeys[i]=0;
33:        for (i=0, j = offset; j<Order; i++, j++)
34:        {
35:            myKeys[i]= new Index(*(array[j]));
36:            myCount++;
37:        }
38:    }
39:
40:    void Page::ReCount()
41:    {
42:        myCount = 0;
43:        for (INT i = 0; i<Order; i++)
44:            if (myKeys[i])
45:                myCount++;
46:
47:    }
48:
49:    void Page::Nullify(INT offset)
50:    {
51:        for (INT i = offset; i<Order; i++)
52:        {
53:            if (myKeys[i])
54:            {
55:                delete myKeys[i];
56:                myKeys[i]= 0;
57:            }
58:        }
59:    }
60:
61:    Page * Page::Insert(Index* pIndex)
62:    {
63:        if (IsLeaf)
64:            return   InsertLeaf(pIndex);
65:        else
66:            return InsertNode(pIndex);
67:    }
68:
69:    Page * Page::InsertNode(Index* pIndex)
70:    {
71:        Page * retVal =0;
72:        BOOL inserted = FALSE;
```

```
73:        INT i,j;
74:
75:        if (myKeys[0] && *pIndex < *(myKeys[0]))
76:        {
77:           myKeys[0]->SetData(*pIndex);
78:           retVal=myKeys[0]->Insert(pIndex);
79:           inserted = TRUE;
80:        }
81:        if (!inserted)
82:           for (i = Order-1; i>=0; i--)
83:           {
84:              if (myKeys[i])
85:              {
86:                 if (*pIndex > *(myKeys[i]))
87:                 {
88:                  retVal=myKeys[i]->Insert(pIndex);
89:                  inserted = TRUE;
90:                 }
91:               break;
92:              }
93:           }
94:        if (!inserted)
95:           for (j = 0; j<i; j++)
96:           {
97:              if (myKeys[j+1] && *pIndex < *(myKeys[j+1]))
98:              {
99:                 retVal=myKeys[j]->Insert(pIndex);
100:                break;
101:             }
102:          }
103:
104:       if (retVal) // got back a pointer to a new page
105:       {
106:          Index * pIndex = new Index(*retVal->GetFirstIndex());
107:          pIndex->SetPointer(retVal);
108:          retVal = InsertLeaf(pIndex);
109:       }
110:
111:       return retVal;
112:    }
113:
114:    Page * Page::InsertLeaf(Index* pIndex)
115:    {
116:        if (myCount < Order)
117:        {
118:           Push(pIndex);
119:           myCount++;
120:           return 0;
121:        }
122:        else       // overflow the page
123:        {
124:           Page* sibling = new Page(myKeys,Order/2,IsLeaf); // make
                                                              sibling
```

```
125:                Nullify(Order/2);                        // nullify my right
                                                                half
126:
127:                // does it fit in this side?
128:                if (myKeys[Order/2-1] && *pIndex <= *(myKeys[Order/2-1]))
129:                    Push(pIndex);
130:                else
131:                    sibling->Push(pIndex);
132:
133:                ReCount();
134:                return sibling;
135:            }
136:    }
137:
138:    void Page::Push(Index *pIndex,INT offset)
139:    {
140:        for (INT i=offset; i<Order; i++)
141:        {
142:
143:            if (*pIndex == *myKeys[i])  // here is the change!
144:                return;
145:            if (!myKeys[i]) // empty
146:            {
147:                myKeys[i]=pIndex;
148:                break;
149:            }
150:            else
151:            {
152:                if (myKeys[i] && *pIndex <= *myKeys[i])
153:                {
154:                    Push(myKeys[i],offset+1);
155:                    myKeys[i]=pIndex;
156:                    break;
157:                }
158:            }
159:        }
160:    }
161:
162:
163:    void Page::Print()
164:    {
165:        for (INT i = 0; i<Order; i++)
166:        {
167:            if (myKeys[i])
168:            {
169:                if (IsLeaf)
170:                    myKeys[i]->PrintKey();
171:                else
172:                    myKeys[i]->PrintPage();
173:            }
174:            else
175:                break;
176:        }
177:    }
```

Answers for Day 11, "Building Indexes on Disk"

Quiz

1. Because a large number of nodes are stored on each page, the tree is wider and less deep. Each page is read all at once, so you must go to the disk far less often than with a deeper B-tree.

2. Typically, page size is determined by the size of the sector on your disk.

3. Each page has 32 nodes. In our case, 31 nodes are used, and a header node is used in the 32nd position.

4. The goal is to speed up disk reads. By writing the entire object into a character array, and then reading those bytes as members of a structure, only one disk read was needed for the entire class.

5. The union could not have members that take constructors. Therefore, a character array was used, and the pointer was used to access that memory as if it were on the heap.

Exercises

1. Modify the index manager to print out whether it gets its page from memory or from disk. Run the program and examine the output.

```
1:      // ***************************************************
2:      // PROGRAM:  diskmgr
3:      // FILE:     diskmgr.cpp
4:      // PURPOSE:  provide i/o for btree
5:      // NOTES:
6:      // AUTHOR:   Jesse Liberty (jl)
7:      // REVISIONS: 11/5/94 1.0 jl  initial release
8:      // ***************************************************
9:
10:     #include "btree.hpp"
11:     #include <assert.h>
12:
13:     // on construction, try to open the file if it exists
14:     DiskManager::DiskManager():
15:         myFile("Robin.idx",ios::binary ¦ ios::in ¦ ios::out ¦
            ios::nocreate)
16:     {
17:         // initialize the pointers to null
18:         for (INT i = 0; i< MaxPages; i++)
19:             myPages[i] = 0;
20:         myCount = 0;
21:
```

```
22:      }
23:
24:      // called by btree constructor
25:      // if we opened the file, read in the numbers we need
26:      // otherwise create the file
27:      INT DiskManager::Create()
28:      {
29:         if (!myFile) // nocreate failed, first creation
30:         {
31:            // open the file, create it this time
32:            myFile.open("Robin.idx",ios::binary | ios::in | ios::out);
33:
34:            char Header[PageSize];
35:            INT MagicNumber = 80589; // a number we can check for
36:            memcpy(Header,&MagicNumber,4);
37:            INT NextPage = 1;
38:            memcpy(Header+4,&NextPage,4);
39:            INT FirstPage = 1;
40:            memcpy(Header+8,&NextPage,4);
41:            Page::SetgPageNumber(NextPage);
42:            char title[]="ROBIN.IDX. Ver 1.00";
43:            memcpy(Header+12,title,strlen(title));
44:            myFile.seekp(0);
45:            myFile.write(Header,PageSize);
46:            return 0;
47:         }
48:
49:         // we did open the file, it already existed
50:         // get the numbers we need
51:         INT MagicNumber;
52:         myFile.seekg(0);
53:         myFile.read((char *) &MagicNumber,4);
54:
55:         // check the magic number. If it is wrong the file is
56:         // corrupt or this isn't the index file
57:         if (MagicNumber != 80589)
58:         {
59:            // change to an exception!!
60:            cout << "Magic number failed!";
61:            return 0;
62:         }
63:
64:         INT NextPage;
65:         myFile.seekg(4);
66:         myFile.read((char*) &NextPage,4);
67:         Page::SetgPageNumber(NextPage);
68:         INT FirstPage;
69:         myFile.seekg(8);
70:         myFile.read((char*) &FirstPage,4);
71:         const INT room =  PageSize - 12;
72:         char buffer[room];
73:         myFile.read(buffer,room);
74:         cout << buffer << endl;
75:         // read in all the pages
76:         for (INT i = 1; i < NextPage; i++)
77:         {
```

```
78:              myFile.seekg(i * PageSize);
79:              char buffer[PageSize];
80:              myFile.read( buffer, PageSize);
81:              Page * pg = new Page(buffer);
82:              Insert(pg);
83:          }
84:
85:      return FirstPage;
86:      }
87:
88:      // write out the numbers we'll need next time
89:      void DiskManager::Close(INT theRoot)
90:      {
91:
92:          for (INT i = 0; i< MaxPages; i++)
93:              if (myPages[i])
94:                  Save(myPages[i]);
95:          INT NextPage = Page::GetgPageNumber();
96:          if (!myFile)
97:              cout << "Error opening myFile!" << endl;
98:          myFile.seekp(4);
99:          myFile.write ( (char *) &NextPage,4);
100:         myFile.seekp(8);
101:         myFile.write((char*) &theRoot,4);
102:         myFile.close();
103:     }
104:
105:     // wrapper function
106:     INT DiskManager::NewPage(const Index& index, BOOL bLeaf)
107:     {
108:         Page * newPage = new Page(index, bLeaf);
109:         Insert(newPage);
110:         Save(newPage);
111:         return newPage->GetPageNumber();
112:     }
113:
114:     INT DiskManager::NewPage(
115:         Index *array,
116:         INT offset,
117:         BOOL leaf,
118:         INT count)
119:     {
120:         Page * newPage = new Page(array, offset, leaf,count);
121:         Insert(newPage);
122:         Save(newPage);
123:         return newPage->GetPageNumber();
124:     }
125:
126:     void DiskManager::Insert(Page * newPage)
127:     {
128:         BOOL inserted = FALSE;
129:
130:         // add new page into array of page managers
131:         if (myCount < MaxPages)
132:         {
133:             assert(!myPages[myCount]);
134:             myPages[myCount++] = newPage;
```

```
135:        }
136:        else  // no room, time to page out to disk
137:        {
138:            INT lowest = 0;
139:            for (INT i = 0; i< MaxPages; i++)
140:                if (myPages[i]->GetTime() < myPages[lowest]->GetTime())
141:                    lowest = i;
142:            Save(myPages[lowest]);
143:            delete myPages[lowest];
144:            myPages[lowest] = newPage;
145:        }
146:    }
147:
148:    // tell the page to write itself out
149:    void DiskManager::Save(Page* pg)
150:    {
151:      pg->Write(myFile);
152:    }
153:
154:    // see if the page is in memory, if so return it
155:    // otherwise get it from disk
156:    // note: this won't scale, with lots of page managers
157:    // you'd need a more efficient search. 10 levels of page
158:    // managers, with 31 indexes per page gives you room for
159:    // 800 trillion words. Even if each page is only 1/2 full
160:    // on average, 10 levels of depth would represent 64 million
161:    // keys alone, not to mention the actual records.
162:
163:    Page * DiskManager::GetPage(INT target)
164:    {
165:
166:        for (INT i = 0; i< MaxPages; i++)
167:        {
168:            if (myPages[i]->GetPageNumber() == target)
169:                return  myPages[i];
170:        }
171:        myFile.seekg(target * PageSize);
172:        char buffer[PageSize];
173:        myFile.read( buffer, PageSize);
174:        Page * pg = new Page(buffer);
175:        Insert(pg);
176:        return pg;
177:    }
```

2. Start with clean data files. Enter this text:

Silent night, holy night, all is calm, all is right, round young virgin mother and child, sleep in heavenly bliss.

Examine the output from exercise 1.

```
d:\day11>ex2 silent night holy night all is calm all is right round young vi
rgin mother and child sleep in heavenly bliss
Page 1 was in memory.
Page 1 was in memory.
Page 1 was in memory.
Page 1 was in memory.
```

```
Page 1 was in memory.
Page 1 was in memory.
Page 1 was in memory.
Page 1 was in memory.
Page 1 was in memory.
Page 1 was in memory.
Page 1 was in memory.
Page 1 was in memory.
Page 1 was in memory.
Page 1 was in memory.
Page 1 was in memory.
Page 1 was in memory.
Page 1 was in memory.
Page 1 was in memory.
Page 1 was in memory.
Page 1 was in memory.
Page 1 was in memory.
 D:\DAY1  all  and  bliss  calm  child  heavenly  holy  in  is  mother
night  right  round  silent  sleep  virgin  young
```

3. Change the header to set the order to 4. Delete the data and index files, and run them again with the string from exercise 2.

```
 1:     ROBIN.IDX. Ver 1.00
 2:     Page 8 was in memory.
 3:     Page 3 was in memory.
 4:     Page 1 was in memory.
 5:     Page 8 was in memory.
 6:     Page 7 was in memory.
 7:     Page 5 was in memory.
 8:     Page 8 was in memory.
 9:     Page 7 was in memory.
10:     Page 2 was in memory.
11:     Page 8 was in memory.
12:     Page 3 was in memory.
13:     Page 10 was in memory.
14:     Page 8 was in memory.
15:     Page 7 was in memory.
16:     Page 2 was in memory.
17:     Page 8 was in memory.
18:     Page 3 was in memory.
19:     Page 1 was in memory.
20:     Page 8 was in memory.
21:     Page 7 was in memory.
22:     Page 6 was in memory.
23:     Page 8 was in memory.
24:     Page 3 was in memory.
25:     Page 4 was in memory.
26:     Page 8 was in memory.
27:     Page 3 was in memory.
28:     Page 1 was in memory.
29:     Page 8 was in memory.
30:     Page 7 was in memory.
31:     Page 6 was in memory.
32:     Page 8 was in memory.
33:     Page 7 was in memory.
34:     Page 2 was in memory.
```

```
35:     Page 8 was in memory.
36:     Page 7 was in memory.
37:     Page 5 was in memory.
38:     Page 8 was in memory.
39:     Page 7 was in memory.
40:     Page 9 was in memory.
41:     Page 8 was in memory.
42:     Page 7 was in memory.
43:     Page 9 was in memory.
44:     Page 8 was in memory.
45:     Page 7 was in memory.
46:     Page 6 was in memory.
47:     Page 8 was in memory.
48:     Page 3 was in memory.
49:     Page 1 was in memory.
50:     Page 8 was in memory.
51:     Page 3 was in memory.
52:     Page 4 was in memory.
53:     Page 8 was in memory.
54:     Page 7 was in memory.
55:     Page 9 was in memory.
56:     Page 8 was in memory.
57:     Page 3 was in memory.
58:     Page 10 was in memory.
59:     Page 8 was in memory.
60:     Page 3 was in memory.
61:     Page 10 was in memory.
62:     Page 8 was in memory.
63:     Page 3 was in memory.
64:     Page 1 was in memory.
65:     Page 8 was in memory.
66:
67:     D:\112\DAY1: Page 3 was in memory.
68:
69:     D:\112\DAY1: Page 1 was in memory.
70:        D:\112\DAY1  all   and   bliss
71:     calm: Page 4 was in memory.
72:        calm   child
73:     heavenly: Page 10 was in memory.
74:        heavenly   holy   in
75:     is: Page 7 was in memory.
76:
77:     is: Page 6 was in memory.
78:        is   mother
79:     night: Page 2 was in memory.
80:        night   right
81:     round: Page 5 was in memory.
82:        round   silent
83:     sleep: Page 9 was in memory.
84:        sleep   virgin   young
```

4. Cut down the disk manager size to 5 pages, and run exercise 3 again, after clearing out the data and index files.

```
1:      Page 1 was in memory.
2:      Page 1 was in memory.
3:      Page 1 was in memory.
```

```
4:      Page 1 was in memory.
5:      Page 1 was in memory.
6:      Page 2 was in memory.
7:      Page 1 was in memory.
8:      Page 3 was in memory.
9:      Page 2 was in memory.
10:     Page 3 was in memory.
11:     Page 1 was in memory.
12:     Page 3 was in memory.
13:     Page 1 was in memory.
14:     Page 4 was in memory.
15:     Page 4 was in memory.
16:     Page 3 was in memory.
17:     Page 1 was in memory.
18:     Page 3 was in memory.
19:     Page 4 was in memory.
20:     Page 3 was in memory.
21:     Page 2 was in memory.
22:     Page 3 was in memory.
23:     Page 2 was in memory.
24:     Page 3 was in memory.
25:     Page 2 was in memory.
26:     Page 5 was in memory.
27:     Page 5 was in memory.
28:     Page 3 was in memory.
29:     Page 5 was in memory.
30:     Page 3 was in memory.
31:     Page 4 was in memory.
32:     Page 3 was in memory.
33:     Page 1 was in memory.
34:     Page 3 was in memory.
35:     Page 4 was in memory.
36:     Page 6 was in memory.
37:     Page 6 was in memory.
38:     Page 7 was in memory.
39:     Page 3 was in memory.
40:     Page 8 was in memory.
41:     Retrieving page 7 from disk!
42:     Retrieving page 8 from disk!
43:     Page 3 was in memory.
44:     Page 4 was in memory.
45:     Page 8 was in memory.
46:     Page 3 was in memory.
47:     Page 4 was in memory.
48:     Page 9 was in memory.
49:     Page 9 was in memory.
50:     Retrieving page 8 from disk!
51:     Page 3 was in memory.
52:     Page 4 was in memory.
53:     Page 8 was in memory.
54:     Page 3 was in memory.
55:     Retrieving page 1 from disk!
56:     Retrieving page 8 from disk!
57:
58:     D:\112\DAY1: Page 3 was in memory.
59:
60:     D:\112\DAY1: Retrieving page 1 from disk!
```

```
61:     D:\112\DAY1  all  and  bliss
62:  calm: Page 4 was in memory.
63:     calm  child  heavenly
64:  holy: Retrieving page 9 from disk!
65:     holy  in  sleep  in  sleep
```

Answers for Day 12, "Records and Parsing"

Quiz

1. The most expensive operation in a database is reading and writing from the disk.

2. Word-Node-Join provides the capability for one key to match multiple records, and provides an extensible trade-off between maintaining multiple word-key connections and repeatedly having to search the disk for new index matches.

3. It is convenient for the user to be able to match *Computer* with *computer* and *COM-PUTER*.

4. It was a design goal to be able to show the record as originally entered by the user.

Exercises

1. Here is the answer:

```
1:   // **************************************************
2:   // PROGRAM:  Expression Evaluator
3:   // FILE:     exprsion.hpp
4:   // PURPOSE:  Class declarations for Expression and UnaryOperation
5:   // NOTES:
6:   // AUTHOR:   Jesse Liberty
7:   // REVISIONS: 02/09/95 1.0 jl  initial release
8:   // **************************************************
9:
10:
11:  #ifndef EXPRSION_HPP
12:  #define EXPRSION_HPP
13:
14:  typedef long ValueType;
15:
16:
17:  // **************************************************
18:  class Expression
19:  {
20:  public:
21:     Expression() {}
22:     virtual ~Expression() {}
23:
24:     virtual ValueType GetValue() const = 0;
25:  };
```

```
26:
27:     // **************************************************
28:     typedef unsigned char UnaryOperator;
29:     class UnaryOperation : public Expression
30:     {
31:     public:
32:        UnaryOperation(UnaryOperator op = '-', Expression * exp = 0);
33:        ~UnaryOperation() {delete myExpression;}
34:
35:        virtual ValueType GetValue() const;
36:
37:        void SetOperator(UnaryOperator op) {myOperator = op;}
38:        void SetExpression(Expression * exp) {myExpression = exp;}
39:
40:     private:
41:        UnaryOperator myOperator;
42:        Expression * myExpression;
43:     };
44:
45:     #endif
46:

1:     // **************************************************
2:     // PROGRAM:   Expression Evaluator
3:     // FILE:      ex1201.hpp
4:     // PURPOSE:   Class definitions for Expression and UnaryOperation
5:     // NOTES:
6:     // AUTHOR:    Jesse Liberty
7:     // REVISIONS: 02/09/95 1.0 jl  initial release
8:     // **************************************************
9:
10:
11:     #include "stdef.hpp"
12:     #include "ex1201.hpp"  exprsion.hpp
13:
14:
15:     // **************************************************
16:
17:     UnaryOperation::UnaryOperation(UnaryOperator op, Expression * exp)
18:        : Expression(), myOperator(op), myExpression(exp)
19:     { }
20:
21:
22:     ValueType UnaryOperation::GetValue() const
23:     {
24:        if (myExpression == 0)
25:           return 0;
26:
27:        switch (myOperator)
28:        {
29:        case '--':
30:           return — myExpression->GetValue();
31:
32:        case '!':
33:           return ! myExpression->GetValue();
34:
35:        default:
```

```
36:          return 0;
37:      }
38:  }
```

2. Here is the answer:

```
1:    // **************************************************
2:    // PROGRAM:  Expression Evaluator
3:    // FILE:     exprsion.hpp
4:    // PURPOSE:  Class declarations for Expression, Number,
5:    //                   UnaryOperation and BinaryOperation
6:    // NOTES:
7:    // AUTHOR:   Jesse Liberty
8:    // REVISIONS: 02/09/95 1.0 jl  initial release
9:    // **************************************************
10:
11:
12:    #ifndef EXPRSION_HPP
13:    #define EXPRSION_HPP
14:
15:    typedef long ValueType;
16:
17:
18:    // **************************************************
19:    class Expression
20:    {
21:    public:
22:       Expression() {}
23:       virtual ~Expression() {}
24:
25:       virtual ValueType GetValue() const = 0;
26:    };
27:
28:    // **************************************************
29:    class Number : public Expression
30:    {
31:    public:
32:       Number(ValueType value = 0);
33:       ~Number() {}
34:
35:       virtual ValueType GetValue() const {return myValue;}
36:       void SetValue(ValueType value) {myValue = value;}
37:
38:    private:
39:       ValueType myValue;
40:    };
41:
42:    // **************************************************
43:    typedef unsigned char UnaryOperator;
44:    class UnaryOperation : public Expression
45:    {
46:    public:
47:       UnaryOperation(UnaryOperator op = '-', Expression * exp = 0);
48:       ~UnaryOperation() {delete myExpression;}
49:
50:       virtual ValueType GetValue() const;
51:
52:       void SetOperator(UnaryOperator op) {myOperator = op;}
```

A

```
53:        void SetExpression(Expression * exp) {myExpression = exp;}
54:
55:     private:
56:        UnaryOperator myOperator;
57:        Expression * myExpression;
58:     };
59:
60:     // ***************************************************
61:     typedef unsigned char BinaryOperator;
62:     class BinaryOperation : public Expression
63:     {
64:     public:
65:        BinaryOperation(   Expression * first = 0,
66:                           BinaryOperator = '+',
67:                           Expression * last = 0);
68:        ~BinaryOperation() {delete myFirst; delete myLast;}
69:
70:        virtual ValueType GetValue() const;
71:
72:        void SetOperator(BinaryOperator op) {myOperator = op;}
73:        void SetFirst(Expression * exp)   {myFirst = exp;}
74:        void SetLast(Expression * exp)    {myLast = exp;}
75:
76:     private:
77:        BinaryOperator myOperator;
78:        Expression * myFirst;
79:        Expression * myLast;
80:     };
81:
82:
83:
84:     #endif
85:

1:     // ***************************************************
2:     // PROGRAM:  Expression Evaluator
3:     // FILE:     exprsion.hpp
4:     // PURPOSE:  Class definitions for Expression, Number,
5:     //           UnaryOperation and BinaryOperation
6:     // NOTES:
7:     // AUTHOR:   Jesse Liberty
8:     // REVISIONS: 02/09/95 1.0 jl  initial release
9:     // ***************************************************
10:
11:
12:     #include "stdef.hpp"
13:     #include "exprsion.hpp"
14:
15:     // ***************************************************
16:
17:     Number::Number(ValueType value)
18:        : Expression(), myValue(value)
19:     { }
20:
21:     // ***************************************************
22:
23:     UnaryOperation::UnaryOperation(UnaryOperator op, Expression * exp)
```

```
24:          : Expression(), myOperator(op), myExpression(exp)
25:      { }
26:
27:
28:      ValueType UnaryOperation::GetValue() const
29:      {
30:          if (myExpression == 0)
31:              return 0;
32:
33:          switch (myOperator)
34:          {
35:          case '—':
36:              return - myExpression->GetValue();
37:
38:          case '!':
39:              return ! myExpression->GetValue();
40:
41:          default:
42:              return 0;
43:          }
44:      }
45:
46:      // ****************************************************
47:
48:      BinaryOperation::BinaryOperation(   Expression * first,
49:                          BinaryOperator op, Expression * last)
50:          : Expression(), myFirst(first), myOperator(op), myLast(last)
51:      { }
52:
53:      ValueType BinaryOperation::GetValue() const
54:      {
55:          if (myFirst == 0 ¦¦ myLast == 0)
56:              return 0;
57:
58:          switch (myOperator)
59:          {
60:          case '+':
61:              return  myFirst->GetValue() + myLast->GetValue();
62:
63:          case '—':
64:              return  myFirst->GetValue() — myLast->GetValue();
65:
66:          case '*':
67:              return  myFirst->GetValue() * myLast->GetValue();
68:
69:          case '/':
70:              return  myFirst->GetValue() / myLast->GetValue();
71:
72:          case '&':
73:              return  myFirst->GetValue() & myLast->GetValue();
74:
75:          case '¦':
76:              return  myFirst->GetValue() ¦ myLast->GetValue();
77:
78:          case '^':
79:              return  myFirst->GetValue() ^ myLast->GetValue();
```

```
80:
81:        default:
82:          return 0;
83:        }
84:    }
```

3. Here is the answer:

```
1:      // ****************************************************
2:      // PROGRAM:   Expression Evaluator
3:      // FILE:      ex1202.hpp
4:      // PURPOSE:   Test classes Expression, Number,
5:      //                UnaryOperation and BinaryOperation
6:      // NOTES:
7:      // AUTHOR:    Jesse Liberty
8:      // REVISIONS: 02/09/95 1.0 jl  initial release
9:      // ****************************************************
10:
11:
12:      #include "stdef.hpp"
13:      #include "exprsion.hpp"
14:
15:
16:      void main()
17:      {
18:          Number *np = new Number(6);
19:          cout << np->GetValue() << "\n";
20:
21:          UnaryOperation * unopp = new UnaryOperation('-', np);
22:          cout << unopp->GetValue() << "\n";
23:
24:          BinaryOperation * binopp
25:              = new BinaryOperation(unopp, '*', new Number(3));
26:          cout << binopp->GetValue() << "\n";
27:
28:          BinaryOperation * binopp2
29:              = new BinaryOperation(new Number(20), '+', binopp);
30:          cout << binopp2->GetValue() << "\n";
31:
32:          // Note that binopp2 'owns' the others, so only it needs
33:          // to be deleted and it will delete its sub-Expressions.
34:          delete binopp2;
35:      }
```

4. Here is the answer:

```
1:      // ****************************************************r
2:      // PROGRAM:   Expression Evaluator
3:      // FILE:      token.hpp
4:      // PURPOSE:   Class declaration for Tokenizer
5:      // NOTES:
6:      // AUTHOR:    Jesse Liberty
7:      // REVISIONS: 02/09/95 1.0 jl  initial release
8:      // ****************************************************
9:
10:     #ifndef TOKEN_HPP
11:     #define TOKEN_HPP
```

```
12:
13:     typedef char token;
14:
15:     class Tokenizer
16:     {
17:     public:
18:        Tokenizer(istream& in, ostream& out, BOOL echoFlag = TRUE);
19:        ~Tokenizer() { }
20:
21:        token Peek();
22:        token GetToken();
23:
24:        BOOL eof()    {return myIn.eof();}
25:
26:     private:
27:        istream& myIn;
28:        ostream& myOut;
29:        BOOL myEchoFlag;
30:
31:        token myPeeked;
32:        BOOL myHavePeeked;
33:        BOOL IsWhiteSpace() const;
34:     };
35:
36:
37:     #endif
38:
39:

1:      // **************************************************
2:      // PROGRAM:   Expression Evaluator
3:      // FILE:      token.cpp
4:      // PURPOSE:   Class definition and test for Tokenizer
5:      // NOTES:
6:      // AUTHOR:    Jesse Liberty
7:      // REVISIONS: 02/09/95 1.0 jl   initial release
8:      // **************************************************
9:
10:
11:     #include "stdef.hpp"
12:     #include "token.hpp"
13:
14:     Tokenizer::Tokenizer(istream& in, ostream& out, BOOL echoFlag)
15:        : myIn(in), myOut(out), myEchoFlag(echoFlag), myHavePeeked(FALSE)
16:     { }
17:
18:
19:     // **************************************************
20:     token Tokenizer::Peek()
21:     {
22:        if (!myHavePeeked)    // If haven't yet peeked, do so.
23:           {
24:           // Skip (and echo) whitespace.
25:           while (TRUE)
26:              {
27:              if (myIn.eof())
28:                 {
```

```
29:                       return EOF;      // Note myHavePeeked is still FALSE
30:                       }
31:
32:                  myIn.get(myPeeked);
33:                  if (!IsWhiteSpace())
34:                      break;
35:
36:                  if (myEchoFlag)
37:                      myOut << myPeeked;
38:                  }
39:
40:             myHavePeeked = TRUE;
41:             }
42:
43:        return myPeeked;
44:     }
45:
46:     // ****************************************************
47:     BOOL Tokenizer::IsWhiteSpace() const
48:     {
49:        return   myPeeked == ' '
50:                 || myPeeked == '\n'
51:                 || myPeeked == '\r'
52:                 || myPeeked == '\t'
53:                 || myPeeked == ',';
54:     }
55:
56:
57:     // ****************************************************
58:     token Tokenizer::GetToken()
59:     {
60:        if (!myHavePeeked)
61:            Peek();
62:
63:        if (!myHavePeeked)         // This could only mean an eof
64:            return EOF;
65:        else
66:            {
67:            if (myEchoFlag)
68:                myOut << myPeeked;   // echo it
69:            myHavePeeked = FALSE;
70:            return myPeeked;
71:            }
72:     }
73:
74:     //#define TEST
75:     #ifdef TEST
76:
77:     void main()
78:     {
79:        Tokenizer t(cin, cout);
80:        char array[50];
81:        char * ptr = array;
82:
83:        while (!t.eof())
```

```
84:     {
85:         *ptr++ = t.GetToken();
86:     }
87:
88:     *ptr = '\0';
89:
90:     cout << array;
91:  }
92:
93:  #endif
```

5. Here is the answer:

```
1:   // **************************************************
2:   // PROGRAM:  Expression Evaluator
3:   // FILE:     parser.hpp
4:   // PURPOSE:  Declaration for Parser functions
5:   // NOTES:
6:   // AUTHOR:   Jesse Liberty
7:   // REVISIONS: 02/09/95 1.0 jl  initial release
8:   // **************************************************
9:
10:  #ifndef PARSER_HPP
11:  #define PARSER_HPP
12:
13:  class Expression;
14:  class Tokenizer;
15:
16:  Expression * Parse(Tokenizer & tok);
17:  Expression * ParseNumber(Tokenizer & tok);
18:  Expression * ParseUnaryOperation(Tokenizer & tok);
19:  Expression * ParseBinaryOperation(Tokenizer & tok);
20:
21:  #endif
22:
23:
```

```
1:   // **************************************************
2:   // PROGRAM:  Expression Evaluator
3:   // FILE:     parser.cpp
4:   // PURPOSE:  Definition and test for Parser functions
5:   // NOTES:
6:   // AUTHOR:   Jesse Liberty
7:   // REVISIONS: 02/09/95 1.0 jl  initial release
8:   // **************************************************
9:
10:
11:  #include "stdef.hpp"
12:  #include <ctype.h>  // for isdigit()
13:
14:  #include "parser.hpp"
15:  #include "exprsion.hpp"
16:  #include "token.hpp"
17:
18:
19:  // **************************************************
20:  Expression * Parse(Tokenizer & tok)
```

```
21:     {
22:         tok.Peek();        // Might need to skip some whitespace.
23:         if (tok.eof())
24:             return 0;
25:
26:         switch ( tok.Peek() )
27:         {
28:         case '0':
29:         case '1':
30:         case '2':
31:         case '3':
32:         case '4':
33:         case '5':
34:         case '6':
35:         case '7':
36:         case '8':
37:         case '9':
38:             return ParseNumber(tok);
39:
40:         case '—':
41:         case '!':
42:             return ParseUnaryOperation(tok);
43:
44:         case '(':
45:             return ParseBinaryOperation(tok);
46:
47:         default:
48:             break;
49:         }
50:         return 0;
51:     }
52:
53:
54:     // **************************************************
55:     Expression * ParseNumber(Tokenizer & tok)
56:     {
57:         ValueType value = 0;
58:
59:         while (isdigit(tok.Peek()))
60:         {
61:             token t = tok.GetToken();
62:             value = value * 10 + t - '0';
63:         }
64:
65:         return new Number(value);
66:     }
67:
68:
69:     // **************************************************
70:     Expression * ParseUnaryOperation(Tokenizer & tok)
71:     {
72:         token op = tok.GetToken();
73:         if (op != '-' && op != '!')
74:             return 0;
75:
76:         Expression * exp = Parse(tok);
```

```
77:        return new UnaryOperation(op, exp);
78:    }
79:
80:
81:    BOOL IsBinaryOperator(char op);
82:    // **************************************************
83:    Expression * ParseBinaryOperation(Tokenizer & tok)
84:    {
85:        token lparen = tok.GetToken();
86:        if (lparen != '(')
87:            return 0;
88:
89:        Expression * left = Parse(tok);
90:
91:        token op = tok.GetToken();
92:        if (!IsBinaryOperator(op))
93:        {
94:            delete left;
95:            return 0;
96:        }
97:
98:        Expression * right = Parse(tok);
99:
100:        token rparen = tok.GetToken();
101:        if (rparen != ')')
102:        {
103:            delete left;
104:            delete right;
105:            return 0;
106:        }
107:
108:        return new BinaryOperation(left, op, right);
109:    }
110:
111:    // **************************************************
112:    BOOL IsBinaryOperator(char op)
113:    {
114:        return (       op == '+'
115:                    || op == '-'
116:                    || op == '*'
117:                    || op == '/'
118:                    || op == '&'
119:                    || op == '|'
120:                    || op == '^'
121:               );
122:    }
123:
124:
125:    // **************************************************
126:    #define TEST TRUE
127:    #ifdef TEST
128:
129:    void main()
130:    {
131:        Tokenizer tok(cin, cout);
132:
```

```
133:    while (!tok.eof())
134:    {
135:        Expression * exp = Parse(tok);
136:        if (exp != 0)
137:            cout << " = " << exp->GetValue() << "\n\n";
138:    }
139:  }
140:
141:  #endif
```

A

Answers for Day 13, "ROBIN, V.1"

Quiz

1. Alpha testing is conducted early in the development process, before the product is feature complete and while there still are many bugs. The purpose of alpha testing is to iron out the design. Beta testing typically is done when the product is feature complete and most of the known bugs have been removed. The purpose of beta testing is to find those bugs that surface only when a large number of users try to use the program.

2. A professional QA team should at a minimum test for compliance with the specification, for boundary conditions in data entry, and for general functionality and robustness.

3. It is virtually impossible for a developer to break out of his or her own mindset about how the program will be used. Time and again QA will come back to you with a totally unanticipated user behavior that crashes your program.

Exercises

1. Only three changes are required. First, change the member variable myIsLocked to be an unsigned short named myLockCount. Then change the two accessor functions (GetLocked and SetLocked) to the following. Note that the interface to these functions doesn't change.

```
BOOL GetLocked() const {return (myLockCount > 0);}
void SetLocked(BOOL state)
    {if (state) myLockCount++; else myLockCount--;}
```

2. This is left as an exercise for the reader.

3. The only trick here is not to count empty lines. Because you are counting lines being inserted into the database, the best place to increment the counter is as close as possible to the Insert function. This will minimize the possibility of a later change in the program flow invalidating your count. The new ParseFile function should look like this:

657

```
// open a file and create a new note for each line
// index every word in the line
void ParseFile(int argc,char **argv, BTree& myTree)
{
   char buffer[PageSize];
   char theString[PageSize];

   ifstream theFile(argv[2],ios::in );
   if (!theFile)
   {
      cout << "Error opening input file!\n";
      return;
   }
   int offset = 0;
   int lineCount = 0;      // Added Exercise 13.3

   for (;;)
   {
         theFile.read(theString,PageSize);
         int len = theFile.gcount();
         if (!len)
            break;
         theString[len]='\0';
         char *p1, *p2, *p0;
         p0 = p1 = p2 = theString;

         while (p1[0] && (p1[0] == '\n' || p1[0] == '\r
            p1++;

         p2 = p1;

         while (p2[0] && p2[0] != '\n' && p2[0] != '\r'
            p2++;

         int bufferLen = p2 - p1;
         int totalLen = p2 - p0;

         if (!bufferLen)
            continue;

         // lstrcpyn(buffer,p1,bufferLen);
         strncpy(buffer,p1,bufferLen);
         buffer[bufferLen]='\0';

         // for (int i = 0; i< PageSize; i++)
            cout << "\r";
         cout << "Parsing " << buffer;
         myTree.Insert(buffer);

         lineCount++;          // Added Exercise 13.3

         offset += totalLen;
         theFile.clear();
         theFile.seekg(offset,ios::beg);
```

```
    }
// Added Exercise 13.3
    cout << lineCount << " lines were added \n";
}
```

Answers for Day 14, "Advanced Data Manipulation"

Quiz

1. The statement A OR B is true if either A or B is true or if both are true. The statement A Exclusive-Or B is true if either A or B is true, but it is false if both are true or if neither is true.

2. Make its value 1.

3. Make its value 0.

4. The stack is a preallocated special area of memory used to keep track of the next instruction pointer and for other compiler housekeeping. It also is where local variables are stored during their lifetimes. The heap is all unallocated memory.

   In C++, you create local objects on the stack and you allocate memory using the new operator on the heap.

5. You can compute this by figuring out what this number is in decimal (189) and converting to Hex, or by dividing the number into two sets of four decimal numbers (11, 13) and using their Hex values (B, D).

Exercises

1. Here is the answer:
```
unsigned short SwapHighAndLowBits(unsigned short I)
{
    // First capture high and low bits
    unsigned short low = i & 0x01;
    unsigned short high = i & 0x80;

    // Now mask off the existing high and low bits
    i &= ~0x81;

    // Move high bit to low position and vice-versa
    // by shifting 7 places.
    low <<= 7;
    high >>= 7;

    // Return with values back into the masked value
    return (i ¦ low ¦ high);
}
```

2. Here is the last part of the answer:

```
Byte 0,  Status byte (Read only)
    D0:     Receive Ready
    D1:     Parity Error Detected
    D2:     Overrun Error Detected
    D3—D6: Unused
    D7:     Transmit Ready

Byte 1,  Configuration byte (Read/Write)
    D0—D2: Baud rate:    0 = 150
                         1 = 300
                         2 = 1200
                         3 = 4800
                         4 = 9600
                         5 = 14.4k
                         6 = 19.2k
                         7 = 38.4k
    D3:    Unused
    D4—D5: Parity       0 = none
                        1 = illegal value
                        2 = even parity
                        3 = odd parity
    D6:    Unused
    D7:    Stop bits    0 = one stop bit
                        1 = two stop bits

[These two lines are used in Exercise 4.]
Byte 2, Last received character (Read only)
Byte 3, Character to transmit (Write only)
```

3. Here is the first part of the answer:

```
const unsigned char ReceiveReady      = 0x01;
const unsigned char ParityError       = 0x02;
const unsigned char OverrunError      = 0x04;
const unsigned char TransmitReady     = 0x80;

const unsigned char BaudMask          = 0x07;
const unsigned char Baud150           = 0x00;
const unsigned char Baud300           = 0x01;
const unsigned char Baud1200          = 0x02;
const unsigned char Baud4800          = 0x03;
const unsigned char Baud9600          = 0x04;
const unsigned char Baud144k          = 0x05;
const unsigned char Baud192k          = 0x06;
const unsigned char Baud384k          = 0x07;

const unsigned char ParityMask        = 0x03 << 4;
const unsigned char ParityNone        = 0x00 << 4;
const unsigned char ParityEven        = 0x02 << 4;
const unsigned char ParityOdd         = 0x03 << 4;

const unsigned char StopBitsMask      = 0x01 << 7;
const unsigned char StopBitsOne       = 0x00 << 7;
const unsigned char StopBitsTwo       = 0x01 << 7;
```

Here is the last part of the answer:

```
class SerialCommunicationPort
{
public:
    SerialCommunicationPort(unsigned char * StartingAddress);

    unsigned char Read( );
    void Reset( );          // Must be called after a read error

    void Write(unsigned char value);

    void SetBaudRate(unsigned char baud);
    void SetParity(unsigned char parity);
    void SetStopBits(unsigned char stopbits);
};
```

4. Write the entire class discussed in exercise 3. Be sure to start the communication port with reasonable defaults for the configuration parameters and be sure to clear any errors it might have pending.

```
class SerialCommunicationPort
{
public:
    SerialCommunicationPort(unsigned char * StartingAddress);

    unsigned char Read( );
    void Reset( )           // Must be called after a read error
        { unsigned char x = myChip[2];}      // clear the error

    void Write(unsigned char value);

    void SetBaudRate(unsigned char baud);
    void SetParity(unsigned char parity);
    void SetStopBits(unsigned char stopbits);

private:
    unsigned char * myChip;
};

SerialCommunicationPort::SerialCommunicationPort(unsigned char *
➥StartingAddress)
    : myChip(StartingAddress)
{
    myChip[1] = Baud9600 | ParityNone | StopBitsOne;    // set default
    Reset( );
}

SerialCommunicationPort::Read( )
{
    if (myChip[0] & (ParityError | OverrunError))
        return 0;

    // (There is actually a gap here where an Overrun error can occur
    //    and we wouldn't detect it.  This turns out to be impossible to
    //    fix completely, with the chip spec'ed as it is, but we could do
```

```
        //    a lot better than we are doing here.)

        if (myChip[0] & ReceiveReady)
            return myChip[2];
        else
            return 0;
    }

    SerialCommunicationPort::Write(unsigned char value)
    {
        // First wait until we see TransmitReady set to 1.
        // (In real life, we would have to declare the space to be
        // volatile.  Let's ignore the whole issue for this exercise.)
        while (myChip[0] & TransmitReady == 0)
            ;

        myChip[3] = value;     // Send it.
    }

    SerialCommunicationPort::SetBaudRate(unsigned char baud)
    {
        unsigned char config = myChip[1];    // get current values
        config &= ~BaudMask;               // Mask away old baud
        config |= baud;                    // OR in new baud
        myChip[1] = config;
    }

    SerialCommunicationPort::SetParity(unsigned char parity)
    {
        unsigned char config = myChip[1];    // get current values
        config &= ~ParityMask;              // Mask away old parity
        config |= parity;                   // OR in new parity
        myChip[1] = config;
    }

    SerialCommunicationPort::SetStopbits(unsigned char stopbits)
    {
        unsigned char config = myChip[1];    // get current values
        config &= ~StopBitsMask;          // Mask away old SB
        config |= stopbits;               // OR in new SB
        myChip[1] = config;
    }
```

Answers for Day 15, "Iterators"

Quiz

1. An *index* provides access to data via keywords. An *iterator* answers the question *What is next in this list?*

2. The deletion of the object must be accounted for, not only by the iterator that does the delete, but also by any other existing iterators that may be walking the same list.

3. The main goal of a good iterator is to hide the details of finding the next object in the list.

Exercises

1. Here is the answer:

```
1:      #include "standard.hpp"
2:
3:      const USHORT DefaultListSize = 20;
4:      class IntListIterator;
5:
6:      class IntList
7:      {
8:      public:
9:          IntList(USHORT size = DefaultListSize);
10:
11:         IntListIterator * NewIterator();
12:         USHORT GetSize() const {return mySize;}
13:
14:     protected:
15:         int * GetArray() const {return myArray;}
16:         int & operator[](USHORT pos) {return myArray[pos];}
17:
18:     private:
19:         friend class IntListIterator;
20:         USHORT mySize;
21:         int * myArray;
22:     };
23:
24:     class IntListIterator
25:     {
26:     public:
27:         IntListIterator (IntList & theList)
28:             : myList(theList), myPosition(0) {}
29:
30:         USHORT GetPosition()   const    {return myPosition;}
31:
32:         // All of the positional methods return TRUE if the position is
                valid
33:         BOOL IsValidPosition() const    {return myPosition <
            myList.GetSize();}
34:         BOOL ToFirst()       {myPosition = 0;  return TRUE;}
35:         BOOL ToLast()        {myPosition = myList.GetSize() - 1; return
            TRUE;}
36:         BOOL ToNext()        {myPosition++; return IsValidPosition();}
37:         BOOL ToPrev()        {myPosition—; return IsValidPosition();}
38:
39:         int GetCurrent() const
40:              {assert(IsValidPosition()); return myList[myPosition];}
41:         void SetCurrent(int value) const
42:              {assert(IsValidPosition()); myList[myPosition] = value;}
43:
44:     private:
```

```
45:        IntList & myList;
46:        USHORT myPosition;
47:    };
```

2. Here is the answer:

```
1:        // Answer to exercise 2
2:
3:        #include "intlist.hpp"
4:
5:
6:        IntList::IntList(USHORT size)
7:            : mySize(size), myArray(0)
8:        {
9:            assert(size > 0);
10:           myArray = new int[size];
11:
12:           for (USHORT i = 0; i < size; I++)
13:           {
14:               myArray[i] = 0;
15:           }
16:       }
17:
18:       IntListIterator *
19:       IntList::NewIterator()
20:       {
21:           return new IntListIterator(*this);
22:       }
23:
```

3. Here is the answer:

```
1:
2:        #include "standard.hpp"
3:        #include "intlist.hpp"
4:
5:
6:        void main()
7:        {
8:            IntList theList;
9:            IntListIterator * iterp = theList.NewIterator();
10:
11:           for (iterp->ToFirst(); iterp->IsValidPosition(); iterp->ToNext())
12:           {
13:               int value = iterp->GetPosition();
14:               iterp->SetCurrent(value);
15:           }
16:
17:           for (iterp->ToFirst(); iterp->IsValidPosition(); iterp->ToNext())
18:           {
19:               cout << iterp->GetCurrent() << "  ";
20:           }
21:
22:           delete iterp;
23:       }
```

4. Here is the answer:

```
1:      #include "standard.hpp"
2:
3:      const USHORT DefaultListSize = 20;
4:
5:      template <class Type> class ListIterator;
6:
7:      template <class Type>
8:      class List
9:      {
10:     public:
11:        List(USHORT size = DefaultListSize);
12:
13:        ListIterator<Type> * NewIterator();
14:        USHORT GetSize() const {return mySize;}
15:
16:     protected:
17:        Type * GetArray() const {return myArray;}
18:        Type & operator[](USHORT pos) {return myArray[pos];}
19:
20:     private:
21:        friend class ListIterator<Type>;
22:        USHORT mySize;
23:        Type * myArray;
24:     };
25:
26:     template <class Type>
27:     class ListIterator
28:     {
29:     public:
30:        ListIterator (List<Type> & theList)
31:           : myList(theList), myPosition(0) {}
32:
33:        USHORT GetPosition()    const    {return myPosition;}
34:
35:        // All of the positional methods return TRUE if the position is
                valid
36:        BOOL IsValidPosition() const    {return myPosition <
        myList.GetSize();}
37:        BOOL ToFirst()         {myPosition = 0;   return TRUE;}
38:        BOOL ToLast()          {myPosition = myList.GetSize() - 1; return
        TRUE;}
39:        BOOL ToNext()          {myPosition++; return IsValidPosition();}
40:        BOOL ToPrev()          {myPosition--; return IsValidPosition();}
41:
42:        Type GetCurrent() const
43:              {assert(IsValidPosition()); return myList[myPosition];}
44:        void SetCurrent(Type value) const
45:              {assert(IsValidPosition()); myList[myPosition] = value;}
46:
47:     private:
48:        List<Type> & myList;
49:        USHORT myPosition;
50:     };
51:
```

```
52:     template <class Type>
53:     List<Type>::List(USHORT size)
54:          : mySize(size), myArray(0)
55:     {
56:        assert(size > 0);
57:        myArray = new Type[size];
58:
59:        for (USHORT i = 0; i < size; I++)
60:        {
61:            myArray[i] = 0;
62:        }
63:     }
64:
65:     template <class Type>
66:     ListIterator<Type> *
67:     List<Type>::NewIterator()
68:     {
69:        return new ListIterator<Type>(*this);
70:     }
```

5. Here is the answer:

```
1:
2:      #include "standard.hpp"
3:      #include "genlist.hpp"
4:
5:
6:      void main()
7:      {
8:         List<int> theList;
9:         ListIterator<int> * iterp = theList.NewIterator();
10:
11:        for (iterp->ToFirst(); iterp->IsValidPosition(); iterp->ToNext())
12:        {
13:           int value = iterp->GetPosition();
14:           iterp->SetCurrent(value);
15:        }
16:
17:        for (iterp->ToFirst(); iterp->IsValidPosition(); iterp->ToNext())
18:        {
19:           cout << iterp->GetCurrent() << "   ";
20:        }
21:
22:        delete iterp;
23:
24:        cout << "\n\n";
25:
26:        List<char *> charList(26);
27:        ListIterator<char *> * chIterp = charList.NewIterator();
28:
29:        for (chIterp->ToFirst(); chIterp->IsValidPosition(); chIterp->ToNext())
30:        {
31:           char * value = new char[5];
32:           value[0] = 'A' + chIterp->GetPosition();
33:           value[1] = '\0';
34:           chIterp->SetCurrent(value);
```

```
35:        }
36:
37:        for (chIterp->ToFirst(); chIterp->IsValidPosition();
           >chIterp-ToNext())
38:        {
39:            cout << chIterp->GetCurrent() << " ";
40:        }
41:
42:        delete chIterp;
43:
44:    }
```

Answers for Day 16, "Synonyms"

Quiz

1. A program is made maintainable with good documentation and clearly articulated design goals, as well as solid, object-oriented design and coding practices. Well-designed, discrete classes with narrow interfaces among them also make a program maintainable.

2. A good comment explains why the code is doing what it is doing and provides an insight into the flow of control.

3. Legacy code is code that you must maintain but you didn't write. Most programmers have a very hard time understanding another programmer's intentions and solutions in detail without a lot of hard work. Well-documented code makes this challenge somewhat easier.

4. The user would like to match on related terms. It is frustrating to search on *automobiles*, for example, and miss articles with the keyword *car*.

Exercises

In order to avoid repeating the same code for each exercise, the complete solution to all exercises is shown at the end of this chapter section.

1. The changes here were to add statics to class BTree, which are defined in BTree.cpp; and to remove unnecessary arguments from these functions and use the statics instead. Page::Find was made no longer inline, because it had to reference BTree statics.

2. The answer is shown in the DoSyn() function.

3. The answer is shown in the modification to main() and the addition of the ShowInstructions().

4. The answer is shown in the addition of the MultipleLines().

5. The answer is shown in the modified `MultipleLines` method.

```
1:      // *****************************************************
2:      // PROGRAM:   R2
3:      // FILE:      r2.cpp
4:      // PURPOSE:   Add synonyms to ROBIN.
5:      // NOTES:
6:      // AUTHOR:    Jesse Liberty (jl)
7:      // REVISIONS: 1/1/95 1.0 jl
8:      // *****************************************************
9:
10:     #include "String.hpp"
11:     #include "stdef.hpp"
12:     #include "btree.hpp"
13:     #include <stdlib.h>
14:
15:     // static definitions
16:     IDXManager BTree::theIDXManager;
17:     DataFile BTree::theDataFile;
18:     WNJFile BTree::theWNJFile;
19:     Iterator BTree::theIter;
20:
21:     int WNJFile::myCount=0L;
22:     int Page::gPage=1;
23:     int BTree::NodeIndexCtr=0;
24:     int BTree::LeafIndexCtr=0;
25:     int BTree::NodePageCtr=0;
26:     int BTree::LeafPageCtr=0;
27:     int BTree::NodeIndexPerPage[Order+1];
28:     int BTree::LeafIndexPerPage[Order+1];
29:
30:
31:     // prototypes
32:     void parseCommandLines(char *buffer,int argc,char **argv);
33:     void ShowMenu(long*);
34:     void DoFind(int, char**, Btree&);
35:     void ParseFile(int, char**, Btree&);
36:     void DoSyn(char *orig, char* syn, BTree& myTree);
37:     void MultipleLines(BTree& myTree);
38:     void ShowInstructions();
39:
40:     // #define shrink
41:
42:     // driver program
43:     int _cdecl main(int argc, char ** argv)
44:     {
45:        BTree myTree;
46:
47:        for (int i = 0; i < Order +2; I++)
48:        {
49:           BTree::NodeIndexPerPage[i] =0;
50:           BTree::LeafIndexPerPage[i] = 0;
51:        }
52:
53:        char buffer[PageSize+1];
54:
```

```
55:        if (argc == 1)
56:        {
57:           cout << "Please provide command line arguments.  Use -H for
           help.";
58:           return 1;
59:        }
60:
61:        // check for flags, if none add text to data file
62:        if (argv[1][0] == '-')
63:        {
64:
65:           switch (argv[1][1])
66:           {
67:              case '?':
68:                 DoFind(argc,argv,myTree);
69:                 break;
70:
71:              case '!':
72:                    myTree.PrintTree();
73:                    break;
74:
75:              case 'F':
76:              case 'f':
77:                    ParseFile(argc,argv,myTree);
78:                    break;
79:
80:              case 'S':
81:              case 's':
82:                    DoSyn(argv[2],argv[3],myTree);
83:                    break;
84:
85:              case 'M':
86:              case 'm':
87:                    MultipleLines(myTree);
88:                    break;
89:
90:              default:
91:                    ShowInstructions();
92:                    break;
93:           }
94:        }
95:        else
96:        {
97:           parseCommandLines(buffer,argc,argv);
98:           myTree.Insert(buffer,argc,argv);
99:           cout << "Inserted.\n";
100:       }
101:       return 0;
102:   }
103:
104:   // concatenate remaining command line arguments
105:   void parseCommandLines(char *buffer,int argc,char **argv)
106:   {
107:       size_t len = 0;
108:       size_t argLen=0;
109:       for (int i = 1; i< argc; I++)
```

```
110:        {
111:            argLen = strlen(argv[i]);
112:            if (len + argLen +2 < PageSize)
113:            {
114:                strncpy(buffer+len,argv[i],argLen);
115:                strncpy(buffer+len+argLen," ",1);
116:                len += argLen+1;
117:            }
118:        }
119:        buffer[len] = '\0';
120:    }
121:
122:    // having found matches, show the menu of choices
123:    // each entry is numbered and dated
124:    void ShowMenu(int *list)
125:    {
126:        int j=0;
127:        char buffer[PageSize+1];
128:        time_t theTime;
129:        int len;
130:        char listBuff[256];
131:        struct tm * ts;
132:        int dispSize;
133:
134:        while (list[j] && j < 20)
135:        {
136:            BTree::theDataFile.GetRecord(list[j],buffer,len, theTime);
137:            dispSize = min(len,32);
138:            strncpy(listBuff,buffer,dispSize);
139:            if (dispSize == 32)
140:                {
141:                listBuff[29] = '.';
142:                listBuff[30] = '.';
143:                listBuff[31] = '.';
144:                }
145:            listBuff[dispSize]='\0';
146:            ts = localtime(&theTime);
147:            cout << "[" << (j+1) << "] ";
148:            cout << ts->tm_mon << "/";
149:            cout << ts->tm_mday << "/";
150:            cout << ts->tm_year << " ";
151:            cout <<  listBuff << endl;
152:            j++;
153:        }
154:    }
155:
156:    // handle -? command
157:    // find matches, show the menu, request choice
158:    // display record and redisplay menu
159:    void DoFind(int argc, char ** argv, BTree& myTree)
160:    {
161:    #ifndef shrink
162:        // create an array of total set of WNJ
163:        // offsets. This will be used to display
164:        // choices and to find actual text
165:        int  list[PageSize];
```

```
166:
167:        // initialize the array to all zeros
168:        for (int i = 0; i<PageSize; I++)
169:             list[i] = 0;
170:
171:        // for each word in the command line
172:        // search for the matching set of records
173:        for (i = 2; i< argc; I++)
174:        {
175:            int offset = myTree.Find(argv[i]);
176:            while (offset)
177:            {
178:              int* found  =  BTree::theWNJFile.Find(offset);
179:              int j=0;
180:              int len;
181:              time_t theTime;
182:              char buff[512];
183:              while (found[j])
184:              {
185:                 BTree::theDataFile.GetRecord(found[j],buff,len, theTime);
186:                 struct tm * ts = localtime(&theTime);
187:                 cout << "Found: ";
188:                 cout << ts->tm_mon << "/";
189:                 cout << ts->tm_mday << "/";
190:                 cout << ts->tm_year << " ";
191:                 cout <<  buff << endl;
192:                 j++;
193:              }
194:              delete [] found;
195:              offset = myTree.GetNext(argv[i]);
196:          }
197:        }
198:
199:         cout << "\n";
200:
201:         if (!list[0])
202:            return;
203:
204:
205:         ShowMenu(list);
206:
207:         int choice;
208:         char buffer[PageSize];
209:         int len;
210:         time_t theTime;
211:
212:         for (;;)
213:         {
214:            cout << "Choice (0 to stop): " ;
215:            cin >> choice;
216:            if (!choice)
217:               break;
218:            BTree::theDataFile.GetRecord(list[choice-1],buffer,len,
                  theTime);
219:            cout << "\n>> ";
220:            cout << buffer;
```

```
221:                cout << "\n\n";
222:                ShowMenu(list);
223:            }
224:    #endif
225:    }
226:
227:    // open a file and create a new note for each line
228:    // index every word in the line
229:    void ParseFile(int argc,char **argv, BTree& myTree)
230:    {
231:     #ifndef shrink
232:        char buffer[PageSize];
233:        char theString[PageSize];
234:
235:        ifstream theFile(argv[2],ios::in );
236:        if (!theFile)
237:        {
238:            cout << "Error opening input file!\n";
239:            return;
240:        }
241:        int offset = 0;
242:        for (;;)
243:        {
244:                theFile.read(theString,PageSize);
245:                int len = theFile.gcount();
246:                if (!len)
247:                    break;
248:                theString[len]='\0';
249:                char *p1, *p2, *p0;
250:                p0 = p1 = p2 = theString;
251:
252:                while (p1[0] && (p1[0] == '\n' || p1[0] == '\r'))
253:                    p1++;
254:
255:                p2 = p1;
256:
257:                while (p2[0] && p2[0] != '\n' && p2[0] != '\r')
258:                    p2++;
259:
260:                int bufferLen = int(p2 - p1);
261:                int totalLen = int (p2 - p0);
262:
263:                if (!bufferLen)
264:                    continue;
265:
266:                // lstrcpyn(buffer,p1,bufferLen);
267:                strncpy(buffer,p1,bufferLen);
268:                buffer[bufferLen]='\0';
269:
270:                // for (int i = 0; i< PageSize; I++)
271:                    cout << "\r";
272:                cout << "Parsing " << buffer;
273:                myTree.Insert(buffer);
274:                offset += totalLen;
275:                theFile.clear();
276:                theFile.seekg(offset,ios::beg);
```

```
277:          }
278:     #endif
279:      }
280:
281:
282:     // add synonyms to the tree
283:      void DoSyn(char *orig, char* syn, BTree& myTree)
284:      {
285:     #ifndef shrink
286:         int offset = myTree.FindExact(syn);
287:         if (!offset)  // syn can't exist
288:         {
289:             int offset = myTree.FindExact(orig);
290:             if (offset) // orig must exist
291:             {
292:                 myTree.AddKey(syn,offset,TRUE);
293:                 cout << "\"" << syn << "\" Added as a synonym for \"" <<
                       orig << "\"\n";
294:             }
295:             else
296:                 cout << "Synonym not added!  \"" << orig << "\" is not in
                       keylist.\n";
297:         }
298:         else
299:         {
300:             cout << "Synonym not added!  \"" << syn << "\" is already a
                   key.\n";
301:         }
302:     #endif
303:      }
304:
305:     // MultipleLines
306:     //     Accept lines of input from cin and insert them.
307:     #ifdef Exercise4
308:     void MultipleLines(BTree& myTree)
309:     {
310:         char buffer[PageSize];
311:
312:         while (TRUE)
313:             {
314:             cin.getline(buffer, PageSize-1);
315:             if (buffer[0] == '\0')
316:                 break;
317:
318:             myTree.Insert(buffer);
319:             }
320:     }
321:     #else
322:     void MultipleLines(BTree& myTree)
323:     {
324:         char buffer[PageSize];
325:
326:         int lineCount = 0;
327:         char * lineText = " Line";
328:
329:         while (TRUE)
```

```
330:          {
331:          cin.getline(buffer, PageSize-1);
332:          if (buffer[0] == '\0')
333:             break;
334:
335:          myTree.Insert(buffer);
336:          lineCount++;
337:          cout << lineCount << lineText << " inserted\n";
338:          lineText = " Lines";
339:          }
340:    }
341:    #endif
342:
343:
344:    void ShowInstructions()
345:    {
346:       cout   << "Supported switches:\n"
347:              << "-? <word>        Find occurrences of <word>\n"
348:              << "-!               Show tree\n"
349:              << "-f <filename>    Parse file\n"
350:              << "-m               Accept multiple lines of input from
                                       keyboard.\n"
351:              << "-s <word> <syn>  Add <syn> as a synonym for <word>.\n"
352:              << "-h               Print this message.";
353:
354:    }
```

Answers for Day 17, "Profiling and Optimization"

Quiz

1. *Optimizing* is performing the time/disk space/clarity trade-offs that maximize those areas of performance or disk-space reduction required. *Profiling* is the exercise that results in a report of the current performance of the program.

2. A() may be the better candidate, but that will depend on how efficient each function is, and how essential each is. If function A() takes 20 milliseconds and performs an essential service, and function B() takes two full seconds and performs a service that can be done more efficiently, then function B() is the candidate for change.

3. It is 6.9 seconds. A millisecond is 1/1000 of a second.

Exercises

Note that the exercises for the profiler are dependent on the specific software provided by your compiler vendor, and the results will vary based on the speed of your computer and its disks.

Answers are *not* provided for these exercises, but you are strongly encouraged to examine your results and to use your profiler sufficiently to become comfortable with its operation and results.

Answers for Day 18, "Advanced Exceptions and Error Handling"

Quiz

1. An exception is an object that is created as a result of invoking the keyword throw. It is used to signal an exceptional condition, and is passed up the call stack to the first catch statement that handles its type.

2. A try block is a set of statements that might generate an exception.

3. A catch statement has a signature of the type of exception it handles. It follows a try block, and acts as the receiver of exceptions raised within the try block.

4. An exception is an object, and can contain any information that can be defined within a user-created class.

5. Exception objects are created when you invoke the keyword throw.

6. In general, exceptions should be passed by reference. If you don't intend to modify the contents of the exception object, you should pass a const reference.

7. Yes, if you pass the exception by reference.

8. Catch statements are examined in the order in which they appear in the source code. The first catch statement with a signature that matches the exception is used.

9. Catch(...) will catch any exception of any type.

Exercises

1. Here is the answer:
   ```
   #include <iostreams.h>
   class OutOfMemory {};
   void main()
   {

       try
       {
           int *myInt = new int;
           if (myInt == 0)
               throw OutOfMemory();
       }
       catch (OutOfMemory)
       {
   ```

```
        cout << "Unable to allocate memory!\n";
    }
}
```

2. Here is the answer:

```
#include <iostreams.h>
#include <stdio.h>
#include <string.h>
class OutOfMemory
{
public:
    OutOfMemory(char *);

    char* GetString() { return itsString; }
private:
    char* itsString;
};

OutOfMemory::OutOfMemory(char * theType)
{
    itsString = new char[80];
    char warning[] = "Out Of Memory! Can't allocate room for: ";
    strncpy(itsString,warning,60);
    strncat(itsString,theType,19);
}

void main()
{

    try
    {
        int *myInt = new int;
        if (myInt == 0)
            throw OutOfMemory("int");
    }
    catch (OutOfMemory& theException)
    {
        cout << theException.GetString();
    }
}
```

3. Here is the answer:

```
1:      #include <iostreams.h>
2:
3:      // Abstract exception data type
4:      class Exception
5:      {
6:      public:
7:          Exception(){}
8:          virtual ~Exception(){}
9:          virtual void PrintError() = 0;
10:     };
11:
12:     // Derived class to handle memory problems.
13:     // Note no allocation of memory in this class!
```

```
14:      class OutOfMemory : public Exception
15:      {
16:      public:
17:         OutOfMemory(){}
18:         ~OutOfMemory(){}
19:         virtual void PrintError();
20:      private:
21:      };
22:
23:      void OutOfMemory::PrintError()
24:      {
25:         cout << "Out of Memory!!\n";
26:      }
27:
28:      // Derived class to handle bad numbers
29:      class RangeError : public Exception
30:      {
31:      public:
32:         RangeError(unsigned long number){badNumber = number;}
33:         ~RangeError(){}
34:         virtual void PrintError();
35:         virtual unsigned long GetNumber() { return badNumber; }
36:         virtual void SetNumber(unsigned long number) ➥{badNumber = number;}
37:      private:
38:         unsigned long badNumber;
39:      };
40:
41:      void RangeError::PrintError()
42:      {
43:         cout << "Number out of range. You used " << ➥GetNumber() << "!!\n";
44:      }
45:
46:      void MyFunction();  // func. prototype
47:
48:      void main()
49:      {
50:         try
51:         {
52:            MyFunction();
53:         }
54:         // Only one catch required, use virtual functions to ➥do the
55:         // right thing.
56:         catch (Exception& theException)
57:         {
58:            theException.PrintError();
59:         }
60:      }
61:
62:      void MyFunction()
63:      {
64:          unsigned int *myInt = new unsigned int;
65:          long testNumber;
66:          if (myInt == 0)
67:              throw OutOfMemory();
68:
69:          cout << "Enter an int: ";
```

```
70:            cin >> testNumber;
71:            // this weird test should be replaced by a series
72:            // of tests to complain about bad user input
73:            if (testNumber > 3768 || testNumber < 0)
74:                throw RangeError(testNumber);
75:
76:            *myInt = testNumber;
77:            cout << "Ok. myInt: " << *myInt;
78:            delete myInt;
79:        }
```

4. Here is the answer:

```
1:        #include <iostreams.h>
2:
3:        // Abstract exception data type
4:        class Exception
5:        {
6:        public:
7:            Exception(){}
8:            virtual ~Exception(){}
9:            virtual void PrintError() = 0;
10:        };
11:
12:        // Derived class to handle memory problems.
13:        // Note no allocation of memory in this class!
14:        class OutOfMemory : public Exception
15:        {
16:        public:
17:            OutOfMemory(){}
18:            ~OutOfMemory(){}
19:            virtual void PrintError();
20:        private:
21:        };
22:
23:        void OutOfMemory::PrintError()
24:        {
25:            cout << "Out of Memory!!\n";
26:        }
27:
28:        // Derived class to handle bad numbers
29:        class RangeError : public Exception
30:        {
31:        public:
32:            RangeError(unsigned long number){badNumber = number;}
33:            ~RangeError(){}
34:            virtual void PrintError();
35:            virtual unsigned long GetNumber() { return badNumber; ➥}
36:            virtual void SetNumber(unsigned long number) ➥{badNumber = number;}
37:        private:
38:            unsigned long badNumber;
39:        };
40:
41:        void RangeError::PrintError()
42:        {
43:            cout << "Number out of range. You used " << ➥GetNumber() << "!!\n";
44:        }
```

```
45:
46:    // func. prototypes
47:    void MyFunction();
48:    unsigned int * FunctionTwo();
49:    void FunctionThree(unsigned int *);
50:
51:    void main()
52:    {
53:       try
54:       {
55:          MyFunction();
56:       }
57:       // Only one catch required, use virtual functions to ➥do the
58:       // right thing.
59:       catch (Exception& theException)
60:       {
61:          theException.PrintError();
62:       }
63:     }
64:
65:    unsigned int * FunctionTwo()
66:    {
67:       unsigned int *myInt = new unsigned int;
68:       if (myInt == 0)
69:          throw OutOfMemory();
70:       return myInt;
71:    }
72:
73:
74:     void MyFunction()
75:     {
76:          unsigned int *myInt = FunctionTwo();
77:
78:          FunctionThree(myInt);
79:          cout << "Ok. myInt: " << *myInt;
80:          delete myInt;
81:     }
82:
83:    void FunctionThree(unsigned int *ptr)
84:    {
85:          long testNumber;
86:          cout << "Enter an int: ";
87:          cin >> testNumber;
88:          // this weird test should be replaced by a series
89:          // of tests to complain about bad user input
90:          if (testNumber > 3768 || testNumber < 0)
91:             throw RangeError(testNumber);
92:          *ptr = testNumber;
93:    }
```

5. In the process of handling an out-of-memory condition, a string object is created by the constructor of xOutOfMemory. This exception can be raised only when the program is out of memory, so this allocation must fail.

It is possible that trying to create this string will raise the same exception, creating an infinite loop until the program crashes. If this string really is required, you can allocate the space in a static buffer before beginning the program, and then use it as needed when the exception is thrown.

Answers for Day 19, "Writing Solid Code"

Quiz

1. Define the macro to test the result and print an error only if debug is defined. Otherwise, define it to disappear.

2. *Side effects* are results of the evaluation in an assert on which your code depends. You prevent side effects by *never* putting an expression into an `assert` statement.

3. Define a VERIFY macro that asserts FALSE if debug is defined, and simply returns the value of the evaluation if debug is not defined.

4. You place the `invariant()` assertion at the beginning and end of every member function except the constructor (where you put it only at the end) and the destructor (where you put it only at the beginning).

5. If you have a pointer to a base class that actually points to a derived object, the virtual destructor ensures that the entire object is deleted.

Exercises

1. Here is the answer:

```
1:      // assert macro
2:      #define DEBUG
3:      #include <iostreams.h>
4:
5:      #ifndef DEBUG
6:          #define ASSERT(x)
7:      #else
8:          #define ASSERT(x) \
9:                  if (! (x)) \
10:                 { \
11:                     cout << "ERROR!! Assert " << #x << " failed\n"; \
12:                     cout << " on line " << __LINE__ << "\n"; \
13:                     cout << " in file " << __FILE__ << "\n"; \
14:                 }
15:     #endif
```

2. Here is the answer:

```
1:     // verify macro
2:     #define DEBUG
3:     #include <iostreams.h>
4:
5:     #ifndef DEBUG
6:        #define VERIFY(x) (x)
7:     #else
8:        #define VERIFY(x) \
9:             ASSERT(x)
10:    #endif
11:
```

3. Here is the answer:

```
1:     BOOL Invariants()                    // class invariants
2:     {
3:          return (
4:             itsLen >= 0 &&
5:             (itsCString == 0  && itsLen == 0 ||
6:              itsCString[itsLen] == '\0')
7:          )
8:     }
```

4. Here is the answer:

```
1:     // Using invariants with listing 3.1
2:
3:     #include <iostream.h>
4:     #include <string.h>
5:     #define UINT unsigned int
6:     enum BOOL { FALSE, TRUE };
7:
8:     class xOutOfBounds {};
9:       // assert macro
10:      #define DEBUG
11:      #include <iostreams.h>
12:
13:      #ifndef DEBUG
14:         #define ASSERT(x)
15:      #else
16:        #define ASSERT(x) \
17:                if (! (x)) \
18:                { \
19:                   cout << "ERROR!! Assert " << #x << " failed\n"; \
20:                   cout << " on line " << __LINE__  << "\n"; \
21:                   cout << " in file " << __FILE__ << "\n";  \
22:                }
23:      #endif
24:
25:     class String
26:     {
27:     public:
28:
29:             // constructors
30:             String();
31:             String(const char *);
```

```
32:                  String (const char *, UINT length);
33:                  String (const String&);
34:                  ~String();
35:
36:                  // helpers and manipulators
37:                  UINT   GetLength() const { return itsLen; }
38:                  BOOL IsEmpty() const { return (BOOL) (itsLen == 0); }
39:                  void Clear();              // set string to 0 length
40:                  BOOL Invariants()  const             // class invariants
41:                  {
42:                    return  (BOOL)(
43:                            itsLen >= 0 &&
44:                            (itsCString == 0  && itsLen == 0 ¦¦
45:                            itsCString[itsLen] == '\0')
46:                          );
47:                  }
48:
49:                  // accessors
50:                  char operator[](UINT offset) const;
51:                  char& operator[](UINT offset);
52:                  const char * GetString()const  { return itsCString; }
53:
54:                  // casting operators
55:                   operator const char* () const { return itsCString; }
56:                   operator char* () { return itsCString;}
57:
58:                  // operators
59:                  const String& operator=(const String&);
60:                  const String& operator=(const char *);
61:
62:                  void operator+=(const String&);
63:                  void operator+=(char);
64:                  void operator+=(const char*);
65:
66:                  BOOL operator<(const String& rhs)const;
67:                  BOOL operator>(const String& rhs)const;
68:                  BOOL operator<=(const String& rhs)const;
69:                  BOOL operator>=(const String& rhs)const;
70:                  BOOL operator==(const String& rhs)const;
71:                  BOOL operator!=(const String& rhs)const;
72:
73:
74:                  // friend functions
75:                  String operator+(const String&);
76:                  String operator+(const char*);
77:                  String operator+(char);
78:
79:                  friend ostream& operator<< (ostream&, const String&);
80:
81:      private:
82:                  // returns 0 if same, -1 if this is less than argument,
83:                  // 1 if this is greater than argument
84:                  int StringCompare(const String&) const;  // used by Boolean
                                                                       operators
85:                  char * itsCString;
86:                  UINT itsLen;
```

```
87:       };
88:
89:          // default constructor creates string of 0 bytes
90:        String::String()
91:        {
92:           itsCString = new char[1];
93:           itsCString[0] = '\0';
94:           itsLen=0;
95:           ASSERT (Invariants());
96:        }
97:
98:        String::String(const char *rhs)
99:        {
100:          itsLen = strlen(rhs);
101:          itsCString = new char[itsLen+1];
102:          strcpy(itsCString,rhs);
103:          ASSERT (Invariants());
104:       }
105:
106:       String::String (const char *rhs, UINT length)
107:       {
108:          itsLen = strlen(rhs);
109:          if (length < itsLen)
110:             itsLen = length;   // max size = length
111:          itsCString = new char[itsLen+1];
112:          memcpy(itsCString,rhs,itsLen);
113:          itsCString[itsLen] = '\0';
114:          ASSERT (Invariants());
115:       }
116:
117:       // copy constructor
118:       String::String (const String & rhs)
119:       {
120:          itsLen=rhs.GetLength();
121:          itsCString = new char[itsLen+1];
122:          memcpy(itsCString,rhs.GetString(),itsLen);
123:          itsCString[rhs.itsLen]='\0';
124:          ASSERT (Invariants());
125:       }
126:
127:       String::~String ()
128:       {
129:          ASSERT (Invariants());
130:          Clear();
131:       }
132:
133:       void String::Clear()
134:       {
135:          ASSERT (Invariants());
136:          delete [] itsCString;
137:          itsLen = 0;
138:          itsCString=0;
139:          ASSERT (Invariants());
140:       }
141:
142:       //non constant offset operator
```

```
143:        char & String::operator[](UINT offset)
144:        {
145:           ASSERT (Invariants());
146:           if (offset > itsLen)
147:           {
148:               throw xOutOfBounds();
149:               // return itsCString[itsLen-1];
150:           }
151:           else
152:           {
153:               ASSERT (Invariants());
154:               return itsCString[offset];
155:           }
156:        }
157:
158:        // constant offset operator
159:        char String::operator[](UINT offset) const
160:        {
161:               ASSERT (Invariants());
162:
163:           if (offset > itsLen)
164:           {
165:               throw xOutOfBounds();
166:               // return itsCString[itsLen-1];
167:           }
168:           else
169:           {
170:               ASSERT (Invariants());
171:               return itsCString[offset];
172:           }
173:        }
174:
175:        // operator equals
176:        const String& String::operator=(const String & rhs)
177:        {
178:               ASSERT (Invariants());
179:           if (this == &rhs)
180:               return *this;
181:           delete [] itsCString;
182:           itsLen=rhs.GetLength();
183:           itsCString = new char[itsLen+1];
184:           memcpy(itsCString,rhs.GetString(),itsLen);
185:           itsCString[rhs.itsLen]='\0';
186:           ASSERT (Invariants());
187:           return *this;
188:        }
189:
190:        const String& String::operator=(const char * rhs)
191:        {
192:           ASSERT (Invariants());
193:           delete [] itsCString;
194:           itsLen=strlen(rhs);
195:           itsCString = new char[itsLen+1];
196:           memcpy(itsCString,rhs,itsLen);
197:           itsCString[itsLen]='\0';
198:           ASSERT (Invariants());
```

```
199:        return *this;
200:    }
201:
202:
203:    // changes current string, returns nothing
204:    void String::operator+=(const String& rhs)
205:    {
206:        ASSERT (Invariants());
207:        unsigned short rhsLen = rhs.GetLength();
208:        unsigned short totalLen = itsLen + rhsLen;
209:        char *temp = new char[totalLen+1];
210:        for (int i = 0; i<itsLen; I++)
211:            temp[i] = itsCString[i];
212:        for (int j = 0; j<rhsLen; j++, I++)
213:            temp[i] = rhs[j];
214:        temp[totalLen]='\0';
215:        ASSERT (Invariants());
216:        *this = temp;
217:    }
218:
219:    int String::StringCompare(const String& rhs) const
220:    {
221:            ASSERT (Invariants());
222:            return strcmp(itsCString, rhs.GetString());
223:    }
224:
225:    String String::operator+(const String& rhs)
226:    {
227:        ASSERT (Invariants());
228:        char * newCString = new char[GetLength() + rhs.GetLength() + 1];
229:        strcpy(newCString,GetString());
230:        strcat(newCString,rhs.GetString());
231:        String newString(newCString);
232:        ASSERT (Invariants());
233:        return newString;
234:    }
235:
236:
237:    String String::operator+(const char* rhs)
238:    {
239:        ASSERT (Invariants());
240:        char * newCString = new char[GetLength() + strlen(rhs)+ 1];
241:        strcpy(newCString,GetString());
242:        strcat(newCString,rhs);
243:        String newString(newCString);
244:        ASSERT (Invariants());
245:        return newString;
246:    }
247:
248:
249:    String String::operator+(char rhs)
250:    {
251:        ASSERT (Invariants());
252:        int oldLen = GetLength();
253:        char * newCString = new char[oldLen + 2];
254:        strcpy(newCString,GetString());
```

```
255:          newCString[oldLen] = rhs;
256:          newCString[oldLen+1] = '\0';
257:          String newString(newCString);
258:          ASSERT (Invariants());
259:          return newString;
260:      }
261:
262:
263:
264:      BOOL String::operator==(const String& rhs) const
265:      { return (BOOL) (StringCompare(rhs) == 0); }
266:      BOOL String::operator!=(const String& rhs)const
267:          { return (BOOL) (StringCompare(rhs) != 0); }
268:      BOOL String::operator<(const String& rhs)const
269:          { return (BOOL) (StringCompare(rhs) < 0); }
270:      BOOL String::operator>(const String& rhs)const
271:          { return (BOOL) (StringCompare(rhs) > 0); }
272:      BOOL String::operator<=(const String& rhs)const
273:          { return (BOOL) (StringCompare(rhs) <= 0); }
274:      BOOL String::operator>=(const String& rhs)const
275:          { return (BOOL) (StringCompare(rhs) >= 0); }
276:
277:      ostream& operator<< (ostream& ostr, const String& str)
278:      {
279:          ostr << str.itsCString;
280:          return ostr;
281:      }
282:
283:      // Listing 3.3 - Exercise the string class
284:
285:      void main()
286:      {
287:          char buffer[255];
288:          String helloStr("Hello");
289:          String worldStr(" world");
290:          cout << helloStr << endl;
291:          cout << worldStr << endl;
292:          helloStr+=worldStr;
293:          cout << helloStr << endl;
294:
295:          String t1 = worldStr + worldStr;
296:          String t2 = worldStr + " series";
297:          String t3 = worldStr + '!';
298:
299:          cout << "t1: " << t1 << endl;
300:          cout << "t2: " << t2 << endl;
301:          cout << "t3: " << t3 << endl;
302:
303:          cout << "\nEnter string 1: ";
304:          cin >> buffer;
305:          String S1(buffer);
306:          cout << "Enter string 2: ";
307:          cin >> buffer;
308:          String S2(buffer);
309:          cout << "\n";
310:          if (S1 < S2)
```

```
311:            cout << "S1 is less" << endl;
312:         else if ( S1 == S2)
313:            cout << "They are the same!" << endl;
314:         else
315:            cout << "S1 is greater" << endl;
316:         try
317:         {
318:            char theChar = S1[3];
319:            cout << "The fourth character of S1 is " << theChar << endl;
320:         }
321:         catch(...)
322:         {
323:            cout << "Unable to display the fourth character!" << endl;
324:         }
325:      }
326:
```

Answers for Day 20, "Debugging"

Quiz

1. A *watch statement* enables you to examine the value of a variable or expression, and a *break point* stops execution of a running program.

2. Typically, the call stack shows you the functions that were called to get you to a particular point in a program. A good stack window also will show the variables and their values, as passed into each function on the stack.

3. A *TRACE macro* prints the values of various variables at different points of your program. A TRACE macro is a good way to create a log of progress in debug mode, as a first approximation of locating bugs.

4. The optimizing compiler will reorganize your code, which will cause confusion when you attempt to step through the operation of your program. Essentially, the symbolic information representing your C++ statements no longer will match up with the blocks of assembler code used to implement your program.

Exercises

1. When copying a C-string, you should allocate one more byte than the strlen, so that there is room for the null.

```
char * retCStr = new char[size + 1];
```

There are two fence-post bugs—both within the for loop. First, the test of the for loop should be i less than NameCount, rather than less than or equal to. The easy way to make sure that you get these right is to imagine that NameCount is 1, so the loop should be executed only once. (Try it. You will see that with the test as it is, the loop executes twice.) The second bug is the use of `getline`. It should be passed `MaxNameLength-1`, or buffer should be allocated with an extra byte.

```
for (int i = 0; i<=NameCount; I++)
{
    char buffer[MaxNameLength];
    cin.getline(buffer, MaxNameLength);
    GlobalNameArray[i] = buffer;
}
```

2. If the test fails and x == 0, then the function will return without freeing `str`.

3. The code here actually is working correctly. The confusion is caused by the `CompareAbsolute` method, however, which takes its argument passed by value. If you add a copy constructor to the class `Complex`, with the appropriate `LOG`, you will see that it is called once just before the call to `CompareAbsolute`. In fact, the destructor for the temporary object is the first destructor called. The Complex object `c1` is destructed after the `LOG("Ending main")` but before the function really is quite ended. The global object is the first one constructed and the last one destructed.

4. The bug here is the test of the return value that is passed back from `CompressCStr`. The comment says that it returns –1 if it fails, and the return value was put into an automatic variable `LenUsed`, and is tested with the following code:

```
if (LenUsed < 0)
    return -1;
```

However, `LenUsed` was defined to be an unsigned int, so it never can have a value less than 0. The value that is passed back from `CompressCStr` when that function encounters an error is instead interpreted as 65,535 characters added to the buffer.

5. The problem is caused by a bug, no doubt, elsewhere in the program, because someone else is passing this function a `MessageID` that is outside the allowed range. A bit of defensive programming, however, would have caught this much sooner. First, the variable `msg` should be initialized to 0. Second, the switch should have a default case, which should assert (FALSE) or output some warning message (assuming that it never was expected to happen). Always put a default case in every switch!

Answers for Day 21, "Next Steps"

Quiz

1. The *trunk* is the continuing evolution of your program. A *branch* is a departure from an earlier version now that the trunk has moved on. If foo.cpp, for example, is now in version 21, you might need to "branch" from version 20 if someone else has 21 locked out of the system.

2. A *named release* is a complete set of files that has been given a release name so that everyone in the project can refer to the same set of files.

3. Tough question. A number of books are suggested in this chapter. My best recommendation, however, is that you read a novel, visit with your family, and take a rest. Then start writing code. After all of that, you probably will want to read many of the books and magazines listed in this chapter.

4. jl@ichange.com

5. 42

B

Make Files

Make Files

A *make file* is a text file that acts as the source of information for the make utility. Modern integrated development environments (IDEs) enable you to create "projects" that track all your files for one program and automatically generate make files.

Although make utilities may differ in some of the specifics of syntax, they all generally work about the same way. Typically, a list of dependencies is created. A dependency describes which files depend on other files that already exist and are up to date. For example, you might write

```
test.exe            string.obj  test.obj
```

This code indicates that in order to create `test.exe`, the `string.obj` and `test.obj` files must be up to date. Other lines in the make file would indicate what each of these files requires; for example, `string.obj` might depend on `string.cp` and `string.hp` being up to date.

The make file also indicates how to create each of these files. For example, under `test.exe`, might be the command

```
test.exe            string.obj  test.obj
        cl test test.cpp string.cpp
```

Note: The syntax for all these commands depends on the make utility you are using. Be sure to check the documentation that comes with your compiler or make program.

Typically, when make starts, it looks for a file named `makefile`, but you can redirect it to another name as well. IDEs often enable you to override which make utility is used, so you can use third-party make files if you feel they offer significant advantages.

Conditional Compilation

The single most significant advantage of using make with large programming projects is that you can avoid recompiling programs that have not changed. You also avoid *failing* to recompile programs that depend on header files that *have* changed.

After the make file is created—either by you or by the project manager in your IDE—it tracks the dependencies. For example, you might write

```
myProg.exe   myprog.o  string.o
      cl myprog  myprog.o  string.o

myprog.o   myprog.cpp myprog.hpp  string.hpp
      cc myprog.cpp

string.o   string.cpp string.hpp
      cc string.cpp
```

If `string.hpp` changes, both `myprog` and `string` are recompiled, but if `myprog.hpp` changes, only `myprog.cpp` is recompiled. If *either* of these recompilations happens, the entire program is relinked.

Make Variables

Make files typically become rather complex, and there is a great advantage to being able to use variable names, macro substitution, and conditional compiles within your make files. Make file hacking is an art in itself, and make files have been known to be some of the more indecipherable collections of indirect code produced.

You can assign strings to variables and then use those variables as a macro substitution for the strings, using the `$()` operator to distinguish macro names from literals. For example, you might assign

```
OBJS = myprog.o string.o
```

and then change

```
myProg.exe    myprog.o   string.o
```

to

```
myProg.exe    $(OBJS)
```

From that time on, every time you need to refer to all the `obj` files, you simply add to the `OBJS =` line, and the substitution occurs everywhere the macro is used.

Built-In Variables

Most make utilities predefine some variables for your convenience. For example, most make files define `$(CC)` as the compiler command.

Make also typically maintains several special variables for parsing the file names. `$@` often is used for the target name, and some clever make files can distinguish between the target name (`myprog`, for example) and the extension (`.exe`, `.cpp`, and so on).

Suffix Rules

It is possible with most make files to create a rule for how certain types of files are created. In most make files, the syntax for these rules is

```
.suffix1 .suffix2:
    commands
```

This states that files ending in `suffix2` depend on files ending with `suffix1` and are created using the `commands`. Thus, you might see

```
.cpp.obj:
    $(CC) $(CFLAGS) $<
```

This says that files ending in `.obj` depend on files ending in `.cpp`. It also says that when these .obj files are to be remade, the make file should use the `CC` compiler line with the flags defined in `CFLAGS`. The final symbol, `$<`, indicates that the depended-upon files (in this case, the `.cpp` files) are to be placed at this point in the command line.

The symbol `$<` is used only with suffix rules. Another symbol commonly used with suffix rules is `$*`, which is the target file without its suffix. The target file is the file being created; in the example used in this section, the `.obj` file is the target.

Next Steps

It is important to check your own make file documentation. Make utilities can be very powerful—some allow you to declare your own suffix rules, for example. Be careful to fully document your make files (almost all make utilities recognize some form of comment symbol).

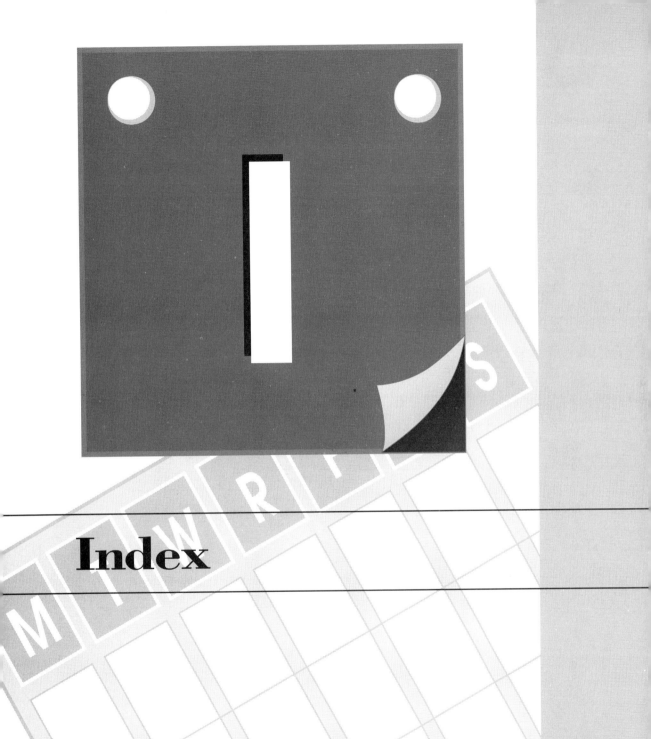

Index

Symbols

& (ampersand) AND
operator, 378
^ (caret) exclusive OR
operator, 379
? (question mark), calling
DoFind() method, 372
{} (braces), alignment in
code, 526
| (pipe) OR operator, 379
~ (tilde) complement
operator, 379

A

abstract data types, 113
access, 18-19
AddKey() function,
273, 435, 470
ADT (abstract
data types), 12
Algorithms in C++, 74
aligning braces ({})
in code, 526
ampersand (&) AND
operator, 378
AND (&) operator, 378
AnimalFillFunction()
function, 38
answers, chapter quizzes
and exercises, 568-689
arguments
command-line, 126-128
sorting, 131-139
sorting linked lists,
134-139
Array class, 498

Array Class Constructor
Template Definition
listing, 29
arrays, 10-11
character arrays,
MyBlock, 287
history structures, 430
sparse arrays,
creating, 255-260
templates, 27-29
unions, 300
asserts, 521-522
Asserts with Side Effects
program, 522
AVL Tree listing, 214-221
AVL trees, 213-225

B

B-Tree Driver Program
listing, 272
B-Tree Implementation
listing, 288-289
B-trees (binary trees),
168, 224, 261-276
balanced, 213-223
disk-based, 281
implementing, 264-276
iterators, 400-401
nodes, deleting, 264
pages, writing to disk, 276
rewriting, 181-188
balanced binary
trees, 213-223
base 2, 390-391
base classes, 11
binary operators, 16, 527
Binary Tree listing, 181-186
Binary Tree of Words
listing, 200-204

binary values (memory),
387-388, 390-392
base 2, 390-391
bits, 391
K (kilobyte), 391
machine instructions,
391-392
BinaryNode class, 180
BinaryNodeWrapper
program, 198
bits, 391
bit field program, 381-382
clearing, 379-380
fields, 380-383
flipping, 380
setting, 379
bitwise operators, 378-379
Booch, Grady, *Object-
Oriented Analysis and
Design*, 562
Bounds Checker
program, 545
braces ({}), alignment in
code, 15, 526
branches, 559
break points,
debuggers, 540
Btree.cpp listing, 313-317
BTree.cpp program,
406-410, 441-445
Btree.cpp program, 347-351
Btree.hpp listing, 308-313
BTree.hpp program,
401-406, 436-441
Btree.hpp program,
342-347
btree.hpp-the B-Tree
Header File listing,
265-266

Bubble Sort listing, 81-82

Bubble Sort program, 482-483

Bubble Sort with a Print Listing listing, 82-83

bubble sorts, 81-88

  improving, 85-88

  optimizing, 88

BubbleSort() function, 82

Bubbling Downward listing, 84

buckets, data location, 165

bugs, 536

  common, 544

  costs, 536-538

  debuggers, 538-551

  design documents, writing, 537

  fence-post errors, 544

  integers, 544

  references, returning to local variables, 544

  release code, finding, 543-544

  specifications, 536-537

building databases, 280-281

C

call stacks (exceptions), 500, 541

calling functions, 383

capitalization in code, 528

caret () exclusive OR operator, 379

case insensitivity, searches, 307

catch blocks, exceptions, 13, 496, 499-503

chapter quizzes, answers, 568-689

char type, bit fields, 380

character arrays, MyBlock, 287

child nodes, deleting nodes, 170

Class Hierarchies and Exceptions program, 503-504

classes, 3-4, 6

  Array, 498

  base classes, 11

  BinaryNode class, 180

  clients, 2

  collection classes, 254

  declaring

    DiskManager, 287

    Index, 287

    Iterator, 430

    Page, 287

  defining, 529-530

  derived classes, 11

  design, 110

  encapsulation, 3

  friend classes, 13

  initializing, 299

  interfaces, 2

  invariants, 522-523

  list classes, 153-156

  Queue, 198-206

  sparse array classes, creating, 255-260

  storage handling, creating, 240-249

  String class, 157-163

  strings, 48-57

  technical specifications, 117-118

virutal destructors, 523

writing, 21

xBoundary, 498

Clear() function, 54

clearing bits, 379-380

CLiDE (command-line directory enhancer), 119-120

clients, classes, 2

code

  braces, 15

  bugs, 538

  capitalization, 528

  comments, 18, 528-529

  extensibility, 434

  identifiers, 17

  indenting, 15

  line length, 526

  long lines, 15

  maintainable code, 434

  notes, improving, 306-308

  optimizing, 474-475

  readability, 527

  reviews, 530-532

  spelling, 528

  style guidelines, 14-15

  switch statements, 16

  text, 16-17

  see also programming

Code Complete, **Steve McConnel, 563**

code reviews, 531-532

code space, 4

collection classes, 254

collections, 113

command-line arguments, sorting, 131-139

Command-Line Arguments listing, 127

command-line flags, 128-129

command-line processing, 126-128

comments, 16, 18, 528-529

commercial software, 561-564

compilers
const function, 524
exceptions, 496
gotoxy() function, 173
optimization, 474-475
profiling programs, 475, 476
templates, support, 26

complement (~) operator, 379

complex data structures, 152-164
list classes, 153-156
Notes, 157-163
saving to disk, 228-229
Strings, 157-163
trees, 166-181

CompuServe, C++ forums, 562

Constant and Nonconstant Pointers listing, 6-7

constants, 10, 19

constructors, placement, 529

containment, inheritance, 12

Count Analysis of Bubble Sort program, 483-484

Count Analysis of the Improved Bubble Sort program, 489

counting function calls, 477-478

coverage analysis profiling, 481-482

Coverage Report program, 481-482

CPUs (central processing units), registers, 4, 384

Create() function, 299

D

data
buckets, 165
complex data structures, 152-164
persistence, object persistence, 231
searches, functional specifications, 106
storage
functional specifications, 105-106
hash tables, 164-166
streams, 13
trees, 166-181
types
abstract, 113
bit fields, 380-383
collections, 113
writing from an object, 230-240

databases
adding notes, 372
building, 280-281
indexes, 281
disk managers, 281-283
disk-based B-trees, 281, 283
leaf-node items, 301
locking pages, 282
LRU queues, 282

marking for deletion, 301-302
page capacity, 283
page size, 282
pointers, 299
iterators, 400-401
statistics, 308

Datafile.cpp program, 317-319, 351-353, 419-420, 452-454

debuggers, 538-551
break points, 540
call stacks, 541
defining problems, 541-543
locating problems, 542
logs, 539
memory
checking, 545
examining, 540
symbolic debuggers, 540
TRACE macros, 538-539
watch points, 540

Declaring a Message, Node, and Linked List listing, 58-59

declaring classes
DiskManager, 287
Index, 287
Iterator, 430
Page, 287

declaring templates, 27-29

defining classes, 529-530

definitions
storing, 152-153
templates, 44

delete keyword, memory, 8

Delete() function, 179, 181

deleting
B-tree nodes, 264
index notes, 301-302
nodes, trees, 170-171

Demonstrating fin and fout listing, 228-229

Demonstrating Potential Optimization listing, 76-77

demonstration program, rWord object, 173-190

derived classes, 11

design, 104
> classes, 110
> creating, 109-113
> documents, writing, 537
> object-oriented design programming, 111
> reviews of code, 530-531

destructors
> placement, 529
> virutal destructors, 523

dictionaries, 254

disk managers
> enhancing perform-ance, 302
> indexes, 281-283

disk-based B-trees, 281-288

DiskManager Implementa-tion program, 295

Display() function, 60, 65

displaying found data, 106-107

displays, 121

documentation reviews, 532

DoFind() method, 372

DoPrint() function, 206

DoSyn() method, 469

Driver.cpp listing, 331-332, 427-429

drivers, linked lists, 58-65

dynamic names, version control, 560

E

Effective C++, Scott Myers, 562

encapsulation, object-oriented programming, 2

enhancements, 560-561

enhancing disk manager performance, 302

environment variables, 140-146

errors, 536
> exceptions, 494-495
>> catch blocks, 496-500
>> compilers, 496
>> hierarchies, 503-504
>> multiple exceptions, 500-503
>> objects, 504-510
>> templates, 510-512
>> throwing, 496
>> try blocks, 495, 499
>> uses, 495-499

event-driven programming, 110-111

exceptions, 13-14, 494-495
> catch blocks, 496-500
> compilers, 496
> hierarchies, 503-504
> multiple exceptions, 500-503
> objects, 504-510
> templates, 510-512
> throwing, 496, 500
> try blocks, 495, 499
> uses, 495-499

exclusive OR () operator, 379

exercises, answers, 568-689

F

false optimizations, 487-490

fence-post errors, bugs, 544

fields, bit fields, 380-383

FIFO (first-in-first-out) queues, 194-212

FIFO Queue Header listing, 195-196

FIFO-Implementation listing, 196-197

files
> branches, 559
> intermediary index files, creating, 306-307
> make files, 692-694
> trunks, 559

filtering, 121

Find() function, 301

FindLeaf() function, 469

FindNote() function, 63

FindObject() function, 70, 181

FindParagraph() function, 17

flags
> alternatives, 130-131
> command-line, 128-129
> IsLocked, 341
> nocreate, 299
> synonyms, 435

flipping bits, 380

friend classes, 13

friend functions, 13

Function Count Report program, 477-491

functional specifications, 104-105
> CLiDE, 119-120
> data searches, 106

data storage, 105-106
help systems, 108
operating systems, 119
user interfaces, 119-120

functions
AddKey(), 255, 470, 273
ADT (abstract data types), 12
AnimalFillFunction(), 38
BubbleSort(), 82
calling, 383
Clear(), 54
const, 524
Create(), 299
Delete(), 179, 181
Display(), 60, 65
DoFind(), 372
DoPrint(), 206
DoSyn(), 469
Find(), 301
FindLeaf(), 469
FindNote(), 63
FindObject(), 70, 181
FindParagraph(), 17
friend functions, 13
GetBigger(), 223
GetCount(), 179
getenv(), 144-146
GetLength(), 50
GetNext(), 430
GetNoteNumber(), 63
GetPage(), 287, 300
GetSmaller(), 223
GetStatus(), 382
GetText(), 249
gotoxy(), 173
Insert(), 179, 205, 287, 372, 469
InsertAfter(), 62

InsertLeaf(), 300
InsertNode(), 469
InsertionSort(), 80
InsertLeaf(), 273
InsertNode(), 223, 273
IntFillFunction(), 38
IsEmpty(), 50
Iterate(), 60, 179
LeftRotate(), 223
MyTemplateFunction(), 34
nonmember (global), 3
Nullify(), 274
operator(), 231
ParseFile(), 373
PrintNode(), 206
PrintTree(), 179, 205
Process(), 129, 131
profiling function count, 477-478
Push(), 273
QuickSort(), 88-101, 131
Recount(), 274
Reset(), 17
Save(), 287
Search(), 17
Serialize(), 231
SetgPageNumber, 299
ShowCursor(), 17
ShowMenu(), 373
SomeFunction(), 33
stacks, memory, 5
standard library rand(), 97
static data, 13
strcpy(), 11
StringCompare(), 51, 55
strlen(), 11
Swap(), 76, 477
templates, 33-45

Write(), 246
WriteToDisk(), 231

G

GetBigger() function, 223
GetCount() function, 179
getenv() listing, 144-146
GetLength() function, 50
GetNext() function, 430
GetNoteNumber() function, 63
GetPage() function, 287, 300
GetSmaller() function, 223
GetStatus() function, 382
GetText() function, 249
Getting Data Out of an Exception Object program, 504-507
global name space, 384
global variables, 4
gotoxy() function, compiler support, 173

H-I

hash tables, 164-166
hashing algorithms, 165
Hashing the Words in ROBIN listing, 165-166
heaps (memory), 384, 386-387
help systems, 108
hexadecimal values (memory), 387-388, 392-394
history structures, 430

identifiers, 17, 527-528
IDEs (integrated development environments), 692-694
IdxManager.cpp program, 454-457
Idxmgr.cpp program, 319-322
IDXMgr.cpp program, 353-356
IdxMgr.cpp program, 421-424
Implementation for the New rWord Object program, 237-238
Implementation of String program, 547-549
Implementation of the Template Array program, 30-31
implementing disk-based B-trees, 288
Improving the Bubble Sort program, 86-87
indenting, listings, 15
indenting switches, 526
Index Implementation program, 271, 294
Index.cpp program, 322-323, 356-358, 417-419, 445-446
indexes, 281
    disk managers, 281-283, 302
    disk-based B-trees, 281
        implementation, 288
        interface program, 283
    leaf-node items, 301

locking pages, 282, 341-342
LRU queues, 282
marking for deletion, 301-302
page capacity, 283
page size, 282
pointers, 281
    initializing, 523-524
    myKeys, 299
splitting pages, 301
synonyms, 434
inheritance, 11-12
    ADT (abstract data types), 12
    containment, 12
    multiple inheritance, 12
    object-oriented programming, 3
    private inheritance, 12
initializing
    classes, 299
    order, 525
    pointers, 523-524
Insert() function, 179, 205, 287, 372, 469
InsertAfter() function, 62
Insertion Sort program, 79-80
insertion sorts, 79-80
InsertionSort() function, 80
InsertLeaf method, 300
InsertLeaf() function, 273
InsertNode() function, 223, 273
InsertNode() function, 469
Inside Visual C++, David Kruglinski, 563
instances, templates, 27

instruction pointers, 4, 384
int type, bit fields, 380
integers, bugs, 544
Interface to String Class program, 546-547
interfaces, classes, 2
Interfaces for a Binary Tree of Words program, 198-200
intermediary index files, creating, 306-307
Internet, C++ newsgroups, 562
IntFillFunction() function, 38
invariants, 522-523
IsEmpty() function, 50
IsLocked flag, 341
Iter.cpp program, 457-459
Iterate() function, 60, 179
Iterator class, 430
Iterator.cpp program, 415-417
iterators, 400
    adding/deleting list items, 430
    B-trees, 400-401
    examples, 401
    static, 430

K-L

K (kilobyte), 391
keyword template, 27
keywords, 16
kilobyte (K), 391
Kruglinski, David, *Inside Visual C++,* 563

labels, 529

large programs, writing,
  14-19
leaf nodes, trees,167
  deleting, 170
  synonyms, 434
leaf-node index items, 301
least recently used (LRU)
  queues, 282
LeftRotate() function, 223
Liberty, Jesse, *Teach*
  Yourself C++ in 21 Days, **2**
line length, 526
line-by-line profiling,
  479-481
links
  lists, 57-65
  command-line arguments,
    sorting, 134-139
list classes, 153-156
listings
  1.1 (Constant and
    Nonconstant Pointers),
    6-7
  1.2 (Using References), 9
  2.1 (Template of an Array
    Class), 28
  2.2 (Array Class Construc-
    tor Template
    Definition), 29
  2.3 (Implementation of
    the Template Array),
    30-31
  2.4 (Passing Template
    Objects to and from
    Function, 34-37
  2.5 (Specializing Template
    Implementations), 39-42
  3.1 (Using the String Class
    Interface), 49-50

  3.2 (Using String Class
    Implementation), 51-54
  3.3 (Using a Driver
    Program to Exercise the
    String, 55-56
  3.4 (Declaring a Message,
    Node, and Linked List),
    58-59
  3.6 (Using the Driver
    Program for the Linked
    List), 63-64
  3.7 (Using a Parameterized
    List Class), 65-69
  4.1 (Using a Selection
    Sort), 75-76
  4.2 (Demonstrating
    Potential Optimization),
    76-77
  4.3 (Using an Insertion
    Sort), 79-80
  4.4 (Using a Bubble Sort),
    81-82
  4.5 (Using a Bubble Sort
    with a Print Listing),
    82-83
  4.6 (Bubbling Down-
    ward), 84
  4.7 (Improving the Bubble
    Sort), 86-87
  4.8 (Using QuickSort()),
    90-91
  4.9 (Sorting Pointers),
    92-93
  4.10 (Using a Parameter-
    ized QuickSort), 95-96
  5.1 (Using the rNote
    Class), 114
  5.2 (Using the Prelimenary
    rWord Class), 115-119
  5.3 (Using rNoteNode),
    116-117

  6.1 (Using Command-
    Line Arguments), 127
  6.2 (Switching on
    Command-Line Flags),
    128-129
  6.3 (Using the Name of
    the File), 130
  6.4 (Sorting the Argu-
    ments), 132-133
  6.5 (Sorting a List of
    Command-Line
    Arguments), 134-139
  6.6 (Sorting the Environ-
    ment Variables),
    140-143
  6.7 (Using getenv()),
    144-145
  6.8 (Using putenv), 146
  7.1 (Using Stdef.hpp To
    Store Standard Defini-
    tions, 153
  7.2 (The Sorted Linked
    List Template), 153-156
  7.3 (Note.hpp), 157
  7.4 (String.hpp), 158-159
  7.5 (String.cpp), 159-162
  7.6 (Testing the Building
    Blocks), 163-164
  7.7 (Hashing the Words in
    ROBIN), 165-166
  7.8 (Using an rWord
    Declaration), 172-173
  7.9 (Using the Driver
    Program), 173-179
  7.10 (Another Way to
    Write a Binary Tree),
    181-186
  7.11 (Using the Driver
    Program), 186-187

8.1 (FIFO Queue Header), 195-196

8.2 (FIFO-Implementation), 196-197

8.3 (Queue Driver Program), 197

8.4 (Interfaces for a Binary Tree of Words), 198-200

8.5 (Implementation of the Binary Tree of Words), 200-204

8.6 (Driver Program to Print a Binary Tree of Word, 204

8.7 (Using Regression To Print the Tree), 207

8.8 (Declaring the AVL Tree), 214-215

8.9 (Implementing the AVL Tree), 215-221

8.10 (Driver Program for the AVL Tree), 222

9.1 (Demonstrating fin and fout), 228-229

9.2 (Writing Object Contents to Disk), 230

9.3 (stddef.hpp), 232

9.4 (String.hpp), 232-233

9.5 (String.cpp), 234-237

9.6 (Implementation for the New rWord Object), 237-238

9.7 (Using the Driver Program for Writing to Disk), 239

9.8 (The Storable Interface), 241-242

9.9 (The Storagable Implementation), 242-243

9.10 (The New Interface to rWord), 244-245

9.11 (Using the Driver Program), 245-246

10.1 (A Modified rWord Header File), 256

10.2 (The Sparse Array Template), 257-259

10.3 (A Driver Program for the Sparse Array), 259

10.4 (Using stdef.hpp-the Standard Definition File, 264-265

10.5 (Using btree.hpp-the B-Tree Header File), 265-266

10.6 (B-Tree Implementation), 267

10.7 (Page Implementation), 268-271

10.8 (Index Implementation), 271

10.9 (The B-Tree Driver Program), 272

11.1. A Disk-Based, B-Tree Interface, 283-286

11.2. The B-Tree Implementation, 288-289

11.3. The Page Implementation, 289-293

11.4. The Index Implementation, 294

11.5. The DiskManager Implementation, 295

11.6. The Driver Program, 298

12.1 (Btree.hpp), 308-313

12.2 (Btree.cpp), 313-317

12.3 (Datafile.cpp), 317-319

12.4 (Idxmgr.cpp), 319-322

12.5 (Index.cpp), 322-323

12.6 (Page.cpp), 323-328

12.7 (WNJFile.cpp), 328-331

12.8 (Driver.cpp), 331-332

13.1. Btree.hpp, 342-347

13.2. Btree.cpp, 347-351

13.3. Datafile.cpp, 351-353

13.4. IDXMgr.cpp, 353-356

13.5. Index.cpp, 356-358

13.6. Page.cpp, 358-363

13.7. WNJFile.cpp, 363-366

13.8. R1.cpp, 366-371

14.1. Using Bit Fields, 381-382

15.1. BTree.hpp, 401-406

15.2. BTree.cpp, 406-410

15.3. Page.cpp, 410-415

15.4. Iterator.cpp, 415-417

15.5. Index.cpp, 417-419

15.6. Datafile.cpp, 419-420

15.7. IdxMgr.cpp, 421-424

15.8. WNJFile.cpp, 424-427

15.9. Driver.cpp, 427-429

16.1. BTree.hpp, 436-441

16.2. BTree.cpp, 441-445

16.3. Index.cpp, 445-446

16.4. Page.cpp, 446-452

16.5. Datafile.cpp, 452-454

16.6. IdxManager.cpp, 454-457

16.7. Iter.cpp, 457-459

16.8. WNJFile.cpp, 459-462

16.9. R2.cpp, 462-468

17.1. Using a Selection Sort, 476

17.2. Function Count Report, 477-491

17.3. Time Report, 478-479

17.4. Profiling by Line, 479-480

17.5. Coverage Report, 481-482

17.6. Bubble Sort, 482-483

17.7. Count Analysis of Bubble Sort, 483-484

17.8. Time Analysis of Bubble Sort, 484-485

17.9. Time Analysis of Each Line of Bubble Sort, 485-486

17.10. Optimized Bubble Sort, 487-488

17.11. Count Analysis of the Improved Bubble Sort, 489

17.12. Timing Analysis, 490

18.1. Raising an Exception, 496-498

18.2. Multiple Exceptions, 501-502

18.3. Class Hierarchies and Exceptions, 503-504

18.4. Getting Data Out of an Exception Object, 504-507

18.6. Using Exceptions with Templates, 510-512

19.1. Using Asserts, 521

19.2. Asserts with Side Effects, 522

19.3. Setting Pointers to Zero, 523

20.1 (Interface to String Class), 546-547

20.2 (Implementation of String), 547-549

20.3 (Driver Program), 550

braces, 15

indenting, 15

lists, 57-65

linked, 57-58

creating, 58-65

sorting command-line arguments, 134-139

parameterizing, 65-70

trees, 167

locking index pages, 341-342

long lines, code, 15

LRU (least recently used) queues, 282

M

M (megabyte), 391

Macintosh, writing for, 563

macros, ASSERT, 521-522

magazines, referencing, 563

Maguire, Steve, *Writing Solid Code*, 563

make files, 692-694

marking indexes for deletion, 301-302

masking operations, setting bits, 379

McConnel, Steve, *Code Complete*, 563

Median of Three rule, QuickSort() function, 97-99

megabyte (M), 391

memory, 4-5

binary values, 387-390

base 2, 390-391

bits, 391

K (kilobyte), 391

machine instructions, 391-392

code space, 4

CPUs, registers, 384

debuggers, examining, 540

debugging, 545

delete keyword, 8

hexadecimal values, 387-388, 392-394

new function, 8

objects, saving to disk, 228-229

organization, 383-384

pointers, 6-8

RAM, 384

heaps, 386-387

stacks, 385-386

references, 9-10

registers, 4

stacks, 4-5

Multiple Exceptions program, 501-502

multiple inheritance, 12
MyBlock character arrray, 287
Myers, Scott, *Effective C++*, 562
MyTemplateFunction() function, 34

N

Name of the File
   listing, 130
names
   declarations, templates, 29
   identifiers, 527-528
   spelling and cpitalization, 17-18
New Interface to rWord
   program, 244-245
new keyword, memory, 8
new operator, 523
No Bugs! Delivering Error-Free Code in C and C++, David Thielen, 563
nocreate flag, 299
nodes, trees,
   deleting, 170-171, 264
   finding, 168-169
   inserting, 169
nonmember (global)
   functions, 3
Note.hpp listing, 157
notes, 157-163
   code, improving, 306-308
   saving, 306
   storage, 306
Nu Mega Technologies,
   Bounds Checker, 545
NULL, pointers, 6
Nullify() function, 274

O

object persistence, 231, 261
Object-Oriented Analysis and Design,
   Grady Booch, 562
Object-Oriented Modeling and Design, 562
object-oriented
   programming, 2-4, 74, 111
   arrays, 10-11
   bitwise operators, 378-379
   classes, 3-4
   encapsulation, 2
   exceptions, 13-14, 504-510
   informational
      references, 562
   inheritance, 3, 11-12
   large programs, writing, 14-19
   passing templates, 34-38
   polymorphism, 3
   saving to disk, 228-229
   sorting, 74
   writing data from objects, 230-240
operator() function, 231
operators
   binary, 527
   binary operators, 16
   new, 523
   overloading, 12
   unary, 527
operatying systems, func-tional specificactions, 119
Optimized Bubble Sort
   program, 487-488
optimizing programs, 474-475

bubble sorts, 88
false optimizations, 487-490
profiling, 475-476
   by line, 479-481
   by time, 478-479
   coverage analysis, 481-482
   function count, 477-478
sorts, 78
OR (|) operator, 379
overloading operators, 12

P

Page Implementation
   program, 268-271, 289-293
Page.cpp program,
   323-328, 358-363, 410-415, 446-452
pages, B-trees, writing to
   disk, 276
Parameterized List Class
   program, 65-69
parameterizing, 26-27
   lists, 65-70
   sorts, 94-99
ParseFile() method, 373
Passing by Reference and
   Using Virtual Function in
   Exceptions program, 507-509
Passing Template Objects to
   and from Function
   program, 34-37
periodicals, referencing, 563

persistence
object persistence, 261
object versus data, 231
Petzold, Charles, *Programming Windows 3.1, Third Edition*, 563
PIM (Personal Information Manager), 19, 104-105
pipe (|) OR operator, 379
pointers, 281
initializing, 523-524
memory, 6-8
myKeys, 299
NULL, 6
sorting, 92-94
polymorphism, 3, 11
print listings, bubble sorts, 82-83
printing
Queue classes, 198-206
recursion, 206-213
trees, 194
PrintNode() function, 206
PrintTree() function, 179, 205
private inheritance, 12
private labels, 529
Process() function, 129, 131
profiling, 475-476
by line, 479-481
by time, 478-479
coverage analysis, 481-482
function count, 477-478
Profiling by Line program, 479-480
programming
access, 18-19
bugs, 536
comments, 18
constants, 19

data searches, 106
data types, abstract, 113
databases, management, 107-108
design, 104, 109-113
enhancements, 560-561
event-driven, 110-111
functional specifications, 104-105
guidelines, 524, 525
initial attempts, 109
managing more than one programmer, 559
object-oriented, 2-4, 74, 111
arrays, 10-11
classes, 3-4
encapsulation, 2
exceptions, 13-14
informational references, 562
inheritance, 3, 11-12
large programs, 14-19
polymorphism, 3
saving objects to disk, 228-229
writing data from objects, 230-240
prototypes, 120-121
specifications, 104-108, 536-537
starting, 111-117
style, 525
aligning braces ({}) in code, 526
capitalization, 528
class definitions, 529-530
comments, 528-529
guidelines, 14-15

identifiers, 527-528
line length, 526
readibility in code, 527
spelling, 528
switches, 526
technical specifications, 108-109
text, 16-17
variables, 14
version control, 558-560
see also *code*
Programming Windows 3.1, Third Edition, Charles Petzold, 563
programs
optimizing, 474-475
false optimizations, 487-490
profiling, 475-476
by time, 478-481
coverage analysis, 481-482
function count, 477-478
qualities
extensibility, 519-520
maintainability, 520
robustness, 519
testing, 340-341, 520-522
initializing pointers, 523-524
new operator return value, 523
protected labels, 529
prototypes, creating, 120-121
public labels, 529
Push() function, 273
putenv listing, 146

Q-R

question mark (?), calling
  DoFind() method, 372
Queue Driver Program
  listing, 197
queues, FIFO (First-
  in-First-out), 194-212
QuickSort() function,
  88-92, 131
    limitations, 97-101
    parameterizing sorts,
      94-99
    sorting pointers, 92-94
quizzes, answers, 568-689

R1.cpp program, 366-371
R2.cpp program, 462-468
Raising an Exception
  program, 496-498
RAM (Random-Access
  Memory), 384
    heaps, 386-387
    stacks, 385-386
RCS (revision control
  system), 558-560
    branches, 559
    trunks, 559
recompiling programs, 692
records
    data, 307
    length, 307
Recount() function, 274
recursion, printing,
  206-213
references, 16, 525
    memory aliases, 9-10
    returning to local variables,
      544
References program, 9
registers, 4, 384

Regression To Print the
  Tree program, 207
release branches, 560
Reset() function, 17
reviewing code
    code reviews, 531-532
    design reviews, 530-531
    documentation reviews,
      532
rewriting binary trees,
  181-188
rNote Class program, 114
rNoteNode program,
  116-117
rNotes database, 280-281
ROBIN, 19-21
    databases, building,
      280-281
    displaying results, 342
    functional specification,
      104-105
    indexes
        disk-based B-trees, 281
        locking pages, 282,
          341-342
        LRU queues, 282
        page capacity, 283
        page size, 282
    management, 107-108
    synonyms, 434-435
root node, trees, 167
rWord Class program,
  115-119
rWord Declaration pro-
  gram, 172-173
rWord Header File
  program, 256
rWord object, demonstra-
  tion program, 173-190
rWord objects, creating,
  171-173

S

Save() function, 287
saving
    notes, 306
    objects to disk, 228-229
Search() function, 17
searches
    case insensitivity, 307
    data, 106
    data types, 113
    displaying found data,
      106-107
    synonyms, 434-435
Selection Sort program,
  75-76, 476
selection sorts, 74-76
Serialize() function, 231
SetgPageNumber()
  function, 299
sets, collection classes, 254
setting bits, 379
Setting Pointers to Zero
  program, 523
Shammas, Namir, *Teach
  Yourself Visual C++ in 21
  Days*, 563
shareware, 561
Shareware Products
  Association, 561
ShowCursor() function, 17
ShowMenu() method, 373
SomeFunction()
  function, 33
Sorted Linked List Tem-
  plate program, 153-156
Sorting a List of Command-
  Line Arguments listing,
  134-139

Sorting the Arguments
listing, 132-133
Sorting the Environment
Variables listing, 140-143
sorts, 74, 121
    arguments, command-line,
    131-139
    bubble sorts, 81-88
    environment variables,
    140-146
    insertion sorts, 79-80
    parameterizing, 94-99
    pointers, 92-94
    QuickSort() function,
    88-92, 97-101
    selection sorts, 74-76
    swaps, 76-78, 78
sparse array classes,
    creating, 255-260
Sparse Array Template
    program, 257-259
Specializing Template
    Implementations program,
    39-42
specifications, 536-537
    functional specifications,
    104-105
        data searches, 106
        data storage, 105-106
        help systems, 108
        operating systems, 119
        user interfaces, 119-120
    programming, 104-108
    technical specifications,
    108-109, 117-118
spelling in code, 528
splitting pages
    (indexes), 301
stacks (memory), 4-5,
    384-386

standard library rand()
    function, 97
starting programming,
    114-117
static data, 13
static iterators, 430
statistics, databases, 308
stddef.hpp program, 232
Stdef.hpp To Store Stan-
    dard Definitions program,
    153
stdef.hpp-the Standard
    Definition File program,
    264-265
Storable Interface program,
    241-242
Storagable Implementation
    program, 242-243
storage, 249
    classes, creating, 240-249
    definitions, 152-153
    hash tables, 164-166
    notes, 306
    objects to disk, 231-250
strcpy() function, 11
streams, 13
String Class Implementa-
    tion program, 51-54
String Class Interface
    program, 49-50
String.cpp listing, 158-162,
    232-237
StringCompare() function,
    51, 55
strings, 48-57, 157-163
strlen() function, 11
structures, 6, 261
style guidelines, large
    programs, 14-15
suffixes, make files, 693-694
Swap() function, 76, 477

swaps, 76-78, 283-288
switch statements, 16, 526
symbolic debuggers, 540
synonyms, 434-435

T

technical specifications,
    108-109, 117-118, 120
Template of an Array Class
    listing, 28
templates, 26
    array objects, 27-29
    classes, 27
    compilers, support, 26
    declarations, 27-29
    definitions, 44
    exceptions, 510-512
    functions, 33-45
    implementing, 29-34
    instances, 27
    keyword template, 27
    objects, passing, 34-38
    parameterized types, 26-27
testing programs, 340-341,
    520-522
    initializing pointers,
    523-524
    new operator return
    value, 523
Testing the Building Blocks
    listing, 163-164
text
    codes, 16-17
    strings, 48-57
thelter static iterator, 430
Thielen, David, *No Bugs!
    Delivering Error-Free
    Code in C and C++*, 563
throwing exceptions,
    496, 500

tilde (~) complement operator, 379
Time Analysis of Bubble Sort program, 484-485
Time Analysis of Each Line of Bubble Sort program, 485-486
Time Report program, 478-479
Timing Analysis program, 490
TRACE macros, 538-539
trees, 167
    B-trees, 168, 181-188, 261-276
    nodes
        deleting, 170-171
        finding, 168-169
        inserting, 169
        printing, 194
        structures, 261
trunks, 559
try blocks, 495, 499

U-V

unary operators, 527
unary operators, code text, 16
unions (arrays), 300
user interfaces, functional specifications, 119-120
Using Asserts program, 521
Using Exceptions with Templates program, 510-512

variables, 14, 17
    environment variables, 140-146

global, 4
make files, 693
version control, 558-560
    branches, 559
    dynamic names, 560
    managing more than one programmer, 559
    trunks, 559
virutal destructors, 523

W-Z

watch points, debuggers, 540
white space, code text, 16
wild cards, searches, 106
Windows, writing for, 563
WNJ (Word-Node-Join) record, 434
WNJFile.cpp program, 328-331, 363-366, 424-427, 459-462
Word-Node-Join (WNJ) record, 434
Write() function, 246
WriteToDisk() function, 231
writing, 114-117
    AVL trees, 213-225
    binary trees, rewriting, 181-188
    classes, 21
    data from an object, 230-240
    design documents, 537
    large programs, 14-19
    Macintosh, 563
    Windows, 563
Writing Object Contents to Disk listing, 230

Writing Solid Code, Steve Maguire, 563

xBoundary class, 498

Ziffnet, C++ forums, 562

Add to Your Sams Library Today with the Best Books for Programming, Operating Systems, and New Technologies

The easiest way to order is to pick up the phone and call

1-800-428-5331

between 9:00 a.m. and 5:00 p.m. EST.
For faster service please have your credit card available.

ISBN	Quantity	Description of Item	Unit Cost	Total Cost
0-672-30602-6		Programming Windows 95 Unleashed (Book/CD)	$49.99	
0-672-30474-0		Windows 95 Unleashed (Book/CD)	$35.00	
0-672-30611-5		Your Windows 95 Consultant	$19.99	
0-672-30685-9		Windows NT 3.5 Unleashed	$39.99	
0-672-30765-0		Navigating the Internet with Windows 95	$25.00	
0-672-30568-2		Teach Yourself OLE Programming in 21 Days (Book/CD)	$39.99	
0-672-30663-8		Visual C++ Developer's Guide, Second Edition (Book/Disk)	$45.00	
0-672-30594-1		Programming WinSock (Book/Disk)	$35.00	
0-672-30440-6		Database Developers Guide with Visual Basic 3 (Book/Disk)	$44.95	
0-672-30453-8		Access 2 Developers Guide, Second Edition (Book/Disk)	$44.95	
0-672-30507-0		Tricks of the Game Programming Gurus (Book/CD)	$45.00	
1-57521-040-1		World Wide Web Unleashed 1996 (Book/CD)	$49.99	
		Shipping and Handling: See information below.		
		TOTAL		

❏ 3 ½" Disk

❏ 5 ¼" Disk

Shipping and Handling: $4.00 for the first book, and $1.75 for each additional book. Floppy disk: add $1.75 for shipping and handling. If you need to have it NOW, we can ship product to you in 24 hours for an additional charge of approximately $18.00, and you will receive your item overnight or in two days. Overseas shipping and handling adds $2.00 per book and $8.00 for up to three disks. Prices subject to change. Call for availability and pricing information on latest editions.

201 W. 103rd Street, Indianapolis, Indiana 46290

1-800-428-5331 — Orders   1-800-835-3202 — FAX   1-800-858-7674 — Customer Service

Book ISBN 1-672-30657-3

PLUG YOURSELF INTO...

THE MACMILLAN INFORMATION SUPERLIBRARY™

Free information and vast computer resources from the world's leading computer book publisher—online!

FIND THE BOOKS THAT ARE RIGHT FOR YOU!

A complete online catalog, plus sample chapters and tables of contents give you an in-depth look at *all* of our books, including hard-to-find titles. It's the best way to find the books you need!

- ● STAY INFORMED with the latest computer industry news through our online newsletter, press releases, and customized Information SuperLibrary Reports.

- ● GET FAST ANSWERS to your questions about MCP books and software.

- ● VISIT our online bookstore for the latest information and editions!

- ● COMMUNICATE with our expert authors through e-mail and conferences.

- ● DOWNLOAD SOFTWARE from the immense MCP library:
    - Source code and files from MCP books
    - The best shareware, freeware, and demos

- ● DISCOVER HOT SPOTS on other parts of the Internet.

- ● WIN BOOKS in ongoing contests and giveaways!

TO PLUG INTO MCP: ➔   WORLD WIDE WEB: **http://www.mcp.com**

GOPHER: gopher.mcp.com

FTP: ftp.mcp.com

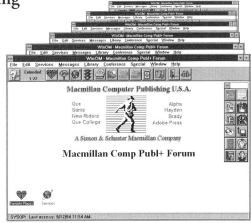